PRIVATIZATION, PUBLIC OWNERSHIP AND THE REGULATION OF NATURAL MONOPOLY

PRIVATIZATION, PUBLIC OWNERSHIP AND THE REGULATION OF NATURAL MONOPOLY

C. D. FOSTER

BLACKWELL
Oxford UK & Cambridge USA

First published 1992

Blackwell Publishers
108 Cowley Road
Oxford OX4 1JF
UK

238 Main Street, Suite 501
Cambridge, Massachusetts 02142
USA

British Library Cataloguing-in-Publication Data

A CIP catalogue record for this book is available from
the British Library.

Library of Congress Cataloging-in-Publication Data

Foster, Christopher D.
Privatization, Public Ownership, and the Regulation of Natural
Monopoly / C. D. Foster.
p.   cm.
Includes bibliographical references and index.
ISBN 0–631–18486–4

1. Trade regulation – Great Britain.   2. Privatization – Great
Britain.   3. Government ownership – Great Britain.   4. Monopolies –
Great Britain.   5. Trade regulation – United States.
6. Privatization – United States.   I. Title.
HD3616.G73F67   1992
338.941 – dc20   91–47004   CIP

Typeset in 9 1/2 on 11 pt Ehrhardt
by Graphicraft Typesetters Ltd., Hong Kong
Printed in Great Britain by T.J. Press Ltd., Padstow, Cornwall

This book is printed on acid-free paper

To my wife, Kay, as always

Contents

Acknowledgements

I would like to thank for their help and comments on draft chapters Sir Lawrence Airey, Prof. Mark Blaug, Michael Bonavia, Ian Byatt, Sir Bryan Carsberg, Lord Chorley, Roger O'B. Davis, J. S. Dodgson, Ian Ellison, Dr Stephen Glaister, Sir Geoffrey Howe, Prof. George Jones, Lord Joseph, Prof. Alfred Kahn, Prof. Ted Keeler, Prof. R. Klein, Roger Knight, Sir Frank Layfield QC; Sir Peter Lazarus, Prof. Norman Lewis, H. C. G. Matthew, Stuart McIntosh, Prof. D. O'Brien, John Palmer, Tony Prosser, the Rt. Hon. Nicholas Ridley, Prof. Richard Shannon, Tom Sharpe, David Stafford, Bevan Waide, Sir Douglas Wass and Stan Webster, as well as a number of serving civil servants, who, following the usual conventions, cannot be named. I owe a debt also to many Coopers & Lybrand colleagues who have worked on privatization and public-enterprise restructuring from whom I have learned much.

Prof. Theo Barker, Dr John Collings, Tony Harrison, Prof. J. L. Jowell and Peter Mackie have wrestled with me though several drafts, often saving me from error. My errors now and my interpretations are my own. I am grateful to my secretary, Mrs Kathy Tedder, for countless retypings and to my wife, Kay, for putting up with all the dislocation and turbulence of this on top of what would generally be reckoned a full-time job.

Introduction

The scope of the book

> Privatization, through exposing former State-owned companies more fully to the disciplines and opportunities of the market ... improves the efficiency of businesses that are crucial to our overall economic performance. As such it forms an important part of the Government's overall strategy for long-term economic growth.
>
> Rt. Hon. Margaret Thatcher (1983)[1]

If any one policy distinguished the Thatcher government in Britain, it was privatization. Although it was canvassed earlier in the United States, by the early 1990s Britain had gone further in carrying it through. This is especially true of the state enterprises on which this book concentrates. Moreover, privatization would seem Britain's most visible ideological export. Like all ideologies, and indeed like the enthusiasm for nationalization against which it was a strong reaction, it captured many blocs of support. Its significance to the Thatcher government can be explained in purely political terms; and the forms it has taken were affected by issues of political tactics. Even so, privatization was meant to leave the bodies privatized more efficient than before. Greater economic efficiency was declared its overriding objective.

Sometimes in this book the word 'monopoly' is used in its common everyday sense of a large enterprise more or less dominating its market or markets; but underlying this is a more formal economic conception of natural and unnatural monopoly in which the first is justified by economies of scale and scope, while the second is not justified by their absence. (*Scale economies* are reductions in unit cost achieved through producing more of an output; *scope economies* are unit-cost reductions achieved through producing several outputs simultaneously.) While some privatized enterprises can be let loose upon a free market to be subject to its disciplines, the old public utilities, when privatized, need be no more under market disciplines as private monopolies than they were as public monopolies. To remedy this in Britain, ministerial control has been replaced by regulation. The form of this regulation has rightly been influenced by the successes and failures of regulation in the United States; but nationalization was preceded by regulation in Britain whose origins were prior to, and influenced, American regulation. Not only was this experience interesting in its own right but the relations that developed between the regulators, Parliament and the courts still have a relevance in Britain, and possibly in other countries with a parliamentary tradition, which the American regulatory system, based on the very different roles of Congress, the executive and the judiciary, cannot match. Therefore chapters 1 and 2 describe a forgotten series of episodes of English regulation from the early nineteenth century until the Second World War. They concentrate on railway regulation, because it repeatedly faced complicated political concerns and economic issues, and because its national problems are more relevant to current problems than are the regulatory problems of those Victorian and early-twentieth-century public utilities whose monopoly was local. This excursion into the past is worth the attention of those whose concern is with the present not only because there is much in that experience that is still relevant to the design of a modern regulatory system, but also because, outside the United States, more-recent experience which will help one conjecture how the new British system will operate is scarce. (The French have not privatized natural monopolies. So they have not needed a new system for their regulation.) Moreover, the relations that developed between regulators, Parliament and the courts still have a relevance in Britain, and possibly in other countries with a parliamentary tradition, which the American regulatory system, based on the very different roles of Congress, the executive and the judiciary, cannot match.

In the first period, discussed in chapter 1, Parliament attempted to be the regulator. In an influential speech to it in 1836, the entrepreneur, economist and MP James Morrison prefigured much of what is essential in the modern theory of natural monopoly. The first regulatory episode discussed is the creation and failure of Gladstone's 1844 Regulation of the Railways Act, which was a far-sighted attempt to write a workable and monitorable licence, as it would now be called, for a natural monopoly. (Gladstone was arguably the greatest British peacetime prime minister, judged by the qualities needed for the long-run well-being of a nation: the ability to govern, to devise and inspire mechanisms and structures which enable others to govern better, sheer administrative capacity and leadership.) In the second period (chapter 2) the courts and then special commissioners took over the same task. They also failed. These failures led to progressive financial and regulatory failure as regards the railways. Among the reasons for all these failures was that Parliament, the courts and the various regulatory institutions were used in ways which inevitably stopped them being effective. At a technical level, there was a failure to define regulatory offences appropriately and to demand relevant information or to understand the kind of jurisdiction a regulator needs in order to be effective. But also underlying these failures, and others of this kind, and largely responsible for them, were the activities of the industries concerned, which frustrated or captured regulation. Especially on the railways, the price paid for this was high in that the frustration of the customer boiled over and a regulatory regime was established that went to the other extreme and acted as a strait-jacket. And its regulatory failure, in turn, led inexorably – so it seemed to many contemporaries – to nationalization and, moreover, helped stop British public opinion accepting that an active government policy to promote competition throughout the economy could succeed or was worth while.

The difficulties of nationalization as a form of regulation originate in some of the reasons – market and regulatory failure, rather than ideological commitment – which explain the occurrence of nationalization in the first place. Unfortunately, the minister mainly responsible for the nationalization statutes, Herbert Morrison, was not a Gladstone. Neither did he have the understanding of natural monopoly that his Victorian namesake, James, had. The vague notions of public interest set up as the objectives of the nationalized industries, the breadth of the discretion given them and the indeterminacy of the relations between ministers and boards amounted to a major step backwards along the road from status to contract which is at the centre of the argument to be developed in this book. Chapter 3 examines why previous, less radical attempts to reform the control and regulation of public enterprise have failed. As do other chapters, it considers both political explanations and those grounded on a behavioural analysis of the interests concerned. Among the shortcomings of nationalization in practice was that, for reasons that seemed good at the time, little attention was given to specifying objectives, to monitoring their achievement or to the motives of the various parties concerned and therefore to the design of appropriate incentives. Nevertheless, until 1979 the political performance of the nationalized industries, despite grumblings, was generally acceptable to ministers.

Chapter 4 discusses the course of British privatization. During the 1980s it moved from being an ill-thought-out option with few backers and many formidable enemies to being a considered programme with widespread acceptance. This chapter considers the reasons why it was advocated, how it overcame initial fierce opposition and why it took the form it did. Besides transforming a substantial section of the economy, it was a political success, possibly changing the electoral balance between the parties. Where there was already competition, privatization was comparatively easy; but the Thatcher government was well aware of the importance of extending competition to the natural monopolies. In this it was generally and naturally resisted by the industries and once by the minister concerned. Nevertheless, the benefits of competition do support the case for allowing free entry into monopoly markets as long as it is realized that this may not be sufficient to achieve competition. Moreover, there is seldom a strong case for delaying the introduction of competition. Chapter 5 discusses the compromises reached and successes achieved. It argues that because economies of scale and scope can be important, break-up will not necessarily be efficient. But neither need growth, merger or acquisition be efficient: a key economic regulatory offence is that of *unnatural monopoly*, where a monopoly or dominant firm is not more efficient but only more profitable, because it can abuse its monopoly power. Moreover, while extending competition is undoubtedly the best form of regulation, until it is successfully achieved, and where it is not available or efficient, an effective regulatory system will be needed to prevent the abuse of monopoly power – for example to prevent a second key economic regulatory offence, *predation*, which is normally easier for large enterprises than for more-competitive firms. The chapter further argues that, since most natural monopolies are intrinsically such because they embody networks or grids, the most ambitious, and intellectually and technically the most demanding, endeavour has been interconnection, that is, creating competitive access to those networks. Here genuine economic progress has been made, though interconnection gives rise to a third key economic regulatory offence: *unfair* or *unequal access*. By comparison with interconnection, yardstick competition – that is, that creation of entities whose performance can be compared – though useful to regulators, is not a real extension of competition.

Chapter 6 is the first of several chapters on different aspects of the regulation of natural monopoly in so far as competition is absent. Besides analysing the issues concerned, they draw on American experience of regulation. Federal regulation in the United States started in 1887. Its form was derived from earlier British regulation. While in the years up to the Second World War it faced many of the same difficulties that British regulation did, it adapted to them better and survived. Chapter 6 starts with the economic paradox that the motive force behind the regulation of monopoly profits is normally envy, not a concern for efficiency. If efficiency were the only concern, and provided that free entry, enforced free-trading laws and the prospect of technical progress existed, natural-monopoly profits might be allowed to rise uncontrolled, to tempt others to enter those markets using whatever product differentiation and technical innovations they could. However, the political requirement to limit monopoly profits seems inescapable. Moreover, in most circumstances monopoly output is in fact less than efficient. While *excess monopoly profits* is the first social regulatory offence to be considered, two more economic regulatory offences are also discussed in this chapter: *allocative inefficiency*, which results from the failure to adopt marginal-cost pricing, and *organizational inefficiency*, which results from the failure to control costs even at the expense of lower profits. Both of these failures tend to occur in monopolies. The issue is whether a regulator can act so as to overcome those sources of inefficiency. To counter these offences of excess profits and inefficiency, American regulation has persisted with rate-of-return regulation, though some regulators in recent years have attempted to combine it with marginal-cost pricing. The new British practice is based instead on a particular form of price control, RPI–X. Economic theory suggests a profound difference between the two, but in practice they can converge. The reasons why US regulators were drawn into greater detail, and therefore longer and more expensive proceedings, to verify rate of return may come to apply to RPI–X. Nevertheless, there are reasons for believing that RPI–X can be kept in an effective form, especially if its procedures can be kept informal and profit envy can be curbed. If so, it should be superior to rate-of-return control, and other forms of profit and price control, as a stimulus to efficiency.

Chapter 7 turns to the neglected topic of regulatory information. While the giving of publicity to relevant information has often been seen as a main, and sometimes as the only, aim of economic regulation, it is argued that, even if there had not been other weaknesses, the persistent failure in Britain and America to require adequate information for regulation would have been enough to undermine its effectiveness, prolong its proceedings and lead to the regulated industry capturing the regulatory regime, as in general it has. Without the passage of sufficient appropriate information to the regulator, regulation cannot be effective. The information must be routine, regular and based on conventions acceptable to the regulator. Where there is monopoly, current cost accounts are desirable and in enough detail to reveal regulatory offences. There is also an economic case for providing actual and potential entrants into a monopoly market with such information. Moreover, it is argued that, as accounting has developed so far, it is only practical to regulate firms that have profit-making objectives, if economies of scale and scope are to be achieved. However, giving publicity to relevant information is unlikely to be sufficient to ensure that natural monopolies do not offend. Regulatory judgements should be enforceable and this implies the deterrent of material penalties, but in its turn this makes acute some issues of regulatory accountability.

The new British regulation, as has often been said, was intended to be regulation with a 'loose rein' (chapter 8). What is generally meant by this is that it should be unlegalistic. While there should be obvious advantages from this in the saving of time and money, it is worth trying to understand why American regulation became legalistic. Some of the reasons relate to American traditions in government, but there are enough other reasons for legalism to make a similar development in the UK not impossible. There are two main kinds of legalism. The first flows from giving the courts a role of review or appeal in regulation. The role of the US courts has always been different from that of the British courts and they have played an important part in shaping the form and, for a time, the substance of the US regulatory system. For constitutional reasons and from tradition, the UK courts are not able to play a similar role – from which they have also been barred by the relevant statutes. However, the European Commission and Court, and because of them the UK courts, could become more interventionist. Avoiding this kind of legalism matters because effective regulation requires the use of more discretion in reaching judgements than courts ordinarily allow. The second variety of legalism comes from any requirement that regulators adopt court-like procedures. While up to a point procedural fairness is sensible and right for meeting the requirements of natural justice, there are dangers – particularly of expense and regulatory capture – if regulators are forced to adopt court-like procedures. It is doubtful whether the regulators have yet found procedures which will ensure that they can protect their independence and discretion from either judicial or political interference.

Social aspects are found in any system of economic regulation. The fact of monopoly itself is likely to lead to requirements for universal service and the prohibition of price discrimination, both of which can be handled as constraints upon efficiency, but can also lead to serious muddle. There are many reasons why regulatory discretion extends economic into social regulation (chapter 9). While there is no logical or inherent reason why this should happen to economic regulation of a rate-of-return or an RPI–X type, the processes through which regulatory machinery is set up or modified encourage this, as may the ambitions of individual regulators. While it is understandable why other, non-economic criteria enter the design and operation of systems of economic regulation, this inevitably leads to an incoherence where it becomes progressively harder for a regulator to defend what he is doing without contradiction. Some forms of social regulation are best handled by imposing them as regulations, that is, as constraints imposed upon the industry and the regulator, as long as a role is left for economic efficiency in the formulation of those regulations. Others are probably best left to ministers, if damaging conflicts are to be avoided. Consumer committees can play an important part in offsetting the influence of the industry upon a regulator; but they may themselves lean towards political or social, rather than economic, judgements. However, a regulator may also have a role in helping strike an efficient balance between profitability and external factors like the environment and safety. A sixth economic regulatory offence then could be when firms consider only their own private interest where there is economic inefficiency caused by a divergence between social and private interests: *externality inefficiency*. In general, success is more likely if regulation can as far as possible be confined to economic issues and, within that category, to the few that are genuine. Much that passes for economic regulation is not that but based on openly avowed or disguised political or social values.

In asserting, as is done here, that the new British regulatory framework should be tested by how far it is likely to increase economic efficiency, one is fortified by several considerations. First, the need for regulation as discussed in this book arises because of an economic phenomenon, market failure. Market imperfections make it impossible for market forces to achieve an efficient allocation of resources. Thus it is natural to assume that regulation is intended to re-create as far as possible what market failure has destroyed (though it does not follow normatively from the fact of market failure that as far as possible regulation should reinstate what market forces would have achieved if they had been able to operate freely). Secondly, the question how far any regulatory system achieves, or damages, economic efficiency is always an important one (though economic efficiency need not be, indeed never is, the unique objective of a regulatory system). Thirdly, in Britain in the 1980s, ministerial statements on the objectives of regulation have defined them as economic and as tending to economic efficiency. (These statements do not, however, have statutory force and are not binding: the statutes provide for other objectives as well and give only indirect hints that economic efficiency is the paramount objective; and, even if they had indicated more clearly that regulation should be economic regulation, this belief would have remained a normative one.) Finally, as will be argued, the pursuit of non-economic objectives by a regulatory body may in many circumstances weaken its ability to serve the objectives of economic regulation and also be undemocratic.

Chapter 10 questions whether a change of ownership was essential to overcome the problems of British, and by extension other countries', public enterprise, and considers how far such problems could have been and can be overcome without such a change of ownership. In doing this it sets out a programme of public enterprise reform. Such an exercise may appear irrelevant when the privatization of public enterprise has progressed further with every passing year and may soon be almost complete, at least in Britain. However, there is an analytical and historical interest in trying to distinguish between what, in Britain, has resulted from privatization itself and what from associated measures which could have been taken without it. The repeated failures of British governments actively to address the problems of public enterprise which had been analysed by a succession of official committees and academic commentators, or to effect the remedies they had suggested, help to explain why public enterprise in the UK was so enfeebled by the end of the 1970s that it enjoyed little active support, but these failures do not show that the problems were insoluble without a change of ownership. Thus one can speculate whether there are circumstances in which the trend towards privatization could be reversed, or whether privatization as a revolutionary movement will not be followed by a restoration. A more practical reason for looking at public enterprise reform as an alternative to privatization is that there are many countries where governments are deciding whether to start, or how far to take, privatization. Rudimentary machinery for channelling domestic savings into privatized industry poses grave difficulties for the securing of inexperienced investors against risks which they do not know how to manage, or may involve foreign ownership to an extent which is not politically attractive. Management competence in the private sector may be low. Especially in less-developed countries therefore, how far public enterprise may be reformed without privatization is a significant issue. Moreover, many of the specific reforms which are entailed by a successful programme of public-enterprise reform are stages which a privatization must go through if it is to result in an economically efficient enterprise. The chapter argues that the difficulties with less elaborate public enterprise reform programmes are that they either concentrate on internal reforms which in the absence of competition will always lapse into organizational failure, or concentrate on external ones, in which case competition in particular may destroy the enterprise before it is strong enough to meet it. The chapter concludes that, if public enterprise is to be efficient in the future, it must be constructed and controlled on a new, very different basis. (It is ironical that Margaret Thatcher, who loathed public ownership, wished to diminish it and did so, may have provided an impetus for devising better forms of public ownership, though this has yet to be proved in practice.) It also analyses what is peculiar to privatization and can reasonably be judged to be achieved by it alone. It considers both the circumstances that favour fundamental public enterprise reform and those that favour substantial privatization. It concludes that in advanced economies the privatization of commercial public undertakings probably has the edge over even the most thorough-going public enterprise reform and that in less-developed countries the first is more likely than the second, though the economic case for either will be less in so far as not enough attention is given to establishing workable competition and regulation. Public enterprise is probably most worth keeping where non-commercial objectives apply; but formidable advances in management and accounting methods are needed before any such enterprise on a large scale can become as efficient as commercial enterprise.

In previous chapters many points have been made about the desirability of, and the difficulty of maintaining, regulatory independence. Chapter 11 asks if any generalization about this is possible. Regulation is generally but not exclusively intended to achieve ends which are those of economic efficiency. This is a normative proposition but, as many have noted, what happens is not always what is intended to happen. A theory is needed to explain what actually occurs. Several are discussed. The most often supported is that of regulatory capture, that is, the capture of the regulator by the industry he regulates. If that theory were universally valid, then economic regulation would be wasted effort, indeed counterproductive. However, there are theoretical reasons for doubting its universal validity, and actual circumstances in which it can be shown to be invalid. Although trying to explain the main episodes in which regulatory capture did not occur or was escaped leads into detailed historical explanations of unique events, some generalizations seem possible which may be helpful in the design of better regulatory systems. The chapter ends with some recommendations on how the new British system of regulation might be altered so as to make it easier to preserve a defensible regulatory independence.

Chapter 12 draws together points from earlier chapters which may be helpful for the design of a regulatory system against which the new British system may be assessed. On balance, it is argued, there are reasons for believing that the new British regulatory system has avoided some of the pitfalls of the past. Though there is a certain amount that was accidental in its construction, it deserves very substantial approval. The nature of the modern British Parliament, the terms of appointment of regulators and their background so far, the limited scope of judicial review and the entrenched position of the consumer's interest suggest that regulatory discretion may be used in the public interest, at least for a time. The new British system fares well by the principles that are set out here. Nevertheless, there are a number of ambiguities and weaknesses in its design which may speed its failure by opening loopholes though which the industries can begin capture. Some could be closed or at least made smaller. Others derive from the general requirements of an effective regulatory system – in particular the discretion that must be given to a regulator and which he must have the freedom to use, and abuse, though possibly within narrower limits – and ultimately cannot be corrected without causing more damage.

Chapter 12 is among those that make some remarks on the international relevance of the arguments of this book. The economic theory as such is of universal application while most of the political observations are likely to reflect the behaviour of elected and non-elected officials in many situations. But it is a theme of this book that the effectiveness of economic regulation will depend on the constitution in which it is embodied. Thus any generalizations for export must be tentative. Nevertheless, the British experience thus far can usefully add to the stock of experience from which other countries can learn. Because so many seem determined to privatize before they have decided how, or even whether, to regulate the resulting enterprises, privatization could become as inefficient an undertaking as nationalization has been. But if the regulation has been thought through and well designed, either privatization, or fundamental public enterprise reform, could represent substantial progress, with privatization having the edge in many, though not all, circumstances.

It has long been pointed out that the classical economists believed in *laissez-faire* rather than competition.[2] It was assumed that *laissez-faire* would lead to competition but this is not so where there is natural monopoly, against which, by assumption, deregulation is powerless. Where there is natural monopoly some competition may be achieved through the prevention of predation and through efficient interconnection; but there is always the rump of natural monopoly, in whatever that may consist – a network, an information system. Both in Adam Smith's time, and in the 1970s and 1980s, the movement for deregulation was intended to, and did, dissolve legal monopolies and other protective devices, but it revealed natural monopoly as impervious to *laissez-faire*. At the heart of the economic theory of value, there is a contradiction:

> In the tranquil view which the modern theory of value presents to us there is one dark spot which disturbs the harmony of the whole. This is represented by the supply curve based upon the laws of increasing and diminishing returns. [If there are increasing returns to scale, that is, falling costs,] consideration of that greater internal division of labour which is rendered possible by an increase in the dimensions of an individual firm is entirely abandoned, as it is seen to be incompatible with competitive conditions.[3]

Thus in 1926 Piero Sraffa pointed to the fundamental inconsistency between the description of the economic world as one in which *laissez-faire* allows economic progress and prosperity to result from competition and the possibility of its invasion, and even destruction, by the limitless aggrandizement of individual firms which, as Sir John Hicks, a Nobel Prize winner, said, undermines economics: 'The threatened wreckage is that of the greater part of economic theory.'[4] How the economy is divided between competition and monopoly is another empirical question. All that one can be sure of is that businessmen will do whatever they can to enlarge their firms and take advantage of every available element of natural monopoly to deter competition. On balance, the regulation of natural monopoly is needed, provided that it can be delivered efficiently enough for its benefits to exceed its costs.

If natural-monopoly profits or prices are to be regulated, can this be confined to a relatively small part of the economy while market forces control profits or prices elsewhere? It is tempting to believe that it can, because much the same few industries recur historically on the roll of natural monopolies: roads, canals, railways, gas and electricity, with telecommunications and airports as more recent entrants. What makes them natural monopolies is that they all comprise networks (or grids) – or are part of one, that is, are nodes, like airports.[5] Their priority on the ground gives them first-mover advantages over potential competitors. These networks and nodes require substantial investment, which results in a barrier to entry, often reinforced by laws which for environmental or other reasons increase the cost of any parallel network or alternative nodes that potential competitors might consider creating and, reinforced by their monopoly status, demand for them is inelastic. However, because technological development may reduce the scale of investment in the network as a barrier to entry, this dominance may not be lasting, as in telecommunications. And there may be a similar erosion of monopoly power, over large users at least, in electricity and gas through bypass. While in other respects all of these industries may be expected to remain natural monopolies, and therefore to require profits or prices limitation if they are in the private sector, together they constitute a generally declining, though still important, proportion of the economy.

However, this may be too simple a story on which to base a prophesy. Adam Smith wrote that, 'the mean rapacity, the monopolizing spirit of merchants and manufacturers, who neither are, nor ought to be the rulers of mankind, though it cannot perhaps be corrected, may very easily be prevented from disturbing the tranquillity of any body but themselves.'[6] In what follows this passage he makes it clear that this is to be done by abolishing legal monopolies, protective tariffs and other obstacles to trade. But it must be doubtful whether even then, when the most efficient scale of operations was so much smaller, this would have resulted in competition in every occupation in every village and market town. More important in creating competition were the various transport revolutions which increased the extent of the markets for goods and services. And no transport revolutions have been more dramatic than those which have cut the costs of maritime transport and road haulage in the last forty years, making it possible in some industries to serve the world from a single factory.

But as falling transport costs have increased the extent of markets, so have economies of scale and scope reduced the number of firms that operate in many of them. As the discussion of scale and scope economies in chapter 5 indicates, there is no necessary technical limit to the size of the firm. In recent years great progress has been made in many industries in enabling a single management to control ever larger firms, largely through the development of better systems for production and distribution. The race will be won by those firms which make most progress in management techniques so as to best coordinate their activities and their service to customers.[7] Multinational operation confers great advantages in enabling firms to hedge supply-side risks, protecting themselves, for example, against changes in labour conditions and taxation. International trade cushions firms against downturns in particular national markets. Firms which rely heavily on research and development, and which therefore need to recover these costs before other products make their own obsolescent, in particular benefit from being able to sell simultaneously in all advanced markets.

Certain industries are already dominated internationally by a small number of very large firms. Because the rewards of size and scope are high in some kinds of industries, more industries can be expected to go the same way. However, even if there is only a handful of firms in an industry, there may still be competition. For any to become natural monopolies there must be obstacles to entry that even similar sized firms find it hard to surmount.

Those industries which look most like providing additions to the roll of natural monopolies are the information-based industries. In some cases, systems architecture may provide the means.[8] IBM has at times devised a systems architecture which has deterred competitors and, in so far as other firms have been able to produce IBM-compatible equipment or programmes, it has maintained a comparative advantage in this way. This is an example of an interconnection problem where regulation is needed – internationally as well as nationally – in order to achieve equal access. Another kind of natural monopoly is based on heavy investment in information and systems which access it. Currently, the most conspicuous examples are the world-wide reservation systems, which only a few airlines have set up, and where there is as much danger of wasted investment if more airlines try to match them as there was when in the nineteenth century new railways were located near old ones in a dense network. Such systems may be extended to hotels, theatres and other leisure facilities. Regulation will be needed in order to provide equal access to information on those hotels, airlines and other facilities that do not belong to the groups that own the information system natural monopoly. One can speculate that information systems may be developed to provide natural-monopoly advantages for other service industries as well.

All this implies that the regulation of natural monopoly as discussed here and in chapter 12 may have a relevance beyond the traditional natural monopolies. Moreover, there will be advantages, in international cooperation between regulators not only in exchanging information and experience but in the joint regulation of international operations with natural-monopoly characteristics.

Let me conclude this introduction with two remarks mainly intended for fellow economists. The notion that successful privatization should improve economic efficiency leads to a corresponding conception of what constitutes an economic regulatory offence. Laws and lawyers define economic regulatory offences in many ways: such an offence is whatever is defined to be one in an appropriate legal instrument. But as an economist I am defining an economic regulatory offence as conduct (which may or may not be deliberate) which prevents or is likely to prevent the realization of economic efficiency. Such conduct reflects one or more aspects of the failure of markets to work perfectly so as to result spontaneously, and more or less continuously, in economic efficiency, both allocative and organizational.[9] By 'economic efficiency' is meant what economists call Paretian economic efficiency, that is, a state of the economy in which no reallocation of resources could make any one better off without making someone else worse off. Such offences as predation, growing or creating an unnatural monopoly and unequal access are likely to prevent the realization of economic efficiency so defined. Inevitably, legal instruments drawn up by those whose habits of thought are different will use words that reflect such economic offences with different degrees of adequacy. Given the ways in which legislatures expect to see words used, one never finds such regulatory offences defined with the precision an economist would prefer; but this may not matter provided that the terms used can be construed to have an economic meaning and that the judge or regulator who interprets the law wants to give them such a meaning. Moreover, from personal experience I have learnt that what seems precise to an economist often seems hopelessly imprecise to a lawyer.[10]

To an economist, laws also often seem to confuse economic and other regulatory offences. I have already said how I am using the term 'economic regulatory offence'. By 'pseudo-economic regulatory offence', I mean one that cannot be analysed as an economic regulatory offence but purports to be one. For example, it is common to consider it such an offence if firms are too large or have too great a market share. By 'social regulatory offence' I mean one which economic regulators are required to consider but which does not even purport to be economic. In general, keeping the law in these respects will lead to a reduction in economic efficiency by comparison with not keeping it, which may or may not be material. 'Excessive' profitability is often regarded as such a social offence, as are undue discrimination and the refusal to provide universal service where it is reasonable to require it. Economic regulation is defined here as regulation which aims at economic efficiency without regard to income distribution, but in practice the apparatus of economic regulation issued to meet distributional objectives. A concern of the economist is how such social objectives may be realized with the least adverse effect on economic efficiency.

The second remark I would make mainly to fellow economists is that what follows is full of hypotheses which ideally one would wish to test by econometric or cliometric methods. In many cases I am sure the data do not exist for this. In others they may well exist, but I do not have them. So the argument is forced back on economic and historical judgements. Thus I am aware that the conclusions I reach rest on experience, *a priori* reasoning and judgement rather than proof. Nevertheless, I offer them as a contribution to the understanding and resolution of the problem of the control of natural monopoly, a problem which, on balance, is not likely anywhere to diminish in importance.

Notes

1 Quoted by Harris (1988), p. 187. He has called privatization 'Mrs Thatcher's lasting social transformation': ibid., p. 189.
2 L. Robbins (1952); Taylor (1972).
3 Sraffa (1926), quoted by Shackle (1967), pp. 13–70, in his superb celebration of the great period of the Cambridge school in which a leading theme is their handling of this difficulty.
4 Hicks (1939), p. 84, quoted in Shackle (1968), p. 10.
5 Aviation can be regarded as a network in which airports are the nodes. Airports will be natural monopolies only if they are prevented from growing to meet demand, usually for environmental reasons. As a result such airports are weak natural monopolies (chapter 5 below). There may be air-traffic constraints also on links in the network. Pigou (1920), p. 252, said that public authorities' attitude to eminent domain was a cause of monopoly.
6 Adam Smith (1802), bk. 4, ch. 3.
7 Chandler (1977), pp. 320–39.

8   The non-spatial nature of information monopolies makes international agreement on their control important. It is also hard to achieve. See DTI (1990), pp. 17, 21, 73, 74.

9   See, for example, Bator (1958).

10 Personal experience in the 1960s showed me that parliamentary draftsmen do not regard as meaningful any duties for anyone to maximize something, because their observance or breach cannot be tested.

Part 1

Historical development

1

Regulation by Parliament

It was said, let matters . . . be allowed to go on as at present, and let the country trust to the effects of competition. Now, for his part, he [Gladstone] would rather give his confidence to a Gracchus, when speaking on the subject of sedition, than give his confidence to a Railway Director, when speaking to the public of the effects of competition.

Rt. Hon. William Gladstone (1844)[1]

That Britain before nationalization had more than 100 years of economic regulation of natural monopoly is now almost forgotten. That period divides into two phases – one in which Parliament tried to regulate, with growing intervention from the courts, and a second from the 1870s in which the regulatory commission became the main instrument. It is worth considering, through looking again at those episodes, whether we have learnt enough to avoid the mistakes of the past: this is the purpose of these first two chapters.[2]

1.1 The railways as a natural monopoly

Most enterprises which are recognized as natural monopolies now were already regulated in the period we are concerned with – toll roads and canals from the eighteenth century, water from the beginning of the nineteenth century, railways a little later, gas, electricity and telephony from soon after their commercial exploitation.[3]

In the eighteenth and nineteenth centuries the sovereignty of Parliament was almost defined by its ability at any time to pass any legislation on any domestic topic it pleased without much regard to consistency. Until late in the nineteenth century there were more private bills than government bills. Almost all of these were only of interest to their promoters and, sometimes, opponents. Many were put forward by local authorities. MPs had to be secured through local or other interests to get a sufficient majority for a bill to pass.[4]

A large number of these bills were for the provision of public works. Roads, ports and later canals were the commonest in the eighteenth century. Their construction or substantial modification needed an act, if only because what was proposed required the compulsory acquisition of land either permanently or in order to lay pipes. Similar private laws were needed in the nineteenth century for waterworks, gas works and later electricity generation because laying pipes and wires required street works and wayleaves. As a matter of contingent fact, not necessity, these monopolies all needed such powers and therefore needed legislation. (Broadcasting would later be an example of a natural monopoly of which this was not true.)

The private acts fulfilled an important purpose beyond that ordinarily associated with legislation. They defined the terms on which the entity in question was to come into being and operate. They were regarded by contemporaries as contracts defining private property rights. Indeed, they were referred to sometimes as 'parliamentary contracts'. They came to be regarded as immune from any later attempts at retrospective legislation. As we shall see, until the 1880s this vital principle of legislative practice was regarded as sacrosanct by almost all MPs. It was well put in 1870 by an MP who was also a leading railway director:

> The railway companies had obtained their Acts subject to certain conditions which had been well considered with a view to the protection both of public and private interests. The bargain had been made: Parliament had already sealed its conditions, and shareholders had invested their money under them, and it would not now be right to impose additional liabilities upon them.[5]

Though in principle each of these private acts could have been drafted with formal provisions entirely different from those of every other such act, in practice there was an altogether understandable tendency for each bill to take as its model an earlier act with a similar purpose. But Parliament strongly resisted attempts to make it commit itself to any definite uniformity in such legislation. It was towards the middle of the nineteenth century before there were real attempts to legislate for common clauses in a class of such bills; and even then their effect was restricted and sometimes overridden.[6] It was three-quarters of the way through the century before the volume of legislation and the growing absorption of parliamentary time by foreign and imperial affairs persuaded it to pass legislation which meant, for example, that not every new gas works and electricity generating plant required a separate act (though every railway development did until 1992). To help explain this, one must remember that the promotion of private bills had become a thriving industry for MPs, as well as lawyers, engineers and others who clustered along Victoria Street.

Given that every bill was discussed by a specially appointed committee likely to be favourable to it, it is perhaps remarkable that some clauses against the obvious interests of its promoters were commonly found. For example, all toll road acts were for a limited term, normally twenty-one years, at the end of which another act would be needed. A twenty-one-year franchise, or one for a longer, though still limited, period, was a common feature of canal, gas, water and electricity acts, though not of railway acts. A provision that dividends be limited to a specified maximum, often 10 per cent, was another.[7]

The omission of a limited-term clause from railway statutes seems to have had two main causes: acceptance of the argument that the risks and extent of the investment needed could not reasonably be expected to be recouped in the customary twenty-one years; and the belief that there would be sufficient competition between trains belonging to different owners on the same route for there not to be the same opportunity for making monopoly profits as on turnpike roads. Both expectations proved wrong. The omission of any review period in the original legislation was to prove a fatal error.

Parliamentary freedom to pass any such act meant that promoters could, and frequently did, succeed in having an act passed to build a waterworks or gas works close to an existing one. The almost inevitable result was a price war which ended with one works buying out the other and putting prices up to earn a satisfactory return on what was then probably an inflated capital stock. As will be considered later, customers tried various, mostly ineffectual, ways of countering this.[8]

Parliament was not helped by the classical political economists in their understanding of these monopolies. Adam Smith argued for the dismantling both of artificial monopolies, that is, monopolies created by law, and of other forms of protection, as part of his general thesis advocating *laissez-faire* to promote economic wealth. He accepted the possibility of natural monopoly but did not stress its importance or analyse its causes. When he came to consider bridges, canals, ports, roads and other public works, he saw that in many, but not in all, cases it should be possible to raise enough revenue from their operation to defray the costs of their provision and maintenance, but that there were dangers that either national governments or private promoters might increase charges beyond what was thus needful and use the excess profits for other purposes. Yet he did not claim a precise solution, saying, of toll roads in particular, merely that,

> If mean and improper persons are frequently appointed trustees; and if proper courts of inspection and account have not yet been established for controuling their conduct, and for reducing the tolls to what is barely sufficient for executing the work to be done by them; the recency of the institution both accounts and apologizes for those defects, of which, by the wisdom of parliament, the greater part may in due time be gradually remedied.[9]

One can deduce that he was among those who looked for discretionary rather than mechanistic regulation, but not much more. Neither he nor Ricardo nor, in the next generation, Bailey, Nassau Senior or McCulloch analysed the problems of local or natural monopoly in a way which illuminated why they were impervious to the beneficial effects of competition. Indeed, in his *Principles* Ricardo did not consider public works, so that he was unable to apply his views on taxation to them as he did to land, mines and private commodities yielding monopoly profits. If he had, the logic of his views would have reinforced the views of those who believed that taxing such profits would deter and distort investment. Even without such an analysis, the building of the Liverpool and Manchester railway was widely seen rather as an example of how technical innovation would sooner or later reduce monopoly profits than as itself the creation of monopoly: for a strong incentive to its shareholders was the knowledge that the Duke of Bridgewater's canal, and other canals collaborating with it, had a virtual monopoly in carrying goods between the two cities and were earning high monopoly returns.[10] McCulloch supported the case for dividend limitation on local monopolies, recognizing, but not analysing, their adverse effects on economic efficiency. John Stuart Mill in 1848 made a clearer distinction between artificial or legal monopoly and natural monopoly. The first was created by the government and the law; its abolition was what the classical political economists believed was essential to stimulate the creation of wealth. But even though that defines natural monopoly to be monopoly which exists irrespective of the promptings of the State and the law, he produced no satisfactory theoretical explanation of it.[11]

Although the problem of how to regulate local monopoly utilities was important in the nineteenth century, the regulation of railways raised the more fundamental issues. Railways were the focus of attention because of their unique importance to the Victorian economy. They of all natural monopolies presented, and arguably still present, the most intractable problems and provoked the most thought and public discussion. Therefore this chapter will concentrate on that experience.

To borrow a term from the 1970s and 1980s, the early nineteenth century was a time of deregulation.[12] That began even before Adam Smith in his *Wealth of Nations* in 1776 sought to persuade educated opinion of the advantages that would result from ending government-made monopolies, tariffs and other forms of economic protection. In the 1820s deregulation accelerated, especially through the inspiration of William Huskisson when President of the Board of Trade until he was run over and killed by a train on the opening day of the Liverpool and Manchester railway, perhaps a unique event in the history of ministerial openings. Nevertheless, after his death pressures for deregulation continued, culminating in the repeal of the Corn Laws in 1846, the debates leading up to which overshadowed the main episode to be discussed in this chapter. That a strong movement for deregulation could coincide, even in the same minds, with a wish to regulate the railways may seem paradoxical; but that would be a superficial conclusion.

1.2 Parliament as railway regulator: its general unsuitability

In the absence of a wide-ranging parliamentary act, such as Gladstone's 1844 Act (considered in the next section), that could serve as a workable basis for the general regulation by Parliament of the railways (even if, because of the aversion to retrospective regulation, only of railways constituted after the passing of such an act), their regulation was, as we have seen, based on the individual acts of Parliament that constituted the governing statutes of each railway. There were a number of factors that rendered this an unsound basis for railway regulation, most deriving largely from the disparate, committee-influenced structure of the process by which such statutes were enacted.

First, there was the regulatory autarky of the committee vetting of the railway bills. As noted above, every such bill went to a committee of the House. And each committee was selected separately, and was jealous of its right to decide exactly what went into each bill. This did not conduce to regulatory coherence and generality. As Gladstone's select committee noted in 1844, 'It is almost impossible to hope that from the separate and unconnected proceedings of bodies whose existence commences and terminates with . . . each particular railway bill, that there should issue any distinct system of sound general rules, uniform in their foundation and varying . . . in a strict and constant proportion to the actual peculiarities of the case.'[13]

Secondly, when a railway bill became law, whatever had been said in committee about the meaning of, or intention behind, the Act's provisions was irrelevant. Enforcement was only possible through the courts, and judges were not expected to exercise any discretion in their interpretation of the law. There was in the United Kingdom no tradition of judicial review by which judges could interpret the meaning of acts to ensure their consistency equivalent to that which was important for the development of regulation in the United States. Frequently, judges overruled the committee's interpretation of the intention behind a provision.[14] One law had to be changed by another.

Thirdly, there was a self-protective tendency for the autonomy of the committees to lead to a disinclination on the part of their members to listen to or take the regulatory advice of informed officials. At various times committees on railway bills were advised by Board of Trade officials or commissioners. The statistics they provided were influential. But otherwise, except on safety, they often complained that not only was their advice ignored but the opposite course of action to the one that they had recommended was taken. It is plain that MPs resented the intervention of such officials and their advice. MPs' intense dislike of being guided by officials meant that even when there was in existence a high-powered board of commissioners, as there was for a year in 1845 (chaired by the Earl of Dalhousie, who went on to become President of the Board of Trade), they would often not be guided by them towards the introduction into railway bills of standard procedures (in accounting, for example) or provisions requiring adequate and accurate information.[15] The result was an utter lack of consistency.[16] Because in these early years Parliament repeatedly resisted any lasting appointment of railway commissioners with status and power, no expert body with experience emerged until the 1880s to counter the expertise of the railway companies or to provide continuous advice and supervision.[17]

Finally, and perhaps most important, the strength of the railway lobby in Parliament and in particular in the committees on the railway bills undermined their ability to decide each bill on its merits. In 1845, at least 157 MPs were substantial railway stockholders. And in 1854, 81 MPs were directors of railways, a figure rising to a maximum of 132 in 1873 – though there were still almost 50 such MPs at the outbreak of the First World War. But, besides these, there were always many more MPs who were strongly influenced to favour the railway interest whether by their being railway stockholders or for some other reason.[18] While more-disinterested members were usually in a majority on the floor of the House and certainly often had the best of the argument, sitting on a bill or select committee was a time-consuming business, so that all too frequently the majority of those on a railway committee had, and often shamelessly deployed, a railway interest, since they had the incentive to endure its tedium.[19] Thus, through their friends on committees and through the extensive teams they employed to present bills to those committees, the railways managed to avoid any process that would control their monopoly effectively.

1.3 Monopoly policy: Gladstone's Regulation of the Railways Act, 1844

In the House of Commons in 1836 – apparently without a lead from any contemporary or earlier economist – James Morrison made a speech on the control of railways which would have been remarkable at any time, but which was extraordinarily perceptive then. It was only eleven years after the Stockton and Darlington railway opened, six years after the start of the first regular steam service (between Liverpool and Manchester) and two years before it was possible to travel by train between

London and Manchester.[20] Nevertheless, there had already been a railway construction boom in the 1830s, and most contemporaries saw railways as transforming communications irreversibly. One thousand miles of line had been built, or less than 4 per cent of the lines that were to exist in 1914 and of course a much lower percentage of the track.[21] The form of regulation was determined from the start by precedent. Like toll roads and canals, each new railway line or extension had to come to Parliament for its own bill because it needed the authority of Parliament to acquire land and execute works.

Morrison was a wealthy self-made draper.[22] Like almost all his fellow MPs in this debate he welcomed the railways which were already lowering the costs of goods, as a powerful force for economic development. It was natural, he said, to see them as roads. (Indeed, the heading of the *Hansard* pages in which his speech is recorded is 'Railroads' when a few years later it would have been 'Railways'.)[23] Instead of a road surface there were rails along which any cart or carriage could move provided it had the right width axle and flanged wheels. Perfect liberty of travel had always existed on roads. Where they were toll roads, 'whoever paid the tolls was at liberty to use them.'[24] In each turnpike act maximum tolls were set which were related to the need to pay the debt incurred. By example, it was unsurprising that the regulatory provision customarily found in the early railway acts was one fixing maximum tolls as in the turnpike acts. Although it was then still known, and would remain so until 1859, for persons and carriers to run their own vehicles on the rails and to provide their own locomotion, it quickly became normal for the railway companies to run their own trains. More to the point, there was nothing in the railway acts preventing companies from contriving a monopoly in this respect through discriminatory charging and service policies, as some of them were already starting to do. Morrison went on to point out that the acts in effect conferred a monopoly. Given that the first railway between two places will choose the most favourable route, 'no company that may be formed at any future time for making . . . a new railway between the same places, could come into the field under equally favourable circumstances.'[25] Moreover, it would be deterred by 'the vast amount of capital required'. Even that was not the end of it.

> [F]or, first, the existing company is in possession of the best line; and, second, were it seriously intended to form a rival establishment, the original company would seek to deter them by reducing their charges; and if, as is probable, they succeeded in this way in getting rid of the threatened competition, they might again raise their charges to the continued injury of the public.[26]

And if despite this a rival entered, 'would not the obvious interests of both parties . . . inevitably bring about some understanding between them . . .?'

Morrison went on to consider what might be done. All future railway acts should, he suggested, have a clause in them allowing Parliament to revise maximum rates.[27] He saw this as necessary for three reasons. First, in the early years there would be doubts over the traffic levels that might be established, but as these rose so profits would increase because most costs were fixed. Secondly, he argued that the cotton trade had been transformed by the cheapening of transport brought about by canals. He imagined similarly that the cheapening of transport caused by the railways would also induce new industries and trade, so raising revenues more than costs. Thirdly, there had already been several changes in railway technology and he supposed there would be more, which would also lower costs. For these reasons, current maximum levels would prove too high even if they had not been, as he supposed, too high from the start. Because of growth in demand, a statutory limitation on rates, as had long been practised on toll roads, was therefore useless.[28] Wiser than McCulloch, he further saw that the limitation of dividends would also be 'ineffectual'.[29] 'The public has no check on the system of management, nor can it explore the thousand channels in which profits may be distributed under other names among the subscribers, nor has it any means of preventing the wanton and extravagant outlay of money on the works, &c.'[30] Thus, like Adam Smith before him, he believed that judgement and discretion periodically exercised were needed to decide what charges were right for each monopoly. His preference was that commissioners should be appointed to oversee the situation, because they could acquire the necessary knowledge and use it with discretion, but he did not press for this, admitting that it would not be politically acceptable at a time when there had been a rash of commissioners – of whom the most famous or infamous were the Poor Law Commissioners – to whom Parliament had been most reluctant to delegate its authority. Instead, he suggested that in each new bill authorizing a railway or an amalgamation, Parliament should reserve to itself the right to review rates periodically. To reserve such a right at this initial stage was important because otherwise shareholders could later complain that any such rates review was an invasion of their property rights because they had not been forewarned of this when they had subscribed to railway shares. He cited the twenty-one-year reviews of the turnpike acts as precedents. However, he did not advocate the railways' becoming national property, as had happened in some European countries for the purposes of development and control, since he saw no intrinsic advantage and strong opposition to it.

His was a remarkable performance. He had the essentials of the problem of natural monopoly in a nutshell. He saw that geography and the need to get a bill and raise substantial capital were what we would now call barriers to entry; that an incumbent railway could engage in what we would now call predatory pricing and in other anti-competitive practices in order to keep or drive rivals out; and that, if that did not work, there would no doubt be a collusive outcome. He predicted that statutory maxima would not work where there was rising demand, economies of scale and technical progress; and that rate-of-return control would be met by the inflation of management costs, stock watering and over-investment. The right answer was to appoint independent commissioners who would have the statutory right and sufficient knowledge to review railway rates periodically. They would do this with discretion, their conclusions on rates depending on the current and forecast circumstances of each railway. And in doing so they should leave enough profit increase with the shareholder not to discourage improvements in efficiency. But he compromised with practicality by suggesting that it might be acceptable if such reviews were undertaken by Parliament, a disastrous weakening of his proposed regulatory regime. Commissioners might have had more hope of success if they had been appointed then and maintained permanently.

By 1844 when William Ewart Gladstone as President of the Board of Trade proposed that the issues be referred to a select committee, while some regulation of safety had been achieved meanwhile, none of Morrison's ideas had been implemented. In making this proposal, Gladstone pointed out that there were already about 2,000 miles of railway.[31] Now the House had a surge of bills in front of it for separate consideration. If all passed, approval of an increase in mileage of about 50 per cent would go through in one session. He believed that conferring so many monopolies required that there should be the prospect of an equivalent advantage to the public. He therefore wished to give the Board of Trade some overall supervisory power so that it could make 'general rules' which would be in such a form that every single private railway bill in future would be passed with its promoters knowing that Parliament had reserved the right to pass future legislation which might alter the profitability of the original investment. He noted that several of the bills before Parliament were for amalgamating existing lines, and that although in 1844 there was a sudden leap in the number of amalgamations proposed several had already happened and had resulted in rate increases. Allowing competition between lines would, he thought, in most cases mean an increase of the evil and turn out to be a mere multiplication of monopoly; for such were the facilities of the union between these large railway companies that competition would lead to amalgamation, such a small number making 'arrangements between rival lines easy of accomplishment'.[32] And then in a manner often to be imitated, he turned from an economic to a social point: should not the poor be protected from the weather, should not their trains achieve a minimum of comfort and punctuality? As so often in the future, economic regulation was entangled with social regulation: it will be a leading theme of this book that this has resulted generally in confusion and inefficiency.

Gladstone prepared for his bill by chairing the select committee that was set up, which examined many witnesses, chiefly from the railways. He began by requiring that the railways should treat their poorer passengers better; but, opposed on this by the railways, he broadened the draft bill out to provide a regulatory framework. In its first report the Committee tried to establish the principle that each new railway bill should contain a clause making the railway in question not exempt from subsequent general railway legislation.[33] The Second Report recommended that all bills should go to a single committee, which should be composed of members who should declare they had no local interest or personal interest in the matter at hand. Both reports were rushed forward because of the Committee's realization that too many bills had already been passed in a form which not only made no mention of the liability to such subsequent legislation, a profound difficulty at a time when the rights of private property were strictly interpreted to disallow retrospective legislation,[34] but also bore the mark of whoever had composed the committee they had passed, resulting in great inconsistency between acts. However, neither recommendation was reflected in legislation, because of the objections of the railway interest, which was already strongly represented in Parliament.

The Third Report was much longer and in effect endorsed many of James Morrison's recommendations of eight years before. It also came up with a novel recommendation which is enshrined in many books on Victorian history as an aberrant nationalization proposal in that *laissez-faire* age. But as reflected in the first draft of the Bill it was more subtle than that suggests. The proposal was

> That whatever may be the rate of divisible profits in any such Railway, it will be lawful ... at any time after the expiration of the ... term of the fifteen years [from the

passing of the Act] to purchase any such Railway with all its hereditaments, stock and appurtenances, in the name and behalf of Her Majesty . . . and upon payment of a sum equal to twenty five year's purchase, of the said annual divisible Profits estimated on the average of the three next preceding Years; provided always that if the average rate of profit for the said three Years exceed the rate of Ten Pounds in the Hundred, it shall be taken at only Ten Pounds in the Hundred . . . or secondly [if the divisible profits are at 10 per cent or over] to revise the fares and charges on the line in such a manner as shall, in the judgement of the Government, be calculated to reduce the said divisible profits, assuming always the same quantity and kinds of annual traffic to continue, to the said percentage: but with a guarantee on the part of the Government to subsist while such scales of forces and charges shall be in force, to make up the divisible profits to the said percentage.[35]

After the Committee had completed all its reports, Gladstone then introduced a railways bill which was in its essentials as enacted the avowed forerunner of the US Interstate Commerce Act, 1887, which was itself the model for subsequent American regulatory statutes as well as for others elsewhere in the English-speaking world.[36] Thus, many of its provisions were of seminal importance. The original bill was specific on the purchase basis proposed, and even on the accounting detail required, though purchase had to wait until fifteen years had passed. It was some of its detailed provisions for purchase that were the cleverest: the Board of Trade in settling the purchase price might claim a deduction for mismanagement and also to make good the railway and the stock so far as they were not in good repair; a railway company was not to increase its capital without Board of Trade agreement, preventing it from avoiding rate revision or purchase through stock watering or over-investment.

There was an unruly opening to the debate in which the railway MPs used many procedural devices to try to block discussion of the Bill. That led to an outburst by Gladstone against all the attempts that had been made to pack his committee with MPs favourable to the railway interest and against the self-interestedness of the objections then being made. After this stormy start, however, the debate, to which many well-known politicians contributed, settled down to a first-rate discussion of the issues. The essential idea of the Bill was ingenious. It was not nationalization; it was a way of dealing with what scholars would now describe as a gaming problem.[37] The point of the provisions was that railways would be caught not knowing which way Parliament would decide to move at the expiry of the fifteen-year period – to purchase or, if 'divisible profits' were not under 10 per cent, to review rates – and so would be induced to declare honest profits of about 10 per cent. The Prime Minister, Sir Robert Peel, declared that the Government could not simply commit itself to nationalization through buy-out, because 'there might be a temptation on behalf of the Railway Companies to swell the amount of divisible profits' in the three years preceding purchase. Therefore, in order to limit any eventual purchase price, profits above a maximum of 10 per cent would not be reflected in such a price.[38] And in addition there was provision that, as an alternative to purchase, if a railway had earned divisible profits of 10 per cent or more in the previous three years, its fares and charges could on review be justifiably reduced – though, as a safeguard against Parliament's setting rates after its review so as to limit divisible profits below 10 per cent,[39] the Exchequer would have to agree to make up such profits to 10 per cent if as a result they fell below that figure. However, as Henry Labouchere pointed out, one still had to have the threat of public ownership. Otherwise, in order to avoid the possibility of a downward revision of fares and charges, railways would have good reason to manipulate their reported costs to keep their declared profits artificially low.[40] He himself believed that rate review was the more likely outcome, though if there were government purchase, the right course, he believed, would be for the Government thereafter to grant twenty-one-year leases to private persons, at the expiry of which further review or the reassignment of those leases would take place, when again the profitability of the monopoly would be considered and any appropriate corrective action taken on rates. Gladstone's own view, privately expressed in 1865, was that he was in favour of buying up the railways and leasing them for short terms 'under stringent conditions'. He said that 'they had too much influence, the present companies, they were becoming a power in the state: and the waste of means by delay and diversion of traffic was intolerable.'[41] He was then sure that he could not only use the 1844 Act to assess whether railways were reasonably profitable and adjust their financial regime accordingly, but also roll this possibility of revision into the future in a succession of leases.

In principle, a periodic review of railway profitability on such a basis could be extremely effective. It is the same in principle as the idea in current British regulation that X in the RPI–X price-control formula should be reviewed periodically and altered to provide for a reasonable profitability over the next period, given experience of the past period and the best possible forecast of what is likely to happen in the next period. Added was a cunning incentive to the railways to declare their profits honestly.

It was well understood by several of the speakers in the debate that in the early years of a railway, profitability was likely to be low. There were usually capital-cost overruns and it would not be unreasonable for a railway thereafter to enjoy some years of high profitability, if it could manage it, before reining profits back to the permissible maximum. This key notion was widely accepted. In an earlier debate, the Radical MP James Roebuck had gone further and suggested what modern accountants would recognize as a 'modern equivalent asset' basis for asset evaluation and therefore what economists would see to be a 'long-run marginal cost' basis for pricing. He noted that, largely because of high capital costs and excessive land purchase prices, construction costs per mile were several times the level experienced in Germany or Belgium. He said he would not be at all surprised if technical progress did not bring these costs down from a current £60,000 per mile average to one of about £2,000 per mile. '[T]he public ought not, under such circumstances, to be called upon to pay the larger sum for practically the same accommodation which the smaller outlay would realise.'[42] Therefore, the allowable rate of return should be calculated in relation to construction and operating costs current at the time of the review, not historic costs.

Overall the standard of debate on the Bill and level of economic understanding shown were high, but they were higher among the majority who spoke for the Bill than among its opponents, most of whom seemed embarrassed by their evident connection with the railway interests. Nevertheless, some of what was said in opposition to the Bill was interesting and even far-sighted. The first opposition speaker, J. Entwistle, made a theoretical objection to any limitation of railway profits, arguing that it would distort investment incentives between one railway and another, if its profits were limited and the other's profits were not – an argument used repeatedly by right-wing economists in their objections to regulatory control of natural monopoly and recently by right-wing economists of the Chicago school. In its essentials it is, as we shall see, Littlechild's argument against altering the value of X in RPI–X, once it has been fixed. A more practical objection was that by Lord Seymour, one of the MPs close to the railway interest, who said, perceptively and prophetically, during the debate that as the Bill stood it would be possible for some companies to adjust, that is, increase, their expenditure so as to limit their returns to under 10 per cent and prevent the interference of Parliament. He made the almost certainly unworkable suggestion that the Government might have the option to purchase extended to cover such cases. However, the general view was rather the contrary, that nothing should be done to discourage investment. John Bright, one of the most famous parliamentarians of his time, a Radical and leading opponent of that set of restrictive practices called the Corn Laws, made what was perhaps among the least happy of the objections to the Bill.[43] He was almost alone in denying that the railways were monopolies, maintaining that, if they had been, they would each by definition only have benefited the promoters of their own particular railway bill, whereas it was obvious that they were conferring a great many economic benefits on others besides. But, aside from this semantically confused objection, he made a shrewd political point in indicating the folly of the Bill's attempting to lay down the precise details of a possible nationalization so far ahead. Not only would the composition of Parliament be different then, but there was the established constitutional practice of ignoring any explanations that might be given by ministers or others in introducing legislation when the time came for those laws to be interpreted. Whatever provisions might be made in 1844 for nationalization, MPs in the future would make up their own mind on the pros and cons of any particular nationalization proposal and act accordingly. In effect Gladstone was caught in a dilemma. On the one hand, a shrewd perception that unless the terms were clear and binding the quarry would escape, as well as the need to avoid the accusation by subsequent investors in railways that they had been misled and the intense Victorian respect for private property, was leading him to be precise in drafting terms of nationalization and in specifying the circumstances in which it could be introduced or rate revenue be revised.[44] On the other, the implication of this would be to fetter Parliament in a manner that was contrary to constitutional usage and might not even then be binding in practice if Parliament chose otherwise. The fact that in the early drafts he tried to make operation of the Act proceed automatically and without significant reference back to Parliament was held against him and the relevant draft mechanisms for this were expunged.

After the debate the Bill went into committee, from which it emerged emasculated, though Gladstone did not acknowledge this. Sir Robert Peel had given way under the pressure of massive delegations of railway directors.[45] The period before review had been lengthened from fifteen to twenty-one years. The precise purchase details had been omitted. And, as important, the Bill's ingenuity had been destroyed. The deductions for mismanagement and for failing to keep the railway and its stock in good repair did not survive. Neither did the limitation on increasing capital or the requirement for annual accounts in a prescribed form. The Bill now provided that any railway which felt that its long-term profitability was undervalued by a proposed purchase price based on its three previous years' profits could take this to arbitration. Thus a rational railway in the last three years before possible purchase or rate review would gain unequivocally from artificially keeping its profits clearly below 10 per cent even if it expected nationalization rather than rate review.

1.4   Reasons for the failure of Gladstone's monopoly policy

It was not long before the 1844 Act and associated legislation were seen to be a failure by those qualified to understand these matters.[46] As enacted, its principal shortcomings were that: it did not apply to railways built earlier than 1844; 10 per cent was an arbitrary figure and, as it turned out, too high a one; rate-of-return regulation could be, and was, evaded by stock watering and over-investment; monopoly power would be increased through amalgamations and other lawful combinations or through collusion; the data required were insufficient for the implementation of the Act. The Act did not protect railway users against particular rates which were felt often to be unfair; and it did not meet enough of the political or social objections to railway fares and services. To take each of these in turn:

Exemption of earlier railways

Almost no MP in the debate had disagreed with the view that it would be an invasion of the rights of private property to impose the 1844 Act retrospectively on railways already built. This view had a narrower and a wider implication, both important. The narrower implication was that it was accepted that, while less than 10 per cent of the eventual length of railways built may not have seemed a great exemption, much of what had been built already might (and in fact did) become main lines, greatly increasing the significance of the exemption. Moreover, while the original bill had foreseen that existing railways would try to evade its provisions by extending their lines rather than creating new ones and had prevented this, the Act left the determination of what extensions were permissible in a less satisfactory state. In 1865, when the Act's prescribed twenty-one years had passed, Gladstone persuaded Lord Palmerston to appoint a royal commission to consider the possible nationalization of the railways.[47] One reason that the resulting Devonshire Commission gave for rejecting nationalization was the impracticality of nationalizing parts of routes over which by then long-distance services ran when other parts of the same routes were exempt because built before 1844. The wider implication was that it was conceded that the more years that passed and the more railways that were built, the less possible it would be to bring the railway system under a satisfactory regime since an increasing part would be exempt from any legislation introduced to impose it.

The 10 per cent maximum return

This figure had been found in many turnpike acts. It was the figure inserted in the Liverpool and Manchester Railway Act, 1826 (with the additional provision, never put into effect, that any excess profit should be equally shared between shareholder and customer.)[48] Later, it was also found commonly in water and gas acts. Once established, it seemed impossible to argue for a different rate or for a rate which varied with circumstances, that is, with inflation and other risks. This was because of the pre-eminent position given to the initial act as conferring a private property right.[49] Moreover, it made no allowance for the very great differences in risk attaching to different railways. Even if it were possible to argue that it was a reasonable return given the risks of investing in the unproved Liverpool and Manchester railway, there were many later to argue that it was too high a rate for many other railways, given their relative lack of risk and the lower yield of Consols. As early as 1848 James Morrison wrote of 'permanently guaranteeing to the shareholder the enormous dividend of 10 per cent'.[50] By 1865 when railways were yielding 4 per cent on average or the decade before the First World War when they were commonly yielding 3 per cent or less, the rate review provisions of the 1844 Act, which provided for government making up revenue to a minimum of 10 per cent, would have been a gift to railway shareholders, and worried those then who considered using the provisions of the Act, which was still on the statute book.[51]

Stock watering and over-investment

Within two years of the passing of the 1844 Act, the report of another select committee, chaired by James Morrison, concluded that the Act had done no good, because 'illusory', because emasculated. The railway companies had been able to distribute profits without increasing dividends, and so avoid rate-of-return regulation, by allocating shares to the principals at par when they stood at a premium. Morrison denounced such stock watering, protesting that no other country allowed it.[52] In 1854, in a masterly paper, the philosopher Herbert Spencer, who had himself spent his youth as an engineer building railways, described many of the tricks the railways used to distribute railway profits other than through dividends and to their own selection of favoured parties, who might, or might not, be shareholders.

> Before this reckless-branch-making commenced, eight and nine per cent were the dividends returned by our chief railways; and these dividends were rapidly increasing. The maximum dividend allowed by the [Gladstone] Acts is 10 per cent. Had there not been unprofitable extensions, this maximum would have been reached many years since; and in the absence of the power to undertake new works, the fact that it had been reached, could not have been hidden. Lower rates for goods and passengers would necessarily have followed.[53]

His own belief, and it was echoed by many both then and much later, was that but for stock watering and over-investment, fares and charges could have been cut to a third.[54] Instead, Spencer pointed out, expenses were overstated: dividends had fallen, as they continued to fall throughout the century and beyond.[55] While in 1844 a few railways had been declaring dividends near to 10 per cent and many were declaring more than 5 per cent, the downward trend was almost continuous throughout the rest of the century until, before the First World War, returns were usually about 3 per cent or less. Yet investment continued at a relatively high rate. Even Matthews, Feinstein and Odling Smee, modern, disinterested historians of the British economy, have observed that, 'since the main railway network was complete by 1881, it may seem surprising that the capital stock in transport grew as rapidly as it did between then and 1914 . . . [R]ailway investment, though its great days were over, was still enough to keep the railway capital stock growing at almost the same rate as Gross National Product.'[56] All told, it is hard to see British railway development as other than an exemplifying instance, perhaps the outstanding one, of the Averch–Johnson hypothesis, formulated in 1962, that rate-of-return control leads to an expansion of the regulated industry's capital base, the danger of which was recognized by Lord Seymour before the 1844 Act was passed, and which was regarded as having already happened by James Morrison less than two years later. By 1854, Herbert Spencer was recommending limiting railway capital expenditure as the only remedy. No railway should be able to spend more than its original authorization without returning to Parliament for approval. Such approval should not be given without examination of the actual expenditure undertaken under earlier legislation followed by a demonstration of the need for additional expenditure and its likely profitability. Thus it emerged that effective rate-of-return regulation required effective controls not only to prevent indirect distribution of profit but also to check over-investment – measures way beyond what the 1844 Act or parliamentary opinion made permissible.

Increases in monopoly power

Through excessive initial costs, stock watering and over-investment, railway dividends were kept down in spite of amalgamations. These amalgamations, especially if end-to-end, could be defended on economic grounds as likely to achieve economies of scale and in particular a reduction of overheads. However, they also increased the railways' monopoly power and induced them to put up rates in so far as they reduced competition. While in principle Parliament could have prevented such amalgamations, since on each occasion a bill was needed, it usually did not, despite the recommendation of an 1846 select committee that amalgamations should not be allowed where they increased monopoly power (though mostly only when they joined railways end to end – not that this distinction was always easily drawn).

However, there were other ways of increasing monopoly power than through amalgamation. It has often been argued that as important were more informal means of combination. Indeed, the increasingly common practice of running trains and despatching goods over several railways made it all the easier for those railways, without amalgamating, to combine so as to limit price competition.[57] There were even cases where one railway paid another not to exercise its running rights in competition with it.

The growth of such pooling arrangements from the 1840s on led, indeed, to the establishment of a special institution, the Railway Clearing House, which survived entire until the Second World War and operated, with a diminished role, until the 1950s.[58] This powerful institution, which in its long heyday employed at any one time more than 3,000 people, was developed to solve the myriad problems which the 1980s came to know as those of interconnection.[59] It proved itself indispensable in, among a host of other matters, ensuring that there were inter-railway connections between the passenger trains of the various railways and that wagons moving from one railway to another were not held up for any undue time, as well as in the task of sharing receipts between the railways over which traffic ran.[60] To achieve this the

Clearing House not only participated in the negotiation of timetables but received and examined every through ticket and invoice. This was interconnection in practice as complicated as any introduced in the 1980s (though done without the help of computers). While it would have been theoretically possible to have apportioned receipts and fixed prices to reflect the costs incurred by each railway so as to produce the possibility of fair competition, the accounting information did not exist to make this happen. Moreover, from the start the railways knew what they wanted to do and did it: they equalized fares and charges between pairs of places irrespective of differences in route and in any other costs.

The history of the establishment of revenue pooling and amalgamation is bound up with the developments needed to establish interconnection. That history shows that whenever a railway had any advantage over those interconnecting with it, it used that power to increase its profits until pressure, generally through the Clearing House, corrected it, but that this was at the expense of setting up collusive arrangements against the customers' interests and in restraint of competition.

Even earlier there had been the elimination by railways of competition from other users of their tracks. In 1839 a select committee noted that it was not practical to insist that a railway be a common carrier in the sense that any carrier could use its own locomotives and stock on it. Some years later the Gladstone Committee was to learn that, while the law allowed everyone access, rates could be set which made it cheaper to use the railway's own locomotives and wagons. Moreover, while the railway acts allowed other carriers access to the rails, the railways 'can refuse them coke, water, the use of their stations and fixed engines, turnplates and any assistance from their servants, unless they come to terms with the company. No parties could run on their lines without their consent and make a profit.'[61] One railway representative explained to Gladstone's railway committee in 1844 that there were economies to be gained in railways running only their own trains and doing their own collection and delivery.[62] Moreover, already some railway companies were starting lawfully to acquire, or reach agreements with, canals, coastal shipping and road carriers in order to limit competition. There were thus many ways in which monopoly power could be increased.

Poor accounting and statistical information

Another reason for the failure of the 1844 Act had also been noticed by James Morrison in 1846. The accounting provisions of the Bill had been watered down in the Act, so that accounts were only needed in the last three of the twenty-one years instead of throughout that period. Gladstone had put a clause into another bill requiring railways to produce accounts, but what was required was so vague and meagre as to be useless.[63] Morrison commented that 'no precautions had been taken to settle the principle by which Parliament could obtain anything like an accurate knowledge of the net profits of railway companies.'[64] In 1849 the House of Lords set up a committee to look into railway accounts. It found that every railway company adopted the form of accounts it chose; none were comparable. Current and capital expenditures were often poorly distinguished. Funds had been misapplied between rail and non-rail businesses. Many works which had been approved by Parliament had not been undertaken; others had been undertaken which had not been approved.

The Committee found that, while the figures were inadequate, the explanations were worse. It recommended separate accounts for separate businesses so that the accounts of the monopoly business could be distinguished, as well as clearer conventions and an independent audit.[65] However, it seems once again that because of the strength of the railway interest in Parliament nothing effective was done to achieve this (though guidance was given in 1868 on how to achieve some uniformity).[66] Certainly up to and beyond the First World War there were still complaints about the fundamental inadequacy of railway accounting and other railway statistics.

These shortcomings had several other practical consequences. There was no recognizable basis for measuring the rate of return for railways or the capital base on which it was measured. It proved difficult to detect from the accounts whether stock was being watered or profits distributed irregularly to parties other than shareholders. As the railway economist Acworth was to say as late as 1912, 'in this Country we do not know what the average rate for goods or the average fare for passengers is. Parliament has not so far thought fit to demand this information.'[67]

Unfair rate making

The notion of a fair price is an ancient one, but had almost disappeared from economic theory by the mid-nineteenth century. It had been replaced by the conclusion of classical economics that the only price worth considering was a market price established by competition. Nevertheless, the issue remained alive for a monopoly's customers. There had been endless complaints that the various tolls different parties paid when using the same turnpike, which included exemptions and restrictions which also varied from one turnpike to another, showed undue preference and were therefore unfair.[68] The same kinds of objection were made to railway rates where it was almost as difficult to justify rate differences by differences in costs. Individual traders were more likely to object to the individual rates they paid than to worry about the railway's excessive or inadequate overall profitability. Each of the early railways had its own rate schedules, which normally differed from those of the others and were complicated in their structure. In his 1845 Act Gladstone legislated at length against discrimination and there was further legislation in 1854.[69] In essence it amounted to a requirement that railways should charge all customers at the same rate in the same circumstances. But customers found little protection in this, especially as there was until the 1870s no obligation on railways to publish their rates.[70] Moreover, the onus was on the customer to take the railway to court, where it could generally find some difference in circumstances by which to defend any difference in rates. While there had been some attempts to give more substance to the law on discrimination, in 1865 Gladstone recognized that the provision remained inadequate when he said 'that what is known as the provision for equal treatment under equal circumstances, is a matter which necessarily, and without the slightest blame to anyone, is full of difficulty in its application'.[71] This was particularly true wherever, as on railways, there was a multiplicity of services with joint costs.

Social obligations

The same reluctance to place retrospective legislation on the railways originally affected safety legislation too. Taken literally, as it almost invariably was until 1893, this respect for the initial statute as a contract was as much a deterrent to safety regulation as to economic regulation, because the imposed cost of improving safety as a result of legislation was seen as an invasion of private property rights, if uncompensated. There were serious railway accidents in the late 1830s. In 1839 a select committee recommended safety regulations and a railway safety inspectorate, which both came into being almost at once.[72] This regulation and inspection applied to new but not to existing railways.[73] The inspectors started early to investigate accidents and recommend safety measures, but they had no powers of enforcement until the end of the century.

It is perhaps harder to see why, given the thinking of the time, the rights of private property were not more of a bar to other social intervention, except that in some cases the railways did receive payment for the services they were forced to provide, and in others MPs gave it as their strong opinion that the services would be profitable if the railways provided them or provided them properly. Most railways were 'high fare' in the sense that they believed that the demand for railways was inelastic, and so raised their prices and restricted output. Where they did provide for the poor, the carriages were often open and little more than cattle trucks, and might not be allowed into platforms. Their passengers might have to get off and on at sidings, or these carriages might be left in sidings while higher paying passengers went through. All this aroused great indignation in the debates on the 1844 Bill. Indeed, the 1844 Act itself was remembered far more as the 'Cheap Trains Act' than it was for its monopoly control provisions, since it introduced the requirement that every railway should run a 'Parliamentary Train' at an average speed of at least 12 m. p.h. for third-class passengers at a penny a mile.[74] In that respect, and in the eyes of some MPs it may have been the most important, the Act was against the railway interest, costly to the railways, and so cannot be said to have been captured. But even this was not the limit of the social regulation of railways. Sir Robert Peel was particularly strong on the rights of private property but he had also been insistent that railways should be required to carry at special rates the royal mails, as well as troops in an emergency. Although the virtual ban on retrospective legislation and a distaste for interfering with railway management prevented Parliament from doing as much as many members seemed to want to do to alter the railways' policies, even so it was ready to load social obligations on railways as another method of keeping profits down. Many of the social obligations found in nationalization statutes, and other policies like those of cross-subsidization which have persisted past privatization in some cases, originated in the personal and political preferences of Victorian statesmen.

1.5 Reconsideration of the 1844 Act: the Devonshire Commission, 1865–1867

All these issues came up in the mid-1860s when the 1844 Act was reconsidered. The twenty-one years were up in 1865 and there was one remarkable element of continuity: as Chancellor of the Exchequer, Gladstone was again in the Government and now dominated it. He had been encouraged to take seriously the maturation of the 1844 Act by the reissue of a book by William Galt which urged Parliament to use the Act to readdress the problems of the railways.[75] But, irrespective of the impact of Galt's book, the prospect of possible nationalization and the importance of the railways to the economy were enough to give the issue some visibility. Gladstone persuaded the Prime Minister, Lord Palmerston, as we have seen, to set up a royal commission. Set up under the Duke of Devonshire, it was intended, as Gladstone said when he introduced it into Parliament, to be a fact-finding body only,[76] though in the event this intention was not realized. Its enemies said that the railway interest managed to pack it.[77] But, even if that was the case, the conclusions it came to were not unreasonable. For various reasons it found nationalization unappealing.

The Commission began its report with a history of the railways and their regulation. It noted the successes that had been achieved through discussion and co-operation between the railways: in safety, in achieving uniformity of gauge and in enabling passengers and freight to travel from one line to another. It observed that since the act authorizing the Liverpool and Manchester railway in 1826 the maximum dividend had been fixed at 10 per cent; but that because of a failure to get any provisions defining either charges or charging principles, there was no uniformity in these among the railways.[78] But apparently more in sorrow than in anger, it concluded that the nationalization and rate-review provisions of the 1844 Act, however praiseworthy its intentions might have been, could not be put into effect.[79] First, many parts of the main lines could not be purchased under the terms of the Act because the acts authorizing them had been passed before 1844; practically, they would have to be bought out, which could involve the State in great and unpredictable expense. Secondly, railway accounts were so incomplete, and were drawn up on such different bases, that it was impossible to decide which railways passed or failed the 1844 tests. No railways had bothered to prepare accounts for the last three of the twenty-one years in the form prescribed in the 1844 Act. While they had therefore broken the law, the Commission did not see what could be done about it. It followed from this that the railways could not provide the information upon which to decide either to nationalize or to revise rates. Moreover, the Commission argued that it did not see how either action would make railway operations more efficient. Its report showed no understanding of the vice within which Gladstone had hoped to hold the railways. Neither indeed did Gladstone seem to remember it. In the circumstances it is hard to dissent from the Commission's conclusion that there was no point in using the Act. The Commission recommended doing nothing. It went further towards *laissez-faire*: it did not 'consider it would be expedient even if it was practicable, to adopt any legislation which would abolish the freedom the railway companies enjoyed of charging what sum they deemed expedient within the maximum rates'.[80] The Commission presented its report in 1867. But, despite being pressed in the House, a succession of governments delayed taking action on it. Even when one year later Gladstone himself became Prime Minister, he did not debate its conclusions. Indeed, its recommendations were never debated and its negative conclusions were fulfilled inasmuch as nothing was done.

As one historian has remarked, the report of the Devonshire Commission rejecting the 1844 Act was a turning-point in railway regulation.[81] It finally punctured the possibility of devising a discretionary form of control through periodic review, a form of control that Morrison had recommended, that John Stuart Mill had endorsed and that Gladstone believed he had secured.[82] It marked the end of the discretionary era, both because it showed the 1844 Act to be unworkable and because thereafter the fierce Victorian belief in the rights of private property made it even more impossible to frame a general railways act which would have had an equivalent retrospective effect upon the mass of railways already built.[83] Given the strict avoidance of retrospection and given that the maximum 10 per cent return which was in many statutes was unattained, unattainable and too high, given, finally, changed economic circumstances, it was impossible to alter the maximum return a railway might make, or to reduce the ill-defined and again arguably excessive maximum charges for which the laws inconsistently provided. Too large a proportion of the railway system had been built for any discretionary revision without retrospection to have been possible. One possibility would have been to insert such provisions into the bills required whenever there was an amalgamation; but that did not happen, partly because of the strength of the railway interest, partly because of this reluctance to disappoint previous expectations even then, and partly because the typical reason for amalgamation was anyway to arrest declining profitability.

To recapitulate: the first period of railway regulation was a failure. It did not meet the complaints that customers of monopolies had against them on price and quality. It did not promote competition – indeed, arguably it encouraged collusion and entrenched the practice of collusion for a century to come, a practice which was copied outside the railways. And it did not secure a reasonable return on capital in the long run, so that further investment was discouraged. The chief financial beneficiaries of its failure were the promoters of railways and their allies, as well as those who received generous payments for their land. Their interests were reflected in the power of the railway interest in Parliament, which prevented effective regulation. Railway regulation in this period was based upon giving each railway an act of Parliament which was formally the equivalent of the modern licence, or more strictly, combination of statute and licence (to be described later).[84] The terms and conditions of these statutes – there were hundreds of them – varied depending on the membership and interests of the particular parliamentary committee considering each bill. This process did not lead to regulatory coherence or generality. And there was no review procedure to ensure that even the inadequate terms of the statutes were being observed: the historian Henry Parris has observed that enforcement of railway legislation including private acts was ordinarily left to local justices of the peace, which meant that it was hardly enforced at all.[85] At various times attempts were made to impose general duties upon railways. They were most successful where they were in the interests of the railways themselves – for example, technical matters of interconnection like standardization of the railway gauge – but in general the railways chose to combine to sort out their own problems. Even progress on safety was painfully slow and impeded by the general presumption that an act of Parliament was a contract concerning private property whose value must not be lowered by retrospective legislation. But despite all this there was in 1844 one advanced general attempt to pass a bill that could act as a workable basis for railway regulation. In its original form it was technically remarkable as an instrument of economic regulation – not far short in its structure of what was to be developed in the 1980s, and in a few respects better. It was emasculated by the railway interest; and when it was brought forward in its emasculated form to be considered in 1865 its defects led to its being easily defeated by the railway interest, which was then probably strong enough to have defeated it even if it had remained in its original form. But it was also prejudiced by the inappropriateness of the reviewing body.

Notes

1 W. E. Gladstone, *Hansard*, 3rd series, vol. 76, col. 500 (1844).
2 In recent times those who have written about the British experience of public economic management have been more interested in the general relations between the government and industry – the tension between *laissez-faire* and government intervention – than they have been in regulatory history. That said, I have found Cleveland Stevens, Parris, Lubenow, Cain, Barker and Savage and Bagwell invaluable sources of material and comment: Cleveland Stevens (1915); Lubenow (1971); Parris (1965); Barker and Savage (1974); Bagwell (1988); see later in this and the next chapter for references to Cain's articles. After sending the typescript to the publisher I became aware of Professor McLean's interest in the 1844 Act, especially in testing it against the various themes of political economy (see chapter 11 below). That aspect is argued more deeply in McLean and Foster (forthcoming).
3 The economist J. R. McCulloch identified these as the industries as well as 'other public works' for regulation (excluding electricity and telephony) in his *Principles of Political Economy* (1849), pp. 299–301, which came out first in 1825; see Robbins (1952), pp. 35, 58–9; Francis (1851), pp. 76–95, on the effect of the Bridgewater Canal monopoly.
4 Webb and Webb (1922), pp. 4–9; Finer (1933), pp. 177–80; Keith-Lucas (1980), pp. 108–11. On the use of private bills for municipal enterprise, see Finer (1941), pp. 68–74.
5 Dillwyn, MP and GWR director, quoted by Alderman (1973), p. 15; see generally Barker and Savage (1974), pp. 72–5.
6 This was mainly Gladstone's initiative, prompted by the Radical MP Joseph Hume. The three main statutes, all passed in the mid-1840s, were the Railway Clauses Act, the Land Clauses Act and the Companies Clauses Act. It was in the 1870s and 1880s that acts were passed allowing government departments to license new gas and electricity undertakings without separate legislation. See Finer (1941), pp. 49–56, 57.
7 Webb and Webb (1920), pp. 118–119; Kelf-Cohen (1969), p. 100. Hannah (1979), p. 5, explains how in some cases the twenty-one years were extended to forty-two on the ground that twenty-one years was too short a term to make a reasonable return on the investments.
8 The Commissioners on the State of Health of Large Towns, *Report*, 1844, quoted by Finer (1941), p. 41; J. Davis (1988), pp. 47–50. Mill (1852), bk. 1, ch. 9, para. 3, argued that because of this there would be economies if all London had single gas and water companies.
9 Adam Smith (1802), vol. 3, bk. 5, ch. 1, p. 98.
10 Barker and Savage (1974), pp. 59–63.
11 Adam Smith (1802), vol. 3, bk. 5, ch. 1, pp. 93–107; Ricardo (1962) (1st edn. 1817); McCulloch (1849). The first major step forward in analysis was by a civil servant in the Board of Trade, T. H. Farrer: Farrer (1883), pp. 61–97. J. S. Mill, like Adam Smith and McCulloch favoured a discretionary approach: Mill (1852), bk. 1, ch. 1, para. 4; bk. 2, ch. 15, paras 3, 4; bk. 5, ch. 11, para. 11. Adam Smith saw that monopolies could be natural. He used the word 'natural' in connection with monopoly (see chapter 6 below, n. 47), as did Bailey. Classifications of different conditions of production which identified natural monopoly as a special case were to be found in S. Bailey (1931), pp. 185, 227–32 (1st edn. 1825), and Nassau Senior (1836), pp. 103–14, but, as the historian of economic

thinking on competition and monopoly in the nineteenth century P. L. Williams has remarked, it is still easy to gain from Adam Smith, especially in his book 1, and these early-nineteenth-century economists the view that government is responsible for the creation or sustaining of monopolies. Smith especially was much criticized by Schumpeter and others for the poverty of his analysis of monopoly. Williams' response is that Smith regarded any disruption of competition as conferring monopoly. See P. L. Williams (1978), pp. 35–6.

12 When deregulation started, whether in the mid-eighteenth century or later, and when it ended in the mid-nineteenth century have been matters much debated by historians. But without question the first fifty years of the nineteenth century saw many measures to free trade. See the excellent discussion in Taylor (1972), pp. 51, 52.

13 Quoted in Cleveland Stevens (1915), p. 155.

14 See Hadley (1890), pp. 135–7.

15 Various attempts were made to set up supervisory parliamentary committees to establish common clauses to go into railway bills, but on regulatory matters these attempts remained limited. Nineteen earlier general statutes (or parts of them) were incorporated in the Railways Construction Facilities Act, 1864, which was a major consolidation of general provisions.

16 Devonshire Commission, *Parliamentary Papers* 1867, vol. 38; Bagwell (1988), pp. 162–4. The Board of Trade did some good in achieving consistency until the Government withdrew its support in 1845: Barker and Savage (1974), pp. 76–7.

17 Lubenow (1971), pp. 112–7. Parris (1965), p. 36, said of the 1840–4 Railways Department at the Board of Trade that, 'its legal powers were sometimes strained to the limit and beyond.' In the terms to be developed in chapter 7 it was a sunshine commission.

18 Spencer (1883), pp. 265, 275. The historian of the railway interest says that the number of its MPs increased at every election from 1832 to 1865 but that its activity was at its greatest from 1867: Alderman (1973), p. 26. See also n. 45 below.

19 In 1845, Richard Cobden complained that there were twenty committees sitting on railway bills, and that he could not escape one as another member had had an accident and he was required for a quorum. He sat from 12 noon to 4 p.m. six days a week. It was, he said, an 'odious committee': Hinde (1987), pp. 152–153. It is the burden implied by this reference that above all persuades me that a new and subversive parliamentary history of a Namierian tendency might perhaps be written of the period after the 1832 Reform Act to about 1890. It would say that most active peers and MPs went to Westminster to line their pockets from the railways. The high-mindedness of so many of the debates one reads about – on electoral reform, welfare legislation and later empire – salved their consciences, bored or entertained them, according to their temperaments. As an American political scientist pointed out many years later, politicians always act in the regulatory game, profiting from it regardless of the outcome: McChesney (1987).

20 Barker and Savage (1974), pp. 59–63; Knowles (1926), pp. 253–90.

21 Barker and Savage (1974), pp. 63–70; Mathias (1983), pp. 257–63.

22 J. Morrison, *Hansard*, 3rd series, vol. 33, col. 977ff *et seq.* (1836). In 1848, Morrison's speeches and tracts were collected into a book, to the worth of which McCulloch testified, and from whose arguments he plainly drew on for his own. Morrison sat as a Liberal MP at various times between 1830 and 1847. He was self-educated. In Parliament he specialized on railway matters. He was a close, life-long friend of McCulloch's: D. P. O'Brien (1970), pp. 20, 106–7. But this does not prove McCulloch's influence on him. They were both members of the Political Economy Club. He was, one of the three members of the club McCulloch valued highly enough to wish to show them his own books in draft. His treatment of the railway question was superior and more detailed than McCulloch's. Hence his was most probably the inspiration of the other. Francis (1851),

vol. 1, pp. 274–81, stressed the political importance of Morrison's speech in 1836 as the first attempt to introduce a general railways bill, an attempt defeated by a fear of deterring investment. See also the reference to him in the *Dictionary of National Biography*.

23   J. Morrison, *Hansard*, 3rd series, vol. 33, col. 977 (1836).

24   Ibid., col. 978.

25   Ibid., col. 979.

26   Ibid., col. 979–80. J. S. Mill (1852), bk. 1, ch. 9, para. 3, developed this analysis in regard to water and other natural monopolies. He also argued for a franchise, rather than outright private or public ownership.

27   J. Morrison, *Hansard*, 3rd series, vol. 33, col. 982 (1836).

28   Ibid., col. 984. Adam Smith (1802), vol. 3, bk. 5, ch. 7, p. 143, was ready to allow a time-limited monopoly for a new venture.

29   J. Morrison, *Hansard*, 3rd series, vol. 33, col. 984 (1836).

30   Ibid., col. 984–5. McCulloch (1849), p. 300, made a similar analysis.

31   W. E. Gladstone, *Hansard*, 3rd series, vol. 72, col. 232–56 (1844). Many authors have discussed the difficulty of describing the first half of the nineteenth century as an age of *laissez-faire*: e.g., Robbins (1952); Taylor (1972). In his discussion of the 1844 Act, Lubenow (1971), pp. 15–29, is most concerned to rebut the view that it was a collectivist measure. He is in a difficulty, because there can be no doubt but that the original bill proposed state intervention in a new form, even though it did so in order to promote competition, stimulate efficiency and deter excess profits. The trouble is that 'collectivist' is too vague a term. Its use assumes that *laissez-faire* is its antithesis, but it can be shown that governments that favoured *laissez-faire* policies often enacted 'collectivist' statutes limiting commercial freedom. The interesting question is why they did so in any given case: whether, in modern parlance, it was to correct or to create market failure. Thus Lubenow's excellent discussion of the railways, like that of Parris (1965), is limited by his not perceiving the crucial relevance of the issue of natural monopoly in justifying this particular intervention as one which potentially could improve the operation of the market by correcting one source of market failure.

32   W. E. Gladstone, *Hansard*, 3rd series, vol. 72, col. 236 (1844). It was in 1844 that railway amalgamations really began: Cleveland Stevens (1915), p. 26; also Bagwell (1988), p. 159.

33   Select Committee on Railways (Gladstone Committee), First Report, *Parliamentary Papers*, 16 February 1844, vol. 11. In 1844, William Galt published the first edition of his influential book on railway reform in which he advocated public ownership: Galt (1844), p. 74; (1865), pp. 52–7. He was a witness before the Gladstone Committee. He wrote later that the 1844 legislation was 'debarred from passing an *ex post facto* law in regard to the companies that had already been incorporated': Galt (1865), p. xii. McCulloch had been ready to consider railway nationalization: D. P. O'Brien (1970), p. 288.

34   Select Committee on Railways, Second Report, *Parliamentary Papers*, 1 March 1844, vol. 11; ibid., Fifth Report, *Parliamentary Papers*, 24 May 1844, vol. 11, which was trenchant on this point.

35   Select Committee on Railways, Third Report, *Parliamentary Papers* 1 April 1844, vol. 11, pp. 5, 6. The actual term of years and rate are suggested later in the report. Gladstone resented the common misunderstanding that his bill just advocated state ownership. See Hyde (1934), pp. 170–2.

36   See Breyer (1982), p. 6. Parris (1965), p. 56, says that, though S. Laing, who had been Labouchere's secretary and was later to be Law Clerk of the Railways Department at the Board of Trade, was said to be the draftsman and had indeed written to Gladstone on railway matters (Gladstone's diary, 27 February 1844: see Foot and Matthew (1974), p. 388), Gladstone's papers reveal that he was himself the author.

In a paper he gave to the Statistical Society of London, Edwin Chadwick claimed that, when working on sanitation between 1838 and 1841, he came up with what he then called 'competition for the field' or franchising. 'The principle was, upon due consideration, extensively adopted and advocated by permanent public offices and commissions and disinterested public investigators for the regulation of the railways then at their commencement.' See Chadwick (1859), p. 385. He may have influenced Gladstone but not Morrison, who had the essential idea earlier. Morrison and Chadwick knew each other. They had first met at Jeremy Bentham's.

37 See Gilbert and Newbery (1988). Parris (1965), p. 24, has observed that 'nothing is more striking in these debates than the infrequency with which the voice of economic orthodoxy is heard.' This was only because orthodox professional political economists had not developed an opinion. As has already been indicated, from Adam Smith on they recognized that natural monopoly was an exception to the natural development of competition but they did not develop an analysis. Many of those who spoke in the debate were well aware of classical political economy and its teachings on competition, particularly as the main economic political issue of the time, the repeal of the Corn Laws, was coming to a head (it was achieved two years later). As he was a member of the Political Economy Club, Morrison's views obviously influenced those who debated there. Though he was not present in the 1844 debate, his *was* the voice of orthodox political economy. While public ownership was a strange idea at the time, Parliament had just reformed the Post Office as a public enterprise. See Galt (1865), pp. 193–7.

38 Sir Robert Peel, *Hansard*, 3rd series, vol. 76, col. 672 (1844). On Gladstone's conduct of the Bill and Peel's influence on it, see Hyde (1934), pp. 179–81.

39 On the use of 10 per cent, see Parris (1965), p. 14.

40 Henry Labouchere, *Hansard*, 3rd series, vol. 76, col. 518, 519 (1844).

41 Vincent (1978), p. 229.

42 James Roebuck, *Hansard*, 3rd series, vol. 72, col. 244, 245 (1844).

43 J. Entwistle, ibid., col. 509–15; Lord Seymour, ibid., vol. 76, col. 635–6 (1844); Lubenow (1971), pp. 121–7. This was the view expressed by the Whig, ex-Prime Minister Earl Grey in the House of Lords. John Bright, *Hansard*, 3rd series, vol. 76, col. 626–35 (1844). A hostile later view of the 1844 Bill was that of J. H. Clapham, who doubted if there was a good point in it: Clapham (1926), pp. 417–21.

44 It is hard to believe that in devising the detail Gladstone did not draw upon his own experience in drawing up commercial and agricultural leases. In the early nineteenth century the question of what were desirable conditions in a lease seems to have received substantial public and political attention. Adam Smith had argued against inserting detailed conditions, because of landlord ignorance, unenforceability and the reduction thereby of tenants to automata; but McCulloch argued the opposite, principally because the tenants' interests were of shorter duration than those of the landlords: D. P. O'Brien (1970), pp. 375, 376. Later, the matter was discussed in detail by Pigou (1920), pp. 172–4. Gladstone's original clauses thus seem to have been ahead of their time.

45 Cleveland Stevens (1915), pp. 142–57. There is a vivid account of the lengths the railway interest went to in Francis (1851), vol. 2, pp. 104–24. Parris (1965), pp. 18–21, Cleveland Stevens (1915), pp. 116–24, and Hyde (1934), pp. 177–81, believe that Peel was the one who backed down. Alderman (1973), pp. 16–17, describes the campaign against the 1844 Bill as the railway interest's first large one, in which it relied heavily on the defence of private property to win support. Interestingly, among newspapers only *The Times* was against the Bill: Roberts (1979), pp. 197–9. Alderman (1973), p. 26, writes of the railway interest then as not having enough MPs who were also railway directors to defeat the Bill; but it is a shortcoming of his analysis that he considers only those MPs: as he says, there are no records of MPs who in 1844 were substantial railway shareholders. But many,

perhaps even a majority, were to, or were tempted to, invest in the new projects in the offing. Many more must have as landowners gained, or expected to gain, from the over-generous compensation that was paid for land by the railways. The railway interest was not the first parliamentary vested-interest lobby – see Adam Smith (1802), vol. 2, bk. 4, ch. 2, pp. 206, 207 – but while it lasted it was perhaps the most powerful single such interest ever. The Gladstone family, and Gladstone himself, derived a substantial income from railway shares: Gladstone inherited railway shares from his father in 1851 (Shannon (1982), p. 246); but he lived on a private income from his father before that. For the Gladstone family's involvement in the Liverpool and Manchester railway, see Veitch (1930), pp. 27, 32, 41. Later, Gladstone invested heavily, and lost money, in Metropolitan and District railway shares: Matthew (1986), pp. 243–5.

46 Barker and Savage (1974), p. 69, say that by 1846 all the caution and basic logic which had previously marked the course of railway building was being thrown to the winds. It was a high price for regulatory failure.

47 Royal Commission on Railways (Devonshire Committee), *Parliamentary Papers*, 1867, vol. 38, pp. xxiv.

48 Parris (1965), p. 14. The merits of this particular solution were rediscovered periodically (e.g., Royal Commission on Railways, *Parliamentary Papers*, 1867, vol. 38, p. viii), and indeed gained considerable backing in the United States in the 1980s.

49 Cleveland Stevens (1915), p. 107, argued that the refusal to put any retrospective legislative constraints on railways was the chief reason for the failure of the Act – an exaggeration given the strength of the railway interest, but a good debating point.

50 J. Morrison (1848), p. 128 who also said that ten per cent was in all acts.

51 Davies (1913), pp. 197–204; Edwards (1897), pp. 207, 208.

52 J. Morrison, *Parliamentary Papers* 1846, vol. 14, p. vi; also Morrison (1848), *passim*. In a private communication the railway historian Michael Bonavia has said that stock watering by railways, up to 1923, is hard to measure. In the early days the main sources were: issuing at a discount (e.g., the London, Chatham and Dover paying its contractors in this way because it could not raise cash on the stock market); charging to capital expenditure what prudent finance would have charged to revenue; and paying dividends out of capital, 'under the counter'. Later came splitting ordinary stocks into preferred and deferred components of a greater total nominal value than the unsplit stock.

53 Spencer (1883), pp. 300–1, referring to the 1844 Act and the Railway Clauses Consolidation Act, 1845. Joseph Hume made a similar point earlier (*Hansard*, 3rd series, vol. 92, col. 822 (1847)), as did William Galt, (Galt (1844), pp. 52–7, and (1865), *passim* but esp. pp. 288–312).

54 Just before the First World War one advocate of railway nationalization wrote that he had never heard anyone doubt that the Belgian and German railway rates were, and always had been, lower than those of Britain: Davies (1913); see also Kellett (1969), ch. 3; Cleveland Stevens (1915), pp. 316. And another, a few years before, had written of these two countries that, with the judgement that the lower rates of their railways were the 'entire cause of their increasing ability to compete effectively with us [,] no one would for a moment seriously contend': Edwards (1897), p. 6.

55 Spencer (1883), p. 301; Cain (1980), pp. 9–28.

56 Matthews, Feinstein and Odling Smee (1982), p. 405; Averch and Johnson (1962). The nub of their idea is to be found in the work of Morrison, McCulloch and Sidgwick. The 'attempt to keep down the profits of such a monopoly, by fixing a maximum dividend, is open to the serious economic objection that when the maximum is reached, the company ceases to have any interest in preventing waste in management': Sidgwick (1887), p. 443.

57 Some strange anomalies and abuses of monopoly power are recorded in Hyde (1934), pp. 129–38.

58 Though the Railway Clearing House's functions petered out in the 1950s, it did not cease to exist until 1963.

59 The Cardwell Committee referred to the same concept as 'intercommunication': Fifth Report, *Parliamentary Papers*, 1852–3, vol. 38, p. 8.

60 Bagwell (1968), *passim* but esp. pp. 1–43. There is an early account of its formation and objectives in Francis (1851), vol. 2, pp. 49–60, and a straightforward account of its activities in the inter-war period in Sherrington (1928), vol. 1, ch. 5. Among the matters that over time were resolved by the Railway Clearing House (which eventually every railway joined) were the following: standardizing the railway gauge, couplings, buffers and braking systems; signals and safety arrangements, such as agreeing on the use of the left-hand track where there were two; letting trains and individual wagons travel over each other's lines; preventing railways holding on to each other's wagons without a charge, or even losing or stealing and repainting them in their own colours; drawing up a standard goods classification and inspecting its use so as to ensure that one railway did not cheat on another by under-recording, or wrongly classifying, goods despatched; preventing one railway from forcing passengers from other railways to walk long distances to change trains, as at Preston (200 yards) and Dover (half a mile); establishing an intelligible time-table with common conventions which made connection predictable and easy; establishing a similar quality of travel, for example, ensuring that foot warmers were always supplied in first- and second-class carriages; ensuring that passengers were not forced to buy first-class tickets if they wanted to make a particular connection; penalizing railways that misled passengers over the destination of the train they had joined; allowing the booking of through tickets; printing standard-format tickets to avoid ticket-touting and other forms of fraud; setting up and operating a lost property office; ensuring that the provision of porters was equitable; preventing penal charges on through traffic; unifying the accounting, collecting and inspecting of all invoices and all through tickets in order to ascertain the net payments the railways needed to make to each other; attempting to avoid terminal and marshalling charges being used to influence consignors; arranging excursion trains and other special trains. As a matter of interest: time had to be coordinated before timetables could be. Before the railways came to them each town or parish generally kept its own time. The railways changed that. See Bagwell (1968), pp. 54–5. On the contrast with the American experience, see ibid., pp. 265–7. The 1839 select committee on Railways (Second Report, *Parliamentary Papers*, 1839, vol. 10) concluded that Parliament expected the main element of competition to be between trains on the same line.

61 Select Committee on Railways, Second Report, *Parliamentary Papers*, 1839, vol. 10, p. vi. Royal Commission on Railways (Devonshire Commission), ibid., 1867, vol. 38.

62 C. A. Saunders, Secretary to the GWR, Select Committee on Railways (Gladstone Committee), Fifth Report, *Parliamentary Papers* 15 March 1844, vol. 11. He was what would later have been called its general manager. On the railways' relations with road coaches as a means to restrict competition, see Parris (1965), p. 41.

63 Railway Clauses Consolidation Act, 1845.

64 J. Morrison, *Parliamentary Papers*, 1846, vol. 14, p. vi. Also J. Morrison (1848), p. 20.

65 House of Lords Committee on Railway Accounts, Third Report, *Parliamentary Papers*, 1849 vol. 10, p. 477. On the inadequacy of railway accounts and statistics, see Pollins (1969), pp. 138 *et seq.* See Acworth (1905), p. 6; also Kellett (1969), p. 61, and Bagwell (1968), pp. 233 *et seq.*

66 Spencer (1883), pp. 265–8.

67 Acworth (1905), p. 6.

68 Webb and Webb (1920), pp. 118, 119. On discrimination in railways rates, see Bagwell (1968); Hawke (1969), pp. 82 *et seq.*

69 Railway Clauses Consolidation Act, 1845, and Better Regulation of Traffic on Railways and Canals Act, 1854; also Edwards (1897), p. 14; Barker and Savage (1974), pp. 91–2. For evidence that the railways also engaged explicitly in predation and that this was easiest for the larger companies, see Cardwell Committee, Fifth Report, *Parliamentary Papers*, 1852–3, vol. 38, p. 7.

70 Bagwell (1988), p. 172.

71 *Hansard*, 3rd series, vol. 177, col. 237 (1865).

72 Select Committee on Railways, Second Report, *Parliamentary Papers*, 1839, vol. 10, p. xiv.

73 Lubenow (1971), p. 116; Bagwell (1988), p. 176.

74 W. E. Gladstone, *Hansard*, 3rd series, vol. 72, col. 236–7 (1844). Peel argued, remarkably, that, 'for a great public benefit, you must, to some extent, give up your rights of private property.' The railways from as early as the Conveyance of Mails by Railways Act, 1838, had to carry the royal mails at a price that was, if necessary, subject to arbitration: Francis (1851), vol. 1, pp. 285–7. The Post Office claimed that it should only have to pay for this service at marginal cost: Hawke (1969), pp. 93, 94. On the controversy over encouraging working people to use trains on a Sunday, see Francis (1851), vol. 2, pp. 42–5, 118–20. On early debates over whether social obligations should be placed on railways created for private profit, see Cleveland Stevens (1915), pp. 315–24. Professor T. C. Barker has pointed out to me that a penny a mile was not cheap enough for the poor, who were earning a pound a week or less. It was the excursion fares later in the century that really made railway travel available to the poor.

75 Shannon (1982), p. 521. The book was *Railway Reform*. First published in 1844, there was a timely and very substantially revised version published in 1865. For his objective of tariff reduction see especially his (1865) preface and pp. 1–115; on competition (1865), pp. 130–56. Galt did not think like an economist. Even then one finds, as so often a century or more later, politicians backing a social preference for cheap fares by arguing in effect that demand elasticities were higher than the railways believed: Hyde (1934), pp. 160, 163. S. Laing, one of Gladstone's aides on the 1844 Bill, had reported to him that fares and charges on the Belgian state-owned system were substantially lower than on English railways: *Parliamentary Papers*, 1844, vol. 11, pp. 631–40, esp. 633.

76 Matthew (1986), pp. 119, 120, and *Hansard*, 3rd series, vol. 177, col. 233 (1865).

77 E. Chadwick, Report to the Social Science Association, 1867, cited by Edwards (1897), pp. 202–3.

78 Devonshire Commission, *Parliamentary Papers*, 1867, vol. 38, p. viii,; absence of unfair-charging provisions, p. xxx. The Liverpool and Manchester Railway Act, 1826, contained a 10 per cent limit on dividends with a 50:50 profit sharing above that, and Huskisson had argued more generally for a 10 per cent ceiling. All railway acts had such a limitation. They all had some maximum rates specified Morrison (1848). The 1844 Act, was however widely seen as setting a 10 per cent maximum, certainly for all subsequent railways, even after the report of the Devonshire Commission in 1867.

79 Ibid., p. xxxiv.

80 Ibid., p. xxxviii.

81 Parris (1965), p. 212.

82 Mill's approval, though not explicit, can be drawn from the 1852 edition of his *Principles of Political Economy*, bk. 5, ch. 11, para. 12.

83 Mill (1852), bk. 1, ch. 9, para. 3, was among the few to oppose this principle in railway legislation. Before 1887 in the USA, there was a similar problem in regard to retrospective regulation: see Pierce, Allison and Martin (1980), p. 91.

84 The Cardwell Committee referred to railway statutes as 'an engagement between the promoters on the one side and the public on the other': Fifth Report, *Parliamentary Papers*, 1852–3, vol. 38, p. 6.

85 Parris (1965), p. 14, stresses the unenforceability of early railway legislation: 'Such vagueness was characteristic of early railway acts. Since it was often difficult or impossible to
enforce them, it is not surprising that they were often evaded or ignored.' Perhaps this
helps explain why the Devonshire Commission did not find the accounts that there should
have been. Hyde (1934), p. 174, has also doubted the enforceability, given the instruments available, of even the first draft of the 1844 Bill.

2

Regulation by commission

[The regulatory commission] emerged in mid nineteenth century Britain as an instrument for regulating the railways in the public interest. It was Victorian capitalist democracy's notion of how to reconcile the public interest in a monopolist service of primary importance with the profit making incentive of joint stock enterprise. The idea quickly spread to the United States

W. A. Robson (1960)[1]

Because they formed a national network linking a large, though dwindling, number of separate companies, the railways remained the natural monopoly that was the focus of most public and political attention at least until after the First World War. A discussion of the tribulations of policy towards railway rate control (section 1) is followed by another, on the handling and financing of the growing burden of their social obligations (section 2). Section 3 shows how even before the First World War the elimination of competition by amalgamation and other means turned many who were not Socialists to nationalization as a solution. And section 4 briefly considers the regulation of the other natural monopolies.

2.1 Regulatory failure: the failure of a legalistic approach to tariff control

After 1867 railway regulation became more judicial and legalistic.[2] On earlier occasions there had been attempts to reinforce the regulatory role of Parliament by setting up civil service advisers to it within the Board of Trade or independently; but they had always been resented and most often ignored. At last Parliament realized that some body was needed with a more permanent interest in railways than it itself or the judiciary had. It departed from the high ground of controlling natural monopoly to more-interventionist but still ineffectual policies. This ushered in the era of the regulatory commission. The early 1870s happened to be a time of general economic prosperity, which also meant relative prosperity for the railways.[3] Thereafter railway prosperity generally declined. The railways' profitability and their public image were adversely affected by the 'Great Depression' of 1873–96, during which employment and output were maintained but general prices fell by a third, squeezing profits, mainly because falls in shipping costs reduced import prices and increased import volumes.[4] Railway revenues rose with the volume of trade but their profitability fell, partly because of a persistent tendency to over-invest, stimulated by low interest rates and abundant savings, but also because of the railways' apparent preference for increasing quality rather than lowering fares and charges. Railway profitability remained low until the First World War, recovered during it, but sank afterwards to levels which contemporaries judged appalling by comparison with what could be earned with certainty on government stocks.[5] Against such a background, rate-of-return control, or any control on profits, seemed irrelevant.

The Joint Select Committee on Railway Amalgamation had washed its hands of rate-of-return regulation for the railways with the gloomy words: 'all motive for economy is gone and nothing is left to prevent extravagance and jobbery except public opinion and the character of the directors.'[6] However, the growing unprofitability of the railways had not lessened passengers' and traders' economic complaints against railway rates. Many traders, especially those adversely affected by cheap imports, found that their transport costs were most likely to rise when they themselves were under financial pressure. While some railways brought about some cost reductions in an attempt to restore profitability, all railways endlessly raised their rates by discriminatory pricing wherever they could. As was economically rational, railways set their lowest rates where competition was greatest from another railway, from a canal or from coastal shipping. Thus railway amalgamations or the acquisition of a canal by a railway commonly led to increased rates where competition had, as a result, declined. Where there was competition from other railways, from canals or from coastal shipping, railway rates would be lower than those charged for similar shipments over similar distances on lines not facing this competition. Such discrimination rapidly increased the number of different railway rates. And there were many commentators ready to follow Galt in pointing out that, in general, foreign railway rates were substantially lower than British ones. Traders were often maddened because they knew or thought that their competitors paid less than they did. But their hopes of redress were limited. The maximum rates in the railways' statutes were too high to be effective at a time of falling prices. So complainants were mostly forced back upon seeking redress through prohibitions on discrimination. The original prohibition on discrimination of 1845 was made slightly less ambiguous in 1854; but given that the railways did not have to publish their rates, proving discrimination was difficult.[7] Traders had to prove their case, starting in the magistrates' courts. But even if they won there they were normally taken on appeal through the higher courts. All this was time-consuming and expensive. Comparatively few cases were brought.[8] And even fewer succeeded, because the railways deployed greater resources and expertise.

The 1872 Joint Select Committee remarked that 'committees and commissions carefully chosen have for the last 30 years clung to one form of competition after another; that it has nevertheless become more and more evident that competition must fail to do for railways what it has done for ordinary trade.'[9] It decided that to fix the same rate per mile for all railways would give the wrong incentives. Neither did there seem any simple way to base rates on costs, given the prevalence of joint costs. Every large company had millions of different rates.[10] The first endeavour, the Committee believed, should be to get the rates published. But even then it did not see how any tribunal could decide what the rates should be unless it were 'invested with absolute and arbitrary powers, which is out of the question, or unless some rules can be laid down by Parliament for its guidance. And it has been shown how impracticable it is to lay down any such rules.'[11] Therefore all such a tribunal could do would be to judge whether rates were 'unfair'. Rather optimistically, given the few cases on that ground that had been brought, and the fewer that had been decided in the customer's favour, the Committee felt that this was more practicable because the decisions of the courts in these cases had, in its judgement, been satisfactory in principle. The case against continuing to use the courts was their expense. But this, the Committee believed, could be reduced by specialized courts with specialized knowledge. It considered the forms that such a tribunal might take. Officials in the Board of Trade would not have the 'required judicial character; a court of law would fail in practical knowledge and administrative facility and a committee of the Houses of Parliament would have no permanence.'[12] Therefore it felt impelled to invent 'a new body ... which might be called the Railways and Canal Commission'. Having reached that conclusion, and invented a body which was to have many descendants, the Committee was sparing in its recommendations on what the new tribunal might do. It should be composed of not less than three persons, one an eminent lawyer and one acquainted with railway management, and its proceedings 'should be as simple and inexpensive as is consistent with giving due notice and hearing questions openly and fairly.' This hope for simplicity and low costs was, however, in vain (as was a further attempt in 1921 to simplify such procedures). One presumes that a legalistic approach was taken because the analogy with the ordinary courts that had previously considered these matters seemed a natural one; because it was thought that the right to demand evidence and to cross-examine railway witnesses was essential given the poverty of published financial information; and because the principal offence, that of discrimination, was more susceptible to legal than to business judgement. The minister introducing the Railway and Canal Traffic Bill did not elaborate and there was no debate over the matter.[13] He said disarmingly that one judge had happened to enjoy railway rates cases but he had retired; others disliked them intensely because they were required to use their discretion to decide the facts and merits in areas where they were technically incompetent. Therefore a special tribunal was needed. This led to the setting up in 1873 of the Railway and Canal Commission, from which there was to be no appeal on questions of fact, only on law. It did not, however, prove satisfactory.[14] The Railway and Canal Traffic Act, 1873, and several others which amended it had themselves been amended by the railway interest in such a way that they were largely ineffective; but, in general, the railways did not in any case find it difficult to demonstrate some difference in circumstances which justified a difference in rates. Moreover, complainants were hampered by the still very limited requirements that the 1873 Act put upon the railways to publish the details of their rates.

The ineffectiveness and expense of this legislation, combined with economic changes in the pattern of trade in the 1880s, led to demands for more-effective legislation. Traders objected with increasing vehemence both to the absolute levels of railway rates – there were always those to recall how much lower overseas such rates remained – and to the distortions in railway pricing produced by discrimination.[15] By 1887 the number of railway rates had multiplied further: there were 13 million different rates on the Great Nothern and 20 million on the London and Northwestern alone.[16] (If that seems extraordinary, in 1969 in the United States it was reported that 43 trillion different railway rates had been filed with the Interstate Commerce Commission.[17]) They reflected every kind of difference in distance, traffic and quality of service, obscuring the extent to which they were discriminatory. By now there remained little price competition between the railways or between railways and canals. In Manchester, for example, all five canals had been bought by railways or had been turned into sewers.[18] Rates might be lower between London and Liverpool than between London and Chester because the shipping lines who provided much of the railway freight at Liverpool could move to use another port. Wilson Cammells, the largest steelworks in Europe, moved from inland Derbyshire to Workington on the coast in 1881 in order to save £60,000 a year in railway charges.[19] Among the commonest and angriest complaints were that imports through the ports to inland cities attracted the lowest rates. It was said that it could be cheaper to transport agricultural and manufacturing products from North America than from inland areas to the major city markets of Britain. That the railways could often reasonably reply that this was true, because of the volumes carried, did not appease the chambers of commerce.

In 1882–3 yet another select committee recommended establishing a more powerful commission with a clearer basis for reviewing rates, one that did not depend upon its having to deal with individual complaints. But because of the activities of the railway interest several bills that set out to achieve this failed. It was during this period that the railway directors who were MPs achieved their maximum power,[20] wiliness and willingness to sit on the frequent parliamentary committees being more important than numbers. Moreover, both inside and outside Parliament, the large number of railway stockholders strengthened opposition to effective railway rate regulation. At 400,000, railway stockholders were the second largest group of stockholders after those who owned government stock.[21] Thus, despite the increasing opposition of the trading interest, an act of Parliament establishing a more powerful railway commission was staved off by the railway interest until 1888. By then adverse public opinion had become so strong, especially among agricultural interests, who were particularly affected by cheap imports, that within Parliament there was a sufficient concentration of effort among non-railway MPs for them to outvote the railway interest.

Gladstone was in office when the 1886 bill for further controlling railway rates was passing through Parliament, as he had been and was to be for the important nineteenth-century initiatives in railway legislation.[22] But by 1886 his main preoccupation had become his attempt to get Irish Home Rule through Parliament. However, one historian has argued that there was a connection between the two controversial measures going through Parliament simultaneously. A key element in Gladstone's Irish proposals was a compulsory reform of land tenure in the tenant's interest. The imposition of railway rate control envisaged in the 1886 Bill was similarly seen as an infringement of private railway statutes and so 'would destroy the value of railway property'.[23] Both were attacked in common, and in common terms, as assaults on private property rights. The traders nevertheless secured an act and an essentially similar act, the Railway and Canal Traffic Act, 1888, was passed by a Conservative government the following year.[24]

Although the new legislation also eventually turned out to be ineffective and as a result no property rights were infringed, the belief that the Liberal Party was less protective of the rights of property than it had been in the era of its commitment to *laissez-faire* was one of the reasons why many Liberals, led by Joseph Chamberlain, started making their move through Liberal Unionism to the Conservative Party, whether the invasion of property rights that they minded most was that associated with Gladstone's plans for Irish Home Rule or the breach, implied by the 1886 railway rate control bill, of the parliamentary convention that the property rights conferred by private statutes should not be abrogated. One result of this was the beginning of a decline in the number of Liberal MPs who were also railway directors, shifting the party balance of the railway interest, which had previously been strong in both parties.

The more immediate and direct outcome of the 1888 Act was what an American commentator has described as the only period in Britain during which the form of regulation became as legalistic as it has remained in the United States.[25] (As it happened, a similar legalistic phase in American regulation began in 1887 with the passing of the Interstate Commerce Act.) The new Railway and Canal Commission, established in 1888, had the authority of a high court. It was presided over by a judge with two lay assessors, and cases in front of it were argued by barristers. It is thus not surprising that it adopted legal procedures and rules of evidence. While there was no appeal from it on points of fact, there were appeals on points of law to the High Court.

It began its career with an attempt at reviewing all railway rates in order to eliminate all which it, and the Board of Trade officials advising it, had been persuaded were discriminatory. Given the multitude of rates, any such attempt to examine them all and reorganize them into permissible, non-discriminatory price schedules was practically impossible.[26] Nevertheless, the work started ambitiously and traders' hopes were high. This inquiry lasted 130 days.[27] The first 85 days were taken up with a preliminary inquiry before Board of Trade officials which was intended to resolve as many disagreements and obscurities as possible before the proceedings proper began. Those lasted 45 days. In all, 211 witnesses were examined; there were 4,000 objections to railway rates from 500 different objectors; 43,000 questions were asked and answered; and the official minutes ran to 4,000 pages. But the onus of proof that a particular rate was unreasonable remained on the objector. Typically, proceedings were made more difficult because Parliament had not managed to avoid inconsistency between the 1888 Act and earlier legislation.[28] And the offences that were actionable, such as discrimination, were not well defined. Nevertheless, the outcome was that many railway rates were brought down. The Board of Trade produced a vast number of rating schedules, which themselves had to be given statutory force. The railways then had the enormous task of working out these schedules for all pairs of stations for every category of goods within five months. This they failed to do. Instead, this task took until 1893, when the companies suddenly decided to raise many other rates that were within the maxima permitted by statute. Neither the objectors nor the Commissioners could prevent the railways from doing this. It was said that for every reduction there were five increases. The traders had not appreciated that, though discrimination was unlawful, the railways retained the freedom under their statutes to eliminate it by raising rates as much as by lowering them. Charges were also introduced for features which had previously been provided free. As Acworth had warned would happen, facilities were sometimes withdrawn and quality reduced.[29] There was no obligation on the railways to publish statistics to show whether the net effect of their rate changes was an increase or a reduction in average rates. The railways maintained that on average they were reducing their rates. Nevertheless, very soon a great many traders found that on balance they were worse off. The Railway and Canal Commission had in effect done nothing for them. The railway companies triumphed, as was said, because of their 'brilliant band of skilled experts'.[30] The protest from chambers of commerce throughout the country was immense and many traders refused to settle their accounts.

So great was the outcry that in 1893 yet another bill for controlling railway rates was brought forward.[31] Gladstone, aged eighty-four, was Prime Minister (for the last time). He thus presided over its introduction, almost fifty years after his first railway legislation, though his thoughts were by now all on Ireland. Home Rule dominated the session and there were many complaints that because of it the new railways bill did not get sufficient debate.[32] But the trading interest eventually felt forced to agree to what it argued was still an unsatisfactory bill, for otherwise, without even this less than satisfactory measure, the railways could have persisted in raising their rates. The passage of the Bill was complicated by its sponsoring minister's having to resign because of a financial scandal. And from weariness and disappointment with the progress on his Irish proposals Gladstone then himself resigned before it reached the statute book in 1894. In the final debate on it, the general tone was one of acute disappointment – at best, it was better than nothing.[33] Yet the committee which had prepared for the Bill – despite the fact that it had a majority of five railway directors – only conceded to the railway interest that there was to be no questioning of the reasonableness of existing rates, only of proposed changes.[34] There was, moreover, an express provision prohibiting any discrimination between the rates for home-produced and foreign merchandise.[35] And finally, not one contributor to the debate mentioned the provision that was to help to make the resulting act, the Railway and Canal Traffic Act, 1894, together with legislation in 1893 (see below), a more important turning-point for railway policy than the Devonshire Commission of 1865–7. For the concession made by the Committee to the railway interest over the questioning only of proposed rate changes was unimportant by comparison with the vital recommendation it made that the burden of proof be shifted to the railways from the objectors: if a trader objected to any rate increase made since the end of 1892, the railways had to justify it.

Because the offence of discrimination was ill-defined and the facts that were available made it hard to prove, the effect of thus altering the burden of proof was fundamental. However, it took some years to become fully effective. Initially, it led to all manner of procedural evasions. If beaten on one increase to one trader, a railway would maintain the old rates to others until each in turn had made its objection. This was a time-consuming and costly procedure for the customers: one historian has estimated that a challenge could cost as much as £2,000.[36]

One effect of this shift in the burden of proof was that it accentuated the controversy between two schools of railway economists.[37] First, there was the 'cost of service' school – generally supported by traders – who argued that all such rates should be based on the costs of the service provided plus some reasonable or normal profit. Among the strengths of their position was that not only was such a charging policy seem commonsensical but it was, they argued, the normal outcome of the competitive process. Another strong argument in its favour was that it appeared to be implied by the legal prohibition against discriminatory charging as it had developed in case law. (Then as now a discriminatory charge was a charge that resulted in an arbitrary difference in rates, that is, a difference not justifiable by a difference in cost or in quality of the good or service.) Therefore it is not surprising that in the early years of litigation before the Railway and Canal Commissioners after 1894, they tried to settle disputes over increases in rates by attempting to decide whether the increases were justified by increases in costs (even where the original differences in rates were not, and could not be, justified by cost or quality differences).

The other school believed in railways charging what the market would bear, as long as short-run costs were covered, and argued that their opponents' views, properly interpreted, were unworkable. This was because of the very high proportion of joint and common costs on a railway, overlaid by all the arbitrary practices of the Railway Clearing House. (In 1956 they were still more than 80 per cent of railway costs.)[38] Extreme examples were that it cost nothing except the cost of the ticket itself to carry another passenger on an already scheduled train; and that if a train was already going from A to B, the extra cost of its return journey was zero on the assumption that it would have to return anyway. Hence the cost of carrying freight by such trains was little more than the handling cost. However, joint costs were more widespread than those examples suggest. Different trains used the same tracks when making different journeys. Rolling stock and locomotives were used to varying extents, often making different journeys at different times. Many of the staff handled many traffics during the course of their work.

Various economists tried to argue that many of these costs could in principle be allocated by working out in advance what was the fully allocated cost of any particular traffic. However, this cost-of-service approach ran into two insuperable difficulties. The first was that whatever volume and pattern of traffic had been forecast when an investment decision was made, the actual volume and pattern would always turn out to differ from these, often substantially, making the *ex post facto* attribution of costs impossible. The second difficulty was more fundamental. It was that this approach disregarded the essential economic principle that 'bygones are bygones.' Once a cost has been incurred, it is economically efficient to accept traffic as long as what it earns exceeds the variable – more properly, the short-run marginal – cost of carrying it. For the railway to be profitable, enough margin over variable cost must be made for the fixed cost to be recouped and at least normal profits earned. There is nothing in economic theory or in ordinary commercial practice to say that such margins should be constant. Far from it – the aim of commercial pricing is to seek out and charge what the market will bear. What limits the possibility of effective discrimination here is competition. The stronger the competition, the less the margin that can be earned. Hence it is not surprising that, as we have seen, rates were lowest where railways competed with other railways, with canals, or with coastal shipping. The railway economist Sir William Acworth, who was an extremist on this point, maintained that railway costs were too complicated to unravel and should be left unanalysed. Railways should divorce rate-setting from costs entirely.[39] Their aim should be to charge 'what the market will bear', irrespective of costs, other than direct 'out of pocket expenses', and hope that the result will cover total costs and make each railway a profit. In this period, as returns fell and some railways went into loss, the economic case for discrimination increased, as some of the defenders of the cost-of-service principle recognized. Provided variable or short-run marginal costs are met, any contribution to fixed overheads is better than none – the enterprise will be less unprofitable than it otherwise would be – unless and until some of these overhead costs themselves can be cut.

There cannot be any question but that in economic terms the 'charging what the traffic will bear' school, led by Acworth, was correct (even though to do as little cost analysis as he recommended was a mistake, and the existence of pooling agreements in restraint of competition increased the possibility of economically inefficient discrimination). Especially where marginal costs are lower than average costs, pure discrimination is an economically efficient policy.[40] Nevertheless, it is frequently outlawed – as by American legal tradition and current EEC legislation – because to charge different persons different rates for the same, or virtually the same, service strikes at the root of what public opinion and frequently the law regard as equitable.[41] The railways were able to evade some criticism by disguising *what the market will bear* as *value-of-service charging*, by which higher valued goods paid higher rates, again irrespective of costs. Thus the carriage of jewellery was dearer than that of coal. The political advantage of this principle was that the goods used by those on higher incomes generally paid more for their transport than those used by the poor. Similarly, relative to cost, the rich paid more for their class of railway travel than the poor did for theirs. Nevertheless, this was far from a complete defence against a charge of discrimination; and it was a poor economic argument.

Thus one can see how the switch in the burden of proof from the objector to the railway had a dramatic effect. Before this switch the objector had to prove that there was not a cost or quality difference underpinning the rate difference; but, given the scrappy statistics the railways published and the jointness of their costs, it was rare that any objector could do this. After 1894 the railways had the equally difficult task of proving in their turn that for any price increase there was a cost or quality justification. For a few years the lawyers and the Commission struggled with this matter and some increases were allowed; but in 1899 the traders finally persuaded the Commission that the railways' statistics and methodolgy could not support rate increases.[42] Thereafter the railways did not dare raise rates. But neither did they lower any either, for fear they would not be able to raise them again, a fear justified by the failure of their appeal to the Court of Appeal on one such case.[43] Thus the consequences of the shift in the burden of proof were that before 1900 the railways were able to raise very few rates and that after 1900, until the First World War, they were not even able to raise them to cover costs, or lower them to meet competition. What made this devastating for the railways was that after twenty years in which prices, including those of railway inputs, had fallen, prices generally started to rise again, just as the railways' fares and charges were frozen. This result helps explain the steep drop at this time in railway profitability.[44]

This episode illustrates another cause of regulatory failure. Quite apart from its increasing the opportunities for discrimination though collusion, the prohibition on the use of discrimination as a method of pricing, though common, runs into two kinds of problems. There is first the clash between economic and legal principles: proceeding legally against discrimination implies a belief that profit rates should be the same on different services; but, while this should be achieved by competition between simple products, there is no efficiency case for this in complex markets where firms produce many outputs with joint costs. The second kind of problem is that using the prevention of discrimination as the touchstone of the success of regulation implies a belief that one can establish the costs of each service so as to decide what is a discriminatory or non-discriminatory price for it. Because logically one cannot do this in so far as there are joint costs, expert argument before the Commission (and on appeal before the courts) was inconclusive, and sometimes the result was determined more by forensic ability than by the merits of a case. Ultimately what mattered, however, was which side had the burden of proof. Whichever side had it, had a near impossible case to make and therefore was prone to fail. The alternative policy adopted in the United States was to construct cost categories and artificial allocations of costs, as was done by the Interstate Commerce Commission. By pretending that costs were what they were not, this found an artificial, but more workable, solution to the problem, though at a substantial cost in economic inefficiency.

Besides the shift in the burden of proof that it brought about, there was, however, another major aspect of the 1894 Act which was arguably of still greater importance: the clear breach in the principle that private statutes were sacrosanct contracts. Previous cases against railway rates had been based on the principle of equity enshrined in the argument that there should be no undue preference or discrimination. The 1894 Act in refusing to allow railways to raise their rates without proving that they were not discriminatory was, and was seen at the time to be, breaching the convention that these statutes were immutable parliamentary contracts. However, the ground for this had been prepared by another act the year before.

2.2   Social obligations on the railways

As the historian of the railway interest has written:

> Prior to 1894 the power of railway companies to raise or lower rates within the maxima laid down by Parliament had never been controlled by statute, save in the cases of undue preference and through rates . . . [W]hether the demands of the unions were for increased wages or shorter hours, the companies found that the Act of 1894, coupled with that of 1893, had driven them into a corner, for they saw little hope of being able to pass on to the public even a proportion of higher labour costs.[45]

The Railway Regulation Act, 1893, was on railway safety. Previously it had been possible to argue that the uncommercial obligations imposed on railways were not uncompensated. The railways might have to carry at special rates troops in times of emergency or the mails, but they would be paid for their carriage. They might think that carrying poor passengers at cheap rates in the parliamentary trains was unprofitable, but it was argued, not implausibly, that they were wrong. Moreover, although since the death of Huskisson at the opening of the Liverpool and Manchester railway, Parliament had taken an interest in rail safety, it had always held back from imposing safety restrictions on existing railways. In 1839 it had given the Railways Inspectorate powers to stop the opening of new railways unless it was satisfied they were safe, but otherwise relied entirely on the railways' self-interest and the power of publicity. In investigating accidents, it was the duty of the Inspectorate to discover causes, apportion blame (if it could) and make recommendations; but, deliberately, it had been given no powers of enforcement. It was held to be in the self-interest of the railways to provide a service safe enough not to deter users – a presumption that became less persuasive as competition declined. The most the Inspectorate and politicians could do was to give as much publicity to the facts and recommendations as possible so as to stimulate enlightened self-interest in the railway boards. In addition, it was repeatedly argued that it was dangerous for outsiders – even the experts on the Railways Inspectorate – to impose technical solutions on the railways; and this was borne out in the 1880s when strong pressure was put on the railways to adopt a system of braking which was then discovered to be technically unsound. Nevertheless, a succession of railway accidents, declining railway profitability, the waning of the political influence of railway directors, especially in the Liberal Party, and changing public attitudes resulted in the 1893 Act, which for the first time gave the Railways Inspectorate powers to impose safety requirements on the railways, to be adopted at the railways' cost.[46]

Coming a year before the 1894 Act, this measure, together with that act, fundamentally altered the basis of railway regulation.[47] It would be convenient if it could be said, though it would not quite be accurate to say it, that the 1893 Act on rail safety was the first occasion when Parliament deliberately broke the convention that private statutes were to be regarded as parliamentary contracts immune from any retrospective legislation that imposed unprofitable or otherwise uncompensated financial burdens on a utility's property. However, what was special about the breach of this convention by the 1893 and 1894 statutes was that it soon had substantial consequences for the railway companies, reducing their already impaired ability to pay dividends; and even more that it set a precedent for the future imposition of uncompensated burdens on the railways and other utilities. These measures destroyed the notion that such a utility has a statutory contract, licence or franchise, entered into subject to stated conditions but with the owners believing that those conditions were not too burdensome for them to be able to make sufficient profit to maintain their business and reward the stockholders to the extent needed to raise the capital required. The change was particularly onerous because many railways were already barely profitable or already unprofitable. But even a profitable utility will find that its stockholders will require higher rewards if it can expect to be suddenly saddled with unpredictable burdens: if the belief that there is a parliamentary contract is replaced by an expectation that Parliament can change the terms of that contract whenever it thinks fit, investment capital will be harder to secure.

It may seem odd to complain if a sovereign legislature uses its power to require railways or any other utilities to be safe; but that is to miss the point. When such a legislature establishes an enterprise which it thereafter expects to be self-financing through its profits, and then decides to change the terms on which that enterprise operates in such a way as to lower its profits, it had better consider what damage the changes may do. This is best seen as an issue not of principle, but of expediency. If in the limit the burdens are so onerous that the enterprise has to run down, or abandon, activities, then that possibility should be foreseen by the legislature. In some circumstances that might be the preferred outcome; but it can never be sensible simply to impose burdens – even more to start a habit of doing so – without calculating the economic consequences.

In the circumstances of the time, what could have been done to avoid the problem? If we accept the view of many contemporaries, from Roebuck in the 1844 debate onwards, that the British railways could have been provided at a much lower cost, as some railways had been overseas – a third of the cost was a figure often given – then a solution might have been found through writing railway capital down to its current-use value, as Roebuck had advised. With about only a third of the capital to be serviced, acceptable returns to shareholders may have been consistent with some combination of lower tariffs and higher safety standards. Such an outcome could have been achieved without public cost by the original, but not the emasculated, version of the 1844 Bill, which admitted the possibility that a railway's property should be realistically valued when the railway's position came to be reviewed. As Gladstone and many other supporters of the Bill most probably intended, a railway, once acquired by the nation, would not have been kept under public management but would have been leased to private management for a term of years on stated terms and conditions which one would expect to have reflected rising social expectations on safety and any other social obligations. In other words, the railways' parliamentary contracts would have been periodically renegotiated. (One may assume that competition and higher profitability would have forced lines built before 1844, and so escaping the provisions of the Act, to devalue their assets as well.) The only other way in which the railways could theoretically have been revalued was if Parliament had not prevented new lines from being built in competition with the old overvalued lines. However, for as long as such new railways had had to incur the heavy expenses of the private bill procedure and offer over-generous compensation to avoid opposition to their acquiring land, they would have been unable to get capital costs down to the lowest overseas levels. Moreover, there would always have been the likelihood, as happened with the early railways and with other utilities, that after a period of fierce competition in which tariffs fell, there would be amalgamations or collusion resulting in tariffs being raised monopolistically in an attempt to service the combined capital.

Some historians have maintained that in the absence of any pressures to revalue to realistic levels and caught in a position where they could not get the rate increases they believed they needed in order to maintain, let alone restore, profitability and with their shareholders' interests in mind, some railways tried to improve their profits by cutting costs and some aspects of quality, where they could, given the regulations imposed on them. This seems plausible. As Acworth said, 'Assume that your tribunal can fix a reasonable rate, what is the use of it unless it can schedule to its judgement a minute specification of the quality of service to be given for the rate?'[48] Falling profits put pressure on costs generally. Railway accidents with loss of life remained fairly common and apparently seemed to be increasing in frequency towards the end of the nineteenth century; and the railways were often accused in this regard of putting the interests of their shareholders before those of their passengers and, even more, those of their workmen. The railway unions indeed got much of their early strength from the political weight of their complaints about safety and the long hours that railwaymen worked in the interests of economy. (The two complaints were related since long hours sometimes made railwaymen too tired to avoid accidents.)[49] There was a bitter strike in Scotland mainly over the excessive hours worked by guards and shunters. And this led to the first parliamentary committee into their hours, which confirmed that some railway workers did work over-long hours and which in turn led to the first legislation on the matter. This gave the Board of Trade the right to demand new work schedules on the railways where its officials judged that excessive hours were being worked. Furthermore, in 1898 railway workers became entitled to compensation if injured in the course of their work. Both of these measures further infringed the notion of the parliamentary contract and interfered with railway management. Then in 1900 there came the first parliamentary act that allowed the Board of Trade to compel railways not to use equipment and stock which its officials thought dangerous. The fears of many who had fought the abandonment of *laissez-faire* were thus realized – though one of the results of these and other measures was the lowering of the accident rate among railwaymen from 1 in 334 in 1875 to 1 in 1,006 in 1899. Another, far from unimport-ant cause of the entry of the State into industrial relations, which later developed into corporatism, was the downward pressure on quality, especially that induced by the inadequacies of railway regulation. Moreover, downward pressure on railways wages continued as the railways struggled against declining profits, and in the decade before the First World War it became normal for Board of Trade officials and then govern-ment ministers to become involved in settling strikes. From these beginnings grew the conciliation services of the Board of Trade, which were later to develop into the Ministry of Labour.[50] The activities of Lloyd George and Winston Churchill in negotiating between employers and employees to settle major strikes so as to avoid disruption of the economy were almost the first examples of what was to become an essential feature of the growing corporatism between 1910 and 1980.[51]

Once such interventions began, there was a growth in the imposition of other social burdens on the railways. Legislation increased the number and the burden of cheap trains, especially those for workmen, until one railway economist was quite reasonably able to claim that 'the workmen's trains are really a special tax imposed on a single industry in the interest of a particular class and for which the railways receive no credit. Control in its present form is in danger of regulating private enterprise out of existence.'[52] The same could be said of safety regulation where, he argued, the statutory requirement to use automatic couplings implied such a large expenditure to avoid so few fatalities and injuries that, on a basis which modern economists will recognize as that of the 'Valuation of Human Life', the implied valu-ation of such a life was the then inordinate figure of £10,000 for each fatality and £600 for each injury.[53] Not only did the State impose many such burdens, which whatever their merits limited railway profits, but the evasive action that railways then took to try to retain, or regain, their profitability led to further intervention.

2.3 Towards railway nationalization

The most effective response to this persistent pressure on railway profits was neither cost cutting nor the lowering of quality. Rather, it was amalgamation and informal combination. As we have seen, amalgamation had taken place since the 1840s or even earlier with the effect of driving rates up through increased monopoly power. In 1853 the Cardwell Committee decided that the main railway lines were already emerging as dominant forces within their sector of the market and recommended that further amalgamations conferring monopoly power should be avoided.[54] But its advice was ignored. More telling than the strength of the railway interest in this was the impossibility of stopping the railways making informal pooling arrangements to avoid competition and raise prices. The Railway Clearing House, founded in 1842, had, as noted above, other purposes – to handle financial transactions between railways and to solve problems of operational interworking – but it also became a place where railway managers discussed how they could work together. And the Railway Companies' Association, founded in 1861, was another such place.[55]

Price competition between railways had been at its peak in the 1850s and was vanishing by 1870.[56] However, even then some realized that competition need not be actual. The 1872 Joint Select Committee on Railway Amalgamation noted that:

> there is one other form in which 'potential' competition on the part of possible railway companies has no doubt had a powerful effect. If an existing railway company makes exorbitant charges, or refuses reasonable facilities, it may encourage other parties to undertake a new and competing line. Such a line is sure, sooner or later, to join the combination of existing railways and to make common cause with them. But in the meantime it may cause great reduction of rates.

Many witnesses told the Committee of the effectiveness of this competition and of it as a reason for preventing amalgamation. However, the Committee decided that it was of declining importance, because experience had shown how unprofitable rival lines were and therefore the threat of entry had a rapidly diminishing influence. And it came close to concluding that amalgamations, of which there were several more pending, were inevitable and probably desirable. Yet so volatile was public opinion on this matter that, the year after, Parliament threw out a major amalgamation.[57] Amalgamations became rarer from then on, but informal combination increased. Such competition as remained – and its extent was much disputed – was in quality. There were many pooling arrangements, arrangements not to compete and working unions which did not require a parliamentary bill.[58] By 1900 the number of railway companies had dwindled from more than 1,000 to about 100. This was still a large number (though some were non-operational),[59] but as evidence of competition it is misleading, since not only had informal combination increased, but there were as well the collusive arrangements promoted by the Railway Clearing House.

In early 1907 the Great Central and Great Northern announced an agreement for the pooling of their net receipts. This was rejected as unlawful both by the Railway and Canal Commission and then by the Court of Appeal. But the boards of directors found a way around this barrier in 1909 by proposing an amalgamation of the Great Northern, Great Central and Great Eastern railways, under which 'almost all the railways in Eastern England from the Humber to the Thames would have been "districted" under one control.'[60] As it happened, the same year a very serious strike on these railways brought in first Board of Trade officials and then both Lloyd George and later Winston Churchill as mediators. Given the strength of public opinion, they were able to persuade these railways not to go ahead with that union. However, Churchill's involvement with the railways led him to the opinion that 'there is no real economic future for British railways apart from amalgamation of one kind or another.'[61]

Settling the strike cost the railways money; and it is said that, in persuading the railway directors to settle, Churchill had agreed to allow them further amalgamation to help meet the cost. But his bill to enable this in 1909 had to be withdrawn because of public feeling against amalgamation. Still another committee was set up, with Acworth as one of its members.[62] It was becoming clear to many people that competition on the railways was over and that some form of control of monopoly was needed. A Board of Trade official told the new inquiry that some thirteen railway companies effectively controlled 88 per cent of the total mileage.[63] The Committee predicted the inevitability of further amalgamations.

It was on this committee also that Acworth, with the greatest difficulty, persuaded the majority, against the railway interests they represented, that railways should be forced to produce statistics of passenger-miles and freight ton-miles so that one could work out average revenues.[64] Yet the railway interest prevented even this from being made law. Thus throughout the nineteenth century and into the 1920s, it was impossible for Parliament, Commissioners or anyone else to know whether average revenues were rising or falling, let alone by how much. It was still impossible to work out intelligible and meaningful rates of return on capital, and it was also impossible to know whether any given set of rate changes was likely to lead to an increase or a fall in revenue, either before or after they were made. But in any case so poor were railway finances by this time that the Government had to pass a further act to allow railways to raise their rates in 1913 by 4 per cent in a totally arbitrary manner, cutting across the machinery of the Railway and Canal Commission and the courts. Railway policy was in complete disarray.

Government intervention in railway rates, operations, safety and even union matters had gradually increased, but without success. No one seemed to be satisfied. Users complained that rates were too high by European standards. Shareholders' dividends almost continuously declined. Workers complained of low pay and unsafe conditions. In 1912 there was a meeting in London of railway economists from Britain and abroad to discuss railways.[65] Against the background just described, it is not surprising that the British contributions were gloomy. Though several books had recently been written on the nationalization of the railways and it was said that at least two British government ministers, probably Lloyd George and Churchill, were known to favour nationalization, the British economists present were all strongly opposed to it both in principle and from their experience. One concluded that there was no definite evidence that private enterprise could not continue to provide an efficient railway service, but the decline in competition and the random actions of the legislature in his judgement made it unlikely that it could unless there were at last developed 'a well thought out scheme of control'.[66] A second blamed Parliament for its irresponsibility, condemned the regulatory regime but argued that there was just a chance that nationalization might be avoided.[67] However, the best known, Sir William Acworth, was far more pessimistic. He spoke of the inefficiency of state railways abroad. They were corrupt. State purchase was never a financial success. State railways' operating efficiency was lower. And except by comparison with Britain their fares were higher. Moreover, private railways had made all the innovations. However, he too saw competition dying on the British railways as the last amalgamations took place. Therefore an effective system of state control was needed. But he could not see either Parliament or the law courts being helpful. How could one draw up statutes which would specify the quality of service to be provided at a price, or how the services of a company are to be judged efficient in the public interest?

> Can anyone imagine the strict technical procedure of a Law Court – with its pre-liminary proceedings and precise issues, its sworn testimony and its rigid exclusion of whole classes of evidence which, though logically irrelevant, are often precisely the considerations which would influence a businessman in deciding a business pro-position – applied to a question as to whether the passenger services of a particular company are reasonably adequate, taking account broadly of the sufficiency of trains, their speed, their punctuality, their comfort, their cross-country connections, the volume and class of the traffic catered for, the financial position of the company and a dozen things more which ought to be taken into account if a fair all round conclusion is to be arrived at?[68]

He argued that the only possibility for state regulation without nationalization was to give executive government ample powers of control, but this he did not believe the public would accept. By experience and temperament what he looked for was an executive with

> wide and arbitrary powers of compulsion. But I quite appreciate that it would be extraordinarily difficult to lay down the precise scope and extent of these powers and to define the organ through which, and the method by which, government should act. That not even the nucleus of such machinery exists at present I am well aware. I see no signs of any public demands for its establishment, and I can appreciate any attempt to establish it would, not unnaturally, be met with the most strenuous opposition by the railway companies. And, logically, they would occupy a very strong position in resist-ing the transference of the ultimate control of a commercial undertaking from their shareholders to their customers ... The conclusion therefore that I most reluctantly arrive at is that we cannot go on as we are, but that there is little hope for the establishment of an adequate and clearly thought out system of state control, and that, therefore, the only alternative – state ownership – is inevitable. I can see on the political horizon no force to stop it[69]

Thus, most unhappily, he reached the conclusion that state ownership was inevit-able, though he believed that the public would lose by it more than they would gain in both financial and operational terms. Another of his colleagues spoke of regulation

> to be in the direction of depriving the proprietors of the power of adjusting their busi-ness with the changes in commerce and industry. The railways had been compelled to spend vast sums without regard to their ability to win a reasonable return on the venture. In other directions the controls stop short, covering only a portion of the field. All this is driving us in the direction of nationalisation. Not because as a nation we wish it or think it would be to our advantage. Not in my opinion because adequate control has proved impossible. It is driving us mainly because the legislator has acted on no guiding principles, but has extended its control in this direction or that, just as popular agitation impelled it.[70]

All were in despair at the random and inchoate way in which regulatory control had developed.

It is interesting that Acworth, like James Morrison about seventy-five years before him, was certain that a discretionary system was needed in which business judge-ments could be made on what it was reasonable for a railway to do and what profits it might reasonably make. This notion, that the regulatory function requires the judgement and temperament of a businessman rather than those of a legislator or a lawyer, we shall come across again. Acworth saw neither Parliament nor the law courts nor the Railway and Canal Commission, with its legalistic procedures, as suited for this. Thus, nationalization, despite everything that he and his colleagues expected to come from it, was also in his view the best of bad alternatives, given regulatory collapse.

In the years just before the First World War, Parliament had no time to give to the railways. They were taken over by the State during the war through legislation which provided for them to stay under state control until two years after it.[71] But they came out of the war in even worse financial condition than they had entered it.[72] And it seemed very likely that they would be formally nationalized. However, though most Liberal ministers, led by Lloyd George, were in favour of it, the Conservatives in the coalition government were against it, and they won.[73] In many respects the public ownership measure that was contemplated was more like nationalization of the (Herbert) Morrisonian kind than is often supposed, for ministers did not like the habit, which Lloyd George and Churchill had acquired, of bringing influence to bear on the railways whenever they believed this politically necessary.

Instead of nationalization the railways, in 1921, were subjected to a forced amalgamation into four main-line railways. Because these amalgamations were forced the act that achieved them was quite different from the earlier amalgamation acts.[74] In a cruel irony it introduced a new form of profit control. The Railway Rates Tribunal, which the act set up, was to ensure that each of the four railways adjusted its rates on average every year to earn a 'standard' net revenue 'equivalent' to the aggregate net revenues earned in 1913 by the companies that it was formed from – adjusted for differences in capital employed. If they had earned less than this in one year, they were allowed to raise their tariffs, provided further that they had operated 'with efficient and economical working and management'. If they had earned more, then they could only retain 20 per cent of their net revenue over the standard, the rest being handed back to the customer through lower prices. As, beyond this, the statute did not make the mechanisms or basic definitions clear, the Railway Rates Tribunal could have developed this form of regulation in various directions. The provisions were consistent with classic rate-of-return regulation as developed in the United States; with the sliding-scale provisions found in the control of other utilities; and even conceivably with their equivalent in real terms, that is, with the earning of a real return on capital or RPI–X. However, they never came into effect. Net revenue never again reached 1913 levels. The railways believed that they would lose more revenue than they would gain through price increases.[75]

The Railway Rates Tribunal, which replaced the Railway and Canal Commission,[76] was an attempt to set up a less judicial body. The presiding judge was replaced by a lawyer. But lawyers still argued in front of it and it remained a division of the High Court. And the railways apparently had almost as much difficulty as before in arguing for a change in rates.[77] Renamed the Transport Tribunal after 1947, the Tribunal's proceedings remained intensely legalistic. Not only were parties were represented by lawyers, but formidable preparations had to be made for it – of the same magnitude as before US regulatory bodies. Its last review of rates, in 1955–6, occupied 44 days of hearings and ran to more than 1,000 pages of evidence.[78] To the end, the conflict between legal prohibitions against discrimination and those who wished to base charges on costs ran up against the fact of joint costs. But this regulatory role was only abolished because at last ministers believed that competition from other forms of transport was strong enough for rate regulation to go.

However, already in the 1920s and 1930s the growth of road competition had posed new questions for such rate control. There has been much controversy over how far the railways were remiss in not lowering their rates to meet road competition and how far the Tribunal stopped them from doing this.[79] But what the course of this competition in this period clearly shows is how natural monopoly may be eroded. A danger any natural monopoly faces is that a competitor may come in and undercut its prices on some line of business, reducing its total revenue more than its total costs. Successive undercutting of lines of business of this kind can make natural monopoly unsustainable by undermining its competitive advantage in one market after another until it experiences financial collapse. In broad terms this is what happened to the British railway system progressively in the first half of the twentieth century. Economic theory says that this outcome can be avoided by appropriate pricing.[80] Prices should be lowered in each market as competition builds up. Provided prices cover marginal costs, genuine natural monopoly will be protected without economic inefficiency. One is in no position to know for how long the railways would have been able to defend their natural monopoly if they had had pricing freedom, but they believed that they had in this respect a justifiable grievance.

The inter-war period, in which there was this enforced railway cartel instead of outright nationalization, was thus an uneasy one for the railways. The cartel was policed on the one hand through political and corporatist relations between ministers, unions and the railway companies, and on the other by a tribunal whose decisions were themselves political and economically incoherent. One can understand how Herbert Morrison, who as a young man had pleaded cases before the Railway Rates Tribunal, could himself find administrative reasons for nationalization.[81] As a minister supported by civil servants, he believed that he would be in a far better position to regulate the railways and match their expertise than any tribunal could be when confronted with the expertise and knowledge of the railways on the one hand and the poverty of the information available both to the railways themselves and to objectors on the other. In his bill for nationalizing the transport agencies of the capital by setting up the London Passenger Transport Board he had provided for the relevant minister to take over many regulatory duties from the Tribunal, but after the fall of the Ramsay MacDonald Labour government in 1931, his Liberal successor in the National government altered the Bill to transfer such powers back to the Tribunal. In 1945–51 ministers sponsoring nationalized industries took over most regulatory functions not only for the railways but also for the other utilities.

Thus the history of regulatory commissions for the railways showed that their development and use could not rescue railway regulation or make it acceptable, politically or to railway customers. The unprofitability of the railway industry – at least to most of its shareholders – showed that the regulation of unprofitable industry was beyond the instruments available then. The tendency of any loss-making operation is to discriminate in its pricing so as to maximize its revenue. The multitude of separate railways, and of journey types and distances for freight traffic, encouraged the development of literally millions of different rates (though passenger fares were generally set on a uniform basis). If done in the right way, it is economically efficient thus to discriminate when marginal costs are below average costs; but the inequity is no less objected to by customers. At the same time, losses encouraged the railways to economize on quality – cutting investment on safety, and keeping wages low with further adverse effects on safety. Liberal governments before the First World War were drawn into intervening in both safety and wage determination so that in effect they levied a tax, in the words of at least one contemporary, on these industries by requiring them to fulfil social obligations that were not in their commercial interest – at a time when their returns were too low for them to maintain their capital intact. This led many people who had no ideological predisposition to believe in it to agree that nationalization was the only way in which to solve the problems of the railways – problems which had been intensified in 1893 and 1894 by the defeat of the railway interest (which became complete after 1900) and the collapse of the convention that private statutes were immutable contracts. There was no longer regulatory capture, only regulatory failure.

2.4 The other natural monopolies and competition policy: regulation by local government

For much of the nineteenth century the control of the other natural monopolies followed the pattern set in its early part. They needed a private bill – or later in some cases a licence conferred after a comparable statutory procedure – which almost always had a term of years – commonly twenty-one or forty-two – after which a new instrument or renewal was required.[82] Such monopolies were local, and at any time statutory powers could be sought by a rival establishment to enter the territory of an existing establishment, lured either by the existing establishment's extreme inefficiency or by rapidly rising demand. The costs of the legislative process and of laying an alternative system of gas or water pipes, or later electricity or telephone cables, were a deterrent to entry, and this increased in intensity towards the end of the century as local authorities acquired more powers to limit or make more difficult the acquiring of wayleaves on the roads by new utilities. As a result, such a potential rival might be bought out before it started construction, or it might begin to compete, driving prices down, before it reached an accommodation with the existing utility and they used their joint monopoly power to service their inflated capitals.

Unlike the railways, however, many local monopolies were profitable and often achieved the maximum dividend, usually 10 per cent, written into their statutes. Therefore, to increase their profits, they increased their capital where they could by watering their capital stock or through over-investment.[83] To try to prevent this, users came increasingly to attempt to use local authorities as a counterweight – this was especially important when the term of a franchise came up for renewal.

During the century there was one technical regulatory innovation of enduring importance. In 1867 a select committee chaired by Edward Cardwell concluded that 'the supply of gas ought to be controlled either by the means of effective competition or if the system of exclusive supply be maintained, by the means of efficient regulation.' To deal with this problem of control, officials at the Board of Trade had invented the sliding-scale rate of return (thought to have been first devised for a bill authorizing a Sheffield gas company in 1866).[84] Its desirability was hotly contested in front of a 1875 select committee chaired by W. E. Forster (better known as the author of the 1870 Education Act). The precise formula that emerged from the Committee prefigured the modern RPI–X formula, except that it was not expressed in real terms. The specific problem it was intended to solve was how to restrain investment to what was really needed and to keep costs down. This was to be achieved by a 'double-acting sliding scale' by which gas companies were allowed to increase their dividends if they had brought their charges down in a predetermined relationship with them.[85] Conversely, if their charges rose, their dividends had to fall in the same ratio. Although the feeling against retrospective legislation was still so strong that the adoption of this control mechanism remained voluntary, roughly half the gas companies did so, persuaded either because they were straining against a ceiling of 10 per cent or because of strong local hostility or both.[86] In London the activities of the Metropolitan Board of Works, which as a local authority was a forerunner of the London County Council, exemplified the extent of this hostility. It had no real authority over the gas companies but found itself a popular role in repeatedly challenging their pricing policies and investment plans,[87] and was among those pressing strongly for the extension of this form of control. In the end this sliding-scale regulation was defeated by inflation during the First World War, but while it disappeared from Britain, until it was revived in inflation-proof form as the RPI–X formula in the 1980s (chapter 6), there were examples of it in the United States in the 1920s and 1930s, as well as a revival of it there in the 1980s.[88]

More generally, the Victorian local authorities usually tried to argue the case of the consumer against the monopolies. Given that there was no lead by national government, it is not surprising that, in different parts of the country, every kind of arrangement was reached between the utilities and local government.[89] The infinite flexibility of the private bill mechanism enabled this, helped by various later pieces of utility and local government legislation. Frustration persuaded an increasing number of local authorities to buy up, or otherwise take into ownership, utilities they found particularly unsatisfactory. Although the hope was often that through greater efficiency and the lower cost of local government borrowing charges would fall, the prices paid on takeover and a failure to achieve improved efficiency meant that often enough charges rose. Moreover, the conflicts that had taken place between local government and the independent utilities were now, with these municipal takeovers, frequently transformed into conflicts within local government between councillors and officers or between the municipal undertakings and the rest of the authority. The chairman of the local authority committee championing users against the private utilities all too easily shaded into the chairman of the local authority water, gas or electricity committee identifying with the views of the general manager and staff of the municipal utility concerned.[90] In some cases several local authorities owned one utility jointly. In others, local authorities participated in the ownership of more than one utility of the same kind within their area. It was in this way that the hopelessly variegated pattern of ownership developed that made the rationalization of the water, gas and electricity industries impossible during the early twentieth century and eventually to seem irresolvable short of nationalization.

One common outcome of this patchwork of ownership and the lack of strong incentives for local authority undertakings to cut costs was that these undertakings indulged their ability to adopt any of a wide variety of equipment and technical solutions, helping to prevent the British engineering industries related to them achieving the technical economies of scale achieved elsewhere, above all in Germany.[91] This individualism also prevented the local monopolies themselves merging or interconnecting to achieve economies of scale from larger operations. There were exceptions to this – for example, in the North-east electricity prices were lowered substantially by the development of an electricity grid. But such exceptions only point up what might have been achieved elsewhere.[92]

The great difficulty Britain had before the Second World War in devising an effective system of monopoly regulation contributed to a general public attitude of tolerance towards monopoly and oligopolistic collusion.[93] As one recent commentator has said, Britain has been more readily susceptible to a revival of Victorian values recently than it would otherwise have been because to a remarkable extent it never lost them, especially in the view taken upon the right relation between government and industry.[94] It is unsurprising that the ministerial and civil service tradition developed in Britain of non-intervention in industry was long maintained in relations between government and private industry, where government in Britain has generally avoided any situation in which it could be criticized for pretending to know more about an industry's affairs than it does itself. But even when the public sector was at its largest as a proportion of Gross National Product, and nationalized industries dominated large sectors of the economy, that tradition of non-intervention remained strong. Whatever ministers said about their policy, the public industries and other public agencies were allowed a remarkable degree of freedom in running themselves.

In the 1890s, and up until the First World War, the United States through the Sherman and Clayton Acts was developing an active government policy towards cartels and other restrictive practices, when nothing of the same kind was attempted in Britain. Alfred Chandler, the distinguished American economic historian, has observed that one effect of the active trust-busting policy in the USA was that firms were encouraged more to merge.[95] As a result industrial giants came into being which were far better able to realize economies of scale than were smaller firms. They were particularly important as the American economy began to move overseas. In contrast, British tolerance of trusts and cartels by Parliament, the courts and to some extent public opinion meant that collusive firms frequently shared a domestic market without any need to rationalize. This has been advanced as yet another reason for Britain's relative industrial decline. There were those who stressed the culpability of the British in this respect and the social impossibility of their preventing such combinations. 'Combination has been accepted without regulation in England because the entire English social system is a series of closed groups . . . English society is stratified and cellular,' observed one American in 1908.[96] Another reason given for Britain's tolerance in this area was the unfriendliness of the English common law to any action against collusion which was not plainly unlawful.[97] A third reason was that there were politicians then who were ready to argue that, even if market forces did result in monopoly or cartels, there was still no economic reason for interfering with them. At the time the economic theory of monopoly was poorly developed and the notion of market failure not well understood.[98] Neither were the railways the only industry able to muster a sufficient body of supporters in Parliament. Others usually found that they could get the support there that they needed to prevent anti-monopoly legislation. Public opinion was somewhat less amenable. Before the First World War, William Lever had tried to establish a cartel monopolizing the soap industry. In this case, it was principally public opinion that prevented him from doing this.[99] After the First World War, there were several attempts to use the force of public opinion to condemn restrictive practices, notably through the Committee on Trusts, established in 1918; but they proved almost entirely ineffective.[100] There was not the same muck-raking tradition which in the United States had been proved so effective in discomforting monopoly. Conversely, the low regard in which regulation by commission was held was one reason why regulatory commissions were not sought by failing industries during the Depression – Conservative dominance of politics from 1931 was another – and why in the 1920s, while there was discussion about whether the newly planned electricity grid should be operated and managed by the Electricity Commissioners, then the industry's regulators – who had, like their railway counterparts, developed legalistic procedures – it had been decided to try public ownership instead.[101]

It is arguable that the regulatory failures described above may have had a further effect – that of helping to retard the competitiveness and growth of the British economy as a whole. Many explanations have been given of the decline of the British economic growth rate after 1870 by comparison with those of America and Germany. Shortcomings in general, business, and technical education, differences in social values and a tendency to prefer overseas to domestic investment opportunities have been among the factors adduced. All of these no doubt made their contribution to this decline in the growth rate; but regulatory failure may also have had its influence. The railways did greatly reduce the cost of transport, especially in the early part and middle of the nineteenth century. One estimate is that real national income would have been 10 per cent less if all people and goods had had to be carried in 1865 by the means available before the invention of railways.[102] By the end of the century the proportion would have been higher. Moreover, this was an underestimate, because it did not allow for the elasticity of demand – for what transport planners call generated traffic. But if British railway capital costs and other overheads could have been kept down to European levels – say to one-third, to cite the often-quoted Belgian figures again – it does not seem extreme to suppose that British transport fares and charges might have been from a third to a half of what they were, quite enough on its own to prevent the entry of many overseas imports and to have enhanced the competitiveness of British exports to the point where Germany, Belgium and France may not have been able to establish an effective international rivalry. Again, to take the most important of the other natural monopolies for industrial costs: by the 1930s it could be said that the British electricity industry was high cost and the most economically inefficient in the world. If it had expanded the electricity grid to cover the whole of industrialized Britain and had realized the economies of scale then available in generation, industrial costs would have been reduced, general economic competitiveness would have increased, a more competitive electricity engineering industry would have been established and, through competition, there would have been knock-on effects on coal and gas, making them become more efficient if they were to survive. However, without detailed studies, these remain hypotheses. It is also unsatisfactory to postulate that these may have been simply additional costs of regulatory failure, for they also reflected a nexus of social attitudes towards competition. But it remains a plausible hypothesis that the forms of regulation adopted in Britain in the nineteenth and first half of the twentieth century did have consequences which amounted to a substantial adverse effect on economic growth, as well as the disadvantages to the industries directly concerned which this book has so far discussed.

It is essential, if a regulatory regime is to be effective and long-lasting, that it meets the need (not met in UK legislation until the 1980s) to give absolute priority in fixing tariff levels to the need a utility has to raise enough revenue and earn enough profit to be able to maintain, and where required, expand its business profitably. (An incidental consequence of this latter need is that the returns theoretically allowed must not be set in nominal terms which take no account of inflation – whether 10 per cent or any other figure – but must be set in real terms, as in Britain in the 1980s.) Or, failing that, there must be available discretion to decide what a reasonable return is. Shoring up a collapsing regulatory regime ultimately pleases no one. Matters go from bad to worse until the only solution seems a radical change with unpredictable consequences. Thus did nationalization follow the collapse of one kind of regulation, and another kind of regulation the collapse of nationalization.

Notes

1 Robson (1962), p. 25.
2 Parris (1965), pp. 213–4.
3 Barker and Savage (1974), pp. 96–104; Cain (1972), pp. 623–6; Hobsbawm (1967), pp. 88–109; Alderman (1973), p. 95.
4 I am particularly indebted to Professor Theo Barker's patient help in unravelling the issues of economic and transport history that underlie this chapter.
5 Barker and Savage (1974), pp. 103, 110; Cleveland Stevens (1915), p. 317.
6 Joint Select Committee on Railway Amalgamation, *Parliamentary Papers*, 1872, vol. 13, p. xxxvi.
7 The first specific legislation was the Better Regulation of Traffic on Railways and Canals Act, 1854 (s. 2). On the early theory of discrimination, see P. L. Williams (1978); and on the history of the requirement that monopoly rates should be reasonable, as well as on the 'common carrier' concept, see Craig (1989), pp. 157–9. Also Shaw Lefevre Committee, First Report, *Parliamentary Papers*, 1893, vol. 4, pp. 435–68; Hyde (1934), p. 141.
8 Robson (1928), pp. 93, 94.
9 Joint Select Committee on Railway Amalgamation, *Parliamentary Papers*, 1872, vol. 13, p. xviii; also Parris (1965), pp. 219–21; Cain (1973), p. 67.
10 Joint Select Committee on Railway Amalgamations, *Parliamentary Papers*, 1872, vol. 13, pp. xxx–xxxiv. As late as the 1930s, the LMS had 445,000 exceptional rates: Bonavia (1981), p. 62; Barker and Savage (1974), pp. 105–7.
11 Joint Select Committee on Railway Amalgamation, *Parliamentary Papers*, 1872, vol. 13, p. xlvii.
12 Ibid., pp. xlvi–lvii.
13 *Hansard*, 4th series, vol. 214, col. 235–6 (10 February 1873).
14 Robson (1951), pp. 90–9; Cushman (1941), pp. 510–12. Parris (1965), pp. 222–3, and Barker and Savage (1974), p. 96, stress economic conditions as a cause of its failure.

15   Davies (1913); Edwards (1897); Bagwell (1988), p. 173; Armytage (1951), p. 241.
16   Barker and Savage (1974), p. 104.
17   C. F. Phillips, *The Economics of Regulation*, 1969, cited by Kahn (1988a), p. 26/I.
18   Armytage (1951), p. 364.
19   The pros and cons of the arguments on this are discussed by Hawke (1969), pp. 557–9.
20   Alderman (1973), pp. 95–107.
21   Armytage (1951), p. 258.
22   He was President of the Board of Trade in 1844, Chancellor of the Exchequer in 1865, and Prime Minister in 1873, 1886 and 1893. Before the 1894 Act was passed, he was succeeded by another Liberal, Lord Rosebery.
23   Armytage (1951), pp. 247–9. His view was challenged by P. M. Williams (1951), who argued that as the majority of traders and farmers supported Mundella, the Bill's sponsor, the exodus of the railway directors can have made little difference to the support for his bill. However, Gladstone's overall majority was insecure and the defection of several Liberal MPs who were also railway directors may have contributed to his defeat on Home Rule. See also Alderman (1973), p. 300.
24   Armytage (1951), p. 265.
25   Keller (1981), p. 67. See also Cushman (1941), p. 512, who saw it as dominated by the lawyers. Shaw Lefevre Committee, Second Report, *Parliamentary Papers*, 1893–4, vol. 14, p. xiii, however, remarked on its unexpectedly light load.
26   Barker and Savage (1974), pp. 104–7; Bagwell (1988), pp. 174–5; also Edwards (1897), pp. 53–78.
27   Cain (1973); Davies (1913), pp. 135–52; Edwards (1897), pp. 136, 137; Bagwell (1988), pp. 174–5.
28   Cushman (1941), p. 512.
29   Acworth, (1905), p. 8.
30   Edwards (1897), p. 137.
31   The contents of the resulting act are described in Barker and Savage (1974), pp. 104–9.
32   Parris (1965), p. 223. Many MPs blamed the railway interest for packing the committees and being persistently obstructive. In the debates on the 1893 Bill, many MPs blamed the railway interest for repeatedly thwarting or neutralizing legislation over many years. The debates show the strength of traders' grievances, especially those of the agricultural interests. See Hansard, 4th series, vol. 28, col. 636–43 (10 August 1894), 785–99 (13 August 1894). Those against the railways believed that the 1894 Act had been captured by them. The debates do not reveal whether speakers saw the significance of the change in the burden of proof envisaged by the Bill. Nor is it plain that the Shaw Lefevre Committee recommended it: cf. *Parliamentary Papers*, 1893–4, vol. 14, pp. xii–xiii.
33   *Hansard*, 4th series, vol. 12, col. 1,045 (16 May 1893); also, on the strength of the railway interest, ibid., vol. 28, col. 636–43 (10 August 1894); ibid., vol. 28, col. 785–99 (13 August 1894). For a general account, see Alderman (1973), pp. 144–57; Cain (1973), p. 78.
34   Shaw Lefevre Committee, Second Report, *Parliamentary Papers*, 1893–4, vol. 14, p. xiii. On competition, see Cain (1973), p. 74.
35   This persisted to puzzle succeeding generations of railwaymen: see Travis, Lamb and Jenkinson (1913), p. 93. Acworth may have influenced the Shaw Lefevre Committee by telling it that in many American states the burden of proving the reasonableness of rates was on the railway companies: Shaw Lefevre Committee, Minutes of Evidence, *Parliamentary Papers*, 1893–4, vol. 14, pp. 430–1.
36   Cain (1978), p. 88.
37   There is a contemporary presentation of these views in Sidgwick (1887), pp. 557–9.
38   Foster (1959).

39 Acworth (1905), pp. 51–98.
40 Sidgwick (1887), pp. 557–9, put the economic-efficiency case for discrimination clearly.
41 See chapter 6 below.
42 Cain (1973); (1978), p. 87.
43 Cain (1978), p. 89.
44 Cain (1972), pp. 626–7; Barker and Savage (1974), pp. 108–15.
45 Alderman (1973), p. 157.
46 Ibid., p. 48.
47 On the central problem of whether public service obligations should be imposed on railways created for private profit, see Cleveland Stevens (1915), pp. 315–24; see also, for the view that the legislation of 1893 and 1894 was a watershed, Alderman (1973), pp. 44–50.
48 W. M. Acworth, *The Railway and the Traders*, quoted in Edwards (1897), p. 146; see also Pigou (1920), p. 364. Is it a paradox that some railways were improving some aspects of quality, as Barker and Savage (1974), pp. 97–100, maintain, while other aspects of quality fell, as Bagwell (1988), pp. 175–6, maintains? Railways varied in their financial positions. Moreover, they may have hoped that some quality improvements would yield more revenue increases, or be more easily sold to shareholders, than others. Furthermore, from 1900 the effective stop on the raising of rates made the lowering any of them unattractive: it was more prudent to attract traffic by improved quality than by lower fares.
49 Bagwell (1988), pp. 184–6. Bagwell argues for the significance of the influence that the unions had in bringing pressure to bear to get safety legislation. M. R. Bonavia (private communication) disputes the reluctance of the railways over this matter.
50 The growth of corporatist relations is well illustrated by the close collaboration that developed between the Railway Companies' Association (which represented railway boards) and Board of Trade officials between 1900 and 1905: Alderman (1973), p. 185.
51 Ibid., pp. 185–6; Middlemas (1979), pp. 55, 61.
52 W. Tetley Stephenson in Acworth (1905), p. 16.
53 Ibid., p. 14.
54 Cardwell Committee, Fifth Report, *Parliamentary Papers*, 1852–3, vol. 38, pp. 3–10. End-to-end amalgamation reduced competition less than other amalgamations, though the larger the railway generally the more able it was to exercise monopoly power against carriers and in other ways.
55 Cain (1972), p. 626. It was for board directors. There had been informal pooling throughout the nineteenth century. The few US pools were killed off by the 1887 Interstate Commerce Act. See Bagwell (1968), pp. 250–68.
56 Ibid. Barker and Savage (1974), pp. 114–5, argue that there was some effective competition among regional railways to the end of the 1890s but not much after that. Cain (1976), p. 191, said that in the 1880s 60 per cent of all rail goods were influenced by sea competition.
57 Joint Select Committee on Railway Amalgamation, *Parliamentary Papers*, 1872, vol. 13, pp. xxv–xxvi; Bagwell (1988), pp. 168–9.
58 Taylor (1972), p. 42.
59 Cain (1972), p. 623. See the arguments for and against economies of scale in nineteenth-century railways in Foreman Peck (1987), and Dodgson (1989). However, the periods they cover do not overlap (by 50 years), so it is possible some scale economics had been realized by mergers by 1900–10. Dodgson did find some economies of density which pointed to the advantages of parallel as opposed to end-to-end line mergers. See also Aldcroft (1968), who argued that low density was a cause of UK railways' high costs relative to those overseas.
60 C. I. Savage (1959), p. 79; Grigg (1978), pp. 112–19 for Lloyd George's role in 1907, and pp. 281–3 for his and Churchill's roles in 1911.

61   Cain (1972), p. 636. Pratt (1908), pp. 421–6, argued that unregulated amalgamation was preferable to nationalization.
62   Board of Trade, Departmental Inquiry into Railway Accounts, 1909–11, Cd. 4697.
63   Ibid., qu. 118, 461–8, quoted by Bagwell (1988), p. 169.
64   Board of Trade, Departmental Inquiry into Railway Accounts, 1909–11, Cd. 4697; Davies (1913), pp. 109, 110; Acworth (1905), p. 6. Bagwell (1968), p. 244, says that these statistics were eventually only conceded to avoid redundancies in the Railway Clearing House in the 1920s because the 1921 amalgamations had reduced its workload.
65   Reported in Acworth (1905).
66   W. Tetley Stephenson in Acworth (1905), p. 18.
67   E. Cleveland Stevens in Acworth (1905), pp. 19–27.
68   Acworth (1905), p. 8.
69   Ibid., pp. 8, 9.
70   W. Tetley Stephenson in Acworth (1905), p. 17. It is interesting that an eminent economist in the mainstream, A. C. Pigou (1920), p. 382, reached the same conclusion.
71   There were a number of abortive nationalizing bills before the war, but as Michael Bonavia has said they showed little depth of thinking about the forms of control to be adopted: Bonavia (1986).
72   Barker and Savage (1974), pp. 145–6.
73   Sir Eric Geddes, who had been a railway deputy general manager, became Minister of Transport, and he drew up this railway nationalization scheme for the postwar coalition government: Bagwell (1988), pp. 229–33.
74   The Railways Act, 1921. A survey of its main provisions is to be found in Kahn Freund (1939), pp. 179–211.
75   Pigou (1920), p. 326; Sherrington (1928), vol. 2, pp. 121–5; C. I. Savage (1959), pp. 105–9; Kahn Freund (1939). There had been a similar provision as early as 1826 (referred to above) when the act establishing the Liverpool and Manchester railway provided that for every increase in dividends of 1 per cent over 10 per cent an equivalent 5 percentage points had to be passed on in lower rates. But even if dividends had exceeded 10 per cent, which they did not, the measure would not have worked, for there was no definition of net revenue. See Pollins (1969), p. 143.
76   Bagwell, (1988), pp. 235–8; Robson (1951), pp. 49, 50, 99.
77   Robson, ibid.
78   Bagwell (1988), pp. 320–1; Foster (1959).
79   Bonavia (1981), pp. 59–69; Milne and Laing (1956), pp. 28–34.
80   See chapter 6 below.
81   Donoghue and Jones (1973), p. 73; H. Morrison (1933), p. 105.
82   The Electric Lighting Act, 1882, which is still the act under which inquiries authorizing new nuclear and other power-stations are set up, introduced a licensing system then operated by the Board of Trade to replace the requirement for a separate private bill each time. There was much argument over how long it was reasonable to give a licence for so as to give utilities the chance of a reasonable profit. See Gordon (1938), p. 84; Hannah (1979), p. 5.
83   There was much discussion of these issues by the Forster Committee, *Parliamentary Papers*, 1875, vol. 12.
84   Ibid; Wickwar (1938), pp. 166–72. These sliding scales became popular in electricity regulation from the turn of the century: Hannah (1979), p. 226.
85   Report in *Parliamentary Papers*, 1875, vol. 12. No one was sure of its origin: ibid., qu. 3, 185. A witness also attributed it to T. H. Farrer, Secretary to the Board of Trade. The railways were not thought suitable for a double-acting sliding scale because they were not profitable enough, a point made by Sidgwick (1887), p. 443.

86 Wickwar (1938), p. 171.

87 J. Davis (1988), pp. 47, 48.

88 Kahn (1988a), pp. 61, 62/II; Bonbright (1961), pp. 263–4, who cites a substantial literature on the subject in the 1920s and 1930s. In the 1980s Kahn himself strongly recommended the adoption of similar devices: Kahn (1990b), pp. 5, 6.

89 Finer (1941): municipal undertakings gained from their low borrowing rates (p. 147), though they were often found to be unwilling to borrow and invest (p. 98); local democracy kept them small (p. 231); and they were often pressed to sell to poor and other customers at favourable rates (pp. 301–3). Because municipal gas undertakings had eliminated excess profit (Hannah (1979), p. 9), many authorities also municipalized electricity: the high point of this municipalization process was in the 1890s (pp. 22–8).

90 Finer (1941), pp. 163–83.

91 Hannah (1979), pp. 22–8. Hannah writes that in determining these decisions local politics was often more important than the prospect of cheap electricity (p. 31).

92 Ibid., pp. 28–33.

93 Hannah (1983), pp. 41–53.

94 Marquand (1988), pp. 146–56.

95 Chandler (1962). His approach to his subject was influenced by his interest in railways (pp. 21–3).

96 T. Williams (1908), p. 248, quoted in Keller (1981), p. 63.

97 The common law gave no protection against cartels and monopoly, though it was used as a basis for proceeding against discrimination. See Keller (1981), pp. 62–4; Horwitz (1989), pp. 13, 43.

98 Although Joan Robinson (1948) (1st edn. 1933) was a breakthrough in the analysis of monopoly, she hardly mentioned problems of the real world. And in so far as she did (ch. 27), it was to cast doubt on the usefulness of economic theory in providing guidance in distinguishing efficient from inefficient monopoly.

99 Hannah (1983), p. 41. The result was that instead of a cartel he built up what was eventually to become one of the largest British firms, Lever Brothers, predecessor of the Anglo-Dutch giant, Unilever.

100 Ibid., pp. 43, 44.

101 Gordon (1938), pp. 86–94, lists many reasons for the inefficiency of the English electricity industry by the 1930s.

102 Hawke and Higgins (1983), pp. 188–96.

3

The failure of public enterprise

The modern development ... of corporate trade has in more ways than one fostered the growth of collectivist ideas. It has lessened the importance of the individual trader. It has transformed the abstract principle that all property, and especially property in land, belongs in a sense to the nation, into a practical maxim on which Parliament acts every year with the approval of the country. It constantly suggests the conclusion that every large business may become a monopoly and that trades which are monopolies may wisely be brought under the management of the state.

A. V. Dicey (1905)[1]

3.1 The background to nationalization

Emanuel Shinwell was the first minister after 1945 to prepare and introduce the nationalization of a major industry – coal. That he found no blueprint in the Labour Party files has often been cited.[2] (There was only a pamphlet in Welsh, entitled 'Glo'.[3]) But when one considers the breadth of support for public ownership, it is less surprising that there was no policy or political blueprint.

Nationalization is widely considered to be a Socialist policy, and its advocacy has been in the constitution of the British Labour Party since 1918. Much of the opposition to public ownership from the Right has indeed been that it was Socialism or would lead to it. But during the inter-war period especially, many non-Socialists, Liberals and even Conservatives, came to support it, particularly among those in, or close to, the industries that were the prime candidates, mainly the public utilities, many of which were municipal. The more important ones – except coal – were thought to be natural monopolies. (However, between 1945 and 1979, public ownership was extended to many which were not.) Without broad support public ownership could not have occurred before the first majority Labour government in 1945. Moreover, the form chosen then and earlier was adopted in large part to appease those who feared Socialism.

To understand why that form was chosen, one must go back to the beginnings of British public ownership between the two world wars. The term 'public corporation' was first used to describe the British Broadcasting Corporation and the Central Electricity Board (CEB), both set up in 1926.[4] The London Passenger Transport Board (LPTB) dates from 1933 and the British Overseas Airways Corporation (BOAC) from 1939. All this public ownership was the product of Conservative governments. And even though Herbert Morrison as a Socialist minister from 1929 to 1931 was the main architect of the LPTB, he took the structure of the CEB as his model.

Moreover, as we have seen, he was out of office before his bill was through Parliament. Little altered, the eventual statute was passed by a Conservative-dominated coalition government of which he was not a member. But because he wrote a well-written and widely-read book justifying the creation of the LPTB, because he called it *Socialisation and Transport* and because he himself later supervised the Attlee government's nationalization programme and modelled that on the LPTB legislation, there has been a natural tendency to think all these to be experiments in Socialism (a notion which the Labour Party did nothing to dispel). However, in each case public ownership had the support of many in, or close to, the industry – as was also true, as we shall see, of most of the Attlee nationalizations. Indeed, Morrison's book glories in the support he had for public ownership from the heads of the private transport undertakings amalgamated into the LPTB.[5]

We have seen how even earlier a group of prominent railway economists who were opposed to nationalization both in principle and from experience had accepted it with varying degrees of reluctance because they realized that competition was impossible and that the old system of regulation had broken down. Some of the more energetic leaders of the railway and coal industries were persuaded of the merits of public ownership by the greater efficiency that those industries achieved when under temporary state control during the First World War.[6] And an ex-railway deputy general manager, Sir Eric Geddes, who had become Minister of Transport, had nearly succeeded in nationalizing the railways in 1919.[7] Besides the examples already mentioned, several commissions and committees of inquiry recommended public ownership of other main utilities in the 1920s. And the Coal Act, 1930, which required efficient mines to bribe inefficient ones through a system of tradeable quotas if they wished to expand production, was very much in harmony with the anti-competitive and clumsy spirit of the old railway amalgamations. It persuaded more people that public ownership of the coal industry was a cleaner, simpler and even more economically rational solution to the problems the Act was designed to deal with.[8] Similarly, what was seen as 'wasteful' and uncontrolled competition between bus operators, trams and commuter trains was a constant source of public and political complaint which led many non-Socialists towards accepting the idea of public ownership.[9]

The objectives of the non-Socialist supporters of public ownership were economic and industrial. And while there were Socialists who put social objectives first they found that the arguments that carried most weight with the electorate were also economic.[10] There was a belief that if the economic problems of transport and electricity could be solved in a depression, then what seemed to be the most pressing social problems of the time would themselves, as a result, be solved. One can search in vain to find a Socialist or other innovative use of a nationalized industry's surplus for social purposes (except in so far as municipal undertakings, where profitable, contributed their profits to help finance other local services). Such industries' departures from commercial practice were normally not original but common to the private monopolies they succeeded. It had long been argued that in return for monopoly power no one should be refused service and so the obligation to provide universal service was often laid down in statutes governing public undertakings. In some cases this had a contemporary importance: a quarter of the population had no electricity in 1936.[11] There was also generally a hope that a public undertaking could be a 'good' employer without loss of viability. The BBC, CEB, LPTB and BOAC were meant to achieve economies of scale and the elimination of 'wasteful competition', though an additional argument for the public ownership of Imperial Airways was that it was already substantially reliant on government subsidy;[12] and, while claims were indeed made for economies of scale in running London buses, trams and underground railways together, the more persuasive argument at the time was that it would end unstable and unfair competition which relied upon misinforming customers, predatory behaviour to drive rivals out of business and the cutting of costs by sacrificing reliability and safety. Similar reasons of scale economy and rationalization were given for the nationalization under the Attlee government of the railways and other transport services, gas, electricity, and iron and steel. Coal was the exception at the time. In the absence of economies of scale, many judged its nationalization to be more a political than an economic act, though at the local level closing down uneconomic pits would have led to a more profitable industry. But even for those other industries economies of scale were of varying importance: from electricity, where they were undoubtedly substantial, to the railways, where they were often alleged but seldom realized.[13] Railway nationalization is indeed best seen as the last of a series of mergers through which the industry tried to reduce internal competition so as to be better able to stand competition from road transport and overcome the millstone of excess capacity which had weighed it down from almost its earliest years.

To the question why market forces had not achieved many of the available economies of scale, as had happened more widely in the United States and Germany, and indeed in some industries in Britain, like chemicals and soap, one answer commonly given is the absence of competition that followed from a long British tradition of regarding *laissez-faire* as either identical with competition or, if the distinction was made, more important than it. Leaving the economy to market forces was widely interpreted and justified as giving businessmen the freedom to cartelize or otherwise collude. Economies of scale which could not be realized in a cartel or other collusive arrangement were therefore discouraged by the prevalence of such collusion, and thus the absence of competition. But they were also discouraged by the prevalence of municipal ownership in some industries, for municipal undertakings were among those most reluctant to lose their identity, and for them local pride and local pressures were far more important than the profit motive.

Thus arguably those on both sides of the argument – those who wished to retain the economic status quo and those who argued for state planning and public ownership – tended to regard competition as unimportant or wasteful or demonstrably wrong, a relic of the past. One does not find the nationalization statutes preserving competition or providing restraints on unfair trading, though there are provisions to prevent nationalized industries competing with private ones, which is not however the same thing. Moreover, at this time the law was being increasingly used to favour one set of interests within a sector of the economy over its competitors, particularly in transport. For example, the major achievement of the railways in Britain, as in the United States, was to get laws which tried to restrict the ability of road to compete with rail in their (the railways') own interest – and that of the large bus and goods-vehicle operators, because they were thereby protected from competition from smaller road operators. Two academic observers referred to this period as one when 'competition, the leading principle of the nineteenth century, began to keep company with the adjective "wasteful".'[14] (Despite its frequent abuse, there is a defensible concept of wasteful competition, which is examined in chapter 6, where it is argued, however, that its practical utility is doubtful.)

Whatever one's view of nationalization now, it then seemed impossible for the 'free' market – which was in fact subject to many legislative and other regulatory restrictions – to bring about needful concentration in many industries. There were 369 municipal and 200 private electricity undertakings. There were 300 power stations, operated by 130 separate generating authorities.[15] There were 1,500 collieries before nationalization, owned by 746 colliery undertakings, of which 640 were limited companies and the rest were in the hands of partnerships or individuals.[16] Iron and steel, and the four main-line railways (joined however in the British Transport Commission – created in 1947 – by numerous bus and haulage operators), were comparatively simple. Gas was the most complicated of all: there were 269 municipal operations, 5 joint boards, 264 non-statutory organizations which in total supplied less than 2 per cent of the market, 509 public utilities all of which, like electricity and the railways, were enmeshed in stringent statutory and other regulatory provisions to restrict profits and to regulate prices and safety.[17] And thus arose an additional reason for nationalization, a reason which was more prominent in the literature before the Second World War than immediately after it, when it tended to be neglected: in all these instances, except that of iron and steel, rescue from the complications that had grown up through successive layers of regulatory legislation and inconsistency in government policy was an important motive for nationalization. Indeed, freeing the industries from a regulatory tangle was even given as the decisive reason for nationalizing the railways, as we saw in chapter 2, although the vestiges of that regulation survived nationalization.[18]

It is important to recognize that when the advocates of nationalization, wherever they came from in the political spectrum, used economic arguments, they broadly agreed what their objectives were; but it was only the more far-seeing who realized that the problems could not be blamed simply on market failure and *laissez-faire*, but had to be blamed also on the shortcomings of the regulatory systems and mixed patterns of ownership that had emerged.

Among the economies of scale sought through nationalization were what were generally at the time regarded as the advantages of coordination, advantages which the 1980s rediscovered and relabelled as those of multiplant operation through interconnection. But the building up of a publicly owned electricity grid after 1926 to be used competitively by both private and municipal distributors was then beyond the competence of the regulators to coordinate and this was a fundamental reason for the eventual nationalization of the whole industry. Between them, the Electricity Commissioners and the Central Electricity Board failed, indeed even did not try, to make a market in electricity.[19] Because different areas had different peaks and troughs in demand for electricity, there were still substantial gains to be made by connecting generators and distributors by a grid network. Public ownership seemed the only way of managing such a system – the computers and computer-based mathematics did not exist which would have made it possible for there to be a truly commercial electricity market buying and selling through the grid. Similarly, among the arguments for the LPTB was the apparent impossibility then (and since) – also related to problems of computerization – of getting the many transport undertakings in London to coordinate their timetables and tariffs, provide through-ticketing and generally make it easy for users to choose the quickest and cheapest route and mode of transport from one place to another. And regulatory failure was also among the reasons for nationalizing water and gas.

As we shall see in chapter 6, similar forces to those that led to the regulation of public utilities in the 1930s in the United States resulted in nationalization in Britain. But in both countries these changes were to a great extent brought about by, and fundamentally for, the industries themselves. Public ownership was what the greater part of the owners and operators wanted, and welcomed, to solve their financial difficulties and achieve greater economies of scale. In Britain, the much-proclaimed industrial opposition to Socialism, though genuinely the position of some of the owners and operators of industries earmarked for nationalization, was for the majority of such opponents tactical – intended to achieve better compensation when their industry was taken over or more power within the new regime.

Thus there was substantial cross-party support for public ownership, particularly among those directly concerned with the candidate industries as workers and managers. Perhaps the clearest statement of the case for public ownership came in the 1920s from the Lloyd George wing of the divided Liberal Party as one component of the new liberalism that they then developed, which was to provide so many of the economic ideas of the 1945 Labour government. Keynes himself said that at the end of the 1920s there was more Liberal enthusiasm for nationalization to promote the rationalization of industry than there was in the Labour Party.[20]

The nationalization programme of the Labour government between 1945 and 1951, though it occupied a high proportion of parliamentary time, was, therefore, not initially politically controversial. The taking of the Bank of England into public ownership was the first nationalization measure in this programme. Remembering the Bank's influence on his own policies as Chancellor of Exchequer in 1925, Churchill declared that he would not oppose it.[21] The second, that of Cable and Wireless, was largely seen as a late imperialistic measure to link the Commonwealth and the colonies by better telecommunications. The nationalization of the civil airlines tidied up earlier Conservative nationalization initiatives – as much as anything it was meant to improve the accountability of bodies already heavily dependent on public subsidies to carry the mails. Churchill was believed to have considerable sympathy for the nationalization of coal and had in 1919 publicly recommended nationalization of the railways. Both the coal and electricity nationalization measures passed Parliament without much difficulty.[22] Transport nationalization was more controversial, but only because there were strong objections to the nationalization of own-account road haulage. The nationalization of gas, in 1948, was vigorously opposed, though not on principle but rather because there was a growing feeling within the Conservative Party that it must oppose characteristically Socialist legislation if it were to win the next general election. The most bitterly fought of these measures was iron and steel nationalization. It was unpopular among many Labour as well as Conservative MPs, for the industry's managers were widely agreed to be more competent than those of the other industries and ready to rationalize their industry without a change of ownership. The Iron and Steel Act was passed in 1949, but was not implemented until just before the Conservatives regained power in October 1951. They then, however, only slowly and only partially repealed it.[23]

There was not much debate about the nationalizations within the Labour Party either. In the 1920s there had been strong disagreement among Socialists over the form nationalization should take.[24] By the early 1930s this had narrowed down to a dispute between those who, like Ernest Bevin, believed that the workers or the trade unions in an industry should be represented on its board and those who, like Herbert Morrison, thought that such worker and union representatives should come from other industries.[25] But after 1932 the disagreement vanished as the unions concerned realized the freedom they would lose if they allowed themselves to be represented on their industry's board.

But, besides this, there was little discussion of the details of nationalization policy, or indeed of the objectives of nationalization, even within the Labour government. As D. N. Chester, the historian of this episode of nationalization has written, the main policy question for the ministers who determined legislation under Herbert Morrison's chairmanship was how to ensure that they took over whole industries. This concern led to lengthy metaphysical discussions about what constituted an industry. As their desire was to eliminate competition, they often tried to exclude bits which were incidental to the industry's core activity, especially when these competed with private firms.[26] In trying to construct relatively simple, isolated abstractions called industries, they were ignoring the findings of the Cambridge school of economists during the 1930s – many of them Socialists or Socialist sympathizers – who had (theoretically) dissolved industries into continuous networks of firms with increasingly differentiated products between which competition may have been imperfect but was often complicated and indirect and thus not open to efficient replacement by methods of uniform coordination. They were also unmindful of the pricing and investment instructions that another, then Socialist, economist, Abba P. Lerner, had set out for the Socialist manager to help him achieve the coordination and integration of public enterprises.[27]

Why did the Labour government go to such lengths to get 100 per cent of each industry under public ownership, even at the expense of great statutory and managerial complication, as well as parliamentary opposition – especially over own-account road haulage and iron and steel? Chester's answer is that there was a long-standing and widespread belief in the labour movement that nationalization was an all-or-nothing process. An 'industry' was not under public ownership unless all of it was. 'Nationalization was based on a denial that a number of competing producers could, even with some central guidance, make decisions individually which would result in as great an efficiency of the industry as a whole than if such decisions were made by a single central body.'[28] When in early 1946 James Meade, later a Nobel Prize winner but then an economist in the Cabinet Office, sought to persuade Morrison that the Ministry of Transport civil servants were wrong to suppose that coordination was best achieved by setting a uniform price per mile for all modes of transport irrespective of cost, and that meaningful coordination could be better achieved by allowing prices to reflect costs of production, Morrison was dismissive: 'But this is not socialisation, it is competition'.[29] Neither was there ministerial support for discussion of whether prices should be based on average or marginal costs.[30] Indeed, ministers at that time took the view that the efficiency of the nationalized industries was no responsibility of theirs and should be left wholly to the boards concerned. Because they had no interest in the pricing and investment policies of the nationalized industries and saw their rationalization as largely a question of realizing technical efficiency, they were not interested in their economics. Because they hoped to exclude competition and profits, which they believed to be the sources of the practices that had led to industrial decay, there was no consideration of the possibility of the newly nationalized industries' indulging in economic regulatory offences like unfair competition and excess profitability, and therefore none of the continuing need for such regulation. One set of regulators – the Electricity Commissioners – was abolished and another, the Transport Tribunal, kept – both, as far as can be judged, idiosyncratically.[31] Virtually no one considered any other form of regulation – for example, the American – as an alternative to nationalization.[32] In every case the intention was to let the new boards, not government, work out the policy for their monopolies.[33] Ministers retained powers – there were, for example, more than 200 under the Transport Act, 1947, to which more were added later – but they were fragmented and were meant as major or minor constraints on policy, not as instruments with which to set it.[34]

Thus one cannot be surprised that Sir Alec Cairncross, writing the history of British economic policy between 1945 and 1951, concluded that, while the nationalization measures were among those most identified with the Labour Party and their detail took up most parliamentary time, they did not contribute to the solution of any of the country's post-war economic problems. They were overhastily designed. They did not increase efficiency or redistribute income. Indeed, they made the solution of some problems more difficult – for example, they had an adverse effect on British standing in the international money markets.[35]

So Shinwell found no policy blueprint for coal, and could not have found one for any other candidate industry (except the railways), because Labour politicians then did not want to define policy. And there was no political blueprint (except for the railways) because it was the achievement of the idea of nationalization then to have gained very substantial cross-party support, and that would have been weakened by giving the measures any sharp political or policy colouring.

3.2 The form of nationalization

Even if there was no policy or political blueprint, there was an administrative model. A few state enterprises had been organized as, or inside, government departments. The most important was the Post Office (until 1969 when it became a public corporation), but there had been ordnance factories, naval dockyards, government printing and publishing operations, government research laboratories and a host of small government enterprises – even prisons. Some early Fabians indeed had recommended the integration of state enterprises into government departments. Those whose main objective was workers' control favoured a form of Guild Socialism or Syndicalism. Municipal ownership – 'Gas and Water Socialism' – already had a substantial history and therefore had strong defenders. But the survivor in the contest for adoption for the post-war nationalization programme was the model chosen by Herbert Morrison for the London Passenger Transport Board, a model which had a long history of practical experience behind it. Its origins have been traced to the many turnpike and port trusts established in the eighteenth and nineteenth centuries. Close ancestors were the Clyde Navigation Trust (1857), the Mersey Docks and Harbour Board (1858) and the Port of London Authority (1908). The last was the direct model for the Central Electricity Board and the BBC in 1926. It was the CEB for which Morrison had responsibility as Minister of Transport in the 1929–31 Labour government, and he used it as his blueprint for the London Passenger Transport Board. The same model of a public trust had been a leading part of the Liberal Party's 1928 programme for Britain's industrial future, where it was warmly supported by Lloyd George and J. M. Keynes.[36] Morrison deliberately chose it as the model most likely to appeal to non-Socialists. And it was widely copied abroad for similar reasons.

The legal model for Labour's post-war nationalization programme was essentially the same throughout. In his account of the 1945–51 Labour government, Kenneth Morgan has said that no alternative blueprint was considered.[37] It was given its classic defence in 1933 by Herbert Morrison, The notion that economic efficiency required national or local monopolies, but that these needed to be managed and their profits used in the public interest was at the heart of his case for nationalization. Morrison saw monopoly as desirable because it was able to achieve economies of scale and eliminate the wastes of competition, but he saw private monopoly as an evil because it 'had as its great incentive the profit-earning motive'.[38] However, although the nationalized monopoly would not be subject to the need to maximize profit, he nevertheless spoke of a requirement on the Board, the top-management executive body of the public-trust enterprise, that it should make a success of its undertaking and that it should fulfil its statutory obligation to pay its way, taking one year with another.[39] Though it scarcely surfaced into the public domain, this was not just a protective measure to avoid losses falling upon the taxpayer, though that was an important element in it, but also a protection of the consumer from the Exchequer's benefiting from profits in a way which could be construed as taxation without representation, that is, not voted by Parliament – the unforgotten principle that had helped cost Charles I his life.[40] This requirement was repeated in all nationalization statutes until the reconstruction of London Transport in the late 1960s.[41] Moreover, according to this conception, the Board was intended to be responsible not only for management but also for the interpretation of the public interest that it was required to serve, though it was to act on that interpretation only after consultation with the minister responsible, who 'may exercise an influence where it is proper and legitimate that he should, without in any way interfering with the management of the undertaking'.[42]

This was the source of the distinction between 'management' and 'policy', 'day-to-day' and 'long-term' responsibility, whose essential meaninglessness was always to obscure the relations between ministers and the undertakings for which they were responsible. It gave ministers an appearance of authority which they did not really have. For these state enterprises were public trusts, in law owned not by the State but by their boards, who were their legal proprietors though appointed by the minister. As Lord (then Lord Justice) Denning said in the definitive judgement on the legal status of public corporations, 'In the eyes of the law the corporation is its own master . . .'[43] In so far as the boards could be described as regulating the industries they owned, they had the power to interpret as they chose their trust to serve the public interest, subject practically to the proviso that they had to listen to what ministers had to say about their interpretation of the public interest and, if they were prudent, to avoid any public controversy over this with ministers. As they were expected to break even, the question of how to employ any surplus funds would sometimes arise, and this matter was also within their discretion. Except that ministers fixed the salaries of the board members, the statutes of such enterprises set few other limits to their use of this discretion. The social obligations imposed on nationalized industries by statute, or volunteered by the enterprises themselves, were few and unenterprising. The main ones fell into three groups:

1 The requirement that they had to provide a service to all. As monopolies they could not pick and choose their customers. The main cost of this to them was the occasionally high cost of connecting their remote consumers. At an extreme, keeping open uneconomic railway branch lines was perhaps the single most conspicuous example of such a policy.

2 Some obligation to be fair and non-discriminatory. This requirement did not prevent the emergence of substantial cross-subsidization, which indeed was often encouraged politically. Thus short-distance telephone callers came to be subsidized by long-distance callers; bulk users of telephones who had private circuits were subsidized by other telephone users; bulk electricity and gas users were subsidized by small users; second-class railway passengers were subsidized by first-class passengers; high-value goods carried by rail for many years subsidized the carriage of lower-value goods. Indeed, at times cross-subsidy was said to be the main objective of such legislation – for example, of the Transport Act, 1933. While sometimes resulting in economically rational discrimination, politically motivated pricing stored up problems for privatization and beyond.

3 The special and generally unremunerative treatment of some small groups, especially the disabled.

However, as might be expected from the discretion given the boards, these new statutory burdens of social obligations were not great, though most social obligations from the past were continued. The choice was meant to be theirs to use such surplus as they earned, or might have earned, to lower prices, give better service, or extend their business activity, even through using the profits on one product to cross-subsidize other, loss-making activities. Or they could tolerate internal inefficiency.

 In the pre–1945 examples, the minister's power to control the boards was practically limited to appointing board members (though even this was delegated for the LPTB to an independent body), to dismissing them – in certain restricted circumstances – to fixing their salaries, and to approving new borrowing. Although the post-1945 nationalization statutes increased ministerial powers, the important formal powers of the minister responsible were still few and, except for the controls over borrowing and capital expenditure, were rarely used.[44] If there was one feature that distinguished post-war nationalization from pre-war public ownership, it was that government controlled all nationalized industry borrowing, on the ground that it necessarily guaranteed that borrowing – a dogma which was to be of the greatest importance both throughout the (post-war) period of nationalization and in bringing about privatization. Theoretically, ministers had powers of direction over the industries nationalized after the Second World War, but they were rarely used, for they required ministers to defend their exercise in detail.[45] Neither in terms of ownership nor through his statutory powers was the minister's position like that of the 100 per cent shareholder the state was widely assumed to be.

This blurred, and rarely referred to, legal position was known to the boards and was part of the price paid for the consent of the various private and management interests to their industry's nationalization. It sat ill behind the façade of Socialism. And it also consorted badly with the practical influence that ministers wished to exercise over the nationalized industries. The result was myth and pretence. Ministers talked blithely of 'their' nationalized industries and behaved as if they, or at least the State, owned them, whereas they had in fact little power over nationalized industries' chairmen, except in so far as they were ready to be influenced. In public it suited all parties to behave as if ministers had more authority than this. The main exception was that ministers had used their powers to restrict borrowing and capital expenditure severely while there were post-war shortages of materials and later to influence the airlines to buy British aircraft.[46] (Only in the mid-1950s were the railways, for example, allowed to begin a substantial investment programme.[47]) In fact, though it allowed them these and other negative powers, the Morrisonian blueprint would have been appropriate only if ministers could have maintained as intermittent an interest in, say, the National Coal Board as they did in the Royal Mint or the Mersey Docks and Harbour Board.

3.3   The attempts to define criteria and set objectives

Ministers had earlier realized the difficulties and drawbacks, from their point of view, of the autonomy they had sought to give the nationalized industries. In a few instances there were issues of macroeconomic policy that were affected by this autonomy. Keynes had argued in the *General Theory* that increased public works and other public investment should be used to raise output and employment in a slump.[48] And James Meade believed that he had made this possible through the newly nationalized industries by getting the original break-even requirement altered to one by which those industries should break even 'taking one year with another'. But in 1949 ministers for the first time became concerned that this still gave them insufficient power to require boards to engineer deficits as a counter-recessionary measure. Asked to give a formal opinion on this, the Attorney-General agreed that they had no such power.[49] However, as throughout that period of Labour government over-full employment was the problem, this legislative defect did not at that time really matter.

More important was mounting public and political criticism of the nationalized industries. In helping to settle the difficulties of post-war Britain, they did not keep their side of the Morrisonian bargain and use their monopoly power to keep consumers, workers and other important interests sweet. Moreover, ministers found that, against their expectation, they themselves were being held responsible for board performance.[50] Thus the issue of how board efficiency should be judged arose first with respect to parliamentary questions.[51] For, though ministers tried to limit the questions they answered about the affairs of the nationalized industries to matters over which they believed they had statutory authority, which as we have seen did not include efficiency, by 1948 dissatisfaction among MPs had forced ministers to answer questions on these matters, which in turn forced them to consider how to judge whether board performance was satisfactory. This led them in two directions.

The first was to revive an old notion of Beatrice and Sidney Webb's which had been a significant part of the apparatus of their envisaged Socialist commonwealth: an efficiency unit to monitor the performance of public enterprises. Although the idea was enthusiastically, if belatedly, taken up by Morrison, it was vigorously resisted by the board chairmen and many of their sponsoring ministers.[52] One of the chairmen indeed used words which were endlessly used in future by those resisting such inquiries into performance: 'Frequent lifting of the young plant to examine the roots inevitably stultifies growth.'[53] It was an inappropriate cliché in the circumstances: a prize tomato grower is likely to measure the growth of his tomatoes; he does not have to uplift the roots. A chairman of the National Coal Board further said 'We none of us feel that we could agree to the suggestion that a common efficiency unit should be set up. Our views on this subject are very definite and, quite frankly, I think they are likely to remain permanently so', while another said that it would distract them from more-urgent problems.[54] The long drawn out discussions meandered helplessly and hopelessly into debates over the meaning of efficiency: whether there could not be something called administrative efficiency, for which ministers could be responsible and which might be subject to monitoring by a common efficiency unit, and something called technical efficiency, whose definition and monitoring could be left to the boards themselves. But in the absence of any clear and precise objectives having been set for the boards, and given the boards' discretion, which was intentionally theirs, the fundamental point was that there was no way of defining efficiency so that it might be properly assessed, measured and monitored. A board's objectives – in so far as they existed – were self-set, various and changing. Therefore there was no well-defined criterion for an efficiency unit to work with.[55]

Faced with implacable opposition from the board chairmen – who indeed were treating the nationalization statutes as 'parliamentary contracts' – and little support from sponsoring ministers, the Government turned towards the second expedient: a select committee of Parliament to oversee and examine the nationalized industries. This eventually came into being in 1957, and produced, especially under the effective chairmanship of Sir Toby Low, later Lord Aldington, a series of reports which were influential in the long haul towards getting it accepted that the boards should have clear, fixed and precise objectives, and that these should be primarily economic.[56]

It was in the mid-1950s that ministerial intervention really increased, when some nationalized industries went into deficit. That those industries had therefore to receive government grants meant they had broken the basic condition of their trust by failing to break even; and, in so far as they were then in receipt of public expenditure to meet the deficit, the sponsoring minister was accountable to Parliament for that expenditure. Moreover, as the guardian of public money, the Treasury also assumed a larger role.[57] The form of intervention used was to investigate and question the industry on its deficit first informally, and then through an apparatus of select committee reports and special inquiries supported by additional inquiries by whatever other general supervisory bodies there might be in existence at the time – for example, the Prices and Incomes Board, the Price Commission and latterly the Monopolies and Mergers Commission. From the mid-1950s, the railway and coal industries were almost continuously in deficit despite various initiatives to get them out, and as a result they were subjected to one inquiry after another. As more nationalized industries moved into deficit, so they became subjected to similar inquiries. In contrast, while a nationalized industry was in surplus, even marginally, its performance was hardly questioned.[58] Thus British Telecom, which even when part of the Post Office found no difficulty in making profits, because of booming demand, was never the subject of a report from a select committee, a Monopolies and Mergers Commission investigation or any special departmental review.

But nationalized industries – for example electricity, for a while, and gas – also got attention because of the demands they made on public funds for investment.[59] Indeed, in the late 1950s both politicians and economists became increasingly concerned that the huge and growing amounts of capital consumed by the nationalized industries were not earning a proper return.[60] Ministers did not use the powers they had to override the industries' capital expenditure recommendations, except by crude forms of rationing. Instead, they set out to educate the industries by giving them guidance. The process began in sessions before the Select Committee on Nationalised Industries, where there was lengthy discussion of how nationalized industries could avoid bad investment decisions through better appraisal techniques.[61] One result of this concern was the 1961 White Paper on the financial and economic obligations of the nationalized industries.[62] Because its language was ambiguous, it was variously considered as a set of instructions to the nationalized industries, for which the statutory backing did not exist; as guidance, which by definition did not have to be followed; or as backed up only by arm-twisting, only to be followed in so far as departments used the powers it gave them over other matters to persuade the industries to take this guidance seriously. But whatever its status its principal message was the need to improve the control of nationalized industry finance, especially investment. It was followed by an academic and departmental enthusiasm for discounted cash flow investment appraisal, which was evangelized by the National Economic Development Office (NEDO) from its earliest days, by House of Commons select committees and by civil service training schemes.[63]

There were nationalized industry activities known in advance to be unprofitable which governments wished to maintain and sometimes to invest in. For example, there was London Transport's wish from the mid-1940s onwards to invest in new underground lines in London, as well as British Rail's plans later to electrify various commuter lines.[64] Partly as a result of this desire, there was keenness during the 1960s to find some economic justification for such unprofitable investment. This led to the sporadic use of social cost-benefit analysis, though there was often a lack of reconciliation between the approval of unprofitable investment which earned a positive social cost-benefit return and the statutory duty to break even.[65] Attempts were also made to require the economic justification of subsidies to nationalized industries in those cases where they were required to provide a social service. This led to the notion of explicit subsidies, preferably supported and justified by social cost-benefit analysis.

Sometimes ministers spoke as if the nationalized enterprises were obliged to adopt particular economic or financial criteria in their decision-making, but, as we have seen, they had no power to insist. In the early 1950s it was clear that the British coal industry was over-expanded and that its prices were far below marginal costs.[66]

Neither the industry nor the politicians took much notice. Indeed, the Coal Industry Nationalisation Act required the National Coal Board to make supplies of coal available 'of such qualities and sizes and such prices as may seem to them best calculated to further the public interest in all respects including the avoidance of undue or unreasonable preference'.[67] Small wonder that a commentator noted that 'nationalised industries strive for simple objectives which have in them a strong uneconomic element.'[68] Thus until the end of the 1950s, the National Coal Board set about maximizing coal output at any price – an activity which it regarded as quite consistent with promotion of the public interest. And the industry went on being over-extended until the onslaught upon it by Ian MacGregor in the 1980s, an onslaught which was not motivated by thoughts about marginal-cost pricing. Similarly, after the Second World War, the electricity supply industry was suffering from severe shortages of capacity. Marginal-cost pricing theory indicated the introduction of peak pricing. Various attempts to introduce it from the 1940s onwards were rebuffed by the industry chiefs because they were anxious both to expand capacity and to keep prices down. It was not until severe power shortages led to embarrassing cuts in supply during the early 1960s that the electricity supply industry itself accepted the principle, though it was some years later before it was realized to the extent needed to affect demand patterns. Meanwhile, in both France and England theoretical thinking on peak pricing had advanced considerably.[69] Again, perversely, for many years the railways charged passengers less in the peak period, when a high proportion used season tickets, than in the off-peak period, when they mostly paid normal fares. Because of the complexity of their cost structure, the railways could not adopt marginal-cost pricing and break even, and it was not until some twelve years after they had been freed from rate control by the Transport Tribunal in 1956 that they actively began to discriminate by charging what the market would bear.

These three notions – marginal-cost pricing, discounted cash flow investment appraisal and, to a lesser extent, explicit subsidies – were, in 1967, enshrined in what at the time seemed a further important white paper, intended to replace the 1961 White Paper in governing the economic and financial behaviour of the nationalized industries.[70] A satisfying framework seemed within Parliament's grasp. Although also expressed with the ambiguity that parliamentary draftsmanship and ministerial prudence seem to require, these ideas became known to, and understood by, a much larger circle of informed opinion than is common for economic ideas. The acclaim for them was much less than for Keynesian notions of demand management in the 1940s and 1950s or for privatization today, but was still widespread.

Perhaps the over-simplification on which such acclaim depends always leads to disappointment. Much had been written on the power of ministers over, and the extent of their interventions in, the affairs of the nationalized industries. Lord Swinton had said that the relations he had had with his board chairmen as a minister were like those he had had with his civil servants.[71] Austen Albu, MP, had written that the encroachment of ministers' influence had become so great that it would merely regularize that position and be more honest if the pattern of the Post Office were adopted and other ministers likewise became the chairmen of semi-independent boards.[72] There were also the countless complaints by board chairmen of ministerial intervention that riddled the reports of the Select Committee on the Nationalised Industries over many years. If ministerial powers, and willingness to exercise those powers, were so great, it ought to be possible to advise ministers to act so as to increase the economic efficiency of public enterprises and improve the allocation of resources between and within sectors. And indeed the endeavour was not without its successes, some of which have lasted. Nevertheless, the failures seem in fact to have outweighed them.[73] And they seem to have derived largely from the fact that not only was the influence of ministers not quite as it was thus portrayed but also the ministers, civil servants and public-sector managers had different primary or real objectives and none of these coincided with economic efficiency as seen by economists.

Civil servants and ministers were prepared to question nationalized industries endlessly and in detail about their investment proposals. But while undoubtedly there were many occasions when the result of the dialogue was an improvement – the gas grid was built, unproductive coal mines and some unprofitable railways were closed, the railways were electrified – and while such discussions could often delay less-favoured decisions for months or more, in the end a resolute board could get its way, if it was ready to hold out and paper over the cracks.[74] Ministers were not helped in this, or any other such task of economic and financial control, by their vague statutory powers (already mentioned). Nor did their clear powers of appointing chairmen and boards help when talent was scarce and the salaries the public sector paid were low. And sacking was a difficult exercise when the appointment was a previous minister's and virtually impossible when the appointment was one's own. Moreover, although ministers had the right to turn down investment proposals, they scarcely ever did so, even when they were sure that the industry's views were mistaken. Partly this was because, in the last resort, they feared to disagree with public enterprise chairmen, whom they saw as the specialists in their field. But they also disliked providing them with an alibi for subsequent poor performance. And it was perhaps even more important that ministers usually wanted favours from the chairmen – something done for a constituency here, some help with opposing a trade union or another industry there. The most important and irritating of these were requests not to close an unprofitable operation, requests not to cut manpower in a certain activity, and requests to locate a new activity somewhere other than the place which would be the most profitable. A prudent chairman would discourage such requests by charm and steeliness, so keeping them down to a manageable number. Yet in the end he would usually yield. Such defensive skills were in fact important enough to decide who were those more likely to succeed as nationalized industry chairman – or indeed ministers. Many of the most highly regarded board chairmen, even within their own industries, were not managers as the private sector would recognize them. Rather, they floated as loosely above the actual running of their industries as ministers did over their departments. In the end, then, weighed against what ministers really wanted from chairmen, financial control and economic efficiency usually had a low priority.

Thus the chairmen and boards of nationalized industries had a great practical independence over the major issues that mattered to them. And they used it to pursue what they believed to be the interests of their public corporation. For them that, not the interests of the public as Herbert Morrison or changeable ministers conceived them, or the improvement of economic efficiency, was the public interest. Moreover, because the strongest pressures upon them were often from the trade unions, those unions came to have a powerful influence not only over the interpretation of the public interest but also, what came to the same thing, a claim on any surpluses. What tended to have less influence upon the way in which the public interest was interpreted were first the consumers, though lip-service had been paid them through the setting up of (rather weak) consumer councils, and secondly the rest of industry, which might contain rivals to the nationalized industries as well as its largest consumers. Suppliers however were usually satisfied, in that they often found they could make persistently high profits in their sales to nationalized industries because of the absence of an incentive for these to economize.

The price that the nationalized industries paid for this practical independence was, as indicated above, a constant irritating stream of interventions, usually on comparatively small matters of passing but intense interest to the politicians. On these they had to make concessions to keep the politicians sweet. Thus, this practical independence coincided with what powerful nationalized industry chairmen called at the time 'intolerable' intervention. The Select Committee on Nationalised Industries concluded in its major 1968 report on ministerial control that the faults were mainly those of the ministers and let the boards off lightly.[75] But it seems to me that the blame and benefits may have lain on both sides, and that both may have largely been able to exercise control in the areas that most mattered to them. From the point of view of the detailed political matters that mostly interested ministers, Swinton and Albu could have been correct in stating that this power of a minister over a nationalized industry was not markedly less than over his department. However, as far as achieving economic efficiency or initiating action to eliminate deficits or preventing unprofitable capital expenditure was concerned, the minister's influence was as weak as Herbert Morrison could have ever intended.[76] Thus what was found was consistent with a hypothesis of 'regulatory capture': however adverse the circumstances, the industries retained the autonomy they really wanted and paid a comparatively small political price for it. Moreover, the ambiguities of the situation gave both sides an alibi. The industries could claim that they were prevented from being economically efficient by endless and frequently political intervention, some of which altered their course, not only from government but also from minister to minister. Nationalized industries with strong engineering backgrounds, for example, tended to substitute technical efficiency for economic efficiency as their guide. Ministers and civil servants, on the other hand, could claim (and did so) that all would have been well if the industries had had the good sense and, occasionally it was alleged, the intelligence to follow the excellent guidance they had been given, a common inference being that, if only higher salaries could have been paid, better people could have been appointed and could have solved the problem. (Such a view of the motives of the nationalized industries had, in fact, little substance; they knew what their statutory duties were and, given those, how they wished to manage their industries.)

Finally, although, as noted above, the vast mass of ministerial interventions were (individually) trivial, there were three other main kinds of occasions when ministers' interventions were more significant. First, there was their involvement in the settling of strikes. From the interventions of Churchill and Lloyd George in the first decade of this century until 1979, ministers of all parties intervened repeatedly to settle railway and other strikes that they believed damaging to the economy. Because even after nationalization they had no real bottom-line responsibility, these were almost invariably settled at the expense both of the industry concerned and ultimately of its consumers, not only because costs were inflated directly, but also because, as often as not, proposed productivity improvements were given away as part of the settlement.[77] The experience my own economists in the Ministry of Transport had in day-to-day monitoring of the 1967 dock strike convinced me that the adverse effect of such strikes on the economy was always exaggerated. Those affected were more resourceful in taking avoiding action than they let on. Those with a hot-line to ministers overstated the peril they were in, releasing their anger and frustration with little regard for fact. Ministers tended to be impressed by such fears and may have become all the readier to cave in. At worst, there was a familiar sequence of events: first, the minister's piling on pressure, unseen if possible, on the board to resist more than it first intended, followed by a strike ending in the minister's either negotiating the settlement himself at the expense of the industry and its customers or pressing the board, invisibly if possible, to climb down. Secondly, ministers hectored nationalized industries over their deficits, leading as often as not to unedifying grovelling by the boards, when ministers played the role of the flinty successful banker or businessman, which they almost certainly were not. The ultimate grovelling came after deficits had accumulated to the point where a special inquiry took place, the chairman left and debts were written off. But, apart from some reorganization, the power relations and performance incentives did not themselves change. Thirdly, ministers blamed nationalized industries, usually electricity, which had failed to invest enough to meet demand. Often their predecessors had stopped or delayed the investment which would have avoided the shortage. In turn, this blame may have encouraged over-investment and the disregarding of the financial consequences, leading to the swinging of capacity from under-supply to over-supply.

We can see then that, given their inexperience, their relatively short periods in office, the scope of their responsibilities and their short-term, essentially political interests, ministers could not be expected to manage nationalized industries and determine in detail how their monopoly profits should be used in the public interest. The boards of those industries were given the power to interpret the public interest as they thought best and to regulate the industry in that light. Rather than attempting to define minister's powers and objectives with precision, the regulatory regime gave ministers discretion in the exercise of their influence over the nationalized industries. Ministerial pride and conventional wisdom required that the supreme power should seem to belong to ministers; but that was only the appearance. It was the extreme difficulty that ministers had in exercising the power that they theoretically had that preserved the discretion in practice of the boards from encroachment by ministers except where the boards believed it prudent to succumb or where a minister was particularly determined. While, most of the time, effective power belonged to the boards, there was fluidity in the relationship. The stronger their characters, the greater their skills in public relations and in doing deals with boards, the more power could ministers wield, while the power of the boards might be weakened by deficits, by their own failures in public relations, by exceptionally heavy investment requirements, by mistakes or by an inability to realize the importance of giving ministers some victories which they could parade as personal achievements.

Still, much energy, diplomacy and intelligence was successfully applied to analyse the nationalized industries' plans and projects during this period and long afterwards until, in the 1980s, the run-down of specialist staff made it harder for the civil service to question them with as much rigour and penetration.

3.4 Improving performance

The net effect of all this was that ministers used their limited influence to serve political ends rather than those of economic efficiency, while the nationalized industries used the great discretion they had – at least while they were in surplus – to respond to their own ideas of good engineering and to other internal stimuli. Regulation through nationalization on the British model was thus as fatally flawed as regulation by Parliament and commission – if, that is, economic efficiency was the prime objective it was said to be. Ministers' political objectives and such internal stimuli were both in fact more powerful than the objectives of economic efficiency. (Hence the increasing number of these industries that fell into deficit.) But in the early 1970s it did not seem to me Utopian to call for the improving rather than the abandoning of public enterprise. My recipe – official bodies and other academics had theirs, containing similar ideas – called for:

Far clearer statutory powers for Ministers and clearer delegated authority to Boards The Select Committee on Nationalised Industries had advised this.[78]

More competition Though with doubts over how far competition could be taken some cases. Competition had been advocated before, but generally for the reverse reason: a belief that public enterprises competing with oligopolistic private enterprises would undermine their competitiveness.[79] An achievement of transport policy in the late 1960s had been to introduce some competition. The National Freight Corporation's subsidiaries were examples of bodies that 'get and give as much competition as they would if they were denationalised'.[80] There was indeed more competition for many nationalized industries than was often assumed; but it was flawed by a lack of proper financial control of public enterprise, so that in those days bodies acting on behalf of industry did their best to keep the nationalized industries away from competition with private enterprises because they believed that public enterprises would compete unfairly whether knowingly or unknowingly. Therefore, to make it less possible for nationalized industries to behave in a predatory manner, it would make sense to create many activities embedded within them as separate accounting entities, so that they could compete fairly. In general, it seemed that competition could be developed to improve the boards' efficiency provided that there was also financial discipline, though at the time natural monopoly seemed more widespread than it does now[81] (and rather less ingenuity had been devoted to undermining it).

Imposing cash limits and in some cases requiring nationalized industries to borrow on their own credit Interestingly, Herbert Morrison had believed that a public enterprise should raise its own capital. As he designed it, the LPTB could have gone into receivership if it had not met its financial obligations. Otherwise, he believed, a board might become slack or even reckless, yielding to a 'travelling public . . . demanding lower fares and uneconomic facilities, and . . . the work people . . . asking for big concessions as to conditions of labour; all might be tempted to say, "Well after all, the Treasury is behind us."' To persuade his followers, he cited how in the Soviet Union workers' control had undermined efficiency.[82] In the 1950s it had become the conventional wisdom that public enterprises had government financial guarantees and could not go into the equivalent of receivership. Yet, while a government might indeed have to meet a public enterprise's outstanding financial obligations, it would give muscle to both boards and ministers if going into the red for more than a set period meant that the board members lost their position, and were replaced by a receiver until there was an organizational reconstruction and the appointment of a new board.

Clarifying the objectives of the Chairman and other board members, individually and collectively It would thus be seen when they had succeeded, or had failed and should offer their resignation. The price for this greater risk should be higher salaries.[83]

A clearer distinction between the commercial and social activities of boards The Select Committee on Nationalised Industries had recommended this. Moreover, any appreciable cost of the social activities should be borne by the government department responsible for the social policy in question, whether ordinary administrative methods were used to control it, or more-sophisticated programme budgeting and cost-benefit analysis.[84]

A strategic approach to financial control Rather than nationalized industries' asking for investment funds piecemeal, ministers would approve and monitor a corporate plan which, among other things, would include all planned investments. Private-sector best practice would be adopted, which would mean the industries' estimating their total earning power and therefore, as a result, the level of investment they could maintain profitably. Relevant cash limits should be set, so that if they failed to meet their net-revenue targets, they would have to economize in order to stay within those cash limits.[85] It would be for the enterprise itself to forecast its overall profitability and performance, the assumption of which would be subject to sensitivity tests. Discussion of the corporate plan would conclude with a series of commitments by the board to achieve the agreed objectives, and its performance in this respect would then be monitored.

At the time Sam Brittan argued perceptively that the impossibility of getting politicians to stand off and adopt proposals such as these made mine 'a more profound tract against nationalisation than anything ever published by the Institute of Economic Affairs'.[86] As was common at the time, my tract did not consider the problem of designing incentives which might motivate the required behaviour. In chapter 10 the possibility of reform on these or similar lines, and therefore the question whether a more rational future for public enterprise is possible, will again be discussed.

3.5   The 1970s

After attempts at reform in the 1960s, there followed several years during which the position of the nationalized industries worsened politically and financially. First, the Heath government, from 1970 to 1974, took ministerial intervention to unparalleled lengths. Instead of the pinpricks of the 1960s, nationalized industries were bullied into keeping their prices down in the supposed interests of its anti-inflationary policy. While the immediate effect of huge financial deficits was bad enough, those of the longer-term erosion of financial discipline and the consequent overestimation of investment needs were worse. Nationalized industries have always had a tendency to over-invest, partly because of the strength within them of engineering interests, which have seen investment as a main object, and partly because of politicians' dislike of bad publicity from interruptions of supply; but this tendency was reinforced in the 1970s when many nationalized industries, but particularly iron and steel and electricity, over-invested on a substantial scale.[87]

Secondly, during the raging inflation of the 1970s, triggered off by the American financing of the Vietnam War, it was a common perception that public-sector pay advanced faster than private-sector pay, or at least exerted a malign influence earlier in the pay round. This was put down to the power of the trade unions in holding consumers up to ransom using the monopoly power of the nationalized industries for which their members worked. And indeed there is evidence that the nationalized industry work-forces were pace-setters in wage rises especially in the 1970s.[88] Public-sector unions were particularly conspicuous in the strikes that helped to bring down the Heath government. And their continuing intransigence over pay policy endangered succeeding Labour governments.

Thirdly, the Wilson and Callaghan governments, from 1974 to 1979, put nationalized industries under greater pressure than they were under in the 1960s, only in the opposite direction to Heath's. The financially stronger public enterprises like the Post Office, were forced to increase their prices substantially in order that public expenditure could be cut. While Heath's policy of keeping postal and telephone charges down resulted in a £300 million loss for the Post Office in 1974/75, the opposite policy put profits up to nearly £400 million in 1976/77.[89] Moreover, an effect of the oil-price increases in 1973 was to confuse the output and pricing policies of many nationalized industries. They also helped bring several lame ducks from the private into the public sector.[90] Nationalized industry managers became a discouraged class. They were less happy with the security of their position as their salaries fell during the great inflation progressively below those of their private-sector counterparts. Meanwhile, the political management of price increases often meant that ordinary consumers, who had votes, were protected at the expense of the larger industrial and commercial consumers, who therefore became resentful.

Ministerial control of the nationalized industries became more difficult and less effective as policies became cruder and more volatile. A NEDO report in 1976 found that the recommendations on economic and financial criteria made in the 1967 White Paper had had almost no impact on what nationalized industries had done.[91] Four industries were examined. None, it was found, based its prices on marginal costs. The report concluded in an opinion (confirmed in several Monopolies and Mergers

Commission reports after 1980) that 'the principle of determining prices in relation to long run marginal cost has been followed to a negligible extent in' gas, rail, telecommunications and iron and steel; and it believed that, in its peak-pricing policy, only electricity among the rest had taken it seriously.[92] It found, moreover, that investment appraisals were often done badly or not at all; that government frequently varied capital programme totals for macroeconomic reasons without regard to the actual rates of return on investment earned or in prospect in particular industries; and that the lines of responsibility between government departments and nationalized industries were confused, trust was absent, performance was poorly measured and there was no established way of agreeing long-term objectives in a corporate plan.

The NEDO report made many radical suggestions for reform, some on the lines indicated above; but they were not adopted. One of these encouraged a fundamentally different, yet attractive, approach to management.[93] What NEDO recommended, and the Government rejected,[94] was that nationalized industry boards should be changed into, or supervised by, policy councils on the model of the supervisory boards found in West Germany. The essence of this participative model is that, besides top-executive management, there should be representatives on the council reflecting all the interests vital to the firm – certainly consumers and workers, but perhaps also representatives of the sponsoring government department, other suppliers of finance such as bankers (where relevant), major suppliers of components and raw materials, and trade unions (if they are not already, as they may well be, the 'worker' representatives). The policy council like any board is then to agree, and as far as possible to reach a consensus on, the firm's objectives, and to ensure that they are transmitted, understood and achieved. Among the attractions of the model are that it is democratic in a meaningful sense, though difficult issues are raised in deciding what interests are to be represented, how many places are to be given to each and what voting system is to be adopted; and further problems arise in attempting to decide how far council members are to be free to vote as individuals or in what circumstances and how they need to have their opinions confirmed by those they represent. And there would be great advantage to management if it had secured the commitment of those interests represented on the council, though unless consensus is achieved, some interests may find themselves outvoted and even in frequent opposition. The system of decision-making that it embodies will be slow and unwieldy unless there is prior agreement on the main issues. If interests change their opinions or the coalitions of interests that will tend to form change, this may be reflected in objectives changing too frequently for there to be clear guidance down the line. In practice, it will only work either where there is prior agreement or where most interests do not press their disagreements. Otherwise, all that may be communicated down the line is confusion. It is likely that, by resorting to ambiguity, which is itself hostile to effective management, the appearance of consensus may be achieved but not the reality.

This participative model still has strong proponents, of whom one of the most persuasive is Tony Prosser.[95] Despite its attractions, however, this model, if it is to be in practice genuinely participative and democratic, seems incompatible with the levels of efficiency international competitiveness now demands. Some relevant arguments to support this are developed in chapter 5 in a discussion of the increasing scope for economies of scale; in chapter 7, where it is argued that effective management requires the definition, setting and monitoring of objectives and targets throughout an organization and this is only possible if such objectives and targets are well defined, simple and persistent; in chapter 9, where it is maintained that mixing economic and social objectives – something which a policy council will be prone to do – is inimical to effective regulation; and in chapter 10, which is specifically concerned with public enterprise reform. Since there is no obviously more convenient place to summarize the difficulties that seem to defeat this model, let it be here: they are that anything approaching genuine democratic participative control (which is a very different matter from top management's securing commitment to its objectives) is consistent with economic efficiency only in very small organizations which are themselves likely to be uncompetitive; in larger organizations it is bound to result in uncompetitive inefficiency; thus, whatever the weight one would like to give to such participative values, they cannot survive in an internationally competitive world. As will be argued later, only simple, persistent and well-defined objectives are consistent with economic efficiency.

In 1978, yet another guidance white paper was issued. However, it too failed to solve the problem, because its precepts, like those of its predecessors, had not the legislative force they were widely assumed to have: the actual powers and duties of the nationalized industries remained untouched. This new white paper was partly prompted by a difficulty which had developed through ministers' trying to control the capital expenditure of nationalized industries by monitoring the returns on individual projects.[96] One project might be better than the base case but the overall return on the programme of which it was a part could still be inadequate. Projects could often be shown to have an acceptable return by careful choice of an unattractive base case, which was seldom scrutinized. Or to put it another way, it had been observed that in several nationalized industries high returns had been predicted from their investments both individually and collectively yet those industries had gone further into the red. The White Paper proposed a required rate of return on a board's total investment, though it demoted long-run marginal-cost pricing, giving each industry the freedom to adjust its prices so as to meet an overall financial target. Therefore it tried to achieve a more strategic control over nationalized industries both by concentrating on the control, through an agreed corporate plan, of entire investment programmes rather than investments in individual projects and by welding together economic concepts and accounting information. However, it was too long delayed, having been bitterly opposed by the nationalized industry chairmen – when it came out, it was as out of touch as ever with the realities of the nationalized industries.[97] One tribute to its mythic quality is that it remained still technically in place more than twelve years later despite dramatic changes in government policy.

My own views on the practicality of such strategic control were affected by my personal experience as a part-time member of the Post Office Board from 1975 to 1978. My first discovery was that few discrete decisions came to the Board and that both the investment programmes and the pricing policies that reached the Board showed little in them that reflected the use of financial and economic criteria – but that was what my 1960s experience had led me to expect. More disquieting was the manner of a development of which I had had high hopes. The Post Office had a corporate plan, and a large part of one day was to be spent discussing it with, the then Secretary of State for Trade and Industry, and with his senior officials. I imagined the copious analysis performed by the ministry officials and the incisive ministerial briefing based on it. I suppose I hoped for the setting out of some well-chosen targets, and some clarifications of policy, that might strengthen the hands of the united, but not powerful, part-time members of the Board. But it was not to be. The Secretary of State was quickly seen to be bored by the corporate plan. There were no penetrating questions and it was only a matter of politeness that there was any discussion at all before he turned to what really interested him, which were some constituency matters. So much for strategic financial control in practice.[98] Ministers in general had neither the personal experience nor the political stomach for it. They did not stand to gain from endorsing a well-defined corporate plan, or securing one from the boards.

By the end of the 1970s, with setbacks of all kinds in the performances of the nationalized industries, and with that of the British Steel Corporation outstanding in that it lost one-sixth of its capital in 1978/79 alone,[99] further discussion of the issue of how to improve the control of public enterprise had become frustrating even for that declining band sympathetic to it. Moreover the fine-tuning of economic and financial criteria seemed mere tinkering when the causes of efficiency in public enterprise appeared deep rooted and tenacious. It was difficult not to believe that more important was substantial, even colossal, X-inefficiency, as economists call it, that is, the organizational inefficiency that arises from the failure to realize cost-reduction opportunities.[100]

During the 1970s, the financial performance of the nationalized industries generally declined; but, as public interest in financial performance increased with general economic decline, there was increasing criticism of their *comparative* financial performance.[101] Such comparisons, however, not only fail to discriminate between the various individual public enterprises, some of which have been far more profitable than others while others have been far less, but also beg every kind of question. To begin with, it has to be decided whether the comparison should be made with subsidies or without them. If the subsidies are payments by the State for the running of unremunerative services or for keeping prices down below costs, then there is a strong case for their being regarded as payments for services rendered. But if instead they are there to plug a deficit, then they reflect an inability to perform and are not income. Yet seldom is this distinction made explicitly. Secondly, such comparisons assume that the public enterprises were allowed to aim for profitability, while in practice all sorts of political and financial constraints, individual and collective, were placed on them. In particular, pricing policies, even marginal-cost pricing policies, may make profits a misleading guide. What is then in principle relevant, though unmeasurable, is the sum of consumers' and producers' surpluses. Thirdly, and even more fundamentally, such comparisons assume that profit is the primary financial objective of nationalized industries, which in general it has never been.

While profitability has thus been a poor guide to public corporations' financial performance (and indeed has not even been intended to be a guide until the last few years), there have been criticisms in parallel of the poor improvement in productivity achieved by the nationalized industries. Those who had pressed those industries to use better economic and financial criteria and techniques believed that the result would be improved productivity. However, one researcher, Richard Pryke, had disregarded criteria and had returned indefatigably to the fundamental question whether nationalized industries had improved their productivity (though even this is irrelevant if their main objective is not held to be economic efficiency). His first verdict, given at the end of the 1960s, was one of qualified optimism.[102] From the first, most nationalized industries had improved their labour and total factor productivity by comparison with the national average, though there were exceptions. But when he returned to consider their performance in the 1970s, his verdict was far less favourable.[103] Rather than improving on the rates of productivity growth of the 1950s and 1960s, there had been a general slackening. This he blamed for the most part on public ownership.

Pryke reinforced this message in a comparative study he published in 1987.[104] He took instances of markets where there was both private and public ownership – civil aviation, short distance sea ferries and the sale of gas and electrical appliances – and found that the publicly owned enterprises had used labour and capital more inefficiently. Several other studies reached similar conclusions.[105] Yet there were as many studies which found either that it was impossible to decide which form of ownership was the more efficient in this respect or in some cases that public ownership was.[106] Millward made the general point that such comparisons ignore the different objectives set, and the constraints imposed on public firms.[107] Moreover, differences in data, in the activities that apparently similar enterprises undertake and in how they are organized mean that the comparative data available to outsiders often make comparison difficult. That would be true even if one were to assume that efficiency was a goal of equal weight in both the private and the public sectors, which in general is a far from reasonable assumption. Furthermore, as John Kay has pointed out, the best comparisons are confined to the comparatively few unbiased situations where there are both public and private firms competing.[108]

3.6   A fundamental attack on public enterprise

While all this experience and analysis discredited nationalization, another more fundamental and theoretical attack, which had started among right-wing economists in America, became increasingly influential in Britain. It was born in the circumstances of American politics and in particular the American practice of regulating rather than nationalizing public utilities. Translated into British terms, it attacked the possibility of the efficiency of public enterprise at a fundamental level, denying the realism of assuming that its managers would act in the public interest.

Economic analysis has generally assumed that firms act to maximize profits, although it has been recognized since at least the 1930s that the interests of shareholder and manager may and do diverge and that, as Sir John Hicks put it then, one of the privileges of monopoly power is to enjoy a quiet life rather than pursue profit to the maximum.[109] As a result, in recent years much attention has been given to incentive schemes to align the interests to managers at all levels with those of shareholders. (It is ironical that collectivists first gained the inspiration to think state enterprise desirable through noting the divergence between ownership and management that resulted from the creation of joint stock companies.)

It was pointed out in this theoretical attack that in the case of public enterprise this problem is compounded because it involves more levels of competing interests. Besides the substantial divergences between the objectives for the firm of manager and 'owner', there are the further interests of bureaucrats and politicians. Bureaucrats came to be accused of wishing to maximize the size of their departments and their own costs of operation – not only their salaries but also various non-pecuniary emoluments, including peace and quiet.[110] By contrast, improving the efficiency of the public enterprises they helped to control did not obviously affect their personal interest. Politicians are assumed to have other objectives again in maximizing the chances of their return to office.[111] While some maintain this leads them too to favour the growth of government, others would see the quest for votes as leading to more-complicated positions.[112] (Indeed, if politicians always favoured bigger government, because of the expansion of patronage this entails, how does one explain Margaret Thatcher's repeated successes at the polls?)

On this basis alone, the problem of aligning the incentives of politician, bureaucrat and public enterprise manager seemed insoluble even on the assumption that economic efficiency, rather than an ill-defined notion of the public interest, is in some sense agreed to be the criterion against which the various objectives should be measured. Thus, although it was from this, perhaps temporary, belief – that the objectives of public enterprise can and should be measured against that single criterion – that much of the thinking and action of the 1980s on this matter sprang, as important was the realization that setting up a structure and a set of criteria to this end is insufficient, that one must also design structures that motivate those concerned to achieve the objectives desired, though to do this at all easily requires that the industries in question seek to maximise profits and give insignificant weight to the interests of particular kinds of consumers, and those of politicians, bureaucrats and the labour-force.

However, there was another possible interpretation of the position, borne of the realism or cynicism which underlay much of the fierce and almost successful early opposition to privatization. This accepted the repeated interventions by ministers in the affairs of the nationalized industries not only as inevitable but as democratically justifiable. If the electorate had given the necessary weight to economic efficiency in the public provision of goods and services, this would have been reflected in the behaviour of politicians seeking votes. Politicians would have seen their giving due weight to it as more important for their popularity and electoral success than were their short-term political interventions in the affairs of the nationalized industries. The lesson such observers drew from the repeated failures to reform public enterprise as well as to make it efficient, was that economic efficiency as a goal was, in terms of electoral advantage, overborne by these short-term political objectives. From this standpoint, the nationalization regime could be judged a success inasmuch as it provided a ground where the Treasury had a good chance of fighting to restrain the worst excesses of politicians and to prevent galloping deficits while politicians were given a power-base which enabled them to exert some patronage and some influence over these industries, in appearance perhaps rather more than in reality but none the less important to them for that reason.[113] In sustaining the self-regard and visible importance of politicians, nationalized industries had stepped in to fill the vacuum left by the loss of the colonies and declining influence overseas.

As long as British politicians were ready to accept the efficiency costs of the situation, the Morrisonian solution to regulating the nationalized industries had enormous political and bureaucratic appeal. It was an arrangement well suited to an easy-going, affluent society where there was an adroit civil service to prevent extreme developments. Arguably, it seemed preferable to the American alternative where, the conventional wisdom had it – at least until the 1970s – as we shall see in chapter 11, the American regulators were captured by the interests of the regulated industries to the virtual exclusion of other influences. Whether the reader accepts the kind of analysis of politicians, nationalized industry boards and civil servants offered in that chapter is important since it affects the likelihood that he will accept the arguments developed later in this book on the sustainability of the new system of regulation that has emerged in the 1980s.

In this chapter we have discussed how and why the third British experiment in economic regulation failed. The seeds of that failure can be seen in the circumstances of its setting up. To solve a political problem and to make the form of nationalization acceptable beyond the labour movement, the nationalized industries had not been given any clear or precise objectives or incentives. Instead, they had been given, in practice at least, the wide discretion which is seen as desirable for a regulator. However, the strongest influences upon the boards as regulators were not from the higher regulatory powers that allowed them discretion but from beneath them: from the managers, who valued technical efficiency and a quiet life; and the work-force, who valued high wages and what were euphemistically called 'good working conditions'. Moreover, the consequence of giving the board that discretion was not only that no precise and binding objectives could under that discretion be defined for them but that other important elements in the managerial paradigm to be discussed in chapter 10 were also missing. There was no effective *monitoring* of performance. The industries were required to produce accounts, but even more than in private industries these long tended to be drawn up so as to serve no other purpose than to measure whether or not there was an overall surplus of income over expenditure. Ministers had powers to call for information on various matters like research and development, but rarely did this information have much relation to the economic performance of the industries. *Ad hoc* studies extracted information from the nationalized industries, with various degrees of reluctance, but they were not much use for monitoring economic performance. Ministers themselves had no general powers to demand information. The industries often used the tactic of being exceedingly slow in providing any information asked for, in the frequently justified belief that ministers would eventually lose patience and turn to some other issue.

The boards' discretion was also inconsistent with any *incentives* to good performance since they can only operate in relation to certain fixed, simple and well-defined objectives, and these could not be imposed in these circumstances. Indeed, the machinery for such a scheme did not exist either. In one respect, the nationalization statutes throughout the period strongly discouraged profit-making because of a technicality: the boards could only use any profits they made either to invest in their own business or to repay borrowing. For all the talk of government being the shareholder, there was in most cases no technical way in which the Treasury could receive a dividend. The theoretical encouragement to over-invest was therefore as great as under rate-of-return regulation.

Dennis Swann has appraised this period of nationalization as if its effectiveness were to be judged as a test of marginal-cost pricing. Given all the evidence in this chapter that the nationalized industries most commonly took all this economic guidance lightly and paid little more than lip-service to the white papers on financial and economic criteria, this cannot be said to describe the situation. Ministers had neither the power nor the will nor any incentive to make nationalized industries observe the formal criteria of economic efficiency.[114]

While most of the elements of the managerial paradigm (to which we shall return much later when we come to consider how privatization and public ownership at their best might compare in terms of improving the efficiency of an enterprise) was absent in nationalization in practice, so were key elements in the other, regulatory paradigm (also to be developed later). The framework within which nationalized industries operated paid no attention to the *control of monopoly* as such; or to *fair trading* either between public enterprises or between public and private enterprises; or to *asymmetric information* – the fact that in this instance a nationalized industry could bolster its monopoly power by having and using substantially more information about itself than was available to the government department that sponsored it, let alone its customers and suppliers. The one element in the regulatory paradigm which is a clear ministerial objective is the improvement of *economic efficiency*, and we have seen how badly adapted the framework of control under nationalization was to helping achieve that. It is hardly surprising that, particularly during the 1970s when old-established political conventions, and especially the long-standing Keynesian consensus, were breaking down in British political life, many people came to believe that, however qualified, the achievement of profitability or economic efficiency should be the main purpose of state enterprise, and that disregarding it had not only led to a substantial waste to resources but had contributed to national economic decline.[115] Ironically the very form of organizational arrangement which Herbert Morrison had believed would distance state enterprise from political intervention was discredited for permitting too much intervention for economic efficiency to be possible. Because there was disappointment over the performance of nationalized industries and pessimism over whether improvement was possible, the way was prepared for the welcoming of a radical solution when one was presented.

Notes

1 Dicey (1914), p. 248.
2 Shinwell (1955), pp. 172–3. However, there were several Labour blueprints for the railways: Bonavia (1971), pp. 38–40.
3 Morgan (1985), p. 105, says that James Griffith's pamphlet was excellent. Sked and Cook (1979), p. 31, suggest that this was a Welsh translation, and that it was present in the archives together with a copy of the English original.
4 Gordon (1938), pp. 1–17. Herbert Morrison adopted the term for the London Passenger Transport Board, though he derived it from the Socialist, William Graham. Technically, these earlier nationalizations were not called such, but I regard the difference as more presentational and political than real.
5 H. Morrison (1933), *passim*. Before 1945, those who wanted public ownership mostly wanted the agreement of those who feared Socialism, so they avoided calling it

nationalization. Nevertheless, forms of public ownership developed before 1945 were the models for post-1945 nationalizations.

6 Bagwell (1988), pp. 224–8.

7 Ibid., pp. 228–35.

8 Robson (1952), pp. 355, 356.

9 Mulley (1983), pp. 7–19.

10 Kelf-Cohen (1969), pp. 15–37, and Clegg and Chester (1953), pp. 3–19.

11 Wickwar (1938), pp. 172–80.

12 Robson (1962), p. 33. Professor Barker has pointed out to me that the rationale for LPTB in its early days was that the very profitable buses could cross-subsidize the underground trains; rationalization as such was secondary.

13 It has been argued that, even if the economies of scale in the nationalized industries were realizable, tradition, conservatism and uncertainty meant they were not realized: Buxton and Aldcroft (1979), pp. 21, 22. Even in electricity, where the grid did realize scale economies, managers otherwise overestimated their ability to make mergers work: Hannah (1979), p. 162. Coal was never a natural monopoly: C. Robinson (1987).

14 Clegg and Chester (1953), pp. 15–16.

15 Hannah (1982), p. 7.

16 Clegg and Chester (1953), p. 50.

17 Robson (1962), pp. 34–5.

18 See Edwards (1897), pp. 213–17, who gives this as the most important reason for nationalization, believing the industry's regulatory problems to be otherwise insoluble. Gordon (1938), pp. 86–99, gave freedom from 'manifold restrictions' as a reason for setting up the CEB. Wickwar (1938), ch. 7, discussed the complexities of regulation. See also Robson (1962), pp. 34–7, 117, 122, on gas and electricity.

19 Gordon (1938), pp. 104–10. When the CEB decided to connect a privately or municipally owned generating station to the grid – a decision it postponed for as long as possible – it became responsible for all of that generating station's capital and operating costs, leaving no risk or financial incentive with the generator: Hannah (1979), pp. 111–13.

20 Keynes (1981), p. 343. He was himself equivocal about monopoly and 'wasteful' competition. He told the Macmillan Committee in 1930 that where there was surplus capacity, forming monopolies or cartels was selling dearer, not producing cheaper, but that 'those methods are very necessary to overcome methods of individualistic production': ibid., pp. 110–11.

21 Morgan (1985), p. 100; Pelling (1984), p. 78.

22 Morgan (1985), pp. 107, 108, more generally, pp. 99–127; Pelling (1984), pp. 79–81.

23 Burk (1988), *passim*.

24 Ostergaard (1954).

25 Pelling (1984), p. 77.

26 Chester (1975), pp. 189–95.

27 Lerner (1944), *passim*. Joan Robinson had undermined the concept of an isolated industry in J. Robinson (1948) (1st edn. 1933), though she did not do so unequivocally: see Shackle (1967), pp. 64–71; Lerner (1944).

28 Chester (1975), p. 1,010.

29 Bonavia (1987): on same prices per mile, p. 9; on Morrison's reaction, pp. 16, 17.

30 Cairncross (1985), pp. 490–2.

31 Chester (1975), p. 960: on the Transport Tribunal, p. 665; on the Electricity Commissioners, p. 1,028.

32 H. E. Finer at the London School of Economics wrote of such alternatives that, 'in the past no fully satisfactory system of control has been devised. There has been far less

experimentation in such devices in this country than in the United States of America, where it is the rule for the municipality to give franchises to private undertakings and then subject them to the control of public utility commissions. Their history is a shocking record of litigious, crafty and sometimes gangster methods . . .': Finer (1941), p. 31. Both the Labour government and the Conservative opposition were explicit in 1946 in wanting not an American-style regulatory commission for aviation but rather a judicial body with full legal powers and sitting under a legal chairman: Baldwin (1987), p. 161.

33 Chester (1975), p. 1,028; Bonavia (1987), p. 20.

34 Bonavia (1987), pp. 165, 166.

35 Cairncross (1985), pp. 463–4.

36 Gordon (1938), pp. 2–4, 257; Liberal Party (1928), pp. 63–83; Keynes (1931), pp. 313–17.

37 Morgan (1985), p. 52. On the failings, seen from very different standpoints, of the Morrisonian public-interest model as applied in Britain, see Veljanovski (1990), pp. 57–8, and Lewis (1989), pp. 231ff.

38 H. Morrison (1933), pp. 78–80.

39 Ibid., pp. 68, 69, 156, 170.

40 For the issue, see Prosser (1986), pp. 62, 63; Bonavia (1987), p. 17.

41 London Transport Act, 1969.

42 H. Morrison (1933), pp. 171–4, 288. I have dealt at some length with these issues in Foster (1971), esp. ch. 1.

43 *Tamlin vs. Hannaford* (1950), cited by Robson (1962), pp. 69–70. Belief in this led the British Gas Corporation, when threatened with privatization, to claim that, since it was its own proprietor, the sale proceeds from privalization should not go to government.

44 Chester (1975), pp. 610–14.

45 Ibid., pp. 958–9.

46 See, for example, Hannah (1982), ch. 2, on the electricity industry's understanding of its relations with government. There were exceptions to the rule that the power over borrowing was not to be used for detailed control – for example, BOAC was made to buy VC10s when it wanted Boeing 707s: SCNI (1968), vol. 1, pp. 115, 226.

47 British Transport Commission (1955): see discussion in Foster (1963), ch. 5.

48 Keynes (1936).

49 Pelling (1984), p. 96. In 1919 Churchill, however, said that 'it does not matter whether the nationalized railways show a deficit although of course every possible economy should be used in their administration': Bonavia (1987), p. 154.

50 Chester (1975), pp. 1,047, 1,048.

51 Ibid., pp. 956–79.

52 Ibid.

53 Pelling (1984), p. 94; Prosser (1986), pp. 26–9; Cairncross (1985), pp. 479–84. Two of the first chairmen had been senior civil servants in the relevant departments: Sir Cyril, later Lord, Hurcomb, who as a young civil servant had been responsible for drafting the model CEB and LPTB legislation, went to the British Transport Commission from being permanent secretary at the Ministry of Transport; and Lord Hyndley, who became chairman of the National Coal Board. The chairmen of the electricity, gas and airline boards had been trade union officials. Only Hardie at iron and steel had been an industrialist. Hugh Gaitskell, who as Minister of Fuel and Power opposed efficiency units, changed his mind when out of office: Gaitskell (1956).

54 Chester (1975).

55 Ibid.

56 The Treasury welcomed the select committee because it got answers to questions which it itself could not always get directly.

57   The Treasury may have spoken generally with one stern financial voice, but internally there were at least five interests, often conflicting: those four divisions separately concerned with nationalized industry financial performance, general prices and pay inflation, public expenditure, economic forecasting; and the economic section with its own interest in economic criteria.

58   L. J. Dunnett, permanent secretary to the Ministry of Transport, in giving evidence to the Select Committee on Nationalised Industries, stressed that going into deficit was the reason for stepping-up government intervention: SCNI (1959), pp. 2, 3.

59   One cause of excessive investment in electricity was that the industry seized on the over-optimistic economic growth forecasts in the 1965 *National Plan*: Department of Economic Affairs (1965). See also Kelf-Cohen (1969), p. 187.

60   From its investigation into the railways from 1959 onwards, this was a constant message of a series of reports of the House of Commons Select Committee on Nationalised Industries, culminating in its report on ministerial control: SCNI (1968), vol. 1, pp. 11–24. See Kelf-Cohen (1969), p. 187; Foster (1971), pp. 146–7.

61   There was lengthy discussion in SCNI (1959); in SCNI (1968), vol. 1, pp. 11–24; and also in most of this committee's reports on individual industries.

62   HM Treasury (1961); Kelf-Cohen (1969), p. 187.

63   NEDO (1965). Also influential was Merrett and Sykes (1963).

64   As the Victoria Line this was realized in the 1960s. Cf. Foster and Beesley (1963).

65   Beesley and Foster (1965).

66   Little (1953).

67   Coal Industry Nationalisation Act, 1946, s. 1(i).

68   Kelf-Cohen (1969), pp. 200–1. On shortages in electricity capacity mentioned below, see Hannah (1982), pp. 33–8, 76–93, 213–17.

69   Perhaps the breakthrough in the British literature was Turvey (1968).

70   HM Treasury (1967). R. H. S. Crossman, then Minister for Housing, commented on the cabinet discussion of this white paper. The Cabinet 'had exactly twenty minutes to consider it . . . As I got up from the table I said to Callaghan, "This is a very poor paper." "What does it matter?" he said. "It's only read by a few dons and experts!" "Well I'm one don," I said, and he replied "You're a don who knows nothing about the subject. Personally, as Chancellor, I could not care less. I take no responsibility. I took no part in composing it." Here was a key issue of socialist strategy and the Chancellor of the Exchequer washes his hands of it.' Crossman (1976), p. 524. This is often considered a reasonable criticism of both the Cabinet and Callaghan; but cabinet ministers are not able to study technical documents, there had been lengthy official discussions and discussions with the boards, and Crossman had not thought out his view that a more Socialist document was needed. He was against the whole tendency of government policy on nationalization at that time.

71   House of Lords Debates, 12 March 1953, quoted in SCNI (1968), vol. 1, p. 14.

72   Albu (1963), esp. p. 111.

73   Foster (1971), *passim.*

74   Ibid. Many British nationalized industries had developed ways of handling outsiders brought in as board chairmen or members using the same skills as civil servants used to guide ministers. The Post Office, which eventually became divided into postal services and British Telecommunications, showed a continuity in this as it changed from government department to nationalized industry. But it is arguable that it was in other nationalized industries a legacy of those first chairmen – especially Hurcomb at the British Transport Commission and Hyndley at the National Coal Board – who created a civil service environment at the top of the organizations they formed. See, for example, Bonavia (1987), pp. 38–59.

75 SCNI (1968), vol. 2, pp. 189, 190, 203. The Committee decided that, while many of the restrictions on nationalized industry freedom of action had been imposed by ministers, others had been accepted voluntarily (p. 150). It was in accord with the Morrisonian tradition in recommending that ministers not boards should decide nationalized industry social objectives (p. 152), and argued that, where ministers wanted them, they should usually pay for them (p. 155). They were convinced that the main cause of the very poor relations they found between ministers, departments and boards resulted from confusion over responsibilities and policies (p. 189).

76 H. Morrison (1933), pp. 140, 141. There is an excellent discussion of the failure to persuade the nationalized industries to adopt economic criteria in G. W. Harrison (1987), pp. 185–8.

77 The first, but far from the last, example of this was when a British Transport Commission fares increase, approved by the Transport Tribunal and the Central Transport Consultative Committee, was stopped on purely political grounds by the minister responsible, with the approval of the Prime Minister. What was unusual was that he used a formal direction to do this: Bonavia (1987), p. 103. Later, more informal methods were usual.

78 Michael Bonavia has remarked to me that the minister's powers in relation to the British Transport Commission were considerable since there were many things he had to approve – for example, area schemes for road passenger traffic and for ports. The effect of this was, in his judgement, that the department's civil servants gained control over organizational patterns, which they enjoyed, and escaped from decision-making on economic matters, which frightened them. See also Bonavia (1987), pp. 94–104.

79 Foster (1971), p. 189. A good example of this were the restrictions in the Transport Act, 1947, which forbade the railways to exploit their manufacturing assets, like rail and bus workshops, commercially.

80 Foster (1971), pp. 138–49; also Robson (1962), pp. 144–6.

81 Foster (1971), pp. 138–48.

82 H. Morrison (1933), pp. 213–24, 269–72. The Mersey Docks and Harbour Board was allowed to go bankrupt in the early 1970s on the ground that it was not explicitly guaranteed by government.

83 Foster (1971), pp. 132–7.

84 Ibid., pp. 200–21; SCNI (1968), vol. 1, pp. 153–5.

85 Foster (1971), pp. 149–61.

86 Brittan and Riley (1978), p. 137. There was an attempt in the early 1970s by the Central Policy Review Staff in the Cabinet Office, to bring in much more business-like arrangements to control nationalized industries, but it foundered when inflation took off.

87 See Pryke (1981) on British Steel; Molyneux and Thompson (1987) on coal; and MMC (1981) on electricity. However, even the fact of such a tendency towards over-investment was questioned by an American economist, W. G. Shepherd, who argued that economic analysis suggested that investment had kept pace with demand: Shepherd (1965), *passim*, but esp. pp. 139–41.

88 See Thomas (1986a), p. 300.

89 Redwood (1980), p. 91.

90 Ibid., p. 156. Many of these were government controlled through 100 per cent or majority shareholdings.

91 NEDO (1976). Lewis (1989), p. 231, refers to this NEDO report as 'a unique attempt to construct a principled system'.

92 NEDO (1976), vol. , p. 31. There is a strong criticism of even the Central Electricity Generating Board's pricing policy for not reflecting long-run marginal cost in MMC (1981), p. 62. See also Wharton (1988).

93 NEDO (1976), vol. 1, pp. 46–8.

94 There were, however, half-hearted nods in its direction when civil servants were put on some nationalized industry boards, and there was a year's experiment with trade union and consumer representatives on the Post Office Board. These first cases – which were not really experiments in participation – involved Treasury civil servants on the boards of the British National Oil Corporation and British Steel Corporation. Usually there were no problems of conflict of interest, but one has told me that there was one occasion on which he was grateful that their chairman withheld information from him, because the Board's policy and the Government's prices and incomes policy differed. I came off the Post Office Board just before the experiment there started. The Chairman was utterly and publicly opposed to it; but even if there had been goodwill on his part, the experiment would still have illustrated some of the inevitable problems posed by such participation. The agenda was difficult to agree and overcrowded, and consumers, trade unionists and the executives wanted to talk about different things and were often bored and uncomprehending of what was the first importance to others, yet getting through such an agenda decisively implies common values and interests so that very much does not have to be said. The routine scrutiny of performance often got short shrift. Decisions were often delayed, or not clearly taken, creating uncertainty down the line. And in some cases board members seem to have departed from the views of those they were supposed to represent. The only recourse of an executive in such circumstances is to take as many decisions as it can itself.

95 Prosser (1986). He sees the policy council as a way of overcoming the failures of past attempts at government, consumer and worker participation in the control of public enterprises. One model he points to is the role of the Transport Users' Consultative Committee under the Transport Act, 1968, in having to go through various procedures to approve rail closures (p. 166). From my own experience, I know that the procedures were made cumbersome in order to make closure as hard as possible; and in that they have succeeded. However, his position is an important one. He believes that the policies of nationalized industries and public bodies should be determined by the participation of the various interests, and that the failure to so determine them was a main reason for both the reality and the widespread perception of nationalized industry failure in the 1970s (pp. 42–4, 58) – on this scheme my only comment here is, how desirable it would be if it were practicable!

96 HM Treasury (1978). For the view that this white paper was not effective because not followed up by legislation, see A. J. Harrison (1988), p. 27.

97 Heald and Steel (1981).

98 In other respects, Varley could be strong-minded. Redwood (1984), p. 32, not a sympathetic critic, refers to his strength of character in supporting Michael Edwardes against the strikers at British Leyland at Speke in circumstances in which most of his predecessors would have moved to undermine management. On the failure of corporate planning in the nationalized industries as a method of control, see Prosser (1986), p. 133, and Lewis (1989), p. 236. But when ministers have to move so quickly, and have such a wide scope of responsibility, can they really be expected to be interested in the detail essential to a corporate plan?

99 Letwin (1988), p. 6; Kay and Silberston (1984), p. 14.

100 Leibenstein (1966). For the view that restructuring within the public sector was much less productive of economies than at Courtauld, Tootal, GKN or ICI in the private sector, see Redwood (1984), ch. 1.

101 Between 1974 and 1983 real rates of return on industrial and commercial companies, excluding North Sea oil, fluctuated between just under 4 and just under 7 per cent, while comparable figures for nationalized industries were between minus 1 and just under 2 per

cent. The countercyclical pattern was similar. See HM Treasury (1985b), p. 6; also Vickers and Yarrow (1988), p. 143.

102 Pryke (1971), pp. 433–42.

103 Pryke (1981), pp. 237–66.

104 Pryke (1987).

105 E.g., Millward (1986).

106 Ashworth and Forsyth (1984) concluded that British Airways had a very poor efficiency record by comparison with other airlines, both public and private. And Millward (1986) reached the conclusion that in electricity supply public firms were more efficient, and that Canadian private and public railways were about equally efficient.

107 Even Savas, who is among the most zealous opponents of public enterprise, has had to allow that in the case of electricity supply the evidence is difficult to interpret and may even be in favour of public enterprise: Savas (1987), p. 150. A careful study of public and private US electricity supply suggests that the difference could be one of the economic and financial criteria employed. In the 1980s private firms moved towards discrimination in the form of Ramsey pricing – that is, broadly, charging what the market will bear in each market, subject to an overall rate-of-return constraint – and away from the favourable treatment of residential and industrial users, while public firms did not: Hayaki, Serier and Trapont (1987).

108 Kay (1987), pp. 21–2; also Bishop and Kay (1988).

109 Hicks (1932). J. A. Kay and D. J. Thompson said this of public enterprise managers in Kay and Thompson (1986).

110 Niskanen (1971).

111 See also Buchanan (1977); Savas (1987), pp. 1–9, 22–31.

112 The Virginian school of political economy in the United States differs from the Chicago school in one important respect. Chicagoans believe that everyone is driven by a wish to maximize income, as much in a regulated as in a competitive market. This holds for ministers, civil servants and those who run industries. The Virginians believe, much more credibly, that many of these involved seek to maximize things other than income. Therefore they would support the second possibility referred to in this sentence, with the addition that they would point out to all not only the sacrifice of economic efficiency involved, but also the undesirability of that sacrifice. See Crew and Rowley (1989), pp. 49–67; also chapter 11 below.

113 Garner has said that he sees nationalized industries as having multiple objectives and as being a reasonable compromise between politics and economics: Garner (1988), pp. 27, 28. See also Commander and Killick (1988), pp. 108–9.

114 Swann (1988), pp. 202–6. On the neglect of incentives, see Littlechild (1981).

115 Marquand (1988), ch. 2.

4

Privatization

The Conservative Party has never believed that the business of Government is
the government of business.

Rt. Hon. Nigel Lawson (1981)[1]

Within a few years of each other there were programmes of deregulation in the
United States and Britain. Because of almost 100 years of regulation by commission,
American deregulation – the lessons of which will be discussed in chapter 11 – was,
though limited in extent, unmistakably a reduction in regulation. British deregulation, as a consequence of the nature of privatization, was deeper and went wider.
But, because of the vagueness and incoherence of nationalization as a system of regulation, it was less readily characterized as deregulation. Moreover, as public ownership fell away, a new system for the regulation of natural monopoly was established.
So there seemed to be, though there was not in reality, the paradox that, while the
governments of Presidents Carter and Reagan were deregulating natural monopoly,
the British Conservative government, in order to achieve the same broad ends, was
establishing a new system to regulate it.

Section 1 considers and rejects the view that privatization as it occurred, with the
political success that it had, can be seen as the realization of a premeditated political
strategy. This matter is worth attention because of the insight it gives into the
necessary politics of privatization. Section 2 describes the actual process of persuasion and improvisation by which privatization was established on the political
agenda. However, it is argued in section 3 that privatization would not have become
the programme it did if it had not been for certain economic factors, not so much
microeconomic issues to do with the control of the industries themselves as
macroeconomic circumstances. The main features of the programme for privatizing
competitive enterprises are outlined in section 4 and for natural monopolies in
section 5.

4.1   An implausible political explanation of privatization

Because privatization became the outstanding and most distinctive achievement of
Mrs Thatcher's administrations, it is tempting to believe that the course that it took,
and the political success that it had, were premeditated. In retrospect, the programme
has arguably been a political masterpiece. As president of the Adam Smith Institute,

Madsen Pirie has been active in the cause of privatization overseas and resourceful in devising schemes for other countries. With the advantage of hindsight, he had no doubt that political advantage on its own was a sufficient justification for the UK programme.[2] He pointed out that those who own shares tend to vote Conservative, as do workers who are given shares in the firm where they work. Managers in the private sector are more likely to vote Conservative than are those in state enterprises. Trade unionists are more likely to vote Labour and they are more numerous in state enterprises than they are in private enterprises. And if there is less state enterprise, there need be fewer civil servants: they were more likely to vote Labour; so there will be a further reduction in Labour voters.

In order to promote privatization, Pirie noted, the Government had had to persuade employees, managers, taxpayers and potential investors, as well as customers, the financial markets, analysts and media commentators, of its advantages. He advised overseas listeners that

> the first task when contemplating an act of privatisation is to list all of those groups and to identify their advantage . . . [T]he golden rule about privatising is always to give people greater advantage than they previously enjoyed. In Britain, we say the rule is: never cancel a benefit . . . however unjust it is . . . especially if you can buy it instead.[3]

He instanced the index-linked pensions enjoyed by British Airways employees. He plainly saw these as unjustly generous yet argued that it was right for the Government to buy them out at a handsome price so as to overcome the opposition of these employees. He went on to criticize those who in 1981 had tried to increase competition by selling the gas showrooms and who had by doing so earned the fierce hostility of the managers of the British Gas Corporation. In his view it was right for the Government to climb down and win them over rather than promote competition by this particular means and suffer their increased opposition. Similarly, it was right to buy off telephone customers by continuing to subsidize those who used payphones and the disabled. Moreover, if people are concerned enough about foreign ownership, it should, he believed, be kept at bay even if it would be more efficient. He promised that when the electricity supply came to be privatized there would be 'carefully written into the bill . . . *ad hoc* measures designed to deal with every single conceivable objection that could possibly be raised against it.'[4] His explanation of the 'underpricing' that has frequently accompanied these flotations of state enterprises was as disarming. The Government should sell cheaply 'because it's very important that the people who buy the shares should perceive an immediate gain'.[5]

Of those whose interests had to be considered during privatization, the trade unions had least influence and lost most power (while nationalization had had the opposite effects).[6] Union officials were generally against privatization, as were their members in the early stages. They have a plausible claim to only two successes: preventing the sale of the gas showrooms and stopping the link between the Ravenscraig steel plant and US steel interests.[7] While the longest campaign was that conducted against the privatization of British Telecom, it had no real effect. Even when there was a strike there after privatization in 1987, union support quickly crumbled. The outstanding strike against the Thatcher government, the 1984–5 miners' strike, was within a nationalized industry for which no intention to privatize had been announced. The effectiveness of union opposition to privatization generally declined after the end of the miners' strike, sapped by the failure of that more general opposition. But another reason was that their members had been persuaded to favour privatization by appeals to their direct interest through giving them opportunities to acquire shares on favourable terms in the companies for which they worked. Extraordinary arguments were used to justify substantial discounts to employees. Some observers tried to argue that because government allowed public-housing tenants a 50 per cent discount when they bought their houses, equity demanded that employees in changing from 'tenants' to 'owners as shareholders' should get the same discount.[8] Such dubious arguments aside, the discounts were pragmatically warranted, and were justified to the shareholders at large as incentives given to employee-shareholders to make them identify their interests with the profitability of their company. The policy has usually been successful.[9]

More formidable was the opposition to privatization of some managers of state enterprises. In some cases, to counter this, a chairman was appointed who was more favourable to privatization (though, as will appear, this was not the only reason for appointing a new chairman in the run up to privatization). However, the Government had other not unreasonable inducements to give boards and managers: the promise that they would be spared the pinpricks and occasional deeper wounds of ministerial intervention; the freedom to raise capital commercially; the greater freedom to set their remuneration in line with that of their counterparts in the private sector; and the ability to give greater weight to financial and commercial objectives. Of these, the most important have been the freedom to raise capital commercially and greater freedom to set their own salaries, though the realization was perhaps less quick that higher salaries would mean less job security.

It remains prudent for a privatizing government to consider what other incentives consistent with its wider objectives it may reasonably offer public enterprise managers. For example, it would be unwise to start, as in Canada, by proposing to sell off chunks of state enterprises to other, private firms, domestic, foreign or multi-national, without expecting stiff management opposition, though such a sale may make sense despite that resistance. As managers of subsidiaries of other companies, public-sector managers could hardly count on any increase in independence or even in salaries, and they might also find their jobs insecure. Hence, the Canadian programme got off to a slow start. British privatization has avoided doing this in all but a few relatively unimportant cases. Individual shipyards have been sold to GEC and Trafalgar House; S. & W. Berisford bought the Government's shareholding in British Sugar and took over the company; Enterprise Oil – British Gas's North Sea and other offshore oil holdings – was wrested from it and sold to the Dorset Bidding Corporation; and various small parts of British Rail and British Steel have ended with other companies.[10] The largest such sale was of Rover to British Aerospace (which had itself already been privatized), where this fate was sweetened by the thought that otherwise the sale would almost certainly be to an overseas car manufacturer. In countries where capital markets are less developed, larger public companies are more likely to resist privatization because of the probability that it will mean their being taken over. Yet ultimately the form of privatization should be determined by what is managerially efficient, which is in itself influenced by the maturity of local capital markets and their effect on the pattern of local ownership. Fear of takeover, particularly by a multinational or foreign firm, is one reason why the British government has usually kept a 'golden share'. And this too can be seen as an inducement to management, though at some cost in efficiency.

There is one price that should not be paid to persuade public enterprise management to welcome privatization. If the price they try to exact for compliance is not confined to their own pay and conditions and to those greater freedoms for their company which are likely to promote greater efficiency, but rather is aimed at keeping monopoly power for their company and stopping competition whenever competition is possible, then that price should not be paid – it would be counterproductive. It is not wrong for them to try to exact this price; it is implicit in their conversion to profit maximization that like management everywhere in the private sector they will hang on to every particle of monopoly they can and will seek to acquire more. Indeed, there have been few public enterprise managements that have not shown their conversion to a private-sector ethos by doing just that. Of course, what matters is whether they are allowed to get away with it. Meanwhile, whatever the means used to persuade them, anti-competitive or not, observers noted that by 1986 there was hardly a voice against privatization within the privatized industries or within the nationalized industries yet to be privatized, certainly not from management.[11]

There has, however, also been much criticism of the 'underpricing' involved in many flotations.[12] Where what is privatized will be subject to competition, this is a problem not so much of efficiency as of income distribution between taxpayers and those who are the initial shareholders.[13] Pirie maintained that such underpricing was necessary in order to attract new shareholders, outside and inside the work-force, and to lock them in, with favourable effects on the size of the Conservative vote.[14] Ministers and their advisers were, moreover, made nervous by undersubscription for some of the earlier sales, like those of Cable and Wireless, Britoil and Enterprise Oil.[15] By comparison with the market, ministers will tend to rate a failed flotation a greater risk than underpricing, because they are politicians and not profit–maximizing shareholders. Therefore they tended to underprice and in general the larger the placing (absolutely and relative to the total value of shares), the greater the underpricing. Thus the immediate gains by initial shareholders were usually highest where the placings were particularly large.[16] Smaller tranches should help here, since more-realistic prices will be realized for further sales of shares.[17] And so should tendering, as was used for the British Airports Authority sale, though the wish for wider share ownership has worked against tendering since small shareholders tend to be frightened off by it. Also, some would argue that the Government's creditworthiness and invulnerability to cash-flow problems should have made it less necessary for shares to be underwritten; and some in the City criticized both the fees paid for underwriting and the profits from underwriting made by many of the financial institutions involved.[18] All these are, however, difficult technical issues, easier to resolve with hindsight than at the time, when the political and commercial risks of a failed flotation bulk large. Against Pirie's view noted earlier, it must be right – indeed it is, I would suggest, a government's duty – to get the highest price for the taxpayer that it can; but, especially with a monopoly, the subjective problems of valuation are such as to admit wide disagreement on what is the highest feasible price. Nevertheless, this underpricing of share issues, coupled with a tendency to be generous in the setting of the price-control formulae, often resulted later on in severe and generally unfair criticism of the regulators when the company profits of privatized industries far exceeded predictions made at the time of flotation.

However unavoidable in practice because of ministerial mixed motives, under-valuation, reinforced, as was logical, by the selection of values in the price-control formulae which similarly understated profitability, had the later effect on public opinion that could have been predicted. Especially in the recession of 1990–2 when other profits and prices were falling and wages were growing less, increasing natural monopoly prices and profits from these two causes resulted in a substantial public and political outcry. That outcry crystallized around the very large percentage increases in salary that most of the chairmen of these companies received as one annual report followed another. Whether anything could have been done to avoid this, besides more-accurate pricing of each issue, is further considered in chapter 6, where it will appear as a serious challenge to the feasibility of independent regulation.

Employment fell in public corporations from 2.046 million in 1978/79 or 5 per cent of the working population to 1.161 million in 1986/87, a fall of 43 per cent.[19] Shareholders increased in total from under 3 million to over 8 million.[20] Various surveys suggested that between 10 and 23 per cent of the population owned shares, but all suggested that the effect of privatization had been to increase individual shareownership two or three times.[21] In 1986 a MORI poll found that of the share-holders in British Telecom who were purchasing shares for the first time 14 per cent intended to vote Labour, 53 per cent Conservative and 31 per cent Alliance.[22] While no thorough analysis has yet been done of the effects of privatization on voting in the 1987 general election, the assumption that there was a substantial influence seems plausible. At the same time, trade union membership fell from an estimated 13.3 million in 1979 to 10.5 million in 1987.[23] After that election, Madsen Pirie was predicting confidently that by the end of 1987 the number of shareholders in Britain would exceed that of its trade union members.[24] That had happened by September 1988, when trade union membership was reported as less than 9 million.

Thus the privatization campaign can indeed be seen as having been politically successful in that it altered the political structure to the point where that alteration contributed to Conservative victories in several general elections. And there may indeed have been a structural shift in voters towards the Right for many of the reasons given. However, this does not mean that the Thatcher government started with such a political master-plan, which it then deliberately unfolded.[25] As will be argued in the next section, the evidence is against there having been any such master-plan. It would be wrong to accept as complete or even accurate such an explanation of the Government's motives from someone like Pirie, who never held an official or influential advisory position in it. Rather, it is probably right to agree with those who maintain that the Government's actions were largely pragmatic and improvised, and that its motives were various.

However, even if there was no such strategic campaign realizing a premeditated political master-plan, Pirie's remarks reflect important elements in the tactics of privatization. A theory may be an invalid explanation of how a policy was adopted while still providing insights on what made for its political success. While Pirie overstated the extent to which interests need to be bought off, a successful privatization programme does need to consider the reactions of the most important interests, particularly those of labour, management and potential shareholders. In this respect it does not need to be peculiarly Machiavellian. Nationalization – both inter-war and post-war – was no different. Ministers introducing nationalizations spent far more time than they had expected in appeasing the various interests, and also realized that they had to be generous enough to avoid prolonged obstruction. Shareholders and other owners were bought out with what was often, but was not always criticized at the time as being, generous compensation (though subsequently those suffered who hung on to the gilt-edge stock they received).[26] Except on the railways, where the regional organizations were kept and change was small and gradual, there was widespread worry among managers in industries being – or in prospect of being – nationalized about what would happen to them as fragmented industries were merged into one.[27] After nationalization those who had been in municipal enterprises were not financially worse off. Some of those who had been in private firms might well have been, but many were reassured by the prospects of rapid promotion as hierarchies were established. While some at or near the top of the larger companies moved away elsewhere in the private sector, others were lured to stay on by 'personal allowances' so that they should not lose financially from the change.[28] In a parallel case, the doctors effected major changes in the National Health Service at its inception before they agreed to cooperate with it.[29] Even those in candidate industries whom the nationalizers thought among the most sympathetic exacted a price: some 150 electricity undertakings, for example, were either in, or entering into, deficit on vesting day because the local authorities who controlled them had used their powers to keep charges down, though their costs were increasing, because of their vexation at the expropriation, through nationalization, of their own influence.[30]

While plainly the interests of the important groups must be considered, as they have been, if there is to be a successful privatization, implicit in Pirie's remarks is the possibility that buying out the various interests could even negate the net gains in profitability from privatization.[31] Though Pirie would still regard such a privatization as politically defensible, it is plain that the Thatcher government would not have done so given the stress it laid on the consequences of privatization for economic efficiency. Therefore, because, as we shall see, that government set itself economic objectives, whether there was likely to be a net gain in economic efficiency was a touchstone of its privatizations, whatever the political case.

4.2 The pragmatic origins of privatization

In order to understand the course of events that led to the development of the privatization programme, one has to consider the influence of a number of disparate factors. In a rich, rag-bag of a lecture entitled 'Curing the British Disease' given to an influential London audience in 1976, Milton Friedman ranged far beyond his ostensible concern with monetary policy. On public enterprises he threw out the observation that

> the obvious thing to do with the steel industry, the railroads and all these industries currently governmentally operated was to get rid of them by auctioning them off . . .

One suggestion [for the steel industry] . . . which I think makes a great deal of sense would not be to auction it off, but to give it away by giving every citizen in the country a share in it.[32]

To the listeners in the crowded hall, this would have seemed irresponsible had it not been practically remote. The easiest explanation was that he was succumbing to the temptation open to clever, distinguished men of believing that a lifetime of contemplation devoted to one set of problems means that they then can solve others, even those of which they know nothing. Aside from the fact that Friedman's international fame was in monetary theory and macroeconomics, his own country, the United States, was almost unique in having virtually no nationalized industry. Moreover, privatization had not been previously prominent on the political agenda anywhere. There had been a few privatizations, not widely remembered. West Germany had sold some shares in a nationally-owned electricity and mining company in 1959, followed by a far more important sale of shares in Volkswagen. In 1965 and 1966 there had been more West German sales, 'in the heavy industrial and communications conglomerate, VEBA, and in Lufthansa.'[33] In Britain in 1951 the incoming Conservatives had undone few of their own earlier nationalization measures or of the Attlee government's. They had denationalized only some road haulage, and iron and steel, neither finishing the first nor until 1963 completing the second (only for it to be renationalized by the Wilson government in 1967).[34] The Heath government sold Thomas Cook's and formed British Nuclear Fuels into a company while starting again on the denationalization of iron and steel; but this modest denationalization had been overshadowed by its nationalization of Rolls-Royce and British Leyland.[35] When Friedman spoke, the great inflation, intensified by the oil-price increases of 1973, was still precipitating other failing firms into the public sector. Moreover, there had been few British Conservatives who had argued for denationalization. One was Rhodes Boyson (to be a minister under Margaret Thatcher) who had edited a book called *Good-bye to Nationalisation*. In the circumstances of the early 1970s, when a Conservative government was still nationalizing, it was singularly ill-timed (as well as less than penetrating in its arguments).[36]

Therefore, at the time, Friedman's suggestion seemed irrelevant.[37] Yet policy change was imminent. One who was later close to Margaret Thatcher suggests that it probably dates from the end of the year in which Friedman spoke or the beginning of the next, soon after she became Conservative leader (in 1975).[38] To detect the change in official Conservative policy one needs a nose for ambiguity worthy of a nineteenth-century biblical scholar or a civil servant. The key difference, perhaps between denationalization and privatization, lies between: 'In some cases it may also be appropriate to sell back to private enterprise assets or activities where willing buyers can be found' (1976), and 'The long-term aim must be to reduce the preponderance of state ownership and widen the basis of ownership in our community. Ownership by the state is not the same as ownership by the people' (1977).[39] Whatever the sense to be given to these coded signals, work went on behind closed doors to discuss privatization. Nicholas Ridley chaired a working-party exploring radical ideas on privatization, whose report was leaked to *The Economist* in May 1978.[40] However, it did not become party policy. And as the 1979 election approached the dominant view within the Conservative Party was that it was not clear that privatization would be a vote winner with either the electorate or most Tory back-benchers. Therefore, the 1979 Conservative manifesto was no more adventurous than those of 1951 and 1970: the only definite elements in it were pledges to sell shares in the National Freight Corporation, to relax bus-licensing controls and to reconsider the scope of the British Shipbuilders, British Aerospace, and the British National Oil Corporation.[41]

Thus, after the election, as one of Mrs Thatcher's advisers, Oliver Letwin, has said:

> We had no coherent policy. It was not the case that we knew that privatisation would bring in millions of new shareholders. It was not the case that we knew all these shareholders would benefit from premiums. It was not the case that we knew companies would do better in the private sector. Almost nothing that has happened since was known in advance. It came upon us gradually and by accident and by a leap of faith. We had a fundamental distrust in the state running things – that we knew . . . It was done in the face of opposition from the industries themselves, from the financial markets and from the Civil Service. As it slowly turned into a success story, the inertia which had acted against us, started rolling in our favour.[42]

Mrs Thatcher from the start had a vehement if unanalysed wish to roll back the borders of the public sector, which she indicated whenever there was an issue to which she believed it relevant. Those close to Mrs Thatcher knew that her ambition was to cut back state power, but they realized that many ministers and Conservative MPs did not agree and found reasons for delay. They also realized that the civil service and nationalized industry establishment had the experience to be able out-manœuvre them. Moreover, other matters continued to have a higher priority – among them the curbing of trade union power, particularly in the public sector. While right-wingers believed that ultimately privatization would itself undermine union power – though they were wrong if they did not also see the need for competition to be created – more-immediate action on this was, they thought, required. Priority was also given to securing enough power over the government machine to be able eventually to be more radical. Mrs Thatcher's advisers had learnt from the failures of outside advisers brought in during the 1966 and 1974 Labour governments, men to whom they often felt personally attached and radically akin despite political differences. Those close to the Prime Minister who believed in privatization soon found that they needed a more detailed policy than the one they had, even a blueprint. But whereas in the United States in 1980 the incoming Reagan administration was embarrassed by the number of schemes prepared by think-tanks for deregulating monopolies, their equivalent did not exist in Britain, both because independent institutions of this kind did not exist, and because politically motivated think-tanks in Britain have long been more interested in politics than in detail.[43]

The time-honoured alternative was to get the civil servants to devise the mechanics of the policies and fill in the detail. But discussion within the civil service of important policy issues has always required copious argument. In advance, this had not been appreciated; nor had it been appreciated that the preoccupation of senior ministers, and particularly the Prime Minister, with other matters meant that they had not the time to give the specialist advocates of privatization the support that they needed to overcome the lengthy defence of the status quo offered by the civil service. This time-honoured tactic of the civil service has much to commend it inasmuch as it proves, or fails to prove, two things: first, that the commitment of the advocates of an important policy change is serious enough, and sufficiently well thought through, not to be a flash in the pan; and secondly – what is not the same thing – that ministers have sufficient commitment to support the advocates of change during a long battle during which those ministers themselves are unlikely to have the time, the application or even, perhaps, the intellectual energy to follow the civil service through all the twists and turns of the argument. Moreover, in British political life one cannot expect the civil service to be enamoured of arguments from party-political advantage.

The advocates of privatization had formidable opponents, besides all the other claims on the Prime Minister and the Chancellor of the Exchequer. As all the possible candidates for privatization were sponsored by particular departments, getting the civil servants even to begin privatization policy formation meant persuading their individual ministers first. And this was especially necessary and especially difficult in the early years. For example, after the 1979 election it would have been possible to sell British Leyland to an overseas manufacturer, but at that time Mrs Thatcher had not achieved the ascendancy within the party and Cabinet necessary to do this. In those early years the Cabinet contained many ministers who were not Thatcherites, several of whom were comfortable with the old relations between ministers and nationalized industries, enjoyed the patronage and illusions of greater power they provided or were too conservative to welcome untried radical change. The chairmen of the nationalized industries would not have been where they were unless, in some part of their being, they had enjoyed, and had been good at, managing and reinforcing those old relations. It took time to persuade individual ministers to be ready to overcome the reluctance of their departments, and when they became ready to do so that was either because they themselves had become convinced of the merits of a particular privatization or because it had become more important to please the Prime Minister. Indeed, the importance of her strength of will in this regard should not be underestimated. It cannot be described as having been based on either political or economic arguments; rather, it was based on a powerful gut-feeling, which at the beginning was more often frustrated than not. The order in which the privatizations came depended not on economic or political logic but on which ministers were persuaded, and their form on how far their sponsoring minister was persuaded by the need for competition.

Gradually, several departmental ministers saw the advantages of particular privatizations. To give their idea substance they turned, as noted above, to civil servants, who to be motivated had to be convinced by the economic merits of what was proposed. As radical a change as privatization fell well outside the bounds of what senior civil servants regarded as the permissible ebb and flow of policy change between one administration and the next. Given as well that they had become used to the old relationships in which they had played an interesting and, they thought, stabilizing role, they had an understandable tendency to doubt whether there was much ministerial commitment to the change, as well as an equally understandable opinion that its supporters were doctrinaire.

However, as they became convinced by the strength of ministerial convictions, they naturally addressed the perennial problems of nationalized industries as they had experienced them – in particular, the difficulties there had been in the past in those industries' avoiding financial loss and improving their economic performance.

In the early 1980s the Monopolies and Mergers Commission was given the power to investigate the nationalized industries and began to publish a series of reports in which it threw a penetrating light on nationalized industry inefficiency – as did the Serpell Report on the railways.[44] These studies and the realization that, unlike previous governments, whose intervention had largely been damaging where it had not been pointless,[45] the Government was interested only in the efficiency of these industries and rarely in intervention for political ends, together with questions raised by litigation begun by foreign airlines against the Government and the British Airports Authority in 1980 and 1981 (see below), all alerted the Treasury to the desirability of altering the duties of the nationalized industries. Thus, in the early 1980s there was a determined, though unsuccessful, attempt to extend the scope of the remit of the Comptroller- and Auditor-General – the House of Commons' financial watchdog – to cover the nationalized industries. And a Treasury consultation paper on nationalized industries regulation was published in 1985. This paper failed to lead to legislation, however, because by then it had been realized that the same changes in their objectives could be achieved by converting them into Companies' Act companies.[46] If nationalized industries had developed simple, persistent and well-defined objectives distinct from those of profitability or economic efficiency, it might have been worth returning yet again to devising reforms in the ministerial control of public enterprise. As they had not, turning nationalized industries into Companies' Act companies was straightforward and satisfactory. In the early stages at least who then held the shares was largely a political issue, though the sale of at least a majority of the shares was needed to prevent ministers or their successors interfering. Outright privatization was simpler. But, even so, the tasks to be performed by the civil servants and by departmental advisers before a privatization could be concluded were formidable except in the simplest cases, as will appear.

The argument that public ownership was needed to enable or stimulate industries to act uncommercially and to continue to meet various social obligations was rarely heard. This was not from any new conviction that these entities should be purely economic in their objectives. Rather, it stemmed from the small part played by the social policies that the nationalized industries did pursue and their generally inconspicuous nature, as well as from the tendency – British Telecom was the outstanding example – to carry through unchallenged into privatization the social burden, particularly the patterns of cross-subsidization, inherited from the past. There was one exception to this lack of a strong explicit reaction to non-economic practices and burdens. The new government was alive to the damaging, even corrupting, effect of previous Conservative interventions to settle strikes. The prevention of that happening again was a considerable reason for privatization. The objective of wider share ownership – which was to influence the mechanics of flotation – developed later.

There is other external evidence for privatization's difficult birth. Privatization was slow to develop. For a number of years the proceeds from public-housing sales – around £15 billion – exceeded the sales of nationalized industry assets substantially.[47] A large tranche of British Petroleum shares was sold in 1979, officially returning the company to the private sector; but, as the Rhodesian crisis had confirmed in the 1960s, British Petroleum (BP) had never been controlled or even substantially influenced by the British government even when it was a majority shareholder.

Moreover, the Labour government had sold BP shares. The Government also sold its shareholdings in ICL and in Ferranti in 1979 and in Fairey, Sinclair and Alfred Herbert in 1980 and 1981, and British Steel sold its stake in its contracting subsidiary Redpath Dorman Long; but these were small and hardly controversial.[48] As late as mid-1981 the informed journal *Public Money* could reasonably say that 'after two years in office it is apparent that implementation runs far behind intention.'[49] A pattern had been established of converting public corporations – like the British National Oil Corporation and the National Freight Corporation – into Companies' Act companies so that they could be sold, but by the end of 1981 only British Aerospace had been sold.[50] The list was eclectic, and the proposed privatizations of various enterprises altered in priority as ministers either were persuaded of their benefits or were changed. Moreover, some of the earliest schemes for privatization – for example, of buses, electricity and gas – were far removed from what eventually happened. In April 1982 a list of twenty enterprises to be privatized was published, but these included electricity, for which in the event firm plans were not to be announced until 1988, and coal, for which even by 1992 only preliminary plans had been made. Furthermore, many of the earliest industries to be sold off were the more immediately competitive not so much because they were easy to sell as because their sale was likely to raise fewer political problems. For example, one of the Government's advisers, Sir Alfred Sherman, was critical of the fact that some of the more competitive state enterprises, like electricity generation, coal and British Airways, were not sold off early; but these privatizations were (or are) late because in each case political or other difficulties prevented them.[51]

In short, it is difficult to maintain that the small number who believed vehemently in privatization would have succeeded in achieving more than scattered, piecemeal privatization, given all the other pressures on the politicians' time and the legislative programme, if powerful economic arguments had not also been developed.

4.3 An economic explanation of the origins of privatization

While microeconomic and organizational arguments for privatization, as well as the strength and persistence of some ministers' intentions, helped persuade some sponsoring departments, that would probably would not have been decisive. The Treasury also had to be won over. It was helpful at first that Nigel Lawson, then a junior Treasury minister, took a keen personal interest in privatization.[52] In the early days of the Thatcher government those who urged the policy directed many of their proposals towards the Treasury in the belief that it would be susceptible to the argument that cutting public expenditure would be anti-inflationary and that privatization, through reducing the size of the public sector, would cut public expenditure. For a long time, and quite rightly, the Treasury resisted the first leg of this argument; the transfer of resources from the public to the private sector did not necessarily have a useful macroeconomic effect. In so far as it reduced the claim upon resources by the public sector, that was cancelled by the corresponding increase in the use of resources by the private sector. And while there was a possibility that greater efficiency and financial discipline resulting from privatization might reduce the use of resources overall, this had to be proved, would take time and, even if realized, would in terms of money be a small gain in efficiency. While this was a difficult argument, against which the advocates of privatization failed to make headway for a while, at this stage the Treasury was not particularly tempted by the putative proceeds of privatization.

What speeded up privatization in 1981 and 1982 was not zeal for obtaining its proceeds but the consequences of the blunt realization that cutting nationalized industry cash requirements was, since other ways were not working, politically the easiest way of cutting public expenditure so as to reduce the Public Sector Borrowing Requirement and control the money supply, a policy to which the Government was committed. Indeed, as soon as the Thatcher government began, there was intense pressure from within the Treasury to achieve the maximum possible public asset sales in order to reduce the Public Sector Borrowing Requirement.

The incoming Thatcher government in 1979 was frustrated in its desire to cut current public expenditure by the need to pay out more in social security benefits because of rising unemployment. Indeed, rather than falling, public expenditure rose (mostly because of unemployment), from 40.5 per cent of Gross Domestic Product in 1978/9 to 43.5 per cent in 1982/3.[53] It then turned to using the External Financing Limits (EFLs) as provided in the 1978 White Paper on the nationalized industries, not to control the industries' cash flow in their own long-term financial interest, as had been intended, but to achieve the maximum reduction in public-sector borrowing (a policy which remained in force through the 1980s).[54] The Government's March 1980 *Expenditure Plans* White Paper provided for a reduction in total nationalized industry EFLs.[55] They were defined as profits plus depreciation minus capital expenditure and any change in working capital.[56] Therefore, except in so far as nationalized industries were able to increase prices – difficult for the more competitive in a recession – or cut costs, the pressure fell on capital expenditure. In the case of the British Airports Authority (BAA), the misfortune that it announced an increase in landing charges on the same day as the Government increased the target for it led eighteen airlines to begin litigation (though it was not pursued) against both the Government and the BAA for putting government policies above the BAA's statutory duties, which they believed had been infringed.[57] And two nationalized industry chairmen resigned in protest against the squeeze on their finances. Yet total nationalized industry EFLs rose not fell.[58] In March 1981 the new *Expenditure Plans* White Paper tried again, forecasting a reduction from £2,500 million in 1980/1 to £50 million in 1983/4.

The financial deficit of the public corporations as a percentage of their contribution to Gross Domestic Product declined drastically in 1981, and persistently thereafter, as a result of the Government's sharply reducing their ability to borrow, forcing them to increase prices, lower costs and cut investment, and leading to a sharp increase in the economic efficiency of many nationalized industries. Cash limits forced cuts in manpower and other savings which had eluded the older methods of control.[59] In this, the public sector was no different from the private sector. For this was the heyday of short-termism, when leaps in productivity were achieved by severe cash control: a necessary stage but not a policy that can be prolonged for ever; sooner or later other ways of sustaining annual increases in productivity had to be found. Despite these increases in efficiency, however, the Treasury saw to it that the nationalized industries were strapped for cash. At one extreme in the spectrum of need, British Gas was in an enviable position: not subject to competition and having completed its massive conversion to natural gas, so that its cash requirements were low, it agreed to lend substantial sums to the Treasury and was given a negative EFL. But at the other extreme British Telecom (BT), while also a monopoly, needed vast sums in order to modernize its network to meet rapidly increasing demand.

The Treasury would not authorize the billions required. Various attempts were made to find the money in ways in which it would not count as public expenditure. But here ministers and boards came up against the intractable Ryrie rules, named after Sir William Ryrie, the Treasury civil servant in charge of public expenditure – though the Treasury's position then remained in essence what it had always been. For according to these any borrowing, or equivalent to borrowing, by nationalized industries directly, or indirectly through subsidiaries or ventures in which they had a majority holding, or through leasing or leaseback, or through numerous other ingenious financial mechanisms, remained public-sector borrowing, because the ultimate risk lay with government. (This is in effect the doctrine of the implicit government guarantee of all nationalized industry which, we suggested in chapter 3, was the key difference between post-war nationalization and previous public ownership, and which, it will be argued in chapter 10, needs to be overcome, though not abandoned, if there is to be worthwhile public enterprise reform.) For borrowing to escape the Public Sector Borrowing Requirement, the risks had to lie outside the public sector. At that time, attempts were made to devise a telecommunications bond whose return would depend on British Telecom's performance; but this was seen through – despite the equity element, while BT was in public ownership its viability was guaranteed by government. So, after various schemes to raise money outside the PSBR were devised and discarded, the conclusion was reached that the only way to hold down the PSBR and control the money supply, as well as secure the very substantial capital expenditure funds most nationalized industries needed, was through privatization. Moreover, there was a correlation between high investment requirements – for example, BT and the BAA compared to British Gas – and a dawning willingness to be privatized.[60]

It was against this background that the beginnings of a policy change towards nationalized industries were signalled by Sir Geoffrey Howe, then Chancellor of the Exchequer, in a seminal speech in July 1981.[61] He noted that private industry had responded to the recession by reducing its overall financial deficit, but that the nationalized industries had increased theirs even though some of their prices had risen more than twice as much as the Retail Price Index. He blamed their immunity from market forces and from effective government control:

> Strangely enough, the nationalised industries are not only shielded from the daily accountability to customers, shareholders and bankers which private industry faces. The Morrisonian constitution grants our nationalised corporations a degree of autonomy which is probably unique in the Western World. In the strict sense of the word they are constitutionally 'irresponsible'. And they are better shielded from Ministerial control than complaints of Government interference may suggest. Their statutes usually prohibit the Minister from issuing detailed instructions to a corporation. He is usually empowered to issue only 'instructions of a general character'. Any specific command like 'make sure the 8.15a.m. to Victoria runs on time' would be legally unenforceable. The Government's only real weapon is the threat to reduce or cut off external funds.

This is far too drastic to be effective. It is like equipping traffic wardens with anti-tank guns but depriving them of the right to leave parking tickets.

A minister had at last in public acknowledged the impotence that lay behind the cloak of the mythical powers of ministers over the nationalized industries. Anticipating a query why there should not be immediate privatization, he sensibly replied that the legislation was complicated and management must be persuaded. Moreover, there were problems with loss-makers. He hesitated over whether they should be kept in public ownership until profitable – which is what happened. He questioned whether it was obvious that public ownership of the natural monopolies was better than private ownership with public regulation, suggesting – probably the first minister to do so in public for many years – 'that our *public* corporations have generally been freer to exploit their monopoly powers than are the *privately* owned utilities of North America and the continent.' He then argued strongly that all the arguments against the squeeze that had been put on nationalized industries' capital expenditure were misconceived. Their investment had in fact been allowed to increase. Moreover, nationalized industries could generate more investment funds by cutting back on operating costs. Because nationalized industries carried an implicit government guarantee, their borrowing was, he argued, rightly included within the Public Sector Borrowing Requirement, since its amount directly affected the interest rates the Government had to pay. And even if new borrowing was used for investment, it was inflationary; for there was a period – often a long one for nationalized industries – before the new output came on stream. Nor, he added, could further increases in their investment be justified on Keynesian grounds as being matched by a reduction in unemployment.

In fact, despite Geoffrey Howe's statement that 'the Government's only real weapon is the threat to reduce or cut off external funds' but that that was 'far too drastic to be effective', this was exactly what the Government was doing, with far more drastic and beneficial results than anyone could have expected. For, even though his attempts in 1981 to control nationalized industries' borrowing were also frustrated by soaring deficits due to the recession, their capital expenditure was cut back, and though with hindsight this operation was not as crippling as it then seemed, the damage it was expected to do and the likelihood that nationalized industry capital requirements would be postponed and not avoided had the effect of encouraging both the Treasury to accept outright privatization as a way of reducing the PSBR and the nationalized industries also to welcome it as a way out of such severe constraints on their cash flow and capital expenditure. As the more an enterprise is sold as a monopoly, the higher its sale value, this emphasis on achieving high proceeds is often thought to have weakened the Government's resolution to achieve more competition and effective regulation.

A crucial intervention in the development of privatization policy was made by Sir Keith Joseph, then the sponsoring minister for British Telecom. As we have seen, BT wanted funds from government for a massive modernization programme. But Joseph, who was seeking to introduce competition, would not entrust a monopoly with so much additional resources. To him this was a further implication of the Treasury dogma that any financial commitment of a nationalized industry was underwritten by government since its borrowings were effectively part of public-sector borrowing.[62] Joseph correctly concluded that there could be no meaningful competition between private firms and an established natural monopoly whose funds were underwritten by a government guarantee. *Ergo* genuine competition could not be established if the incumbent monopoly holder existed within a framework of public ownership. So the wheel turned round: the public ownership that had been created in order to eliminate competition was eliminated in order to create it. At this juncture, the political need to be seen not to be increasing public expenditure, and by implication to be seen to be reducing the public sector's perceived contribution to inflation, as well as the political embarrassment that would occur if the queues of those waiting for telephones grew even longer and the quality of service continued to worsen, overcame the scruples of the Treasury with regard to the privatization of BT, and this led to a switch in its thinking in regard to the other candidates.

Thus privatization overcame the strong resistance to it, not through the workings of a premeditated strategy to shift the country's political structure to the Right; nor as the result of the persuasions of a more pragmatic wish to reduce the size of the public sector; nor because of the manifest shortcomings of the apparatus for controlling nationalized industries; but principally because of the power of certain more or less questionable macroeconomic arguments in the difficult economic circumstances of raging inflation and high unemployment at the start of the 1980s. In the absence of these difficult economic conditions it is doubtful how far opposition to privatization in Westminster and Whitehall would have been overcome. It is not part of my plan to evaluate those macroeconomic arguments, but they were or they adduced:

the effect of the control of the money supply on suppression of inflation;
the belief that, to this end, the money supply should be reduced still further given the high unemployment and interest rates of 1981 and 1982;
the extent to which reducing the Public Sector Borrowing Requirement makes open-market operations to control the money supply easier; and,
in part, the effect of privatization proceeds in reducing the money supply, interest rates and inflation.

4.4   The competitive privatizations

Yet another indication of early pragmatism is that in the first years of privatization there was no clear or comprehensive government statement of its objectives. In 1982 some observers scrutinizing the evidence that was available decided that four objectives were paramount.[63] Two were related to economic efficiency. They were to increase consumer choice and to open up nationalized industries to the discipline of the capital and products markets. The third objective was to help break the stranglehold that the public-sector unions had over public-sector pay and so lessen the influence they had on inflation. And the fourth was also economic: 'to reduce public expenditure and the public sector borrowing requirement.' As we have seen, following a Treasury convention the sale of public assets was regarded as negative public expenditure.[64] The Treasury also allowed that, when an enterprise formerly owned by government had sold more than a stated percentage of its shares, its borrowing no longer counted against the Public Sector Borrowing Requirement. Hence the PSBR was sharply reduced. These objectives of privatization were very important until the mid-1980s, since the main motive the Treasury had in marshalling a succession of flotations had been to put continuous downward pressure on net public expenditure and the PSBR.[65]

As it happened, the comparative lack of publicity given to financial and economic objectives did not matter much with the earlier privatizations.[66] While some big public monopolies featured in the list of twenty candidates for privatization published in 1982, the privatizations of the largest monopolies and competitive candidates were postponed, principally when their financial position worsened because of economic recession.[67] Instead, the enterprises privatized early tended to be small and found their way into competitive markets. Their own competitiveness was improved by the disciplines of the market and the withdrawal of the government safety net. For example, Amersham International, which had been a government laboratory specializing in the development, manufacture and sale of radioactive materials for medical research and industrial uses, was in the middle of international competition – as indeed were ICL, Ferranti, and the various shipyards privatized.[68] One of the larger enterprises sold early, British Aerospace, was in competition with other aeroplane manufacturers. And the sale of shares in British Petroleum made no difference to a concern already competing with other major oil internationals. Another, Associated British Ports, was a collection of ports that the public sector had inherited from the old railways, but its monopoly power was non-existent since they were all competing with private and municipal ports here and abroad. Enterprise Oil and Britoil's producer interests were relatively unimportant by comparison with the other major oil producers.[69] Similarly, when the Government sold its shares in Cable and Wireless in 1981 and 1983, that company operated solely in various overseas countries.

The National Freight Corporation (NFC) was exceptional in the form of its privatization. The Corporation represented the tail end of a policy, begun in 1947, designed to nationalize all road freight haulage and so create a public monopoly. Other public road haulage had been denationalized. The NFC remained the largest road haulage operator. Since the road haulage licensing regime had been liberalized in 1968, the NFC had struggled to find a new role, for basic road haulage operations were as effectively carried out by undertakings with only one or two vehicles. Indeed, in 1978 it had lobbied a committee of inquiry into road haulage in an attempt to persuade it to recommend reintroducing a quota system into road haulage so as to give it protection against competition from small hauliers. Its model was the form of regulation that existed in the United States to protect motor carriers. It wanted such protection because its viability was under threat. Though it had developed other businesses, it had realized that the road haulage business from which it started was without economies of scale – or, more strictly, that the only scale economies lay in the greater ease the larger firms had in deriving benefit from the restrictions of the old road haulage licensing system before it had been liberalized in 1968. It became instead an organization specializing in distribution and providing transport and distribution services to firms. Emerging from a history of recent losses, it was barely profitable in 1978/9. Avoiding break-up because the resale value of vehicles in a recession would have been low, it proved impossible to sell in any ordinary way. By a brilliant stroke, it was instead sold in 1982 to a consortium of its managers and employees for a net figure of £6 million (£53 million raised minus the £47 million used to remedy its under-funded pension scheme).[70] Thus 82.5 per cent of its shares came to be held by its employees, though the risks were such that initially only 36 per cent of them bought shares.[71] Unprofitable before privatization, since then it had a history of amazing financial success, so that it has been called the 'Jewel in the Crown' of privatization.[72] Mainly from property sales, its pre-tax profits rose almost ninefold from £4.3 million in 1981 to £37 million in 1986. It diversified and cut costs. By 1984, the number of employee-shareholders had risen from 10,000 to 16,500, and in 1986 to 19,500. The original shareholders had seen the value of their shares increase thirty-one times. A particular tribute to the incentive effects of employee motivation was that when the company came to shed 1,000 out of 4,000 of its parcels division employees, it was able to do so without a reaction from its work-force even though no special preference was given to shareholders in choosing those to be made redundant.[73] In 1989 it was successfully floated as a public company. As has already been indicated, this was a triumph for its management, under Sir Peter Thompson. But there was no question but that it was in a competitive industry from the start. And several later privatizations, for example of Rolls-Royce, Jaguar, the Trustee Savings Bank and British Steel, fall broadly into the same competitive category.

Thus, it is not surprising that when John Moore, who as Financial Secretary to the Treasury was in overall charge of the privatization programme, at last made in 1983 the first comprehensive statement of the Government's objectives in privatizing he was able to deal with the efficiency objectives lightly.[74] He referred first of all to the flaws in the original establishment of many public enterprises as public monopolies, pointing out that the monopolies in most cases were artificial rather than natural. He went on to argue that the financial and economic performance of the nationalized industries was generally not satisfactory. He mentioned the extent to which their pricing policies had been distorted by ministerial action. And he listed a number of comparative studies to the disadvantage of the public sector. He did not blame the managers or the employees, but rather the confusion of commercial and social objectives, as well as the constraints the public sector set upon the nationalized industries' ability to raise capital. He referred also, briefly, to the kinds of difficulties of control discussed in chapter 3.

He then went on to discuss the benefits of privatization. He mentioned the post-privatization financial success of Cable and Wireless, Associated British Ports, Amersham International and the National Freight Company. He referred to the ease with which they were now raising money; their pleasure in their new-found freedom from intervention, and the lack of second-guessing by civil servants. Employees had gained from their shareholdings in their companies. He thought that pay bargaining was less constrained by politics. He argued that, overall, jobs would not be lost – competition would create new opportunities. And he promised that there would be more attention to promoting competition.

Certain of the Government's plans for privatizing, however, ran into opposition through their inattention to the promotion of competition. This was not from the general public, the managers or the employees. Rather, it came from academics and from a number of back-bench MPs who put economic efficiency above realizing the highest proceeds for the Treasury. Possibly the strangest of such aberrations where the competitive principle was, or seemed for a time not to be, given due weight were three small examples. British Steel was allowed to join in a joint venture with Guest, Keen & Nettlefolds in rod and steel bar production which amounted to some limitation of competition. The previously nationalized Seaspeed and the private company Hoverlloyd were merged, with the effect of reducing competition across the Channel. And, the most anti-competitive, a bid for nationalized Sealink was considered from a serious major competitor, European Ferries, which would have given the latter 80 per cent of the cross-Channel market. While this was eventually rejected by the Government on the advice of the Monopolies and Mergers Commission, after an eight-month inquiry, it is remarkable that such a solution was ever considered seriously.[75]

There were three areas of privatization where it was not as easy to maintain the view that the public enterprises could be privatized into a competitive market.

Express coaches

In 1980, express coaching was liberalized.[76] National Express – a subsidiary of National Bus – lost its local monopolies. Ten independents grouped together to compete with National Express on the main inter-city routes. As a result, fares about halved, frequencies increased and there was a large increase in demand. Nevertheless, the new entrants' challenge was declining in 1981 and by 1983 was nearly over. They had been defeated not only by the investment that National Express could put into publicizing its already known name and more generally into marketing, but also by its keeping its competitors out of its terminals, most notably Victoria Coach Station, and as a consequence benefiting from the ease with which its passengers could change coaches, a high proportion of whom did this – for example, 24 per cent of those using Victoria Coach Station. Thus, by far the largest operator in the market, National Express, declared its intention to match any entrant's lower fares – by implication without regard to its costs or to the fact that its response would be predatory if its fares were then below cost – and did so match the independents' entry. National Express became a monopoly again. Its fares then generally increased, arguably to previous levels.[77] But frequencies and usage were also higher. The net result was that coach users benefited from higher quality and improved frequencies, as well as some lower fares. National Express, separated from National Bus, increased its profits, and some rail passengers gained from the greater restraint on rail-fare increases to help meet the competition. British Rail lost from the competition with its services, and so may some coach users who suffered from the cutting back of the more lightly used services. On balance, despite the monopoly's continuing, the outcome was almost certainly a net economic gain.[78] However, the issue is now whether the market will be kept efficient because of the potential for competition. In the pre-liberalization assessment of the likelihood of competition and the effectiveness of potential competition in keeping National Express efficient, it would have been better if it had been recognized that it had the natural monopoly characteristics which have since have become apparent.

National Express consists of the network and the associated marketing arrangements, which are able to realize economies from networking and the brand name. It buys capacity from many other bus and coach operators, who can be changed and who have little opportunity for making anything more than normal market profits themselves. But potentially there are still many small independents which would be able to enter into competition with it on a particular route if National Express were to make substantial monopoly profits on that route.[79] To use the jargon, its monopoly has become more 'contestable'; for since the Transport Act, 1985, it cannot keep other operators' coaches out of its bus and coach stations. And presumably any obstacles to entry from its preventing the resale of its old vehicles to any of its competitors, if they exist, will be challenged as unfair trading. However, National Express may have been able to drive out some rivals by predatory practices which were not policed effectively: 'UK competition policy attempts no clear statement of proscribed practices and so gives National [Express] little cause to worry whether or not its behaviour might reasonably be judged predatory.'[80] Yet, provided that the 1985 Act's prohibition against keeping rivals out of its bus and coach stations is effective, it is likely that National Express will have to stay reasonably efficient, otherwise competitors will, as noted above, be able to seize opportunities on particular routes – though this threat may be weakened by the expectation that National Express will react immediately to any intruder. But it is instructive that there are some routes where there still is actual competition. They tend to be long-distance routes, where fares are therefore a large absolute amount, and differences between fares offered by one company and another are perceptible; where the problems of getting to and from terminals are less important, again because of the distance travelled; and where for the same reason there tend to be a few sensible times of departures so that a cluster of coaches leaving within a short time of each other can still serve the market.

In David Thompson's view, express coaching has provided doubtful evidence of the effectiveness of contestability, that is, of relying on freedom of entry to allow potential competitors to deter incumbents from being inefficient or making excess profits.[81] He contrasted National Express and the Scottish Bus Group's express-coaching operation, the first of which had, unlike the second, invested in advertising its name to the public and was in a financially stronger position to resist new entrants. Where there is fear of competition, one would expect prices to be similar on similar routes whether or not there is actual competition. This held for the Scottish Bus Group's operations, but in the case of National Express's operations fares were definitely lower where there was actual competition, reflecting a continuing readiness to keep fares above marginal costs unless and until competition actually materialized.

Local buses

The National Bus Company was itself a small holding company with substantial devolution of responsibility to local companies with separate identities. There were no persuasive economic arguments for privatizing it as a whole, so a strong minister and a less resolute board resulted in the business's being broken up. The minister was Nicholas Ridley who, as we have seen, had led a working-party examining the possibilities of privatization even before the 1979 election, and was ideologically committed to liberalization; while the chairman, a businessman and ex-Labour minister, Lord Shepherd, was recent to the industry. Moreover, the resistance of the National Bus Company's chief executive was undermined by the keenness of many of its constituent local bus companies to be independent. The bus industry had previously been divided between the nationalized National Bus Company, Passenger Transport Executive operations in the largest conurbations, the nationalized Scottish Bus Group, London Transport and other municipal bus operations. The effect of the regulatory regime established in the 1930s was that, despite this pattern of ownership, each route was a local monopoly, while almost all the entities had a sufficient number of routes to practise cross-subsidization, which was indeed in large part forced on them by their regulators, the Traffic Commissioners. All claimed elements of natural monopoly to justify their local monopolies. It was argued that the competition that had undoubtedly existed for a century before regulation was not only imposed, but was inherently unstable, created uncertainties for customers over routes and frequencies, stopped them enjoying the benefits of integrated timetables and through-ticketing, and led to long or uncertain waits for connections. Those evils, it was said, had been eliminated, or much reduced, by monopoly.[82] Aside from the unmentionable possibility that as with road haulage the chief advantage of size was in being able to deal more effectively with government and the regulatory authorities, they claimed that it gave the advantage of their being able to provide concessionary fares and integrated timetabling. They argued that the elimination of competition meant that profits on some services could meet losses on others and that therefore more services could be provided.

These arguments were met and dismissed by a trenchant white paper in 1984, which estimated substantial cost reductions from competition.[83] However, that was after initial attempts at liberalization which had not worked well. The Transport Act, 1980, had shifted the burden of proof from the potential entrant, who had been required to show that it was in the public interest for it to operate, to the incumbent, who had now to show that it was not. Fares were no longer to be controlled, and three small trial areas of unfettered competition were introduced experimentally. But, following the Act, up until 1984 there had been applications to run competitive services on less than half a per cent of all routes, of which two-fifths had been turned down by the regulators, and only one-fifth of these services were still operating in that year. Ian Savage, who reviewed the cases, found that almost always there had been unfair competition by the incumbent operator which the regulator had not wished or was powerless to police or prevent.[84] Fares were slashed without regard to cost, though when the new entrant withdrew, fares often went up again. Bus times were altered so that the incumbent's buses would run just in front of those of the new entrant. Litigation was used to drive competition out through its financial cost. And the competition was not helped by being banned from bus stations, or by arrangements which made it difficult for them to buy or sell second-hand vehicles because of the purchasing power of the incumbent.

The Transport Act, 1985, made competition easier by abolishing the need to apply for a licence to run buses over any given route. It broke up the National Bus Company and privatized its parts, so limiting their ability to cross-subsidize and compete unfairly. The Passenger Transport Executive buses and other municipal buses were transferred to separate companies. And the Traffic Commissioners were turned from regulatory authorities into mere registrars of particulars. It is still too soon to know how great an effect this act will have on competition.[85] Competitors have been slow to take advantage of freedom of entry. Those studies which have appeared suggest that competition is now more over frequencies than over fares.[86] But there remain obstacles to effective entry. While anyone can buy some second-hand buses and start a service, new entrants find it difficult to maintain their viability, because the existing operator tends to retaliate immediately, not so much with fare cuts, though experience suggests that it can often drop its prices, as with retimed schedules and the substitution of minibuses for larger buses, so as to force a newcomer out. Overall, it seems that fares are in fact higher, that subsidies are much lower, that in general frequencies are greater, but that use has not risen as had been expected. The bus user has not lost from the disappearance of either the National Bus Company or the conurbation monopolies. But whether consumers are better off is disputed. However, it is clear that there would have been more competition if there had been a quicker and more effective regulator. Since the specialist regulators, the Transport Commissioners, do not have the power to prevent such predation, complaints can only be made to the Office of Fair Trading which, after investigation, may refer them to the Monopoly and Mergers Commission. It is too long and cumbersome a process for this industry, made more difficult by flaws in the fair-trading legislation.[87] Before it reports the new entrant may have retired, defeated or bankrupt.

Deregulation has had the effect of creating or reinforcing natural monopolies not only in bus operations. Airlines in the United States created them by concentrating their operations on particular airports or hubs, and the largest also by employing computerized reservation systems which, because of the cost of reproducing them, conferred elements of natural monopoly. And, as we have seen, British coaches also found natural-monopoly advantages through networking. If, in such cases, competition does not prove effective, even with specialist regulators to stop predation, then the stronger is the case for franchising as an alternative. It was considered in Britain for buses.[88] Its merits are discussed further in chapter 6.

British Airways

The privatization of British Airways was delayed until 1987, first by its un-profitability and then by litigation against it after the collapse of Laker Airways. Its privatization raised issues for competition policy, and the Government was criticized for not breaking the company up before sale. Critics pointed to the active competition that was being promoted in the early 1980s in the United States between a large number of airlines through policies of deregulation. Though British Airways, which was as resistant as any of the nationalized industries to break-up, had within a year of its privatization absorbed British Caledonian, the second-largest UK carrier, the Government's policy of not breaking it up was defensible in that not only were many of British Airways' overseas rivals operating in a highly regulated market in which on most routes airlines, many subsidized, divided the slots available arbitrarily, but there were also substantial economies of scale. However, strict policing was necessary to prevent British Airways behaving predatorily towards its small domestic rivals or the charter operations. A regulatory body, the Civil Aviation Authority, already existed to do this domestically so that it should be possible to keep competition on domestic routes. However, overseas, workable competition requires international cooperation, either worldwide or, for example, regionally within Europe, and that is inevitably much harder to achieve.

4.5 The privatization of natural monopolies

When John Moore returned in 1985 to consider the results of the Government's privatization programme, he said that privatization had shown itself to be of such benefit that, 'we have decided that it is right to extend it progressively to the so-called natural monopolies.'[89] He cited the sale of British Telecom as an example of such a privatization and pointed to the privatization of gas, airports and water in the future. While sensibly not venturing an opinion on how far competition could be developed to pare away what was artificial in any natural monopoly, he reached the conclusion that, 'I firmly believe that where competition is impractical, privatisation policies have now been developed to such an extent that regulated private ownership of natural monopolies is preferable to nationalisation.'[90] He argued that even as monopolies they would be invigorated by shareholder pressure, scrutiny by analysts and the freedom to go to the capital markets.

Yet the issue was not simple. One could not declare that there was a determinate class of nationalized industries which, if privatized, would have to be comprehensively regulated because competition was impossible. There was to be a succession of cases where it was necessary to consider, and in most cases to achieve, some structural change to promote competition rather than to have to rely entirely on regulation. They were the privatizations of British Telecom (1984), the British Gas Corporation (1986), the British Airports Authority (1986), the National Bus Company, by the sale of its constituent companies (1986–8), the water authorities (1989) and the electricity supply industry, excluding nuclear generation (1990–1).

While most writers on privatization have seen more competition as the main stimulus to efficiency, others – particularly Michael Beesley and Stephen Littlechild – have maintained that privatization should result in greater efficiency even without competition.[91] The stock market will exercise its discipline through share-price movements, and the prospect of a hostile takeover is a powerful incentive to management, one unaffected by the finding that actual takeovers on average do not improve net worth. Moreover, while most privatized companies were meant to be protected against takeover by a golden share, nevertheless Britoil disappeared into British Petroleum, against the Government's wishes (because the provision was defective),[92] French water companies have bought their way into British ones and are interested in acquiring water authorities where they can, and the Government deliberately did not use its golden share to prevent Jaguar being bought by Ford. However, the discipline of the market will have least effect on the large privatized natural monopolies, where the threat of effective takeover is least, and where the golden share is most likely to be used, for some as yet not very well defined perception of the national interest. Thus, one could not rely on the threat or fact of takeover to make natural monopolies efficient. It was realized that there would have to be regulation, and a model was needed. Because the control mechanisms of nationalization had nothing to offer the new regulatory regime; because the lessons from the old regulatory regimes discussed in chapters 1 and 2 had been forgotten or had not been learned; because no blueprints had been prepared by the Conservative Party, by policy or research institutes, or within the civil service; because the American system was seen as a model to be avoided; because the settling of the policy after 1979 was spasmodic and unplanned; because of all this, the form and details of privatization and the new system of regulation of natural monopolies were largely improvised.[93] But the contrast with nationalization is instructive. The one, a long-standing commitment rubbed smooth to achieve consensus and mapped onto a already-used civil service blueprint that reflected mainly administrative and some political considerations, quickly ran into difficulties and ended by pleasing no one. The other, cobbled together in its formative stages mostly by hard-pressed civil servants under severe deadlines and at a time when they were most reviled by politicians who believed that among the other aspects of corporatism for which they were responsible was an over-regulated economy, was in the end more systematic and penetrating.

A result of Sir Keith Joseph's decision to privatize British Telecom – though the work was completed under his successor Patrick Jenkin and Jenkin's deputy, Kenneth Baker – was that a cluster of civil servants in the Department of Trade and Industry set to work to turn a flickering idea into legislation. What they put together then for the privatization and regulation of that natural monopoly provided the model for the privatization and regulation of the other natural monopolies. Without knowing it, they had rediscovered the secret lost since Gladstone that, in so far as marked forces do not work, a contract between the State and the privately owned natural monopoly is needed to define the terms on which the second may reasonably expect to be profitable, though they lacked a clear notion of what retrospective changes were permissible. The instrument Gladstone had wanted to devise was a parliamentary contract or statute. More sensibly, given some of the reasons described above for the failure of the nineteenth-century approach, its functions were instead to be divided between statutes and secondary legislation, though again there was unresolved doubt over the immunity of these from retrospective legislation and regulatory action, a marked difference from most of the nineteenth century. The essential structure now devised was later imitated not only because of its merits, but also because all subsequent privatizations came under the influence of the Treasury Privatization Unit, which meant also that some uniformity was achieved. (Oddly though, different words were used to describe the secondary legislation: 'licences' for telecommunications and electricity; 'authorizations' for gas; 'permits to charge' for airports; and 'appointments' for water authorities, while similar instruments for radio and television were called 'franchises'. Hereafter, we will generally call them licences.)

There were various sources for the elements of this structure.

1   In turning British Telecom into a private company whose shares were sold to the public, the creators of this structure were following precedent.

2   As it happened, British Telecom had inherited from the Post Office the duty to issue licences to many private and public entities which were connected to or used its systems. It was a small step to conclude that, if it entered the private sector, it too should have a licence.

3   The licence's contents were adapted from materials close to hand: a schedule in

the Competition Act, 1980, prepared in the same department, which provided a model set of specifications for firms found to be in breach of the fair-trading laws. Its detail was negotiated between civil servants and British Telecom officials.

4 If British Telecom were to be licensed, its licensing of others – with some of whom it would be in competition – would be inequitable. So it lost its licensing responsibilities.

5 It was a political decision that British Telecom should not be regulated by ministers. Instead, analogy suggested that the job should be done by the Director General of Fair Trading, who was in fact pressed to take it on. However, he decided that he had enough to do, so a specialist look-alike was invented, the Director General of Telecommunications. (A model followed subsequently, except that an existing body, the Civil Aviation Authority, was used for airports. As the CAA was a well-established body, headed by a chairman and several members, which had been used to holding quasi-judicial hearings, the way in which it conducted economic regulation was to differ. It had important non-regulatory functions.)

6 In certain circumstances, the Monopolies and Mergers Commission was to be an appeal body from the Director General of Telecommunications, as it was from the Director General of Fair Trading.

7 The decision to keep the courts out of the regulatory process was made not because of a wish to avoid the legalistic procedures of American legislation, though that it was was maintained later, but because at about the same time the Cabinet, considering changes to employment legislation, was persuaded of the harm past increases in the regulatory role of the courts had done to employer–employee relations.

8 The extent of the competition to be introduced was contested bitterly and a compromise reached: ministers decided to retain the discretion to review, that is, increase, its extent later.

This listed account, and much of the earlier argument in this chapter, may seem only to corroborate J. A. Kay and D. J. Thompson's accusation that the goals of privatization were not only various but also ill thought out and sometimes conflicting, and that as a result it has not achieved any of them. But, though it is true that there has been no blueprint and that the policy, its objectives and its details developed over time, their charge, to my mind, misses the target. No earlier policy described in this book came about in a closely premeditated and carefully organized way. And that nationalization was a long-standing policy commitment whose execution was based on a tried form of organization did not mean that it was any the better adapted to the actual circumstances it had to confront. Large changes do not occur according to plan even in authoritarian societies. It will be argued in the rest of this book that on balance what occurred through improvisation was by most standards surprisingly well adapted to the needs of the occasion, though some aspects need to be developed further.[94]

A stimulus to economic efficiency that is derived from the process of privatization is that it results in fundamental thinking about the organization to be privatized, especially where it is a natural monopoly, and even more when there is to be structural change. If the entity is important the decision will be set out first in a white paper. This will say something about how the privatization is going to be done, and to that extent will reflect the conclusions reached by the minister responsible after what will often be lengthy arguments with the board and with ministerial colleagues. On the assumption that there is no substantial modification of what is in the white paper, there will next be a period in which legislation is prepared. Profound changes may be needed in management and in accounting systems, and these improvements take time. But even thereafter it is not uncommon to keep a public company, once it has been formed from a public corporation, as wholly owned by government for some length of time.[95] Thus it is the Act that sets the objectives, powers and duties of a privatized company; but under the new regime there is also the Licence. This sets down the constraints upon the privatized company's freedom: who is to regulate it, what criteria he is to use and what procedures are to be adopted.[96]

As important as legislation in the privatization process is the work of the accountant, who first prepares what is called a 'long-form report' on all aspects of the company's business, covering production, management and employees, management information systems, accounting systems and its marketing. Accounting systems and practices that are satisfactory for a public monopoly will probably not do for a private company. Some of the reasons for this are to do with legal differences in accounting requirements, but the legal differences are a symptom rather than a cause. A nationalized industry in a monopoly position with only government as *de facto* shareholder does not need as comprehensive accounting systems as a private company does. Neither does it normally need this information as quickly at the month, quarter and year end for management and reporting purposes. Yet accounting systems become the better the more they are needed and used. Having been drawn up, the long-form report, and then a short-form report, become the basis of a prospectus, which is the document written to induce investors to subscribe for the sale of shares. If the shares are to be placed in several overseas stock exchanges as well as in London's, they will have their different requirements which have to be reflected in different prospectuses. Moreover, not only do the accounting systems of the company that is to be privatized therefore have to be of a standard both to satisfy the relevant stock exchanges and to produce the information required to underpin the various reports and a prospectuses, but also to that end assets have to be valued realistically. All this prompts penetrating questions about their earning power, their depreciation profiles and their replacement. Where after the privatization several enterprises must rely on the adequacy of long-lived investment, as with the electricity grid, or where the same is essential to meet consumer demands and there is no probability of competition, as with water, mechanisms will have to be established to ensure that investment is, and continues to be, adequate. But settling a balance sheet, and then a price for a flotation, also means asking fundamental questions about the health and direction of the company. Forecasts have to be made and supported. And definite statements have to be given on the objectives and major risks of the business. The financial markets are less impressed by distant prospects and are likely to take a far sharper attitude towards risk than either government or the enterprise's management did.

More-recent privatizations – for example, of water and electricity – have involved much more stringent requirements for regulatory accounting than did their predecessors, but throughout the programme there has been a requirement for both regulated and unregulated businesses to prepare separate accounts within a short time. A similar intensity is present in the negotiations, in which managers are also involved, over the exact wording of bills and licences, since the wording can substantially affect the powers and therefore the profits of the privatized firm. If the privatized business is to be regulated, at some stage there will have to be negotiations over the price formula involving discussion of the business's revenue and cost forecasts, and the tendency here too has been to require the organizations to produce more-detailed information in each successive privatization. Finally, not the least of the pressures on the organization subject to the privatization process is the continuous selling of the organization to potential analysts, potential financial intermediaries at home and, in the larger cases, abroad and potential investors which means that senior managers have to be equipped to answer all manner of questions about the financial and operational health of the business and its performance as well as to accept that in the future they will continue to be subject to such appraisal and criticism.

During the final year to year and a half before privatization there is a crescendo of work for management. Managers are both running the business and preparing for the flotation. In addition, they may be reorganizing or even, as with electricity, splitting the business up. Thus, while this process can be stimulating, it strains top management to pay as much attention as usual to running the business. The quality crisis that affected British Telecom in 1987 was in part due to a relaxing of attention to quality during the privatization period. Board members and senior management find themselves surrounded by many merchant banking, legal, accounting and other advisers working in committees with each other, with the sponsoring government department and the Treasury. In many ways, the pressure has the same intensity and excitement as, and in many respects is similar to, what goes on in a government department when any major piece of legislation is being prepared.

All this casts an intense searchlight upon the enterprise that is subject to this process, and this should improve its self-knowledge and its potential for good management. It provides an opportunity for an enterprise to know itself to a remarkable degree. An ongoing business does not usually stop to consider what it is doing, why it is doing it or whether it could not do it better. Anyone who has been through the process of privatization will recognize the release of intellectual energy, even occasionally euphoria, that occurs when managers recognize a better way of doing something, a way round an old organizational problem, the prospect of a clearer and cleaner operation or the opportunity to replace complex and irrational rules and procedures with those of a better design. The process of privatization in face of competition creates a great awareness of the potential for change, of the need for it and of how it might be achieved. Like the act of nationalization, it is an almost unique opportunity; but the process of privatization asked the subject enterprises more-penetrating questions than they were asked during nationalization, or than were asked of them in the many parliamentary committee, departmental or independent reviews that occurred before privatization (chapter 7).

Those who have been through a privatization – even those sceptical about privatization as such – agree that the process has revealed, as we have noted above, fundamental issues arising from the management of the natural monopolies under the old, nationalization regime which then had to be solved under, or before the installation of, the new regime. Examples are: (a) airport pricing, which was supposed to be based on the principle of congestion pricing (marginal social-cost pricing) but did not follow the theoretical principle rigorously; (b) water investment, where it was found that starvation of funds by the Treasury had led to more-serious under-investment than had been visible to anyone; (c) the high cost of nuclear energy, where old nationalized industries' asset-valuation procedures and cost apportion-ments had led to a profound underestimation of the costs of nuclear generation in England; (d) the shortcomings of the Central Electricity Generating Board 'merit order', which was supposed to ensure that at all times that combination of power-stations ran that generated the cheapest electricity, but in some significant respects fell short of this; and (e) the introduction of special low-price off-peak electricity, which when it came on in the middle of the night created a new peak, which increased the need for generating capacity.

Let us now consider in outline the privatizations of the main natural monopolies that were achieved in the first decade of the programme. In each case a main issue was how far the Government strived to establish whatever competition was possible so as to reduce the burden placed on the regulation that was to reflect the consumer's interest. One may believe that what stopped the further extension of competition in the 1980s was only the weakness or disinclination to proceed of some ministers when opposed by the monopoly-preserving machinations of some nationalized industry chairmen. But it was not as simple as that.

Telecommunications

Of the privatizations of the main natural monopolies, that of telecommunications drew the most comment and criticism. In 1980 Sir Keith Joseph announced an intention to liberalize telecommunications. In 1981 Michael Beesley wrote a path-breaking report to help Joseph to decide how.[97] His inquiries led him to believe that those who leased private circuits from British Telecom should have an unrestricted right to resell their leased capacity to others for all value-added services. He noted that the main BT argument against this was that it itself would lose revenue and therefore would not be able to fund investment.[98] He countered that this was only a product of the then government policy of putting stringent limits on nationalized industries' External Financing Limits in order to control the PSBR. He objected that, even in BT's own terms, putting up prices, which he believed to be possible given the inelasticity of demand, would be a more efficient means of raising funds for investment. Moreover, putting up prices would have the advantage of not pre-venting the competitive benefits which he believed consumers would gain from un-restricted resale. Neither did he attach weight to the argument that restriction was needed here to protect BT's ability to continue cross-subsidization, which he believed should decline anyway. He admitted that his argument that consumers would benefit was partly theoretical in that he maintained that they would always benefit from more competition, but he also adduced as evidence the fact that data-transmission services had advanced most in the United States, where there had already been the most liberalization.[99] He also pointed out that BT itself admitted that the restriction of resale to circuits for non-voice services was not practical, even if it had been desirable, because it could not be policed.[100] Neither did he believe that telecommunications was really a natural monopoly. And even if it were, in the sense that unit costs would rise if its existing network were divided between more than one operator, that would be irrelevant to the issue. Traffic was growing fast, and what in general mattered at the margin was whether any new operator could match BT's costs. He believed that they might, principally because of their ability to draw on low-cost producers at home and abroad, and to adopt new technology.[101]

In the event, the Government did not go as far as Beesley recommended, confining resale to circuits for data services for the time being while promising to reconsider this decision in 1989 (when it allowed unrestricted resale – chapter 5). Meanwhile, the British Telecommunications Act, 1981, established British Telecom as a public corporation separate from the Post Office and liberalized competition in customer-premises equipment. That act took away BT's statutory monopoly but gave it an exclusive privilege. However, early in 1982 the Government gave a new enterprise, Mercury, a licence to operate a telecommunications network. In doing so it may have picked up the hint in Beesley's report that in his opinion there were no economies of scale in BT's network at the margin. In mid-1982 the Government announced its intention to privatize BT, an intention which resulted in the Telecommunications Act, 1984.

Writing in 1984, in the year when British Telecom was privatized but before the new regime had started, John Kay felt anxious that the proposed checks on BT's abuse of monopoly power were merely Mercury and the regulator, the Director General of the Office of Telecommunications (Oftel), 'the two newest and as yet weakest participants in the game'.[102] Writing a year later, John Vickers and George Yarrow developed these criticisms further, noting, as we have, that Beesley in the report commissioned by Sir Keith Joseph had argued for unrestricted resale of leased capacity and that this had been rejected.[103] They argued that, despite appearances, the Government had listened too much to the management of BT, which was set on protecting its own monopoly, and to a Treasury anxious for the highest proceeds possible from the sale of shares. They worried that BT and Mercury, as the only two competitors, would become a cosy duopoly. And they asked, as they were to again in 1988, for more competition and also advocated splitting up BT as the Bell System had been split up into AT&T and the Regional Bell Operating Companies in the United States. However, no one had studied the real problems of interconnection that would have followed from a greater degree of break-up and more competition. Neither had there been careful consideration of the economies of scale and scope that might be lost.

What would have been easier would have been to restrict or eliminate British Telecom's power to run value-added services, from chat-lines to information services as well as mobile telephones and cable television. Other nationalized industries had been so treated – for example, British Rail lost its ships and hotels – on the grounds that they had no particular advantage in providing them and that they were a distraction from their main operations. Arguably, BT might have overcome its internal inefficiencies and capital-programming and quality problems sooner if it had concentrated on its main network and had not been distracted by many much smaller businesses, and indeed towards the end of the 1980s BT itself seemed to realize the wisdom of this. Another reason for stripping it of such services is the difficulty, especially for small services, of the incumbent's rivals establishing themselves even if competition between the incumbent and its rivals, using its networks, is fair. But, as will be argued in the next chapter, the argument for retaining a natural monopoly is that it has sufficient scale and scope economies to provide its customers with services at a lower cost than if it were disintegrated. Sir Bryan Carsberg, the telecommunications regulator, increased competition in the network in stages, until in 1989 the original Beesley recommendation that simple, unrestricted resale should be allowed was implemented, and in 1991 everyone was given the right to build his own network with access to BT's.[104]

Gas

The least satisfactory privatization was that of the British Gas Corporation, where there was a minister, Peter Walker, whose heart was not in the policy, in combination with a strong chairman, Sir Dennis Rooke, whose working-life had been spent in the industry and who was determined to keep it together.

The industry not only had the advantage of a chairman who believed in public enterprise and never seemed to be swayed by any blandishments he was offered, but was of all the nationalized industries in the strongest economic position. When it had substituted natural gas for manufactured gas and had built the gas grid in the 1960s, it had sharply reduced the delivered price of gas (as building the electricity grid had that of electricity in the 1930s). Thereafter, its capital requirements were low. It had benefited from the increases in inflation between 1973 and 1980. And keeping its prices down it had greatly extended its markets. Before the end of the 1970s, it had repaid back all its debt.[105] As its status in law, like that of most other nationalized industries, provided no way in which it could pass on its excess profit as a dividend to government, it entered the 1980s with a negative External Financing Limit, agreeing, as noted above, to lend substantial amounts of money to the Treasury, since it had already invested in all the projects which it regarded as reasonable. For all these reasons British Gas was in the strongest position to resist privatization and, even more, break-up.

The issues raised during the five years that British Gas took to wind its way towards privatization illustrate virtually every possible difficulty that can arise from the process. As early as 1981, the Government said that it would privatize gas showrooms.[106] It seemed simple. The showrooms lost money, so their sales were arguably predatory in that they undercut private-sector competition, the not unexpected result being that British Gas dominated its retail competitors – for example, it sold 80 per cent of all gas cookers. Opponents of the sale began by using the Monopolies and Mergers Commission report on which the Government had relied. The Commission had not made a choice between its two preferred alternatives of ending retailing by British Gas and allowing it within a financial framework which prevented the cross-subsidization of retailing by its other activities. But under neither option need the showrooms go, since British Gas said it would keep them as information and bill-paying centres. The issue of whether to allow British Gas to continue retailing turned on difficult problems of cost apportionment. British Gas argued that, on an avoidable-cost basis, its retailing was profitable and that the showrooms were justified given also the other activities that took place there. Moreover, by engaging in retailing it had put pressure on, and would put more pressure on, manufacturers, in Marks and Spencer's style, to improve their efficiency. Finally, there was the worry that privatizing all retail sales would mean less attention to safety. In the end, whatever the reason for the campaign's success, both the clarity of the Government's case and its commitment dissolved. When British Gas went private, its showrooms were still with it.

At the same time as the debate raged over the showrooms the Government attempted to sell off British Gas oil reserves. From 1981 to 1984, when it eventually succeeded, it fought to persuade British Gas to sell its 50 per cent share in the small Wytch Farm oilfield. And in 1982 British Gas had its offshore oil interests transferred to Enterprise Oil, though even in 1988 it was reported as on the acquisition trail to get them back.

Arguably, a high price was paid for securing the Corporation's agreement to privatization. As one commentator put it, 'British Gas has been transferred to the private sector with its monopoly and monopsony powers intact. The philosophy of "regulation with a light-hand" has been implemented in an extreme form and major opportunities to improve incentives in the industry have been missed.'[107] In deciding if this is fair, the key issues are whether the privatization of British Gas as a single entity was the most economically efficient solution and, even if it was, whether an efficient regulatory regime was devised. In effect, it has been treated as a natural monopoly.[108] That implies the judgement that the technological conditions of the industry are such that it cannot be efficient for more than one firm to exist in it: unit costs of supply would rise if there were effective competition at any stage in the supply of gas. And there is indeed such a natural monopoly in the gas grid, in the sense that it would not be efficient for more than one such grid to exist in the industry.[109] It has also been argued that, while it is theoretically possible to imagine consumers having a choice of suppliers transmitting through the grid, the costs of the metering then needed rule this out as an economically efficient solution. On the other hand, this could still be feasible for the largest gas consumers: the act privatizing the industry, the Gas Act, 1986, allowed this in principle while ruling out the possibility for most consumers.[110]

British Gas kept the right to be the sole purchaser of all gas produced in the UK gas and oilfields and of gas landed in Britain (on behalf of its largest consumers).[111] This monopsony power enabled it to sell the gas on at average rather than marginal cost, so artificially increasing gas's market share and making it difficult for any other energy supplier to compete. This monopsony power could have been replaced by competition, even if British Gas had otherwise been privatized as a whole. It would have been possible to privatize the regional boards separately, as was later done for electricity. And not only could this have been associated with giving them the power to make separate supply contracts with producers, but it would also have introduced some possibility of competition across boundaries, as well as allowed price differences to reflect the different costs of supplying gas in different regions. Thus it might have been possible to introduce more competition into the structure of the industry, even while admitting a residuum of unavoidable natural monopoly in the grid as well as a local monopoly in distribution to all but the largest consumers. Realistically in the circumstances, the original bill did not give the regulator the duty of promoting competition, but that was inserted by Parliament.[112] However, because British Gas started without effective competition over most of its market, because technological change is unlikely to provide a base for competition and because the arrangements prescribed did not make it easy for a regulator to police the competition there is, the gas regulator's ability to promote competition seemed exceptionally weak. What was lacking was a thorough analysis of the difficulties of interconnecting more than one supplier through the grid with more than one customer, so as to test the practicality of competition. Rather, the Government wasted its energies on issues (like the showrooms, Wytch Farm and the other oil reserves) which were negligible from the standpoint of competitiveness and left too little time to campaign to win far more important victories over monopoly.

Nevertheless, despite the weakness of his powers, the gas regulator was able to increase competition, both through the Office of Fair Trading's general fair-trading powers and by securing a Monopoly and Mergers Commission report which forced British Gas to abandon price discrimination. Industrial price schedules were to be related to cost and open to all users whose objective circumstances were similar. Thus, in principle, British Gas was no longer to trim prices so as always to give a better deal in order to keep any customer without regard to cost. At the same time, the regulator established a principle of open access to the gas grid for other suppliers – which in its turn raised the difficult problem of determining what prices those others might pay for use of the network – and gave a ruling that 10 per cent of all gas from new fields was to go to suppliers other than British Gas. And in 1991 and 1992 British Gas was threatened with references to the Monopolies and Mergers Commission if it did not allow effective competition. Although this progress towards competition in principle was remarkable, by 1992 it was still unclear how effective it would be in practice.[113] (This endeavour to introduce competition is discussed further in chapter 5.)

Airports

The British Airports Authority was privatized in 1986. While there were many other private and municipal airports, when it was privatized it continued to own the most important: Heathrow, Gatwick and Stansted, as well as the leading Scottish airports. Opponents argued that its London airports should have been sold into separate ownership. However, that would not have achieved the greater competition hoped for.[114] Because of the importance of interlining, Heathrow was the preferred airport for most airlines; Gatwick was for Heathrow's overspill and the package airlines. There could still have been workable competition between the two if there had been a genuine auction or some other market pricing system by which landing slots at both could have gone to the highest bidder; but the use of such slots is determined by means of international agreements and other arrangements which will continue to preclude competition until they are changed. Moreover, planning laws backed by public hostility prevent the growth of competition through the expansion of either airport. Meanwhile, investment in developing Stansted as a third London airport will take so long to earn a return that on its own Stansted would not be viable. Within each airport, however, most services are franchised. (The particular problems of controlling airport profits are discussed in chapter 6.)

Electricity

The electricity supply industry also resisted reorganization. When Nigel Lawson had been Energy Minister, there had been an exercise to test how far it would be possible to replace the bulk-supply tariff by which the Central Electricity Generating Board (CEGB) sold its electricity to the independent area boards by market-based arrangements. When Peter Walker replaced him, he (Walker) was as unkeen to break up electricity as he had been to break up gas. In this he was supported by Lord Marshall, chairman of the CEGB, who like other nationalized industry chairmen favoured privatization as long as his board would remain intact. In 1988 the issue was decided against him. The CEGB was to be divided into two generating companies and a third entity to own and operate the grid. One of the generators, National Power, was to be twice the size of the other so that its fossil-fuel power-stations could enable it to carry all the CEGB's nuclear stations into the private sector and provide a strong enough financial base for it to build more nuclear stations. Each area board was to be privatized separately, though they would jointly own the grid company. They, and large consumers, would have the freedom to buy either from the heirs of the old CEGB – National Power and PowerGen – or from independents, which were free to enter the industry. There was argument over whether the CEGB should have been broken into more parts and whether the grid should have been made independent. In 1989, to the Government's embarrassment, the unprofitability and future uncertainties of nuclear generation had risen so high that they prevented the flotation of National Power. So a separate Nuclear Company was formed to be retained in the public sector. After buses, this was the Government's most ambitious attempt to create competition; and it was even more ambitious in the sense that the technical problems of establishing competition were far greater.

An issue which had rumbled inconspicuously since the privatization of British Telecom and which had been stifled at the birth of the privatized British Gas, became the focus of the most complicated financial engineering: the establishment of workable contractual relationships between the various parts of the electricity supply industry so as to effect fair competition, a process of *interconnection* which came in this industry to be called 'use of system' (discussed further in chapter 5). Without doubt, this was amongst the most ambitious attempts made anywhere to create competition in the presence of natural monopoly. The complexity of what turned out to be needed in the case of electricity was the main reason why in the autumn of 1989 the privatization and break up of the railways were postponed by the Government. There the interconnection problems are even greater.

Water

The privatization of the water and sewerage industry turned out to be complicated for other reasons, of which the chief was the realization that during the process of privatization the industry was being subjected to increasing environmental standards from Brussels, which were likely to be raised still further later on. Water privatization might not have been attempted if the industry had not been starved of capital funds by successive governments – though another tenable view was that it would have had enough investment funds if it had tackled properly the problems of leakage and other forms of waste. While the decline in the quality and reliability of the water mains and sewers was hidden for many years as the demand for water increased, it began to be realized that the spending of larger sums could not be delayed indefinitely, especially given the pressure for higher environmental standards. Privatization was a way of protecting the Public Sector Borrowing Requirement. A regime had to be found which would enable the industry to meet these standards while remaining viable and without passing on undue costs to the consumer. Competition between water authorities was technically impossible, though lip-service was paid to its possibility by allowing those industrial consumers near the border of one authority to purchase water from over it.[115] Instead, the suggestion was made that the setting and monitoring of standardized-performance measures between authorities could lead to another form of competition: *yardstick competition* (also to be discussed in the next chapter).

The rump

The enterprises that remained in the public sector by the early 1990s were still there for a number of related reasons.[116] Among the more important were that:

1 Coal was not a natural monopoly. Competition could have been created at any time by break-up and by allowing the free import of foreign coal. But the miners were the workers most devoted to public ownership, until after the 1984–5 miners' strike. Moreover, there was an economic case for first rationalizing electricity, coal's major consumer. And there was also a difficult and potentially very large overhang of financial obligations stretching into the future from possible subsidence claims and from concessionary coal for former employees. However, in 1991 the Major government announced that it intended to privatize coal.

2 Nuclear electricity was overshadowed to an even greater extent by an unforeseeable amount of financial obligations, in this case from the future dismantling of its power-stations – some of this caused by political unwillingness to decide how its waste and how its power stations were to be disposed of.

3 The Post Office in its more-than-a-century-old commitment to a single letter-postage rate – only varied by the split into first- and second-class post – practised cross-subsidization to a far greater extent than British Telecom; and its profits after privatization were expected to be less buoyant. A privatized Post Office must be expected to want to vary letter-postage rates by route and volume so generally raising rates to people as against business, especially in remote places, and thus creating acute political problems.

4 British Rail and London Regional Transport were the prime examples of operations that did not have ordinary commercial objectives and were heavily dependent on subsidy. While economic principle supposes that they or their component parts could be franchised to whomever could run them for the lowest subsidy, the problems of quality definition are great. Besides, the conventions of British public expenditure do not easily provide for a certain enough subsidy over a long enough period of time to reassure investors. On the other hand, the widespread belief that huge investment is needed to improve capacity, quality and

safety, and the difficulty of investing the necessary public money for this, given Treasury public-sector borrowing conventions, have increased the impetus for a privatization of the water authorities' type. Indeed, in 1991 the Major government said that it intended the privatization of the railways, though it had not decided on its form.

5 Beyond these, there were a great many publicly-run activities – from the BBC to HMSO to the Vehicle Licensing Department – for which it needed to be decided what their objectives were. In some cases, they might be agreed to be sufficiently commercial for privatization to be possible.

What principally distinguished those enterprises left in public ownership is that, for social or political reasons, they could not easily be given commercial objectives and be expected to be profitable. It will remain difficult to privatize an enterprise with a substantial burden of social obligations unless, like British Telecom, it is expected to be profitable enough to shoulder such burdens. (This will be discussed further in chapters 7 and 10.)

Less than a decade of commitment to privatization – though with substantial privatization occurring only in the last five years – has brought about profound changes in the UK economy.[117] The borrowing requirement of the public corporations, which rose in the early 1980s, reversed from £1.10 billion in 1984 to a positive contribution of £1.35 billion in 1987, mainly reflecting a reduction in their deficits.[118] Nationalized industries' net claim upon the Treasury – the planning total, which is mainly composed of grants, subsidies and borrowing less profits – rose from £2,140 million in 1982/3 to £3,827 million in 1984/5, but thereafter fell to an estimated £355 million in 1987/8.[119] Their gross domestic capital formation fell from £7.3 billion in 1983/4 to £4.6 billion in 1987/8, but only because of privatization.[120] While it is too early to estimate the efficiency gains, the 1980s have plainly seen a substantial change in economic structure.

Notes

1 *Hansard*, 8th series, vol. 1, col. 440 (November 1981).
2 Pirie in Walker (1988), pp. 3–10. K. Wiltshire gives an interesting account of privatization's origins in Wiltshire (1987), pp. 6ff., believing in the influence of New Right ideologues and academics more than I do.
3 Pirie in Walker (1988), p. 6.
4 Ibid., p. 9.
5 Ibid., p. 10.
6 While it is true that over the last ten years the position of the public-sector trade unions has been enormously weakened, privatization has probably only been a small contributor to this. Arguably, high unemployment, the greater readiness of public- and private-sector employers to sit out strikes, and the decline of the more unionized manufacturing in favour of services and self-employment have had a greater effect.
7 See Thomas (1986a), p. 300.
8 Oakeshott (1983), pp. 15–18.
9 HM Treasury, quoted in Veljanovski (1987), p. 104. Exceptions were BP, where the effect of privatization was negligible, and Jaguar, where both the overseas risks facing it

and its recent financial and labour history had an adverse effect on its employees' willingness to buy shares in it. In 1991 a much larger concern, the smaller of the two electricity generators, PowerGen, was nearly sold to Hanson, but terms could not be agreed.

10 Vickers and Yarrow (1988), pp. 160–7.

11 Likierman and Bloomfield (1987), p. 111; Bishop and Kay (1988), pp. 22, 23.

12 E.g., Mayer and Meadowcroft (1986), pp. 322–40; Vickers and Yarrow (1988), pp. 178–81; Bishop and Kay (1988), p. 29. In Britain there is no law that demands that the State sell assets at market value. In France it was held that its constitution prevented privatization sales below the assets' 'true value'. While this seems to have reduced the extent of underpricing, it has not eliminated it: Graham and Prosser (1991). However, the fact that the French privatized no natural monopolies may have reduced underpricing: Craig (1989), pp. 165–6 (established independently).

13 Mayer and Meadowcroft (1986), p. 333; Vickers and Yarrow (1988), pp. 171–94.

14 Pirie (1988), p. 10.

15 It has been calculated that, up to 1987, the Treasury had forgone £3 billion in underpriced asset sales: Vickers and Yarrow (1988), p. 178. The sales of Britoil in 1982 (where 70 per cent of the shares were left with the underwriters), and Enterprise Oil in 1984, were adversely affected by sudden oil-price movements, while the prospectus for the sale of the tranche of shares in British Petroleum in 1987 was published only four days before the October stock market crash: ibid., p. 179.

16 Ibid., pp. 176ff.

17 Ibid. See also Beesley and Littlechild (1986), p. 12. A mixture of fixed prices for small investors and tendering for large investors might have helped.

18 Vickers and Yarrow (1988); National Audit Office (1988), p. 11. One commentator instanced the 33 per cent profit made by the British Telecom sale's underwriters overseas: Chown in Walker (1988), pp. 19–20.

19 HM Treasury (1988), p. 83.

20 Butler and Kavanagh (1988), p. 20; Vickers and Yarrow (1988), pp. 181–5.

21 Vickers and Yarrow (1988), pp. 181–9; Veljanovski (1987), p. 103. The smaller shareholders tended to sell their shares from after flotation so that numbers began to decline: Buckland (1987). In one case, that of the British Airports Authority, the profits distributed to a majority of the shareholders were exceeded by the cost of keeping them on the register: Bishop and Kay (1988), pp. 31–6.

22 Veljanovski (1987), pp. 68–9.

23 Central Statistical Office (1990), table 6.20.

24 Pirie (1988), p. 4.

25 Wiltshire (1987), pp. 25, 26, writes 'privatisation is an extremely cleverly constructed piece of ideological weaponry.' While true in retrospect, this implies forethought which, I believe, was not there.

26 On the generosity of inter-war Conservative compensation, see E. Davies in Robson (1937). On compensation by the Attlee government, see Robson (1962), pp. 278–82; Kelf-Cohen (1969), p. 198.

27 Kelf-Cohen (1969), pp. 237–48.

28 Hannah (1982), p. 10.

29 Fraser (1973), pp. 216–21; Abel-Smith (1964).

30 Hannah (1982), p. 32.

31 While such inducements may merely result in a redistribution of the benefits from privatization, given imperfect information the net effect may be a reduction in viability and efficiency, as may have happened with some early railways (see chapter 2 above).

32 Friedman (1977), p. 51. For an account of federal privatization the the United States, see Utt (1991).

33 Letwin (1988), p. 8. A consequence of there being almost no American nationalization was that there was nothing much to privatize. An exception was Conrail, which was sold in 1987: Swann (1988), pp. 183–4. A large part of the US electricity supply industry remains in public ownership, but it is mostly non-federal.

34 On steel, see Burk (1988); Kelf-Cohen (1969), pp. 135–52. On road haulage, see ibid., pp. 71–3.

35 Redwood (1980), pp. 156, 157. Another exception was the curious case of the public houses around Carlisle which became publicly owned during the First World War because of worries about drunkenness among armaments workers. The Heath government denationalized them.

36 Boyson (1971). However, in it George Polanyi argued well that it was better to go for the single objective of profit maximization. And Russell Lewis seemed to believe that competition could be achieved through break-up. A rare early academic attack on nationalization was Wiseman (1969), though he stopped short of advocating the privatizing of gas and electricity.

37 Sam Brittan and B. Riley argued for the particular form of privatization that Friedman had most advocated when in 1978 they suggested that shares in North Sea oil should be given away to the whole United Kingdom population instead of reduced taxation so as to give visibility to the benefit from it while bringing home to all that it would be a declining one: Brittan and Riley (1978). Nevertheless, journalistic and academic argument in favour of privatization was sparse.

38 Letwin (1988), p. 10.

39 Ibid.

40 *The Economist*, 27 May 1978. Prosser (1986), p. 55, summarizes what he says were its contents. In 1976 Sir Geoffrey Howe and Kenneth Baker attacked the Chancellor of the Exchequer, Dennis Healey, when in order to meet the conditions of an International Monetary Fund loan he proposed to sell £564 million worth of government shares in BP, on the grounds that it made nonsense of the Government's previous argument that national ownership had no adverse effect on the Public Sector Borrowing Requirement, and that he was dispersing valuable assets to unknown foreigners: Harris (1988), pp. 181–2.

41 Veljanovski (1987), pp. 65, 00; Pirie in Walker (1988), pp. 3–10, 15.

42 Letwin in Walker (1988), p. 50.

43 Michael Beesley, Stephen Littlechild and Sir Bryan Carsberg were important academic influences on the course of telecommunications privatization. Beesley and Stephen Glaister, in opposition to Ken Gwilliam, Christopher Nash and Peter Mackie, had an influential debate on the course of bus deregulation.

44 The Competition Act, 1980, extended the MMC's terms of reference to include nationalized industries. Its reports concentrated on efficiency: Wharton (1988), pp. 55–71; Serpell Committee (1983). See also National Audit Office (1984). A very senior civil servant who had been closely involved in many earlier railway reviews told me that it was only the Serpell Report that persuaded him that the railways were substantially inefficient and could be run better with fewer resources.

45 Dunleavy and Rhodes (1986), pp. 133–5, argue that the Thatcher government was more interventionist than earlier ones and acted in ways which were dubiously lawful. However, intervention was economic and macroeconomic rather than to serve political ends. The 1979 Conservative manifesto had promised that nationalized industry management would be protected from interference. However, nationalized industry managers were reported as feeling that they were more constrained and interfered with in their commercial management than before. There is an account of relations between departments and nationalized industries which stresses the greater interventionism in Prosser (1986), pp. 57–63.

46 HM Treasury (1985a). On this and its reception, see Prosser (1986), pp. 71–4. The House of Commons Public Accounts Committee initiated the move to extend the scope of the Exchequer and Audit Department. On the abandonment of the view that nationalized industries should have different objectives from those of privately owned ones, see Graham and Prosser (1991), p. 12.

47 Bishop and Kay (1988), p. 3.

48 Vickers and Yarrow (1988), p. 167. See also Heald and Steel (1986), pp. 59–63; A. J. Harrison (1981a), pp. 59–61; on the role of the BP directors, see Prosser (1986), p. 33; on ICL, see Redwood (1984), pp. 86–96; on Ferranti, ibid., pp. 96–9.

49 A. J. Harrison (1981a), p. 59. See also A. J. Harrison (1983), p. 29, for criticism that the Government was still failing to think through what it wanted innovatively. On delays, see Likierman (1988), p. 118. Many of the privatizations of subsidiaries – for example, of British Rail's hotels – were primarily done to raise cash to meet the External Financing Limits. Lewis (1989), p. 225, has questioned how far the Government met acceptable criteria of public accountability in thus privatizing sizeable assets without reference to Parliament.

50 A. J. Harrison (1981a); Heald and Steel (1986).

51 Cited in Veljanovski (1987), pp. 10–11.

52 On becoming Financial Secretary to the Treasury, Nigel Lawson asked the Chancellor, Sir Geoffrey Howe, if he could take a special interest in privatization and was allowed to do this: Harris (1988), p. 182.

53 Veljanovski (1987), pp. 65–6.

54 Heald and Steel (1981).

55 HM Treasury (1980).

56 Barnato (1981). On cash limits as a crude method of control, see A. J. Harrison (1988), pp. 28–9.

57 Likierman (1981). Prosser (1986), pp. 66–9, questions the legality of this use of EFLs.

58 Heald and Steel (1981). They also altered unpredictably during the year, causing the Government acute embarrassment in the management of the public finances. Nationalized industry EFLs rose from £3,200 million in 1981/2 to a maximum of £4.5 billion in 1984/5, before falling to £560 million in 1986/7: HM Treasury (1985b).

59 A. J. Harrison (1988). Various authors have noted that as a result of harsh EFLs during the 1980s the productivity of many nationalized industries improved far more than it did after they were privatized: e.g., Kay (1987), p. 26; Bishop and Kay (1988), pp. 37–46. This was another sign of a greater concentration of the Government on performance indicators (Prosser (1986), pp. 176–83), which was itself a belated recognition of what NEDO (1976), vol. 1, p. 49, had strongly recommended. And in the specific circumstances of economic crisis, with a government which for the first time concentrated the nationalized industries upon efficiency and did not distract them with the ministerial interventions of the past, and with chairmen in some cases put in to prepare them for privatization, this rare improvement in productivity cannot be attributed to public ownership.

60 HM Treasury (1981), pp. 166–71. Even in smaller public-sector industries where capital requirements were less, like the bus industry, the prime motive for privatization may have been to gain the freedom to raise more capital: Glaister (1991).

61 Howe (1981).

62 Cf. Brech and Whiteman (1982). Joseph's dilemma provides the practical answer to David Heald's contention – which I had myself shared in 1971 (see chapter 3 above) – that there was surely no necessary contradiction between competition and public enterprise: Heald (1985) p. 9. Graham and Prosser (1991), p. 75, show that privatization proceeds in France did not count as negative public expenditure.

63 Heald and Steel (1986); also Beesley and Littlechild (1986), p. 10; Vickers and Yarrow (1988), p. 157. For an analysis of privatization objectives and agenda derived from a study of speech material, pamphlets and interviews, see Wiltshire (1987), *passim*.

64 Discussed by Rees (1986), pp. 20–1.

65 Heald and Steel (1981).

66 J. Williams in Walker (1988), p. 32.

67 Heald and Steel (1986), pp. 61–2.

68 Vickers and Yarrow (1988), p. 160. For ICL's achievements in the public sector, see Redwood (1984), p. 95.

69 Even as stern a critic as Redwood allows that the British National Oil Corporation acted with verve and distinction under the Labour government: Redwood (1984), pp. 111, 112.

70 Vickers and Yarrow (1988), p. 164. The NFC had earlier almost been sold entire, before it lost a major contract, which destroyed its profitability. Hence the unusual measures that had to be taken.

71 Coyne and Wright (1982).

72 Veljanovski (1987), p. 112; on the increase in employee-shareholders, see ibid., pp. 138–9. While its performance undoubtedly improved, its initial terms were attractive given the earlier difficulty in selling it. The gearing was high and it had substantial property assets. If it had not been sold, it would have gone broke.

73 Thomas (1986b), p. 9. Between 1979 and 1989 there had been more than 100 management buy-outs. There were also some bus-company employee buy-outs: Wright, Chipton and Robbie (1989).

74 Moore (1986a), pp. 78–93.

75 Heald and Steel (1986), p. 66.

76 Vickers and Yarrow (1988), pp. 372–7; E. H. Davis (1986).

77 Robbins and White (1986). Rather later, Victoria Coach Station was transferred to London Regional Transport as a neutral umpire.

78 Douglas (1987) reached the conclusion that on balance deregulation resulted in a net economic gain.

79 E. H. Davis (1986), p. 154.

80 Ibid. There is considerable concern within the industry that the MMC is propounding rules which do not make economic sense – another argument for specialist regulation.

81 Thompson (1988). Jaffer and Thompson (1986) attempted to show empirically that the express-coach market was not contestable because fare levels depended on the actual number of competitors on a route.

82 The original proposals said little about competition: see A. J. Harrison (1983). The Scottish Bus Group was not privatized until 1990. On the pre-1930s bus industry, see Glaister and Mulley (1983). For an analysis of the instability issue, see Foster and Golay (1986).

83 Department of Transport (1984). A detailed analysis is to be found in Banister (1985). For evidence that private buses can have lower costs than public ones, see Savas (1987), p. 174, n. 3.

84 I. S. Savage (1985), pp. 21, 22. Evans (1988) strongly confirms this for Hereford. I like to believe that the far greater role of academics in advising on bus deregulation than on other areas of deregulation and privatization reflects the establishment over many years of a strong academic tradition in transport economics – in Britain stronger than in any other brand of microeconomics, except labour economics.

85 Vickers and Yarrow (1988), pp. 375–84. On the effect on fares, costs, subsidies and frequencies, see Gwilliam (1989); White (1990); Glaister (1991); Evans (1990).

86 Mackie and Preston (1988).

87 See Preston (1991). By 1991 there had been five Office of Fair Trading reports and two

140   *Historical Development*

MMC reports on the Badgerline takeover of Midland Red and Stagecoach/Hastings. After the second, the minister responsible ordered divestment only to find that on judicial review his decision was overturned because of the provision in the Fair Trading Act, 1980, that mergers can be prevented only where they affect a significant part of the United Kingdom. This no doubt will be remedied. As safety regulators, the Traffic Commissioners are widely respected within the industry. On the fair-trading laws as they affect the bus industry, see Beesley (1990). On the failure of the anti-trust authorities to police airline deregulation, see Kahn (1988b), p. 318. The case of the savings and loan associations in the USA is cited as an outstanding example of how removing the regulators has defeated deregulation: Kahn (1990a), pp. 349, 350.

88 See Gwilliam, Nash and Mackie (1985a) and (1985b). Franchising has been used in London. Glaister (1991) says it has worked well.

89 Moore (1986b), pp. 94–7.

90 Ibid., p. 95.

91 Beesley and Littlechild (1986). A different argument relates to the taxpayer as owner. Ray Rees has argued that a disadvantage of nationalization is that it is involves forced saving, a form of saving which does not allow individuals to change their portfolios freely: Rees (1986).

92 On golden shares, see Graham and Prosser (1988), pp. 84, 85; (1991), pp. 141–50.

93 H. Parris, met in chapter 1 as a historian of railway policy in the nineteenth century, was indignant that the long history of public-utility regulation before 1945 had been ignored: but his was probably a lone voice and it was not heard until Parris, Pestiau and Saynor (1987), p. 162; neither did he develop his thoughts. (Improvization less happily also marked deregulation in US telecommunications: Faulhaber (1987), p. xvii.) It looked as if the early versions of the Broadcasting Bill, 1990, which provided for the auction of television licences and the regulation of the industry, might be amended so as to be recognizably of the same family; but, perhaps because it was not under the influence of the Privatization Unit, after amendment its cousinship actually became more distant.

94 Kay and Thompson (1986).

95 Before they could be privatized, the water authorities had first to be converted from bodies which reflected their local government into something closer to nationalized industries. This was done in the Water Act, 1983. Graham and Prosser (1991), p. 48, contrast this with the position in France, where the main work was done by one statute.

96 See for example Coopers & Lybrand (1988). Wiltshire (1987), pp. 30–57, has a useful account of the process of privatization.

97 Beesley (1981).

98 Ibid., p. 4.

99 Ibid., p. 10.

100 Ibid., p. 11.

101 Ibid., p. 17.

102 Kay (1984), p. 85. See also A. J. Harrison (1982), *passim.*

103 Vickers and Yarrow (1985), pp. 38, 39; (1988), pp. 195–241.

104 DTI (1990). By 1990 Mercury claimed 4 per cent of the telecommunications market. The slow development was not Mercury's fault. As Coll observed of MCI, a US telecommunications entrant, it was difficult to get it to increase its competition against AT&T once its own objectives had been met: Coll (1986) pp. 200–8.

105 A. J. Harrison (1988), p. 35.

106 A. J. Harrison (1981b), p. 29. Another distraction was that British Gas argued at length that the Government had no legal right to sell it since under statute, it maintained, its assets belonged to it not to the Government – a view that had some justification given

Denning LJ's judgement in *Tamlin vs. Hannaford* (1950), cited by Robson (1962), pp. 69, 70.

107   Vickers and Yarrow (1988), pp. 267–8, also pp. 163, 321.

108   The concept of natural monopoly is briefly examined in Vickers and Yarrow (1985), esp. p. 85. There is a full treatment in Sharkey (1982) and Berg and Tschirhart (1988).

109   Hammond, Helm and Thompson (1986).

110   Ibid., pp. 259–60; Vickers and Yarrow (1988), p. 257 Cramer (1989), pp. 137–54, discusses the problems of creating competition through pipelines.

111   Vickers and Yarrow (1988), p. 256.

112   Likierman and Bloomfield (1987), p. 112.

113   Vickers and Yarrow (1988), pp. 257–81. In 1991, the Office of Fair Trading reported that measures taken thus far were insufficient to achieve 'self-sustaining competition' to British Gas: OFT (1991), p. 24. The Director General of Fair Trading recommended an MMC inquiry unless British Gas agreed to release a significant proportion of the gas it had contracted for sale by others; to allow more competition for customers consuming less than 25,000 therms a year; and to allow customers more variation in the contracts they can choose, including allowing more interruptible contracts and contract aggregation. The most striking recommendation was that gas storage and transmission should become a separate, arm's-length subsidiary whose charges should be non-discriminatory and cost related. John Wakeham, the Energy Secretary, was earlier reported as saying that there would be no break-up of British Gas: *The Times*, 16 April 1991, p. 22. The Office of Fair Trading reported its view that this would be necessary to prevent abuse by British Gas but did not recommend it.

114   Starkie and Thompson (1986) described the dilemma facing the minister responsible, Nicholas Ridley, who did not want Heathrow and Gatwick to subsidize Stansted and therefore rushed through investment appropriations for Stansted just before privatization.

115   There were further attempts to extend the possibility of competition in the water industry by encouraging new entrants: *The Financial Times*, 9 October 1991, p. 14. But they look likely to remain marginal.

116   One of the most penetrating criticisms of privatization is David Heald's where he says it is a 'challenge to the legitimacy of public policy objectives themselves, not just to public enterprise as a defective instrument': Heald (1985), p. 8. Why it is that experience has failed to come up with a detailed blueprint for delivering non-commercial policy objectives efficiently is a question to which this book will return at various points, though without providing a remedy for that defect.

117   Vickers and Yarrow (1988), p. 155.

118   HM Treasury (1988).

119   Ibid., p. 78.

120   Ibid., p. 83. While in the end it is the efficiency gains that matter in a contest of economic efficiency, their calculation is both conceptually and statistically difficult: see Jones, Tandon and Vogelsang (1991); Hutchinson (1991).

Part 2

Policy issues

5

The extension of competition

The long-term success of the privatisation programme will stand or fall by the
extent to which it maximises competition. If competition cannot be achieved, an
historic opportunity will have been lost.

Rt. Hon. John Moore (1983)[1]

Academics as well as politicians have stressed the case for extending competition to
avoid regulation: 'Competition where possible, regulation where necessary'; 'The
introduction of competition is the most effective policy to improve the efficiency of
the nationalised and formerly nationalised industries'.[2] The arguments for preferring
competition to promote efficiency are powerful. Competition's invisible hand is the
best regulator because it draws competitors into a market to remove excess profits.
Under the pressure of competition firms reveal more facts about their costs than can
ever be extracted from them by law or regulation;[3] they will reduce their costs to the
minimum for fear that they will otherwise be undercut by rivals; to stay in business
they must plan yearly productivity improvements at least to match those their competitors might achieve, or else their short-term profitability might evaporate; and
they will innovate more and there will be more-diverse goods and services. And if
there is enough competition, it will be harder and less rewarding for firms to engage
in anti-competitive practices. Moreover, even the possibility of competition may be
enough to stimulate the incumbents to greater efficiency.

By contrast, regulation is a difficult, imperfect, and often expensive, time-
consuming and ineffective activity, easily spreading from economics into politics.
Therefore it is worth considering every feasible extension of competition. However,
the fundamental extensions of competition in the presence of natural monopoly
which are to be considered in this chapter are not alternatives to regulation. Rather,
it will be argued that these extensions of competition generally need regulation in
order to be effective. The regulation required in this context and which is discussed
in this chapter is generally that prescribed in Britain under the fair-trading laws, in
the United States under the anti-trust laws, and in Europe principally under Articles
85 and 86 of the Treaty of Rome.[4]

This chapter considers the more important issues raised by the extension of
competition. They are conflicts between it and the realizing of economies of scale
(section 1); the culture of public-sector industry (section 2); unnatural monopoly, as
distinct from some pseudo-regulatory offences, and its control by break-up or otherwise (section 3); difficulties in relying on freedom of entry (section 4); and the
problems of interconnection (section 5). Section 6 discusses yardstick competition.

5.1   Break-up and economies of scale

Although it has been argued that all monopolies can be broken up into smaller businesses, it does not follow that the outcome will be greater efficiency or even more competition. But it is not surprising that many observers, rightly conceiving that competition is far more effective than regulation can be, argue for more-rapid liberalization. Why did the Government allow in England and Wales only one new entrant into the telecommunications market? Why break up the electricity supply industry into only two fossil-fuel generating companies? Why not make every coal-mine a separate enterprise? Or break up British Airways or British Rail into routes or clusters of routes? Or British Steel into separate plants?

Such a ruthless economic Darwinianism relying on the survival of the fittest was easier to endorse at the end of the nineteenth century when there were vast numbers of firms in Britain mostly of small size with the 100 largest responsible for only 15 per cent of national output. There are now far fewer firms and the top 100 account for 41 per cent of national output.[5] Thus the fittest that survive may well be based, or controlled from, abroad, leading to a growth in imports or more foreign control or both – which would be good for the consumer but may mean fewer UK jobs. Nevertheless, many large British firms have been successful in meeting the more intense competition from overseas during the last ten years. And in the recent past many of the most successful British firms have been large and have grown larger, usually adding also to their production overseas. But some have been hampered, and even possibly prevented, from becoming major internationals by the concentration of UK anti-monopoly policy on preventing any UK firm acquiring 'dominant size' in the home market even when there is substantial competition from overseas. The argument that any one firm should be so restricted in size as not to be able to dominate the domestic market is, however, not valid *per se* in an open economy like the United Kingdom's.[6]

A way of illustrating the importance of not being over-impressed by the dangers of bigness is by taking the argument to an extreme. Why is not all economic activity undertaken by self-employed individuals working through contractual relationships with others? Why instead do partnerships and firms (consisting of more than one individual) exist? In the famous first three chapters of Book 1 of Adam Smith's *Wealth of Nations*, on the division of labour, there is no reference to a firm, to management, or to any form of partnership or management hierarchy.[7] At the centre of his argument is the well-known example of pin-making, where what used to be done by one worker combining many operations was later done by many, who divided the eighteen or so operations between them. He considered the possibility that they might work together in a factory, yet what he describes is as consistent with a group of self-employed workers entering into contractual relations with each other so as to secure the production of pins as it is with their being managed within a firm. Even where there is a substantial piece of equipment, one individual might own it and rent out its use to others, as, for example, was common in the United States after the Civil War. The relevance of this here is that it poses the question: in what circumstances, and why, should a firm or partnership be more efficient than the contractual interaction of self-employed workers? In Oliver Williamson's penetrating analysis of this question, the key is not technology.[8] However large the equipment and complex the operation, all engaged could theoretically be self-employed, working together on the basis of contractual arrangements between them. Rather, what is crucial is what makes for the more efficient transaction. If all workers were omniscient and able to make a complete and rational evaluation of their best course of action at all times and in all places spontaneously, all could be self-employed: there would be no firms or partnerships; and everyone would safeguard his economic interests in every respect by making appropriate contracts with all other parties with whom he has economic relations. But in reality the 'capacity of the human mind for formulating and solving complex problems is small compared with the size of the problems whose solution is required for objectively rational behaviour in the real world'[9] It is because of lack of information and bounded rationality – that is, an inability to weigh all factors relevant to making a rational decision between all feasible alternatives – that firms develop as alternative ways of completing a related set of transactions. Which arrangement is best in any given circumstance depends upon the capacities of the human beings involved, the nature of the markets in which they operate, and the complexity and rate of obsolescence of the technology they employ.

The boundaries that separate one firm from another will generally come where there is greatest market certainty so that transactions between them can be made contractually on the most certain basis. The more complicated the transaction and the greater the uncertainty, the more likely it is that the transaction will be internalized within a firm.[10] As increasing competition and other factors make the external environment less certain, there is a persistent tendency towards the integration of firms: horizontally by joining with competitors and vertically by joining with others in a chain from retailer through to the supplier of raw materials. For example, assume that a firm makes contracts with its suppliers. If each side had all the relevant information available to the other, that is, if there were transparency of information, it would be a matter of chance, as well perhaps as of comparative intelligence and foresight, which party in any given contract would do best out of it when, for instance, given an inevitable lack of sufficient knowledge, the future turns out to be different in several respects from that forecast. And of course, if there were no uncertainties about the future also, each party knowing all possible future courses of events and the probabilities to be attached to them, then, given equal intelligence, it should in every case also be possible to write an absolutely satisfactory contract. Such uncertainties, however, obviously abound – knowledge is limited and rationality is bounded. Moreover, it is also obvious that external transparency of information is almost unknown in business. Every firm or individual operator tends to divulge as little as possible, and may also deliberately mislead. Frequently, knowledge is not symmetrical – for example, buyers must expect to have less information about their suppliers' production costs than the suppliers have.[11] And opportunism too must be expected, where someone takes advantage of a situation to further his own interest openly or surreptitiously.[12] Hence a party to a contract who has superior knowledge may use it to distort or reinterpret the contract as best he can, taking advantage of every mistake, piece of misinformation or change in the environment. Finally, although in the absence of transparency something equivalent could be gained in any competitive situation where there are many buyers confronting each supplier, and vice versa, because between them they would generate enough solutions for one to be preferred by each buyer, such large numbers are in fact rare – for it is in the interest of both buyers and sellers to differentiate their products – and even if there should be a large number of potential suppliers initially, they will probably decline in number with time, since those who failed first time would know that the incumbent supplier will have an advantage in subsequent negotiations, and they are therefore less likely to bother to compete and will chase after market niches of their own, so that there is usually only a small choice of parties on either side when contracts are made.[13]

One can hardly be surprised therefore that in such circumstances firms have grown in size, particularly vertically, and have dwindled in number. Such a powerful stimulus to vertical integration has made firms grow from individual operators to complex organizations. When a firm finds that it is having persistent difficulties in devising satisfactory contracts and monitoring them successfully, its next step will be to take on the activity itself.[14] This difficulty in making transactions externally has directly or indirectly led to public enterprise in some cases – because it is just such complex organizations which find it hardest to maintain, or even to initiate, competitive market relations within a fragmented industry. In such circumstances, rationalization may easily lead to internalizing such relations within a large command structure.

Although, as we have seen, the tendency for firms to grow larger will be less when operations and the environment are comparatively certain and simple, in recent years uncertainty and complexity have generally increased. One cause is the growth of international competition in most markets. Examples of changes which one would expect on average to cause firms to grow in size are the huge reduction in international sea-freight transport rates since the 1960s, the substitution of floating for fixed exchange rates in the early 1970s, and the recent deregulation of many industries. (Indeed, the deregulation of airlines and buses in the United States has already led to an increase in firm size there.) And certainly, the abolition of retail price maintenance in 1962 was a direct cause of the gradual concentration of most of the retail trade into mammoth undertakings.

Provided that the firm is efficient, internal transactions, between individual employees, departments and divisions, are simpler for several reasons. One is plainly that the sanction hanging over an internal transaction is usually no longer a contract which is ultimately only enforceable at law. Instead, firms develop their own procedures and codes to govern internal behaviour. For example, they normally establish principles and procedures to govern transfer pricing between operations as well as to reward and penalize performance.[15] If a firm were to try to align management incentives so that they reflected every change in each manager's environment and efficiency, that would become as complicated as any external contract and would be certainly unworkable. Rather, managers and (other) employees learn to accept as fair something which is much more crudely related to performance and which they know to be something less than perfect justice, because they have enough trust in the firm and those who operate the reward system.[16]

Another reason for the greater simplicity of internal transactions is, or should be, the comparative ease of establishing transparency of information within the firm.[17] The firm's supply of information is a common property of the organization and should be available to all who need to know. Managers and employees within the same business should be expected to speak the truth to each other in their business transactions. The possession of relevant information should not be kept deliberately asymmetrical. Colleagues should not be opportunistic towards each other in their business relations whatever their behaviour towards the world of business outside. Internal disciplines and the trust of colleagues in each other should prevent this opportunism. When there is a change in the external or internal environment which rationally should alter an internal transaction, contracts do not usually have to be renegotiated. When making the changes required, managers should cooperate in the firm's interest rather than pursue their own.

In order to ease the supply of information and make it more useful, in an efficient firm there will be management information systems well related to business objectives at all levels. They will be audited internally and where there are disputes there will be procedures for resolving them.[18] An important part of the function of managers at all levels is indeed deciding disputes. As Williamson suggests, the exercise of authority is often a more effective way of deciding them than haggling or using the courts.[19]

In order to help achieve such honesty and transparency firms will generally strive for a high proportion of lifetime employees, whom they will expect to be loyal. By being 'good' employers, they will strive for loyalty in all staff. They will get to know staff so that their experience, strengths and weaknesses may be rated and used. A high turnover of labour is rarely found in efficient firms that use labour that needs to be trained. A high turnover of management at any level is a sign of an inefficient firm, though possibly one trying to be more efficient.

Though management systems and computers have in recent years greatly increased the possible rationality of firms, none of these techniques can so overcome the problem of bounded rationality as to make an organization act and react as if it were a single comprehensive omnicompetent brain. Firms still have to remain aggregations of individual intelligences cooperating with each other. Complicated tasks must be broken down into a number of different sequential operations by means of which organizations adapt themselves to change.[20] For example, in any complicated organization selling related products in different markets, pricing is likely to be a decentralized task because of an inability to determine all prices simultaneously, though ideally this is what should be done. This achievement of simultaneity and integrity in the performance of such tasks is perhaps particularly difficult in a regulated environment where complicated enough commercial decisions taken low down must compromise with political reality as seen at the top.

The most difficult set of decisions a company must make is generally on its capital expenditure. Textbook models tend to assume that a firm can make many separate investment decisions where it considers a large number of options against several future scenarios. While this may reflect the reality in some cases where individual independent decisions can be taken for distinct parts of the business, many are those cases where it does not. This tends to be especially true of large public enterprises, which are often capital intensive, where investments typically take a long time to plan and undertake, and then have long economic lives far into an uncertain future, and where, moreover, there is very considerable interdependence between major investments. Such interdependence is most true of large network businesses like telecommunications, gas, electricity and railways.[21] Rationally, all investment decisions should still be taken simultaneously with full recognition of all the interrelationships;

but they cannot be. Instead, major investment decisions are taken incrementally on the basis of an incomplete appreciation of limited facts. They tend to be made sequentially and with relatively few degrees of management freedom at any one time. Such a sequential process, vital (as the world is) for a network business, cannot easily be achieved contractually between separate businesses. This is probably a major reason why networks tend to be kept within one monopoly enterprise whatever other bits of such enterprises may be hived off. But, as will be argued later, that is not an argument for keeping such networks or grids in public ownership; or necessarily together if appropriate interconnection rules can be found to achieve equal access across networks or grids.

More generally, the most important and difficult problem to be overcome when a public monopoly is broken up is to discover how far the transactions previously internalized can be effected contractually between the divorced parts, that is, to establish that the rules of common carriage, as it used to be called, or interconnection, as it is now called, are capable of being put on a fair and effective enough basis to ensure that enough capacity is provided, that its provision can be profitable to the provider, without being over-profitable, and that no party will be able to discriminate in its use against other parties. The power of Williamson's analysis in this regard is that it concentrates on the question of whether the individual transaction is best accomplished within the firm or contractually between firms.

His analysis has been worth developing here for three main reasons. There is first its general applicability to issues of firm size in relation to the extent of the market and therefore the economic desirability or not of breaking up monopolies into competing parts. It secondly prepares for our later analysis of a crucial regulatory problem: the policing of interconnection. Lastly, it points up the fact that the contracts or licences between the regulator and the regulated which are essential to effective regulation are an alternative to, or intercede within, other, private contractual arrangements. Difficult though the facts may be to decide, in principle the choice between monopoly and competition in any given case can thus become an empirical one. In particular, his analysis introduces the possibility that the fragmentation of a market into units which are numerous enough for effective competition may create contractual complexities at the interfaces of those firms with each other and with other economic agents which create more inefficiency than is destroyed by the greater competitiveness. There has been a tendency in the more complicated privatizations involving interconnections to underplay this point. But it also explains why the break-up of firms like British Airways and British Steel, which do not imply solving difficult problems of interconnection, need not result in greater efficiency, especially, but not necessarily, in so far as there is competition.

However, the power of Williamson's analysis is such that it can also help us understand why competition is generally not enough to make either privatization or public enterprise reform effective for monopoly. Public or private monopoly confirmed by barriers to entry provides an environment within which firms may grow without the disciplines that make them economically efficient. While such monopolies could put their owners first and maximize their net revenues, that never happens. To a greater or lesser extent they use their immunity from market forces to develop a comfortable inefficiency. Productivity improvement in substantially inefficient organizations commonly goes through three stages. There is first the cash squeeze, which prompts the easy labour-savings and improves cash and stock control. There is then the determined attempt to break down the organizational inertia that is the inheritance of the past before embarking on the third stage. This last stage is complete when through judicious research and product development, strict attention to quality and careful planning an enterprise is able to sustain sufficient productivity improvement every year to stay profitable. As we have seen, the first stage often occurred in public enterprises before privatization; and the third, even at the beginning of the 1990s, was only being realized by the best British companies. It is the second stage which is the real target of successful privatization, especially of the large monopolies.

The laborious process of privatization will therefore have thrown light upon the reality of the abstraction that economists call X-inefficiency or organizational failure: the culture of the organization which has developed within a protected monopoly.[22] The output of the earlier privatizations of natural monopolies could be seen mostly as only various kinds of paper: statutes, licences, long- and short-form reports, interconnection agreements, where relevant, and prospectuses. Although the actual behaviour of the privatized monopoly enterprise, its culture and probably its organization must change profoundly if it is to become a vigorous, dynamic firm, this may not happen where the enterprise remains substantially intact. Privatization can be a paper exercise if competition is slow to develop and regulation can be kept at arm's length by the privatized enterprise. At the worst, the whole effort of privatization could have fallen foul of one of the snares endemic to the public sector. One has repeatedly seen how in moments of minor crisis some body or other has been called in to write a report on the situation. When there has been a major crisis there has been a similar, if more intensive, exercise, dignified as a fundamental review and often leading to legislation, if only to write off bad debt. A few heads have rolled. Government has possibly elaborated new policies. But even so the enterprise survives more or less intact because its fundamental status as a self-regulating monopoly, and the disciplines and incentives to which it is subject, have not materially altered. The privatizations of competitive industries did avoid this pitfall, because the industries in question became subject to competition as they never had before – they were no longer protected by a deficit safety-net or hampered by government intervention. However, in so far as competition was not introduced when natural monopolies were privatized, they could, of course, try to carry on as they had before, shrugging off the weight of new paper as they had many times in the past. Indeed, there may be a long period during which such an enterprise believes it can rid itself of those who joined to help privatize it and return to its normal sluggish, bureaucratic calm. Furthermore, if competition does not develop and regulation proves no more effective than ministers used to be, then in the worst cases nothing may in fact change – except that privatization will have given those natural monopolies even more discretion to be inefficient. A corollary of this is that, wherever there is little or no competition and as long as that remains so, it is the regulator who must bear the brunt of bringing about increases in efficiency (this will be discussed in chapter 6). Where, as in the case of water, no appreciable competition is to be expected, this becomes the main rationale of replacing ministerially-controlled public enterprises by *regulated* private companies.

Where there is break-up, on the other hand, paper cannot be the only output.

Many managers and staff will have to behave differently, report to different people, even change their place of work, cutting off some relationships and establishing others. Various transactions which were internal and informal must be replaced by external relationships, which must be better defined and will often lead to the transfer of money on stated principles. The main difficulties and delays experienced by electricity privatization had as their cause the novelty of the commercial and organizational relationships needed; and these had to work if the new regime was to be a reality. However, while break-up necessitates change, that change (for reasons other than those to do with resulting contractual complexity) need not lead to greater efficiency. To instance the case of the railways alone, the British Transport Commission, created in 1948, was broken up in 1962; one of its parts, the British Railways Board, had some of its activities passed in 1968 to the National Freight Corporation, which itself was a reconstruction of another of the Commission's constituent parts; and further organizational changes were made in 1974: but, although in each case there were reasons of efficiency for what was done, they left intact the objectives, incentives and styles of management that were themselves in large part sources of inefficiency. What matters for natural-monopoly privatization is that the besetting sin of the past – the reorganization or break-up an organization as a way of affecting behaviour below because of a lack of effective reporting-lines and accountability, one of the few ways in which ministers or nationalized industries' top management had of doing this – is replaced by the minimum reorganization needed to achieve the efficiency that is required in order to meet greater competition and respond to the new regulation.

5.2   The culture of public-sector industry

The least easily surmountable barriers to efficiency are the entrenched habits of the past which in one form or another are common in monopolies insulated from market forces. Because their origins have been different, British nationalized industries have varied in their habits. Those which came from the private sector, particularly if recent arrivals, have been more likely to retain private-sector attitudes and procedures. There have been some which, like British Leyland, apparently inherited the habits of a private bureaucracy, while others were welded out of a diversity of private and municipal enterprises and have borne the marks of their first nationalized leaders, who may have been civil servants, trade union leaders or managers. Others, like the Post Office and British Telecom, evolved from government departments and have been suffused by that inheritance. Still, in general, those nationalized industries that have been monopolies acquired a bureaucratic culture despite differences in style and degree, and this is likely to have been the more entrenched the larger the organization.

Such a culture tends to be marked by management attitudes in which individual accountability is not highly valued, and achieving consensus is. This can lead to excessive reliance on committees and the provision of too little management information by which individual managers and units can be held accountable. Objectives are often vague and, so far as they exist, tend to be laid down at the top after insufficient consultation with those down the line who, if they are to be effective, need to be committed to these objectives. Such a management often divides into an elite of high fliers and a mass of administrators and executives. The former move rapidly form job to job: their success depends on knowing the system, understanding the internal politics and becoming agile in dealing with the external environment, as well as, some would say, keeping on the move. Indeed, this unhappy division of labour may be reflected in a hierarchy which is a denial of sound management practice. Those at the top who have learnt their trade and earned recognition by managing and serving externally imposed chairmen and ministers turn their talents to managing the media, city opinion, as far as they can, and other external communications. They spend little time on the internal executive tasks of private-sector chairman and chief executives, confusing, as several nationalized industries have, the difference between the controlled delegation of authority and the uncontrolled diffusion of it. Very great freedom may be given to managers without there being set up an apparatus of target-setting and monitoring to discipline that freedom. Too little attention is paid to ensuring that the people, systems and external vigilance are in place to identify quickly something that is going wrong and take rapid and effective corrective action.

Instead of clear accountability, and management systems by which performance can be set and monitored, one finds a culture in which almost the main weapon those at the top have to deal with those lower down is organizational change. Moreover, hard-pressed managers in large organizations tend to be able to react only to the pressure of immediate business, so that, unless there is an intelligent, well-defined process that draws together the decisions they make in a way which gives coherence to the whole, the organization will not be able to achieve the objectives it sets itself without luck or by giving itself in the first place ample latitude to achieve them. Instead, one may find a system where lower management and staff are more likely to learn what is really happening above them from the press or their trade unions than down the management chain, and where those above them have responsibility without power. Since in organizations with such a culture objectives are poorly defined, such incentive payments as exist cannot align with them. Instead, they may become a form of patronage; and, though through this supervisors may bring a good influence to bear on those that work under them, even at best how they reward them will not then be bedded in an overall conception of their objectives, so that, when these people move, the objectives they set and the assessments made will change, and the likelihood is that many managers will sooner or later leave because they are not congenial to their new superiors, since the objective information is lacking which ought to be their best defence. At worst, uncontrolled discretion in remuneration can deliver managers to the mercy of unscrupulous or blinkered bosses. But in general, because of the sparsity of managerial information, those who follow the rules are rewarded. The bringers of bad news, however, are not, and there is little frankness and objectivity in bringing problems to the surface, until they are forced into the open, probably too late for remedial action. Such an organization is over-layered. Too many people have jobs which are coordination and liaison rather than management. Innovation is resisted on the ground that, whatever it is, 'it is not done here'. Many intelligent, well-meaning and professionally skilled individuals can get trapped in such structures, believing in their inevitability. Such cultures tend to mark private as well as public monopoly. As Sir John Harvey-Jones has said in describing such an environment, 'the curious thing about industry is that if we think for ten minutes and draw a picture of the kind of organisation we would least like to work in, and hence the one where we are least likely to be effective, we often look about and see just such an environment around us'.[23]

Instead of trust, here there is dissimulation; instead of transparency of information, people hang on to what they have and will not share it. Managers behave opportunistically, scoring points off each other at the expense of the firm rather than collaborating to face the outside world. Transfer pricing does not work and results in internal conflict. Profit centres find it easier to make a profit at each other's expense rather than for the whole firm. Rapid turnover of staff and poor selection procedures mean that loyalty is doubtful and experience may not be rated correctly. Too many managers are unknown quantities with poorly designed and monitored objectives. An internal market may exist which individual managers use to attract managers from elsewhere within the organization but which may not be in its best interest. Codes of conduct either do not exist or become excessively detailed and bureaucratic.

No enterprise will have all those faults, or perhaps any one of them throughout its organization. Bureaucracies commonly find a place for the virtues of professional integrity and a tradition of public service. Nevertheless, any tendency an enterprise may have to possess the characteristics described limits the extent to which the internalizing of transactions within it produces a more efficient outcome than would be gained by freely negotiated external contracts. Whatever the extent of such organizational failures, they reduce the efficiency of internal transactions by comparison with external contractual ones. A mistake of nationalization, as well as of the rationalizations of private industry into monopolies and cartels, has been the opinion that there would be no special problem in achieving internal efficiency. While break-up or demerger may be the appropriate response in part, internal efficiency is also needed to meet competition. How to get it is an issue for the privatized enterprise.

One reason for organizational failure is that the firm has become too large to provide an efficient internal environment, giving some hope to smaller and more-vigorous competitors. But another cause may lie in the existence of monopoly itself and in the resulting lack of financial discipline traditionally associated with much public enterprise. Sir John Hicks' much quoted phrase that one of the privileges of monopoly is the enjoyment of the quiet life may be amplified to comprehend not only the monopolistic or deficit-financed public enterprise but all monopolies. It is demanding work to run an efficient firm at all levels and even harder and more demanding to turn an inefficient firm into an efficient one, whether private or public. It is easier to perch on or near the top of a firm where there is little personal accountability, that is, where, what happens to one does not depend upon one's performance. Then the cut and thrust of debate at committees not only provides the pleasures of intellectual argument but blurs accountability. Rather than empower an individual to settle a dispute, it is often more comfortable to introduce another level into the hierarchy to coordinate or liaise. For this and other reasons support staff multiplies. This helps account for the large administrative overheads characteristic of so many old-style public enterprises and private monopolies. Those used to the competitive private sector may find such an atmosphere stifling – to others it will seem one in which there is far more personal freedom from pressure and scope for individuality.

Some public enterprises may be less bureaucratic than others because they have been more recently private or because, though public, they are in competitive markets. In general, those where engineering skills are powerful are most likely to maintain standards of excellence, even though they may tend towards technical rather than commercial excellence, and therefore to over-investment, as repeated investigations have suggested. And where there has been a recent revolution in the method of supply, as in gas, or rapid technical innovation, as in electricity, there may be great technical efficiency. Yet it is not accidental that, in many instances in Britain in the 1980s, radical changes to rectify organizational faults were brought about in nationalized industries by determined and vigorous chairmen before privatization. Often these chairmen were brought in from outside – Sir Ian MacGregor with steel and then coal, Lord King at British Airways, Sir Michael Edwardes and Graham Day at British Leyland, and Sir George Jefferson at British Telecom – though MacGregor's work at steel was completed by an insider, Sir Robert Scholey, and another, Sir Peter Thompson, did the same at National Freight Corporation, as did the first Sir Robert Reid on the railways, while yet another, Sir John Egan, turned round Jaguar.[24] However, in most of these cases it was the first rather than the second, and certainly not the third, stage in productivity improvement on which they naturally and rightly concentrated.

It is possible to draw the moral that privatizations often require a revolution in the enterprise's culture before they can become effective. If that revolution does not happen, and the enterprise is not already efficient, there must be a chance that it will be less able to respond to any other changes and to the competition or regulation or both that emerges. Indeed, such a culture change is perhaps the *sine qua non* of efficiency. One aspect of this which becomes important as competition through privatization threatens is that there is a tendency for managers steeped in a monopoly culture to see their main objective as keeping their market share at, or as near as possible to, 100 per cent. Therefore, despite the possible loss of profits, they may be more likely to resort to predation where they can. Another danger from their past, in the shape of the Morrisonian conception of their relations with ministers, is that their interpretation of the light rein of regulation will be that the regulator is a weaker minister, to be similarly handled. There will thus be a limit to what privatization, as well as public enterprise reform, can achieve unless such bureaucratic arrangements are slimmed down into hierarchical efficiency. One can just about admit that it may be in the consumer's interest for British Airways, British Steel, British Telecom or the National Freight Company, in the absence of a sufficient degree of hierarchical efficiency, to be competed into the dust by new entrants – consumers should benefit from the survival of the fittest. But that would be a lesser national success, not necessarily in economic but certainly in political terms, than if they were to survive as effective competitors among other, similar-sized or smaller firms, domestic and foreign.[25]

Thus the conclusion at this stage is that, whether by way of privatization or by another route, public enterprises have to go through similar stages of debureaucratization if they are to achieve competitive efficiency. As has already been observed, in circumstances of economic crisis when the Government allowed them to concentrate on economic efficiency several achieved this even before privatization and even in some cases before privatization was contemplated. As John Kay noticed in 1987, 'the most marked productivity gains have been made not in the privatisation candidates but in the traditional nationalised industries – posts, steel, rail – where no privatisation was (then) in prospect . . . Each of these industries has experienced senior management changes which have introduced a more commercial and a more abrasive management style'.[26] Thus the greater the importance of economies of scale and scope in an industry, and therefore the greater the presumption that efficient firms in that industry must be large, the more important it is to create therein as much competition as possible. If the firms are large, that generally means opening their markets to overseas competition. But in so far as competition cannot be created the principal instrument for reducing *organizational inefficiency* is the independent regulator (chapter 6); for historical experience of private monopolies not subject to competition shows that one cannot rely on the profit motive alone in such circumstances.

So we reach a number of tentative conclusions on this section and the previous one:

1 Bigness does not necessarily imply inefficiency. The US courts in the end decided against breaking up IBM, because there is no presumption now against bigness as such in US law and because, by every test made, IBM was a highly efficient firm.[27]

2 However, many very large firms are inefficient. This used to be true of large sheltered private monopolies. But the enormous recent growth in international competition has made this unsustainable in open economies.

3 Many of these large private monopolies became large in order to enjoy economies of scale and were then nationalized in the public interest. Probably in all cases, they used their sheltered position to become inefficient and stayed so after being brought into public ownership, in general because of their protection from home and overseas competitors by restrictions on market entry, or through the availability of deficit subsidy, or both.

4 It does not follow from this that break-up should go with privatization. If a privatized enterprise is subject to market disciplines and international competition, as British Airways and British Steel are in overseas markets, then keeping it intact may improve its competitive potential and it will have all the incentive it needs to be efficient.[28]

5 Some weight should be given to the argument that firms like British Telecom and British Gas, while they have as yet competed in only a limited or indirect way in overseas markets, will be the better able themselves to enter those markets if they have a strong home market which gives them the critical mass to become world players; and therefore to help their suppliers, or, in BT's case, value-added network services as well, to enter those markets.

6 It is, moreover, possible that where international competition is not possible, the efficiency lost through breaking up an enterprise in an industry where scale and scope economies are actually or potentially important may substantially exceed that gained from domestic competition thus introduced.[29] If the scale economies are sufficiently large the enterprise capable of producing an output at lowest unit cost in any one market may be a natural monopoly. Moreover, such a natural monopoly may also enjoy economies of scope which enable it to produce more than one good or service, possibly many, at lower unit costs than can other,

smaller-scale producers. By assumption, creating competition entails break-up or other restrictions on the scale or scope of operation of the dominant firm, which in turn implies higher unit costs, at least for some outputs. Thus, despite the inefficiencies of regulation, using it to prevent or punish the anti-competitive practices that natural monopoly is heir to may result in greater efficiency overall than would competition.

5.3 Some pseudo-regulatory offences and unnatural monopoly, a key economic regulatory offence

At this point we may start to distinguish some pseudo-regulatory offences from genuine ones.[30] *Bigness* as such is not sensibly regarded as an economic offence.[31] Neither are related phenomena like *dominant size* or *too large a market share* in relation to a particular market, domestic or global. *Rationalization*, whether through takeover, merger or even nationalization, may be associated with either greater or lesser efficiency depending on the circumstances, particularly the extent of, and potential for, competition. *Cartels* are likely to be relatively inefficient because they cannot easily achieve scale economies, but they may also find it more difficult than do monopolies to concert predatory behaviour.

Nevertheless, there is a first key economic regulatory offence to be established in relation to natural monopoly. A regulator needs to be able to distinguish between increases in size, whether through growth or by acquisition or merger, which are consistent with the falling unit costs that characterize natural monopoly, and those which do not have such an effect and thus amount to *artificial* or *unnatural monopoly*. By assumption, that task cannot be achieved by a fair-trading or anti-trust regime which works in terms of maximum market shares. It is a factually more demanding task, since it requires the analysis of whether a given change is consistent with natural monopoly; but it seems an inescapable one if economic efficiency is the overriding object.

The UK natural-monopoly legislation provides that such powers in general should be exercised by the specialist natural-monopoly regulator jointly with the Director General of Fair Trading. Oftel, for example, advised ministers to prevent British Telecom joining with IBM to run a joint venture providing managed data network services;[32] and to ask the Monopolies and Mergers Commission (MMC) whether BT's acquisition of Mitel, a Canadian apparatus manufacturer, might not entail unfair competition with other apparatus suppliers;[33] and, with the Department of Trade and Industry, has prevented BT using its cable systems for home entertainment because it believes that that would not assist market entry.[34] This last decision was justified by the important argument that while as an efficient natural monopoly BT might be able to provide these, as well as telecommunications services, more cheaply than an independent cable operator could, as an inefficient natural monopoly its being able to this could not be taken for granted – BT needed competition in its local monopoly from combined telecommunications and entertainment independents to stimulate its own cost reductions.[35]

But, while such powers in the armoury of specialist regulators will remain important, it is more important still that the regulatory authorities retain the power to break up entities if they believe that their size and market dominance are not justified by natural monopoly. The most important example of this was in the United States where the courts decided that they did have the right to break up AT&T on anti-trust grounds, because the Federal Communications Commission did not seem able to control it.[36] In this spirit, it is worth noting that the MMC rejected British Gas's argument that, because of the terms of its privatization, it was in a different position from that of any other body under investigation for unfair trading and could not be broken up.[37] Thus, merger is not the only event which may create an offence of unnatural monopoly. A natural monopoly may grow past the point where it realizes economies of scale or scope, either in general, or in particular areas or in relation to particular activities. Although this will open it up to competition if there is free entry, another solution would be break-up – preserving the natural monopoly and detaching the rest. The British competition laws may be presumed to cover this offence and to allow for this solution, though it would be a novel one, rather than a more arbitrary break-up. A natural monopoly may also grow units producing value-added services or goods which should be subjected to the same test. If they involve economies of scope, then they will be in the consumers' interest; if not, they may be demerged, especially if they are in actual or potential competition with other firms in circumstances in which the natural monopolist can abuse its monopoly power and where it is difficult to get routine accounting information to monitor the exercise of that power.

5.4   Free entry: contestability and predation

However, some economists maintain that regulation of anti-competitive practices is not necessary even where there is no competition. Natural monopolies, they say, may be kept efficient by free entry. Two main issues arise from this claim: Is free entry always desirable? And is it sufficient to ensure the efficiency of natural monopolies?

Is free entry always desirable?

It is a natural implication of any system – such as the new British system of regulation, but also many others – that allows only licensees to trade that some would-be entrants do not get licences. But where there is a need for conditions of trade to be written down, as with a natural monopoly, or with enterprises whose safety, environmental impact or other features make this sensible, why not make the licences freely available to all who are ready to meet the conditions? Adam Smith heralded the deregulation of his times by calling for the abolition of all legal monopolies in restraint of trade whether granted or imposed by the Crown, by Parliament or by the merchants of a borough. Some economists in recent years like William Baumol have reached a similar conclusion.[38] To perhaps over-simplify their position: they have suggested the abandonment of regulation wherever possible, which in general means where there are not heavy sunk costs or other technical obstacles to entry, though even then the threat of competition will do more good than harm; there should be no restrictions on entry. In short, all markets should be 'contestable'. Not regulation, but competition and potential competition should, as far as possible, be the policeman.

Most public enterprises, private monopolies and cartels have been protected from competition by restrictions on entry. Removing such restrictions can create competition, as happened initially in the case of express coaches and more permanently, if patchily, in the case of buses. Requirements that industries divest themselves of various ancillary activities or allow outsiders to compete in their markets have permanently introduced competition into such activities as the manufacture and maintenance of telecommunications equipment and the provision of value-added services in telecommunications. Free entry may also be an effective competitive discipline even if it does not result in competition, as we have seen with express buses. One company alone may run buses or aeroplanes on a route, but be kept reasonably efficient by the threat of potential competition to the point where no special regulation is required in order to prevent abuse of its (apparent) monopoly. The theory is that the incumbent will know that, if it becomes demonstrably inefficient or sets too high fares, another firm can enter and take a share, or all, of its market from it.

There are three main arguments against absolutely free entry:

(1) Many of the British disputes in the 1980s over the extent of competition were deflected into dispute over its timing. It is possible for competition to develop so slowly that monoploy profits are hardly eroded, especially when business is as buoyant as demand for telecommunications was in the 1980s. Industries that have been monopolies, which, as we have seen, have many changes in management, organization and working practices to undergo if they are to be able to compete, may not change fast enough if competitive pressure is too light – from this standpoint it is unfortunate that Mercury's competition with British Telecom lagged several years behind what it was promised to be in 1984. And there is also a danger that the slow development of competition, especially where it is restricted to two parties, may make the growth of collusion easier, even without any explicit arrangements, once the new entrant has reached a significant scale of operations. On the other hand, competition can be introduced too quickly for an industry suffering from organizational failure, making it unable to react at all, so that it gradually crumbles, failing to realize the scale and scope economies that timely, efficient management could have gained. Alternatively, to admit many small competitors at once in a complex situation may make it easy for the incumbent to continue to dominate the market. This is most likely when the initial-entry investment is substantial and not readily saleable, as it has been for Mercury, which has had to build its own network. To have admitted other networks to interconnect with BT's before Mercury was established would probably have harmed Mercury and benefited BT. However, Mercury's experience suggests that the protection of it and BT against any third entrant has not ensured the effective and quick development of Mercury into a substantial competitor; while the contrasting effectiveness of Racal in competing against BT in the car-phone market raised the equally worrying possibility that, unless there were more entrants, that market might settle down into a cosy duopoly even if the basis for agreed coexistence were tacit.[39] The admission of many new entrants into the telecommunications market from 1991 will test the proposition that prices have been high because of duopoly.

It is a fine act of political judgement to decide what rate of introduction of competition is best.[40] Commentators from the outside will almost certainly underrate both the structural and cultural changes that are needed and the damaging effects of rapid change; while those within are likely to overrate them. On balance, however, it is better to move too quickly than too slowly. Long experience of trade tariffs, and other avowedly transitional protections, has shown that, once established, the forces for keeping them increase their influence and they become progressively harder to dismantle. What is needed – and this is what in Britain the regulatory regime and government intentions provide – is an ability and willingness to allow competitive pressures to increase periodically.[41] To that end, and to avoid shareholders' and early competitors' expectations being seriously damaged, a general policy of introducing competition where possible, and at suitable times, needs to be announced in advance. (As we saw in chapter 2, failure to do this caused insuperable problems in the nineteenth century.)

(2) The second argument is that free entry should not be allowed where it will result in wasteful or destructive competition. This may arise, it is alleged, because of the over-provision of assets. For actual or potential competition to be effective, entry and exit must be relatively easy.[42] To that end, any capital costs may be fixed, but not sunk. There is, for example, a new and second-hand market in buses and aeroplanes which ought to make entry and exit easy in that any firm can add to or reduce its fleet quickly as market circumstances change. However, by comparison, railway track and buildings, power-stations and transmission lines, and water-treatment works and sewers are sunk costs. Even if there were free entry, they would be barriers to effective entry; for providing such new plant adds substantially to the cost of entry. Moreover, such plant is not easily disposed of once a new entrant has provided an alternative, and it therefore pays an incumbent to drop its prices to cover only short-run marginal or variable costs – in cash-flow terms, it will still be better off. Therefore there will be a period – how long depends on the resources of those concerned – during which all involved must respond to each other by dropping their prices to a level which will not be profitable until someone retreats; or alternatively, if they are few, until they come to some anti-competitive arrangement.

  Therefore substantial sunk costs introduce the possibility of destructive competition where a new firm makes substantial sunk investments that duplicate those of incumbents; where all will be led to cut prices, and all may be unprofitable while the fight lasts; where the loser will be worse off than if the contest had not happened; where, if incumbents win, they will be worse off than if there had been no contest and may, as so many nineteenth-century railways did, stagger along on the edge of bankruptcy; and where, even if the new entrant wins, it may never achieve a satisfactory level of profitability. In such situations, entry may well entail such a high risk of loss that it can seem to be explicable only in terms of ignorance.[43]

  What needs explaining is why rational investors should risk their money in excessive investment. It is possible that the enterprise is substantially over-optimistic about the growth of demand; where investments take several years to make, mistakes may be made. Yet for a regulatory body to prevent such investments is to imply that its forecasting ability is better than that of those who risk their money, which is generally an absurd proposition. Perhaps an investment that started in a boom, matures in a slump – certainly, outcry against wasteful competition has been greatest at such times. But, again, the proposition that a regulator should act to prevent this in advance overstates his forecasting ability. Moreover, at any time, restricting entry will tend to keep in place old, obsolescent investments and discourage innovation. Finally, methods of managing and shortening recessions, of doubtful value in the past, could be now more effective and they, as well as international competitiveness in a world of more-open economies, make restrictions on entry even less relevant.

Another explanation for the over-provision of assets, and therefore for wasteful or destructive competition, is that, through ignorance, promoters of a rival project may have overstated the profits, present or prospective, of the incumbents. Otherwise, the most likely cause of such ignorance – one that provides the most likely explanation of destructive railway, water and gas competition in the nineteenth century – is that it is in the interests of the promoters, of the lawyers involved, and of those who sold land and supplies to encourage and exploit the gullibility of shareholders through misinformation. However, because disclosure requirements and accounting standards have improved, it is a plausible conjecture that wasteful or destructive competition caused in either of these ways is now less likely.

As it happens, most clamour against wasteful competition has occurred in industries like buses, trucks, farming and financial services, especially in the 1920s and early 1930s, where assets were not sunk and both entry and exit were easy. The classic objection was to a presumedly ignorant and over-optimistic ex-soldier who bought a second-hand bus, truck or taxi-cab cheaply, underestimating its operating costs and overestimating traffic, and who ran the vehicle into a dangerous condition before becoming bankrupt. What is the moral of such stories? It may be sensible to have strict enforcement of safety regulations in order to prevent 'cowboy' operators as far as possible, forcing operators to keep their vehicles in good condition and to drive safely. But, once that is done, this case for restrictions on entry disappears; it comes down to recognition that some operators are readier to work for lower remuneration that others. And regulation to prevent such 'wasteful' competition is even less in the consumer's interest than is no regulation.[44]

(3) A third argument is that there are circumstances in which a natural monopoly may not be sustainable and that there may then be a case for restricting entry. To be sustainable a natural monopoly must be what is called 'strong', that is, its unit costs must fall as its output increases (whether it has one output or many).[45] A natural monoploy is 'weak' where it has exhausted its economies of scale and scope, so that its marginal costs are rising over a range of outputs.[46] This case may be exemplified by a single-product natural monopoly whose unit costs begin to rise past some level of output: scale economies are replaced by diseconomies. Why this should happen has been extensively discussed in the literature. The more persuasive, long-run explanations are in terms of the limitation of management – when what Oliver Williamson calls control-loss diseconomies begin to operate,[47] when management is over-extended in its risk-taking, its entrepreneurship or its ability to communicate with and control lower levels of management. However, these features of management are not immutable – vast progress has been made in techniques to expand the scale and scope of effective management. Indeed, it seems unlikely that rising unit costs in a natural monopoly for this, or indeed any other, reason need be a long-term phenomenon. Yet this may provide a period during which a smaller-scale operation may enter at lower unit cost. Commonly, this happens during the difficult period

when a natural monopoly is considering whether, and if, a market is more vulnerable to entry; but, concomitantly, marginal-cost pricing is profitable, because average cost is below marginal cost. However, if there are no barriers to entry, the weak natural monopoly is only sustainable if it can charge marginal-cost prices and not make any excess profit. It will thus be under some internal pressure to reduce its profitability by pricing down to marginal costs where it can; [48] otherwise, it can only make a normal profit overall if it drops at least some of its prices below marginal cost, and that implies cross-subsidization, which opens up the possibility of entry in its more profitable markets. However, it may not be easy for a would-be new entrant to determine that such a weak natural monopoly is in the vulnerable range before the monopoly makes additional investment to reduce its marginal costs below its average costs.[49]

A multi-product natural monopoly may also be non-sustainable if, for example, it practises, or is forced to practise, cross-subsidization for political reasons. This cannot be a rational economic policy for a profit-maximizing firm, so it may then need regulation of entry to protect its cross-subsidization. Such a monopoly is being used to pursue political or social ends rather than economic efficiency.

Underlying this third argument for restriction of entry is an economic domino theory. A new entrant successfully invades one part of a natural monopoly's market, undercutting it in one product or one geographical area. As a result, the monopoly's average costs rise since the same fixed costs must be recovered from smaller total sales. This enables another entrant to enter another part of its market and undercut it there, so reducing still further its total sales and increasing still more its average costs. By successive invasions, the natural monopoly is progressively destroyed. This will be economically inefficient if the final outcome is that average costs throughout the market are higher than under the monopoly. And if that is likely to be the result, the argument runs, a natural monopoly should be protected against free entry. However, such a collapse cannot happen if a natural monopoly has declining average costs and the freedom to discriminate in its pricing, since it then pays it to protect itself against such entry by lowering its prices sufficiently in that part of its market where it meets such competition. Since it is not economically efficient to prohibit price discrimination, in practice the issue only arises either when marginal costs are increasing or where criteria of fairness, or politics, override considerations of economic efficiency. An example is provided in telecommunications where, over the years, political forces have kept the profit margins of long-distance and international calls high and those of local calls low. Under free entry, a new entrant could cream off the international and long-distance markets;[50] this would prevent the incumbent cross-subsidizing the local-call market, so local-call charges would have to rise. If British Telecom had pricing freedom, it would react by rebalancing its charges to prevent this kind of entry. In so far as its freedom to rebalance is practically limited by the regulator or by its own inclination to carry on meeting the social obligations of the past rather than to maximize profits, that is, given price controls, free entry makes it vulnerable to domino invasion and thus leads to the possibility of an increase in economic inefficiency in that market.

Regulatory policy needs to decide what matters most: politically preferred prices entailing cross-subsidization, or economic efficiency through competition. A profitable new entrant is bound to lead to there being a closer alignment of prices and costs in that market. Where average cost is below marginal cost, so that the mono-poly concern could make a greater profit than regulation allows, many different price patterns for its different products may be consistent with a price ceiling. But from experience it may be said that the forces determining the actual pattern are more likely to be political than economic. Yet, as technical progress increases the scope for competition from outside, and if free entry is allowed, the difficulty grows of defending prices which have been distorted by politics or social policy. We have already seen how, from at least as early as the 1840s, politicians have tended to impose political and social obligations when they grant licences, and how, later, industries came sometimes to accept uncompensated obligations as part of a wider deal which they thought was in their own, if not the consumer's, interest – it is now clear, however, that there are circumstances in which the cross-subsidization entailed can significantly undermine an industry's viability. (The damaging effects that social obligations can have on economic regulation are further explored in chapter 9.)

Free entry is also important because technical innovation has in many industries reduced technological barriers to entry. In telecommunications, copper wire is chal-lenged by radio telephony, optic fibre, satellite communications, laser and wave guide technology; and, while cost still favours land routes, there are circumstances when radio and satellite are competitive.[51] To leave such developments in the hands of a monopolist makes it almost certain that the rate of innovation will be slow, so that consumers will benefit less from cost reduction. Free entry increases the likelihood that competitors will innovate and erode the established monopolist's monopoly power. With hindsight, it is remarkable how long AT&T and the British Post Office were able to hang on to a monopoly of terminal equipment, insisting that all tele-phones were much the same. Now there are hundreds of different models with an ever-growing range of facilities widely spread in price. And there are similar eco-nomic arguments for encouraging entry to stimulate innovation in electricity supply, broadcasting and railways.

The conclusions of the first part of this section are comparatively straightforward. First, while a theoretical case can be made for restricting entry in the interest of eco-nomic efficiency, the circumstances in which it would be relevant are rare; and even then the remedy is likely to be worse than the disease. Even if employed transitionally, the restricting of freedom entry should be used with restraint. Secondly, almost all examples of restrictions on entry (of which there are many) exist because of a polit-ical unwillingness to tolerate efficient pricing systems. Thirdly, when free entry is permitted, such politically determined pricing patterns will sooner or later be threatened, and when that happens it may lead to political difficulties and customer protests, as happened after the privatization of British Telecom. The regulator may believe it part of his duty to prevent moves towards efficient pricing. But, as will appear, there are better ways of doing this than through entry restrictions.

Is free entry sufficient?

Although free entry is thus a necessary condition for economic efficiency, it is not always a sufficient one. While in general the contestability that free entry provides is desirable, it will not work in so far as an incumbent firm can through predatory action prevent it from working, as has been shown by experience in bus and coach deregulation in Britain and in airline deregulation in the United States. *Predation* is therefore arguably the most important economic regulatory offence: in broad terms, it is charging low prices to deter entry or force out new entrants before they are established, though price is not the only instrument – quality differences may also be used.[52]

In the case of competitive markets, where there is no dominant firm or collusive arrangement, it can plausibly be argued that the ability of any incumbent to resist new entry will be limited, and that therefore the costs of regulation may easily outweigh the benefits. Indeed, one may plausibly go further than this and contend that, where there is abundant information, it is never rational for an incumbent to retaliate in this way in a competitive market. The same argument has been attempted for a natural monopoly. It runs to the effect that, in a rational world with perfect information, predatory behaviour never pays.[53] In the first place, no new entrant would enter a natural monopoly's market unless it knew that that monopoly was unsustainable either because of the incumbent's excessive profitability or internal cross-subsidizations, or because technical progress or inefficiency had undermined that natural monopoly to the point where it no longer existed in some parts of its market. And in the second place, no incumbent would drop its prices to undercut the newcomer unless it knew that it could sustain those prices in the long run, for it would know that, in the perfect market that is being supposed, it would pay the newcomer to drop its prices even more, or hold out longer, as the comparative advantage that had encouraged it to enter in the first place would enable it to do. Therefore, if the new entrant has a real advantage over the incumbent, which should alone tempt it in if it is rational, the incumbent cannot win the price-cutting game in the end, and, knowing that fact, will not begin it. Moreover, even if it should be able to see one entrant off, another will take its place because of the same real advantage. Indeed, predation is also never a rational policy, it is said, because taking over a new entrant will always be more profitable than fighting it to a finish.[54]

While such arguments may have some plausibility in highly competitive markets, they neglect the highly imperfect information characteristic of natural (and statutory) monopoly markets.[55] Any new entrant in such a market will know little of the incumbent's costs and therefore of its powers of retaliation. For example, where, as is common, natural monopolies provide a variety of goods or services with the same capital, or even the same service to different consumers in different places and at different costs, the prevalence of joint costs makes the establishing of marginal cost in relation to any market an almost impossible task for a would-be entrant.[56] And the same difficulty in establishing costs to prove or disprove discrimination that we have seen in the case of the nineteenth-century railways applies also in the case of present-day railways, as well as in regard to buses, telecommunications, gas and the distribution of electricity. Moreover, once one new entrant has been seen off by an incumbent, others will, in the absence of sufficient information, be discouraged from taking its place, though it would have been rational for them to try to do so if they had had enough information.[57] The more one sees predation as a dynamic process by which an incumbent wards off or chases off any who would threaten its market, the more predation appears a comparatively easy activity for an incumbent to engage in, especially if its natural monopoly covers many goods and services and the entry niche for any given new entrant is small. Moreover, the alternative policy of merging with the new entrant will in many cases not be open to the incumbent in a natural monopoly because of its prohibition in the anti-trust or fair-trading laws.[58]

A regulated natural monopoly may also be able to engage in predatory behaviour if its position is strengthened because licences are not freely available to would-be competitors. But perhaps most important, it may be able to recoup the costs and forgone revenues of predation by smuggling them into its next round of price or profits negotiations with its regulator.[59]

While predation may well benefit a natural monopoly, unregulated or regulated, preventing predation is made hard by the difficulties involved in defining the offence. A broad conception is that it is the sacrificing of current profits for future (monopoly) profits. That may seem to imply that any drop in price when there is a new entrant is predatory. Yet, as Alfred Kahn has observed, no one drops his prices when he does not have to.[61] Competition works through new products or new entrants competing away excess profits. Those already in the market may rationally, that is, non-predatorily, drop their prices in response to competition, provided that prices do not fall below marginal cost. Areeda and Turner see the problem as one of comparative statics and condemn prices when they fall below short-run marginal cost: if a dominant incumbent or a large new entrant drops its prices below short-run marginal cost, there is a presumption of predatory behaviour.[62] Posner, alternatively, has argued for the relevance here of long-run marginal cost.[63] So, what is the relevant marginal cost? One may suppose that normally it is the long-run marginal cost, which includes the cost of keeping the business going through investment. But what if there is recession? Economic theory and common sense suggest that it may be rational then for a firm to price down to short-run marginal cost – covering its outgoings – whether or not there is a new entrant. And even if excess capacity exists because of past investment mistakes rather than recession, the same policy remains rational, though not if the over-investment was deliberate.

However, whatever definition is used, proof remains difficult. The problem is greatest when a multi-product firm is accused of predation in one of its markets where there are substantial joint costs of provision in common with other goods or services.[64] For example, to prove that a British Telecom value-added service – say, a weather information or stock market dealing service – is not being subsidized and is therefore not being priced predatorily to discourage competition is more difficult than a similar case for a single-product firm would be.

It will be argued in chapter 7 that there is a strong case for requiring transparent information on a historic and current-cost basis from a natural monopoly which among other matters should reveal relevant long- and short-run product marginal costs. But while that may solve the measurement problem, or greatly ease it, it will not meet the further difficulty that there are circumstances in which every such test can be argued to be an invalid test of predation. The Areeda–Turner rule has triggered debate among academic economists and lawyers who have found circumstances in which it is economically efficient for prices to be below marginal cost.[65] The most powerful objection to marginal-cost rules, however, is that they ignore strategic behaviour where, for example, a dominant firm alters its plant from the optimal size to make entry more difficult by making operations more capital intensive and short-run marginal costs lower.[66] It then follows a sub-strategy of keeping prices at monopoly level between competitive entries, lowering them as a rival enters and raising them when the danger is over. (This is another reason for over-investment in natural monopoly.) Other approaches to testing for predation construct models of the whole market in order to estimate marginal costs, or simply use pragmatic methods intended to look at 'all relevant' information.[67] One approach, where there are joint costs, is to check if prices lie between marginal cost and stand-alone cost (the cost at which the good or service could be provided on its own): between these two extremes there may be a wide range of equally defensible prices. Williamson has suggested that rather than devise a regulatory rule for predation in terms of prices – which is difficult to apply and enforce – a better rule would be that a drop in price where there is new entry should not be followed by an increase in output for, say, twelve to eighteen months.[68] And a variant which has been used in telecommunications policy is to allow a price discount in a market which has been entered only if there is evidence to suggest that the net result will be an overall increase in output taking the market as a whole.[69] However, all such expedients suffer because in many circumstances output change and price change are both rational (non-predatory) responses to new entry.

What standards of evidence and proof are reasonable and attainable will be discussed in chapter 8 for all regulation. Meanwhile, a provisional conclusion for predation is that a regulator's overall objective should be to prevent a monopoly incumbent increasing its long-term monopoly profits at the expense of competition. He should do his best to assess whether the new entrant promises long-term economic efficiency. What is most relevant is whether the new entrant promises the possibility of lower-cost or higher-quality production through either the use of new technology or lower organizational inefficiency. As experience in Britain with bus operations and experience in the United States with airline operations indicates, specialist knowledge is needed in order to be able to form a sound opinion on this. The regulator should apply whatever models and tests he believes will help him form a sound judgement on what is a justified and what is an unjustified response by an incumbent. He should analyse the information provided but should not forget that rapid action is usually needed to protect an entrant. And he should have the power to stop allegedly predatory behaviour while he makes an investigation. No one with experience doubts the existence of predatory behaviour, though ultimately its identification may not be capable of proof that would satisfy legal or academic standards. And if there has to be proof, then, as under the 1984 Act discussed in chapter 2, it will be more fruitful if the incumbent has to prove that it is not acting predatorily rather than the burden being on the entrant to prove that it is, because inevitably the incumbent has the superior information. What the regulator eventually needs to use his judgement and discretion to decide is which promises to be the more efficient, the market with the new entrant or the market without it, though he should avoid taking a firm long-term view of the industry which may restrict its development.[70]

Specialist knowledge is thus invaluable in complicated regulatory situations where natural monopolies are able to conceal essential cost information. Indeed, the more information a natural monopoly is required to produce, the less strong the argument for the specialist regulation of predation. Nevertheless, because predation is usually hard to prove this is itself an argument for a specialist regulator, who will know more about the businesses, be able to act more rapidly and may feel more certain in his convictions.[71] Specialist regulators inherited from the past were in fact terminated for domestic airlines in the United States and the bus and coach industries in Britain. But there is a strong case for saying that, though terminating the Civil Aeronautics Board and the regulatory role of the Traffic Commissioners seemed a victory at the time, the absence of specialist regulators made it easier to establish hub monopolies in the domestic airline industry in the United States, to resurrect National Express as a coach monopoly, and for many bus lines throughout Britain to keep newcomers out of the bus industry by markedly predatory practices. Not to bring back into economic regulation the Traffic Commissioners, who were not equipped for it, but rather to provide some equivalent tribunal with instant powers to prevent predation, would be a major move towards more-effective bus and coach competition in Britain.

In conclusion, the power to investigate and remedy the key regulatory offence of predation – normally found among fair-trading or anti-trust offences – is in regulatory terms more important for natural monopoly than for competitive businesses, and indeed the need to deal with the offence is a sufficient reason for the economic regulation of natural monopoly.

5.5 Competition through interconnection

As noted above, some economists have argued as if free entry were all that is needed to stimulate enough competition to avoid regulation. But free entry, though a necessary condition for economic efficiency, is not always a sufficient one. Especially where there is sustainable natural monopoly, there is a need to consider imaginative means of extending competition.

The most important innovation in American telecommunications policy, and in the British privatization of telecommunications, electricity and gas, has been the realization that there is no compelling reason why the monopolist should have an exclusive right to use his distribution network. As we have seen, all comers once had a right of access to the railway system in Britain; but, though the notion of a railway as a public highway open to all was never taken away in law, that right was removed in effect through safety regulation and various management initiatives that made entry impractical through denying the right to coal, water and the use of stations. The Railway Clearing House provided interconnection; but at the expense of competition. As it was developed in the 1930s, the interconnecting electricity grid was open to all generators and distributors; but the actual financing and operation of that grid was uncommercial and bureaucratic, preparing the way for the rigidities of nationalized operation.[72] The gas grid did not exist until the arrival of natural gas in the 1960s and 1970s;[73] and when it did competition was not attempted. In the United States electricity and gas grids are localized and normally privately owned; but any transmission of one utility's electricity or gas over another's network is for ordinary commercial negotiation, as it is for oil pipelines in the UK.[74]

That one firm should be given the right to use the property of another without its consent seems a considerable innovation. In the form in which it was decided by the Federal Communications Commission (FCC), it seemed less radical and no infringement of the Fifth and Fourteenth Amendments to the Constitution, protecting property rights (whose importance for regulation is discussed in chapter 6), because AT&T like other telecommunications companies normally leased private lines to subscribers, and these were lines, and even networks open at the ends, along, or through, which those who leased them could send their own calls and data freely, having paid connection and annual rental charges. It was, moreover, arguable that AT&T's pricing of them was discriminatory in that the implicit price per call was far less on private, that is, leased, lines than through the public network and lower than could be justified by any difference in cost;[75] a subscriber did not have to divert many calls to a private line for it to pay. However, the telephone companies did not allow private-line capacity to be resold to others – and that was a restraint on trade. When in 1969 the FCC allowed MCI, a new carrier, to develop a microwave service connecting a number of cities, AT&T's monopoly over long-line communications was infringed.[76] And other, similar licences were granted. However, the lifting of a restriction on entry was not offset by allowing AT&T to lower its prices to meet the competition, mainly because this would have meant departing from the FCC requirement that it should adopt uniform pricing. In 1974 the new entrants were further allowed to access customers via what were then AT&T's local lines. And in 1976 the FCC allowed the newcomers to share and sell private-line capacity that they had leased from AT&T, though that right was not widely used.[77] Finally, also in 1976, the last step was taken when the courts overruled the FCC and allowed the operation of Execunet, a service by which ordinary subscribers could use their telephones to make calls over AT&T local lines, as well as MCI long lines, at MCI prices.[78]

Interconnection is such an important means of promoting competition where there is natural monopoly that the problems associated with it are worth comment. In the UK, the Energy Act, 1983, apparently broke the nationalized electricity and gas suppliers' monopolies in that it allowed private generators and gas suppliers to use the publicly-owned electricity and gas distribution systems to supply consumers directly with power.[79] However, in the case of electricity supply this was undermined by there being no restriction on the Central Electricity Generating Board's ability to set tariffs in a discriminatory manner so as to keep private generators out. And the same result was reached for gas by predatory British Gas pricing policies which enabled it to undercut its competitors' prices in any market it pleased, even by dropping its prices below marginal cost, and so to build up a discriminatory pattern of pricing which depended as much on differences in customers' competitive positions as pricing did in the later-nineteenth-century railways. For this reason, the apparent freedom given in the Gas Act, 1982, and extended in the Gas Act, 1986, allowing others to use British Gas's pipelines as a common carrier was not effective.[80] The Monopolies and Mergers Commission (MMC) found that British Gas managed in effect to keep a monopoly position in gas by itself using a system of charging related to the marginal cost of carriage through the grid while requiring other carriers to pay average cost. Moreover, British Gas was able to control the outflow from new gas fields because of its dominant power. Unhappily, the Gas Act, 1986, had omitted the relevant large suppliers, that is, effectively, British Gas, from natural-monopoly regulation altogether. Thus, the only powers the regulator could adopt were those under the fair-trading laws. Nevertheless, with the MMC broadly in agreement with the regulator, lengthy attempts were made to replace discriminatory pricing by tariffs which were open to all who met stated characteristics – the main problems being that any such banding creates losers as well as gainers, and that difficulties in cost apportionment, over which there was lengthy debate, made it hard to relate prices to costs. Moreover, the regulator, as we have seen, also imposed a rule that 10 per cent of all new gas should be available to go to suppliers other than British Gas. Time will tell whether competition can be increased without either statutory change or further reference to the MMC; or whether those commentators were right who believed that the gas industry should have been broken up as the electricity industry was.

An altogether more ambitious attempt at interconnection was made in the Telecommunications Act, 1984, which, among other things, tried to bring about more competition for long-distance calls (and car-phones). The basic principle, which would have astonished the Victorians, was that (in both cases) another operator was to have a retrospective right to use the established operator's network – its property – at a price to be determined ultimately by the regulator. Though I believe this was nowhere said, it may have been easier to establish this principle because, at least in the public mind, the property belonged to the nation (though legally it may not have) before privatization. And it would be interesting to speculate on whether the same principle could be introduced or even substantially expanded in the case of a private or privatized company without provoking the counter-argument that this was an infringement of ownership and of profit expectation for which, at the least, compensation should be paid.

The Act fell short of what Beesley had proposed in the report he had made to Sir Keith Joseph when he had argued for unrestricted resale of leased capacity for all value-added services.[81] He recommended (as we saw in chapter 4) that anyone should be allowed to lease a private line at the appropriate tariff rate and resell its capacity to others. British Telecom's response was that this would undermine its tariff structure through which various customers were cross-subsidized by others; overall, its profits would fall and it would have less cash for investment. But it was, of course, in order to get rid of such pockets of monopoly power that Beesley wanted unrestricted resale; he saw it as the most direct means of introducing effective competition given the natural monopoly of the network. Instead, the Government allowed resale of leased circuits of data services, but not for live speech and telex – until 1989, when unrestricted resale was allowed. Moreover, it restricted competition in ordinary telephony to BT and one newcomer, Mercury, which had been given a licence in 1982 to operate its own network but which now was to be allowed access to BT's network so as to be better able to compete against it. The underlying idea was that it would compete where BT made its highest profits – particularly with its long-distance traffic – and so help bring down BT tariffs there to the level of profit obtaining on local calls, which was lower.

When eventually Mercury in 1986 announced its own tariff, it had just that effect in prompting British Telecom to lower its trunk-call tariffs in reply.[82] So far as can be judged from outside, Mercury ought to have been able to make a very satisfactory return because of the large margins between even these prices and those which it paid for the use of the BT system. Crucial therefore in this interconnection, as they are in any such interconnection, were the prices at which an agreement was reached. In 1985, BT and Mercury had spent some months trying to negotiate a particular agreement – one which was favourable to BT by comparison with what was decided later. Somewhat to its surprise, BT failed to conclude that agreement, because Mercury was able by using its licence to bring in the regulator to determine those parts of the deal which were still not agreed – which included prices. BT's first proposal had been that Mercury should pay the same for its use of the BT network to convey its customer's traffic as any other caller less a due proportion where Mercury used its own network. The argument was that otherwise BT would be discriminating in favour of Mercury. Of course, such pricing levels would have left Mercury no margin out of which to meet its own costs and give a discount to attract customers. The 'Determination' of the issue (as it was called) by the regulator, Sir Bryan Carsberg, was based on different principles.[83] Mercury would pay BT the normal charge for a local call, because Mercury at that stage was not expected to compete locally. And it would pay BT International the normal charge for that part of the call that went over BT's own network.[84] But on inland trunk calls Carsberg gave Mercury a much lower tariff than that normally applying, without however explaining the reasons why he set it at the level he did. At that stage his motive for not giving reasons was presumably the familiar one that, the least said by way of justification under English law when justification is not explicitly required, the less such a judgement is open to legal challenge. However, a not unreasonable interpretation of the charges set was that Mercury was being required to pay around the marginal cost for its use of British Telecom's network, perhaps with a small element of profit as well. Economic theory would suggest that taking on more traffic through its network is profitable for BT, as long as it at least covers the marginal cost of carrying such traffic. But marginal cost is never an easy concept to define, and an issue here might have been how it should be measured – whether short or long run.

At that early stage it was hoped that Mercury would be carrying some 5 per cent of total telecommunications traffic within a few years (in fact, it took until 1991 to reach above 5 per cent), and it was intended that, in achieving this share of the market, it should rely largely on BT's investment rather than on its own – Mercury was planning to spend £200 million on its network in total while BT spent up to £3 billion a year. And indeed in principle there was no economic reason why it should have made any network investment of its own. That it was required to do so may be seen as the charging of a price for entry, a test that it had financial strength and was a serious competitor, as well as a device for slowing down the effectiveness of its competition. Moreover, in public relations, though not in economic, terms it may have needed to make such an investment in order to show that it was making a real contribution to the development of a national telecommunications network.

As long as Mercury remains a small carrier, the short-run cost to British Telecom of carrying its traffic is not likely to diverge greatly from long-run marginal cost, in the sense that on average BT's capital expenditure needs are not likely to be greatly affected by the addition of marginal Mercury traffic, except at and around the points of interconnection themselves; and in fact its Licence and Determination provide that where – as, for example, at such interconnection points – BT has to incur extra expenditure which can be attributed to Mercury, that must be paid for by Mercury.[85] However, while this is not unreasonable while Mercury remains small, an increase in the volume of interconnection traffic from Mercury, or from Racal car-phone traffic or – as is likely from 1991 – from subsequent new operators could reach such a level that it could have significant effects on the capacity of the network required. To a limited extent that problem was met by a requirement in the Determination that Mercury, and presumably other operators, forecast their requirements three years ahead.[86] However, there is nothing which requires this to be more than indicative. Provided that Mercury gives six months' notice, BT is obliged to supply whatever interconnection capacity Mercury asks for, wherever required. It is arguable that, if Mercury and others were to abstract, say, half or more of the market from BT, it would be unfair for BT both to continue to compete in using the network and to provide it – just as it would not be possible to safeguard fair competition if National Power also owned and operated the national electricity grid. As has been shown with MCI and other long-distance operators in the United States, there are many ways in which an AT&T or a BT can adopt anti-competitive devices to impede an MCI, Sprint or Mercury. One AT&T device was to give its US competitors long and unmemorable telephone numbers – a tactic which the BT Licence may prevent in Britain;[87] others were to delay interconnection, to provide inadequate connection or not to provide an equally high quality of line. Any of these problems may be accidental or the responsibility of engineers down the ling juggling priorities as they make connections and maintain their systems, but any situation in which a competitor has access to an operator's network will give rise to such complaints and requires extreme vigilance from the regulator in case they stem from the employment of an anti-competitive policy.

There were in fact many disputes between Mercury and British Telecom both over the terms of interconnection and over delays in effecting it.[88] Part of the problem lay in the difficulties, referred to above, of establishing fair charges for the use of the BT network.[89] For the basic economics of interconnection, in this as in many other cases, have not received sufficient attention. It will be found that they vary with the nature of the system involved. The costs are different where, as on the railways, traffic in general goes by one route from a given origin to a given destination from what they are where, as in telecommunications, it moves from a given origin to a given destination but may change its route depending on congestion in the network; and they are different again where, as in gas and electricity, there need be no identity between input into the network and the actual output any given customer consumes. Moreover, there can be queues and congestion on the railways, which are a form of short-term storage, and gas can be stored, but there are severe limits to the extent to which electricity can be stored. And there are also conceptual difficulties in deciding what cost-reflecting pricing policies provide equal access to all users.

The regulatory problems presented by interconnection become greater as the numbers interconnected increase and as the proportion of traffic carried by additional users rises. Nearer the other end of this spectrum from British Telecom and British Gas is the new (post-1989) British electricity supply industry. The 1989 Act provided, as we have seen, for the division of the old Central Electricity Generating Board into two generating companies and a grid-owning and -operating company,[90] the National Grid Company, which was to be a subsidiary of the twelve area boards, which would themselves continue as local distribution and sales monopolies (though privatized) except in so far as generators were to have the right to make direct sales to larger customers. The grid now carries the power supplied by the two new generating companies, further supplies from area boards (who are free within limits to generate their own electricity) and from independent generators, as well as supplies imported from Scotland and France. Unlike British Telecom and British Gas, the National Grid Company is not a producer, apart from a small amount of pumped storage. Instead of the interconnection agreements each being between one producer who happens also to own the grid or network and another who does not, there must be agreements between every producer, the grid and every area board or other direct customer. And in relation to each of these there have to be legally binding arrangements to ensure that there is sufficient grid capacity available. These cover the terms and conditions upon which interconnection is provided between every generator and the grid; and between the grid and every distributor or direct customer.

Joskow and Schmalensee have analysed the difficulties that have arisen in the United States from similar arrangements.[91] The reasons why independent generators there want to be connected to each other are the same as those that underlay the construction of the British electricity grid in the 1920s and 1930s. Demand fluctuates and grows at different rates in different parts of the country – an interconnected system would enable supply to match it better. Any breakdown or any other reason for the non-performance of one generating set may be more fully offset in such a system by supplies from elsewhere. Some sets are most efficient if used all the time for base load; others are better used for peak load: in general, as power-stations age and newer models come on stream, the older sets can be shifted from regular base use to irregular peak use and this can be better achieved the larger the system of connection. Where a connected system uses a diversity of fuels, there will also be a different pattern of use if the relativity of fuel prices changes: interconnection can be seen as providing some insurance against such changes, since power-stations are able to switch more easily from base load to peak load, and vice versa, the larger the interconnected system.

Thus an interconnected system can be operated with greater technical efficiency and requires smaller capacity to meet a given demand than a series of separate local systems. In general, the larger the system the more efficient it ought to be in these terms. The cost of producing and supplying electricity should therefore be lower. However, in order to use any interconnected system efficiently in the face of demand conditions which might alter as often as every half hour, not only do those who operate the grid need to ensure the provision of sufficient capacity to carry the power from any given generating set whenever that may be called, but rules have to be drawn up to govern which generating sets are introduced or withdrawn from use as demand changes, as well as how any changes in their characteristics or availability should alter their priority. Such a 'merit order' was at the heart of the British electricity supply system under nationalization, where it was possible to introduce it as part of a command system.[92]

Joskow and Schmalensee have shown how much more difficult this has been in the United States, with separate ownership, both private and public. Because interconnected generating systems there have had to rely on contractual relationships rather than a command system, their pooling agreements have been on a much smaller scale and more limited in their extent.[93] Moreover, these agreements have been constant sources of friction. A reason for this is that who generates electricity when, and how much the generator generates then, is a main determinant of individual power-firms' profits. Thus, the merit order needs to be totally predictable in its selection procedures and fair. And fairness means that the detail of the generators' costs must be reflected in the merit order. For example, if one were to assume that the marginal cost of bringing a coal-fired power-station into operation was in every case the same, one would get one result; but in reality such stations could be the same in every respect except that one is cheaper than another if it can be brought into operation slowly, while the other's marginal cost is lower if sudden generation is needed from it. In principle, the problem can be solved by ever more accurate description of the dynamic parameters of the operation of each power-station; but there will be a constant tension between the cost, complexity and controversial nature of the software required and the requirements of fairness.

Moreover, the detail of the generators' costs must be reflected also in a financial settlement system which is sufficiently reliable and transparent for all parties to agree that they have been fairly treated – though, as operating costs vary according to how sets are used and with the speed and warning with which they are brought into or taken out of service, as well as with other changes in their costs, such agreements have been hard to negotiate and harder still to sustain. The reason such a system is needed is that the profitability of a generating set will be affected by what other parties do. Thus, if for any reason there is congestion on some part of the grid so that supply has to be switched from one generator to another, the finances of both will be affected. To take an extreme example, a moratorium on the use of one kind of power-station – nuclear, say – while a possible fault is being investigated will alter the pattern of use of all other stations, as well as put limits on the capacity of the grid, and this will require treatment within the financial settlement system.

This flexibility in use is, however, combined with very long lives over which the capital costs of the plants must be recovered. As there are major risks of technological and economic obsolescence, how these risks are borne becomes an important financial issue in an integrated system of separate companies. Because they represent a very substantial sunk cost in a highly capital-intensive industry one cannot expect power-stations to be built commercially without contracts safeguarding profitability over a substantial number of years.

Thus the contractual relationships that need to be established to make privatized electricity firms work together are more complicated than were needed within a nationalized system, where what ultimately mattered was the financial viability of the whole. The contractual arrangements reached must cover what happens to the merit order and to the financial return to each generator when there are changes in the level of demand and the time or geographical distribution of demand; changes in the capacity of the transmission system and of particular links in it; changes in relative fuel costs, and absolute and relative operating costs; changes, short and long term, in the availability and capacity of particular generating sets; and disruptions in demand and supply during various kinds of short and more-lasting emergencies. Information must be provided of sufficient quality and independence for it to be accepted as reliable by all parties. It must be sufficiently detailed to be an adequate basis for invoices between parties and for establishing the extent of liability where there has been failure in performance. Contracts must determine whose is the liability upon various contingencies and how it is to be estimated.[94] One result is that in general the risks become more unmanageable the more the system is broken up between competing generators. In the absence of prolonged experience it is impossible to know what the optimum number of competing power companies would be, but theoretically it could be a small number.[95]

Unsurprisingly, American experience has thus shown how very difficult it is to build up and maintain pooling arrangements. Pools break down frequently or become collusive; contracts are often renegotiated;[96] arrangements far simpler than those proposed are the more likely to last. The situation is an excellent example of that analysed in section 1 of this chapter. There, Oliver Williamson was cited as pointing out the critical difference in terms of efficiency between a command structure and contractual relations. If the factors involved are particularly complicated, contractual relations may not be able to cope. What has been done in the British electricity supply industry must be near the limits of what is contractually negotiable, but four factors make its success more likely than that of the interconnection attempts in the United States. First, the American situation is complicated by the existence of both state and federal regulators: pools are usually confined within states so as to avoid federal regulation, and because pools are smaller risks are less easily spread. Secondly, the new British situation has the advantage of long experience of the successful operation of a sophisticated merit order, although not on a commercial basis and with a considerable amount of rough justice. Thirdly, the agreements in Britain come under regulatory scrutiny, and indeed are not likely to come into existence without their most critical terms being decided either by government or by the regulator. Fourthly, in Britain there has long been a separation between generating company (CEGB) and area boards.

From this description of the difficulties which, it is believed, have been surmounted in electricity interconnection in Britain can be deduced the problems that the Victorians would have faced if they had created a genuine railway market rather than the Railway Clearing House; or, though with the indispensable benefit of computers, would have to be faced today in the creation of such a market. Most heavily-used railway systems have interlocking train-paths which are harder to alter than the timetable in a large school and for the same reasons. Even changing the speed of a train may have ramifications throughout the timetable. Railway general managers have lost their positions for trying to change their commuter timetables in order to release more capacity and having failed to foresee some complications which defeated their endeavour. Every train-path – that is every slot in the timetable – would in a true market have to be auctioned to the operating company making the highest bid. But because of the interdependence of the time-table it would be impossible to conduct a first auction. Re-auctioning could only be a rare event, and this would pose difficult financial forecasting problems for bidders. (Where services are deliberately loss-making, bids would be negative: the bidders would have to be paid to operate.) Further complications would arise if all or some of the operating companies owned their own parts of the route-system (as British Telecom operates and also owns the BT network) – but regulation would be essential to prevent a single separate owner of the track having too much monopoly power.

Moreover, an associated financial settlement system would also have to be created. Every day trains are late, and a late train often requires a consequential decision: Shall following trains be delayed? Whose train? Who then should compensate whom for lost traffic? If compensation is paid for loss of traffic, should it also be paid to passengers or freight transporters for delays? Such problems may be soluble –

perhaps not logically in every respect but with goodwill – but they should not be regarded too lightly.

What is most relevant to this chapter in all these examples of attempts at interconnection is that competition through interconnection is not an alternative to regulation – one presupposes the other. In Britain, in telecommunications, gas and electricity, the parties were unable to come to a freely negotiated agreement, because one party had dominant power. If the network arrangements had been left to the free workings of the market, those dominant parties would have abused that power in their self-interest. Thus, how the relevant transmission prices are to be established and maintained – whether on the basis of long-run marginal cost or on some other basis – as well as how those charges are to be passed on to customers, will need to be externally agreed and monitored. And the terms on which a grid or network transmits, the quality of that transmission and the provision of sufficient capacity will all require regulatory intervention. Whether the grid or network is separate or part of one supplier, it too will need regulation as a natural monopoly. It must not be allowed to give into a natural temptation to economize on capacity in order to increase its profits.

If one conclusion is thus that interconnection requires a regulator, and the more complicated the interconnection and the larger the number of units interconnected, the more difficult is the regulatory task, another is that this reinforces the earlier conclusion that arguments for and against break-up ought to be judged empirically. While it is understood that there may be technical economies and diseconomies of scale affecting the case for break-up, what is much more likely to be important in making the best decision in such a case are the relative organizational and management costs at the interfaces associated with a command structure on the one hand and contractual relations on the other. In any given instance such costs need careful examination before a decision is taken for or against break-up. It would be over-dogmatic to believe in a particular case without such an examination that competition through regulated interconnection is likely to be more efficient than an internalized command solution through vertical integration. However, the very activity of attempting to achieve a contractual solution will result in a greater understanding of the factors that should affect commercial relations between the parties than that which will have shaped the command solution it sets out to replace. Potentially, the passing of money between separate entities should give operators greater incentives to efficiency. But if it proves impossible to model all the factors which are financially significant, so that rewards are thought to be unfair and some parties even find themselves worse off than before, the instability caused may result in a worse outcome than that achieved either by more-independent operations, as in the United States, or within a nationalized industry, as in Britain. Various remedies for this may be attempted. The regulator may, for example, impose more-workable and more-acceptable arrangements in place of freely negotiated contracts. However, if he has to intervene at all frequently, there is a real sense in which he may end up managing the industry – in effect replacing the old command structure, at least in part, by a new one. It is also possible that the nature of the risks which can be pooled by integrated operations will result in a pattern of cooperative working between the separate entities which in reality is no different from vertical integration – where, that is, there is little real competition, except possibly in the comparatively rare event of the construction of, say, a new major power-station. And it is not impossible that the end product of this risk pooling will be as integrated as many Japanese component and service suppliers are with the large conglomerates which dominate them, or as much as some large retailers in Britain are with their suppliers. Where such integration is a major way of ensuring against risks because a larger entity is better able to pool those risks, formal break-up may have less real effect than might be at first imagined. Moreover, it may not be easy to maintain that such formal or informal vertical integration is a less efficient outcome than one which allows for more competition in use.

While, as we have seen, the policing of predatory behaviour is needed in an interconnected system, there is another economic regulatory offence which, it has been argued, is practically even more important: *inefficient interconnection* or *unfair access*. It arises because of the superior knowledge and bargaining power of one party to the interconnected system – and especially needs to be watched for where, as with telecommunications and gas, the network provider is also a user of it competing with others. Where a natural monopoly like an area electricity board has a contractual relationship with an enterprise with less monopoly power like a generating board, it is unlikely that the negotiations pursued through ordinary commercial relations will have resulted in a contract that provides a level playing-field. The specialist knowledge needed to understand such contracts is likely to be sufficiently important to justify specialist regulation. A regulator may here add to efficiency, not simply redistribute income between the parties, because an efficient contract resulting in effective competition will add to overall economic efficiency.[97]

The main requirement of equal access is that there should always be enough network or grid capacity to meet all demands without congestion. This may present problems. As we have seen, British Telecom has the duty to provide whatever capacity Mercury needs, wherever it needs it, six months after it is requested by Mercury. In order to be in a position to fulfil this duty, British Telecom has to cushion itself with a margin of spare capacity. But as the number of those wanting to interconnect rises – as with the electricity grid and as will happen as the number of competitors using the British Telecom network increases – so will the problem increase of forecasting the capacity needed to avoid congestion. In some cases, moreover, it is beyond the power of the network provider to ensure sufficient network capacity, especially at nodes. For instance, the need to get planning permission, and strong local resistance to airport expansion, especially to new runways, together imply that such congestion will be an increasing feature of airports. In order to achieve economic efficiency in this case, a system of pricing will be needed (which is not clearly provided for in statute or licence) to allocate to airlines airport time-slots in such a way that the airports do not make excess profits. And the railways would have the same problem if more than one operator could use the railway network, for there are often severe planning constraints on the local expansions of its capacity, coupled with difficulties in funding. But even where there are no such constraints on network expansion, provision needs to be made to avoid local capacity constraints affecting network users. For example, while the electricity grid has ample spare capacity, there are circumstances and configurations of use which cause local bottlenecks. Economic efficiency requires that investment planning be used to avoid this in so far as it is efficient to do so. But also, in order to achieve fairness here, the rules of the electricity grid provide that generators should be paid as if there were no such constraints, while supplementary arrangements ensure that no generator is worse off because of the mix of generators actually called.

Economic efficiency also needs to govern the prices users are charged, so that the network is most efficiently used. However, given the joint costs involved in the network, and the complicated and varied routings possible, especially in networks like the gas and electricity grids where inputs are not matched by specific outputs, the basis of cost-based pricing is not always easy to ascertain. The presumption is that, since such a network is a natural monopoly, long-run marginal costs should be covered, including whatever profit rate is needed to maintain and develop the network; but the long-run marginal cost involved in the use of the network by any particular new generator, source of gas or telecommunications operator may be difficult to establish. Estimating the long-run marginal cost of a network dedicated to one user is comparatively easy; but the precise geography of expansion needed by, say, a telecommunications operator whose precise calling pattern is not easy to predict is another matter. Moreover, even the principle of long-run marginal costs is not appropriate where there is congestion or excess capacity. And it may also sometimes make sense to discriminate. For example, a number of large users of electricity may benefit by combining to provide a dedicated spur to the electricity grid, but their willingness to pay may vary, so that, unless discrimination between them is allowed, the spur may not be provided.

5.6 Break-up and yardstick competition

As we saw above, even if it is true that all monopolies can be broken up,[98] break-up will not necessarily create much additional direct competition. But there may be a case for breaking up a national or regional monopoly into smaller, local monopolies even if the only competition then possible is for customers not far from the new boundaries. An extreme case of this kind was the trust-busting of Standard Oil of New Jersey, where the pieces into which it was split did begin to compete in each other's markets. Again, in peripheral services, the regional Bell Operating Companies can compete with each other (though not in telephony). And in Britain the break-up of the National Bus Company may have the same outcome, since a well-run operation can not only invade its neighbours' territories but operate further away (though local knowledge may be specific to a local bus company and does confer some comparative advantage).[99] It has, moreover, been argued (again, as we have seen) that even when there is no additional direct competition break-up may still be beneficial. Smaller natural monopolies will have less ability to cross-subsidize than larger ones; thus, break-up may increase the possibility of competition by making predation less possible. Furthermore, there will be more innovation and greater diversity of operation if there are several operators than if there is one. All such arguments pose the question how far any additional costs from breaking up a monopoly offset the advantages of doing so. And the same is true of a different argument for break-up without the prospect of much additional direct competition, that it is justified in so far as it makes inter-firm comparison possible – for a regulator is helped by being able to compare performance.

It has been suggested by Stephen Littlechild that it may be possible to build this 'yardstick' into the price formula by requiring that the costs which a firm is able to recover are based not on its own costs but on those of an average or above-average firm.[100] Now, if all units resulting from break-up were similar, no doubt the comparisons would greatly help the regulator, especially in revisions of the price formula. But the more different these bodies are, the harder the comparisons. British Telecom districts, water authority areas, electricity board areas, railway regions – within each of these groupings the areas vary greatly in size, in their demographic and geographical character, in their populations' consumption per head, income levels and growth rates, in historical investment patterns, in industrial mix, and even in temperature and climate, and do so in ways which can lead to considerable differences in unit costs and other measures of efficiency.[101] To devise comparative-performance indicators by which to judge the relative efficiency of such undertakings is always difficult. It is indeed common for many business operations – perhaps particularly, though not exclusively, public bodies – not even to have developed such indicators as can be used to track their own performance over time. Moreover, the management accounts of such undertakings may not be sufficiently detailed, or appropriate enough, to yield the necessary information, and where current cost accounts which have been properly and carefully constructed exist, deciding the appropriate measures of capital use will still be difficult. And even if each enterprise to be compared produced meaningful statistics for its own use, differences in definition and in conventions of measurement and of apportionment (particularly in so far as there are differences in the range and mix of products), as well as variations in the sources of inputs which are produced internally, would make such comparisons frail, even though all agreed to make such comparisons and to exchange information for their common benefit. Where the consumer of such information is a sponsoring government department or a regulator, the parties to be compared have no interest in producing consistent, compatible and intelligible information – rather the reverse.

Comparative studies using econometric techniques are a useful exercise. They can often come up with illuminating insights on comparative performance between firms, and for individual firms over time (though the results are normally qualified because of doubts over the quality of the data). However, one must remember that such studies have a limited purpose so far as the firms are concerned. Besides being of possible interest to the firms themselves, they may on occasion be used as evidence against them at public inquiries; but they are not normally used as part of the formal machinery for their control.

The UK Audit Commission, meanwhile, has inherited and developed a tradition of using such studies for comparing the performance of local authorities; and to that end there has been a long tradition of requiring local authorities to provide statistics and accounts according to certain appropriate conventions. What has tended to make the Audit Commission successful, though the interpretation of its studies is still often disputed, is that it is not a regulator – it instead works through publicity. It has no executive or quasi-judicial power, except in comparatively rare cases; but it is able to collect its own data on its own terms as part of the audit process.[102]

This is a different position from that of a regulator seeking to rely on such comparative studies for determining enforceable price formulae, permissible rates of return and whether or not costs could be lower. He is likely to find himself confused and frequently obstructed in the use of such comparisons; and if he ties himself too closely to figures whose interpretation is disputed he opens himself up to challenge – thus he needs to use his discretion. And, while in theory it would be possible to establish forms of accounts – that is audited statements based upon appropriate conventions – which would make comparisons possible within statistical limits, such an endeavour is far beyond anything yet attempted in regulatory accounting in Britain.[103] A sensible regulator will make the best comparisons he can between firms, and for individual firms over time, to help him reach a decision, but he would be unwise to rely on them in detail, particularly in public. It is just the kind of matter which, even in Britain, might tempt a judicial challenge, though if it ever got to the courts it would lead to the most difficult and extensive discussions requiring judgements disliked by judges.

In the end, then, where there are good economic reasons for break-up – as in buses and electricity – the inter-firm comparisons it makes possible may be helpful to the regulator, even if they will not be decisive; but, where substantial economies of scale will be destroyed by break-up, the fact that it will enable one to make inter-firm comparisons will not be a strong reason for it. Moreover, break-up will only provide a restricted field for comparison. An alternative (or additional) strategy would be for regulators worldwide to pool their information and analysis. If they did this systematically, they could be of the greatest help to each other.

Extending competition meaningfully is not always possible. Neither has it always been extended as far as it could have been. In the circumstances discussed in this chapter, competition will not be a substitute for regulation; regulation is needed to make competition effective. And even when competition is taken to the limits of what is efficient, and both predation and unfair access are effectively dealt with, there may still be substantial natural-monopoly profits.

Notes

1 Moore (1986a), p. 92.
2 Kay and Vickers (1988), p. 287; Kay and Thompson (1987), p. 193. Also Veljanovski (1990), pp. 38–40; Heald (1983), p. 8. See also Bishop and Kay (1988), who stress the need for extending competition and argue for combining it with public enterprise reform.
3 Vickers and Yarrow (1988), p. 47.
4 Breyer (1982), pp. 158–61, points out that anti-trust controls and natural-monopoly regulation are distinct traditions in the United States. There is even a well-established tradition by which the two are taught separately in law schools. No such hard and fast distinction is yet made in Britain, partly because neither is comprehensively taught there. The distinction may also be related to a difference in theory between the Austrian school, which stresses competition, and the neo-classical school, which stresses market failure and therefore regulation. The use of the word 'regulation' in this book is not confined to natural-monopoly regulation but generically covers anti-trust laws, or fair-trading laws as they are called in Britain. However, this chapter deals with fair-trading offences as they might apply to natural monopolies, while chapter 6 treats of natural-monopoly regulatory offences as such. For a shrewd view of differences between American and European uses of the word 'regulation' and attitudes towards it, see Majone (1990), pp. 1–4. Graham

and Prosser (1991), p. 32, show that, because natural monopolies were not privatized in France, regulation there was not important.

5 Hannah (1983), p. 92.
6 Neither is it sensible to discourage the Monopolies and Mergers Commission from investigating local monopoly by a legal requirement that the area affected must be a significant part of the United Kingdom – a policy which, it will be seen, has had serious consequences for bus competition.
7 Smith (1802), bk. 1, chapters 1–3, cited in Williamson (1983), p. 50: 'each of these activities could be performed by an independent specialist.'
8 Williamson (1983), p. 42.
9 Simon (1957), p. 198; Williamson (1983), pp. 23, 32.
10 Williamson (1983), pp. 29, 35, 36; on integration, see pp. 82–105.
11 Ibid., p. 14.
12 Ibid., p. 26. Williamson distinguishes opportunism from stewardship, where someone acts conscientiously for another person, and from agency, where someone does what he is told.
13 Ibid., pp. 27–9.
14 Ibid., p. 29.
15 Ibid., p. 107.
16 Ibid., pp. 77, 129; see also Waterson (1988), p. 52.
17 Williamson (1983), p. 102.
18 Ibid., p. 104.
19 Ibid., p. 101.
20 Ibid., pp. 67–70.
21 Ibid., p. 25. A regulator can destroy economies of scope by insisting on segmentation. Berg and Tschirhart (1988), p. 434.
22 Although neither phrase is perfect, they both refer to the failure of organizations that are imperfectly subject to competition to develop the incentives necessary to achieve the maximum possible efficiency. There is an interesting discussion of the relationship between organizational changes and privatization in Dunsire (1991).
23 Harvey-Jones (1988), p. 50. I have drawn deeply in this section on what he has said on the problems of bureaucracy in a private company: ibid., pp. 48–59. See similar criticisms of introverted companies in Kanter (1984): 'True freedom is not the absence of structure – letting the employees go off and do whatever they want – but rather a clear structure which enables people to work within established boundaries in an autonomous and creative way' (p. 248).
24 Bishop and Kay (1988), pp. 37–46. A second Sir Robert Reid, who came from Shell, succeeded the first as chairman of the British Railways Board.
25 Foreign ownership can be an economic disadvantage – that is, Gross Domestic Product (GDP) may be less – even though the goods and services are provided at lower cost, if the effect on the balance of payments is adverse. Even if the goods are produced in the country of consumption, more components may be imported. And even if no less value is added domestically, a higher proportion of foreign management or of research and development undertaken in the country of ownership may directly, or indirectly through spillovers, have an adverse effect on GDP. Whether the failure of any given British firm reduces GDP is in principle an empirical question, though the effect is hard to measure. One can always hope that the stimulus given by privatization will so transform an enterprise that it could do at least as well as under foreign ownership.
26 Kay (1987), p. 26; also Bishop and Kay (1988), pp. 37–46.
27 For the story of how the Department of Justice gave up its anti-trust suit against IBM, see Coll (1986), p. 316; Thurow (1980), pp. 148–50.

28 Graham and Prosser (1988), p. 74. argue that allowing British Aerospace to acquire the Royal Ordnance Factories, and so create the largest defence company outside the USA, caused a reduction in competition. Not so, since international competition is intense.

29 Cf. Chandler (1977).

30 I have found Stephen Breyer's classification of justifications for regulation a useful reference point: Breyer (1982), ch. 1; also Waterson (1988), pp. 2–6, and Utton (1986), ch. 1.

31 Faulhaber (1987).

32 Oftel (1985a), p. 11. Later, Oftel was similarly concerned that BT was cross-subsidizing its apparatus supply service, Centrex, and value-added services: Oftel (1987a), pp. 2–4.

33 See Oftel (1986a), pp. 37–8; (1987a), p. 14. As a fair-trading case, the Office of Fair Trading (OFT) took the Mitel case before the MMC, advised by Oftel. OFT and Oftel were given the task of negotiating a satisfactory implementation of the MMC recommendations with BT.

34 DTI (1990), pp. 28, 29.

35 As interesting a decision was that of the MMC, advised by the Office of Water Services (Ofwat), when three small water companies wanted to merge, that this should occur only if it could be shown that there would be a reduction in unit costs which would be passed on to customers. There are specific provisions in the Water Act, 1989, for mergers or acquisitions among water authorities to proceed only if there are demonstrable benefits to the customer. It is unique among the natural-monopoly statutes in that it specifically refers to mergers (s. 29, 30). This hostility to horizontal cartel-like arrangements which raise prices and reduce quantity is characteristic of Chicago thinking: see Eisner (1991), p. 106.

36 Coll (1986), p. 192.

37 MMC (1988), p. 96.

38 See Baumol, Panzar and Willig (1982). Some 2,000 licences were issued before 5 August 1984 by the Post Office or BT: Oftel (1986a), p. 41. Later, the Government was explicit in saying that in general there need be no restriction on the number of licences execept where there is an absolute shortage, as, for example, with radio frequencies: DTI (1990), p. 26.

39 Vickers and Yarrow (1985) p. 46; Oftel explained the case for duopoly in Oftel (1985a), p. 8, but the end of the duopoly was signalled in DTI (1990), p. 4.

40 On this, see Carsberg in Oftel (1985a), p. 8. Alfred Kahn, on the other hand, refused to admit only one new entrant at Midway Airport when requested on similar grounds to do so. He defended his reasons for his refusal in Kahn (1979), pp. 7–9. Williamson (1987), p. 237, suggests that twelve to eighteen months should be long enough for a new entrant to establish itself.

41 Some of the privatization statutes, notably those for telecommunications and electricity, gave powers to ministers to increase competition later, while all gave the regulator a duty to promote competition – whose meaning it was up to the regulator to interpret.

42 Kahn (1988a), pp. 173–8/II.

43 On the importance of information, see Sappington and Stiglitz (1987).

44 For a not unsympathetic account of wasteful competition which reaches similar conclusions to mine, see Kahn (1988a), pp. 220–33, 246–50/II. There is also a concern in these cases where entry and exit is easy about unstable and volatile markets. If such instability or volatility persists, the market's solution is that new entrants will only be tempted in if they expect high short-run profits; while those already in will work to construct any monopoly protection they can. If they cannot secure legal protection – as they did in the 1930s, because of the power of vested interests and the absence of any strong pro-competitive tradition – they will try to differentiate what they do to the same end.

45 See Berg and Tschirhart (1988), pp. 238–51, for a discussion of strong and weak monopoly; also Waterson (1988), ch. 2.
46 Berg and Tschirhart, (1988), pp. 251–4. Mankiw and Whinston (1986) discuss the case where natural monopoly is optimal but there is more than one firm in equilibrium.
47 Williamson (1983), ch. 2.
48 Kahn (1988a), p. 224/II; Breyer (1982), pp. 29–32.
49 Berg and Tschirhart (1988), pp. 26–9, 252–4. Subsidy affects the feasibility and perceived fairness of competition: see chapter 9 below.
50 Political and technological considerations resulted in similar cross-subsidization in the USA: Faulhaber (1987), pp. 15–18.
51 Kahn (1988a), pp. 64, 65, 165/I; Berg and Tschirhart (1988), p. 460; also Hazlett (1985).
52 Kahn (1988a), p. 149/II. British Gas was strongly criticized for non-price predatory practices. For example, in using its faster planning powers to give notice that it intended to build new pipelines 'possibly pre-empting bridging and other crossing points': OFT (1991), p. 18.
    A strong case against recognizing natural-monopoly predation as a regulatory offence is made in Faulhaber (1987), pp. 115–25. His three main arguments are: (a) Though subsequent entries will be discouraged by predation, they will not be prevented by it (Kreps and Wilson (1982); Milgrom and Roberts (1982). However, this assumes that the conditions of entry remain relevantly similar for successive entrants. (b) Where there is high rate of technological innovation and many potential competitors, some of them large, (a) is particularly true. This could be a reason for believing that predation will be less successful in, for example, some branches of telecommunications than in, say, bus operations. (c) Since there are many ways in which a regulated industry can persuade a regulator to allow it higher profits, the need to do so to fund predation is not material. If a regulated firm believes it can always make marginal adjustments to secure a predetermined profit level, it will be unbothered by the cost of predation, particularly if the need is confined to one market or area out of many in which it operates. Faulhaber also argues that the regulation of predation can be so distorting as to be worse than predation itself.
53 McGee (1958), p. 137; Breyer (1982), p. 32; Scherer (1980), pp. 335, 340.
54 McGee (1958).
55 Utton (1986), pp. 37–75. On unnatural monopoly, predation and the effect of regulation, see Berg and Tschirhart (1988), p. 245. While in general the Chicago school has not believed in the possibility of predation, it is, as an abuse of dominant or joint-dominant power, consistent with their position.
56 Competition makes it far more important to get cost causation right: A. E. Kahn quoted by Breyer (1982), p. 300. Proving that an industry is a natural monopoly where it has many products is difficult: Waterson (1988), pp. 19–26.
57 For the argument that predatory pricing may aim to deter future entrants, see Yamey (1972).
58 On the illegality of mergers as a fact refuting McGee's argument that predatory pricing is irrational, see Posner (1976), p. 185, n. 3.
59 Williamson (1987), pp. 225–81, discusses firms' lowering and raising prices predatorily.
60 In the United States, the Sherman Act proscribed predatory pricing in so far as it made all combinations in restraint of trade: Williamson (1987), pp. 231, 232. Areeda and Turner (1975) and Posner (1976) define it by whether it excludes a more efficient firm than the dominant one.
61 A 1910 amendment to the US Interstate Commerce Act, 1887, provided for the investigation of companies which raised rates again after they had lowered them, to discover whether the original lowering was anti-competitive: Kahn (1988a), p. 165/I.

62 Areeda and Turner (1975).
63 Posner (1976); Kahn (1988a), p. 176/I, argued for long-run rather than short-run marginal cost as the criterion here except briefly where there is excess capacity. Practical concerns inspired theoretical discussions in which AT&T and the regional telephone companies backed either historic or current cost accounting, long-run marginal cost: Faulhaber (1987), p. 75.
64 Williamson (1987), p. 246. Although British Telecom and British Rail produce the greatest variety of such joint products, all the traditional natural monopolies yield examples.
65 See, for example, the discussion in Williamson (1987), pp. 225–81; Kahn (1988a), p. 176/I. For situations in which economic efficiency requires prices below marginal cost, see Kahn (1988a), pp. 190–2/I. On the danger of arbitrary restrictions on price competition to discourage predation, see Kahn (1988a), pp. 246–50/II.
66 Williamson (1987), p. 226, argues against Areeda and Turner (1975).
67 For the view that regulators should establish 'all relevant' information, see Kahn (1988a), pp. 176, 177/I.
68 Williamson (1978), pp. 236–40.
69 The origin of this lay in the discount tariffs AT&T was allowed by the Federal Communications Commission (FCC) in 1959: Faulhaber (1987), pp. 24, 25. See also the controversy over WATS (a charging plan) in ibid., pp. 69–71.
70 For a useful discussion of the difficulties of proving predation, see Martin (1989), pp. 407–43.
71 Breyer (1982), pp. 158, 161. A larger part of the activity of Oftel against British Telecom has focused on alleged predation than on anything else except individual complaints.
72 It is significant for the course of US deregulation in the late 1970s and 1980s that, in trucking and airlines, the various road networks and airports were separately owned.
73 Estrada et al. (1988), pp. 145, 146.
74 Joskow and Schmalensee (1983).
75 Faulhaber (1987), pp. 24, 25. The attempt to establish costs and rates of return on businesses that shared joint costs was an endless, and almost hopeless, exercise; AT&T argued that many different cost apportionments were equally arbitrary: Kahn (1988a), p. 132/II.
76 Tunstall (1986), pp. 96–9; Kahn (1988a), p. 317/II.
77 Breyer (1982), pp. 308–11.
78 Coll (1986), pp. 83–91; Tunstall (1986), pp. 96–9; Faulhaber (1987), pp. 68–9.
79 Vickers and Yarrow (1988); Vickers and Yarrow (1986), pp. 201–6; Hammond, Helm and Thompson (1986), p. 242.
80 MMC (1988), pp. 64–6; Ofgas (1988), pp. 8–21; Ofgas (1989), pp. 27–8. Ofgas was at a disadvantage because the minister under the fair-trading laws imposes the recommendations on British Gas. Though he could have allowed the regulator to do this, he used these powers to require Ofgas to negotiate a voluntary solution with British Gas: Ofgas (1990), pp. 2–4, 13–16. For the view that British Gas should have been broken up, see Sykes (1985). However, Ofgas believed that separating out the area boards may have weakened them against the network: Ofgas (1988), p. 2. MMC (1988), p. 111, recognized that there was a strong case for separating out the network. On the steps by which regulators and the courts allowed the interconnection of US gas pipelines, see Kahn (1988a), pp. 152–71/II.
81 Beesley (1981).
82 Oftel (1987a), p. 9.
83 Oftel, *Determination of Terms and Conditions for the Purposes of an Agreement on the Interconnection of the British Telecommunications Telephone System and the Mercury*

Communications Ltd System under Condition 13 of the Licence granted to British Telecommunications under Section 7 of the Telecommunications Act, 1984, 1985, Oftel. (Carsberg's description of the terms and conditions of the Determination was also opaque: Oftel (1986a), pp. 15–16.)

84   At that stage Carsberg was more concerned that otherwise the anti-competitive practices of some overseas governments might lead to their grabbing a larger share of a smaller total charge. See chapter 6 below, n. 80.

85   Oftel, *Determination*, s. 3 and 4.

86   Ibid., s. 2.8.

87   The BT Licence, condn. 34, gives the regulator power to approve BT's telephone numbering schemes and therefore presumably to disapprove any part of them which seems to him anti-competitive.

88   For complaints from Mercury over interconnection, see Oftel (1989a), pp. 5, 6, 19. Progress on this was reported in Oftel (1990), p. 4, and again in Oftel (1991), pp. 12, 13. In 1991, interconnection charges were raised to cover BT's social obligations, which raised further difficulties in deciding what was an appropriate charge. See also Faulhaber (1987), p. 74.

89   DTI (1990) nowhere considers the other form of interconnection, duct-sharing, as Beesley and Laidlaw (1991), pp. 4, 5, complained.

90   On the difference between telecommunications and electricity interconnection problems, see Joskow and Schmalensee (1983), p. 43. Gas posed a very difficult problem, since British Gas charged a single price irrespective of distance for the transportation of gas. Because competitors did need to recover their costs from any pipelines they laid, this made competition much more difficult: OFT (1991), pp. 15–19.

91   Joskow and Schmalensee (1983).

92   MMC (1981), pp. 123–9.

93   Joskow and Schmalensee (1983), pp. 145–6; Kahn (1988a), pp. 74–7/II.

94   Kahn (1988a), pp. 47, 64–70/II.

95   On why it may not always be sensible to increase the number of generators, see Joskow and Schmalensee (1983), pp. 63, 64.

96   Goldberg, (1976); Lee (1980).

97   Williamson (1983), pp. 82–105; Vickers and Yarrow (1986), p. 223. Faulhaber (1987), pp. 128–47, argues that inefficient interconnection is the most important regulatory offence, though he is scathing in his condemnation of the distortions the US regulators have here imposed on regulation. This offence is not well defined in the relevant British statutes or licences. The Government has said that it is not keen to define new anti-competitive offences and has drawn attention to the fact that there is a clear distinction between conveyance and provision in the Broadcasting Act, 1990, s. 72(2), which enables the right to interconnect to be more precisely defined, e.g., in relation to more than one user of a duct or cable: DTI (1990), pp. 42, 73. Beesley and Laidlaw (1991), p. 11, note that over the previous year the notion of equal access had been as much discussed in the United States as in Britain. DTI (1990), p. 55, defines 'equal access' as an opportunity to use a trunk carrier of one's choice without bias. See also Peacock Committee (1986).

98   A. J. Harrison (1983). Vickers and Yarrow (1988), pp. 69–76, 268–71, p. 286, discuss the various reasons for break-up. Veljanovski (1987), p. 148, argues for regionalization.

99   See Button (1988), p. 85.

100   Littlechild (1986), p. 32; Shleifer (1985); Vickers and Yarrow (1988), p. 115. An extreme example was an argument that, if Pacific Telesis were divested, comparisons with the remainder of the Bell System would still be possible: Coll (1986), pp. 143, 144.

101   On the difficulties of such comparisons, see Joskow and Schmalensee (1983), pp. 22, 55, 56. Essentially the same points were made long ago in Pigou (1920), p. 385.

102 It also benefits from the tension between the elected council members on the one hand, who are usually grateful for anything that helps them to a greater understanding of the factors which should influence the performance of the local authority, and the permanent council officers on the other.

103 Uniform systems of accounts have been developed in the USA in which particular items are, in principle, always recorded in the same way, but not always to an extent which allows for statistical comparison.

6

The economic regulation of monopoly

Competition is indisputably the most effective means – perhaps ultimately the *only* effective means – of protecting consumers against monopoly power. Regulation is essentially a means of preventing the worst excesses of monopoly; it is not a substitute for competition. It is a means of 'holding the fort' until competition arrives.

Stephen Littlechild (1983)[1]

Thus far, regulation has not been defined beyond our saying that it is what is needed when competition is absent. In its widest conception it is state intervention in the economic decisions of companies. There are various ways of doing it and styles in which it may be done. At one extreme there is the flexibility, procedural informality and ministerial discretion characteristic of government departments regulating nationalized industries. At the other is the use of legislation enforceable through the courts, which ensures inflexibility, procedural formality and almost no discretion. Between, there is a range of regulatory processes. Among them are the American tradition and the old British procedures (before they were overtaken by nationalization), both of which changed over time and the processes of which eventually became hard to distinguish from legal ones, as well as the current British procedures, where the intention is to regulate with a 'light rein'. (The significance of such differences will be discussed in chapter 8.)

What regulation is for also varies. The same regulatory agencies often have several purposes and many industries have been subjected to regulation by bodies with different purposes. A useful and convenient distinction is between economic and social regulation. Economic regulation may be defined as that concerned with monopoly and competition; social regulation with the promotion of social objectives like safety and environmental protection, the achievement of fairness between various interest groups, the enhancement of the status of certain groups, the redistribution of income, or the service of some other end favoured by government. (The implications of social for economic regulation, though it will be impossible to avoid discussing them before then, because the different objectives are practically, though not logically, inextricable, are more fully discussed in chapter 9.)

The objectives of economic regulation are then the promotion of competition and the control of natural monopoly, both to serve the end of greater economic efficiency.[2] The first of these types of economic regulation, discussed in the last chapter, includes all that is covered by fair-trading laws in Britain and by anti-trust laws in the United States. It assumes that monopoly power can be reduced, and that economic efficiency can often be increased, by breaking up cartels and other forms of collusion or by reducing the size of dominant firms. It entails preventing or mitigating anti-competitive practices like predation and unfair or unequal access by which dominant firms use their monopoly power to keep others out of their markets, such prevention or mitigation of anti-competitive practices being normally a central government or judicial function maintained in relation to all markets. This is the only type of economic regulation needed for those privatized industries like car manufacturing, airlines and iron and steel which become, or can be made, competitive upon privatization. But special arrangements, employing specialist knowledge, are then needed where such policing of competition is hard because of large local differences in product and quality, as happens with buses and express coaches, or where there is natural monopoly, with its attendant potential for anti-competitive behaviour. Thus fair-trading responsibilities in Britain have been mostly transferred to the specialist regulators of the telecommunications, aviation, gas, electricity and water industries, who must work with, or in consultation with, the Director General of Fair Trading. But another reason for this transfer is that these specialist regulators are better qualified to perform the other economic regulatory role, the control of natural monopoly itself, than the general regulatory authorities can be.

What distinguishes these two branches of economic regulation is that there is a presumption in the case of the first that competition can be realized and monopoly dissolved; while in the other it is accepted that economic efficiency sometimes requires monopoly, and that fair trading may induce enough competition to reduce market dominance and restrain monopoly profits but not enough to eliminate either. As we have seen, several nationalized industries have been built around such natural monopolies. And though much ingenuity has now been devoted to introducing competition into telecommunications and electricity there will remain an irreducible element of natural monopoly in the networks, at least for the foreseeable future.

In Britain the control of natural monopoly as it stands at present is a problem created by privatization, one which has been met by the creation of new regulatory bodies that will, it is intended, avoid the mistakes of the past. That past involved both the control of public monopoly by government departments, a method whose shortcomings were discussed in chapter 3, and the regulation of private monopoly, whose past and mistakes are generally seen to be American. (Lessons from that American experience will be drawn in this and the next three chapters.)

American experience of rate-of-return regulation as a method of controlling monopoly is discussed in section 1. In the light of that and of the old British experience, section 2 considers the consequences of doing without the control of natural monopoly, and, if it is to be employed, whether its aim should be the curtailing of profits or the promotion of efficiency or both. Section 3 considers RPI–X's strengths and weaknesses as a form of such control, while section 4 considers the problems of its revision.

6.1 The American experience of rate-of-return regulation

While American regulation has had among its objectives the achievement of fair rates of return, and actions against such offences as undue discrimination and predatory behaviour, a regulated monopoly in the United States has also had to pass another test of fairness inasmuch as it has been required that its revenue should yield no more than a fair return on its capital. By contrast, the new British regulation has made a virtue of avoiding any consideration of rate-of-return control, preferring a particular form of price control (RPI–X), because this does not provide the incentives to the distortion of management behaviour that rate-of-return control does. Why should the United States have persisted with its approach? At the heart of the approach, historically, would seem to be envy of high, secure profits, as well as an inescapable weight of precedent.

The centring of regulation on the control of a monopoly's returns goes back a long way in the United States. As in Britain, maximum rates of return were often written into statutes and charters, often the same 10 per cent.[3] But in 1876 the Supreme Court overthrew as unconstitutional this notion of a maximum rate of return.[4] (One can argue that Britain in the nineteenth century would have benefited in this instance from a similar constitution if it would have broken the strangle-hold that such maxima had imposed on the effective control of its monopolies' profits.) That decision was based on the Fifth and Fourteenth Amendments against taking property 'without just compensation' and 'without due process of law'. It reaffirmed the right of a regulated monopoly to a 'reasonable' return on its capital, as well as the right of the judiciary to review the question of what a reasonable return is in any given circumstances. Moreover, subsequently, the Fourteenth Amendment was often used to justify challenges in the courts to regulatory commissions' decisions on rate-of-return control.[5]

What a reasonable, or 'fair', return was inevitably much argued over. The Supreme Court discussed the issues at length in *Smyth vs. Ames*, 1898, a case which dominated US regulation for almost the next fifty years.[6] Consideration of the Fifth and Fourteenth Amendments led naturally to a concentration on determining the value of a monopoly as that which constitutes its property – and then using this value as the 'rate base'. Like Gladstone's committee in 1844, the Court recognized in that decision that the original cost of a railroad would scarcely ever be the same as its current value. The current value could be less, because the stock may have been watered, or outlays may have been extravagant; the property may have been badly maintained; and some expenditures may have been abortive. Or current value could be higher, because there may have been subsequent capital outlays, or because the value of the asset in the market may have increased. However, unhappily, the Court cut across these observations with the irrelevant consideration of the difference between original and replacement costs and of the effects that different interest rates have on value. Indeed, its conclusion on how to value a railroad consisted of a list without its being stated either what weight should be given to each item on the list or how they were to be related:

> We hold . . . that the basis of all calculations as to reasonableness of rates to be charged by a corporation . . . must be the fair value of the property being used by it for the convenience of the public. And in order to ascertain that value, the original cost of construction, the amount expended in permanent improvement, the amount and market value of its bonds and stock, the present as compared with the original cost of construction, the probable earning capacity of the property under particular rates prescribed by

statute, and the sum required to meet operating expenses, are all matters for consideration, and are to be given such weight as may be fair and right in each case.

'What else?' one may ask. But the judgement went on:

We do not say that there may not be other matters to be regarded in estimating the value of the property. What the company is entitled to ask is a fair return upon the value of that which it employs for the public convenience. On the other hand, what the public is entitled to demand is that no more be exacted from it . . . than the services rendered . . . are reasonably worth.[7]

In consequence many lawyers and others were kept in active employment arguing over the total present value of a monopoly company whenever a rate case came up. Not that it was the only matter in dispute in such cases. As the great American jurist Mr Justice Brandeis said, a decision by a commission or a court on fair rates required, not only such a calculation of the 'rate base', but also a prediction of the gross earnings at any given rate, a prediction of operating charges and expenses, and a determination of what rate of return should be deemed fair.[8] Before the inflation of the 1970s, neither of these two predictions caused much difficulty since each was normally extrapolated from the recent past, though occasionally expenditure was disallowed, and there was a convention that capital expenditure during the construction period of, say, a power-station could not be charged to the consumer until the power-station was completed.[9] Deciding what constituted a fair or reasonable rate of return, however, required highly subjective comparisons with returns from other companies whose comparability was much argued over. Nevertheless, it was the calculation of the rate base which in these first years provided the most dispute. As one long-time expert said in 1961 (some fifteen years before the movement towards deregulation started), regulation under the influence of the *Smyth vs. Ames* decision was 'an experience so dismal that, in my opinion, it constituted a serious threat to the long continued survival of regulated private ownership'.[10]

The outcome of the *Smyth vs. Ames* decision was thus endless wranglings over figures to fix the net present values of monopolies, wranglings in which the superior information, resources and expertise of the companies involved, as well as the reluctance of the courts to second guess matters of detail, generally tended to give the advantage to the regulated. As Brandeis said in 1923:

The rule of Smyth vs Ames sets the laborious and baffling task of finding the present value of the utility. It is impossible to find an exchange value for a utility, since utilities, unlike merchandise or land, are not commonly bought and sold in the market. Nor can the present value of the utility be determined by capitalising its net earnings, since the earnings are determined, in large measure, by the rate which the company will be permitted to charge; and, thus, the vicious circle would be encountered. So . . . it is usually sought to prove the present value of a utility by ascertaining what it actually cost to construct and install it; or by estimating what it should have cost; or by estimating what it would cost to reproduce, or to replace it. To this end an enumeration is made of the component elements of the utility, tangible and intangible. Then the actual, or the proper, cost of producing, or of reproducing, each part is sought. And finally, it is estimated how much less than new each part, or the whole, is worth. That is, the depreciation is estimated. Obviously each step in the process of estimating the cost of reproduction, or replacement, involves forming an opinion, or exercising judgement, as distinguished from merely ascertaining facts. And this is true, also, of each step in the process of estimating how much less the existing part is worth, than if it were new.[11]

Whole treatises were written on single components of this value.[12] But, despite improvements in accounting, for which regulation was often responsible, there was no convergence on an agreed approach.[13] An academic accountant has recently argued that enlightened firms would estimate their net present value regularly; and appraise important changes – investments, acquisitions, mergers – by calculating the probable change in net present value.[14] And indeed, a firm may well gain from such an approach where the issue is important and be able to reach its own practical conclusions on how to value its assets, what interest rates to choose and what other current cost accounting policies to adopt. But there is all the difference in the world between a firm's being able to reach agreement on these matters internally in order to make its own decisions and their being openly justifiable in a regulatory arena. It was this latter task that the American courts demonstrated to be hopeless.

The end of this period came in 1944 when the Supreme Court in *Federal Power Commission vs. Hope Natural Gas Co.* reversed its view on this matter. That case showed up the shortcomings of *Smyth vs. Ames* (in what may have been an exaggerated form). Among the many interesting details of this 1944 case, two are worth mentioning here. First, a substantial proportion of the original investment had been expensed inasmuch as customers had paid for it through charges as it was incurred. Thus, to reflect this in the value of the gas field, as had been done, was blatant double accounting to the disadvantage of the customer. Secondly, a huge part of the net present value of the monopoly was the capital value of its gas, and since this natural gas could not be reproduced, and had no original cost, its value depended on current market values for gas. The monopoly's net present value could then vary annually depending on market demand and the discovery of new gas reserves elsewhere. The Supreme Court was forced into a recognition that the shareholders had done extremely well out of the company even on its old basis and that anything approaching the increase in net present value that the company was asking the regulator to recognize would lead to returns that might be judged extortionate. The Court bowed to pragmatism:

> We held in Federal Power Commission vs. Natural Gas Pipeline Co, that the Commission was not bound to the use of any single formula in or combination of formulae determining rates. Its rate making function, moreover, involved the making of 'pragmatic adjustments' . . . Under the statutory standard of 'just reasonable' it is the result reached not the method employed which is controlling. It is not theory . . . but impact of the rate order which counts. If the total effect of the rate order cannot be said to be unjust and unreasonable, judicial enquiry under the [1887 Interstate Commerce) Act is at an end. The fact that the method employed to reach that result may contain infirmities is not then important . . . .[15]

The immediate effect of this ruling on the regulatory process was that, for the most part, commission and court proceedings turned on discussions of what Brandeis had recommended in 1923, when in quest of certainty he had recommended that, instead of net present value, the original cost of any outlays made by a regulated company should be its rate base, never to change,[16] arguing, in effect, that someone investing in a utility was in a similar position to someone investing in a government gilt. However, he was wrong to think that this would lead to less uncertainty in rate-of-return regulation. The character of the debates that followed the 1944 decision may not have been as wide-ranging or abstract as that of those in the period of *Smyth vs. Ames*, but they threw up as many reasons for uncertainty. One reason why the return on an investment in a utility could not be regarded purely as equivalent to a return on an investment in a gilt was that economic circumstances might change so that a utility could not raise money for subsequent investment on the same terms as for its original investment either because of inflation or from some other cause or causes. Replacement costs were also smuggled in where they were much higher than original cost. Capital expenditures were not still allowed until the works undertaken had been completed. Moreover, there were endless arguments about the appropriate form of depreciation. When an asset was acquired from another company should its cost be the original cost when formed or the cost when acquired? If the former, that would be a severe discouragement to any such acquisition; if the latter, that could mean that identical assets of identical age could have different values in the books. One can thus see why regulation in Britain and America has been a principal cause of developments in accounting. (Indeed, it has been said that the regulatory initiatives of the 1930s in the United States made the modern accounting profession.[17]) But, despite many accounting developments, and despite the great advantages that would have flowed had it done so, the regulatory process failed to come up with an acceptable and standard conception of what we would now call current cost accounts (chapter 7). And as inflation increased from the 1950s onwards the limitations of the use of original cost as the rate base in rate-of-return regulation became more obvious.

Thus, whatever may have been hoped for by those who welcomed the judgement in *Federal Power Commission vs. Hope Natural Gas Co.*, the outcome was not greater certainty in the determination of the rate base and, in so far as there was a similar approach to the discussion of what was a fair rate of return, the uncertainty was necessarily transferred there. The rate of return had to reflect not only differences in risk and in the opportunity cost of capital, but also judgements about the future rate of inflation. Discussions of rates of return had, moreover, as insecure and vague a basis in law as had those of the rate base. Since 1923 they had been based upon the opinion of the Supreme Court in *Bluefield Water Works Improvement Co. vs. West Virginia Public Service Commission*:

> A public utility is entitled to such rates as will permit it to earn a return . . . equal to that generally being made at the same time and in the same general part of the country on investments in other business undertakings which are attended by corresponding risks and uncertainties, but it has no constitutional right to profits such as are realised or anticipated in highly profitable enterprises or speculative ventures.[18]

But, whereas in the past there had been a tendency to treat it as a conventional 6 per cent, though this was not a legal maximum, now that attention had shifted from the rate base to the rate of return itself, 'litigants have become increasingly skilled and assiduous in developing prolonged, complex and inconclusive testimony about its proper measurement'.

The American regulatory system has in fact wobbled between three views of what constitutes a fair or reasonable return. There is first the view that the property right of the shareholder is defined by the market or net present value of the business on which he then should earn a return as from a business of similar risk. Arguably, that is the view that flows most naturally from the Fifth and Fourteenth Amendments. The second view stresses the historic value of the actual investment as made: it is on the original value of those outlays, whenever and wherever made, that he should earn a return, whatever the rises or falls in their value that occurred subsequently. The difference between these two underlying views of the utility is one between the utility as an equity and the utility as a gilt. The third view is managerial and puts first the notion that the utility must have a sufficiently high return to raise whatever capital it needs to maintain its operations (which raises the further problem of how far a regulator may help define the scope of these operations). The difficulty here is that, while each of these three views is defensible, they are not the same, and they do not lead to the same result (except in the unlikely event that the *ex ante* expectations of all parties are realized).[19]

Mediating between these different conceptions of a fair return is so much a matter for interpretation of the facts and of subjective opinion that no rules or methods have been found to define the notion of fairness involved in such judgements at all narrowly.

> Efforts to obtain economic precision in the regulatory process – estimates for example of a 'proper' rate of return carried out to one or two decimal places – are unlikely to be worth the effort expended.The standard to which such efforts implicitly appeal is that of overcoming 'distortions' produced by competitive market failure – the standard of trying to replicate what will occur without such failure. Yet in trying to overcome such failures the regulatory process introduces so many distortions of its own, that one should be satisfied with gross estimates and not insist upon refined economic calculations. . . . Insofar as cost of service rate making is advocated as a 'cure' for market failure, one must believe that the unregulated market is functioning quite badly to warrant the introduction of classical regulation.[20]

Thus, in the end, the courts have had little choice other than to give the regulatory commissions a wide measure of discretion.[21] The discretion given is not unfettered, because the price that has to be paid is obedience to the Administrative Procedures Act, 1946, and the other appropriate statutes. But provided that a commission goes through a full set of hearings during which evidence is produced and tested, provided that its own findings can be regarded as being mindful of that evidence and are consistent with its various duties and the precedents it has set itself, and provided that its own arguments are internally consistent, its conclusions are unlikely to be challenged successfully in the courts. Yet commissions try not to intervene too frequently:

> Commissions . . . have tended to let the existing rate levels stand, subject to minor revisions in the rate pattern, until there appears to be impelling reason for a new general rate case . . . Quite aside from the recognised undesirability of too frequent rate revision, commissions recognise the 'regulatory lag' as a practical means of reducing the tendency of a fixed profit standard to discourage efficient management.[22]

The origin of the lag lay in the regulators' desire to avoid regulated firms returning annually to increase their return if it was unexpectedly low, or their customers as frequently demanding price reductions if it was unexpectedly high, so greatly increasing the resources involved in regulation, though it has since been justified as a (crude) means of encouraging utilities to be efficient, for any excess returns they get during the lag they generally keep, even though they may lose them when their return is next negotiated.

In all this adjudication, 'rate of return' is an organizing concept, enshrining the experience of a century. If it had been employed mechanistically, then it would have had the effect that Averch and Johnson predicted for it in 1962 and which we have seen it have in Victorian England. That theory predicted that any attempt to set a maximum rate of return would encourage expansion of the rate base. Dilution through stock watering has, however, been stopped by legislation, and American commentators suggest that in practice there has been relatively little recent movement towards real over-investment in regulated industries. Moreover, what there has been, has been disguised. For example, Alfred Kahn has argued that poor quality of service has rarely been an issue in American regulation; there has been a tendency, other things being equal, for regulated industries to invest continually in raising quality in the expectation that regulators would sanction such expenditure.[23] He also finds this preference a reason for resistance to peak pricing in the electricity supply industry: both regulated and regulator have preferred to provide enough electricity production capacity to avoid the need for this even though to do so is less than optimally efficient.[24] Moreover, utilities have shown a willingness to maintain more standby capacity than is economic. They may have not been over-keen to drive hard bargains with their suppliers and may have been more willing than is economically prudent to take on business at below marginal cost. And they have gone in for more research and development than is economic. Furthermore, in recent years especially, among the most difficult regulatory problems has been how to treat multi-product firms where some products are provided competitively and others are not; for, under rate-of-return regulation, it pays the firm to shift as many of its costs as possible onto its regulated output so as to be allowed to increase its regulated prices to realize whatever rate of return it is allowed. (Regulators have had to resort to various rules of cost apportionment to limit this tendency, though these have produced their own inadequacies and inefficiencies.) Where a natural monopoly has set up separate companies, for example, to supply the basic monopoly with inputs, it has every incentive to over-price those supplies where it can get away with this.[25] This will also tend towards over-investment in the core monopoly. Indeed, for all these reasons it is arguable that natural monopolies will have invested more than competitive firms would have done. However, empirically the Averch–Johnson effect is not supported; in general, there is no evidence of much real recent over-investment due to rate-of-return regulation.[26]

What has happened instead is that regulators have been drawn ever more deeply into examining and questioning the capital expenditure plans, as well as other aspects, of the industries they regulate to ensure that the investments undertaken and other costs are economically defensible.[27] In that respect, they have tended to extend their discretion as well, despite complaints that this inevitably draws them into second guessing in the province of management – a tendency that was once strongly resisted both by regulators and by the courts and is still resisted by many.[28] And indeed it is not surprising given the multiplicity of federal and state regulations in the United States, often with overlapping jurisdictions and all subject to the courts, that rate-of-return regulation has been applied in various ways and with different degrees of intervention into the business decisions and other internal affairs of regulated firms. But one can understand why Michael Beesley and Stephen Littlechild have suggested that rate-of-return regulation might be as bad as nationalization.[29] There is great uncertainty over how it may be applied in detail, little consistency in the attention given in it to economic efficiency and great differences in the extent and nature of regulatory intervention, depending on the interests and pertinacity of the regulator as well as the evasive skills of the regulated.

Thus the outcome of about a century of federal regulation has been a model generally called 'classical regulation'. It is based upon establishing the cost of providing the good or service and incorporating in that a reasonable return so as to fix a reasonable price. The interpretations and measurements involved here have proved, as we have seen, fraught with difficulties. Different regulatory commissions have interpreted the notion of a reasonable rate of return very differently. Price, quality and entry are variously controlled.[30] Just as nationalization in Britain has been applied to competitive as well as monopoly industries, so has rate-of-return regulation, and with similar limited appropriateness. Great difficulties have arisen in preventing multi-product firms that produce both competitive and monopoly products assigning costs to inflate the rate base and even acting predatorily. In fact, for various reasons a natural monopoly will find it easier to engage in predatory activity if under rate-of-return regulation, unless the regulator intervenes to prevent it; but though he can almost certainly do this he can do so only through arbitrary cost-apportionment rulings or other arbitrary decisions, because of the slipperiness of the facts with which he must deal.[31]

Indeed, it has been pointed out that, in the 'landmark' legal cases, that is, those which have determined the form of rate-of-return regulation, one can find no trace of an understanding of the relevance of the concept of natural monopoly.[32] As is unsurprising when one considers the legal domination of the American regulatory process, concepts have been used in that process to achieve not the efficiency of the industry from the standpoint of the consumer but rather fairness. Thus most action to improve the efficiency of monopolies has been an unintended by-product of a regime seeking to achieve fairness. For example, we have seen how regulatory lag in fact arose from the impracticality of forcing monopolies up or down to a reasonable rate of return annually but has been justified *ex post* as an incentive to achieve efficiency. As two commentators have said, 'In essence this blandishment to reduce costs is mainly an ironic and ephemeral product of a major operational defect in profit level regulation.'[33] Other attacks on inefficiency, such as the scrutiny and disallowance of excess operational or capital costs and interference with cost apportionments and transfer prices, have had their impetus in a need to provide a defensible fair return and only incidentally may have improved efficiency. Often though, they have not. Instead, the solutions adopted have served social or political ends, not economic ones.[34] Indeed, a useful way of characterizing the main fault of rate-of-return regulation is that it gives undue weight to one symptom of the state of competitive efficiency – the equality of a firm's average revenues and costs, leading it to earn no more than a normal profit. For that equality is consistent with any amount of production inefficiency or organizational failure, as well as with an infinite variety of price structures where such a regulated firm sells more than one non-competitive product.[35]

The economists' fear that rate-of-return regulation would cause over-investment has therefore been widened into a more general fear that the incentives given by so indeterminate a process must themselves have indeterminate consequences. As two commentators have said, 'The requirements on an economic regulatory agency that tries to do its job properly according to traditional public utility regulatory concepts are not very different from the requirements on a central planning agency in a socialist or communist country.'[36] Or, for that matter, the requirements on those who tried to induce nationalized industries to adopt marginal-cost pricing in Britain and elsewhere. Experience shows that all such agencies have an equally impossible task – omniscience is needed. Thus the collapse of regulatory commissions to a point where neither they nor anyone else can always rationalize their decisions or find in them a consistent pattern cannot be an unexpected outcome. As Alfred Kahn expressed it when he became chairman of the Civil Aeronautics Board, in a directive to his staff which criticized its past decisions: 'If you can't explain what you are doing to people in simple English, you are probably doing something wrong.'[37] Or as another distinguished economist and close observer of regulation summed it up in a symposium on regulation: 'The views expressed in the papers presented in this session seem, where they overlap, to be broadly in agreement: what the regulatory commissions are trying to do, is difficult to discover; what effect these commissions actually have is, to a large extent, unknown; where it can be discovered, it is often absurd.'[38]

As in recent years public-utility economics and natural monopoly have received more attention from mainstream economics, and economic thinking has had more influence over regulatory processes, many US regulators have reinterpreted *Federal Power Commission vs. Hope Natural Gas Co.* as introducing economic efficiency, instead of the central elements of classical regulation, as the touchstone of the regulated firms' behaviour. And that means in practice elevating marginal cost to be the pre-eminent test of that behaviour, as for example in the actions of those influenced by Alfred Kahn's writings and in his own actions as a regulator.[39] Just as he characterized aeroplanes, when chairman of the Civil Aeronautics Board, as 'marginal costs with wings', so a regulator of this persuasion may treat telephone calls or electricity output as marginal costs on wires, natural gas and water as marginal costs through pipes, and airport landing slots as marginal costs on the ground.[40] Regulatory interest thus turns to considering whether the departure of prices from marginal costs distorts competition. With strong monopolies where marginal costs are less than average costs, this means regulatory interest in accepting multi-part tariffs or even price discrimination in order to allow such monopolies to be as efficient as possible while earning an adequate return. With weak monopolies, on the other hand, where marginal costs are above average costs, efficient pricing constraints may be needed to limit the return to what is acceptable.

Throwing more of the risk on the regulated by diverting regulatory attention from the task of achieving an exact rate of return means allowing them to vary the returns on their activities according to their relative risks and even management abilities.[41] The periodic rate-of-return renegotiation can thus become what has come to be called a 'social compact'. That – if confined to economic stipulations – secures promises from the regulated that they will adopt specified marginal-cost pricing and investment policies, while limiting their ability to discriminate to what is agreed with the regulator as promising an adequate return. However, the economic arguments for allowing discrimination – that it will achieve a return that is both acceptable and efficient in a strong monopoly – clash with widespread limitations on discrimination. And regulators who are not economists are often tempted to include new, non-economic stipulations in their social compacts or contracts. Indeed, as Alfred Kahn has pointed out, no complete reconciliation between classical rate-of-return regulation and the criteria of economic efficiency is possible, since there remains the requirement of:

> review within a few years of how the schemes are working – which means primarily how rates of return are behaving – and a more or less automatic correction if profits are too high or too low. This means that these new methods do not eliminate, only mitigate, the possible distortions of traditional regulation . . . they do not eradicate the possible incentive . . . to engage in uneconomic investments in modernisation, if that has the effect of keeping rates of return from exceeding the implicit ceilings.[42]

To recapitulate: the intellectual basis of US monopoly regulation has had a curious history. The objectives set out in enabling statutes have generally been brief, vague and ill-defined (at least until the 1970s), requiring the agency to decide in the 'public interest' for the 'public good'.[43] Thus, originally, regulators had great discretion. Early on, the primacy given to private property by the Fifth and Fourteenth Amendments was imported into the regulatory agencies' objectives through a Supreme Court decision. This was done by requiring the determination of a reasonable or fair return on capital. That objective, arguably appropriate to natural monopoly, was, however, extended inappropriately to industries where the alleged problem was one of wasteful competition, the protection of weak or small producers or whatever. By another Supreme Court decision, the decisive influence of which persisted for the first fifty years of this century, the measuring of the net present value of the regulated firm was required as part of that process – but this was something which it was impossible to do with sufficient objectivity. When the difficulties of such measurement had become patently absurd, the Supreme Court once again intervened decisively. Much greater flexibility was allowed in the determination of the value of a regulated firm. Provided that a regulatory agency conformed to increasingly well defined procedural requirements, it now had great discretion in deciding what return was fair on what measure of capital. Because they had such discretion, regulatory agencies were able, so far as they chose, to take action to blunt any of the regulatory scheme's tendencies towards the distortions that Averch and Johnson, and others, said would flow from a rigorously defined rate-of-return criterion. More recently, some regulators, rightly believing that the touchstone of economically efficient investment and operation is marginal cost, have used their discretion to persuade the industries they regulate to reflect marginal costs within the limits of the requirement to allow a fair rate of return. Where marginal costs are falling below average costs, which is a defining characteristic of strong monopoly, this forces those regulators to allow price discrimination, in so far as the relevant law allows such discrimination, in order that the industries they regulate might achieve a fair return. But this is only one attitude among many. It is how some regulators choose to use their discretion within the constraints the system places on them. Others are closer in their decisions to classical regulation. Many are political.[44] Moreover, because there are many regulatory commissions, almost all composed of more than one person, because their members change as they are elected or appointed politically, because they have wide discretion within a legal tradition of working by precedent and because most firms are subject to both federal and state regulations, the decisions and the reasoning of US regulatory agencies have tended to be inconsistent and often inexplicable. All these inconsistencies have been held together, and prevented from becoming grotesque, by a glue of administrative procedures enforced by the courts.

6.2   Why regulate natural monopoly?

If the regulation of natural monopoly has proved to be tortuous, prolonged and easily side-tracked away from economic efficiency, might we be better off without it? Might it not be more efficient to allow a monopoly freedom over pricing and profits if that avoided the costs involved in regulating monopoly profits? These costs are particularly heavy in the United States, because of the legalistic nature of the American regulatory processes, but already in Britain the costs of regulation are not small and may, as is suggested in chapter 8, increase.

There is a powerful economic efficiency argument against the regulation of monopoly profits where there is free entry, enforced fair trading and the prospect of technical progress and competition: the higher the return to the incumbent, the more the incentive to potential competitors to overcome the barriers of natural monopoly. We have seen, for example, how the monopoly profits earned by the owners of the canal between Liverpool and Manchester stimulated its replacement by a railway. In the nineteenth century, and even in the earlier parts of the twentieth, consumers may have been forgiven for discounting the incentive to internal efficiency and competitive entry that high profits provide; it is possible that, even if it had been further stimulated by unrestricted profits, the rate of technical progress was then too slow to be a threat to the monopolies enjoyed in water, rail, gas and electricity, though that cannot be proved. In recent years, however, technical progress has been increasing too rapidly to allow (most) natural monopolies to remain immune from potential competition. This is most obvious when there are alternatives to a natural-monopoly grid or network, as in telecommunications, where the use of satellite and the use of radio telephony are feasible options, while cable-television companies can carry voice and data. Thus there is a strong probability, given free entry, possibly combined with allowing BT ducts to be a common carrier of cable and telecommunications for all parties, that British Telecom's trunk and local monopoly would disappear.[45] Again, combined-cycle gas turbines are reversing some of the advantages of scale in electricity generation, and in both this and gas it may eventually prove cheaper for a large customer to bypass the natural monopolist's distribution system. Only with water supply and sewerage can one not easily imagine alternative systems, though the drinking-water market in time may be threatened by bottled water.[46] To be pragmatic, there is no strong economic argument for profit control in telecommunications, broadcasting or any other industry with a high rate of technical innovation, as long as there is free entry, interconnection is regulated, predatory behaviour can be controlled effectively, there is no ban on price discrimination and it is sufficiently technically feasible for the enterprise to get near enough to the economic efficiency implied by competitive output levels for any remaining inefficiencies to be of less cost than the probable costs to the consumer of regulation.

Against this incentive effect of unconstrained profits may be placed the *waste of allocative efficiency* that may result if marginal-cost pricing is in consequence not adopted. For economic efficiency will be greater the closer output and input prices are to marginal costs. This is the first economic offence to arise from the matters discussed in this chapter, and is the first monopoly, as opposed to anti-competitive, offence.

Thus the economic case for the regulation of natural monopoly derives fundamentally from the propositions that there are monopoly industries where such an advance in competition cannot be relied on and that, in so far as price discrimination is technically impossible or legally impermissible, that means, in the absence of regulation, under all circumstances higher prices and under almost all lower outputs than under competition if the firm sets its prices and output so as to maximize its profits.[47] Therefore, in order to simulate competitive levels of price and output, the monopolist should be induced by the regulator to set prices equal to short-run marginal costs (except in so far as discrimination can achieve a similar result) and expand output until price equals long-run marginal cost.[48] However, while weak monopolies may be profitable with such policies, strong monopolies will not unless they are allowed to discriminate since by definition a strong monopoly's marginal costs will be below average costs and therefore its revenues from prices equal to marginal costs will fall below its total costs. In order to remedy this unprofitability without inefficiency price discrimination is essential, allowing the enterprise to price down to marginal cost in all its markets while making intra-marginal profits by discriminatory pricing wherever it can so as to make at least enough overall profit to maintain its capital.[49]

Indeed, provided that enough price discrimination to earn them a profit is legally permissible and technically possible, economic theory suggests that for natural monopolies economic efficiency can in theory be as well achieved by price discrimination as by marginal-cost pricing.[50] And since any privatized monopolist has profit incentive enough to discriminate as much as he can he does not need a regulator to reinforce his natural tendency to discriminate wherever he can.[51] It is, of course, an empirical question whether a natural monopoly, strong or weak, could in fact approach economic efficiency through having the pricing freedom to discriminate wherever it chose. But in so far as it could not a profit-maximizing natural monopoly in classic textbook fashion would normally restrict output below the levels achieved in a competitive market so as to eliminate loss and raise its profit to a maximum. It is another empirical question how high a monopoly return a strong monopoly would be able to earn if it had such a freedom to discriminate. But if the monopoly return were higher than that which the regulator believed necessary, then he could use his powers to make the regulated industry lower its prices on average or according to some other politically or socially attractive plan or in whatever way was most conducive to economic efficiency.[52]

However, in practice, such freedom does not exist, and legal obstacles to discrimination are imposed which further reduce output below competitive levels. As we have seen, the strong, and occasionally violent, resentments against pricing structures regarded as unfair have been handled mostly through the development of the regulatory offence of *price discrimination*. Indeed, whether the monopolies are strong or weak, most regulatory systems contain prohibitions against discrimination (though confusingly, they also continue pricing policies which are themselves discriminatory).

From the endeavours made in the nineteenth-century railway legislation to define it, the offence has developed to the point where it is now most often characterized as the use of a difference in price that is not justified by a difference in cost or quality as valued by the consumer,[53] and is thus a social regulatory offence, not an economic one.

The political and ethical principles behind the prohibition on discrimination by monopolies will be examined in chapter 9. For now it is enough to say that they are rooted in long-established notions of fairness. But the disallowing of discrimination has also in some circumstances been a (crude) way of limiting profits so as to make them more acceptable on average to customers (if the cause of the rise in profits is a lack of competition, this is logical, as is argued in chapter 9, but not otherwise – competition eliminates the ethical case against discrimination). What matters if there are not to be accusations of unfairness on one side and disappointed expectations on the other is (as will also appear) that the extent of discrimination does not vary over time, and that this is understood to be so.

As indicated above, if it were not for such bans on discrimination and monopolists had their head under conditions of both strong and weak monopoly, charging what the market would bear with as much skill and intricacy as the late nineteenth-century railways did, efficiency might be greater. As long as they are profit-maximizing monopolists, they will have an incentive to be efficient in all their markets. As long as there are economies of scale to be realized, their profit rates should be low while the enterprises themselves continue to expand. Historically, allowing this freedom would probably have meant that, through a process of merger and amalgamation, local monopolies in each major public utility – water, railways, gas, electricity and telecommunications – would have grown till they formed a national monopoly (as came about in Britain through the different route of nationalization). If – and, given the attitudes and techniques available, it like the rest is a big if – if there had been free entry and a satisfactory regulation of predation, arguably this could have been – in so far as it realized economies of scale while avoiding the Averch–Johnson tendencies to over-investment and the diseconomies of the regulatory process – a more efficient solution than the regulated monopoly.

However, scale and scope economies are not the only reason for the growth of a firm. Where economies of scale and scope are exhausted or not realized, a firm may still increase its prices and profits through absorbing its competitors and increasing its monopoly power without further increases in efficiency. Hence the need also to be able to prevent or mitigate the offence of unnatural monopoly (as discussed in chapter 5), though to determine what is the optimally efficient size and what size is the most profitable for a firm is (as that earlier discussion showed) a difficult, empirical question.

Although technical and legal obstacles to perfect discrimination do thus create an additional justification for economic regulation, nevertheless, historically, the most potent motive for such regulation has been, not the desire to increase the potential for economic efficiency by reversing whatever output reductions have resulted from those obstacles, but rather the dislike and envy of the fact or prospect of 'excessive' profits, reinforced by political rebellion against discrimination, leading to the limitation or attempted elimination of discrimination. However, the various forms of profit or price limitation adopted have in fact given incentives to further inefficiencies

as firms have striven to maximize profits under these constraints, reinforcing whatever previous case may have existed for the regulator to try to stimulate, or require,
the industries he regulates to become more allocatively efficient, that is, to adopt
marginal-cost pricing. Thus, once there is economic regulation, there is in economic
logic a strong case for conducting it on marginal-cost pricing principles identical with
those that, as we saw in chapter 3, ministers attempted to induce nationalized industries to adopt as their pricing and investment criteria.

Some measures which improve allocative efficiency, such as the introduction of
peak pricing, ought to be unequivocally beneficial, since they can be introduced so as
to cut costs and prices while allowing profits to increase. However, many other
measures to improve allocative efficiency do involve profits sacrifice, so that, because
all the new British statutes governing the privatized industries include duties which
fulfil the same function as the Fourth and Fifteenth Amendments to the American
Constitution in requiring economic regulation to secure the regulated industries'
profitability, the ability of regulators to get those industries to implement such
measures is limited. Where either a strong or a weak monopoly is not sufficiently
profitable to maintain the capital it needs, the regulator has no leverage to induce the
regulated industry towards marginal-cost pricing except in cases like the introduction
of peak pricing where the measure will increase its profitability. But even such cases
are not straightforward. We have already seen how both public and rate-of-return
controlled private monopolies would rather not adopt peak pricing reflecting the
different marginal costs of peak and off-peak provision. They would rather over-
invest, to the consumer's detriment, since average prices will then have to be higher
if costs are to be covered; public monopoly because of inertia and a fondness for
investment, private rate-of-return controlled monopoly because of the incentive that
rate-of-return control gives to over-investment. Since they would have adopted such
pricing anyway, without regulatory intervention, had they been profit-maximizing
monopolists, this implies they are not. The regulator's task then becomes that of
stimulating a privatized firm to overcome its organizational inertia. (This inertia
defines the second offence for the economic regulation of monopoly, organizational
inefficiency.)

Where, on the other hand, a strong monopoly is excessively profitable, a regulator
can use the power he has to limit those profits through striking a bargain or compact.
An economically efficient bargain is one which requires the firm in forgoing profit to
move some or all its prices to or towards marginal cost in advance of competition.
Although none of the UK or US statutes requires this – though there are statutory
duties in the former which cover the need to be economic and efficient which could
bear this meaning – the regulator could nevertheless use his influence to this end –
though, of course, he could, and often does, use it, contrary to economic efficiency, to
perpetuate or even increase the social or other non-economic pricing policies of the
past by making a social rather than an economic contract (chapter 9).

The regulator may pursue the same economic or social policies in relation to
excessively profitable weak monopolies, but this can run into other problems. Weak
monopolies are such generally for either of two reasons. First, they may be temporarily weak because they have under-invested. This may be either deliberate or
because, given the long investment gestation periods characteristic of many natural
monopolies, they have been caught out by booming demand. In the latter case,

allocative efficiency would suggest raising prices in the short run to choke off demand. Indeed, that is the market solution. But this may result in higher prices or greater profitability than is allowed under one or another of the different forms of regulation.[54] The real problem, however, is with deliberate under-investment, which comes about because, in so far as it can raise prices and profits, a weak monopoly has an incentive to under-invest, and while this is offset under rate-of-return regulation it is not under many forms of price and profit control. The regulator can, through negotiation, try to force the industry to invest enough. But a better solution is that the risks from under-investment be transferred from the customer, who otherwise would suffer from higher prices or shortages or both, to the firm itself. And the most efficient way of doing this is, not to allow the increases in short-term prices that result from under-investment, but rather to make the regulated firms liable for damages where they do not supply or where there are delays or where other aspects of quality fall below a predetermined standard, so that then profits do not increase from the under-providing of capacity or in some cases, like gas, from the inelastic supply of a scarce commodity.

The second common cause of weak monopoly is that there is one or more scarce factors causing costs to increase with output. To try to reduce prices in such circumstances will lead to long-run inefficiency, so that in the circumstances price control is not desirable, nor is liability an appropriate remedy since the shortage *ex hypothesi* cannot be overcome. In such circumstances, some methods of profit control have less damaging effects on efficiency than rate-of-return control has. Their superiority follows directly from Ricardo's teaching that the most efficient form of taxation is the taxing away of the monopoly rent earned on land.[55] His argument depended on the proposition that, though the rent of any given piece of land as a scarce factor should be determined by supply and demand, and that therefore to force a reduction in the rent of any piece of land below that which would be achieved by market forces would lead to its inefficient use, it would be efficient thereafter to tax away any portion of the monopoly element in that rent or price, defined as the difference between the rent received in the land's most profitable use and that received in its next most profitable use. Such taxation is not usually politically acceptable in so far as it means assessing different profits tax rates for different enterprises, probably through some sort of excess profits levy. But it is the most appropriate form of profits limitation for weak natural monopoly elements which are in fixed supply (like natural gas, or land at a particular airport), though not for those where supply is not fixed, for it will then distort investment incentives.

The same aim of taxing monopoly rent efficiently could be achieved in another way, as James Morrison and Gladstone foresaw – through franchising. Let a natural monopoly make as much money as it can for a finite period. Then let it be put up to auction to select the highest bidder from those who are interested, including the incumbent – as licences for North Sea oil and, from 1991, UK independent television franchises are auctioned.[56] Such an intended use of franchising has a long history going back before Ricardo – it was the intention behind giving a franchise of twenty-one years, or of a similar length of time, in toll road statutes from 1706 (the year of the first toll road) onwards. In theory, franchising is thus an efficient way of taxing the profits of any monopoly enterprise, since it allows prices to remain at levels determined by supply and demand, and therefore to be efficient, while allowing potential franchisees to compete periodically, reducing long-term profitability to competitive levels. Yet in practice the renewal of such franchises has tended to become automatic, as was generally the case with public-utility franchises throughout most of nineteenth century, and as has been the case with cable television franchises in the United States. What in particular seems to limit the practical effectiveness of franchising is both the great advantage an incumbent possesses because of superior information and the fact that, if the franchised business has substantial assets, the valuation, replacement or transfer of these assets from a losing to a winning franchisee poses great practical difficulties.[57] But there is also the difficulty of continuing the business between the losing of a franchise and its being taken over by the next franchisee; for a franchisee who has lost, or does not expect to retain, the franchise has no incentive to be efficient or give good service and every reason to strip as much value out of the business as he can. Moreover, though the policy of taxing monopoly rent through franchising can be applied to both strong and weak monopolies, whereas a weak and profitable monopoly will yield a profit to the franchisee, where a monopoly is strong and unprofitable the policy may entail the franchisee's being paid, if, as is common, strong monopolies are expected to yield a profit. Thus, this application of the policy may have to be at the expense of some allocative inefficiency. Furthermore, though one can write quality requirements, social obligations and other restrictions into the franchise specifications, once a franchisee has been chosen those constraints cannot reasonably be altered without compensation if that would result in a loss of profit.

Both of these Ricardian ways of efficiently reducing profits have, moreover, a political drawback which is arguably more fatal than the practical problems of implementing them: they do not keep prices down.[58] While rational people ought to be indifferent as to whether they receive the gain from controlled profits through lower prices or through taxation, there is ample evidence from experience that they prefer the first. Therefore, while it is important to resist this preference in the case of weak monopolies dependent on some scarce factor, it is not surprising that almost the only area in which franchising has become established is commercial broadcasting, where those who pay the price are, not the mass of mostly voting viewers, for whom reception is free, but the much smaller group of advertisers.

It is not remarkable that the growing interest in marginal-cost pricing for regulated private industries has resulted in a body of economic literature which advances propositions generally identical in principle, though not necessarily in their elaboration, to the propositions about allocative efficiency advanced in the literature on public enterprise pricing.[59] It seems natural to an economist who assumes that allocative efficiency is in the public interest to believe that, in tracing out the implications of that criterion, he is not being normative, merely logical, since his prescriptions are implied by the assumed goal. Rightly, he believes that, in most of the circumstances that are likely to arise, following these prescriptions will result in greater benefits to consumers.[60]

However, there is a case to be mounted on the other side. Aside from the possibility that any regulation of monopoly profits would be worse for efficiency than none, and accepting that the drive to achieve allocative efficiency should not be taken to the point where it jeopardizes profitability or results in unlawful price discrimination, to give regulators a remit to improve the economic efficiency of the industries they regulate is to introduce an additional source of conflict between the two. For, as we have seen, virtually all requirements that regulated industries adopt marginal-cost prices and outputs will tend to reduce their profitability. Moreover, whereas the intention of privatization in the UK has been to establish and liberate the profit motive, the regulation which has been recognized to be necessary has had as its objective not only the stimulation of competition in most cases, but also the prevention of the taking of excess profits at the consumer's expense. Thus, for regulators to force allocative efficiency on the industries they regulate will be seen by those industries as a return to policies they faced and fought when nationalized. Indeed, the conflict, arguably, should be greater than it was when they were nationalized, because the commercial objectives of private companies are definitely not the same as those of allocative efficiency whereas nationalized industry objectives were more indeterminate.

Yet, if the industries were wrong then to resist, why should they be less wrong now? Regulated (as well as unregulated) firms recognize that government rightly requires them to restrict their profits in the interests of safety and the environment. Why should it not do so also in the interest of allocative efficiency? Besides there being the usual difficulty of measuring marginal costs, part of the problem in gaining acceptance of the policy has tended to be the abstract terms in which the argument has been conducted – allocative efficiency and marginal-cost pricing are not slogans to match calls for safety or the protection of the environment. Nevertheless, they can be better presented, since the ultimate purpose and result of achieving economic efficiency so defined is that consumers will get the goods and services they want at lower prices.[61]

More fundamentally, there is an underlying source of conflict, which may be analysed both at a common-sense and at a more theoretical level. At the common-sense level it may be seen that, since there is a conflict of objectives between the regulator and the regulated, the regulated may be expected to use its superior information, its ability to draw a veil over its operations and its superior resources to mislead, and if possible outwit, the regulator.[62] As is discussed in the next chapter, this may become harder if the regulator has better information than he has had in the past. But suppose that he hasn't. If he over-specifies what he requires from the managers of a regulated industry, he removes their freedom to manage. And he will be criticized for trying to manage the enterprise (as was the constant refrain of nationalized industries against ministers and civil servants, by comparison with whom he has more power) as if he were the principal and they the agents. As they will complain, he is not a management expert and he does not have the legal responsibility for management. He may nevertheless insist on their acting in ways they do not believe feasible for their industry. They will then have two, or three, courses of action they can adopt. They can fight every inch of the way, complaining and appealing whenever they can. Or they can use the dictatorship of the regulator as an alibi: if they do not hit their targets, they blame the regulator even if it is their own bad performance which is at fault, so possibly destroying his credibility. Or they can do both.[63]

At the theoretical level, analysis of this source of conflict raises the question of what motivates the regulator. It was because governments became dissatisfied with nationalized industries' own interpretation of the public interest that the industries were instead to be given the incentive of profits, while regulators perform that interpretative task. But why should a regulator serve the public interest any more or better than a Morrisonian board or a minister? Moreover, since, as we saw in chapter 3, they did not define it as equivalent to economic efficiency – not that they were consistent in their interpretations – why should a regulator? It will be argued later that the new British system of regulation is in fact broadly consistent with the pursuit by its regulators of economic efficiency as their main goal through the promotion of competition and through price control – but it is not their only lawful objective. Other systems of regulation have had many social objectives. Economic efficiency as such has rarely been an explicit objective.

Moreover, there is the further issue that, whatever may be the stated objectives of economic regulation, the lessons of the past underline the importance of incentives in achieving them; and they are as relevant to regulators as to other parties. Experience suggests that regulators have their own other objectives and interests (chapter 9). But even if economic efficiency could be assumed to be their overriding objective there is no evidence that the most efficient division of labour between a regulator and the regulated would be for the regulated industry to seek profit maximization while the regulator constrains it to achieve economic efficiency.

If it is agreed that it is neither in the public interest nor economically efficient for the regulator to manage, control or dominate the industry (or industries) he regulates, then the right analogy for the relationship between them is not that of principal and agent, especially as their objectives are by assumption different. We will consider how their relationship might be best regarded when we come later in this chapter to consider RPI–X in detail, but in general a regulator is sensible if he relies on analysis and persuasion, and concentrates on what is important. He will be on comparatively sure ground if, in setting his profit or price controls, he aims to reduce organizational inefficiencies, because their existence is usually more obvious, especially in recently privatized industries, and their elimination can result in both lower prices and higher profits. However, if he believes – and can show by example from elsewhere – that substantial capital expenditure can be saved, as for example by peak pricing, so that average prices will be lower, then he should do his best to persuade all concerned – public, political and consumer opinion, as well as the industry itself – that he is right and his suggestion reasonable. He should listen and respond to counter-arguments. But in the end he will be wise if he insists only on what he can demonstrate and what is widely accepted to be reasonable. He will, moreover, avoid imposing his will on detailed issues where of his constituents only the regulated industry will follow him, since that way lies regulatory capture, either because he becomes the prisoner of the facts as presented by the industry or, worse still, because he loses his credibility through imposing what turns out not to be feasible. Furthermore, even if the regulation of natural-monopoly profits is primarily motivated by profit envy rather than the desire to promote efficiency, it should be devised and operated so as to improve efficiency, though, again, not in such detail as to jeopardize the regulator's credibility. To that end, a regulator should insist that as much economic efficiency as is consistent with the enterprise getting an *ex ante* return sufficient to finance its operations is his criterion, in so far as the law allows, and in so far as it is in the consumer's interest. He should also demand that he be provided with sufficiently precise economic and financial analyses but must avoid requiring such precision as might result in regulatory failure and a consequent loss of credibility. However, he is more likely still to lose credibility if his motives are regarded not as economic, but as political or personal. And it is in this context that the merits of RPI–X as a means of controlling profits and increasing allocative and organizational efficiency should be discussed.

6.3 RPI–X

When in 1984 it was decided not only to privatize but also to regulate British Telecom, a method of profit or price control had to be found. As seen from Britain, the main shortcomings of rate-of-return regulation as it operated in the United States were that it was in itself at least partly responsible for the complexity, cost and legalistic nature of American regulatory proceedings, and that it provided no inherent incentives for a regulated firm to become more efficient. Stephen Littlechild was asked to suggest an alternative, and his recommendation was decisive in providing the formula which has been followed subsequently. He made plain his view that 'competition is indisputably the most effective means – perhaps ultimately the *only* effective means – of protecting consumers against monopoly power.'[64] He noted that the decision to allow only Mercury to compete with BT as a public carrier restricted competition; and that, in general, because of BT's dominant size, to protect the 'emerging competition will require a vigilant policy with respect to anti-competitive practices (such as price discrimination, predatory pricing, tie-in sales, loyalty discounts, etc.).'[65] He then went on to argue, *contra* some forms of price regulation, that controlling prices was not in itself desirable, because keeping prices down may deter the entry of competitors. Therefore the underlying aim of price control had to be one of keeping prices, as well as profits, to levels which were seen to be not unfair but which would not remove the firm's incentive to improve its efficiency. To that end, regulation, he said, needs to distinguish between the various sources of profit: 'superior performance, monopoly power or sheer good luck'.[66] Littlechild's idea was not entirely new. The use of price-control formulae was widespread in nineteenth-century British gas regulation, though they were expressed in nominal not in real terms; and it has been not uncommon in the United States. It is the linkage to an inflationary price index, the Retail Price Index (RPI), that is the real novelty, though even here there were some innovations in the United States which had RPI–X characteristics.[67]

The difference between rate-of-return regulation and most other forms of profit control on the one hand and the RPI–X system on the other is fundamental, even stark. As Hillman and Braeutigam have put it in their valuable analysis:

> A shift from profit to price level regulation effects a shift of risks and benefits between the firm and its consumers. In purest theory profit level regulation assigns to consumers the risks of cost increases and the benefits of cost reductions, while price level regulation reassigns both to the firm.[68]

If each were adopted without compromise, the difference between them could not be more stark. Pure rate-of-return regulation guarantees profits to the shareholder, though they can only be increased through expansion of the rate base or by arguing the regulator into conceding a higher return. The consumer gains from any cost reduction, but the enterprise has no profit incentive to make it. Pure RPI−X means that, though an absolute prohibition is placed on raising average prices by more than is allowed by the price formula, any increase or fall in revenue from any other cause, and any cost change, flows through to profits.

To keep RPI−X pure in that sense, Littlechild objected to its employment as a form of price control on all services indifferently, competitive and non-competitive. His objection to a price ceiling for British Telecom based on such a formula used indiscriminately was that, if it were set so as to constrain severely BT's ability to make profits, then it would have almost the same disincentive effect as rate-of-return control, while on the other hand, if it did not bite, it would serve no useful purpose except as some check against the abuse of monopoly power.[69] He therefore recommended a price ceiling applied only to the prices which he thought it likely BT would want to raise because they continued to have monopoly power over them – for example, local-call charges, connection charges and rentals. While the logic of his position may seem to have indicated separate price-caps, one for each monopoly service, the demands of practicality and flexibility led him to suggest a single 'basket', as it came to be called. BT would thus have an incentive to be efficient on its monopoly services, for it could keep any profit it made from reducing the costs of those services, while competition would keep it efficient on the remainder of its services.

What happened was significantly different in that charges for trunk calls, where competition was then expected to develop quite quickly, were included in the basket. (Charges for international calls on the other hand, where competition was not imminent, were not. They were brought in later, in 1991, when competition there had increased. And this again was against the spirit of what Littlechild had recommended.) The difference meant that British Telecom now had the option, apparently, of recouping any lost profits from competition, or the threat of it – if that threat led it to lower prices on its competitive services – by raising prices on non-competitive, or less-competitive, services within the basket, while keeping all these changes under the RPI−X ceiling, the increases and reductions cancelling one another out.

British Telecom took full advantage of this freedom in 1986. But while a substantial rebalancing was then achieved the public reaction to the increase was so strong that BT did not rebalance further despite its legal right to do so, fearing adverse publicity and a reference to the Monopolies and Mergers Commission. Since the policy of privatization appears to be based on the aim of achieving more economic efficiency, it should also be based on the acceptance that economic efficiency implies more-competitive pricing. Then a refusal to rebalance merely stores up problems until the pressure from external competition makes it inescapable. Alternatively, if the Government wishes to maintain cross-subsidization with the political aim of keeping some prices low at the expense of others, this aim should be made explicit and be provided for (as was in part done, as we shall see, in the BT Licence by providing for the possibility of 'access charges' or as was actually done in 1991 by making a comparable adjustment to the interconnection rate).[70]

To provide competition, a single other operator, Mercury, which became a wholly owned subsidiary of Cable and Wireless, was allowed to provide its own fixed links to interconnect with, and use, BT's trunk network. It was not subject to a price formula or any other form of profits limitation. It was not appreciated early how slowly competition would develop. If it had been, it might have been realized earlier that there are broadly only two satisfactory approaches to the setting of price-caps. The first is to set an initial value for X taking into account the likely development of competition but also assuming that the regulated firm will take every opportunity that its licence obligations allow to increase its profitability by raising inelastic prices within the RPI–X constraint. The second, much simpler approach is to set a separate price-cap for every different service which is not yet competitive. Undoubtedly, if this had been proposed in the beginning it would have been resisted strongly as over-regulation, but it was the direction in which BT price regulation went during the 1980s.[71]

The basic notion of RPI–X of a limit to price increases related to changes in the Retail Price Index is common to all the UK licences.[72] In the BT Licence there is first a description of the charges which are to be included within the price formula, the basket. The excluded charges are in principle, though as we have seen not always in fact, those judged to be sufficiently subject to competition as not to require regulation; and one-off charges, such as connection and installation charges, which, it is prescribed, are to be 'cost plus' with a reasonable return on capital. (Small charges may also be excluded on the ground that they would have such a small weight in the formula that their increase would not effectively be controlled by it. This was argued for connection charges. Their eventual inclusion in 1991 was more presentational than real.) A year is specified as the period over which the increase in British Telecom's revenue is to be measured.[73] The relevance of the Retail Price Index is stated and it is said that the annual revenue from the basket may not increase by more than the increase in the RPI minus, or sometimes plus, some percentage, X.[74] That percentage figure is given in almost every licence in the context of a formula, or formulae, showing exactly how the actual increase is to be measured and compared with the permissible increase. If in any year the licensee increases its prices by more than the formula allows, it must hand the excess back the next year through reduced prices. In every year, it must provide forecasts and such other data for each charge as will show why it believes that it will stay within the formula's maximum. It may aim at less than the maximum. If it does, it may carry forward some of the price increases it has forgone, at least for a number of years. Interestingly, Littlechild also recommended a licence clause committing British Telecom not to reduce quality on its 'monopoly routes'.[75] This did not materialize, but all licences after British Telecom's and British Gas's had some provisions attempting to provide the regulator with what he needs to monitor quality and take that into account in reviewing price changes. From 1992 Oftel's and Ofgas's powers in this regard were altered so as to be the same as Offer's and Ofwat's.[76]

The principal reason for the exclusion of charges from the basket is clear enough and politically manageable: if the services (or goods) in question are subject to competition it would already have exerted a downward pressure on their prices and might be expected to do so in the future. It is when competition is expected soon, but has not yet arrived, that the political worries arise. Though British Telecom international calls were starting to experience substantial competition from 1989, there had still been enough monopoly power from 1985 to allow their prices to be increased generally and easily outside the basket, and this led to their inclusion in 1991.[77] One consequence of including local calls within the basket, though presumably not a motive for this, was that it became possible for BT to increase their prices while making corresponding reductions in charges for long-distance calls because profit margins were lower.

Every exclusion from a price formula admits the possibility of a misallocation of costs, the avoidance of which was the main practical argument Hillman and Braeutigam gave for preferring price-level to profit-level regulation.[78] British Telecom was until 1991 allowed to exclude private circuits from the RPI–X basket, yet calls on those circuits used lines and other equipment also used for calls and value-added services within the basket. The same was true of international calls, which were given a separate cap in 1991.[79] While some of these costs are merely not easy to allocate, others are genuinely joint costs in that they would not be saved if, say, any of the services within the basket that shared them were discontinued. In these circumstances there is likely to be artificiality in cost apportionment which will affect the calculation of RPI–X. Moreover, where, as in electricity supply, industries have been broken up vertically, the calculation and the problems of cost apportionment will become yet more complicated, because costs have to be tracked through different companies in the production chain.[80]

If the costs associated with an operation within a firm under RPI–X regulation are wholly or substantially separate, a strong case can be mounted for the exclusion of the operation from the formula if it is arm's length and competitive; or for separate regulation with a separate price formula where the value of X would depend on the particular circumstances of that part of the enterprise. There may, on the other hand, be significant costs that cannot be allocated, and which are joint to two operations, one regulated, the other not. Cost apportionment in such a case would be subjective. While Oftel (and Ofgas) had followed this line of seeking to apportion joint costs, by 1991 the Government and Oftel had, it seemed, come to appreciate that it is not a worth while exercise and that it is sounder to rely on cost causation.[81] How the firm then deals with joint costs, whether by discriminating and charging what the market will bear, or through non-discriminatory uniform transfer charges, depends on the attitude taken to discrimination (chapter 9). In either case, the operation in the basket should be ring-fenced and provided with separate accounts. If the regulator believes substantial unapportioned costs remain, then he will need to investigate, if he has the power to do so, whether or not unreasonable cross-subsidization is taking place to the unregulated from the regulated operation, allowing excess profitability or even predatory behaviour in the former. An advantage of RPI–X price control over rate-of-return regulation is that it makes the handling of joint costs easier where there is a mixture of regulated and unregulated businesses.

Closely related to this problem is that of devising a statistically robust index with appropriate annual weights to measure any group of heterogeneous prices' annual movements against an RPI–X formula.[82] While this has been achieved for telecommunications, the diversity of prices in electricity seems to have meant that there has been no real attempt to construct a statistically significant basket there. Instead, RPI–X is to be measured by a simple rule of tariff yield divided by output. This is the first main difference which distinguishes the operation of the price-control formula used for British Telecom from that of the formulae used for gas, the British

Airports Authority and electricity. This simple rule may be adopted because output appears homogeneous or because an industry's pricing schedules are so complicated as to make the construction of a weighted basket intractable. The problem would be even greater for an industry like the railways where the diversity of prices is several orders of magnitude greater. How output is to be defined for this purpose itself becomes either the subject of a massive negotiation or simplified.

In licences subsequent to British Telecom's there is a tendency to leave certain costs outside the formula for 'cost pass through'. The underlying idea is that certain costs – for example, of fuel, of raising environmental standards or of meeting other regulations – are beyond the control of the industry and should therefore be passed through, usually at 100 per cent, to the consumer (though in fact that is never the whole story, since industries always have some control over the proportions in which they use inputs and the prices at which they buy them). No such exemptions were made for BT. In later licences, therefore, there is a description of any costs where the increases are to be passed 100 per cent through into the final price. (Only a percentage pass through is allowed with airport security costs – of which 25 per cent was allowed through, increased to 85 per cent in 1991 – and the gas pass through was reduced from 100 per cent in 1991.) The relevant prices, price increases, quantities and quantity increases as well as the costs that are passed through are to be verified. And there are to be means of ascertaining that the costs set against any basket of price increases are only those properly attributable to it, and that any costs passed through are ring-fenced from those that are not, so that the regulated industry can be seen to be not passing through costs at 100 per cent which should be subject to productivity improvement.

Among the reasons for cost pass through is that the intrinsic difficulty of choosing a value for X is greater where technical progress is less rapid than it is in, say, telecommunications and there is therefore less scope for productivity gains and therefore less of a case for preferring RPI–X control to rate-of-return control since the practical difference between them may vanish. Indeed, in the case of water and the distribution businesses of the area electricity boards, the values for X that were chosen were to be added to RPI, not deducted from it, reflecting the finding that increased levels of investment would be needed by them, mainly for environmental enhancements.[83] This may be shown in many ways. Revision of X may be delayed – in the case of water for up to ten years, though by consent for five years – to give the industry a longer period in which to enjoy any profit gains it may make. Where demand growth is low, or productivity improvement difficult, tougher negotiation of X is likely.[84]

However, perhaps the strongest case for cost pass through is where a particular factor of production is in fixed supply. An approximation to the same is to allow only a cost pass through of less than 100 per cent. By Ricardian principles, the full price should be determined by demand, and any excess profitability in relation to this one factor be expropriated by a suitable tax or levy – as is broadly the case with gas. The same principle ought to apply to airport landing charges in so far as they are high, since airport capacity is artificially constrained because of environmental restrictions on airport growth. But in this case, as also in the similar case of the railways, if they were to be privatized, it is harder to put this principle into practice. (A different reason for cost pass through – for example, in the electricity industry – is to avoid controlling price increases that have already been controlled in relation to one stage of production at another stage, that is, to avoid controlling the same cost increases twice.) It might be an advance if a clear, or clearer, distinction could be made between demand and cost changes which are within the firm's control and those which are not.[85] Because of the absence of competition most demand – one could reasonably say except possibly that for genuinely new business lines – is outside the control of large monopoly utilities, so that it is reasonable to assume that all increases and decreases in demand are due to external factors. Therefore, one could construct an RPI–X formula which would standardize for changes in demand. Thus one would be seeking to reward companies for shifts in their cost curves, not for movements along them. To do this effectively would inevitably require measures of capacity utilization which are detailed and difficult to establish. RPI–X formulae in later licences do designate the costs a firm does not control and therefore where there is to be cost pass through. Such a designation on the demand side might remove some of the arbitrariness in the present RPI–X approach – though not without difficulty in measurement – and give the formulae a longer life, since there must be a real danger that a given price formula, tolerable while a regulated industry is profitable due to buoyant demand, will not be so if economic circumstances suddenly change.[86] A sudden fall in demand, for example, may affect profitability, leading to urgent demands for a change in the price formula. In this respect RPI–X is more vulnerable than rate-of-return regulation, since a fall in demand should lead the rate-of-return regulator to allow price increases to restore profitability (though as we have seen, in practice US regulatory reluctance to do this, especially in the power industries in the 1970s, has led to financial difficulties for utilities, even bankruptcies.)

Some years after it had become accepted in practice in Britain that rate-of-return regulation is inferior to price control, there were hearings by the National Tele-communication and Information Administration within the US Department of Commerce to consider whether in the United States RPI–X should replace rate-of-return regulation. Evidence in its favour was provided by Oftel and British Telecom, among others.[87] While there had been some initiatives by the Federal Communications Commission and other regulatory agencies towards some forms of price control which were arguably variants of RPI–X, in general the arguments against change and tradition were strong. There were both more and less noble reasons for a reluctance to change. Many lawyers and others depended for a livelihood on the nature and length of the existing procedures. The regulated industries preferred a system they knew and which some said they could manipulate. Most situations that were likely to lead to dispute were covered by precedents based on established rules and methods. And it was not a straightforward task to find a consistent and legally unchallengeable path to RPI–X from previous regulatory and court decisions.

In their excellent critique of RPI–X and how it might be used in the United States, Hillman and Braeutigam are amazed by the informality of the British process of choosing a value for X. They observe that British Telecom described the process in the following way:

The BT Licence was granted on 22 June 1984 for a period of at least twenty-five years. The text was drafted by the Government [Department of Trade and Industry] before

Oftel was formally created, in negotiation with BT and was designed to balance the needs of competitors, customers and the public against the need of the potential shareholders who would soon be asked to buy shares in the new company.[88]

And on this they comment,'This model of direct private negotiations between firm and government is hardly a candidate for adoption in the United States. While it meets the tests of efficiency and direct political oversight, it fails the test of due process.' They assume that in the United States whoever was given this task would have to consider alternatives, reveal the calculations involved and give reasons for the recommendation made, with opportunities given to the interested parties to express their views. But there is more to this than just due procedure, for, as we have seen, the more the basis of such a decision is revealed, the more likely it is that there will be discussions of the rate of return assumed. Because of the weight of precedent and the force of habit, it must be likely that such hearings would result in conclusions that gave more weight to fairness than to efficiency, that is, to rate of return than to productivity improvement, with the consequence that risks would be shifted back from the regulated firms to their customers.[89]

But, besides such procedural complications, there were fundamental arguments against such a change to the US system. RPI–X might not satisfy the Fifth and Fourteenth Amendments inasmuch as it would not necessarily provide even a well-managed business with a fair return on its capital – though in Britain there are express provisions in the relevant statutes requiring the regulator to respect the need for regulated firms to be financially viable.[90] What if under an RPI–X regime the regulator or the courts were wrong to believe that a utility could improve its productivity by a given value of X? One might then make the mistake that Brandeis had made in that decision against the railways in 1910 when he persuaded the Supreme Court that the railways ought to be able to achieve a given improvement in productivity where it seemed they could not.[91] The 1876 Supreme Court decision had made it clear that regulation should not be confiscatory, as it could be held to be if it thus prevented a utility earning a fair rate of return.

Moreover, the discretionary nature of regulatory hearings avoided the distorting effects suggested by the Averch–Johnson hypothesis and other kinds. From this it is but a step to maintain that, in practice, if not in theory, the substitution of RPI–X would make little real difference. We have argued that this convergence could easily have developed from Carsberg's original contentions concerning the criteria he would use to revise the BT formula. Such a convergence may arise for several reasons. One is that no productivity improvements are possible, though it would be unwise to assume, as this implies, that technical progress is impossible. Another is that too generous a privatization deal leads to excessive profits so that regulators find that they are under inescapable political and public pressure to bring down returns, irrespective of productivity improvement. A third is that, though the possibility of productivity improvements exists, all parties find it easier to argue about the proper rate of return than to get to grips with technical progress and other sources of productivity improvement. If that were to happen, it would be a major defeat of the purpose of the new British system of regulation. What is important is that such a convergence is not a necessary consequence of the use of regulatory discretion under the British system, though it might be under US procedures. That is the apparent difference that is possible under the UK system. A regulator can use his discretion to revise RPI–X for the sake of efficiency rather than fairness, though as it is his discretion he does not have to use it so.[92]

US regulation has in fact shown comparatively few signs of abandoning rate-of-return control, though some academics there pay less attention than in the past to classical regulation.[93] It is, however, not to RPI–X that they tend to turn, but away from the control of monopoly profits, to the control of anti-competitive behaviour. Nevertheless, the fact that the new regulation in Britain also requires that profits be limited, though in a different way, shows how powerful a political imperative is behind this long-standing view.

In conclusion then, RPI–X, though not without its difficulties, is a promising initial organizing concept for the promotion of natural-monopoly efficiency. The more risk and opportunities for increasing profit that attach to the firm, the more incentives for productivity improvement the formula provides.

6.4   The revising of X

The initial negotiation of X before the flotation of a natural monopoly requires that all parties to it take a view on what improvement in productivity is possible, with government, still in effect the owner and regulator at that stage, deciding ultimately what the initial value of X should be. In practice there are three reasons why a government in such a position is likely to chose a lower value for X than that suggested by its mean forecast of what is possible. First, the information relation between it and the natural monopoly is *asymmetric*: the monopoly has much better knowledge of the productivity gains it can make than has a government and its advisers; and it has every profit incentive to understate the gains it can reasonably be expected to make.[94] Secondly, a more immediate and important aim for a government and its advisers than that of improving efficiency is a successful flotation. And this, other things being equal, is helped by a lower value for X (chapter 4). Thirdly, if the value of X is too demanding, then even the minimum productivity improvement the formula then requires may be more than the enterprise can deliver, with the result that it will become increasingly unprofitable. But the relevant statutes give the regulator what may be interpreted as a duty to ensure that the firm is viable provided it is reasonably efficient; for if a firm is not viable it can apply to the regulator for a revision of X in its favour.

Before the flotation of BT, government and British Telecom negotiated a value for X in the formula. As noted above, to police the situation thereafter, a new regulatory body, Oftel, was set up under a Director General, Bryan Carsberg.[95] It was given substantial enforcement powers backed up by powers to call for information from BT.[96] It was required to scrutinize BT to prevent it acting in an unfair or predatory manner.[97] It was to investigate cross-subsidization between BT's different businesses (for example, of apparatus supply by profits from telephony). It was to act as a channel for complaints by consumers.[98] And above all it was to modify the BT Licence before five years had passed. (Similar review arrangements now obtain for the other regulated privatized industries.)

Under the RPI–X regime, each regulator is to have access to sufficient information to allow him to determine a sensible revision of X. And though each licensee is to be protected from too frequent changes in X, in some of the licences there is provision for a change in X if there are unexpected changes in circumstances outside the control of the licensee which have a severe effect upon its profitability. In every case, the Monopolies and Mergers Commission is to act as a court of appeal if the regulator and the licensee do not agree,[99] except that any change in the price ceiling in the airports' 'permit to charge' (their equivalent to a licence) must be referred to it.[100]

Government and regulators have been persistently embarrassed by the excessive profitability of many of the regulated firms. In the case of British Telecom, within a few years of its having been initially set, Carsberg made it clear that its X value was in his judgement too low.[101] The high profitability that resulted from the low value for X was fed by two other factors. First, not only was the 1980s a period of unprecedentedly booming demand for telecommunications, considerably increasing revenue, but given the fixed nature of so many of the company's network costs – a characteristic shared with other natural monopolies – much of this increased revenue went straight through into increased profits. Secondly, the failure to restrict the formula to monopoly services meant that in 1986 BT was able to compensate itself for the reduction that it felt it needed to make in rates for long-distance calls because of imminent competition by raising local-call rates (where its monopoly was not under threat), which it could not have done if the basket had been confined to monopoly services. (The fact that it turned out that significant competition was not imminent and developed far more slowly than was expected in 1986 is another reason why BT's profits were higher from 1985 onwards than had been expected when X was set at 3 per cent.)

A robust reaction to all this would have been to follow the advice offered by Littlechild when he recommended the RPI–X approach. This would have been to accept that mistakes had been made in choosing the initial value for X but to have stuck with the 3 per cent that was chosen, using the argument that unduly high profits were as such no disincentive to efficiency and that increasing the value for X because profits were thought to be too high, or inhibiting increased profitability in other ways, would be a signal to British Telecom not to expect that it could retain all the profits it could make, acting as a disincentive to efficiency as well as discouraging Mercury, its competitor. The reason for not doing this can only have been profit envy, leading to the embarrassment the regulator would feel at BT's making 'too high' a profit, as well as a belief that BT had not as yet acquired a culture hungry enough for profit to cut costs.

For a few years it looked as if Carsberg was undermining the spirit of RPI–X and reintroducing rate-of-return regulation by the back door. In 1986, he approved British Telecom's proposed price increase but warned that when he renegotiated X in 1989 (as he was required to do by the BT Licence) he would have in mind what rate of return BT was earning. He said he felt that he had no choice, given its low level of risk.[102] In 1986, BT's profitability increased and, moreover, BT, as we have seen, lowered its long-distance prices and increased its local prices to compensate. If that were an economically rational policy, it would have had to have been assumed that it would result in further increases in profitability. In his report for 1986 (issued in 1987) Carsberg again threatened intervention, strengthening his warning.[103] (There was in fact considerable public outcry against the increase in local-call charges. The package was rightly seen as generally more favourable to business than to residential customers – though the last were increasing their long-distance calling on average.) All this revealed the incoherence in policy noted above. If the new regime had really been interested in encouraging BT to abandon its old public-sector stolidity and respond to market forces, then whatever mistakes had been made in setting X too low or in creating too large a basket, it was arguably still right to allow BT every opportunity to make a profit, rather than to reinforce its hankering for the status quo ante.

In a sense, the situation was saved by the 1987 quality crisis. In early 1987, British Telecom experienced a widely supported strike during which its managers, quite remarkably, were able to maintain operations almost intact until the men came back. After the strike, though, faults increased, as did the backlog of new customers to be connected. At the same time, BT was having the greatest difficulty introducing some new model exchanges. Several failed in a blaze of publicity. During the summer BT was rarely out of the headlines at just the time when it was considering further price changes, including more rebalancing between long-distance and local calls. The main causes of the crisis, however, went back before the strike. BT had for several years been improving its productivity by calling upon its local districts to reduce their labour forces – leaving it largely to them to decide how to do this. Every year the districts complained they could not both cut their labour force and deal with booming demand, as well as cope with a difficult period of substituting new for old technology. For several years they were wrong but by 1987 they were right. BT reversed its policy and began to increase the numbers of its staff. While this was not the way in which the New York Telephone Company had met a similar crisis – it had moved quickly to install labour-saving equipment – BT in this way eventually overcame the quality crisis.[104]

But, for the regulatory regime, the experience of the quality crisis had two other important consequences. In the first place, it was realized that a major shortcoming of the British Telecom Licence was that, despite Littlechild's recommendation, there was no provision in it which plainly stated that the choice of a given value for X implied an obligation to maintain or improve its service to stated standards. While under rate-of-return regulation the profit to be gained from additional investment usually protected quality and might mean that customers would get a higher quality than they would have paid for freely, a firm under RPI–X control had a profit incentive to reduce the quality of service provided, as long as in doing this it could cut its costs more than its revenues. Thus, subsequent licences had provisions that the regulator could use to require a firm to reimburse its customers through compensation if it tried to increase its profits by reducing its quality.

The second, more fundamental consequence was that British Telecom was deterred from raising prices by as much as its RPI–X formula allowed. While in 1987 this could be, and was, presented as a public-relations price it had to pay for the collapse in quality – though not a price that it was required by law to pay – this could not explain BT's reluctance to raise prices by as much as the formula permitted once the quality crisis was over. Reasons were not given in public, but the combined effect of a loss of service due to the quality crisis and an apparent belief that the levels of profit it was earning were not in its long-term interest seen to have led BT to forgo immediate profits and fall back on public-sector canons of reasonable behaviour. Thus, the embarrassment that flowed from (among other things) too low a value for X was not only curtailing high profitability but blunting the incentive to move to a commercial motivation and reduce organizational inefficiency.

No wonder that Hillman and Braeutigam, observing this from across the Atlantic and used to more-robust profit-seeking, wondered what was up. Was Carsberg's 1986 statement that further price increases were, though allowed by the formula, not to be expected a declaration through his mouth of British Telecom's own policy, that is, a reflection of a 'unilateral political act' by the firm out of concern for 'excess' earnings in advance of its 1989 licence review or 'the product of a prior understanding reached with British Telecom'?[105] Overwhelmed by the quality crisis, and as yet not free from immurement in a political world where the avoidance of public embarrassment is a more important incentive than profits, BT had apparently accepted Carsberg's suggestions that the value for X in the formula should be set by reference to a rate of return, as if this were a necessary implication of the RPI$-X$ formula, which it was not. It would have been better for the sake of efficiency if Carsberg had merely pointed out how easily the profit increases had been won or had said nothing at all. Either would have given BT an incentive to improve its productivity as much as possible in the short run (or, at least, would not have taken it away).

One danger to this system of regulation will be if a regulated industry becomes unprofitable and seeks to revise its X so as to restore its profitability. If this unprofitability is the result of a failure to take the opportunities to reduce costs or expand demand which were foreseen by the regulator at the last RPI$-X$ operation and which have been successfully achieved elsewhere, it ought to be seen as the management's fault. Although in such a case one would expect the board to change the management, the management will take every chance that it can to blame the regulator. Therefore his ground had better be well prepared.

In the early years of the new system of regulation the opposite danger of the formula's working over-generously seemed the greater. Experience and common sense suggest that governments will tend to be over-generous to newly privatized monopolies, both in their initial balance sheets and in the initial setting of the price-control formula. The robust response would be simply to accept the windfall profits that will tend to accrue, and for the regulator to delay action until the first agreed time for revision. However, the public and political outcry against 'excess' profits may in reality be too great. Moreover, these extra profits cannot, by assumption, be said to have resulted from greater efficiency. Probably the best tactic would be for the regulator – perhaps after presenting a prima facie case to the Monopolies and Mergers Commission – to agree to review the price-control formula but not earlier than two years after flotation. He then should suggest only such revisions as can be justified by there having been undue pessimism in the financial information used when the prospectus was written and the initial price-control formula set. By 1991, it had come to seem that in some industries such a revision was a likely event.

The periodic review of X written into the licences inevitably creates problems in ensuring that the main or overriding objective of the regulatory regime remains the stimulation of efficiency. An expectation that X will be reviewed periodically will encourage a firm to make all the money it can quickly after a review and then increase or play up its costs and other difficulties as the period of the next review approaches. The games that result are very similar to those which take place under rate-of-return regulation, where regulatory lag has much the same effect in inducing gaming.[106] If RPI–X is indeed operated as if it were rate-of-return regulation, then many of the shortcomings of that form of regulation will follow. Analysis shows that the relative efficiency in gaming of rate-of-return regulation and RPI–X depends on a regulator's ability over time to reward a regulated industry more for productivity improvement under one regime than under the other. The superiority of the RPI–X regime in this respect is demonstrable but could be offset by an expectation that under it the regulator will draw off as much or more profit than under rate-of-return regulation.[107] Under both regimes the regulator and the regulated will both be concealing their true intentions. As the facts which matter and forecasts for the future belong to the regulated industry, it is bound to have the advantage. If a regulator feels outwitted in one regulatory review, then, if he survives until the next, there will be a tendency for him to punish the regulated industry by a more severe settlement the next time. The realization that, because of that, it may not in the long term be able to keep the gains of a previous period will be a further disincentive to efficiency. Moreover, in order to establish what is reasonable, a regulator will be drawn more deeply into analysis of the industry and detailed intervention in it. He will also know that active intervention between review periods for other regulatory reasons will be helpful in eliciting useful data to store away for later renegotiation of the price formula.

When a value for X is first set, the calculation on which the Government bases its decision must imply an assumed return on capital, though the UK government has never disclosed what it was in relation to any of the industries thus regulated. A robust approach, as we have said, would have been to stick to the value for X once chosen, whatever return was subsequently earned. If a reasonable increase in efficiency had been estimated in the first place, only consideration of 'fairness' require an upward revision to a more stretching figure if returns are high. For, even an acceptance that X should be revised, as all the relevant licences require, does not imply that this must be done so as to achieve a more acceptable rate of return. The regulator in setting a new value for X does not have to disclose his calculation or his reasons, but what is necessary given the nature of the RPI–X concept alone is that he should consider what future improvements in productivity may be possible over the period until the next revision, without taking into account past profits or altering the rate of return. Intellectually, there is the further problem that what a reasonable rate of return is depends on taking a view of the risks facing the business and these will change over time, even in part as a result of regulation. Predicted competition will alter them. Its actual realization may be different. As the discussion in this chapter has indicated, exact discussion of the appropriate rate of return is pointless given the wide variety of views on the risks confronting an industry.

The ideal outcome of any RPI–X negotiation would be, first, that in deciding on a new value for X the regulator has confidence that with effort the enterprise will be able to achieve the implied increase in productivity over the required period, because he knows that such a performance has been achieved elsewhere at home or abroad; and, secondly, that the firm, though feeling that it will be stretched to get there, accepts that it can do so profitably, so that, thirdly, if it fails to do so, the non-executives on the board are more likely to replace the executive than to castigate the regulator.

Even so, given Carsberg's previous arguments that implied the importance to him of the rate of return, it seemed highly probable that in 1989 the revision of British Telecom's X would hinge upon the view taken of what this rate should be. The negotiations with BT were private: X was increased to 4.5 per cent; and BT waived its right to appeal against this to the MMC, so the reasons for the change were not publicly investigated or reported. However, Hillman and Braeutigam were told informally by BT that it resulted from 'a specific reflection of *projected* productivity gains resulting from current and continuing modernisation programmes rather than as a general limitation on earnings'. They were right to observe that:

> If such is the case, then Oftel is to be commended, especially for not converting the productivity factor into a mechanism for expropriating a large share of the firm's efficiency gains from prior periods . . . The ultimate ability of price level regulation to generate its potential benefits [will] depend importantly on the refusal of regulators to judge its success or failure primarily by comparative profit levels rather than comparative price levels. Absent such resolve, these benefits could be lost. In natural monopoly markets the efficiency benefits of a price level regime would be dampened. In the case of diversified public utilities, fully distributed costing would continue to distort prices and managerial decisions both in regulated and unregulated markets.[108]

In 1991 there was a further increase to 6.25 per cent but its intention was to be neutral, that is, equivalent to the previous 4.5 per cent given that international calls were now included in the basket.[109] This was the result of a set of negotiations in which both British Telecom's reluctance to accept some new international price-caps and the Government's reluctance to have an MMC reference which would have delayed the sale of its remaining 49 per cent shareholding may have influenced the outcome.[110]

In general, where productivity improvement is hard to come by, it is not surprising that discussion of changes in the formula in fact centres on the rate of return chosen. Thus it was not surprising that in 1991 Ian Byatt, regulating water and believing that underpricing and flotation and apparently over-generous initial price-control formulae were resulting in too high profits, revealed the rate of return which he believed was publicly supportable. Under the British system in its first ten years the regulator had sufficient discretion to avoid doing this. (In chapter 8 arguments are given as to why this could change.) However, the more formal and open the procedures, and the more a regulator has to disclose the detail of his calculations and give reasons for the assumptions he has made, the more probable it is that there will be argument over the choice of a rate of return. This may have the effect that, if *ex post* the rate of return has been unexpectedly high in the previous period, the regulator will be under pressure to assume that it should fall in the next period to a more normal level for that type of business, given its risks. There was such a difference in approach when airport price-control formulae came before the Monopolies and Mergers Commission (as they had to according to the airport licences). In 1987 the MMC determined X for Manchester Airport.[111] In that case it concluded that the value for X could be more demanding than the airport contended but did not reveal any particular expected rate of return. However, when it reviewed the British Airport Authority's south-east airports' price formula in 1991 its conclusions relied almost entirely on what it thought a reasonable return on the airports' existing and projected assets. This one might have expected, since the MMC customarily sets out its reasons in more detail than does a specialist regulator and is not expert in airport or any other productivity improvement. But, apart from other objections, it ignores the relations between changes in risks and profitability. To achieve similar *ex post* profitability, very different *ex ante* rates may be appropriate and at different times. The only reassurance a regulator could reasonably give is that the *ex post* rate of return should not be unreasonable given a reasonable improvement in efficiency.

Another approach to the periodic review would be to concentrate upon competitiveness – to analyse the areas where competition has been effective and where it has not, and to consider what measures might increase competition by allowing more entry or make profitable entry more likely. It may also be useful to recommend further interconnections or break-up.[112] Moreover, it seems reasonable that the utilities should explain *ex post* how far any increase in profitability was the result of improved productivity and how much due to external demand. British legislation normally reserves the duty of adopting measures to increase competition to the Government, possibly acting on the advice of the regulator.[113] Unfortunately, this makes their adoption problematic since what is done will depend upon the political circumstances of the time.

In conclusion, despite the important differences between rate-of-return regulation and RPI–X both require negotiations between regulator and regulated which, though they can be used mainly to create pressure to increase organizational and allocative efficiency, may also be distorted to reflect any social objectives that the regulator has over and above any laid down specifically in statute or licence. The role of the Fifth and Fourteenth Amendments in RPI–X is played by stability provisions that require that the regulated firms be enabled to make a profit, though this is to be interpreted as a right only if the firm is reasonably well managed. The ability of the regulator to conclude such negotiations in the consumer's interest depends crucially on the information available to him.

Notes

1   Littlechild (1983), p. 7.
2   This classification is related to economic notions of market failure and has been influenced by Breyer (1982), ch. 1; also Utton (1986), ch. 1; Waterson (1988), p. 2. On broader and narrower definitions of regulation used in economics, see Romer and Rosenthal (1987), p. 108. Many economists have said that the fundamental challenge is not privatization but regulation: Veljanovski (1987), pp. 16, 171; Rees (1986), p. 26. For the view that regulation is only warranted where there is serious market malfunction, see Kahn (1988a), pp. 54–7/I; and for the belief that, after AT&T's divestiture, the main obstacle to improved performance is US telecommunications was regulation, see Faulhaber (1987), p. xvii. Breyer (1982), p. 285, however, says that, 'where natural monopoly is at issue, regulation remains appropriate'; see also Craig (1989), pp. 147–8, 156–7.
3   McCraw (1984), p. 12.

4 Breyer and Stewart (1985), p. 26, n. 30. The key case, *Munn vs. Illinois*, 1876, established that some private economic activities were clothed with a public interest because they were monopolies or for other reasons; and, as a result, they had certain obligations – for example, not to discriminate – but also the right to a reasonable return: Horwitz (1989), pp. 59–62.

5 Breyer and Stewart (1985), p. 222.

6 Ibid., pp. 226–7.

7 Quoted in ibid., p. 227.

8 Quoted in ibid., pp. 228, 229.

9 Ibid.

10 Bonbright (1961), p. 159.

11 Quoted in Breyer and Stewart (1985), p. 229.

12 Bonbright (1961), pp. 148, 164; Keller (1981), p. 87. There were endless additional complications: for example if a utility started buying in its own debt (Pierce, Allison and Martin (1980), pp. 220, 221), let alone those arising from various asset-revaluation assumptions (Kahn (1988a), pp. 112–14/I).

13 Kahn (1988a), p. 26/I.

14 Rappaport (1986).

15 Quoted in Breyer and Stewart (1985), p. 234. Despite the common sense shown, and the overwhelming importance of this precedent for the future, in this instance the decision reached by the Supreme Court was the wrong one since it meant that natural gas was to be priced far below its market value. The misfortune was that at that time – and until recently – the US regulatory armoury did not enable the taxing of rent on natural gas and thus the expropriating of monopoly profits in a rational way. The problem is discussed in Breyer (1982), ch. 13; Kahn (1978), p. 15. The attempt to deregulate the gas industry in the early 1980s at first failed (Derthick and Quirk (1985), pp. 208–12), but was retrieved later. For the view I have followed on the significance of this case, see Bonbright (1961), p. 148.

16 Bonbright (1961), p. 189; Pierce, Allison and Martin (1980), pp. 212ff.; Breyer, (1982), pp. 38–40.

17 McCraw (1984), pp. 188–92; Hays (1981), pp. 141, 142.

18 Pierce, Allison and Martin (1980), p. 218.

19 Ibid., pp. 217–34.

20 Breyer (1982), pp. 58, 59.

21 Horwitz (1989), pp. 83–9.

22 Bonbright (1961), p. 147. On the economics of the regulatory lag, see Joskow (1974).

23 'Price really has no meaning except in terms of an assumed quality of service . . . Price regulation alone is economically meaningless': Kahn (1988a), p. 21/I; Hillman and Braeutigam (1989), pp. 38, 39. On the difficulties quality provides for regulation, see Spence (1975). In his discussions of turnpikes, Adam Smith has seen that a monopolist would charge more and let the quality deteriorate: Smith (1802), bk 5, ch. 1, pp. 97–8.

24 Kahn (1988a), p. 98/I.

25 Ibid., pp. 27–30/I; ibid., pp. 50ff./II. Hillman and Braeutigam (1989), pp. 16–35, discuss various aspects of this in detail and make it the most important reason for considering adopting RPI–X.

26 Vickers and Yarrow (1985), p. 24; Kolbe and Read (1984); Breyer (1982), p. 49.

27 Kahn (1988a), pp. 26–8/I.

28 Pierce, Allison and Martin (1980), pp. 251–7, 260; Kahn (1988a), p. 77/II, cites particularly the willingness of many regulators to substitute their own judgement on capital expenditure for that of the companies.

29 Beesley and Littlechild (1986), p. 41.

30 Kahn (1988a), p. 13/I.

31 Horwitz (1989), p. 236, gives as an example the monumental task of deciding if AT&T was pricing predatorily, a task that resulted in endless arguments over cost-apportionment methodology.

32 Kahn (1988a), p. 118/I. Aviation in 1938 was regulated as if it were a natural monopoly: McCraw (1984), p. 262.

33 Hillman and Braeutigam (1989), p. 38.

34 Ibid., ch. 2.

35 Sharkey (1982), p. 40.

36 Cornell and Webbank (1985), p. 44.

37 A. E. Kahn, cited by McCraw (1984), p. 271.

38 Coase (1979), cited by Kahn (1988a), p. 109/II.

39 This is the outstanding message of his powerful *Economics of Regulation* (1988). Kahn and Shew (1987), for example, is a particularly powerful demolition of specious arguments against marginal-cost pricing, at least from an economist's standpoint. O'Leary and Smith (1989), p. 224, conclude that this view was most influential in the 1970s, when economists' influence was at its height. Earlier, US public utilities were no more receptive to marginal-cost pricing than were UK nationalized industries: Shepherd (1966), pp. 62–3.

40 McCraw (1984), p. 222.

41 On the regulator's greater readiness to accept rate-of-return differences related to risk differences, see Kahn (1990a), p. 337.

42 Kahn (1990b), p. 6. In order to encourage efficiency through profit-seeking, Kahn would extend the provision found in some US states – and which we found in the Liverpool and Manchester railway statute – that allows for 50/50 profit-sharing above a certain maximum return: his profit-sharing would start above a level which would vary depending on the real cost of capital. On the Liverpool and Manchester Railway Act, 1826, see Parris (1965), p. 14.

43 McCraw (1984), p. 19.

44 State public-utility commissioners are especially liable to continue older styles of regulation and to be political: Kahn (1990a), p. 340.

45 DTI (1990), ch. 7.

46 Dasgupta and Stiglitz (1980) argued that, in general, monopoly promotes R. & D.: the monopolist will use it as a deterrent and potential competitors will use it as a means of effecting entry. However, regulators may disallow R. & D. expenditures that they believe unnecessary and are rarely able to force technological change: Berg and Tschirhart (1988), pp. 385–427.

47 Adam Smith (1802), bk. 1, ch. 11, used the word 'natural' – a word he quite often used – in his description of monopoly conditions: in particular, land rent is 'naturally a monopoly price'; see also bk. 1, ch. 7. John Stuart Mill is credited with the concept of natural monopoly ((1852), bk. 2, ch. 15, paras 3 and 4; but also bk. 1, ch. 1, para. 4; bk. 5, ch. 11, para. 11), but he did not analyse it. Farrer (1883) gave a useful account of the circumstances in which natural monopoly is likely to arise. The concept was first analysed in English by Marshall in 1890 (Marshall (1920), ch. 12). He derived his thinking from Cournot (1838), who had first correctly defined natural monopoly, in terms of a downward-sloping demand curve facing a seller. Marshall related it to his apparatus distinguishing between industries with increasing, constant and decreasing costs. For a further account of the history of the concept, see P. L. Williams (1978); Sharkey (1982), pp. 12–20; also Lowry (1973) and, for a different perspective, Hazlett (1985).

While the geometry for a single-product firm has been well understood for a long time, most natural monopolies are multi-product. The relation of economies of scope to natural monopoly was analysed in a number of path-breaking works in the 1970s: for example, Baumol, Bailey and Willig (1977); Panzar and Willig (1977); Faulhaber (1975). Further accounts are to be found in Sharkey (1982) and Berg and Tschirhart (1988), which also go into more complications than are needed for the intuitive understanding of the concept required here.

In rare circumstances monopoly output can be greater than competitive output: J. Robinson (1948), pp. 152, 153. Baumol and Klevorick (1970) analyse the circumstances in which rate-of-return regulation may increase output, though it will still be inefficient. There is a useful review of the effect of rate-of-return control and other regulatory constraints on efficiency in Berg and Tschirhart (1988), pp. 323–84. Pigou (1920), pp. 375–7, analysed the distortions created by sliding-scale profit control and shared profits.

48 These are the same as the Lerner rules for the Socialist manager referred to above in chapter 3: Lerner (1944).

49 The theoretical case for marginal-cost pricing is to be found in any microeconomics textbook. For strong arguments that regulating a contestable natural monopoly so as to get marginal-cost rather than average-cost pricing may be worth while, see Braeutigam (1989) and Brown and Sibley (1986), *passim*. The arguments abstract from second-best considerations, but in practice those rarely undermine the case for marginal-cost pricing: Kahn (1987), p. 3; Kahn (1988a), pp. 241–3/II.

50 Cf. J. Robinson (1948), pp. 179–208. The classic discussion, largely fired by the railway problem, is in Pigou (1920), ch. 17. For a modern treatment, see Martin (1989), pp. 373–406. As Pigou shows, only what he calls discrimination of the first degree leads to as efficient an output as does marginal-cost pricing. Kahn (1988a), pp. 130, 131/I, has argued that discrimination should be allowed to loss-makers (p. 123/I), but not where there is competition, except where it allows prices to move to long-run marginal costs (p. 172/I). There have been attempts to distinguish good and bad price discrimination with the last based wholly on demand elasticities, but any such distinction is political, not economic: Nelson (1959), pp. 96–7. There is a useful discussion in Braeutigam (1989), pp. 1, 309–15.

51 Natural monopolies can often split up their markets by area, or by type of user, so as to achieve sufficient discrimination to be profitable, both because competition is limited and because those who buy cheap from them cannot resell to those who would otherwise have to buy dear, either for technical reasons – gas, electricity, airport landing slots and telephone lines cannot be conveniently shared or resold – or because there are prohibitions on doing so – for example, the prohibitions on resale of British Telecom's line capacity that continued for some years after its privatization. Among the mechanisms that are used to discriminate are two-part tariffs: most natural monopolies employ a mixture of standing charges or line rentals with variable usage charges that can be used to help practise discrimination.

52 On the regulation of strong monopoly as being about getting prices as near marginal cost as possible, see Kahn (1990b), p. 1.

53 A difference in price may sometimes be allowed to be justified only by a cost difference. That is, a difference in price due to a quality difference may only be allowed where there is a cost difference also.

54 Short-run shortages always provide a problem for price control. RPI–X is no exception. Altering the formula cyclically would be as likely to lead to indeterminacy as the nationalized industries' formula of breaking even taking one year with another: Breyer (1982), p. 67; Kahn (1978), pp. 7, 8.

55 Ricardo (1862), ch. 12. Pigou (1920), pp. 373–5, analysed this issue. Posner (1969), p. 548, held the view that natural monopolies should be deregulated and taxed on their profits.

56 Kay and Vickers (1988), pp. 326–8. The economic case for franchising was first developed rigorously by the Victorian reformer Sir Edwin Chadwick as a contribution to the

1867 debate on railway regulation. This was recognized by the main modern advocate of the idea, H. Demsetz: Demsetz (1968). Telser (1969) argued that, though franchise bidding would eliminate monopoly profits, it would not result in marginal-cost prices. Demsetz (1971) pointed out that it would be possible to negotiate a contract that would do this too, but that it could easily become very complicated and arguably impractical. On the use of franchising in the case of roads, see Webb and Webb (1920), p. 116.

57 See, for example, Hillman and Braeutigam (1989), pp. 5–6; Goldberg (1976). For an analysis of the difficulties involved in franchising natural monopolies, see Williamson (1976), who notes its tendency to degenerate into rate- of-return regulation; also Vickers and Yarrow (1988), pp. 110–15.

58 It is possible to require bids at predetermined nominal or real price and output levels but this is only practical where the enterprise produces a few simple products without complex joint costs and unit costs, and where therefore the rate of profit does not alter markedly with demand. On the difficulty of reflecting quality in franchises, see Baumol (1975), p. 287.

59 See, for example, the citation of authors who wrote about the pricing problems of public enterprise, in Braeutigam (1989); also Brown and Sibley (1986).

60 By the 1960s the public interest had come to be seen as underlying older notions of the rationale regulation being the protection of consumers, but it was displaced in the 1970s by the tradition that developed out of Stigler (1971) (see chapter 11 below). Another way of putting the argument in the text is to say that, rationally, one cannot simultaneously advocate regulators' detailed involvement to secure marginal-cost pricing and accept the Stiglerian or any other predictive theory of regulation: see, for example, Nowotny, Smith and Trebing (1989). In Schmalensee and Willig (1989) discussion of the theories is separated: one chapter discusses theories of regulation; another normative precepts based on economic efficiency (see therein p. 1,299).

61 See, for example, J. R. Hicks' remarks on the limited help that economic theory has given to anti-monopoly legislation, in his preface to Hicks (1959), pp. xi–xii. Economic efficiency maximizes consumers' surplus, with the usual caveats about income distribution and the second-best. There is a useful discussion on the welfare implications of competition and regulation in the context of the American anti-trust laws in Martin (1989), pp. 16–43.

62 E. Sanders refers to the climate of antagonism that is normal between regulators and businesses, in Sanders (1987), p. 117. On the difficulties of applying this 'principal and agent theory', see Sappington and Stiglitz (1987), pp. 6–11. The FCC found difficulties in agreeing to marginal-cost pricing as it was 'difficult to use': Hillman and Braeutigam (1989), pp. 20, 21.

63 See, for example, Noll (1989), pp. 1,277–81. The matter will be taken further in chapter 11 below. Sometimes regulators have to interfere in what seems extreme operational detail – for example, over the design of meters to permit pricing flexibility: see Kahn (1978), p. 10. The accuracy of meters has been a repeated concern of regulators: see, for example, Ofgas (1988), pp. 7–8; (1989), pp. 15–16; (1990), pp. 8–9; (1991a), p. 31; also Oftel (1988a).

64 Littlechild (1983), p. 7. On pp. 12–13, he made it clear that he saw equity – the protection of the domestic and small-business subscribers – as the justification for profit limitation. See also Beesley and Littlechild (1986), pp. 40–1.

65 Littlechild (1983). Because of its price ceiling, an RPI–X regulated firm will have a strong incentive to increase its profits by increasing price discrimination, multi-part tariffs, etc.: Hillman and Braeutigam (1989), pp. 38–9. It may also find it profitable to price below marginal cost on competitive goods and services so as to take more advantage of inelastic demand for non-competitive goods and services: ibid., pp. 40, 41, 59.

66 Littlechild (1983), p. 8.

67 Wickwar (1938), pp. 170–3; Kahn (1988a), p. 61/II. Hillman and Braeutigam (1989), p. 115, n. 143, make some reference to the practicalities of such advances in the United States. There is no particular virtue in choosing the Retail Price Index to be the price index used. What is important is that the index chosen is not one which the industry itself can directly influence and therefore that it is recognizable as a general price index.

68 Hillman and Braeutigam (1989), p. 37.

69 Littlechild (1983), pp. 32–3.

70 DTI (1991).

71 As early as 1984, Oftel reacted to complaints against special services price increases by stating that BT could not be free of all control on them, but that it would not investigate except where it suspected an abuse of monopoly power so bringing in the fair-trading laws where there were omissions in the licence: Oftel (1985a), p. 12; also (1986a) pp. 11–14. An example of this was the draft licence amendment agreed between Oftel and BT imposing price-caps on charges for private circuits. Oftel's reason for requiring this was their 'excessive price': Oftel (1989b). The FCC at the end of the 1980s came to subject AT&T's basic and non-basic interstate services to separate rate-caps, and followed a similar policy with local companies: see Kahn (1990a), p. 338. Also Oftel (1992a).

72 BT Licence, condn. 24; Gas Authorisation, condn. 3; Public Electricity Supply Licence, condn. 3; Airport Permit to Charge, annex B; Water Appointment, condn. B.

73 For calculation difficulties, see, for example, Oftel (1986a), p. 9.

74 This formulation means that it is more favourable to the firm as inflation increases than if it decreases. Neutrality with respect to inflation would be achieved if X were a multiplicative constant. Regimes adopting price-control formulae are best advised to adopt them in the X.RPI, rather than RPI–X, form if possible, so as to avoid stimulating excessive profits during a period of depression or recession when business profits generally will be depressed and to avoid the controlled firms having to hand back real profits just because of inflation. RPI–X was apparently chosen because of its (superficially) greater intelligibility; but the consequences eventually came home to roost when, during the recession of 1990–2, it helped edge regulated-monopoly profits higher when business profits generally were depressed.

75 Littlechild (1983), p. 35.

76 Competition and Services (Utilities) Act, 1992.

77 Although the Government wished to increase international competition and so reduce prices, it was frustrated, where the government of the other country did not want the same, by a set of international agreements which often secured that, when one country lowered its call charges, the actual revenue payable to the country at the other end increased, even if it did not also lower its charges. For all the brave words in DTI (1990), pp. 56–64, the imposition of an international price-cap or the inclusion of international calls within the basket recognizes that international calls remain a monopoly in so far as there is not international competition: Oftel (1992a), pp. 10, 11.

78 Breyer (1982), pp. 66–8; Berg and Tschirhart (1988), pp. 449–53; Faulhaber (1975).

79 Oftel (1988c). As early as 1987 Carsberg gave notice that when he had to renegotiate X in 1989 he might extend price control to private circuits, though he did not give his reasons for wanting to do so: Oftel (1988a), p. 10, and again in Oftel (1992a), pp. 10–12.

80 Vickers and Yarrow (1988), pp. 69–76. Hillman and Braeutigam (1989), p. 54, have suggested that because of these complexities, these details of the formulae should be negotiated with the regulator rather than with government.

81 Cf. Beesley (1981), p. 14, who argued that eleven years of attempting to allocate costs under the FCC had been a complete failure.

82 See Hillman and Braeutigam (1989), pp. 70–3, on problems in allowing for inflation.

83 Littlechild (1986), pp. 28–30, 35, 36.

84 Where the formulae become complicated, cost pass through is bound to encourage the misallocation of resources: Waterson (1988), ch. 2.

85 Hillman and Braeutigam (1989), pp. 55–7, have discussed some of the difficulties.

86 Carsberg concluded that such adjustment for demand would be too complicated and hard to understand, and noted that some demand changes result from good management: Oftel (1988c). Also Oftel (1992a), pp. 27, 28. Some of the distortion would have been avoided if the formula had been X.RPI rather than RPI–X. On this effect, see Oftel (1992a), p. 3.

87 The comprehensive review of rate-of-return regulation in US telecommunications was announced by A. C. Sikes, Assistant Secretary for Communication and Information, Department of Commerce, Nov. 1986, NTIA docket no. 61091/6191.

88 Ibid., n. 2, quoted by Hillman and Braeutigam (1989), p. 84.

89 When the Duopoly Review of BT and Mercury took place in 1990–1, there was a difficulty of fairness in reconciling the government proposals, presented in DTI (1991), with the licence amendments then negotiated with BT and Mercury which were then themselves rejected and replaced.

90 They probably do not protect unprofitability due to inefficiency or declining demand. The wording varies considerably, perhaps being clearest in the Water Act, 1989.

91 McCraw (1984), pp. 91–4. Hillman and Braeutigam (1989), pp. 78–81, discuss the constitutional issues. Presumably, they were unaware of the UK statutory duties to safeguard the regulated firms' returns, or saw them as an insufficient safeguard.

92 Presumably because effective competition was absent, the Director General of Ofwat was explicit in regarding it as his duty to consider what was a reasonable return on capital: Ofwat (1991c), p. 9. See also Littlechild (1986). Carsberg said, incorrectly in my view, that the difference between the use of price-caps and rate-of-return control is exaggerated: Oftel (1988c).

93 See Kahn's reference to applied microeconomics, quoted by McCraw (1984), p. 243.

94 Ofgas was particularly disadvantaged by asymmetrical information. An earlier annual report had disclosed how hard it was to get cost data from British Gas to explain the non-gas cost base for RPI–X. This led to a cost-apportionment exercise. Disagreements with British Gas over this led to prolonged delays. It was not completed until 1990. And even then the outcome was not fully satisfactory. Part of the problem was that it attempted to apportion joint costs fairly rather than to establish cost causation. See Ofgas (1989), pp. 23, 24; (1990), pp. 19–20, 36–7; (1991a), pp. 48–9.

95 The regulator is appointed by the relevant Secretary of State, for not more than five years (Telecommunications Act, 1984, s. 1(1), 1(2); Gas Act, 1986, s. 1(1), 1 (27); Water Act, 1989, S. 5 (1), 5 (2); Electricity Act, 1989, S. 1 (7), 1(2)). The regulator is one person, a 'Director General', under all statutes (except that the regulator is a body, the Civil Airports Authority, under the Airports Act, 1986, as are the National Rivers Authority under the Water Act, 1989, and the Independent Television Commission under the Broadcasting Act, 1990). He, or they, may be removed only 'on the ground of incapacity or misbehaviour' (Telecommunications Act, 1984, s. 1(3); Gas Act, 1986, s. 1(3); Water Act, 1989, s. 5(3); Electricity Act, 1989, s. 1(3)). The regulator appoints his staff within a budget provided by the Treasury, a budget over the size of which he has no control (Telecommunications Act, 1984, s. 1(5); Water Act, 1989, s. 5(3); Gas Act, 1986, schedule 1; Electricity Act, 1989, schedule 1).

96 On enforcement, see Telecommunications Act, 1984, s. 11, 16, 17; Gas Act, 1986, s. 28, 29; Airports Act, 1986, s. 40, 48, 49, 50; Water Act, 1989, s. 20, 21, 22; Electricity Act, 1989, s. 25, 26, 27.

97 On fair-trading powers, see Telecommunications Act, 1984, s. 50; Gas Act, 1986, s. 34 (4); Water Act, 1989, s. 28; Electricity Act, 1989, s. 43; also Airports Act, 1986, s. 56, if the need arises.

98 On complaints, see Telecommunications Act, 1984, s. 49, 52, 54; Gas Act, 1986, s. 31, 38; Airports Act, 1986, s. 48; Water Act, 1989, s. 162; Electricity Act, 1989, s. 45. All these were to be strengthened in the Competition and Services (Utilities) Act, 1992.

99 On review by the MMC, see Telecommunications Act, 1984, s. 13, 14; Gas Act, 1986, s. 24, 25; Airports Act, 1986, s. 43, 44, 45; Water Act, 1989, s. 16, 17; Electricity Act, 1989, s. 12, 13.

100 While the relevant words in the Airports Act, 1986, seem consistent with the view that the MMC is a court of appeal, the Civil Airports Authority in 1991 showed that it took another view of it, as a body advisory to it (the CCA), when it set a more demanding value for X than the MMC's recommendation: MMC (1991). For further discussion, see chapter 8 below.

101 Hillman and Braeutigam (1989), p. 84, citing National Telecommunications and Information Administration docket no. 61091/6191, 'Response by British Telecommunications plc to the NTIA's request for Comments dated 10 Octber 1986', p. 2. Helm (1987), p. 49, says that, if nationalized industry cost targets had been extrapolated, the original value for British Gas's X would have been 3 or 4 per cent rather than 2.

102 Oftel (1986a), p. 9. Carsberg's belief in the relevance of rate of return to RPI–X is evident in, for example, Oftel (1985b); (1986b); (1987a); (1987c); (1988c). However, in announcing the result of his 1989 review of X, when he increased it to 4.5 per cent, (Oftel (1989b)), he altered his previous message by allowing that excess profitability might be carried forward for two or three years, rather than proceeded against at once as he had earlier suggested, in Oftel (1988b). However, while stressing the primary role of RPI–X, he understood also the role of rate of return Oftel (1992a), pp. 12, 13, 15–17, and (1992b).

103 Oftel (1987a), pp. 12–13.

104 It was not until 1990 that it heralded the resumption of its staffing reductions, believing that it had an improved management structure and systems which would at least enable it to save on staff numbers without jeopardizing quality: BT (1990a), pp. 2, 3.

105 Hillman and Braeutigam (1989), p. 77.

106 Gilbert and Newbery (1988).

107 Beesley and Littlechild (1986), p. 41. When Littlechild came to consider the application of RPI–X to water he saw its regulation as permanent, and conceded that rate-of-return considerations were implied in the choice of a value for X: Littlechild (1986), pp. 28–30; Ofwat (1991a), p. 9; also Ofgas (1991b) and Oftel (1991b). For the argument that RPI–X is vulnerable to deliberate inefficiency to build up the cost base before renegotiation of X, see Sopengels (1982). As Kahn has said, 'Profit envy is simply incompatible with a true transfer of investments risks from ratepayers to investors': Kahn (1990b), p. 6.

108 Hillman and Braeutigam (1989), p. 98.

109 DTI (1991). There was bitter correspondence between the regulator and BT's chairman: *The Financial Times*, 19 April 1990; 23 April 1990; 24 April 1990.

110 *The Financial Times*, 23 October 1991, p. 20.

111 MMC (1987).

112 For Carsberg's repeated interest in the need to extend competition, see, for example, Oftel (1987a), pp. 2–4. Breyer (1982), pp. 160–1, also raises the question how far a regulator ought to be able to take structural decisions.

113 Hillman and Braeutigam (1989), p. 84.

7

The uses of information

With perfect information the three approaches of regulation, nationalisation and control via tax or subsidy are equivalent . . . With perfect information none of the controversies about the efficiency of government control or its form would arise.

D. E. M. Sappington and J. E. Stiglitz (1987)[1]

Without adequate information, as experience has shown, regulation cannot be effective.[2] A state of unbalanced or asymmetric information benefits the regulated by comparison with not only the regulator, but also actual and potential competitors and customers. However, an attempt to define the information generally needed to equalize the positions of the parties in this respect would lead readily to an impossible, even infinitely demanding, programme. Rather, the course adopted here is to consider what information is needed for a regulator to be able to confirm the existence in any particular case of the economic regulatory offences already described – unnatural monopoly, predation, unequal access, and allocative and organizational inefficiency – as well as some of the social regulatory offences that have been mentioned. Yet however amply one defines the information thus required from a natural monopoly, what is actually available to the regulator will be less than he needs for proof – it is for example in the interests of the regulated to withhold significant information. This means that regulatory offences cannot be precisely defined and monitored. Hence, regulators need to be able to use their discretion. But information affects regulatory competence in many different ways. There is for example an inverse relation between the simplicity of the objectives of the regulator and the regulated and the ease with which relevant information can be extracted. And there is also commonly in democracies an inverse relation between the discretion regulators are allowed and their powers of enforcement which has at its root an important democratic safeguard. There are understandable reasons why in a democracy the relations between the availability of information, reliance on publicity and the power of enforcement are complicated.

This chapter deals with a number of topics (which are more closely related than they may at first appear). Section 1 looks at an American regulatory episode in order to illustrate the strengths and weaknesses of the policy of basing regulation entirely on publicity. It is a particularly pure example of an attempt to regulate by extracting and publicizing information without licences or powers of enforcement. However, there has been a long-standing tendency in Britain to try to regulate through a similar reliance on investigation and publicity rather than on clear contractual arrangements involving powers of enforcement, though it has often not been explicit that this was its nature (section 2). One incidental result of the disconnection between information and power was that the regulator or investigator commonly imputed objectives to the bodies under control or inquiry which were not their own. Moreover, their real objectives were often complicated and shifting. It is argued that effective regulation requires that, as far as possible, the regulator and the regulated should have substantially the same objectives for the firm; and that these objectives need to be simple and, as far as possible, unchanging (section 3). It is argued in section 4 that the only objectives that can be realized efficiently in large organizations are commercial ones, aimed at the goal of financial profitability. This is not a logical point. It so happens that the appropriate accounting and other control mechanisms have not yet been developed in the detail and rigour required to serve objectives other than commercial ones. This has profound consequences for the effective regulation of large bodies. What information can be regarded as adequate for regulation is discussed in section 5, where it is argued that it is never enough.

7.1 Regulation through publicity: American experience

An influential view holds that, especially in a democracy, a regulator should work through publicity; and that it is harmful if he has powers of enforcement. There was practically no US federal regulation before 1887 but there was some by the states.[3] One example was a model of the discretionary approach that relies on publicity without enforcement. Charles Francis Adams was a Boston patrician – great-grandson of the second, and grandson of the third, US president, and scion of perhaps the most famous American family.[4] After fighting in the Civil War, married and past thirty, he was looking for an occupation grand and demanding enough for an Adams. Banking and the professions he found unexciting. Going into business in the ordinary sense was not then an occupation for a gentleman. And standing for election in the family tradition was too demeaning when the tone of public life was declining as faction, porkbarrel politics and corruption were entering it after the Civil War. 'Surveying the whole field . . . I fixed on the railroad system as the most developing force and largest field of the day, and determined to attach myself to it.'[5] Since it provided so much of the dynamic for American economic growth and cultural change, he was undoubtedly right about its economic importance. He himself still hankered after public recognition. So his decision was, not to join the railroad interest, but to wage a war against what he saw as the corruption of the financial interests behind the railroads and their sacrifice of both the customers' and the shareholders' interests. He had recognized that he was a good writer. His many articles on railroad policy and regulation drew in part on British experience, his British contacts being excellent. (His father had been a popular and effective US ambassador to London during the Civil War.) He thus formed a view of the history of British railway regulation, drawing upon what he had read and on those contacts. But he put his own slant on it. As a commentator said, he was 'too active and rational a man to be quite ready to accept some of the facts of modern English history'.[6] In his writings he made the success of the British committees and commissions of the 1860s, and later of those of the 1870s, seem greater than it had been. He also used British experience, real and elaborated, to show what to avoid. As in Britain, a 10 per cent rate-of-return ceiling had been adopted in Massachusetts. He criticized not only that but any ceiling on profits as a disincentive to business growth and innovation except in so far as it could be evaded by stock watering and over-investment. He blamed this use of a 10 per cent maximum on the example Gladstone had set in the 1844 Act. His main target, however, was stock watering, which was even commoner in the United States than in Britain. Wealthy companies did it to evade profit control, poor ones because otherwise they could not pay dividends on existing shares. Massachusetts had tried to check the tendency to water stock by encouraging railroad competition. And as a result of its policy of competition Massachusetts had sixty-two railroads and the densest railway network in the country. Adams argued against this over-provision not only because of its evident results in defrauding shareholders, but also because, in his judgement, the railroads' high fixed and low variable costs made competition inefficient and unsustainable.

He wrote many articles – some journalism, some substantial – but what gave him a prominent and lasting reputation was his essay 'A Chapter of Erie' (1869), one of the first classics of muck-raking. As such, it stands comparison with Upton Sinclair's 1906 onslaught in *The Jungle* on the inhumanity and insanitariness of the Chicago stockyards or Rachel Carson's *Silent Spring*, which had an enormous effect in drawing attention to the growing devastation of the environment in the 1960s.[7] It stayed in print for more than a hundred years. Its satire is based on sustained sarcasm and boundless contempt for the Vanderbilts, Jay Goulds, Jim Fisks and others who made their railroad fortunes at the public expense. Undeterred by the possibility of libel, it catalogued the lengths that the rival factions went to gain control of the railroads and how they defrauded the stockholders in the process. For example, he described the Board of the Erie Railroad as a 'throng of panic-stricken railway directors – looking more like a frightened gang of disturbed thieves, disturbed in the division of their plunder, than the wealthy representatives of a great corporation'.

Rather than statutory controls, he recommended the setting up of a regulatory commission. But he believed that he had learnt a curious lesson from the failure in Britain to establish a commission or commissioners with any real power: such a commission should have no powers of enforcement, only the power to demand what information it needed. He was in fact recognizing a necessity, given the deep reluctance of contemporary regulators in Britain and Massachusetts to give officials who were not judges real power. But he turned this into a virtue. His commission would work through publicity, shaming the railroads into compliance. That appealed to Adams, the writer. So was born what came later to be known in America, by a happy turn of phrase, as a 'sunshine commission', one whose power came only from the light that it shone on ill-doings.

He had already been working on the Massachusetts legislature to persuade it to set up his commission when he wrote his classic essay, and in the month that it appeared he was made the first chairman of the new Massachusetts Board of Railroad Commissioners. He is possibly unique among regulators in that he had diagnosed the evil, proposed the solution and persuaded the legislature to adopt it and then was given the top regulatory job in it. All this just after he had published 120 pages of sustained invective scorching the class he was about to regulate. As a younger contemporary reported:

At first many people were disposed to treat it with good-natured ridicule. It had really no power except the power to report. But its reports were strong enough to command respect, and even obedience. The commissioners were by no means infallible. Some of their theories were wrong. They were in favour of a partial state ownership of railroads ... but the commissioners had something better than correct theories: they had practical business sagacity.[8]

As Adams put it, 'the Commissioners have no power except to recommend and report. Their only appeal is to publicity. The Board is at once prosecuting officer, judge, and jury but with no sheriff to enforce its process.'[9]

In their search for material the three Commissioners were often out of the office inspecting the property and services of the railroads. Safety drew their attention. There were many accidents, some spectacularly gruesome. After each, Adams and his colleagues would arrive at once to make a report. For instance, after one major accident he spent ten days piecing together the evidence. His report found that the Eastern Railroad had been lax and negligent in regard to safety. He then recommended improvements to avoid such accidents in future. He persuaded railroad representatives to join him on a working party to inspect safety devices and later on another to draw up more-adequate rules and regulations. Such was the publicity, the railroads had no practical alternative but to agree.

He adopted a similar approach to rate regulation. He rejected maxima, objective tests and flat, across-the-board increases. He recoiled from the establishing of costs in individual rate cases, maintaining that the work would be endless. Typical of his approach to rate regulation was that shown in an 1871 letter from him. In it he pointed out to the Massachusetts railroads that locomotives which had once cost $30,000 could now be bought for $12,000.[10] What did they propose to do about it? If they did not pass on some of the benefit to the customer through reduced rates, he would advise the legislature to force it. He also pointed out that lower rates should result in increased demand. Questionnaires followed the letter. As a result of this badgering, he claimed, the railroads reduced their rates selectively so that users gained by an amount of up to half a million dollars. And whether or not his commission was mainly responsible rates did decline sharply during the last third of the nineteenth century. As Professor Hadley wrote in 1885, the strength of the Massachusetts commissioners was that 'They abandoned courses which proved wrong; they followed up with successful persistence thoughts which proved right. Gradually but surely they introduced improvements in accounting which since 1878 have been further extended by the commissioners of other states.'[11]

The sunshine approach that Adams and his colleagues had pioneered worked best where the regulated firm's faults were visible and cried to heaven; where a certain amount of devilling and bullying to extract fact otherwise hidden made good copy which the regulators had the talent to make into headline material; and where they had the prestige and the contacts in the legislature to make it a credible threat that they had the influence to persuade it to do something about the abuse if the railroads did not do something about it first. Inevitably, it was an approach to railroad regulation that worked best with safety, though their protests against rail tariffs gained force from the agricultural distress that led to the start of the Granger movement, which had as a focus the discriminatory, and allegedly high, rates railroads set for agricultural produce. By contrast, the sunshine approach did not work well where the issues were ones of detail, and public opinion could not be engaged.

Adams had himself become bored and pulled out of the Board in 1879. Thereafter, his career was less focused and in old age he became embittered. He had been proud that the sole statutory duty his commission had had was to interpret the public interest and its only power, publicity. He saw this approach to regulation break apart in disputes, and his and other such commissions become enmeshed in rule-making and judicial reviews. No one with as much influence and ability to raise public opinion was found to replace Adams, so that the Board's effectiveness declined. (A regulator's influence it always enhanced by the strength of his personality and gift for communication; but this is particularly so where that influence has to rely for its effect on publicity.) The railroads, moreover, developed ways of counteracting the effectiveness of this and other state railroad commissions. Amalgamation increased their ability to influence legislators who, as political standards declined towards the end of the century, were more vulnerable to corruption. As railroads spread over more than one state through amalgamation, they were also able not only to play one state regulator off against another, but also to use the constitutional provision that interstate commerce was a federal matter in order to challenge state decisions, which increasingly brought regulatory matters before the federal courts.[12] The result of this was the Interstate Commerce Act, 1887, which, while it set up a federal regulatory commission for railroads, brought about a development of still greater consequence: regulation in future was to be under the aegis of the courts.

7.2   Sunshine regulation in Britain

The principle that a regulatory commission should rely on publicity for its effect had a longer but, because of the stronger laws against libel, dimmer history in Britain. Outside the relatively few industries like transport and electricity where legalistic commissions were established, there was a tendency to rely on variants of the old nineteenth-century Blue Book tradition of occasionally establishing a committee to write a fact-finding report. Depending on the public and political reception of that report (and of course the relevance of legislation to solving the problems it delineated), legislation might follow. The sunshine principle was behind the Standing Committee on Trusts as it operated in the early 1920s.[13] However because of the libel laws and the expectation that a report would not cast blame unless it could prove an offence, the Standing Committee on Trusts and other such bodies could do very little to prevent the growth of the collusive arrangements and anti-competitive practices preventing competition and outright merger from improving the efficiency of British firms but appealed to the consensus-seeking instincts of a society of top industrialists and politicians – most of whom knew each other.[14] Protected from litigation, they were robust enough to ignore the criticism made by the Standing Committee on Trusts and other bodies without power.

At a more fundamental level, the tradition of giving regulator, whether minister, civil servant or independent body, little or no effective discretionary power other than that of information gathering and publicity, reflects a deep-seated reluctance to give executive or enforcement power to individuals unless their constitutional subordination and the bounds and nature of the power thus granted are clearly specified. To quote John Locke at the end of the seventeenth century:

> The executive power placed anywhere but in a person that has also a share in the legislative is visibly subordinate and accountable to it, and may be at pleasure changed and displaced . . . Of other ministerial and subordinate powers in a commonwealth, we need not speak, they being so multiplied with infinite variety in the different customs and constitutions of distinct commonwealths, that it is impossible to give a particular account of them all. Only thus much which is necessary to our present purpose we may take notice of concerning them, that they have no manner of authority, any of them, beyond what is by positive grant and commission delegated to them, and are all of them accountable to some other power in the commonwealth.[15]

There is a telling episode in which Parliament departed from this tradition, and which James Morrison indicated was a reason why it proved impossible to persuade it a few years later to allow official commissioners to have real power to regulate the railways.[16] The original bill for the Poor Law of 1834 provided for there to be independent commissioners to administer the reformed poor law; and it laid down in detail what their objectives, powers and criteria were to be.[17] But in debate, controversy and impatience with detail led to a watering down and blurring of that detail (just as happened ten years later with the passage of Gladstone's railway bill). The unintended result was that the three Poor Law Commissioners were given wide authority and discretion, which they used to the full. They, and their assistants, rode up and down the country forcing parishes to amalgamate so as to provide workhouses, and bullying them to limit outdoor relief and to segregate the sexes within the workhouses, breaking up married couples and families. Thus they became the most hated officials in the land – the Three Bashaws of Somerset House. Yet, because of the high cost of the old system of poor relief, reaction to the riots that there had been against them in rural districts and the importance of the cost savings they could make for the landed interest, they continued, despite complaints against their unbounded power, until 1847, when they were hounded into subordination and made responsible to a new minister. This was the kind of approach to commission-building which, running against tradition as it did and because of the notoriety and unpopularity of the agency that it empowered, re-established the old wisdom for a long time to come. (Indeed, there is still hesitation about creating separate executive agencies.) Parliament was prepared to have judges and judge-like officials, fact-finders, inspectors and officials who were ministerial advisers, but in peacetime remained reluctant to give substantial authority and discretionary power to officials.

Somewhat disguised by the different forms it took, the sunshine approach – again with the less-than-burning light expected in the British climate – was at the heart of relations between government and the nationalized industries. For even when ministers were the regulators there remained traces of the reluctance to confer the power of enforcement as well as that of publicity, to give ministers substantial power where, as over the nationalized industries, they could then exercise it arbitrarily to affect the activities of substantial numbers of people and the expenditure of large sums of money. Though, as elected politicians, they were politically accountable, prudence recognized that while they might be sensible, judicious and restrained, they might also be inexperienced in the direction of large organizations, or they might be temperamentally impulsive, grandiose in their ambitions or motivated by a host of political or other short-term ambitions. In other words, the ability to gather facts and the use of his influence to persuade a regulated industry or political or public opinion, as might be relevant in the circumstances, of the need for changes in the business behaviour of the industry was a safer power to give even a minister than any exact powers to enforce those changes. Hence from the 1930s on there was a tendency for ministers frequently to set up committees and commissions to investigate matters when they believed there to be something wrong with a nationalized industry, culminating in the standing remit given to the Monopolies and Mergers Commission in 1980.[18] At times Parliament – as through the Select Committee on Nationalised Industries in the 1950s and 1960s – established similar fact-finding procedures, with various powers of extracting information. Where a matter was popularly judged to be one of great public importance – not unexpectedly, a major accident or a damaging strike was the most likely – a judge or other senior lawyer was often chosen to run a quasi-judicial inquiry, but again without power of enforcement. Alternatively, a vigorous minister, believing that changes were needed, might make the running himself, whipping up public and political opinion to the point where his political colleagues agreed that legislation was needed. However, because the legislation never proscribed the kinds of behaviour deemed to be regulatory offences, the nationalized industries were never brought before the courts on such matters, so that the effectiveness in regulatory terms of any such initiative – whether prompted by a report or a minister – depended more on the public endorsement it received and on the willingness of the nationalized industry, or other public body, to be influenced by it, than on the force of law. This was true even where ministers changed the heads of nationalized industries or where new legislation reorganized the industry. Undoubtedly these measures would result in some significant changes, but whether the economic or other policy changes the fact-finding commission, minister or, by implication, Parliament wanted were translated into changes in behaviour depended ultimately on whether the nationalized industry was persuaded to make those changes. As we have seen, though many excellent reports were written, many ministerial guidelines given and much legislation passed, the nationalized industries were repeatedly not persuaded to adopt the techniques, or take the other steps, needed to improve their efficiency, often despite considerable enforced changes in organization. (It was an inevitable consequence of the approach that there tended to be more disruptive changes in organization than were desirable on efficiency grounds, a tendency which survived in some even after privatization.)

Experience of the British version of the sunshine approach shows that it too works best when safety, working conditions, quality or more recently the environment is involved, because it is on these matters that public and political opinion can be most readily and persistently engaged. Indeed, another way in which the sunshine approach can work is by the regulator's becoming a bureau dealing with the complaints of the many, which may be fed to it directly by the aggrieved or through representative organizations, pressure groups or members of the national legislature or local government. In such a role of ombudsman, its power over the regulated will be much greater if it also has legal powers to extract information and powers to enforce its decisions. (It is more likely to be given these, if only because its decisions over individual complaints are unlikely to affect the overall policies or profitability of the enterprise. Moreover, the facts may be more tractable in such cases.) But even here, whether or not it has powers of enforcement, its authority will be increased by the knowledge that it can and will give damaging publicity to some newsworthy complaints, so building up its popular and political reputation, as happened over phone boxes and gas disconnections.

Where a regulatory commission cannot enforce its findings, there will be a greater readiness to allow the information that it uses to be more incomplete and less thoroughly tested than there will be for a body that can, which has commonly been expected to weigh evidence carefully and adopt more court-like procedures. But over-reliance on publicity, often based on inadequate information, goes to the root of the reason why the regulatory regimes described in the first three chapters all failed. None of them found a way of giving the regulator enough power of enforcement to be effective. The United States found a way out of this dilemma through the courts, but that, as we shall see in the next chapter, had other disadvantages.

There are lessons to be learnt from the sunshine tradition which should not be forgotten in the design of a new regulatory regime.

(1) A gift for publicity helps explain the effectiveness of unofficial reports like those of Ralph Nader in the United States in the 1960s and 1970s. Whatever the form of regulation, a compelling and vivid prose style is a formidable aid to a regulator. Carsberg's effectiveness has been surely increased by his ability to convey his thinking, even nuances of his judgement, with great clarity and well-chosen words in a style which perfectly fits his personality; as in his time Alfred Kahn's was by his wit and command of the medium of television. Moreover, just as Charles Francis Adams' impact was strengthened by the forcefulness and lucidity of his annual reports, so would be that of any other regulator issuing annual reports with those qualities, as Oftel does.[19] A modern British independent regulator, equipped as he is with considerable powers, would if prudent still rely more on publicity, and threats of publicity, than on legal enforcement, as Carsberg has often done, for example over the publication of quality statistics and in limiting individual price increases.

(2) The value of the occasional report which relies on persuading public and political opinion that effective action is needed is greatest where something is plainly and visibly wrong. It is not an effective way of controlling an enterprise as a matter of routine, or of improving its efficiency. Such a conclusion has been repeatedly demonstrated by the problems there have been in controlling nationalized industries and other public bodies.

(3) Because public and political opinion is usually more interested in social issues like safety, working conditions and more recently the environment, an independent regulator who seeks publicity for the reasons given above will be pulled constantly towards using whatever powers he has to act for the consumer against the regulated firm in these matters. But consumers have repeatedly shown themselves to be more readily concerned over quality than over price. And experience of UK shareholders' meetings since privatization shows that they are readier to complain as consumers than to press for higher profits, though that could alter if profits dip. Hence another reason for the tendency for economic regulation to broaden into social regulation (discussed in chapter 9).

(4) Because many consumers' concerns are immediate, an independent regulator will gain greatly in his ability to persuade consumers that he is doing a good job if he is able to investigate emergencies and remedy consumers' complaints.

(5) While sunshine commissions in Britain and elsewhere have commonly had extensive powers to demand information, the information made available in this way has always fallen far short of that which could be made available (see section 4). Although a sunshine commission might be effective if it had abundant information (to an extent that will be described), yet no powers of enforcement, it would still seem unwise for it to rely on publicity shaming the regulated firm into compliance on economic and other detailed matters which cannot readily be made to attract publicity. Moreover, the regulated firm would probably use its ampler resources to build up its own publicity and lobbying to the extent necessary for it to be able to out-gun the independent regulator, unless it permitted serious accidents or allowed a visible and substantial decline in quality.

(6) What underlies the importance of communication to an independent regulator is that he exists to mediate between the consumer and the producer. He has to know the producer well. And if it is wise the regulated firm will take every opportunity to get to know him. But too close a relationship between them, unbalanced by as strong an understanding on his part of the consumer's needs, can result in regulatory capture – that is, in the regulator's becoming too identified with the interests of the regulated firm. To counter this, and discharge his duty to the consumer, a regulator has to work hard at establishing communications with consumers and their representatives. This balance can be achieved by associating formal machinery with the regulator to institutionalize the consumer's interest. The new British system of independent regulation, as will appear, has done this. (In most cases the machinery is substantially more promising than was that for the nationalized industries.) Thus, the regulator also needs publicity not for self-advertisement but in order to ensure that he has consumer support for the issues he has taken up with the regulated firm. Otherwise, his position may be weak. He has to expect that the regulated firm will use the resources of its publicity and lobbying machines against him. But support gained through judicious publicity can help him to maintain a stand against a firm. More important still, even with the breadth of discretion an independent British regulator has, there is always the possibility of new legislation that will amend, transform or even abolish his position, but here too publicity can help him. For in preventing the success of lobbying by the regulated firm for such changes to the law (lobbying that may be invisible and inaudible to him) his greatest strength may be evidence that he has consumer support. (But more on this in chapters 9 and 11.)

(7) As we have seen, there has always been reluctance to give regulators substantial powers of enforcement which could result in significant policy or financial consequences unless they adopted court-like or similarly constrained procedures. In general, this has been true of ministers, as of other regulators. However, the new British system of regulation has departed from tradition in giving regulators considerable powers of enforcement over breaches of licence conditions. And where they have such powers they may be expected to demand more information to support their

judgements. But, as will appear, it would be a mistake to suppose that they can acquire enough exact information to achieve the standards of proof required in a court of law.

7.3 The preconditions of adequate information: alignment of objectives

One can read widely in the literature on regulation – whether written by lawyers, economists, political scientists or experts in public administration – without finding much on precisely what information a regulator needs. One reason for this is the strength of the public-inquiry and the judicial traditions. In Britain, the occasional commission, committee or other review into a natural monopoly before or after nationalization called for, or occasionally demanded, evidence. What it wanted in this way depended on the questions implied by its terms of reference; and, depending on its resources, it also did its own investigations or commissioned them from others. Yet the bodies under investigation customarily produced fewer, and less revealing, data than required. Attempts were then made to get more data. But in the end, if the inquiry were not to be spun out too long a conclusion had to be reached, and recommendations made, on the basis of whatever evidence there was. In the United States (and in Britain in times gone by) the production of information before regulatory commissions and the courts was similar, though reflecting differences in procedure – the two sides were likely to be extracting information from each other. There would be certain formal procedures for admitting and for not admitting evidence, and for allowing for its testing. But again, and for the same reasons, in the end a judgement would have to be reached on the basis of the evidence made available.[20]

Regulated bodies commonly resort to one or more of the following tactics when asked to produce information that they are reluctant to disclose:

(1) They may produce little information even for their own purposes, especially in sensitive areas, so that they can believably deny their ability to produce anything more than that for the regulator or court, or they may keep it back-of-the-envelope and informal, so that they can use its lack of quality as a reason for non-disclosure. Thus, it was common to find during the process of privatization that many public enterprises had less, or worse quality, management information than one would have expected them to have if they had been private and working in a competitive environment. (Sheltered behind barriers to entry, this may have been a rational use of their monopoly power.)[21]

(2) They may produce superabundant information, much of it opaque or irrelevant. This is a common tactic before the US regulators and courts, where complicated and obscure data are frequently produced in barrow loads as the inquiry progresses. Under the rules of evidence of such bodies, it is often impossible to rule out any of it as misleading or useless until after patient examination. This can be a way of prolonging hearings, usually thought to be in the interest of the regulated firm since it has the longest purse and can spend the most on lawyers. But it may also confuse

the regulator or the opposition unless they are particularly experienced, persevering and nimble-witted. Until 1963, both British Rail and London Transport published vast amounts of monthly and quarterly data for many categories of traffic, output, price and even cost; but the rules of cost apportionment were so disguised or artificial that one could never work out from the data what a regulator really wanted to know: the marginal cost of carrying certain traffic and the profit earned.[22]

(3) Whether or not the regulated firm has sparse or overflowing data, a third tactic is to produce the required data slowly. Withholding information to the last moment improves the bargaining power of the regulated firm. There are many ways of doing this. (One advantage the 1970's inflation gave the regulatory process was that it reduced the regulated firm's incentive to delay the decisions of the regulator. The longer the delay, the less the effect of any price increase granted.)

(4) The regulated body may claim that the purposes it serves are various and that any given information – particularly accounting and other financial information – is misleading as a test of its stewardship. (This may be a not unreasonable defence for a multi-product firm or one whose services have many different quality dimensions – for example, speed, reliability, comfort, cleanliness.)

To overcome these problems, three particular advances are needed:

1   As far as possible the information produced must be relevant, periodic and produced as a matter of routine and on the basis of agreed or established conventions. It has been said, as we saw above, that advances in regulation have often been responsible for advances in, as well as greater consistency in, accounting policies.[23] While this may be so, the great difficulty regulators have invariably had, until recently, in getting the financial data they need suggests that, as with the Owl of Minerva, dusk is already falling before the bird takes flight. This is understandable, because accounting improvements have usually been brought about at the instance of firms, including regulated firms, and not at that of the regulators. This leads us to the second advance needed, which is in fact a prior condition of the first.

2   There must be clarity over the purposes for which the information is wanted. This means that both the regulator and the regulated firm must have clear objectives. The firm's primary or overriding objective had best be simple, measurable and communicable, as is profit maximization, and no other objective, in the present state of the art. And the regulatory offences, which it is the independent regulator's aim to prevent or mitigate, need as far as possible to be clearly defined so that it can be seen what constraints they impose on profit maximization. Then information requirements can be tailored to illuminate those offences.

3   As far as possible – and it is virtually never wholly possible – the regulator and the regulated should have substantially the same objectives for the firm. The more diverse and conflicting the objectives and constraints upon the firm, the greater the difficulty, even to impossibility, of providing the information to monitor them.

These three points, essential for this chapter's argument, may be illustrated by returning to the problem of the control of UK nationalized industries; and asking how far privatization was necessary to improve efficiency.

Those who in the past have argued for the reform of public enterprise have tended to regard a multiplicity of objectives and a departure from profit maximization in seeking them as inescapable features of public enterprise, and possibly its justification.[24] Reformers have therefore concentrated on trying to devise machinery for clarifying and better implementing these objectives, in the belief that they could then be achieved with greater efficiency.

Such objectives have been complex not because a single politician has had multiple and shifting objectives, though that is commonly true of individual politicians, but because they have been decided upon through a political process mediating between different politicians, who have themselves been under diverse political pressures. Hence the confusion over objectives and responsibilities which has been blamed repeatedly for nationalized industry inefficiency.

Many devices were used to try to resolve this confusion. It provided the rationale of pure Morrisonianism, that is, the notion that a board should interpret the public interest and derive from that its operational objectives. The hope was that the board would distil the political messages it heard into clear enough objectives for efficient management. It was also the reason behind what one might call 'impure' Morrisonianism, where the board shares this responsibility with ministers and their officials – a process so cumbrous and unlikely to lead to clear management objectives that one only mentions it because it is what happened. Several later suggestions for reform amounted to various unpromising devices for resolving conflicts. One idea was that economic objectives should become dominant, with either the Treasury or a special 'ministry for nationalized industries' acting as a holding company or an umbrella for state holding companies.[25] But that never seemed politically possible. Another notion was that there should be a functional sponsoring department – for example, transport or energy – which would be responsible for the social and political policy for a public enterprise. But that would be to shift the conflict without resolving it. There seems no reason why the resulting objectives for the nationalized industry should be any less confused when it is responding directly to two, or even more, ministers rather than one. Alternatives to such devices for resolving the confusion through government intervention were amplifications of the Morrisonian principle intended to make it easier to resolve the conflicts within the boards themselves. One was to import the (West) German concept of a supervisory board, which would have trade union, consumer and government interests on it (chapter 3).[26]

While such changes may act as palliatives, they cannot achieve sufficient clarity in an industry's objectives to provide clear guidance to middle and junior management. The parties concerned represent different interests and therefore have substantially different objectives, and while they may agree to compromise-objectives in order to take action the result will not be clarity or permanence in objectives, and their underlying objectives will remain uncompromised. Thus, as long as unreconciled objectives remain, what is at work is inevitably a political process. And if the management of a public enterprise is seen primarily as such a political or otherwise representative process, accountability will necessarily run in several directions – indeed to all interests represented in policy-making. Now, as Day and Klein have argued, there is

a basic distinction between political and managerial accountability. 'Political accountability is about those with delegated authority being answerable for their actions to
the people . . . directly . . . or indirectly . . . Here the criteria of judgement are themselves contestable and reasons, justification and explanation have to be provided.'[27]
And this is as true of the politics at the top of a politically driven and representation-
al enterprise as it is of central or local government. 'In contrast, managerial accountability is about making those with delegated tasks answerable for carrying out agreed
tasks according to agreed criteria of performance.' The almost endless attempts to
separate policy or strategic control from day-to-day management, wherever the line
is drawn – whether between minister and chairman, supervisory board and executive
board, executive members and non-executive members of the same board – are
attempts to reconcile 'political' and managerial accountability.[28] But what is always
missing is any engine for turning these complex and shifting objectives, or
compromises between objectives, at the top into clear instructions down the line by
which management's performance can be monitored. This is inevitable. While it is
conceivable that complicated objectives at the top could be translated into clear
instructions down the line, this cannot be done if compromise agreement is achieved
at the expense of clarity, or alternatively, if even clear objectives are frequently
changed under political pressure, with a management whose actions were initiated
under one set of objectives finding itself judged later by different objectives or by
different interpretations of ambiguous objectives. It is now axiomatic in a well-run
firm that it is necessary to translate objectives into clear guidance which can be used
to set individual objectives at all lower management levels as well as to set the objectives of subsidiaries and divisions.[29]

Objectives should also be capable of being monitored. That is a further demanding
requirement but one which helps define what is meant by clarity of objectives. In its
absence one can understand why attempts to establish meaningful and monitorable
accountability have failed in the public sector.

All this is why political bodies are necessarily less efficient at doing what they are
meant to do than are competitive private bodies, which need to have an overriding
commitment to their simple objective if they are to survive. Long ago Aristotle said
that for a state to be democratic it must be small enough for all its citizens to be able
to crowd into its market-place to hear their leaders and join in debate.[30] A modern
equivalent of this proposition is that complicated objectives are only consistent with
efficiency in small organizations, because only in small organizations can the personal
discussion take place that is then needed in order to avoid misunderstanding and
achieve a common purpose. Thus, when public ownership was decided upon, public
corporations were established in the hope that, as bodies with objectives less complicated than those of the body politic, though subordinate to it, they could greatly
extend the scope of efficient political administration. The Greek city-state of course
had slaves, who were not citizens and were outside the democratic process, but
whose work in industry and the home enabled the city-state to possess a larger economy than it would have had if it had had to rely on citizen labour. Now, while
one can hardly call public corporations slaves, it was the intention that in some sense
they should be servants carrying out the will of political masters efficiently, and in
that sense their own operational objectives were to be clearer, less complicated
and interpreted with less discretion. The masters, meanwhile, would have greater

freedom to discuss what was to be done and establish policy. As Attlee said when as Postmaster-General he was asking for a shift in the status of the Post Office away from being a government department, in such a department 'the minutiae of administration come right up to the highest officials diverting their minds from broad matters of policy.'[31] Public corporations were therefore established in the hope that they would be able to achieve greater management accountability than is possible within government departments; and it was the further belief that this had not been achieved or that, where it had, even more could be achieved in the private sector which underlay civil service and some other support for privatization.

Therefore any reforms which can be achieved in public enterprise without privatization must start with the assumption that all but small public enterprises are to be given the clarity and singleness of purpose of private enterprise. From that standpoint, what has been extraordinary in the 1980s is the shift in the political mindset towards agreement on giving a preponderant influence to economic objectives. It could then be assumed that the objectives of public enterprises before privatization and of regulated enterprises after it were to be financial and economic. As Beesley and Littlechild expressed it: they were to maximize 'the present value of aggregate net benefits to UK consumers.'[32] This does not mean that such enterprises were not to engage in political or philanthropic activities, but, rather, that when they did those activities were to serve as means to the enterprise's long-term profit-making objectives, not as separate objectives in their own right.

Just as governments tended to impose targets on nationalized industries rather than reach agreement on them, so they tended to regard the monitoring of nationalized industry efficiency as primarily an arm's-length function to be conducted by externally devised criteria. There was a multiplication of bodies auditing the efficiency of public enterprises (with varying degrees of formality). Among the bodies with this function have been the sponsoring government departments, usually through special reviews; the external auditors, in so far as they carry out value-for-money audits; the Monopolies and Mergers Commission, since 1980; the National Audit Office, for whom greater powers have at times been proposed; select committees; and regulatory bodies. Many penetrating and useful reports have resulted.

But a key issue arises here because the case for efficiency auditing rests on one or other of two not equally satisfactory bases: it may try to correct a divergence of interests or objectives between a body and a superior body to which it is accountable; or it may check on the fulfilment of the intentions of the accountable body itself. Unhappily, the first tradition has dominated. Auditing which is undertaken by a body with one set of objectives for the body to be audited on a body with its own, substantially different set can hardly encourage efficiency in the second. Only confusion could arise if, for example, the auditing body assumes that profitability or economic efficiency is the goal while the accountable body in the Morrisonian tradition has a much more diffuse interpretation of the public interest. It may not happen where there is broad agreement on the objectives but will tend to otherwise. A more-specific example is that generally the Monopolies and Mergers Commission has followed the economic tradition in stressing the importance of systematic investment appraisal and cost-based pricing (as if these were mandatory, whereas in fact they are not) while the accountable bodies it has investigated have not accepted them as instruments to an end. Moreover, even where there is agreement on targets and objectives, or the financial objectives of an enterprise are specified with enough precision for there not to be misunderstandings arising from ambiguity, an efficiency audit which presumes to judge performance by externally-imposed indicators will often find the accountable body substantially ignoring its criticisms unless they have a very secure legal basis. Efficiency auditing is only likely to work if the objectives have been set by the body itself. One cannot correct substantial divergences of interests or objectives by auditing.[33]

This is almost as much a problem of language as it is of power. To illustrate the difficulties, I shall use a parable based on an example given by Elizabeth Anscombe.[34] A man draws up a shopping list based on his expectation of what he and his wife need. On his return his wife finds that against her expectation he has bought margarine instead of the butter that the list specified. How should he react? He might admit the discrepancy and say that he changed his mind, that he prefers margarine after all, or he might admit a mistake and return to the shop to change the item, or say that he will pay more attention to his list next time. If, on the other hand, it is her shopping list rather than his, his reaction might be more complex. He might concede that the shopping list expresses his wife's orders, but argue that the price of butter has so risen that he could keep within the budget only by buying margarine, or that there was no butter of the right quality, or that what there was did not look fresh. Thus, while his objective was still to obey orders, he aimed for an acceptable course of least disobedience; and had used his discretion to that end. Or he may have learnt over the years that the shopping lists his wife gave him were incomplete, and he always used his discretion to fill in what was missing. Surely, there were rows, but what was the alternative? That he should telephone his wife every time a difficulty or an opportunity struck him? Or that his wife should do the shopping herself? But she had other things to do, and there would be no benefit from a division of labour.

How could an outside observer help? Probably best by staying far away, but let us be fanciful and call in a marriage-guidance counsellor. He or she might observe that, despite all the conceptual and potentially real difficulties, there was enough of a marriage of minds for the rows and disappointments on this score to be few. But what should be the advice if they were many? Even if there were available a complete series of shopping lists with expected prices and also itemized bills with actual prices, it would be a devilish job to establish what went wrong and why. Rather, it would be sensible to listen in order to establish what the wife's underlying principles were, so that better guidance could be given to the husband. It might have to be pointed out that the husband has some wishes of his own which diverge from those of his wife; and that either those of one must dominate or an accommodation must be reached.

What distinguishes this from the problem of the efficiency auditor is not the detail – all of which *mutatis mutandis* could be paralleled from experience of efficiency auditing – but the fact that the relationship between the efficiency auditor and the audited is (fortunately) more remote, even with the most interventionist government or regulator – though, on the other hand, 'divorce' is scarcely possible. The moral is that those who run enterprises whose overall objectives are set externally should draw up their own shopping lists and be judged by what they said they would buy, if they promise to reach the overall objectives set. If an approximate harmony of interests does not obtain and the systems do not exist for self-accountability, then, of course, the Monopolies and Mergers Commission, or another external auditing body, will have to be relied on much more. Many bodies accept such dependence not only as normal but as a satisfactory state of affairs. Yet, without denigrating particular cases or denying the achievements of such audits, it must be said that there were significant limits to what is achieved. The successes are often based on criticisms of procedures at a conceptual level independent of their real effect or importance. Sometimes, for example, it is crucial to criticize investment appraisal techniques but there are occasions when this criticism seems almost perfunctory. Moreover, practical difficulties may prevent the recommendations being carried out. And analysis is not always deep. As my reminiscent gloom over the ancient history of British Rail's investment indicated in chapter 3, the use of good procedures and good external analysis is not in itself a guarantee of an acceptable use of resources.

Occasional inquiries are often at their most effective where they are investigating causes of inefficiency which are open to criticism in similar terms wherever found – from project management and inventory control to overmanning and capital expenditure controls. One should not underestimate the importance of such inefficiency in the use of inputs – sometimes called 'X-inefficiency', as we have seen, but here called 'organizational inefficiency' to avoid confusion with RPI-X – yet there are aspects of inefficiency which are not common and can only be defined in relation to a specific objective or technology of a public body. The more such a body departs from a classic public monopoly the truer this will be.

We may be deceived by the appearance of a report into believing that action will be automatic, not realizing the likelihood of the non-enforcement, and indeed sometimes the non-enforceability, of external inquiries' recommendations. Unless action is quickly taken on receipt of a report, both inertia and a strong perception of the difficulties of implementation from within will all too often mean that nothing much is done on difficult issues. Governments often have few powers and incentives to impose the reports' recommendations on boards even where they back them. Time passes and the report is forgotten. In some cases such recommendations may be buried within the organizations by arguments – right or wrong – that the report writers in question 'got hold of the wrong end of the stick', 'did not see our problem', 'did not appreciate the cost' or 'did not recognize the progress already made'. Unless the management is prepared to digest the good criticisms made, implementation will be imperfect.

Experience suggests not only that not too much should be expected from efficiency auditing by external inquiry not also that there is a better state of affairs in which the audited body sets its own efficiency auditing policies and provides the resulting data to those who have a right to it. Where this is possible, the extraction of information by external inquiries or audits will be not only easier but also less necessary.

Ever since it started after the Second World War, efficiency auditing has had in many cases repeated failures. Repeated government and parliamentary reviews and inquiries into a public enterprise have reached the same or similar conclusions and made the same or similar recommendations, deploring the lack of progress since the previous review. These failures were not the result of bloody-mindedness or stupidity. Their fundamental cause was that the efficiency auditor and the audited firm did not have substantially the same objectives for the firm, so that management actions and systems were, unsurprisingly, not adapted to fit the other's objectives.

Nevertheless, audit on behalf of government as the owner is necessary if government is to have the information necessary for control.[35]

If the industrial objectives of a minister and a nationalized industry are substantially different, as was commonly the case, and the power of the minister to impose incentives is limited, the situation could become as conflict-ridden as that of a landowner and his estate manager in a nineteenth-century Russian novel. Privatization has clarified the objectives of the industries, though some seem to have been slow to realize that their mission now is to maximize profits within the regulatory constraints imposed on them. And an independent economic regulator's industry objectives should be less diverse, diffuse and changing than those of (a succession of) ministers, though they will not be precisely the same as those of the industry he regulates, for its objectives of profitability and his of economic efficiency will only coincide in the absence of the market failures which give rise to the economic offences for the prevention or mitigation of which independent economic regulators are needed, in which case there would, of course, be no need for economic regulation.

Confusion of objectives in either party or a substantial difference of objectives between them, or both, not only complicates the relations between them, but is mirrored is the difficulty of providing information both for internal management purposes and beyond that for external regulation. For example, the financial accounts of nationalized industries and the internal management accounts from which they derived, though adequate for the sake of probity, to control cash, or to prove whether an overall surplus or deficit was earned, were not of much use for management, because the clear and simple profit-making objectives of a private firm, to which financial and management accounts should be well related, are not those of a public enterprise. Indeed, it was not uncommon to find that the processes for getting information to meet ministers' inquiries and customers' complaints were better designed and speedier – though often skill congested – than the processes for producing routine financial and management information. This was, of course, because this first set of information needs was the more important one from the perspective of top management, sometimes even vital for its survival.

Often one found that in fact the accounting systems of nationalized industries were designed not for their more effective management, but as a way of balancing the books in the process of negotiating and renegotiating External Financing Limits with the Treasury.[36] As within government departments, various bits of the enterprise bid for more resources to meet operating shortfall, or to fund investments.

What then should be the proper purpose of financial and efficiency auditing be for public and regulated bodies? Where industry objectives remain confused, complicated and varying, the function of auditing is likely to be palliative, making the relationship between ministers and boards politically acceptable while illuminating particular matters of concern, rather than providing an audit in any precise sense. But where the information is more adequate and regularly provided, auditing can be given a more precise role. Broadly speaking, *internal auditing* is the process, independent of line and ordinary financial management, by which the top management is assured that its financial or management information is reliable; that its financial systems work well to ensure that the objectives of the firm are being met effectively; that processes for recording and explaining any departures from these targets exist and are understood, so that, where appropriate, they may be corrected as soon as possible; and that procedures exist that will prevent fraud and waste. *External auditing* performs the same functions for financial information and systems on behalf of the owner: the shareholders or, in the public sector, the government or another public body.[37] In a political context, there is room for another activity, more loosely called *political auditing*, by which government or the legislature occasionally or regularly tests the objectives of the body and considers whether for political reasons they should be changed. In the past, in practice 'efficiency auditing' has confused the last two of these activities.

7.4 The preconditions of adequate information: objectives

There have been many advances in the specification, systematization and design of objectives for public-sector management in recent years. But by comparison with the development of best-practice financial and management information systems in the private sector, together with the development of the battery of management techniques and incentives that can be made to depend on them, the race is at present like that between a real hare and tortoise. This is not surprising if, as the argument of the last section indicates, the only objectives which can be set, incentivized, monitored and regulated in a fully auditable sense are commercial, that is, ones which, whether or not subject to constraints, aim at profitability by some financial test. This is because accounting has been most developed to reflect such objectives. These are not necessary facts. The public sector could have developed routine accounting information and incentives to reflect well-specified social objectives. That it has not is one 'unnecessary' reason why the public sector has been losing out to the private sector as a form of organization – and is at present an additional reason for privatization. For without suitable calendarized accounting and other management information, one cannot begin to exercise effective control over large organizations whatever the machinery of control.[38]

This may seem such an extreme position as to require some defence but its basis can be set out briefly by the choice of three examples of non-commercial objectives:

(1) *Passenger-mile maximization per unit of subsidy* is a well-defined objective for a subsidized public transport undertaking. It was adopted by London Transport in the 1970s for planning purposes. A rational undertaking with such an objective will change its services or its policies so as to increase its passenger-mileage except in so far as to do so will have an adverse effect on receipts – some passenger-miles with lower fares than others but with a less than commensurate reduction in direct costs, for example, those bought with season tickets, bring in lower net receipts per passenger-mile. Though such an objective could have been operational for every London Transport underground-railway line and bus route, this did not happen. Consequently, neither was it reflected in periodic – monthly or quarterly – budgetary review sessions. Instead, actual performance was, in so far as that happened then, monitored by the ordinary financial accounts, with accountable units treated as profit or cost centres, which Glaister and Collings have shown to be inconsistent with passenger-mile maximization per unit of subsidy received.[39] However, it would be relatively easy to develop for this objective a financial-planning, budgeting and

performance review system with management accounts which showed forecast and out-turn passenger-miles carried by every accountable unit as well as revenues and costs. In general, where there is one objective to be maximized subject to a net revenue or cost constraint – for example, the saving of lives, job creation, tree-planting per unit of subsidy, or whatever – it can be handled in this way.

(2) The issue is more complicated where the maximand covers more than one objective. Health is the outstanding example of this, and the one for which perhaps most work has been done on objective formulation. A 'Qaly', standing for 'quality-adjusted life years', is defined as a weighted average of several objectives of health care – the saving of lives, the avoidance of continuing disability or impairment, the avoidance of days off work or any other form of financial loss, to be multiplied by some estimate of the avoidance of recurrence or further complication.[40] Where a money figure can be placed on these, including the value for a human life, then, taken together with the costs of alternative patterns and policies of health care, they can be made commensurate and the resulting net-output measures, a Qaly, can be maximized. Normally this is suggested only for planning purposes: the accounts of accountable units within hospitals are kept as those of cost centres. But it would be possible to construct financial-planning budgets and to perform quarterly reviews on the basis of the achievement of Qaly targets, probably subject to a financial-planning budget constraint for, say, a whole hospital. This would require periodic information (which might well include standardized estimates of human life values, income losses from days off work, and so on) as well as revenues and costs. Given that some at least of the weights and values will be arbitrary, one can expect the formulation of plans to include exercises to reflect changes in weightings and in such matters as the value for a human life to be used – decided at some appropriate higher level. Such an exercise should lead to procedures which result in higher levels of measured efficiency, as the adoption of such practices has done where profit is the objective and for the same reasons.

(3) More commonly, the situation arises where a public body knows its budget and has several objectives, but most of these are unquantifiable and therefore cannot be made commensurate. Suppose a body that owns historic buildings has among its objectives the ownership of as many as it can, their physical preservation, the maintaining of their decoration and contents to as high a standard of authenticity as it can, the preservation of the rural areas that it owns, the protection of farming and other rural pursuits in these areas and the attraction, not of as much revenue as it can from visitors, but of enough visitors to give it widespread public support. Then while relevant information on several of these may be collected for each accountable unit – house, monument or piece of countryside – a weighted combination of these objectives cannot be produced for their financial-planning, budgeting and performance review unless work is put in to make them commensurate, if that is possible, in the context of either cost-benefit or cost-effectiveness analysis. In default of this, such a body has to fall back on more-traditional methods of trying to ensure that all of its accountable units strike a balance between these objectives which is acceptable to the board – through discussions, review, comments on plans, visits and the monitoring of complaints.

Many private and public enterprises have used the absence of competition to see their objectives and monitor them at all levels by administrative or political methods, relegating their accounts to the minimum functions prescribed by law – that is, to ensure that money is properly spent and that properly drawn-up accounts are eventually prepared for the business as a whole and any subsidiaries. But to do this is to throw away the enormous potential for control of properly-used financial systems. These are a prerequisite for a large efficient enterprise, an essential tool enabling organizations to grow very large indeed without losing management and administrative efficiency (chapter 3).

The principal desiderata of such a control system, the features which give it such current advantage by comparison with even the most sophisticated control systems devised for enterprises with non-profit-maximizing objectives, are:

1   that, as far as possible, all of the firm's principal activities can be subdivided into profit centres, not only for every good or service, but also differentiated geographically down to individual plants and other facilities; that, as a corollary, activities that are cost centres, that is, not earning any revenue (or not enough to be profitable), are kept to a minimum and are open to external competition from outside the firm;

2   that the financial accounts for profit and cost centres are sufficiently developed to be used as management accounts, so that every manager has routine, calendarized information that refers to the activity by which his objectives are set and monitored; and that, as a corollary, every such manager is not just formally accountable but also actually able to take full responsibility for that activity while everyone else is an assistant or an adviser, however eminent in the firm;

3   that any interdependencies between profit centres, which almost invariably exist and most certainly do in natural monopolies, are carefully defined and costed, with clear and economically efficient procedures covering the ways in which joint costs are incurred and allocated, such interdependency being kept to the minimum that is efficient;

4   that there is an annual dialogue that sets for each management activity an annual budget by which it is to be managed through the year, these budgets being vertically and horizontally consistent with a full understanding, supported by sensitivity analyses, of the risks facing each manager, and of how he would expect to deal with the more important risks in so far as these lie within his control; that higher management also has contingency plans to deal with the most important unpredicted changes an external circumstances;

5   that the necessary management accounts and other information for each unit are available, though not audited, and are ready soon enough after each month's end for significant variations to be detected and explained and for any corrective management action to be taken;

6   that, as far as possible, all management action centres on periodic discussions around these accounts so that all decisions are taken with a view to their effect on the unit and other parts of the firm's profitability; and that managers are selected, rewarded and promoted to a large extent according to their results so measured.

Privatization solved the 'objectives problem' for regulated firms by making their general aims no different from those of any other commercial company. It should therefore follow that their financial and management information will become more relevant to managers and therefore worth development. One would expect them to follow as far as possible the example of other large commercial organizations and break down their activities into separate businesses or profit centres with their own accounts by which their managers' performances may be judged. It should be axiomatic that a unit is to be a profit centre only if those who manage it have very great influence over its revenue and costs so that they are truly responsible for the profits made or their absence. One often found in nationalized industries that lower-level managers of units did not have control over most of their costs – often pay rates, staff numbers, and assets were determined for them at a higher level – or their revenues – since they had no control over price or advertising, or market share as a monopoly. To call such units profit centres is a misuse of language. To reward their managers according to the rise or fall of profits over which they have no control is no more an incentive to good management than if their managers' earnings depended on a lottery. If their managers control their costs but not their revenues, units can be made into cost centres (though if possible this should be avoided by units' charging for their services where their customers are internal). Where their managers influence some aspects of their revenue as well, they can be made into contribution centres. All centres can have their own accounts as separate businesses. A profit centre, however, is a microcosm of the business as a whole.

Left to its own devices, a privatized natural monopoly would produce all these accounts as historic accounts, which broadly record revenues at their values when received and costs at their values when incurred.[41] And where there is inflation it would not revise the book value of its assets to reflect their changing values. Historic cost accounts thus systematically overstate the real return on capital, especially when assets are long-lived. Especially during the 1970s, there were attempts to persuade, and indeed require, all businesses to produce some accounts which were adjusted for inflation. These attempts aroused remarkable passions, generating endless debates over the correct conventions to adopt and the compromise to be struck between correctness and the cost of producing more-perfect accounts. Underlying this controversy are two fundamental objectives:

(1) Though the successful predator is often the one that spots historic cost accounting weaknesses, especially over property valuation, in competitive markets current cost accounts may produce considerably more information that is valuable to an enterprise that is deciding whether or not to expand its share of a market or enter it, or is on the acquisition trail. A sensible board will find it useful to have some current cost calculations to reassure it that it is putting enough into depreciation provisions to maintain the firm's operating capital. (After takeovers, flotations and substantial fund-raising, modified historical cost accounts are often produced in which various asset classes are revealed.) Real numbers will help determine what its investment and disinvestment strategy should be; but it will keep these numbers to itself.

(2) Governments have often had a hidden agenda. From the 1950s to the 1970s, different governments engaged in various forms of price and wage control to try to check inflation. Current cost accounts would have made it easier for these governments to decide how small a price increase a firm could be allowed and still make

enough profit to stay in business. But what was in a government's interest here was not in a firm's. The limited transparency of historic accounts made it easier for a firm to maintain profits, if it was skilful.

It is a characteristic irony that it was only as nationalized industries were starting to pass out of existence that the proper basis for their accounting was at last argued and exemplified in a government report – one whose clarity, pertinence and originality make it deserve to rank as a classic. If the Byatt Report had been written in, say, 1945, and had been adopted from the start as setting the accounting rules for that and subsequent waves of nationalization, much pain and anguish might have been avoided.[42]

The Report of the Byatt Committee gave a number of reasons why it is important for nationalized industries to produce formal current cost accounts: pre-eminently, the absence both of competition and of a need to compete in the market for capital. When there is no independent check upon the value of an enterprise, then the strain needs to be taken up by an accounting system which attempts to measure changes in its real value. 'If accounts are to show resource use and economic performance they must allow for general inflation, for fluctuations in specific prices and costs, and for technical progress resulting in changes in the value of capital equipment.'[43] Such accounts would have made it easier to ensure that nationalized industries competed fairly in competitive markets and were not in receipt of subsidy in so far as they did not earn enough revenue to maintain their operating capital. Because so many had long-lived assets, adequate provision for replacement would have been particularly important so as to avoid one generation of managers apparently making good profits while actually storing up problems for their successors. But current cost accounts should also have made it possible to detect whether a nationalized industry was making excessive profits. A particularly important point was that 'nationalised industries are already required to make a specified rate of return on their investment programmes. Monitoring the performance of the industries could be done on a more arm's length basis than at present if the return on capital in the accounts could be used to indicate whether the specified return on investment was being achieved.'[44] The more real the financial information produced by a nationalized industry, the less argument there should be over the measurement of its performance and therefore over whether its agreed objectives have been reached.

In New Zealand, legislation took the principle one stage further:

> To ensure that information is publicly available on the value of the taxpayers' investment in each state enterprise, each board will be required to report their estimate of the net worth of the enterprise and the method used to reach that estimate. A comparison of consecutive measures of net worth will be an important indicator of the performance and efficiency of each enterprise. The statement of corporate intent will also indicate when comprehensive net worth and efficiency audits will be undertaken.[45]

The methods that were used to estimate their net worth by discounting future net earnings could also be used regularly to evaluate future policies – for example, of acquisition and investment by estimating the resulting prospective change in net worth. Thus, what is proposed in New Zealand is the logical step beyond what was recommended in the Byatt Report. (And it is also what is correctly suggested by Rappaport as private-sector best practice, though, because of competition and because there is no need for regulation, there is for that sector no need for publication.[46])

Precisely these arguments may be used to support the view that there should be a requirement in all natural-monopoly licences that current cost accounts be produced. In all the licences the regulator is given the power to demand from the regulated companies the information he believes relevant for regulation but, as we have seen, many regulators, though not all, have had that power since Charles Francis Adams had it. It is not effective if it is the only power on which a regulator can rely to correct the asymmetry of information between himself and the regulated – if he has not also the power to ensure that the right kind of information is available.

So unpopular are current cost accounts with industry that a belief that they are necessary for natural-monopoly regulation must be defended. Any system of accounting is dependent upon the basis selected for valuing assets and liabilities, the capital maintenance concept adopted and the unit of measurement used. The most commonly adopted system of accounts is historical cost accounting, which is based on the valuation of assets and liabilities at historical values, employs the financial capital maintenance concept and uses the 'nominal pound'. However, it is recognized generally that, where a concern's results and financial position are materially affected by changing prices, historical cost accounts are insufficient.

Current cost accounts adopt the current-cost method of asset and liability valuation, and may be drawn up using either the financial capital maintenance concept or the operating capability maintenance concept of profit determination.[47] Their purpose is to provide a means of enumerating and reporting the effects of changing prices on a concern's financial performance and financial position. The 'nominal pound' is usually adopted.

The current cost of a business's assets is also known as their 'value of the business' – this is not the same as the value of a business as a whole. Generally, unless there is a need to provide for a permanent diminution in its value, an asset's current cost will be its net replacement cost. This does not mean that it is being assumed that the asset will be replaced by an identical asset; for practical or economic reasons this will seldom be the case. It is the replacement of the 'service potential', or capacity to produce similar useful output or service, which is assumed.

Where there has been technical progress, the valuation of assets at net replacement cost will involve consideration of the 'modern equivalent asset'.[48] For example, it would appear, certainly where traffic volumes are substantial, that copper wire is generally being replaced in telecommunications by optic fibre.

Where there is a reason, such as the existence of spare capacity, for believing a configuration other than the existing configuration of assets to be optimal, then the 'modern equivalent asset' based valuation should be based on the competitive price required to acquire the optimal configuration. For example, a decline in a localized use of water, gas or electricity because of the decline or closure of some heavy industrial users may make parts of the local networks of pipes or wires under-utilized or spare. Another example would be that of a telecommunications network or electricity grid which has grown up piecemeal and therefore has spare capacity in some links which it would not have had if planned from the start.

If the modern equivalent asset values should fall below historical values because, for example, technical progress means that the same output could be produced more efficiently with a lower value of capital, then it is reasonable to allow the concern in calculating its profits to adjust the *depreciation profile* of the relevant assets so that it can recover as much of the historical costs of those assets as market conditions permit during the remaining period in which those assets are in use. Where monopoly conditions and price controls permit, this could result in price increases which by definition would not be discriminatory.

Both of the alternative bases for calculating profits are relevant to natural monopolies. The notion of *operating capability maintenance* is that a concern retains enough profit to maintain the operating capacity it requires in its existing businesses. Thus a natural monopoly is reasonably required to set aside enough of its profits to ensure that it maintains the capital it needs to serve its customers, given the growth in demand forecast and its quality standards. One would expect discussion between it and its regulator over these forecasts and quality standards, and over the capital expenditure required in their light to maintain operating capability. That it is the regulator's duty to ensure this is made clear in the Water Appointment, but it is arguably implicit in any negotiation or renegotiation of RPI–X.[49] In so far as there is technical progress the profits to be retained will be less, whether that technical progress is original or attained by following the example of other firms.

By contrast, a policy of *financial capital maintenance* is one which at least maintains the real value of a business as a whole. That this should be the policy is the normal expectation of investors. It is of most relevance to a natural monopoly where technical progress or increasing competition means that the profits required to be retained for operating capability maintenance are falling, as has happened in telecommunications, gas and possibly electricity. Then it is not unreasonable that sufficient profits should be retained to permit diversification of the business so as to achieve real financial capital maintenance or that enough real profits should be returned to shareholders to compensate them for the real fall in the value of their assets. Virtually by assumption, any such profits not required for maintaining operating capability, but retained to maintain the real value of a firm's capital, will be invested in its unregulated business. One would expect the regulator to ask whether any such diversification threatens the ability of an enterprise to maintain its operating capability. Byatt did just this in 1991 when he proposed licence amendments to ensure that any diversification by the water and sewerage companies did not affect their ability to maintain their operating capability.[50]

Those who argue against current cost accounts – including most companies and their auditors – reject them on the ground they are too subjective. Much in accounting has an element of subjectivity in it, but what makes current cost accounting especially subjective is that the modern equivalent asset method of valuation that it employs requires a view on what assets a firm would use to produce its output if it were to replace what it has by the most efficient modern technology available to it.[51] To provide this, subjective judgements must be made on any surplus it should shed, any additional capacity it should acquire or what business it should be in.

One can see why the market dislikes these accounts: it has neither the time nor the opportunity to check the approximations made in their calculations; and it cannot rely on the auditors alone because the underlying issues are technical. However, these disadvantages do not apply to a regulated industry. Over time, the regulator can establish the validity of any particular asset valuation, its fairness and the likely opportunities for productivity improvement, as well as the long-run marginal cost of the industry's various activities – though the necessary subjective judgements to be made are ones which he must be able to check with authority. Thus, current cost accounts will provide the new regulatory regime with a better basis for the detection of economic regulatory offences in many relevant circumstances than any previous system of regulation has had. Indeed, I would also argue as an economist that current cost accounts are needed generally if accurate quantitative microeconomic analysis is to be possible.

7.5   Adequate information for regulation

However, it would be mistake to believe that even regularly produced current cost accounts will generally produce all the data needed to convict or clear regulated firms of regulatory offences. To consider the information relevant to some of the economic and main social offences we have discussed:

Predation   If a natural monopoly produces separate products using separate capacity then – as most of the British licences allow – its separate businesses should have their own current cost accounts, assisting the detection of cross-subsidization. Since the modern equivalent asset method of valuation yields, in effect, the long-run marginal cost of supplying the product, it makes it easier to detect workable predation defined as the supplying of goods below long-run marginal cost when so calculated (and to measure short-run marginal cost where relevant). The detection of cross-subsidization is thus harder where, as in value-added services in telecommunications, their number makes it impracticable to provide separate accounts for each or, more generally, where there are joint costs, as between first- and second-class rail travel, which prevent the calculation of marginal cost. However, as was indicated in the previous chapter, and as is beginning to be accepted in telecommunications regulation, it never makes economic sense to apportion costs where there is not causation. In the United States there is a tendency to give an advantage to newcomers by insisting on cost-apportionment rules which work to the disadvantage of the incumbent, and the same has been true in relation to British Telecom. While not making economic sense, both may be justified in so far as they encourage effective and efficient entry. American regulators have in fact in recent years taken a greater interest in these rules. And most of the later British licences give regulators powers to veto rules of cost apportionment which they believe to be anti-competitive. Where products produced using separate capacity do not have separate accounts, the regulator will have to rely more on his general powers to extract relevant information than on its extraction from current cost accounts. Moreover, accounts only refer to past periods. And even in the most advanced regulatory regimes, regulators are unlikely to have relevant accounts less than three months old. Therefore, a regulator needs to be given the power to act upon his judgement of what may have happened since the last audited accounts he has. (The need for speed is particularly important for dealing with predation; but the point stands for all the offences listed below.) He needs to have the power not only to decide whether there is excess capacity but to discover why it exists (which indicates the possibility of deliberately predatory investment discussed in chapter 5) so that he can then decide whether short-run marginal cost or long-run marginal cost or indeed any other aspect of conduct is the more relevant test of predation.

Unequal access The most convincing principle underlying the determination of this offence is that interconnection should be allowed at long-run marginal cost, and this is something which current cost accounts can help reveal. However, difficult issues may be raised by a decision over whether entrants should be allowed to use the network or grid at a generalized long-run marginal cost or at the long-run marginal cost particular to the route or routes they use. The regulator must also secure that, where possible, there is enough capacity to allow equal access to all without raising short-run marginal costs. This leads him beyond the accounts to the natural monopoly's capital expenditure plans. Where capacity expansion is not freely available, as at some airports and on rail routes, he particularly needs information which will help him enforce an equal access charging policy.

Price discrimination In so far as this is an offence to do with fairness, not economic efficiency, current cost accounts can help in its detection. However, other information may also be needed to decide whether a price difference insufficiently supported by a cost difference may nevertheless be justified, by a difference in quality. Since discrimination commonly means charging different prices for the same good or service without there being a justifying difference in costs or quality, it is likely to escape measurement by the ordinary processes of cost causation. On the other hand, small quality or cost differences in good or service provided can justify price differences even though they are unlikely to be reflected separately in routine management accounts. As an extreme example, one could not have expected the millions of different railway rates that used to exist in Britain and the United States to be reflected as separate items in the accounts; yet, given complicated patterns of joint costs, there may have been differences in the costs or service quality underlying many of these rate differences.

Excess monopoly profits If, despite the sorts of criticisms of such a shift made in the previous chapter, the revision of X in RPI–X were to become an exercise in rate-of-return control, such calculations would be easier and more meaningful in an operating capability maintenance, current cost accounts context. Argument would then mostly be limited to the choice of a rate of return, which will be the easier the more the firm in question is a natural monopoly from which risk is largely absent. In a regulatory regime like the American one where rate-of-return control is formally the aim of regulation, having available current cost accounts would be a great advance. It would not remove the subjective element in asset valuation, but it should then be easier to specify precise rules which, if obeyed, should determine their calculation. There are two safeguards against a regulated firm rigging the rules in its own favour. One is that, while it is possible to do this in any one year through a choice of favourable asset revaluation and depreciation methods, consistency will tend to mean that they will have to be persisted with even when circumstances alter to make them less advantageous, though it would not be unreasonable for a firm faced with new data on technological obsolescence to adjust its depreciation method to recover as much profit as it reasonably can. Secondly, the regulator can draw on best practice elsewhere in resisting unreasonable depreciation. However, because in rate-of-return regulation future investment plans, judgement over the dissemination of technical progress and agreement over any change in quality will be relevant, accounting information will not be enough.

Organizational and allocative inefficiency Revaluing assets on a modern equivalent asset basis which reflects the latest available technology operated in an optimal configuration to meet prospective demand should help the regulator order his thoughts on how investment could reduce costs and prices. However, deciding how to increase efficiency requires more than accounting information. In order to determine possible productivity improvements, for example, the regulator will benefit from being able to make inter-firm comparisons, nationally and internationally, on labour productivity. Regulators around the world share a common interest in exchanging information which will enable them to compare efficiency. The regulator should be provided with enough resources to be able to do this.

Most of these offences can be perpetrated through quality changes as well as price changes. Therefore quality also needs monitoring. The regulator will find it easier to maintain quality if the regulated firm becomes liable to pay damages if it infringes stated quality standards, as has happened with British Telecom.[52] Quality standards are more easily measured, maintained or improved where the product is comparatively homogeneous, as gas and electricity are. With both gas and electricity it is simple to set standards in production and distribution where the regulated firm pays damage if it falls below them. There is greater difficulty in telecommunications, where there are more services and where installation, repair and maintenance on customer premises affect the previewed quality of those services; and in water, where there are many health and environmental dimensions to quality. In all these cases and in that of airports, where quality affects passengers directly, as well as other users, and where consistent geographical quality differentiation is possible, the statistics which the regulator needs to monitor quality may be as abundant as the accounting information required. Quality is still more difficult to monitor for buses and railways. On the railways especially the quality dimensions that concern users are numerous – speed, reliability, comfort, cleanliness, smoothness of ride, and so on – and the satisfactoriness of the service varies not only by route but also for each journey.

Thus, while a requirement to produce current cost accounts – so far as possible for separate businesses – is perhaps the most important help a regulator can have in trying to detect economic offences and some social offences, it does not provide all the information usually needed. The information required cannot always be provided regularly and on a routine basis. Hence the general licence provision allowing a UK regulator to ask for whatever information he needs in addition to that regularly provided. But even then the information seldom determines clearly whether an offence has been committed and, as Vickers and Yarrow have said, the more numerous the goods and services provided, the harder the information asymmetry makes the regulator's role.[53] In the end, the decision has to be left to regulatory discretion, not proof.

There are two important further points to be made about information transparency. The first follows from the fact, implicit in the problem of entry, that information is asymmetrical not only between regulator and regulated, but also between a natural monopoly and its potential competitors. It is this: where there is a monopoly there seems no economic case against the proposition that its costs – expressed in current cost accounts form for each activity, good and service with published cost-apportionment rules where imposed – should be transparent so that any potential competitor can see what it must beat if it is to enter and survive.[54] If the monopoly is truly a natural monopoly and is more efficient than an entrant could be, then a potential competitor with such knowledge will be deterred from making what would be an unwise entry. But if technical progress or superior efficiency are seen to give the potential competitor a chance, then transparent cost information will help him to take it. The consumer will be better off whichever is the case: either a monopoly is more efficient than any potential entrants, who then have the knowledge not to enter, but whose knowledge and potential will provide the monopoly with greater incentive to remain efficient; or it is less efficient, in which case it will either need to improve its efficiency or be undercut by more-efficient entrants. But could one not say that, even where there is effective competition, all would gain from similar transparency? One could, but there are arguments on the other side. Information is expensive, and the extraction of information to help actual and potential competitors compete with each other is arguably a less useful expenditure of resources than to publish that information about a monopoly. One competitor is more likely to know what is relevant to him about his competitors than a possible new entrant who is contemplating entry into a market dominated by a monopoly. Moreover, there is the further argument that too much transparency where there is already effective competition can result in, or increase, instability.

Such arguments against requiring transparency in cost information can support the second point, which is that, while the publication of current cost accounts is reasonably required of a monopolist, it is not where there is effective competition. This implies – as holds for the later British licences – that, to meet the case where the market for a good or service becomes competitive and the erstwhile monopolist is no longer dominant, there should be provision in a licence to discontinue any requirement that current cost accounts for it be produced and otherwise to reduce the amount of information required to be published on it, as well as to eliminate it from future negotiated revisions of X.

The British Telecom Licence was sparing in its information requirements by these standards – though it required separate accounts for separate businesses, it did not ask for current cost accounts. Subsequent licences demanded more information until in those for water and electricity the standards were reached which have been defended in this chapter. (In the Water Appointment the requirements went even further, for reasons which will be explained in chapter 9.) The information requirements of the later licences represent a development of the first importance in the history of regulation. Though Carsberg has said that he believes that the information provisions of the BT Licence are sufficient, he has also said that his regime could benefit from more.[55] One may expect the information conditions of the earlier licences to become more like those of the later ones.

How reasonable is it for a monopoly to be required to provide information about its future (beyond that which the regulator needs for the valuation of its assets on a modern equivalent asset basis)? Where other firms depend on interconnection with a natural-monopoly network (or grid), it is necessary that the regulator on their behalf should know what investment is intended so that he may ensure its adequacy and that it is to be provided efficiently. And individual firms will themselves need to know for their own business planning how much and where their own capacity in the networks will be, though care must be taken before allowing them to know what is to be made available to their competitors. And a regulator will need such information in order to make a proper judgement if an interconnecting network tries to persuade him that, added together, the forecasts of the competitors who will use the network are over-optimistic.

A particularly difficult problem arises with technical information and research. In 1956 the US courts required that Western Electric make its research available through licences available to all, and this, it has been said, led to a boom in technological development in telecommunications.[56] Where a monopoly whose natural monopoly is evaporating for reasons discussed in the previous chapter has a strong research and development tradition, it may be efficient to make its laboratories give its information to the whole industry, including potential entrants. However, there is a dilemma here. If this service is not funded by a levy, it may not raise sufficient funds to continue, as some users decide that it is more in their interests to become free-riders, getting the benefits of the research and development done by others without paying for it. On the other hand, it may be difficult to devise a levy that does not give more independence to the laboratories than is consistent with their having as their objective the commercial advantage of the whole industry. An alternative approach is to accept that research and development facilities belonging to such a natural monopoly are to be retained by it as its exclusive property, in the belief that the possibility of entry and bypass will lead it to use its research and development to cut costs more than if the results were freely available to all. There is no obviously most efficient approach to this matter, even though there has been substantial discussion in the literature of the circumstances in which one would expect a monopoly market to do more research and development than a competitive one and of the circumstances in which one would expect the opposite.[57]

Notes

1 Sappington and Stiglitz (1987), p. 5.
2 Breyer (1982), pp. 26–8; Utton (1986), pp. 37–75, who attributes to the public-good characteristics of information the regulatory problem it presents (p. 10); Vickers and Yarrow (1988), p. 99: 'Asymmetric information is at the heart of the economics of regulation.'
3 On the early history of American regulation, see Breyer and Stewart (1985), pp. 22ff.
4 McCraw (1984). I have drawn heavily from his pp. 1–56. What it meant to be an Adams, and the pressure put on a young Adams by the weight of family tradition in an age less friendly to it, is described in his brother's classic autobiography, *The Education of Henry Adams*, 1907).
5 Quoted in McCraw (1984), p. 4.
6 Hadley (1890), p. 166n.
7 McCraw (1984), pp. 16, 17. Adams' essay was first published in the *North American Review* in July 1869. It was republished in C. F. and H. Adams, *Chapters of Erie and Other Essays*, Osgood, 1871, pp. 1–99.

8   Hadley (1890), p. 136, 137.
9   Quoted in McCraw (1984), p. 20.
10 Ibid., p. 35.
11 Hadley (1890) p. 137.
12 The state regulatory commissions also declined in effectiveness because interstate transit increased and there came to be strict federal limitation on state powers regarding interstate shipments: Breyer and Stewart (1985), p. 26; Cushman (1941), pp. 29–34.
13 Ministry of Reconstruction, *Committee on Trusts Report:*, 1918, Cd. 9236, HMSO.
14 Whereas during the first years of this century large numbers of American firms were brought before the courts for regulatory offences, from 1895 to 1935 only 22 British firms were. And whereas in the early 1900s 11 out of the largest 50 US firms were brought before the courts in government-initiated actions, none of the largest 50 British firms were. See Keller (1981), pp. 64, 69; Hannah (1983), p. 44; Hannah (1979), pp. 75ff.
15 Locke (1947), quoted in Day and Klein (1987), p. 12.
16 J. Morrison, *Hansard*, 3rd series, vol. 33, col. 984–5 (1836).
17 On the controversy over the role of the Poor Law Commissioners, see Bagehot (1933), pp. 164–8; Lubenow (1971), pp. 30–68; Gregg (1973), pp. 186–92; Checkland and Checkland (1974), editorial introduction, esp. pp. 42–7; Dicey (1914), pp. 203, 204; Young (1953), pp. 39–42; Halévy (1928), p. 225.
18 A. J. Harrison,(1988), p. 33; Wharton (1988), *passim*.
19 McCraw (1984), p. 23. Carsberg has often stressed, as indeed might the other regulators, how much can be achieved by consent. For example, 'In practice it is usually possible to persuade the PTO [public telecommunications operator] concerned to change its practices voluntarily': Oftel (1987a), p. 9. By contrast with Carsberg, James McKinnon, the gas regulator, found it far harder for several years to get public attention. While his public image was boosted by an MMC report in 1988, he was complaining that many thought that his office was the body that carried out disconnections: Ofgas (1988); (1989), p. 31. Ofgas was confused with Offgas. But he had achieved widespread public recognition by 1991. Unlike the rest of the regulators, the Civil Aviation Authority did not attempt a full account of its regulatory activities: one page in its annual report was enough.
20 The problems of extracting relevant, comparable information are still greater where more than one firm has a single regulator, especially if their interrelationships are relevant to an alleged offence. Competition between them reduces the need for information, but where particular relationships are not competitive – as over issues of interconnection – this does not help.
21 In *West Yorkshire Road Car vs. Pinnacle Motors*, the Office of Fair Trading decided that West Yorkshire Road Car's management information was so poor that their price cutting in response to Pinnacle's entry into their bus market was not predatory, because they could not have known whether it was costing them money. Such an unhappy decision can only encourage a company to misinform itself.
22 There was a rapid escalation of statistical requirements in 1910, 1919 and 1921. For a description, see Ede et al. (1925), vol. 1, pp. 104–12. Ofgas persistently complained at British Gas's slowness in producing information: Ofgas (1987a), p. 8; (1988), pp. 12, 13, 15, 16; (1990), pp. 1, 8, 9, 19, 37.
23 Many commentators attribute the growth of the UK accountancy profession to the railways. See Hays (1981), pp. 141, 142, who sees regulation as 'the history of economic accounting'. Annual reports were required by law for the railways from 1868, for gas from 1871 and for electricity from 1882: see Gourvish (1988), p. 31. McCraw (1984), pp. 188–92, says that the new US financial regulations of the 1930s made the accountancy profession. On the influence of rate regulation in achieving consistency in accounting, see Bonbright (1961), p. 183.

24 Day and Klein (1987) argue that the objectives of accountability are necessarily various. They also distinguish between political, management and professional accountability, which they see as normally coexisting in public bodies. Accepting this complexity as a fact, they conclude by asking that those accountable should sit down with board members – nominated and elected – and work out 'tools of accountability' (p. 242). My own argument owes much to their stimulating and penetrating analysis. My departure from their position arises because I do not believe that any but the smallest public bodies can construct their own accountability tool-kit on the basis of discussion. Workable accountability in a sizeable organization implies appropriate management accounts, by which relevant performance is monitored in the context of an appropriately designed budgetary system. My disagreement with them is purely practical.

25 SCNI (1968), vol. 1, pp. 191–2.

26 NEDO (1976), vol. 1, pp. 46–8. See also n. 94 to chapter 3 above.

27 Day and Klein (1987), p. 26.

28 Ibid., p. 27.

29 Ibid., pp. 59–63.

30 Aristotle (1946), p. 292.

31 Harris (1982), pp. 90, 91.

32 Beesley and Littlechild (1986), p. 36; also Moore (1986a). Day and Klein (1987), p. 42, trace this brief that in the public sector the objective of accountability is to increase efficiency: they cite the 1969 Fulton Report on the Civil Service as one source of this. While this move for efficiency was a powerful one from the 1960s onwards, it did not become identified with economic efficiency or accepted as such by ministers until the 1980s.

33 This paragraph is based on Foster (1983).

34 Anscombe (1957), p. 56.

35 'Principal and agent theory' is much used to analyse relations between regulators and regulated and to determine what incentives could be used to make the agent do what the principal wants, as well as the changes in comparable relations and behaviour that may be expected from privatization. Sappington and Stiglitz (1987) provide an excellent summary, which is far too subtle to fall into assuming that principal and agent must have the same objectives. See also Berg and Tschirhart (1988), pp. 507–20. For discussion of this theory in regard to its relevance to privatization, see Vickers and Yarrow (1988), pp. 9–15, 92–120. A very useful inference that follows from this theory is that, however well designed these incentives, and even given that the regulator has the power to impose them, if the principal (for example, a minister or regulator) has less information than has the agent (for example, the board of a nationalized or regulated industry), then it can always be shown that there will be inefficiency as the agent uses its superior information to serve its own interests at the expense of those of its principal.

36 Prosser (1986), pp. 177, 178.

37 Williamson (1983), p. 30.

38 This is the nub of my disagreement with the conclusions drawn by Day and Klein (1987), esp. pp. 227, 249. One hopes that time will tell whether a programme can be effected to develop management tools for the complex objectives of some public bodies that are as good as those that exist for the simpler objectives of private firms. Because of its size and social importance, the needs of the National Health Service in this regard are outstanding.

39 Glaister and Collings (1978).

40 A. Williams (1985).

41 Kahn (1988a), pp. 39–41/I, has noted the tendency of regulators to favour historical accounts in periods of inflation and reproduction costs during deflation. Brandeis made the same point in 1923: Pierce, Allison and Martin (1980), pp. 177, 178.

42 HM Treasury (1986b), vol. 1. On the superiority of current cost accounts for the purposes of regulation, see Oftel (1988c); also Accounting Standards Committee (1986). I have been much helped here by Roger Knight, my colleague at Coopers & Lybrand. Ofwat (1990), p. 14, has stated that current cost accounting information will generally be needed to support pricing proposals. It is interesting that several of those who played an important part in helping to create the new regulatory regime formed the first generation of regulators. Byatt in 1989 became the first water regulator and Littlechild the first electricity regulator. Carsberg, also on the Byatt committee, had helped formed the telecommunications regime, and he became its regulator from 1984. McKinnon, the gas regulator, came from industry.

43 HM Treasury (1986b) vol. 1, pp. 9.

44 Ibid., p. 10.

45 State Owned Enterprises Act (New Zealand), 1986, p. vii, para. 32.

46 Rappaport (1986), *passim*. In principle this is what the best entrepreneurs do when considering big deals, though the methods they use may be more informal. In short, if discounted cash flow appraisal techniques are appropriate, as they are, for considering the effects of its investment upon an enterprise, so are they for measuring the consequences of all other significant changes on its overall net worth. If the current cost accounting output is appropriate and well done, and if the forecasts made are conceptually consistent with the accounts as well as made on the basis of clear assumptions, then control should be much easier.

47 For the distinction between these two concepts, see HM Treasury (1986b), vol. 1, pp. 20–4; vol. 2, pp. 29–39.

48 HM Treasury (1986b). One can find the genesis of the 'modern equivalent asset' method in Brandeis: 'what it would cost to establish a plant which could render the service, or in other words, at what cost could an equally efficient substitute be produced', *Southwestern Bell vs. Missouri Public Service Commission*, 1923, quoted in Pierce, Allison and Martin (1980), pp. 181–2.

49 The Water Appointment gave regulators most power over capital expenditure. But Oftel can be seem moving in the same direction: Oftel (1992a).

50 Ofwat (1991a).

51 Individual assets should not be considered separately. Rather, the whole configuration of assets that would replace existing assets at the existing levels of activity is to be valued. That is the main step in the calculation of the 'operating capability maintenance' value or 'financial capital maintenance' value of a regulated firm.

52 Oftel (1988a), pp. 3, 4.

53 Vickers and Yarrow (1988), p. 105.

54 One way of putting the argument for the transparency of a monopoly's cost information is that it would help meet the Bertrand–Nash assumption that potential entrants are able to evaluate the profitability of entry at the incumbent firm's pre-entry prices: G. W. Harrison (1987), pp. 191–225.

55 By 1990 the Government was signalling that it believed that Oftel needed to extract more information, especially to prevent cross-subsidization: DTI (1990), p. 72. Carsberg had also earlier said, faced by complaints over many specific prize increases, that he could do with relevant routine accounting and other information: Often (1986a), pp. 11, 12; (1987a), pp. 7, 11; (1988a), pp. 1, 8, 11; (1990), p. 9; also Oftel (1992a), pp. 4, 16, 17. On the use by the Director General of Walter Services of his right to get independent certification, see Ofwat (1991a), p. 36.

56 Faulhaber (1987), p. 23.

57 Dasgupta and Stiglitz (1980); Berg and Tschirhart (1988), pp. 385–427; Cohen and Levin (1989).

8

The limits to the regulator's independence

There have been wide differences between [regulatory] commissions and in their legislative mandates, and changes over time in the political environment in which they operate. Both . . . are illustrated, for example, in the oversimplified but illuminating generalisation that regulatory commissions tend to go through a life cycle, setting out as vigorous, imaginative and enthusiastic protagonists of the public interest, reflecting the public concern and ferment that had to be mobilized to legislate them into existence in the first place, defining their responsibilities broadly and creatively, and gradually becoming devitalised, limited in their perspective, routinised and bureaucratised in their policies and procedures, and increasingly solicitous and protective of the interests of the companies they are supposed to regulate, resistant to change, wedded to the *status quo*.

Alfred Kahn (1971)[1]

This chapter deals with the almost insoluble problem of how one can ensure the necessary independence for a regulator while making him accountable.[2] It attempts to find a way through difficult territory which is primarily the province of lawyers, political scientists and experts in public administration and where an economist is at risk – but so important is the topic for this book that something must be ventured.

Already, two reasons have been given why a regulator needs discretion: the difficulty of giving the main regulatory offences a precise definition; and that of finding the evidence to prove they have been committed. 'Discretion' means room for decision or for manœuvre. It does not involve the idea of the unlimited power of sovereignty – one would not say that Parliament had discretion. The word itself suggests constraints upon the use of power. The great Victorian constitutional lawyer A. V. Dicey, who is still influential, tried to eliminate discretion by invoking the Rule, or supremacy, of Law. He saw it as a glory of British public life that all, from ministers down, were equally subject to law. Ministers and officials could not act except to remedy 'a distinct breach of the law established before the ordinary courts of the land. In this sense the rule of law is contrasted with every system of government based on the exercise by persons in authority of wide, arbitrary or discretionary powers of constraint'.[3] An attempt was made at the end of the nineteenth century to subject British regulation to the rule of law by making the discretion of the regulator as narrow as possible.[4] But it has been in the United States, especially since 1887, that there has been the most prolonged series of attempts to conduct regulation within a tight framework of law. Its effects and the lessons to be drawn from it are discussed in section 1. However, there are other ways of limiting the discretion of officials and ensuring their accountability while still allowing them the requisite independence. Reasons are given in section 2 why neither the rule of law nor parliamentary supervision nor the preferred British route of ministerial responsibility is the appropriate way for the regulation of natural monopoly. Nevertheless, under the new British system of independent regulation, ministers do have powers, some more defensible than others. Section 3 considers the case for the adoption of procedures within the new British system to ensure fair hearings with limited appeals on procedure to the courts. However, it is arguable that the further safeguard is needed for parties before the regulators of appeals on matters of substance. The new system provides for this in part. The pros and cons of extending this right of appeal are argued in section 4.

8.1 American legalism

There were various technical reasons why in the United States in the late 1880s, a new initiative was needed in the field of railroad regulation. As we have seen, though the Massachusetts Board of Railroad Commissioners remained effective after Adams left, it operated with diminishing force in the absence of his personality and style. As a regulatory body relying on publicity, it needed an outstanding leader, and at all times they are hard to find, let alone replace. With less inspired leadership other state railroad commissions found their task harder. Moreover, many states had fewer railroads than Massachusetts had or even, in some Western states, only one, so that the railroads in those states had at least as much influence over the state legislature as had the regulator. However, the main technical reason why a new initiative was needed was that there were strict federal constitutional limits on the power of the states to regulate inter-state shipments.[5]

Far more important than any technical reason though was the growing resentment against the railroads' discriminatory pricing, which they practised in order to approach nearer to their statutory entitlement of 10 per cent, whether or not this was justified by real investment. As in Britain the railroads often appeared less profitable than they were, because of over-building and stock watering.[6] But that many railroads appeared, or in some cases were, unprofitable seemed irrelevant to their customers, who had become familiar with the view put out by Adams in *A Chapter of Erie*, and subsequently by many others, that, even if many small investors had not made money, the promoters and subsequent owners had, through their various manipulations. Moreover, there was little trust in railway accounting. In so far as they were controlled, it was through the maximum rate of return.

Railroads in the United States could discriminate more than could those in Britain because of the greater distances and lower densities involved and the much greater variations in local competitiveness between railroads, and between railroads and other forms of transport. As the frontiers moved west, the farmers especially felt that they were badly treated by the railroads on whom they were dependent for getting their produce to market. Farmers saw the railroads 'arbitrarily' deciding how much to charge them by calculating what they could bear without going out of production, reducing them all to a common level of border-line poverty however far or near they were from their markets. Thus any improvement they made that increased the fertility of their land could result in higher railroad charges. Only those relatively few in a catchment area between two railroads, or between a railroad and a canal, might benefit from rates kept down through competition. But the railroad amalgamation movement ended even that opportunity for most.

As the Collum Report, which preceded the 1887 Act, said, the United States had 'the most efficient railway services and the lowest rates known in the world . . . at the cost of the most unwarranted discrimination'.[7] And it was an explanation of that unwarrantability that was at the centre of the argument on which its case for federal regulation rested (though that argument might easily have supported a case for state ownership). It stated that, as – for the most part – local monopolies, 'the only reason for the existence of railroad corporations was that they might undertake a duty which the State was unable or unwilling to perform.' They should get a due return on the private capital invested, but as monopolies their revenue was as much a land tax as any impost of government. Therefore, it was said, as taxing authorities they were 'under the same obligations to deal fairly and equitably with all its citizens [,] without favouritism or discrimination, as [was] the State itself'. The Committee rightly concluded that, when analysed, all the apparently different sorts of complaints against the railroads amounted to objections to discrimination in one form or another. Indeed, a modern authority has said that ever since 1887 discrimination has been the only railroad regulatory problem. Because of low profitability, the possibility of railroads earning too high a return has, since 1922, not even been mentioned in US regulatory proceedings.[8] The Report concluded that it had had no party before it that did not agree that discrimination should be reduced. Indeed, as in Britain at about the same time, it seemed as if for once popular agitation had overwhelmed the concentrated power of the railroad interest and had stopped it avoiding new legislation.[9]

The Interstate Commerce Act which followed set up the Interstate Commerce Commission, the model for subsequent US regulatory agencies. As one scholar has said, while the Act owed much to Gladstone's 1844 Act, it relied also on a highly idealized account of the British system for which Charles Francis Adams was partly responsible.[10] The Act defined the duty of the new commission in the widest possible way as simply to establish the public interest. The only practices specifically condemned by the Act were discrimination and pooling.[11] The Commission was intended to have the wide discretion that the Massachusetts Board had, and that in Britain the Railway Commission was thought to have had under the Railway and Canal Traffic Act, 1873. It was always assumed that it would be subject to the courts.[12] And that was in fact its undoing. During its first twenty years, it fought many battles with the courts – and these it mostly lost. The clash was at one level political. The courts reflected an older view of the rights for private property than that which was intended by the 1887 Act to be embodied in the workings of the new commission. Repeatedly, the railroads used the Fourteenth Amendment – concerning the taking of property without due process – against the Commission, as well as state commissions, the Commission reaching conclusions in particular cases on what fair rates should be, the railroads refusing to obey and appealing to the courts, who frequently overturned the Commission's decision. But the underlying difficulty was that involved in making justiciable any view on what constituted 'undue' discrimination given the complexity of railroad joint costs, which remained considerable despite the prohibition of pooling.[13] It was not until 1906 that the Commission was able to act unhindered by such challenges when it was given the statutory power to prescribe maximum rates.[14] And a few years later it was allowed to hold up any proposed increases for a year while it investigated them.[15] However, while these changes made it possible for the Commission to become more effective, a high price was paid. It had to bind itself with rules in order to pass the test of judicial reviews, and these rules were often arbitrary and economic nonsense, because they tried to establish economically-unsound cost tests that distinguished between good and bad discrimination. Later, similar tests were applied elsewhere, as unsuitably, and in 1936 the Robinson–Patman Act established similar principles, generally to the dismay of those who preferred legal rules to be based on economic logic (though a partial defence may be made of the tests as some protection against predation).[16]

The main US attempt to establish discretionary regulation had thus practically ended before the First World War. Indeed, in the discretionary form first intended, modelled on the Massachusetts Board, it was never effective at the federal level. As we shall see, there were attempts in the 1930s to establish agencies with wide discretion, but their activities were from the start cramped by established rules and procedures, by the active practice of judicial review and by the fact that a far greater emphasis on restrictions on entry – expressed in many different ways – increased the importance of rules and rule-making.

The reasons for this greater emphasis on restrictions on entry were revealed by the dealings that underlay the acquisition by the Interstate Commerce Commission at this time when many new regulatory duties and agencies were born of the responsibility for regulating motor transport. Several commentators have found no clearly stated reason why the Motor Carrier Act, 1935, was adopted. There was no mention of any intention to use competition to regulate between modes of transport.[17] Rather, it was railroads and the large truckers that were the main forces which secured that legislation, and neither were keen that the reasons for requiring such control should be stated. As scholars have said subsequently, the main impetus behind the new regulatory duties and commissions of the 1930s derived from the economic troubles of capital-intensive industries at a time of acute depression. Falling demand meant excess capacity and therefore a tendency for marginal costs to fall below average costs, the resulting depression being particularly severe in the railroads. Because the courts had made discrimination more difficult, many industries contrived regulation which made entry more difficult in the hope, generally realized outside the railroad industry, that restrictions on entry and 'destructive' competition would raise returns to a level where capital invested could be profitably maintained. Thus, it was in order to try to restore the desperate state of railroad unprofitability that the railroad lobbies in Congress contrived to restrict entry into motor transport as a close substitute for rail – raising profitability in both to some extent.

It was to be in the courts' reviewing of the decisions of the early regulatory agencies that the foundations of US administrative law as it applied to these were laid.[18] We have already seen how the courts paralysed the Interstate Commerce Commission until a change in the laws enabled it to act more effectively but then only in a context that they regarded as acceptable. Still stronger was the influence they exerted over the next important federal regulatory agency to be set up, the

Federal Trade Commission. This was created in 1914 to implement provisions of the anti-trust laws, which previously the courts had frequently neutered. But even so for many years to come they often paid little attention to its findings, seeing it as essentially a subordinate fact-finder.[19] Some of the early statutes provided for judicial review, others for trial-type hearings, as in Britain; but, where the statutes did not provide for either, the courts asserted that they had such a right. For example, in a commonly cited case the Supreme Court refused to allow the Highway Administrator of Virginia to enforce a state statute which allowed him to require a railroad to replace a level-crossing by a bridge even though in the interests of safety without a hearing and without an opportunity for a review.[20]

Just as in Britain, there had in the United States been strong political and industrial forces in the 1920s anxious to protect monopoly and restrictive practices.[21] A manifestation of this was the series of battles fought in the courts to maintain that price regulation was illegal. Borrowing from English as well as American precedents, the Supreme Court had argued that private undertakings were free to charge what prices they liked, though the courts could proceed against discrimination.[22] Nor could a state prevent free entry into a market.[23] However, after 1933 the Roosevelt government had a reforming mandate, and this led it to create, as we saw, dozens of regulatory agencies.[24] Because of the Depression, there was a widespread disbelief in the powers of the free market. Many of these regulatory agencies were born to correct what were seen as deficiencies in competition and the market. There were some sharp conflicts here between government and the courts, but there was also a rapid revision of the previous judicial view that the Constitution only allowed regulation of a monopoly or of excessive competition.[25] In the classic case of *Nebbia vs. New York*, 1934, the Supreme Court, in allowing the State of New York to regulate milk sales by preventing a retailer discounting milk below a minimum price set by the Milk Control Board, veered round and denied that there was such a restriction:[26] though superficially the Court gave its decision as it did because it found that the setting of the price had been based on very detailed inquiries, as well as because of trade depression and a need to maintain milk quotas.[27] While there were other attempts by the courts to restrict the scope of the new agencies, Roosevelt was eventually able to replace the members of the Supreme Court whom he had inherited by others readier to accept Congress's right to give regulatory agencies whatever terms of reference it was ready to legislate.[28] As a result, there was a period of judicial deference to the exercise of substantial discretion by the agencies both in procedure and in content – but it did not last. In 1937 the Brownlow Committee reflected a widespread legal and administrative opinion in its view that 'independent regulatory commissions constitute a serious and increasing problem'.[29] A reason for this opinion echoed a problem of Victorian England: set up under various statutes, the different agencies proved to have widely differing powers and duties, often differing for no obvious reason. That is, there appeared to be little 'consistency or functional logic' in what Congress had provided, though perhaps lawyers were too ready to condemn a lack of uniformity as inconsistency.[30] Another reason was the size of the substantial financial sanctions that the new agencies could impose in the 1930s, especially those regulating the securities industries.[31]

Several attempts to constrain the agencies were defeated by Roosevelt but ultimately the pressure behind such attempts resulted in the Administrative

Procedures Act, 1946, which has since then controlled the behaviour of both federal and state regulatory agencies.[32] It required that the rules and regulations proposed by an agency be published first in the Federal Register, while other documents – subsequently strengthened to include virtually all documents – were to be otherwise published or made available. But the heart of the Act lay in a distinction between rule-making and adjudication.[33] Where an agency proposed rules or regulations, its procedure was to be to publish them in the Register and then to invite those affected to submit written or spoken comment on them, which might in some cases be at a public hearing. Where an agency was adjudicating cases where there was a dispute, it would normally be required to hold trial-type hearings. They were to be conducted first by those of its officials with independent standing (now called 'administrative law' judges), but with appeal to the head of the agency. There was also to be a distinction drawn within the agency between those officials who judge and those who prosecute. Where a statute did not require a hearing on the record neither did the Act.

The Act went on to codify the provisions for judicial review of agency decisions by the courts. Besides testing whether those decisions complied with the relevant statutes, the courts had the function of deciding whether any action was 'arbitrary, capricious, and [an] abuse of discretion'. Where a decision was reached after a trial-type hearing, they were to consider if it was reasonably based on the evidence presented.

In the years that followed the passing of the Act, the courts generally used a light hand in interpreting it.[34] They left the agencies substantial discretion. But after 1965 the courts became more constructive, imposing more-stringent requirements, striking thereby more of a balance between regulatory expertise and the need to recognize principles of fairness, and reversing their previous leanings towards conservatism. Ralph Nader's consumerism was an important influence here. Based on the premise that the regulatory agencies were often captured by those they regulated, it demanded that the courts intervene to ensure that consumers' interests were safeguarded. There were demands for more openness and more-court-like procedures, as well as for the exposure and elimination of conflicts of interest. As a result, consumers and their representatives have been given greater rights to be represented at hearings and submit evidence; regulators have been required to document their actions carefully and reveal the reasons for their decision-making in a way that opens them to challenge; and the courts have increased their previous willingness to engage in judicial review and have broadened its scope.

What has emerged from these developments of administrative procedure is a process, with criteria and models for action. Unlike practice in many European countries, there is no special court to deal with the behaviour of government agencies and officials – they are under the surveillance of the ordinary courts. While there is a special law, the Administrative Procedures Act, the courts can also use the statutes establishing an agency, any rules and regulations that an agency establishes, the Constitution and the common law, as may be relevant. The criteria they use are in general that an agency's decisions do not break its own or any other relevant laws or its own regulations, are not unsupported by evidence, are not arbitrary and are not 'unreasonable'. A vital difference between the role of the courts before the 1930s and since is that they now avoid reviewing, and therefore revising, the regulatory judgements themselves.

The models for action as described by Stephen Breyer are four in number, or more strictly two by two, since the two models that derive from the initial distinction between adjudication and rule-making are each subdivided into a formal and an informal version.

Formal adjudication   This is where an agency makes a decision on the basis of evidence presented to it at one or more hearings where witnesses are subjected to cross- examination. No evidence is relevant unless it has been introduced into the process and is open to testing by other witnesses. The issue may be a case arising out of a complaint or some other breach of a licence, regulation or other stipulation. Or it may be a dispute between parties. Or it may concern the awarding of a licence or franchise, especially where there are contenders. The procedures here resemble those of the courts, the strength of this being that, if they have been followed correctly, the outcome is that much less easy to challenge in the courts.

Formal rule-making   Though it is not unknown for agencies to establish rules progressively, through a series of adjudications, adjudication usually proceeds on the basis of rules known in advance. Thus, agencies will often wish separately to decide the rules under which the regulated parties are to operate.[35] Formal rule-making requires that any such rules be published in draft and brought to the attention of interested parties. (Rate determinations are regarded as an example of such rules.) There are then to be hearings on record where witnesses will be heard and cross-examined. And only then will the rules be issued. The strength of this process lies in its being difficult to overturn the rules provided that the appropriate procedures have been followed. It is also a test of 'reasonableness'. On important issues, such rule-making was rare until the 1950s and 1960s because of an old lawyer-like practice that regulatory agencies had of not issuing guidance – which is what such rules normally are – in advance. For many years the rules of such an agency tended to be what emerged by precedent from its individual decisions. As agencies had shifting personnel, who in any case did not have the same legal tradition as judges did of deciding cases by the interpretation of statutes and by precedent, this was another cause of inconsistency.

Informal adjudication   This covers the lesser decisions made by regulatory agencies. These can still be reviewed by the courts for their reasonableness but the procedural requirements are slighter. The border-line between what requires formal and what informal adjudication is hazy. Because the Fourteenth Amendment disallows the taking of property without due legal process, one test is whether the decision in question involves taking a significant amount of property from someone. Deciding this may involve not only the question of the amount but also that of whether what is to be taken is a privilege given by law in the first place, like a licence, rather than a firm's own property.[36]

Informal rule-making   This is common; most agency rules do not require hearings and the other trappings of trial-like procedures. Any other proposals for rules and regulations must be published in the Federal Register, so an index of regulatory activity is the number of pages per annum of such proposals thus published. It has risen from 1,500 in 1936 to 10,000 in 1950, 14,500 in 1960, 20,000 in 1970 and 60,000 in 1975.[37] All interested parties are to be invited to comment, and when these comments have been considered the final rules can be issued. At one time these agencies were free to consult, or not consult, whom they pleased. More recently there has been a tightening up to require a written record of such comments with opportunities for the parties to comment on each other's submissions. The rules as issued must be supported by written justification and publicly published information.

With all its faults, the American tradition of judicial review saved the American regulatory system from incoherence and, as a result, decay. If the courts in Britain had been able to intervene similarly, they might have done the same for British regulation – American regulatory statutes and practices were at least as various and inconsistent as the British ones. It is also not fanciful to suppose that if the courts had not saved it American regulation might also have slid into nationalization – no more for ideological motives than in Britain, but, rather, because of regulatory failure and the unavailability of obvious alternatives. Even as early as the 1890s there were those in the United States, like Richard Ely, the first president of the American Economic Association, who advocated nationalization, and there were renewed calls for it in the 1930s.[38]

One outcome of a legalistic and adversarial process is expense. And in the USA such a process can absorb enormous resources. For example, MCI, the main and first challenger to AT&T in its long-line businesses, found that 80 per cent of the costs of its first microwave service were legal and regulatory costs; and an estimate has been made that the price of gas in the United States is from 5 to 6 per cent higher because of regulatory costs.[39] But such costs are inherent in some kinds of regulation, and will be considerable even if the process is efficient in its own terms. As the Federal Communications Commission has said:

> Cost of service regulation . . . even if done correctly and well . . . imposes significant costs on regulated firms and those they serve. The policies and rules we have developed to make this method of regulation work are complicated: their application and enforcement are a resource intensive activity for the regulator, the regulated firm and other interested parties.[40]

While judicial review has been the most important channel through which the law has influenced US regulation, two others are worth mentioning. First, there was, until recently, the pervasive influence of lawyers on the regulatory agencies themselves. From their origins to 1969, the percentage of the members of the Interstate Commerce Commission who were lawyers was 75; the Federal Trade Commission 82; the Federal Power Commission 58; the Securities and Exchange Commission 70; the Federal Communications Commission 54; the National Labor Review Board 54; and the Civil Aeronautics Board 66. Secondly, reinforcing this, lawyers have been preponderant in Congress.[41] From the 1790s to the 1980s, two thirds of senators and about half the House of Representatives have been lawyers. Quite apart from external pressures from the courts, it is hardly surprising then that the regulatory agencies have tended to adopt quasi-legal procedures and that lawyers have usually appeared before them. As Stephen Breyer has said: 'there is an American social or political tendency to think, and to act, as if business and consumers were in a basically adversary relationship. The procedural context and use of lawyers further encourages the framing of issues in an adversary manner'.[42]

By their training, lawyers are inclined to interpret the law in the way that allows them to argue as strongly as they can for one side of the case. And legal advocacy may overcome the facts. In the years before the First World War there was an outstanding example of this in the regulatory arena, when Brandeis, the leading advocate of his generation and possibly the most distinguished American lawyer to have had a persistent and active interest in regulatory affairs, won a case in the courts in 1910 against the railroads, even though they had a very strong empirical case for raising prices, by parading a number of management theorists to give hypothetical reasons why and how the railroads should be able to save at least a million dollars a day through more-scientific management.[43]

But, aside from his wish to win his case, Brandeis was also moved by his own social values. He was an idealist with a hostility to big business:

> I am so firmly convinced that the large unit is not as efficient – I mean the very large unit . . . as the smaller unit that I believe that if it were possible today to make the corporations act in accordance with what doubtless we would all agree should be the rules of trade, no huge corporation would be created, or if created, would be successful.[44]

He was a strong influence upon President Woodrow Wilson, who was persuaded by him among others to see the fight against big business as necessary to restore equality of business opportunity, to 'look after the men who are on the make rather than the men who are already made'.[45] Brandeis was behind the founding in 1914 of the Federal Trade Commission to enforce the anti-trust laws; and its remit 'to put down unfair methods of competition' was in his spirit.[46] What was in reality a social or political principle – arising from a hostility to bigness in business – was paraded as an economic proposition. It was not the first nor the last occasion on which the scope of a regulatory agency was extended beyond the province of economics by disguising a distributional value judgement as a matter of economics. As it happened, the effect of this strengthening of the anti-trust legislation was the reverse of what Brandeis wanted. By making combinations and informal cartels more difficult, it actually encouraged merger and the emergence of very large corporations.[47] And Alfred Chandler has argued that this actual encouragement of bigness was a major contri-bution to US economic growth; and that, by analogy, Britain's toleration of com-bination was an additional reason for its relative economic decline.[48] But whatever the consequences here Brandeis was among the many lawyers who imported alien political concepts into economic regulation, a process particularly common in the 1930s and again in the 1970s. And as we shall see the complications these concepts introduced were important stimuli to the growth of the campaign for deregulation, as was indeed the pervasiveness of legalistic, adversarial procedures run mainly by lawyers with their own, rather than business or economic, canons of relevance.

Since the American judiciary has been more involved than has the judiciary of, say, England in reviewing the actions of the executive and has had a clear con-stitutional basis for this, one cannot deduce from United States experience whether it is inevitable that legal practices and procedures will invade economic regulation and constrain its discretion. But there are other reasons why legalism became pervasive there that are easy to see as universally operative. The main one of these is the fact that large penalties and sums of money turned on regulatory decisions. The regulated firm thus had every incentive to bring in the law whenever it could if decisions were going against it, as indeed had other parties. However, an important realization since the passing of the Administrative Procedures Act, 1946, has been that, provided that legal procedures have been followed, it is unwise for the courts to challenge a regulator's actual decisions on their merits, that is, on such matters as fair prices or rates of return, because of the difficulty of devising exact laws – a more prudent conclusion than that of the earlier American and British judiciaries, who often preferred exact laws even where they led to economic and commercial nonsense.

Thus there are two kinds of legalism in American regulation. There is that of the courts using their powers of judicial review to strive after some consistency and procedural equity, as well as at times attempting to go further and review merits or alter the law; and there is that with which each agency conducts its affairs. The two are connected because the existence of the first is a powerful, though not the only, reason for the development of the second. But this legalistic framework does not eliminate regulatory discretion. It constrains it. Discretion remains an essential element if regulation is to be workable, because of the difficulty of defining and proving most regulatory offences. The crippling legalism is that which ignores this. The division of labour between the US courts and regulators which has gradually emerged over time does provide a framework of accountability within which regulators may use their discretion – in particular in interpreting the facts – with the interests of the parties safeguarded by the right of appeal to the courts and by legalistic procedures. However, the financial and time costs of the American system are great, and many concepts, like that of rate-of-return regulation, and many precedents seem to be set in concrete. Neither has it kept regulation purely economic; it has frequently strayed into social issues (chapter 9). And the elaborateness and cost of the procedures have made it easier for the industries to capture the regulatory process.

8.2 The accountability of the regulator

There was a conscious decision in Britain to keep the law and the courts out of the new system. It was to be regulation 'with a light rein'. The Government and its civil service advisers who drafted the 1984 Telecommunications Bill and the British Telecom Licence were determined to avoid creating a legalistic system, one which would employ lawyers to present cases and which could lead to endless delays in hearings and on appeal. This was not so much because of the consequences of legalism in the American system, though the draftsmen knew it existed and wanted to avoid it and Patrick, later Lord, Jenkin, the minister responsible for the Telecommunications Act, 1984, returned with this intention strongly reinforced by a visit to the United States. More immediately influential, especially among the Cabinet, was another piece of legislation of this period. When this bill was being drafted Norman Tebbit in his Employment Protection Act was introducing new regulations to get labour relations out of the courts as far as possible; this was mere coincidence, but the reasons that seemed compelling in that case flowed over into the other.

The instinct was wise. To be effective, history suggests, regulators need ample discretion, that is, power to act in the way they see fit. In Britain ministers have power, but their freedom to use it is subject to their commanding a majority in the House of Commons. A majority in the House of Commons has power subject to the periodic vote of the electorate. The House of Lords has influence ultimately subject to veto by the House of Commons. The judiciary has power based on, but limited by, its constitutional role under such principles as the separation of powers and the rule of law, and has a system of reasoning that prevents it entering into areas of policy, in addition to well-defined procedures and a structure of appeal. And civil servants' power is checked by their direct accountability to ministers (while the boards of nationalized industries are principally constrained by their statutory duty to break even and, if they do not, their accountability through ministers to Parliament for deficit or other external finance). All are accountable to someone; to Parliament as a whole, to the electorate, at the House of Commons, to superior courts of appeal and Parliament through changes in the law, to ministers.[49] Similar arrangements limit the power of such bodies in the United States and other democratic nations.

By contrast, to whom are regulators accountable? In Britain, they are appointed by ministers; in the United States, by the President or by state authorities. But, once appointed, they are generally not easily dismissed.[50] Appeals from them in the United States may be over law, process, consistency and fact, though, as we have seen, the American courts have become more reluctant to question regulators' interpretations of facts. In Britain, regulators' powers under the law are more widely defined. (As we shall see, this follows from the narrower scope of judicial review that obtains in Britain compared with the United States.) In Britain, their discretion to determine right or wrong within the scope of their powers is almost absolute. Indeed, British ministers' formal powers over the independent regulators are less, though not markedly so, than over the financially self-sufficient nationalized industry boards – except on appointment and reappointment their formal accountability is unlimited.[51]

History suggests reasons for this development. It shows how both Parliament and Congress often failed to be consistent in devising regulatory policies. It shows how both were prevented from achieving consistency by the pressure of vested interests. And it shows that more important even than that pressure from vested interests in preventing consistency was the changing composition of committees in Parliament and Congress. In contrast, though that pressure also helps explain why Congress has not pursued a fully satisfactory policy of deregulation, vested interests have had less influence on the content of the privatization statutes and subordinate legislation in Britain (chapter 11); and though there are differences between those statutes they have reflected an evolution of regulatory policy in the mind of government more than they have the idiosyncrasies of particular ministers. Moreover, in developing the privatization programme, ministers have had the benefit of being able to rely on civil servants who have more time to achieve continuity, and more interest in doing so, than their nineteenth-century predecessors had or than their American counterparts have had. Later we will consider how far what has emerged may be described as a consistent regulatory policy and legal basis for economic regulation, but however it may be described it does not involve Parliament itself being the regulator.

As we saw earlier, the nineteenth-century attempt to use Parliament, and its committees, to act as regulators was as hopeless as its essays in regulatory policy; even if the influence of the railway interest had been negligible, no regulatory consistency could have been expected from this variable source of control. There were also attempts to use as regulators ministers (and others who seem indistinguishable from ministers since they were MPs appointed by government to a regulatory position), and these failed for similar reasons of vested interest and inconsistency of approach. Later, arguably the most prolonged attempt to use ministers as regulators was nationalization. But it also failed, and for similar reasons, its shortcomings, which eventually led to its being displaced by privatization, being displayed as much in the failure of ministers to regulate the nationalized industries as in the failure of the industries themselves to be efficient. Nationalization in fact involved a variant of the regulatory capture of the regulator by the industry. The silent majority in the industries concerned welcomed nationalization as a way of overcoming their difficulties, particularly apparent during the Depression, while a minority worked actively for it; and although there was negotiation over terms, and strident opposition from other minorities within, the form of nationalization adopted in each case was generally one that was acceptable to the industry; with the resulting operation of ministerial control over nationalized industries being generally consistent with regulatory capture inasmuch as even when they were in deficit and their relations with ministers were uneasy they survived, as they might not have continued to do in the private sector. What distinguished nationalization from US-style regulation in this respect was that the capture was not solely to the benefit of the regulated industries; the regulators, that is, ministers, also got what they wanted, though in a form that did not involve much interference with management decisions. Indeed some US regulators, in questioning capital and other expenditures, intervened more than did the civil servants directly controlling the nationalized industries. Another difference, of course, was that the ultimate enterprise objectives for the securing of which a nationalized industry wished to capture the regulator were not commercial.

In nineteenth-century Britain, as we have noted, there were many attempts to set up commissioners as regulators subordinate to Parliament or to ministers. They never lasted long. However eminently the commissions were led, Parliament or ministers or both seemed to take pleasure in making it clear that they saw their role as advisory, and then more often than not they disregarded that advice. (Over time, American regulators were distanced from a dependence on a similar presidential and congressional caprice.) Committees and royal commissions were used from time to time into the twentieth century to help produce or revise regulatory policy, but their role was limited to that advisory function. As for civil servants, as the experience of nationalized industries shows, they cannot *qua* civil servants be effective economic regulators, because they do not have enough independence from ministers. Ultimately, they have no interest in maintaining a consistent regulatory policy when it becomes clear to them that ministers do not want it, or there is a change of minister or government. Although the House of Lords is able to take a less political and deeper view of what matters, it and its committees are also affected by changes in those participating from one debate to another, and even more from one committee to another, as well as by the realization that they can only hold out against the Commons temporarily.

The realization that the opinions and decisions of legislatures are transient is of course a reason why changes to the law in most countries involve ministers in substantial effort; and why the interpretation of that law is given to a judiciary whose inclinations concerning the temporality of the law are almost exactly the opposite of those of legislators. Judicial procedures combine to ensure that the legal system, as far as possible, reaches the same decision in the same circumstances. And if any human institution can achieve consistency and continuity until the law is changed, this is it. Thus one might suppose that a regulator should be a judge or a judge a regulator. The argument which was used against this in 1873, 1893 and 1921 in Britain was that a quicker, cheaper process was needed; and the same was argued in 1887 in the United States and often since. Experience shows that this is not in fact a good argument, because regulatory processes under the existing American and the old British systems were not noticeably quicker or cheaper than judicial processes would have been. But there are, as we shall see, strong arguments against regulation by judges and against allowing for appeals on merits from regulators to judges. (The two are interrelated, for the practical effect of the second is the invasion of regulatory bodies by legalistic processes and attitudes.)

Discussion of the American experience of legalistic regulation poses the question whether it would be desirable, in other countries, to adopt aspects of that tradition and, even if it would not be, whether a move in that direction is not in fact inevitable. What alternatives are available that offer the required accountability with discretion? The American administrative lawyer K. C. Davis, and the tradition flowing from his work, have concentrated on devising appropriate structures which constrain officials, among whom are regulators, to act in ways which reflect the laws they serve. Since under most responsible regulatory regimes they cannot be given financial incentives to do this, the instruments used must be procedural. He has distinguished three main techniques: confirming their discretion by rules; structuring it through procedural requirements; and checking it by appeals or other forms of review.[52]

But before developing ideas on these for the new British system of regulation, let us consider the classic British approach to accountability, which is to invoke the doctrine of ministerial responsibility. Fortunately, for reasons that will soon appear there is no need to venture far onto this battlefield. On the one side are the ministers and officials who sincerely and often vehemently uphold it as the corner-stone of the constitution, that which in diverse ways, and with various limitations and provisos, keeps the State upright.[53] (As a matter of fact they are right to say this.) On the other side are those lawyers, political scientists and other critics who point to the frequent flexibility and obscurity of the doctrine. At worst it may seem so flexible as to allow ministers to assume responsibilities when and where they want them while disclaiming the penalties of ministerial responsibility when things go wrong.[54] It has been suggested that the obscurity of the doctrine could hardly be greater than it is among the quangos, the non-departmental public bodies (NDPBs) which are the indirect responsibility of ministers. Norman Lewis has observed the most interesting indication of government thinking on them is the HMSO publication *Public Bodies*, which lists the public bodies for which ministers have a degree of responsibility, dividing them into nationalized industries, certain other public corporations, health service authorities and NDPBs, the last being divided into executive bodies, advisory bodies and tribunals.[55] However, as Lewis points out, one cannot get a lead on the nature of the accountability of these bodies from this classification. Among the bodies that are of interest to us, Oftel, Ofgas, Ofwat and Offer, as non-ministerial government departments, are in fact outside the classification, the Civil Aviation Authority, another regulator of natural monopoly, is a nationalized industry (presumably because it also provides services to aviation like air-traffic control) and the Monopolies and Mergers Commission is down as an executive body, though, as Lewis notes, it could as well be classed as an advisory body or tribunal (while the Securities and Investments Board, a regulator, though one outside the scope of this book, is a company limited by guarantee). But while little help lies there, or in any other publication, there are two reasons why the obscurity and flexibility of this doctrine do not matter in this context.

The first is that most, though not all, of the powers over the regulated firms under the new system given ministers in the relevant statutes are consistent with conventional and intelligible notions of ministerial responsibility.[56] Their most important task here is to issue licences, where these are needed (though they may delegate this to the appropriate regulator), the most important implication of this being that it is their duty to decide the timing and extent of the progress of a natural-monopoly industry towards competition. An excellent exercise in such policy-making is that contained in the white paper issued in 1990 on the Government's proposed policy for the extension of competition in telecommunications.[57] Ministers also commonly have powers in relation both to the powers of compulsory purchase, and even criminal powers,[58] that natural monopolies tend to retain even when privatized, and to the various codes that are intended to constrain the behaviour of the various firms in the natural monopoly. And they have the right, or may ask some other body, to review the operations of a regulator; and can, of course, initiate legislation to alter it. Thus, most of the relevant ministerial powers resemble other well-known applications of the doctrine of ministerial responsibility. However, there is also written deep into the traditions of Whitehall an informal doctrine of ministerial responsibility or power. It is that, except where the law expressly provides, ministers, as democratically accountable agents, must get their way, not necessarily immediately, perhaps only after deliberation and challenge or after testing whether there is cabinet agreement, but nevertheless in the end.

The second reason why that obscurity and flexibility do not matter in this context is that the doctrine of ministerial responsibility cannot be meant to cover all the regulator's activities. Indeed, the statutes, with varying degrees of clarity, provide for the regulators' independence in specified circumstances. There are other instances where tribunals, inspectors and other officials have such a quasi-judicial independence, one which is fiercely cherished, but almost invariably a minister has the power to take the ultimate decision or decide the consequent course of action either on their advice or on appeal. What marks out the Telecommunications Act, 1984, for example, is that the Director General of Telecommunications is given the power and the duty to decide whether there have been breaches of licences quite independently of ministers and without any process of appeal from his decision. Moreover, when he, or another party, seeks a licence amendment, the Monopolies and Mergers Commission has the duty to agree or disagree with or modify that amendment if agreement cannot be reached, and Oftel to implement it, in all material respects independently of ministers. Thus by inference in this case (as, with rather different scope, in that of gas regulation) there is not ministerial responsibility for these regulatory decisions. Thus a fairly clear demarcation of responsibility has emerged for the major decisions in these areas:

ministers give licences and, as a result, determine the extent of competition; and they also decide the initial content of licences unless they delegate this power to the regulator.
the regulator decides whether there has been a breach of a licence;
the Monopolies and Mergers Commission decides a licence amendment if regulator and regulated cannot agree.

Unfortunately, the clarity that was in the telecommunications legislation became blurred in aspects of later legislation, which can be variously interpreted as allowing ministerial responsibility back into the area of licence amendments. (As there exist other ministerial powers which could be abused, as well as the informal doctrine referred to, it will be argued in chapters 9 and 11 that ministers could be a more serious threat to regulatory independence than are the courts.)

This independence of the regulator (and the Monopolies and Mergers Commission) not only shows that the traditional doctrine of ministerial responsibility cannot apply to these aspects of natural-monopoly regulation, but also bolsters the case for considering ways – other than through the courts – of making it more likely that the decisions of regulators acting independently and with discretion will reflect the purposes of the laws they serve. This is the more desirable where the penalties and other financial consequences of a regulatory decision may be considerable; the interests of the parties then need safeguards, the lack of which will cause the courts to intervene more often. Of K. C. Davis's three suggestions, the setting down of specific rules to guide the conduct of regulators has not been a feature of British practice, and also can lead to arbitrary decisions.[59] Neither is it possible to imagine Parliament or ministers doing this without materially compromising regulatory independence. This leaves procedural requirements (section 3) and appeals on issues of substance (section 4) as the main ways in which legalistic procedures, as in the United States, can restrict regulatory independence so as to make it more acceptable.

8.3   Procedural constraints

In considering the procedural requirements that may make it likely that regulators will use their independence and discretion to serve the purposes of the relevant statutes, one needs to find a middle way between the over-legalistic procedures found in the American system and the informality that has often been associated with the exercise of ministerial responsibility. We have seen that in the United States the courts and Congress have taken an interest in regulators developing procedures which are regarded as legally and politically defensible; and that the procedures that have been developed are similar to those of a court. We have also seen that some American observers, commenting on how the value for X was set in 1984 for British Telecom, found that by their standards the procedures were indefensible.[60] Behind closed doors the value for X was decided by a cabal of government officials and representatives of the monopoly to be regulated, without other parties being present and without anyone being required to state publicly the reasons for the value for X

adopted, and with no question of the Secretary of State being questioned over the procedures that were adopted by his officials. In the United States a similar exercise would have been open to legal challenge and might have been expected to get it.[61]

It is usual to discount the relevance of judicial review in Britain by pointing to its more limited scope – by noting that British judges are reluctant to question or interpret the intentions of politicians as expressed in law, and do not have a constitution to interpret here. Yet the development of the judicial review of administrative decisions in Britain over forty years has been dramatic. While the application of the broad rules of natural justice to such decisions goes back to the 1860s, at the end of the 1940s a comparison between the United States and Britain in regard to the state of judicial review was all to the advantage of the former.[62] In a celebrated case in 1948 a minister of town and country planning called a public inquiry into a development in Stevenage, as the law required, visited the town before it opened and expressed publicly his opinion that the development should happen despite considerable objections, and then after the public inquiry, authorized the development.[63] Fought up to the House of Lords, the minister's decision was upheld. Many lawyers – including one of the House of Lords' judges on the case – thought that the right to challenge the administrative process was a mockery if the palpable injustice of a minister's activities could not be overturned in such circumstances. In 1987 the author of the comparison that found British judicial review so wanting returned to the subject and found that in the previous twenty years British practice had caught up with, and in some respects had overtaken, American practice.[64] (Though it may justly be pointed out that there are other respects in which British practice has not even tried to start to catch up.) That was also the view of several British judges. Lord Diplock, for example, said, 'that progress towards a comprehensive system of administrative law ... I regard as having been the greatest achievement of the English courts in my judicial lifetime'.[65]

In *Council of Civil Service Unions vs. Minister for Civil Service*, Lord Diplock set out the three possible grounds for judicial review: illegality, irrationality and procedural impropriety.[66] An administrative action is illegal if it is not within the power allowed by the relevant statutes. And an administrative decision is irrational if it is so illogical or contrary to normally accepted moral standards that no reasonable person could have reached it. The concept of irrationality or 'unreasonableness' employed here is in principle the same as under American law, but British judges until recent times have not used it to anything like the same extent or with as broad a scope. It tends to be defined only in relation to logic, not in relation to the evidence deployed or the conclusions that might reasonably be drawn from the evidence.

An administrative decision is taken without procedural impropriety if it is taken with fairness or natural justice; and it is on this that the revolution of the last twenty years has concentrated. Of most relevance would seem to have been:[67]

(1) A requirement since 1958 that certain categories of administrative bodies – particularly public inquiries and tribunals – give reasoned decisions. (All are required to do so in the United States: 'The discretion vested in an administrative agency is not the naked, unfettered power to turn thumbs down or thumbs up', *People vs. United States*, 1973, which may be contrasted with an aphorism of Lord Sumner's: the record 'speaks only with the inscrutable face of a sphinx'.[68])

(2) A requirement that there be fair hearings, which since *Ridge vs. Baldwin* in 1963 has grown to mean that any person with 'legitimate expectations' has a right to be heard by an unbiased tribunal, to have notice of a charge of misconduct, and to be heard in answer.[69] After the hearing is closed the person who conducted it must not hear one side without the letting the other know. And he must not accept from third parties what supports one side's case without giving the other an opportunity to answer it.[70] At the root of this change has been the development and application of the concept of 'natural justice', which has its origins in the common law, to parallel the American notion of 'due process' which in part has its origin in the Constitution.[71] (An application for a licence does require a hearing but British practice still regards an applicant for a licence as having a lesser interest than someone with a licence under threat.)

Indeed, public inquiries in Britain have come to be run under procedural rules similar in nature to those laid down by the United States Administrative Procedures Act, 1946. For example, the inquiry into the proposal to build a nuclear power-station at Sizewell was a formal adversarial adjudication and was required to adopt procedures very similar indeed to those required of formal adjudication in the United States. Such elaborate procedures are not what the Government intended for natural-monopoly regulation since they can be extremely lengthy and costly when matters are complicated, can employ legions of lawyers and have strict rules governing the provision and testing of evidence.

There is no question but that the new regulatory bodies are subject to judicial review. This was illustrated in 1990 when for the first time the courts used their power of judicial review to investigate the proceedings of one of the new independent regulators, reaching an adverse opinion on Carsberg's failure to refer back for comment by the parties concerned a revised decision he had made in the light of comments by one party on a draft he had circulated to all.[72] It should also be noted that, because the new British regulatory agencies have limited sanctions of their own and generally have to use the courts for enforcement, the likelihood is increased that parties will use judicial appeal to avoid the enforcement of punishment by the courts; and that in any case, given the commercial and financial consequences of regulation for the regulated firms and the lawyers they employ, such firms must be expected to weigh the chances of successful judicial review at all stages.

If that is so, why not wait for the courts to act at the instance of interested parties, for inconsistency to result, as in the United States, in an administrative procedures act or for some extension to regulatory bodies of the requirements placed on public inquiries and tribunals by the Council on Tribunals?[73] The compelling reason against what may seem a natural progression is that there must be a severe risk that the outcome would be the emergence of expensive trial-like procedures where cases are argued at length by lawyers with highly developed rules of evidence. Even if the procedures required were to go no further than what is required at public inquiries like Sizewell, the legalism and procedures would have arrived which the British legislation of the 1980s studied to avoid. In that regard, the regulatory process could become as expensive and time-consuming as those of the American or the old British regulatory commissions. Moreover, experience shows that such procedures always work to the advantage of the regulated: they provide another route to regulatory capture.

The best defence against excessive legalism would seem to be to do what Sir Bryan Carsberg has attempted to do. This is to devise procedures that avoid the possibility of legal challenge. Based on his experience as a regulatory staff member in the United States, he would seem to have adopted methods similar to American methods of informal adjudication and rule-making, pressumably for the very reason that the more defensible his procedures are the less opportunity there will be for the courts to enter, or for Parliament to be persuaded to require the courts to enter. And the other new British regulators have sometimes adopted the same tactic. However, as we shall see, while the degree of informality here is perhaps understandable in the early, formative stages of the operation of a new regulatory system, it would be wise, as the system matures, to institute the practice of making available, in so far as is possible, the reasons for decisions, and of doing so before the decision is finalized, so as to set clearer precedents for others and to ensure that third parties affected by those decisions are able to question them intelligently in draft.

Because as yet in Britain there has been no equivalent to the United States Administrative Procedures Act, 1946, the choice of the procedures to be adopted has been among the matters left to the discretion of the regulators. The style the regulators should adopt itself raises important issues: it may be contrasted with the bureaucratic style. For example, the British Telecom Licence was, more than its successors, a characteristic civil service document. It was elegantly drafted in some respects, but within it – as within many civil service papers – coexisted both ambiguity and over-scrupulousness in drafting. Among the reasons for ambiguity in white papers and other vessels of civil service prose is that ministers may have not yet decided quite what to do, and may indeed await public reaction to help them decide what to do. Elsewhere in the same document carefully chosen, even pedantic, language may be used because one party to the drafting wants to chalk up beyond doubt a victory won in preliminary meetings. Other wordings – clear and unclear – may represent concessions made to achieve a consensus. The drafting of the licences had some of these characteristics because they were the product of the negotiations of (more or less) equals around a table, who referred matters upon which they could not agree to a higher level, even – if necessary – to ministers. That is, at all lower stages a consensus would have been sought, failing which in the end ministers would decide. This is the unvarying method of Whitehall.

These meetings, which as we have seen were so foreign to the American style of regulation, created a climate of expectation within the industries themselves, certainly in the early days, that a similar relationship would be established with the regulator – not with government, for it was well understood that they were about to win their independence from government. If it is surprising that this was what most officials within the nationalized industries thought would be the atmosphere of regulatory meetings after privatization, one must remember that in many cases they had limited experience of other styles of meeting. That is how relations between government and nationalized industries, as well as those within Whitehall, had always been conducted. If there was another model in their minds, it was probably that of the legalistic proceedings which they knew it was the Government's intention to avoid, as it was their own.

It was Carsberg's need and achievement to convert such meetings at which everyone still sat in similar chairs on the same level around an ordinary civil service table exchanging views and consensus-seeking into a quasi-judicial process or fair hearing which was subtly, but powerfully, different. (It was not a coincidence that he had experienced American regulation at first hand.) The regulator must behave to some extent informally but also quasi-judicially, proceeding deliberatively without the apparatus of the law or a tribunal. He must use his talents and tact to hold fair hearings and communicate aspects of natural justice in a way which persuades parties before him, government, and public opinion that what he decides is reasonable and appropriate. His decisions must be consistent with the duties he has been given, consistent with each other and inconsistent with regulatory capture.[74] This was an atmosphere for which many in the regulated industries were unprepared and which quickly seemed inconsistent with what they expected from regulation 'with a light rein'. It has not been unknown for a regulated industry chairman to be found waiting on the regulator's doorstep in the morning to catch him as he came in, believing that a few reasonable, off-the-record words between sensible men could settle a matter which otherwise would, rightly as he saw it, take several months and exchanges of paper be settle. (Neither has it been unknown for a chairman to refuse to meet his regulator again after an initial meeting.) Some of the regulated industries took years to realize that the civil service practice of getting someone with whom one wants to do business to sit at a table with one to try to establish common ground would not do either. Not that a regulator would refuse to attend such a meeting, but natural justice demanded that he be only a listener at it. He could not easily respond without falling into the Stevenage trap of appearing to indicate what his views might be before a hearing.

The point of departure in determining a regulatory style is indeed the recognition that the activity of a regulator is quasi-judicial, and that there are two common kinds of event and one less common kind with which a regulator has to deal. They are: complaints; proposals by the regulated industry whose consistency with the licence needs testing; and possible licence changes.

(1) There are likely to be many complaints, or other reasons to suppose that there has been a breach of a licence condition. Every complaint may disclose such a breach. Because of their number, a wise regulator will be anxious that as many as possible are settled bilaterally between the industry and those who complain, unless the issue is serious or raises a new or difficult principle. He will therefore arrange that as far as possible he is brought in only in such circumstances or on appeal. Where the issue is serious or new or comes to him on appeal, the model behaviour indicated by natural justice would seem quite simple. An accusation having been made, the regulator will convey that to the accused party in as clear and comprehensive a form as seems necessary, together with any observations he may choose to add on the nature of any rebuttal or other information that he may require or suggest be supplied. If he thinks it appropriate, one way of expressing the charge is as a draft enforcement order outlining the action he would regard as reasonable and as likely to be enforced by the courts if the rebuttal is not successful. It is then for the industry complained against to seek any clarification it needs before preparing a written defence, which may lead to a hearing. If there is a hearing between the regulator and one side, then there should also be one with the other side and possibly with other parties whom the regulator believes have a standing in the

matter or whose views would be helpful to him. He will then reach a preliminary decision, upon which, if he is wise, he will give each side an opportunity to comment before publishing his final decision. And if he changes his mind on the basis of these comments and changes his decision materially, he should then give the parties a further opportunity for comment.

The principles underlying such procedures – and there might well be acceptable variants of them – are, as noted above, those of natural justice. There should be some clarification and testing of a charge before it is formally made. Those charged should know of what they are accused and have an opportunity of increasing their understanding of it. And they should have some idea of what kind of evidence would be accepted in defence. Any opportunity one side is given to state its case should be matched by an equivalent opportunity given to the other side. And any other parties considered by the regulator to have a sound reason for expressing their opinion should be given the opportunity to comment on the decision before it is finally published.

Those who chose the value for X for British Telecom in 1984, as we have seen, did not give their reasons for their choice. Neither did Carsberg for his first important decision, concerning the financial and operational basis for Mercury's right to interconnect with BT. Unlike American law, British law has repeatedly refused to demand that ministers and administrators give their reasons for their decisions, as we have seen.[75] Plainly, their not having to do so makes it less likely that they can be called to account for the irrationality of their decisions. On the other hand, as we have also seen, since 1958 those conducting public inquiries and tribunals have had to give their reasons. The greater readiness from the mid-1980 onwards of regulators to give reasons – which should be expressed as clearly and accurately as possible – may reflect the sensible view that this second way of proceeding is the wise model to adopt here if legal challenge is to be avoided.

Among the practices a wise regulator should avoid when dealing with complaints are:

1   not giving to the defending party, or anyone else specified by him as having a relevant interest, written warning of a possible offence or complaint that he is going to investigate, with a clear indication of what the alleged offence is, the licence condition, or other requirement that may have been breached and an indication of the remedy that might be suitable – without any indication of whether or not he believes that the offence has in fact been committed;

2   giving any preliminary or provisional views on what his final recommendations might be at any stage before delivering them in draft;

3   altering the charge as specified in his initial statement of it without giving good reason for doing so (if he has to alter it, even then he should be ready to go back almost to the beginning of the process);

4   not giving reasonable time and opportunity to those that he thinks have any relevant interest in doing so to supply evidence in relation to any alleged offence, complaint or permission granted him, though he does not have to reveal the principles which lead him to decide who has and who has not such an interest;

5   omitting to consider in time any written evidence presented and give the main

party or parties an oral hearing if so requested, unless he believes that it is plain that it would not be relevant to his decision;

6 indicating at any such hearing or other meeting what his opinion of any piece of evidence is, or what his attitude to the decision he has to make is, before he has provided all the parties that he believes have a relevant interest with his written decision in draft – any questions he asks should be of fact or otherwise elucidatory;

7 not providing such a draft decision to give the defending and any other main party an opportunity to comment – thereafter, he may consider their representations but no other evidence, and if he makes a material change as a result he must circulate the draft again for comment, and so on until what is seen by all is substantially the final decision as it is to be published;

8 being inconsistent in the procedures he adopts between apparently similar cases;

9 reaching different conclusions in what may appear similar cases without explaining why;

10 giving illogical or over-elaborate reasons, or reasons not easily justified in terms of his powers;

11 allowing himself to be put under undue, informal pressure by any party – he can always listen to what anyone may say without thereby being compromised, but he must not let himself be manœuvred into a position where he can be quoted as having favoured one side of a case;

12 where a charge is being levied or altered, not ensuring that there is enough factual information to make sure that no regulatory offence is being committed, or not being ready to communicate the fact that this has been ensured to those charged so as to reassure them, unless there is genuine competition.

(2) The regulator would be wise to follow similar procedures when dealing with the second common kind of regulatory event: a regulated firm wanting to be allowed to do something where there is doubt about whether it is a breach of the licence (or a failure in some other area where the regulator has standing: for example, fair-trading issues). Every traditional nationalized industry instinct, engendered in its past relations with Whitehall, prompts the regulated firm to try for approval in principle before working up a complete scheme. Nothing could be more dangerous for a regulator, who could easily be accused of bias or prejudgment. He may indicate the criteria he will use and other factors he may take into account in reaching a decision here, though if he is wise he will avoid giving an exhaustive list. He will demand a worked- up proposal, and will not act until such a proposal has been put to him. Having received it, he will state any data deficiencies or other shortcomings in it. And when they have been put right he will give any other parties he believes have a reasonable interest in the matter a chance to improve their understanding to it, and then call whatever hearings he believes necessary. Finally, having given the parties a chance to comment on his draft decision, and to comment on any changes made because of comments, he will publish it with his reasons.

(3) Where the issue is a possible licence change, which may originate with either the regulator or the regulated, an appeals process is normally provided for, but in his handling of the preliminary stages the regulator must similarly protect himself by ensuring that his actions accord with the requirements of natural justice.

The dictum that what the appropriate procedures to ensure fairness are depends on the particular circumstances was exemplified by the UK Duopoly Review of 1990 to 1991.[76] This was especially complex in that it involved both the Secretary of State for Trade and Industry, because of his powers in regard to the extension of competition, and the regulator; and also because it resulted in an intricate set of licence modifications whose effects would be felt by many parties besides British Telecom. Several of the issues of substance raised by this review are considered elsewhere in this book; here we are concerned only by those of procedure. The process began in 1990 when the Secretary of State and the regulator issued a joint consultation document. [77] (A careful reader could tell which parts of it related to the duties of one and which to those of the other.) After a series of consultations, a further document was put out by the Secretary of State and the regulator in 1991, a week before the Budget, as it happened. It was in effect a draft proposal stating their joint intentions concerning the licence modifications they proposed covering the extension of competition; the revised terms on which others could use BT's network and help finance BT's social obligation in doing so; and various other matters, including another revision of the price formula and changes in policy on price-caps, all of which had been duly covered by the previous consultation document and the consultation process. Up to this point there is no procedural criticism to be made of the process. But then, unfortunately, the fact that the Budget announced that the remaining 49 per cent of BT shares owned by government would be sold in the autumn gave rise to a widespread impression that the licence amendments were to be as proposed in this second consultation document, even though in fact BT had objections, which quite properly had to be taken account of. There were then negotiations which culminated in a weekend meeting at which the Secretary of State and the regulator sat down to negotiate with the chairman and other members of the BT board, a meeting from which the board members went away believing that they had secured a deal which had become more favourable to BT, although it was said that the other side made it clear that there would, rightly, have to be consultations on the revised terms with the other parties. As it turned out, these parties objected strongly to some of the changes, on the ground, principally, that the higher cost now proposed for their use of BT's network would make their competitive entry into the network financially impossible. Persuaded of this, the regulator produced a further revision of the proposed licence amendments, which was greeted by BT with astonishment as a breach of faith, destroying the deal which it believed had been made – a view which it expressed publicly. What BT seems to have failed to see was that it would have been unfair and against natural justice if the deal reached had not been referred back to the other parties before adoption. Unquestionably, if there had not been further consultation, it might have been subjected to judicial review, which, from precedent, would probably have overturned it.

To account for these misunderstandings, one may argue that the procedures were too informal, given the complexity of the issue. It would have been wise if the regulator had held hearings at which each of the parties could have heard the cases presented by the others. Such hearings would not have needed legal representation for the parties, or a process of examination and cross-examination.[78] What would have mattered was that there should have been no doubt in the mind of any party about what evidence had been put in by any other party. Every party would have had an opportunity for making its representations on the evidence of any other. To the end of ensuring such fairness, it might be wise to adopt the procedure available in the proceedings of the European Commission whereby there is always a hearing at a late stage at which an official – who is not the one who takes the final decision – goes over the evidence and procedures adopted with the parties in order to ensure that all are reasonably satisfied that the proceedings have been fair. It might also be wise if what is the Secretary of State's business and what is the regulator's were to be kept separate so that there should be no confusion at any stage over the role of each. Thus, in this particular kind of joint review, the regulator might first hold hearings to determine any changes in the basis for interconnection – if there should not be agreement between the parties over this, the nature of the disagreement should still be clearly established. Then, whether agreement has been reached or not, the Secretary of State might form a provisional view on the extension of competition to be made, if any. If the parties still disagree, or have come to do so, then is the time to go to the Monopolies and Mergers Commission. As far as possible, any extraneous matters should be kept away from this set of proceedings and dealt with separately. With some such procedures in cases whose complicated nature makes them appropriate, one may hope that regulation can find a mean between procedures that clog up the regulatory process and those that may be criticized as producing complicated ex-parte deals – a mean whose results are judge-proof and publicly acceptable.

However, all this having been said, one must not overrate the importance of procedural justice. Even the best procedures may not in the end avoid palpable injustice and irrationality. Alfred Kahn has argued that, in the United States, operating good procedures has not avoided bad, because impenetrable, decisions. The Civil Aeronautics Board before he became chairman would often go through the correct open procedures but then,

> I have been told ... that in the past the Board would often choose among competing applicants for the right to operate a particular route in secret sessions, held in a closed room from which all staff were rigidly excluded; that somehow out of that process emerged a name attached to the route in question; that the Chairman – or perhaps his assistant – would then pick up the telephone and call the General Counsel and tell him who the lucky winner was, and nothing more; that then a lawyer on the General Counsel's staff, amply supplied with blank legal tablets and a generous selection of clichés – some, like 'beyond-area benefits,' 'route strengthening' or 'subsidy need reduction,' tried and true, others the desperate product of a feverish imagination – would construct a work of fiction that would then be published as the Board's opinion. Need I add that any resemblance between it and the Board's actual reasons for its decision would be purely coincidental? And then the courts solemnly reviewed these opinions, accepting the fiction that they truly explained the Board's decision, to determine whether the proffered reasons were supported by substantial evidence of record.[79]

Moreover, he added that the expectation that there would be detailed, extensive hearings itself acted against the free granting of route licences. It had constrained the exercise of the discretion that he believed the statutes had granted the Civil Aeronautics Board. Instead, when he became chairman, he used that discretion to overturn the procedures and grant licences freely despite an uproar that gave voice to the view that he was violating due process. Fortunately, as he would admit, the statute under which he operated was repealed before his decisions were tested in the courts. The main point here, however, is that, while there should be procedures that reflect natural justice, they can become a prison preventing the objectives of regulation policy being realized; they can be obeyed and yet be subverted by self-interested or otherwise ill-intentioned regulators; and it surely remains true that, 'while some beneficial changes can be made in purely procedural matters, the really significant potential for improvement [in regulatory systems] lies in the area of substantive policy.'[80]

What underlies this search for appropriate procedures may seem paradoxical, but it is sensible. Given that the opportunities for legal challenge in the British system are, and are meant to be, narrow, a wise regulator will adopt procedures which would be defensible if they were challenged. If British regulators do not do this, then the resentment of those who feel they have not been handled fairly will accumulate. It is likely that there would then be frequent judicial reviews, and, even if most were not successful, that sooner or later something like the US Administrative Procedures Act, 1946, would be enacted, unless the European Court of Justice stepped in first with similar effect. Then a truly legalistic system with all its costs, opportunities for delay and heightened likelihood of regulatory capture would be inescapable.

8.4   Appeals on matters of substance

There have been times, as in the 1930s and 1940s, when American courts have been in general as reluctant to question congressional decisions as the British courts have been to question parliamentary ones. And even before that American courts had to retreat before the clearly expressed intentions of Congress and successive presidents to make the early regulatory commissions more effective. On the other hand, the old British commissions, such as the Transport Tribunal and the Electricity Commissioners, were as much subject to judicial review as have been the comparable American institutions.[81] Although they could not be appealed against on merits, they could be on a point of law or standing, that is, on the right of any particular interest to be heard.[82] But the British courts did not use their review powers to interpret the laws passed by Parliament;[83] they exposed the inconsistencies between successive pieces of legislation, but left it to Parliament to resolve them. Because Parliament did not do so, and given its practical powers could not have been expected to do so, this inaction of the courts was a powerful reason why that system of regulation deteriorated rather than improved.

That disposition of the British courts has persisted, and for that reason, and for all the other reasons given for confining their role in regulation to procedural issues, there is no question of finding a way of getting them to review the legislation that bears on regulation so as to achieve legislative consistency.

One of those other reasons is that many of the central facts and concerns in regulatory cases are not amenable to legal scrutiny. For instance, the real reason why legislatures have shied away from letting regulation be done by judges is the intractability of the relevant facts. The facts needed to establish whether a regulated firm has been guilty of abusing its natural monopoly, or of discrimination or of such unfair practices as predation, are often elusive and complicated. Indeed, as was argued in the previous chapter, in the absence of a system of accounts detailed enough to isolate and measure them exactly, the data on these facts cannot be said to exist. And even if that were not the case – and it has always been true that the availability of accounting data and other kinds of information has lagged behind regulatory needs – some of these facts are inherently ambiguous or subjective to a greater extent than are the facts of criminal and even commercial law. For example, one cannot value a company without choosing an interest rate, as economists have proved in other contexts, but in a regulatory context where society's valuation of a company is as relevant as the company's own, the choice of an interest rate, though it should be influenced by the facts, also depends on an evaluation of risk and uncertainty, as well as possibly on an ethical judgement – the weight to be given to the interests of different generations – which cannot be decided objectively.[84] One reason indeed why the old school of regulatory economists fell into disrepute with their more academic colleagues was that they had to form definite opinions, willingly or unwillingly, on matters which their colleagues knew were essentially indefinite. Moreover, as if this were not enough, regulatory decisions often require a regulator to take a view of the future, if only because he cannot continually be revising his decisions as circumstances change. He has to set a rate of return, agree a break-up or allow a tariff with a view to its suitability for the future. Therefore he has to make his own forecasts, and assess those of the regulated industries, whereas almost invariably judges confine their conclusions to events that are past.

So much difficulty over the facts has an effect on the rules – that is, the 'laws' – that regulatory processes make. There is no logical reason why regulatory offences should not be as clearly delineated as most criminal offences are – even with the simplest of criminal offences there are difficult cases. What prevents the clarification of most regulatory offences is the slipperiness of the relevant facts. Even within the legal system, where through their application in various cases to a variety of circumstances offences like murder and theft come to have a definite and carefully limited meaning, wherever the facts of a case are harder to establish – as with a complicated fraud or rape – so is the law likely to be less developed.

Those regulatory commissions in Britain and the United States which behaved as if they were courts differed from ordinary courts in that they were specialists and in so far as there was an appeal from them to the ordinary courts. But they still found themselves in the difficulty of defining regulatory offences, and then of establishing innocence or guilt clearly enough to stand up to an appeal. The significance of *Federal Power Commission vs. Hope Natural Gas Co.* was that it marked the point at which the Supreme Court acknowledged that a fair return on a fair valuation was not a precise concept; and that therefore departures from it could not be precisely established.[85] It could not sensibly be formulated in such a way as to be capable of precise evaluation and measurement. The result of that decision was that the regulator came to be given, not discretion over law or process, but the discretion to determine the facts of a case. It was tantamount to an admission that regulators could not proceed as judges do by the interpretation of well-defined laws or rules, relying as far as possible on well-specified precedents.

The same difficulties with facts are another reason for avoiding adversarial procedures either originally or on appeal. Where adjudication turns on complex calculations, as for example in setting the terms and conditions of interconnection, or otherwise involves testing detailed evidence, some opportunity for the parties to meet together under the regulator's chairmanship will probably be inescapable, though it should be possible to avoid a formal legal process of examination.

As Craig has emphasised in his work on administrative law, the procedures that each body adopts should be tailored to its individual circumstances.[86] As a corollary, it may be logical for a body to adopt different procedures for its different activities and for the same activities in different circumstances. Where there is a regulatory issue which materially concerns many parties, and as the issues become more complicated, a regulator is prudent if he emphasises the necessity of establishing the relevant facts in a form available and reasonably acceptable to all the parties. Every party must be able to discover what the others are saying. Where written cases are put in – as is sensible where the issues, and particularly the figures, are complicated – papers should be available to the other parties except when it can be shown there are genuine issues of commercial confidentiality. But even then it may be sensible to have recourse to independent assessors able to view information in confidence.

Judge Breyer has said that a regulator needs the qualities not of a lawyer but of a businessman.[87] Those qualities are to be sharply differentiated from those of the politician, the lawyer, the civil servant and the academic – from those of the lawyer and the academic because the skill or art of the businessman, like that of a general, is to be able to make up his mind in the absence of all the relevant facts yet in a way that still, in effect, accounts for them. In so far as his success is not due to luck, it implies an ability not only to learn from experience but also to recognize a new situation quickly by an intuitive understanding of its affinity to past situations. A regulator similarly needs in the absence of all the facts to form a view on whether an offence has been committed. Whatever administrative procedures he does or does not go through to be fair, a judicial system is inappropriate here, even more an appellate one, because no more than a businessman can he demonstrate the facts or fully explain the grounds upon which he decided that there was, or was not, an offence committed. Because of this, a regulator may well reach a different conclusion in what appears to be the same kind of situation without its being possible to convict him of inconsistency or error, just as a businessman may reach different decisions in what appear to be the same circumstances.

What is supposed to motivate or condition a businessman to exercise his discretion properly is that he either is risking his own money or is directly accountable to shareholders who may remove him. In this respect a businessman is in a similar position to a minister, who is removable by the prime minister of the day or, in a different way, by the electorate. The regulator, however, is not similarly motivated or accountable or as readily seen to be a success or failure – he cannot put his mouth where his money is. Of course, there may be some process that allows for his removal and he may be restricted in the procedures he uses, but if he is too readily accountable to someone else – particularly a minister, a court of law or a civil servant – he will lose that very discretion that allows him to reduce to order the facts with which he has to cope. Thus the question of who or what motivates the regulator becomes a vital one. (This issue will be further considered in chapter 11.)

If difficulties will arise if a regulator is, or tries to behave like, a judge, then similar difficulties will arise when appeals on merits or law lie to a judge. Experience suggests that conscientious courts try to mould (intractable) regulatory offences so that they have the certainty of laws and evidence. This will tend to eliminate the discretion of regulators; and the system will become as ineffective as if regulators were themselves to be, or behave like, judges. It has been this aspect of legalism that the new British system of regulation has been keenest to avoid, and has sought to prevent by barring all appeals to the courts other than on procedures.

It has been helped in this by the British tradition of judicial review. Despite various attempts to persuade the judiciary that they should question the policy underlying administrative decisions, they have largely resisted this.[88] They have been helped in this by a narrow view of their powers to consider the legality of any administrative decision: they confine their attention to what is needed to establish the absence of *ultra vires*, avoiding any tests of the consistency of a decision with decisions taken by the courts or by other regulators. Where they do consider policy, they limit themselves generally to establishing that there is no evidence that a minister or administrator did not have a policy or if he did, that he went against his own guidelines or was irrational in interpreting that policy.[89] They have avoided challenging in judicial review the merits of administrative decisions.

However, the requirement that there should be a right of appeal on matters of substance from a regulator does not seem unreasonable. The purpose would be two-fold: to help ensure consistency between regulatory decisions where appropriate and to allow parties the safeguard of a right of appeal. And as will appear the discretion that the statutes allow for this development is considerable. A possibility only to be considered to be dismissed is that appeal should be to a minister. While common in other areas of administration, it is difficult to see how one could avoid such a relationship relapsing into one closer to that between ministers and nationalized industries, for ministers would inevitably bring their political and social objectives to bear on appeals. And as inevitably the regulator would be drawn into a position more similar to that of a departmental civil servant.

Where a licence condition is to be changed or there is a fair-trading offence, the new British system already gives leave of appeal – to the Monopolies and Mergers Commission. There is much sense in this arrangement which means that appeal lies from one discretionary regulatory body to another. Because the Commission too is not a court and is comparatively informal in its procedures, this should help avoid the legalism lurking in this area. It should also help build up a body of opinion on the wording most appropriate to the various licences, as well as on what it is reasonable and appropriate to lay down in licence conditions. And it also provides a form of review, since many other regulatory issues may well come up in the course of hearings before the Commission and be reflected in its reports.

However, it can be argued that it remains a defect in the system that no appeal lies from a regulator – who has ample discretion which he can use arbitrarily or capriciously and on the use of which very large sums of money could turn – when he is interpreting, rather than considering a change in, a licence. That is, besides operating with natural justice backed by the availability of a corresponding scope for judicial review, and with a system of appeal where licence amendments are proposed, regulation would be more robust if appeals were extended to, first, regulatory decisions on a breach of licence, where there might be first a screening procedure to establish that the appeal was reasonable (as with judicial review, where parties have to make a case for it on the basis of written affidavits) and then an appeal procedure in terms of agreeing or not agreeing that the regulator's decision was not unreasonable given the facts and the nature of the breach committed. And, secondly, regulatory determinations or formal decisions under a statute or licence, where there might operate a similar process. (There would be no such right of appeal where the regulator is brought in as a mediator between the parties.) And the obvious body for all these appeals is again the Monopolies and Mergers Commission.[90]

Such a change from practice that has evolved in the 1980s may be desirable, but should not be necessary except in circumstances to be described in chapter 11 where the regulatory system has been captured or has otherwise decayed. A second possibility is that the Monopolies and Mergers Commission or some other body should occasionally review regulatory decisions, not to overturn them but in an attempt to draw out principles and inconsistencies as guidance for the future. At the same time, it would be helpful if in all cases the statutes were revised to make it utterly clear that the relationship was one of appeal, by narrowing the apparent discretion the regulator has in implementing the Commission's recommendations.

It is not the business of this book to try to appraise the Monopolies and Mergers Commission in all its capacities – natural-monopoly regulation is not the only reason for a substantial increase in its activity recently. But it may well be sensible to consider whether its procedures in relation to natural monopoly are themselves sufficiently structured to ensure that all parties see the evidence given by others and have sufficient opportunity to comment on it; and whether there is not a case for a special hearing before the Commission reaches its recommendations at which parties may comment on how satisfactory they believe the procedures have been; as well as any other measures as may reinforce the consistency of the Commission's decisions as its work load becomes heavier and more complicated.

However, one must remember that holding fair hearings, so defined, may not protect regulation from judicial or legalistic influences. Sooner or later the courts are likely to enter, or try or be forced to try to enter, by other routes. One possibility – for example, in the regulation of airports – is that international agreements will permit the challenge of regulatory decisions in the UK courts. More likely to succeed is challenge in the European Court of Justice. If such a successful challenge were to happen and cast its shadow over the regulator in the new British system, his freedom from judicial and legalistic intervention, by comparison with his American counterparts, could again be short-lived. All this increases the good sense of such a regulator's behaving so that he avoids legal challenge. For his independence, and therefore his ability to use his discretion, provide not only the strength but also the vulnerability of the new British system. Yet even so time may be expected to show some erosion of that independence – though that should be resisted – and experience shows that regulatory systems tend to decay and that on average later regulators are likely to be less able than earlier ones, as well as more fettered by bad precedents and other mistakes of the past. The new system may then edge towards legalism or relapse into a set of relations similar to those between ministers and nationalized industries. In the long run, it is unlikely to stand still unless, as is suggested in chapter 11, the regulatory structure can be built up and given sufficient robustness.

Though the historical circumstances are very different and the focus now is narrower, I do not think it too fanciful to draw an analogy between the position of the independent regulator, and that of the ruler as described by Plato in one of his discussions of statesmanship. He said that there was a sense in which the king, or his highest advisers, ruled best if they were able to rule without, or above, the laws, because 'the differences of human personality, the variety of men's activities and the inevitable unsettlement attending to all human experience make it impossible . . . to issue unqualified rules holding good on all questions at all times.'[91] The art of the ruler (or a judge within a system of common law) is to modify laws to fit new or otherwise difficult circumstances, or to override them where they cannot be modified. This is not the same activity as that of a judge deciding cases on the basis of standards set for him and embodied in laws which he then aims to interpret impersonally. [92] In the hands of badly intentioned or inept rulers, the danger of the misuse of such discretion is obvious. Better such a society should stick rigidly to the laws it has, even though the cost of that in difficult cases – such as some regulatory offences – is a stupid or biased outcome.[93] But in contrast, by upright and under-standing rulers 'no wrong could possibly be done so long as they keep firmly to one great principle, that they must always administer impartial justice to their subjects under the guidance of their intelligence and the art of government.'[94] Only the select and most enlightened individuals can be entrusted with such a use of their discretion. By analogy, deciding how one can help secure a good regulator and avoid a bad one becomes an important issue. If a regulatory system can be designed so as to secure and retain able, even outstanding, regulators, then the nature of regulatory offences is such as to make this the best solution; but it may be better that a bad or indifferent regulator be shackled within the cage of law despite the undoubted shortcomings of a legalistic regulatory process.

The regulatory regime under which a British regulator can use the discretion the new legislation has undoubtedly given him may not survive. Sooner or later the shadows may lengthen, removing his independence, because there are many ways to his capture by the regulated industry. If UK law does not remove his discretion, challenges will probably come under international law where applicable, or before the European Court of Justice, making it likely that sooner or later, if steps are not taken, regulators in the new British system will find their discretion constrained to a greater extent than is desirable for an effective and impartial regulator.

Notes

1 Kahn (1988a), p. 11/II; also Bernstein (1955).
2 I have been much helped by Jowell (1989), pp. 3–23; and by Lewis (1989), pp. 219–45; as well as by Prosser's writings, referred to elsewhere. I am also grateful for Professor Jowell's willingness to help my lack of expertise here with his advice, though he is, of course, not responsible for my arguments or conclusions. There is an excellent discussion of the development of administrative law in Britain in Craig (1989), of which chapters 7 and 8 are particularly relevant to the development of notions of natural justice and of fair-ness and chapter 10 to the scope of discretion.
3 Dicey (1959), p. 788 (1st edn. 1885), cited by Jowell (1989), p. 5, who traces the historical and current influence of Dicey's views.

4   There was also a strong party in the USA in 1887 in favour of leaving state regulation to be enforced by the courts which failed in this attempt only a few weeks before the passing of the Interstate Commerce Act: Cushman (1941), p. 45

5   Breyer and Stewart (1985), p. 26; Cushman (1941), pp. 38–9; Hilton (1982), pp. 45–7. M. Keller has said that the political pressures were similar to those behind 1894 Act in the US: Keller (1981), pp. 66, 67.

6   Hadley (1890), pp. 100–3; Kahn (1988a), p. 46/I; McCraw (1984) pp. 13, 14. In *A Chapter of Erie* it was noted that many of the investors that lost were British, so distancing themselves further from sympathy. Adams noted that Gladstone's 1844 Act contributed to the 1845 railway mania in Britain: McCraw (1984), pp. 12, 13

7   Quoted in Pierce, Allison and Martin (1980), p. 872. On the relevance of the Granger movement, see Horwitz (1989), p. 58

8   Kahn (1988a), p. 55/I; Nelson (1959), pp. 193–230.

9   Cushman (1941), p. 44.

10 Ibid., pp. 34–6, 50. For the influence of the 1844 Act, see Breyer (1982), pp. 6, 199.

11 Keller (1981), p. 66.

12 Cushman (1941), pp. 34, 36, 50; also Eisner (1991), pp. 48–64.

13 Breyer and Stewart (1985), pp. 26–9. The Supreme Court established discrimination as a common law offence by referring to a seventeenth-century opinion given by Lord Chief Justice Hale. The same development did not happen in Britain. See Horwitz (1989), pp. 59–60. See also chapter 9 below.

14 Cushman (1941), p. 65; Hilton (1982), p. 46.

15 Cushman (1941), p. 70.

16 Cf. Bonbright (1961), p. 381. Kahn (1988a), pp. 142–150/I, discusses the cases for and against the prohibition of discrimination on this ground and defends discrimination more generally as sometimes the best way of ensuring the financial viability of monopoly.

17 Nelson (1950); also Breyer and Stewart (1985), p. 136, for a citation of Professor Jaffe on this.

18 Breyer and Stewart (1985), p. 27.

19 Ibid., p. 29.

20 Ibid., pp. 551–4.

21 Keller (1981), pp. 74–85.

22 Pierce, Allison and Martin (1980), pp. 98–111.

23 Ibid., pp. 111–19.

24 McCraw (1984), pp. 210–12.

25 Kahn (1988a) pp. 3–11/I.

26 Pierce, Allison and Martin (1980), pp. 119–27.

27 Ibid. p. 119.

28 These terms of reference often explicitly required the regulator to serve social as well as economic ends: Breyer and Stewart (1985), pp. 31, 32. On the social tendencies of New Deal regulation, see Horwitz (1989), p. 7.

29 Breyer (1982), p. 2.

30 Breyer and Stewart (1985), pp. 26–32.

31 McCraw (1984), pp. 172–6.

32 Breyer and Stewart (1985), pp. 33–5; Breyer (1982), pp. 6, 7; McCraw (1984), pp. 283–4.

33 Breyer (1982), appendix 2.

34 Breyer and Stewart (1985), pp. 35–40: McCraw (1984), p. 283.

35 For the view that case by case decisions will generally favour the regulated, while regulatory rule-making will not, see Noll (1989), p. 1,280. However, by 1990 BT was asking for rules rather than a series of decisions from Oftel, to help it for planning purposes: BT

(1990b), p. 10. Jowel (1986), p. 289, cites H. A. Simon's discussion in his *Administrative Behaviour* of rule-making within an organization which helps control through the specification of factual and value premises for subordinates. Perhaps Noll is more likely to be right where there are numerous regulated firms. It is worth noting also that in Jowell's opinion, (p. 299) adjudication is quite clearly adversarial since it invites cross-examination, demands that one party wins and another loses, and may generally cause antagonism.

36 Breyer and Stewart (1985), pp. 274–89.

37 Breyer (1982), appendix 1.

38 See Hazlett (1985), p. 9; McCraw (1984), p. 37. Alfred Kahn has said that fear of state control, even as a remote possibility, has been a discipline upon natural monopolies in America: Kahn (1988a), pp. 104–6/II.

39 Faulhaber (1987), p. 146, also, more generally, pp. 85–7; Gerwig (1962).

40 ' "In the Matter of Policy and Rules Concerning Rates for Dominant Carriers" *Notice of Proposed Rule Making* Adopted Aug 4, 1987', cited by Hillman and Braeutigam (1989), p. 65.

41 McCraw (1984), pp. 136–7, 244–5. G. J. Stigler has hypothesized that lawyers in the USA are particularly likely to become regulators or legislators, because their professional business is conducive to their receiving financial rewards in those roles through patronage. 'Why are so many politicians lawyers? – because everyone employs lawyers, so the congressman's firm is a suitable avenue of compensation, whereas a physician would have to be given bribes rather than patronage': Stigler in (1971) in Stigler (1975), p. 127. On US regulators' backgrounds see O'Leary and Smith (1989), pp. 225–7. Both the American Bar Association and the regulated industries themselves were strong supporters of the Administrative Procedures Act, 1946: Horwitz (1989), p. 164.

42 Breyer (1982), p. 6.

43 McCraw (1984), pp. 91–4.

44 Quoted in ibid., p. 108.

45 W. Wilson (1913), pp. 13ff.

46 McCraw (1984), pp. 109–12.

47 Keller (1981), p. 63.

48 Chandler (1977).

49 Not that these accountabilities are without problems. The claim that ministers are responsible for the actions of civil servants has long been contentious; and in other respects actual accountability is far more complicated than the formal positions suggest: Day and Klein (1987), pp. 4–29; also Turpin (1989), *passim*. However, there is no one to whom a regulator is even formally accountable except the law – until his reappointment. Baldwin and McCrudden (1987), pp. 35–45, discuss how regulatory agencies may be made accountable, but natural monopoly requires more discretion than is easily consistent with the adoption of any except procedural requirements.

50 For a discussion of their independence, see Breyer and Stewart (1985), pp. 95–126.

51 Foster (1971), pp. 68–76.

52 K. C. Davis (1969), cited by Jowel (1989), p. 10. There is some discussion of other incentives in chapter 11 below.

53 There is a balanced account of the doctrine in Turpin (1989), pp. 53–85. I have myself often heard it invoked by senior civil servants as the 'corner-stone of the constitution' or in a similar phrase.

54 See the references cited in Turpin (1989) and Lewis (1989).

55 Lewis (1989), pp. 221–2.

56 Turpin (1989), pp. 58–60. Quite commonly in 1990 and 1991 the view that ministers must be responsible was expressed in the press. See, for example, *The Financial Times*, 7 February 1991: 'the regulator of such a vital national industry must be 'accountable to

the public and to Parliament.' But this was not what was intended when independent regulators were established.

57 DTI (1990). Under British practice, applying for a licence does not entitle the applicant to a hearing.

58 Lewis (1989), pp. 220–1.

59 Jowell (1989), pp. 8–13, and (1986), pp. 293–6, discusses the function of such rules, pointing out how they may lead to arbitrariness. Rules may be used by regulators as guidance to clarify their incentives. Statutes contain criteria but they are normally not precise enough to act as rules binding the regulator or the regulated. Rules may also be devised, as Carsberg, for example, did for BT, to determine the regulated industry's liability where quality of service falls below a certain standard; or as McKinnon did for British Gas, to define its policy on unpaid bills: but such rules are generally reached by agreement. However, it is worth noting Lewis's observation ((1989), p. 227) that the Independent Broadcasting Authority, whose existence ended in 1990, was empowered to dispose of lucrative franchises without public hearings, without having to give reasons in public for decisions, and without there being an appeal mechanism or any public review or monitoring.

60 Hillman and Braeutigam (1989), p. 84.

61 Norman Lewis and Tony Prosser in Britain have also criticized the informality of the procedures adopted: Lewis (1989), pp. 220, 221, and Prosser (1986), pp. 226–7. Prosser recommends the model of the Civil Aviation Authority (CAA) licensing system. The CAA, which is the economic regulator for airports, is a decendant of one of the last of the old family of such commissions, set up by the Attlee government, and has a wider range of functions than the other regulatory bodies. Its procedures are consequently different. Its hearings, for example, involve trial-like procedures. See Baldwin (1987), pp. 164–76.

62 Schwartz (1949), chs. 3 and 7; (1987), p. 2.

63 Schwartz (1949), pp. 270–6; (1987), pp. 15–17. A reason why the development of judicial review in Britain at this time was slow was that during the Attlee government many matters which had previously gone to the courts, including appeals, were moved to newly created tribunals, which took time before they threw up important concerns for judicial review.

64 Schwartz (1987) pp. 2, 3.

65 *Regina vs. Inland Revenue Commissioners* ex parte *National Federation of Self-Employed and Small Businesses Ltd.*, 1982, quoted in ibid., p. 3.

66 Schwartz (1987), p. 3.

67 Pannick (1988), pp. 23–37.

68 Both quoted in Schwartz (1987), pp. 37, 38.

69 Lord Hodson in *Ridge vs. Baldwin*, quoted in ibid., p. 32; also Craig (1989), pp. 386–7.

70 Lord Diplock in *Bushell vs. Environment Secretary*, 1982, quoted in Schwartz (1987), p. 36.

71 Schwartz (1987), p. 4; Craig (1989), pp. 199–239; Wade (1982), p. 413.

72 On the scope of judicial review, see Pannick (1988). Oftel and Ofgas have both been admonished under judicial review. The Director General of Ofgas had not misdirected himself in law, not exceeded his powers, nor acted irrationally, but had acted unfairly in not offering a complaining customer a chance to comment on the note of its interview with a British Gas employee: Ofgas (1990), pp. 27, 28. An important related case was Mr Justice Otton's reversal of the Secretary of State's decision, following an MMC recommendation, to order South Yorkshire Transport to divest itself of four bus company acquisitions which increased its share of the Sheffield bus market from 73 per cent to 87 per cent, on the ground that the Sheffield bus market was only 4 per cent of the national bus market and so could not be the substantial part of the UK market that the Fair Trading Act, 1973, required for forced divestiture: *The Times*, 23 March 1991, p. 25.

73 The stimulus was given by the Report of the Franks Committee on Administrative Tribunals and Inquiries, 1957. On its consequences, see Craig (1989), pp. 55–6.
74 In chapter 11 it will be argued that the new British system of regulation has not been captured before birth; that the founding legislation gave regulators ample discretion to resist capture.
75 The classic statement is the opinion in *Associated Provincial Picture Houses vs. Wednesbury Corporation*, 1948: see Craig (1989), pp. 221, 222; Jowell (1989), p. 20.
76 For this dictum, see Craig (1989), pp. 213–7.
77 DTI (1990).
78 On the courts' resistance to any rights of legal representation at such hearings, see Craig (1989), p. 220.
79 Kahn and Roach (1979), pp. 101–2.
80 Ibid., p. 103, quoting W. T. Jones (1962).
81 Some important developments in the modern use of *certiorari* to bring regulatory decisions before the courts began with the Electricity Commissioners: Craig (1989), pp. 382–7.
82 The UK tradition of judicial review developed no firm position on *locus standi*: Schwartz (1987), p. 4.
83 Note that this was not always so: in the eighteenth century the judiciary achieved consistency out of great diversity in local rating. See Cannan (1927), pp. 103–11.
84 Kahn (1988a), pp. 45–54/I.
85 320 US 591, pp. 601–3, 1944, cited by Breyer and Stewart (1985), pp. 233, 234.
86 Craig (1989), pp. 213–7.
87 Breyer (1982), pp. 80, 81.
88 See Oliver (1988), pp. 73–91. Not that laws are unambiguous. Often they are deliberately so. As Jowell indicates ((1986), p. 258), they may be not clear initially because the expectation is that their meaning will only become clear in practice.
89 Contrast the extent to which the American courts have become involved in trying to ensure consistency in US regulatory policy and have failed, as described in Breyer (1987), pp. 45–72. He describes the tension between the need to control regulators, to make them accountable for their policy-making, and the reluctance to challenge specialist knowledge. US judicial review has however led to greater attempts to achieve consistency on general, non-specialist matters, while challenging regulatory agencies where they have failed to achieve well-reasoned and well-evidenced opinions on specialist matters.
90 Breyer (1987), pp. 66–7, comes to the conclusion that it would be desirable to develop the District of Columbia Court of Appeal into a special administrative appeal court, but impracticable to do so, because it would need special investigative and other expert staff and the right to get off-the-record information from regulators – a right which in general terms the MMC has. His suggestion is to borrow from France the model of the Conseil d'Etat, except that he believes that its working in private would be unacceptable. The Conseil d'Etat would more easily be an appropriate model for a review forum for a country with a French legal tradition, just as the MMC might be for one with a British legal tradition. See also Brown and Garner (1983), pp. 30–57.
91 Plato (1952), p. 196.
92 Ibid., p. 209.
93 Ibid., p. 203.
94 Ibid., p. 220.

9

The dangers of mixing social with economic regulation

The truth is that public service and private profit go hand in hand. Public service means serving the public and giving them what they want. Marks and Spencer, Sainsbury, the local newsagent – they all give an excellent public service but they are all trying to make a profit.

Rt. Hon. Cecil Parkinson (1987)[1]

More than any other, this chapter could itself have been expanded into a book. Once one leaves the relatively certain area of economic regulation with its five key offences, and the information, institutions and regulatory discretion required to deal with them, the possibilities are infinite. Social regulation is defined to be that regulation which is not economic regulation. The view that regulated firms serve the public best by following their own self-interest is not reflected in regulation. The motives of those who set up and alter regulatory systems are not purely economic. And the relevant laws almost always admit other objectives besides economic ones, often inconsistently. Neither do those who operate regulatory systems have only economic objectives or motives: they have various interests and are under various pressures. Nevertheless, this chapter argues that, while doing so is practically inevitable, straying into social regulation should be kept to the minimum.

Section 1 discusses the justification of some non-economic pricing policies. Because this book is about natural-monopoly regulation, it can concentrate on the prohibition of price discrimination, which is endemic to it. Section 2 considers how the resulting financial burdens may make a natural monopoly unsustainable. Section 3 discusses quality and section 4 the valuation role of consumer committees in representing consumer interests, though it also argues that this may distract attention from economic efficiency. Section 5 uses the environmental problems of the electricity and water industries as the main illustration of circumstances in which economic regulation could be expanded to handle the sixth economic regulatory offence – of a firm's considering only its private interest where there is divergence between public and private interests. Finally, section 6 returns to the relation of the social role of the regulator to his accountability and the dangers of social for economic regulation.

9.1   Non-market pricing policies

In chapter 6 it was argued that to allow price discrimination should lead to higher profitability. Competitive firms discriminate wherever they can; and it is also profitable for monopolies to discriminate, and their opportunities to do so are the greater in the absence of alternative sources of supply for their customers. Moreover, there are many circumstances in which treating discrimination as a regulatory offence will be visibly inefficient. However, in various guises and with varying degrees of consistency, discrimination has been widely condemned. In the United States, though not in Britain, the common law notion – derived from the English seventeenth-century judge Lord Chief Justice Hale – that enjoying a monopoly confers an obligation to use it in the public interest, and that by virtue of its being a monopoly its charges are not prices but taxes, has been developed into the requirement that a monopoly's charges must, like taxes, by equitable, that is, non-discriminatory.[2] And in Britain, through more-pragmatic measures, some prohibitions on discrimination have been imposed on regulated industries under both public and private ownership;[3] and privatization has increased and, in certain respects, clarified these requirements. Universal-service requirements and uniform charges are also anti-discriminatory – though they sometimes involve discrimination, as we shall see – while the privileged treatment of particular consumer groups reflects other notions of what is equitable. Other things being equal, all reduce profits and often reduce economic efficiency.

Universal service

By refusing to supply his good or service to a potential customer, a legal or a natural monopolist can deny him his only means of obtaining that good or service.[4] In the limit, a monopolist of, say, salt – to take an example common up to the eighteenth century – or a railway, by refusing to trade or by setting a price that a potential customer cannot afford, can deny him the means of continuing his livelihood or even his life. It is mistaken to argue, as many economists would do, that this would not happen, just because it would be irrational for a profit-maximizing monopolist to deny himself a profitable sale. The history of toll roads in the eighteenth century showed monopolists revenging themselves on their enemies by excluding them from the toll roads they owned. And in practice there is little to distinguish this from those nineteenth-century railways who extended their monopoly onto the roads by allowing access to their stations and goods yards only to their own or to tied carriers, excluding or discriminating against others – early examples of unequal access. Such behaviour, which need not be irrational and may be profitable, can be discouraged, though not stopped, by imposing universal-service, common-carrier or equal-access obligations – different terms for similar restrictions. Such requirements without further qualification were common in publicly-regulated and publicly-owned industries, and have in general been carried over into privatization.[5]

Prohibition on discrimination

On its own, a requirement to provide universal service may achieve nothing. A monopolist could exclude potential customers he does not want, or cannot be bothered to serve, by setting too high a price or by imposing other conditions which effectively bar them.[6] However, the comparison of a monopoly price with taxation leads to a comparable principle of equity to that expected of a tax: just as the incidence of a tax should be the same on all taxpayers in like circumstances, so monopoly prices should only vary when such 'circumstances' as cost or quality vary. Therefore, a not unexpected additional requirement placed on monopolies is that they must not discriminate in their prices or their terms and conditions; that any differences in, say, electricity prices should only reflect differences in the costs of connecting customers and supplying them thereafter, or differences in the quality of the service produced – for example, in the likelihood that the supply might be interrupted.[7] Thus, as the cost of supplying electricity – or indeed gas, telecommunications or water – to a remote farmhouse or country cottage will be greater than to a suburban home, a higher charge would not be discriminatory. Indeed, British Gas has argued successfully that it would be discriminating if it did not charge the full cost of connection, (though this has raised in the regulator's mind a further possibility, that gas connection costs are high because of British Gas's expensive pipe-laying techniques.[8])

Such a ban on discrimination might seem to imply that different consumers should pay different amounts for, say, telephone calls, depending on when the equipment that serves them or their area was installed: the technology might be newer, and cheaper and better because of technical progress; or it might be the same but with its price having risen or fallen over time. But that is not so. This implication can be avoided through the use of current cost accounts – illustrating again their importance for the regulation of monopoly (chapter 7).[9] They allow consumers to be charged prices based on long-run marginal cost, established by calculating what the cost of supplying them would be if their calls used the latest equipment (modern equivalent assets) optimally configured. And this removes the problems posed by equipment of different ages and technologies. If technical progress is leading to falling costs, then the regulator, when he reviews the RPI$-X$ formula, should form a view not only on what the modern equivalent asset and its optimal configuration are, but also on what is a reasonable time-path to achieving that configuration; what are appropriate depreciation provisions, given the obsolescence of old technology caused by new; and what reasonable rate of return, providing the enterprise is reasonably efficient, should earn the company enough funds to raise the capital it needs. Just as this will draw him into detail, so will the further problem of how to handle mistakes. Suppose that equipment costs more in one area than in another even on a current-cost basis because it was installed less competently or optimally. Should the unfortunate consumers in the one area bear its higher cost? That should not be implied by a prohibition on discrimination. For example, costs may be expected to be higher in early installations of new equipment because of teething difficulties. Such costs are properly spread over the whole investment because the presumption is that the later installations learn from earlier mistakes. But suppose there is no learning and equipment is put in less efficiently in one place and results therefore in higher operating costs there also. Some allowance for risks of this sort will have been made by the regulator when he last fixed a value for X, but particular consumers should not be allowed to suffer because of local inefficiencies for which they are not to blame: in general, the intention of privatization would seem to be that such risks, and therefore the costs of a monopoly's inefficiency, should be borne by its shareholders. For these reasons, discrimination may sensibly be tested in relation to current rather than historic costs.

If a regulator is required to, or does, adopt a policy of no price discrimination, must this imply that all cost differences – other than those just dealt with – should be reflected in price differences (unless offset by differences in quality)? The statutes and licences often fudge this, prohibiting 'undue' discrimination – sometimes called undue preference – rather than all discrimination, and leaving the working definition of 'undue' to regulatory discretion. Thus, the substantive question often still survives. Sometimes cost- or quality-based pricing seems impossible because the charging methods used are not flexible enough to reflect the relevant differences in cost on quality. Electricity, telecommunications and gas meters commonly suffer from being unable to record many price differences; while water charges, normally unmetered, are therefore almost totally insensitive to differences in cost or quality.[10] Yet there is some circularity here: if those industries while nationalized had wanted to develop more-sensitive pricing mechanisms, they could have done so – though there will always be refinements in pricing to reflect cost or quality differences which it will be inefficient to provide because of high equipment or staffing costs. So regulators are drawn into discussions of metering not only because particular customers complain that their meters give false readings, but also because in the absence of competition, it is said, companies derive profit from metering that is too crude or too refined or just biased. Moreover, most of the privatized industries inherited a patchwork of uniform charges and discounts, which are not based on costs and are therefore discriminatory, and these have tended to survive.

Uniform charges

A no-discrimination policy interpreted in a current-cost sense can provide a reasonably robust basis for determining this regulatory, even if social, offence if joint costs do not make it too difficult to allocate the relevant costs. As we saw above, cost-based pricing becomes progressively more difficult where there are complicated overlapping joint costs – or where costs are unanalysed. This last may be because the monopolist has followed, as many natural monopolies have done, Acworth's advice not to try to unravel complicated costs but simply to raise as much revenue as possible, charging what the market will bear, that is, discriminating.[11] To avoid the charge of discrimination, frequent, non-economic attempts have been made to apportion costs using essentially arbitrary procedures to allocate what are really joint costs, so as to try to justify prices which monopolists believe customers will stand. This disguises rather than eliminates discrimination.[12] While more cost analysis than natural monopolies have attempted in the past can often be used to attribute costs rationally, network industries particularly retain extensive joint costs whose apportionment can only be arbitrary.

In such circumstances – whether the cause is jointness or lack of cost analysis – a natural interpretation of the principle that monopoly charges should, like taxes, be equitable is that they should be the same. That is, uniform charges are required not only where costs are the same, but also where they cannot be shown to be different. Moreover, while also sometimes justified in terms of marketing simplicity, uniform charges often have a social or political appeal. Whether or not there are differences in the marginal cost of supply, the political judgement would seem to be that all or most citizens are entitled to gas, electricity, telephony and water at a common rate. This entails cost apportionment, not cost causation; but on a simple basis which can be justified by the principle of equal ignorance. (In some circumstances, complex joint costs affecting goods or services differently may each be apportioned uniformly, but together result in non-uniform prices.) Such uniform apportionments are discriminatory, however, where they suppress known cost differences. For example, local-call charges, domestic maintenance and installation charges and telephone rentals are generally uniform despite apparent cost differences (which had been under-researched, since British Telecom before privatization had been under little external or internal pressure to research them). But this discrimination is given its warrant by the principle of common entitlement referred to above, expressed through the traditional practice of allowing the same access through price no matter the locality. Indeed, one may wonder whether any utility would find customers in the remotest areas if it were not for this sort of protection. Again, the tradition of providing access to all within the Greater London area at local-call rates is almost certainly a discrimination in favour of Londoners, though difficulties of cost causation may make it difficult to prove it. Except for some telecommunications charges, such uniform charges are usually not explicitly allowed for in statute or licence.[13] Their support is the common licence condition that requires that tariffs be published showing the terms and conditions on which they are applicable, which itself encourages simplification.[14] The traditions of an industry may thus inconsistently support uniform charges, which may be discriminatory, while the statute or licence prohibits discrimination.[15]

The problems that can result are shown by the history of the gas contract market since privatization. The boundary between this market with its specially negotiated rates and the ordinary tariff market with its higher uniform charges was written into the Gas Act, 1986, at 25,000 therms per annum.[16] This arbitrary distinction was a problem inasmuch as some large users found it profitable to flare gas rather than let their annual gas consumption fall below 25,000 therms, a state of affairs which conflicted both with common sense and the regulator's duty to promote energy efficiency. A further serious issue was that British Gas had over many years discriminated in its tariffs to large users, in many cases lowering tariffs simply in order to retain customers. The regulator used the prohibition on discrimination to bring this in front of the Monopolies and Mergers Commission, who substantially found against British Gas in 1988, recommending that it should publish schedules at which it was ready to supply interruptible and non-interruptible or 'firm' gas to all who qualified, and not discriminate in its pricing and supply.[17] For example, it should not refuse to supply interruptible gas because of the use that would be made of it. While widely heralded as a victory, suggesting that the regulator had more power than many supposed the Gas Act, 1986, gave him, it was only the start of a long negotiation between Ofgas and the industry.[18]

Thereafter, though less visible politically, there were many echoes of the railway tariff disputes of a century before (chapter 2). British Gas made it clear that it believed that the RPI–X formula gave it the right to raise a tariff for every tariff it lowered, in order to maintain its expected rate of return.[19] When eventually the schedules were published, the losers complained against what was in effect the averaging of many tariff schedules into a smaller number. There were more changes to meet objections; but there remained losers who still complained. The regulator, however, said that he had no statutory basis to intervene on price charges below the ceiling. What neither he nor the Monopolies and Mergers Commission mentioned was that the joint costs were so complicated that, as on the railways, the underlying problem was that it was virtually impossible to identify the costs attributable to each user. Ofgas had begun a cost-apportionment exercise in 1986 which it had still not completed in 1990 – largely, it said, because of the obstructiveness of British Gas, which had refused to provide enough cost information or to clarify differences in the levels of service it provided, which, it held, justified many of the price differences. Moreover, there were theoretical disputes between those who argued that all indirect costs should be apportioned between users on various bases and those who would base attribution on peak use, with British Gas coming somewhere between the two.[20] The truth may well have been that the discounts to contract users could not be justified by differences in the costs of supplying them. But where differences in costs could not be distinguished, taxation-like equity would have required uniform apportionments, and bulk users already complained that their charges were up to 20 per cent higher than those paid by their competitors in Europe.[21]

In so far as high profits and costs were the cause of high charges, prices could have been reduced if the long-run marginal costs had been determined for the contract and ordinary tariff markets (and any other identifiable sub-markets) on a modern equivalent asset, current-cost basis.[22] What was needed was a revision of the Gas Authorisation – British Gas's licence – not only to extend the principle of no discrimination to the contract market, as the Monopolies and Mergers Commission requested, but also to clarify that that implies cost-based or, if that is impossible, uniform apportionments, to be achieved over a stated short period. Thus one might expect uniform charges where differences between the schedules could not be justified by differences in long-run marginal costs; and different charges where they could – for example, where the costs of interruptible supply and those of non-interruptible supply differ, or different costs of transporting gas over different distances affect customers differently. A modern equivalent asset basis revaluation might not result in lower prices immediately but could well do so after the re-negotiation of X, allowing British Gas to provide appropriate depreciation meanwhile. As it was, political and commercial pressures in the past and overvaluation of assets at privatization – as if indeed British Gas had been gold plated – resulted in a tangle of discriminatory practices whose logic was not easily defensible before or after the changes achieved by regulation. Just as with railways in the nineteenth century, the sheer complexity of the joint costs involved in supplying gas made the avoidance of discrimination technically impossible. That gave further strength to the opinion prevalent within British Gas that it should not be forced away from discrimination towards fallacious so-called cost-based tariffs which were economically unsound, for the reasons given in chapter 6.

British Telecom provides another example of the difficulties of price regulation. It inherited a price structure in which trunk-call charges (in different distance bands), local-call charges and domestic and non-domestic exchange-line rentals were uniform. In 1987, BT de-averaged trunk calls on some (B1) routes as low cost, with the blessing of the regulator.[23] And in the same year it proposed to charge for priority maintenance for emergency services on the ground that it would be discriminatory not to do so, because it cost more.[24] (Carsberg persuaded it to halve the increase, because in his opinion the extra costs had been overestimated.) But a more central issue was the proper relationship between BT's charges for local and trunk calls, and between them and exchange-line rentals. Over many years, BT had for political reasons kept its trunk-call charges up and its local-call charges down, so that business callers, who once made almost all long-distance calls, might cross-subsidize residential callers. Thus, trunk calls were much more profitable than local calls according to the cost-apportionment methods used. In 1985 and 1986, BT rebalanced its charges, bringing down its long-distance rates in 1985, and then to a much greater extent in 1986 in anticipation of price competition from Mercury's new services to be introduced in 1987.[25] While conscious of public and consumer protests against this, Carsberg agreed in both years that BT was within its rights, but warned that he might go the Monopolies and Mergers Commission if rebalancing resulted in higher profitability in local calls than in trunk calls – a position that seemed unwarranted given the apparent freedom BT had to rebalance within its basket. As we saw in chapter 6, the 1987 quality crisis persuaded BT not to continue rebalancing; but it believed that its licence, properly interpreted, would allow it to resume when it wished. BT had also expected that long-distance charges would be excluded from the basket.[26] But not only did these stay within the basket; a separate price-cap was proposed for international calls – which had previously been uncapped – because the duopoly in international calls was not creating enough competition.[27] BT objected strongly to this as an infringement of the regulatory regime, and therefore of the terms, under which it had been privatized.[28] The argument that competition would develop most quickly for long-distance calls was the initial (unavailing) argument for excluding them from the basket; but, given that substantial competition was in fact slow to develop, hindsight has shown that their exclusion would have been a mistake. The realization that price-caps are needed wherever BT is a pricemaker explains the very different approach that the Government took in 1990 and to which BT objected. Its logic is that price-caps should remain until the regulator decides in each case that competition has reached the point that BT is a pricetaker. Its fundamental drawback is that it may prevent price changes even where there is an upward cost justification, as with some private-circuit provision.[29]

That the underlying regulatory justification of this approach was the prohibition on discrimination is shown more clearly by the development of regulatory policy on exchange-line rentals.[30] These were meant as a fixed annual charge paying for the customer-specific costs of the network plus a contribution to overheads. But British Telecom could show, on the basis of cost allocations which were defensible at the beginning of the 1980s, that they far from covered these costs. Carsberg accepted this, admitting one opposing argument: that, to some extent, reducing the number of subscribers, as would happen if rentals were raised, would be a cost to all since it would reduce the population any subscriber could access.[31] Yet despite the strength of its case BT was persuaded to accept a voluntary price-cap on rentals of RPI+2 until the Duopoly Review in 1990/1.[32] By 1990, however, the regulatory argument had changed. The old cost allocations which BT had used were no longer accepted.[33] New digital technology had made the old distinction between operating costs (to be raised from call charges) and fixed costs (to be raised from rentals) less supportable.

There were still operating costs attributable to calls (and fixed costs attributable to trunk calls) but they were a much smaller proportion of the total.[34] Moreover, the regulatory view, shared by government and regulator, maintained that, even if the cost apportionments had been valid, the call charges and the rentals taken together could alternatively be regarded as a two-part tariff whose relative size should optimally be determined by the ratio between them that would raise the most revenue subject to any price constraint.[35] On that basis, BT could only have justified a change in the ratio if it could argue that this would increase revenue towards that maximum subject to the RPI–X price constraint. The counter-position, which had come to be plainly stated by 1990, was that apparent freedom to price within an RPI–X constraint had been replaced by an implied requirement that BT prove a cost difference to justify a price change – as it had with B1 trunk routes, emergency maintenance services and some private-circuit price increases – otherwise, the price change would be regarded as discriminatory, irrespective of whether it removed or diminished any discrimination inherent in the status quo ante. Thus BT was put into a strait-jacket. It was arguably a defensible interpretation of a no-discrimination policy given the prevalence of joint costs in some instances and insufficient analysis of costs causally allocable in other instances; but what it allowed was far from the pricing freedom that had been envisaged and which the regulator had once admitted.[36]

The underlying issues are complicated. Arguably, the politics of the problem started with BT's negotiating too favourable an X in its initial RPI–X. With booming demand added in the 1980s, BT's high profitability threatened to embarrass regulator and government. They were saved from having to act by the 1987 quality crisis, which dissuaded BT from price increases to which it had a right. But the regulatory arguments against such rebalancing sat uneasily, legally and morally, with the rationale of the new regime. They may arguably have reflected a higher wisdom: very high BT profitability might have damaged, and might have continued to damage, the regime's credibility, and undermine its chances of survival. As was argued in chapter 6, a no-discrimination policy can be used as a brake upon excess profitability, though an inefficient and crude one. And if BT had not been prevented from discriminating and otherwise de-averaging, its profitability could have been even more embarrassing than it had threatened to be. Yet, properly quantified, a long-run marginal costs basis for raising rentals could have been demonstrated. If BT had done it, would government and regulator have accepted it, or would they have found another reason to avoid political embarrassment?[37]

Oftel had travelled during the same number of years the same distance as railway tariff regulation had travelled after the no-discrimination rule had frozen railway prices at the end of the nineteenth century (chapter 2). Again the principle that charges always have to be proved to be non-discriminatory by demonstrating a related cost difference had to be used to sustain the existing pattern of charges and prevent any de-averaging. Given the political antipathy to price increases, its high profitability, the complicated joint costs and the lack of a long tradition of cost analysis in British Telecom, it was almost inevitable that its pricing freedom should be reduced by the burden of proof being shifted to it, as had happened to the railways a hundred years before. Oftel's general power – common to all the natural-monopoly regulators – to ask for information enabled it to shift that burden of proof.[38] The main differences now are first that modern cost analysis may demonstrate more cost differences, and therefore justify more price differences; and secondly that gas, telecommunications and electricity are profitable industries. If their profitability becomes unsustainable, then there is a way out – which was not adopted on the railways until it was too late – through invoking the principle of competitive necessity.

But before we take up that topic we should not leave this one without noting that, while uniform cost apportionments of joint costs may result in intelligible pricing structures, even if at the loss of some economic efficiency, where joint costs vary in complex ways over time and distance as often happens on the railways, such intelligibility may be elusive. The conflict between non-discrimination, as well as discrimination due to non-economic objectives, and profitability or economic efficiency often makes a consistent, intelligible reconciliation between them impossible. In such circumstances, what is and what is not discriminatory may not be subject to any objective test.

Competitive necessity

In the United States a way out of the dilemma has sometimes been found for competition caused by uniform telephone tariffs through 'option calling plans' by which large users of telephone calls pay an up-front flat charge or annual rental plus a lower calling-charge rate.[39] For those large users this results in a substantial discount. Sometimes a two-part tariff of this kind may be justified by a difference in costs between such large users and other users – and to that extent it is a move away from discrimination. But it is rare for there to be a cost difference that provides a sufficient justification.

However, there is another argument which has been accepted in the United States; an option calling plan is justified if it results in an increase in traffic. This entails showing *ex ante*, and proving *ex post*, that it was aimed not at protecting an existing market through predation but at tapping a new market available only at a lower price. No one is worse off; and the large users and the provider of telephone services are both better off. The difficulty is that, while it is economically efficient, it is still discrimination, if there is no justifying cost difference.[40]

Such discounting is often justified in the United States under a plea of *competitive necessity*.[41] And this illuminates further the nature of the issue. In telecommunications, commonly one starts – as in Britain – with high profit rates resulting from high uniform charges for long-distance calls. A cream-skimming entrant provides some users – usually large business users – with such calls at much lower prices – which are still above the incumbent's marginal cost. If the incumbent retains uniform charges, it either brings them down, losing profit elsewhere, or it stays where it is, losing output. In either case the cross-subsidy structure will sooner or later be eroded. Discounting through option calling plans is a way of slowing down that erosion by bringing down the profit rate earned from one group of traffic after another rather than at once from all. The practical difficulty that arises is how to distinguish price cuts which are predatory. And this generally means that the regulated industry must have a defensible estimate of long-run marginal cost. While non-predatory discounts can be defended as revealing what economic entry prices really are to actual and potential entrants, they imply that those uniform charges that are not as yet assailed by competition must be earning high profits. And from that it follows that the probability is that underlying the regulator's decision concerning such discounts is a political consideration: how quickly to let the profit basis erode which is being used to cross-subsidize uncommercial services. But, however this issue may be resolved, there is a contradiction between the commercial objective of economic efficiency, which would encourage measures like an option calling plan, and a non-commercial objective of no discrimination, which would bar them.

One is here on the threshold of an important principle for economic regulation. A no-discrimination rule is no necessary part of it; it means less efficiency and may drive some firms bankrupt. But it appeals to widespread notions of equity towards monopoly customers. It can only be enforced as such where costs are allocable, and should otherwise lead to uniform charges. Before competition arrives, the insistence on an industry's proving a cost difference to justify a price change is a way of slowing down its use of pricing freedom to increase its profitability; if a monopoly is allowed to change its charges – whether this means more discrimination or more cost-based pricing – it is only likely to do so, if it is rational, to increase its profits. Rate-of-return control easily provides a pragmatic compromise, though an illogical one in terms of economic efficiency: firms may discriminate to improve their returns to the permitted level, above which non-discrimination becomes mandatory. But it is yet another arbitrary, non-economic solution. Logically, the extent to which the monopoly can use pricing freedom should be anticipated in the setting of the value for X in its RPI–X formula; but, besides having unattractive political implications, this also requires difficult predictions – for example, of the growth of competition. The monopoly's grievance will be that this was not understood from the start. However, the situation should be transformed when competition approaches or arrives. It would be a preferable and efficient principle, then, if licences did not ban discrimination where there is effective competition. For by assumption there is no longer an equity case for it, as the customer has a choice.

There is no question but that to allow a profit-seeking firm to discriminate is likely to result in greater economic efficiency. Where joint costs are prevalent and compli-cated, any attempt to ban discrimination is likely to result in nonsense charges: often a spurious uniformity that is itself discriminatory without being efficient. Where an enterprise is finding it difficult to make enough profit to maintain its capital, there is the further reason for allowing discrimination that doing so improves its profitability. As an insufficient level of profitability must directly or indirectly result from com-petition, allowing discrimination in such circumstances can be reasonably justified in terms of competitive necessity. Where an enterprise practising discrimination is making excessive profits, the most efficient solution is for government or regulator – in so far as he has the power – to take every opportunity of increasing competition. If competition cannot be extended sufficiently, the next most efficient solution is to allow discrimination subject to a ceiling on prices or profits set at all levels which allows for the enterprise's practising such discrimination as lies within its power. Unfortunately, granting such pricing freedom is consistent with the enterprise's rais-ing some prices to a high level. Particularly if done quickly, this will stimulate strong protests from those affected which may be translated into effective political protest. Because such protest has existed from almost the earliest times on the railways it has become customary to prohibit undue discrimination or preference, as has happened again in the licences under the new British system of regulation and as is enshrined in EEC competition law. This fundamental conflict between economic efficiency and legal principle has been, and will continue to be, a constant source of friction between regulator and industry.

Protected customer groups

Like other licences, the British Telecom Licence allows the regulator discretion in the weight he gives these different objectives, though it too constrains the weight that can be given to economic efficiency where protection is given to consumer groups. In fact, the BT Licence – and statute – protects more such groups than do the others, partly because it was less sure in its treatment of discrimination, but also because it inherited them from the past. For example, British Telecom has to provide various services to the disabled and blind at no extra cost.[42] Pricing policies that cause cross-subsidization may be distinguished from other provisions which require utilities to provide services or consider various interests without specifying whether they are to be subsidized.

Besides such constraints on economic efficiency, which are explicit in statute or licence, there are others which are simply an implicit inheritance from the past.

The poor

It would not be discriminatory simply to disconnect those who do not pay their bills (though it could be said to be an infringement of the universal-service provisions). Nevertheless, since they were established, the regulators have been at pains to agree uncommercially tolerant procedures to help those who cannot pay. While part of the justification is the harm done to the poor by absence of heat, light or communication, there is also the more abstract deprivation that lies in there being no alternative source of supply.[43] In telecommunications, there are also agreements by BT that those with low bills shall receive a rebate on their rentals,[44] a policy which was meant to help the poor, but in fact also subsidizes other low users, such as those with country cottages and burglar alarms, who cannot easily be distinguished from them.

9.2 Social obligations and the unsustainability of natural monopoly

All the cases discussed so far can result in cross-subsidization that may, if the financial burden becomes heavy enough, result in a non-sustainable monopoly. An entrant gives priority to entering those parts of the monopoly's market where profit margins are high – from which other of its goods, services or groups of customers are being cross-subsidized. If the cross-subsidization is voluntary, then the monopoly may react by lowering its prices, while keeping them above marginal cost so that they are not predatory. If the new firm has entered, it may then be forced out at a loss because its marginal costs are higher than those of the natural monopoly, or alternatively its profits may be much reduced. (If its revenue covers short-run marginal costs, it may stay for a time and then go, creating further instability, a cause of wasteful competition.) If the incumbent cannot so lower its prices, because this is vetoed by the regulator, then the new firm may be tempted in as by a false prospectus, only to be driven out later when the incumbent becomes free to alter its prices. If, either by the terms of statute or licence or because the regulator will not accept the principle of competitive necessity, the incumbent cannot move its prices towards cost then it will find its ability to cross-subsidize eroded. Its ability to sustain high profit margins in some markets to cross-subsidize others will decline; and if the regulations that bind it are not relaxed, then progressively more, and ultimately the whole, of its business may become non-viable. This is the essence of what is called the 'cream-skimming' argument (which in the previous section we looked at briefly in the context of option calling plans in telecommunications).[45] Perhaps the most persistent and damaging example of it in Britain and the United States was the undercutting of the railways' value-based or otherwise inflexible tariffs by road hauliers. It took twenty-five years in Britain and twice as long in the United States for the railways to get the freedom to discriminate in response. In the rail passenger market as well, discrimination has come to be accepted – principally because of the extent of competition from other modes of transport. Both in Britain and in the United States, it is the telecommunications industry that has been saddled with most such price distortions, but they exist in other industries too.

As we have seen, where the regulator is given discretion on how far to restrain firms from moving towards economic efficiency, he is largely free to strike a balance between the objectives of social and economic regulation. He is making policy on those matters – a responsibility which under nationalization was usually seen as belonging to ministers but was actually shared with nationalized industry boards. What are the alternatives open to a regulator? What should he do first if he inherits an industry where some or all of its cross-subsidization is voluntary and historical, rather than required by statute or licence? Economic regulation would require that he allow, or even encourage, such disaggregating and rebalancing of tariffs as would align prices with marginal costs. This would give the correct signals to potential and actual entrants. The main economic argument against this is that many users who have made locational or other business investment decisions based on the old relative prices would have their expectations disappointed.[46] This might well justify gradualness of change, but it cannot be efficient to persist with such cross-subsidization. Rather, the steps by which more-efficient prices will be reached should be indicated, so that further mistaken customer decisions are not taken. (In some cases, short-term congestion may justify only gradual change before new capacity is provided if demand elasticities are high.) What was not made clear before privatization was which of such economically irrational patterns of cross-subsidization the Government wished to continue. And as we have seen they have tended to be preserved. If efficiency through fair competition is the ultimate aim, too much delay because of public and political sensitivity is a dangerous game. In so far as there is no competition it is more supportable, but even then it will distort the emerging pattern of competition.

The regulator is in a different position where the statutes or licences specify pricing or other constraints that imply cross-subsidization. In general, the social obligations laid down in statute are not as precise as those defined in the licences,[47] but none of the relevant statutes or licences makes it clear in what circumstances those social obligations may be abrogated, so that a regulator must be expected to sustain them for as long as possible, setting a lower value for X than otherwise required. A serious regulatory issue will arise when competition advances to the point where uniform charges, or the costs of other social obligations, undermine competitiveness, and where in a normal market a firm would alter its pricing policies so as best to compete – which as we have seen is what one must expect a utility to do where it can.[48] For the promotion of competitiveness is also a regulatory objective set out in the relevant statutes. Moreover, there is the further possibility that these social obligations will clash, because of their cost, with another statutory requirement, that the regulator ensure that the regulated firm can earn an adequate return on its capital (which may be defined sensibly as one sufficient to allow it to maintain and develop its regulated business).[49] If the regulator is brought, by the need to balance these various duties, to seek the relaxation of the social obligations, he must, where they are defined in the licence, get the agreement of the regulated industry, which in the circumstances indicated would presumably be forthcoming; but where they are laid down in statute, first ministerial and then parliamentary approval would be needed.

There is, however, in one case another way of managing these conflicts: the British Telecom Licence does provide an alternative route by which any stated cross-subsidization may be allowed to continue to finance a social obligation without undermining the regulated firm's position. This is through implementing a provision in the licences which allows the levying of access charges upon British Telecom's competitors, who are not required to bear such social burdens directly, the purpose being to share the cost of such burdens that fall on BT, though what social burdens may be so financed is not clearly expressed.[50] The access charge is equivalent to a tax or levy on all firms within a market sector. It will not directly affect competitiveness where it is equitable; but where there are complicated joint costs equity may be hard to define. And there may also be difficulties in determining jointness on the consumers' side: low user and rural telephones may be loss-makers if regarded only as originators of calls, but they also receive calls. However, if this provision were greatly relied on, it could blunt the effect competition would otherwise have in increasing BT's efficiency.[51]

A similar policy underpins the financing of nuclear power and renewable energy resources. Since neither provides cheaper electricity than fossil fuel does, they can only be justified as serving some long-term social objective. The shortfall in their revenue is financed by a levy on all consumers of electricity (except, however, those who generate their own). And this is formally analogous to BT's access charges. There is a crucial difference, however: whereas it is the regulator who negotiates access charges with the relevant licensees, the policy governing the non-fossil-fuel levy is the concern of the government.[52]

The regulator's role in respect of social regulation could be *passive*: taking account of the claims of this inheritance while allowing competition and market forces to prevail. Or, put differently, allowing these social obligations to continue until competition makes them no longer supportable. And, indeed, though it cannot be pinned down, the government intention behind privatization and the new regime of regulation would seem to have been to reduce social obligations and concentrate on commercial objectives – though in those early stages ministers acted as if they thought they could have it both ways. By contrast, since little capital is involved one reason for not privatizing the letter post in many countries has been that allowing any competition could quickly make uniform charges untenable as prices related to cost might be expected to vary greatly. Thus there is a contrast between BT, where it is unclear how far competition can go before the statutory, licence and voluntary constraints on its pricing become unsustainable, and the letter post, where the present structure could well be unsustainable from the beginning.

Costly social policies imply cross-subsidization, which will tend to lead to the unsustainability of the regulated firm as competition develops, unless those social obligations are relaxed or reduced – or unless they are financed in some other way. And here access charges give the regulator freedom to develop an *active* policy of social regulation because they insulate such a policy from competition, though at the likely expense of a reduction in economic efficiency.

9.3 Quality

Considerations of quality need not force a departure from economic regulation. As has earlier been observed, low quality is rarely an issue under rate-of-return regulation: because firms under such a regime have an incentive to expand their capital base, they have an incentive to invest in quality wherever they can. The regulatory problem there is to prevent companies making a noticeably higher investment in quality than consumers would freely pay for. While there is no competition, consumers generally do not have a choice; but when competition is introduced their choices will tend to disclose such over-investment. For example, when after de-regulation there was airline competition, quality fell by various measures:[53] planes were fuller; more seats were crowded into aircraft; in-flight facilities were of lower quality. But prices fell and frequencies generally increased. While some consumers no doubt would have paid more for comfort, the presumption in a competitive market must be that the majority preferred lower fares and less comfort. As Alfred Kahn has said, in such circumstances falling quality is not a criticism.[54] Rather, it is proof that the market is working. Similarly, competition in long-distance telephony in the United States has shown that there is a market for a lower cost, lower-quality service than was given by AT&T as a monopoly.[55] And one can question whether the luxurious space standards of many trains, or the high expenditure to achieve exceptionally high standards of reliability in electricity generation, would be the outcome of a freely competitive market.

By contrast, as we have already noticed the incentive under RPI$-X$ is to reduce quality.[56] Once its value for X has been fixed, an undertaking has an incentive to cut costs by lowering quality so as to increase its profits. But the problem has been increased by two further factors common among nationalized industries. Because their borrowing in Britain was guaranteed by government and controlled by it, nationalized industries persistently got less capital than they wanted – the exceptions being electricity and gas.[57] This meant, first, that most of the nationalized industries to be privatized were over-reliant an old and insufficient capital assets and were particularly liable to a fall in quality from congestion where demand was rising rapidly, especially during the 1970s, when there were policies of keeping nationalized industry prices down, in the 1980s when there were severe constraints on capital expenditure. (As we have seen, the need to invest for demand and quality was a powerful impetus to privatization for some industries.)[58] And it meant, secondly, that most had to rely on what would have otherwise been excessive labour to maintain quality. However, as regards this last point, because trade unions had acquired more influence than in competitive firms and, just as important, because many of these industries were poorly organized, preventing its being well deployed and managed, labour tended in fact to be in excess of what was thus additionally required, but for the same reasons it was often difficult to estimate how far numbers could be reduced without adversely affecting quality. This was particularly apparent in the case of British Telecom, where – as we saw in chapter 6 – such ignorance helped cause a quality crisis in 1987.[59] But though this was the most dramatic example many privatized industries inherited management and labour policies and practices that were obstacles to maintaining and improving quality while also improving productivity, especially where there was rising demand.

Among Carsberg's reactions to the 1987 quality crisis was the acceleration of the conclusion of long-standing discussions with British Telecom – whose hand was forced by adverse publicity – on what quality measures it should provide and publish.[60] Those who drafted its licence had not provided for this, not appreciating the connection between RPI–X and quality levels. Later licences – prompted by the BT quality crisis for the most part – paid more attention to quality.[61] An issue here is how appropriate quality levels should be determined. In principle there should be no difficulty. Under economic regulation the objective should be to produce the quality which would be freely chosen by consumers in a competitive market (subject to provisos about safety and the environment, to be considered later in this chapter).[62] Experience suggests that this means a greater range of choice than public and private monopolies have habitually provided. (The classic lack of choice in telecommunications was revealed in the provision of telephones for many years that were almost all black.) But it also means raising the quality of many existing services. To do this quality must be monitored, which is often more difficult than giving a greater range of choice. Some yardsticks are simple to construct. Others are not, requiring complex measurements and surveys. But even if quality is measurable, how is an acceptable standard to be established? How, for example, should one determine the security-of-supply standard in electricity generation? This has always been defined in terms of ensuring enough generating capacity to avoid more than a certain very small number of disconnections (nine years per century).[63] (Customers may also be disconnected because of failures in transmission.) But it is possible that the implied extra cost of having some plant available which is used only a few times in a century imposes a larger extra cost on the price of electricity than users would be willing to pay for. Here as elsewhere there is a strong case for the regulator's periodically conducting consumer research to help him establish what standards are efficient, in the sense that they, first, are what people want (as against quality as perceived in the eye of the provider, which so often leads to over-engineering) and, secondly, are what they would pay for.[64]

Another worthwhile development is the altering of standards from regulations which are enforced by the regulator upon complaint into contract conditions whose breach carries an automatic liability to a penalty.[65] This gives a far stronger incentive to any regulated firm to improve its procedures than a mere complaints procedure can. Again Carsberg pioneered this in 1987, when he got British Telecom to agree that late installation and repair would be so penalized.[66] But such penalties must be realistic, not an inducement to provoke a liability.

However, where the goods, services, and dimensions of quality are many it will be difficult – even impracticable – to set, and monitor, all the quality standards that are relevant, or prescribe appropriate penalties, so that one may be forced back to a less rational approach. One might simply demand that existing quality standards should not fall, though this would beg the question, for it would leave undetermined how effectively they can be measured and whether they were too high or low in the first place – it is likely that some would be too high and others too low by any market test. That is, one might use the time-honoured practice of defending the status quo until external pressures and adverse publicity become so uncomfortable as to force a change. For example, the Public Service Obligation, the form of control which defines the additional services British Rail is expected to provide for its main subsidy, has more or less been fixed in terms of maintaining past levels of service.[67] Or one might try raising target standards by some percentage each year, though this would be arbitrary in its implications for both benefits and costs. If done without regard to cost, it could become very costly since in general the cost of securing each extra increment in a standard would increase progressively. And such a policy would be bound to result in a combination of quality and price that is higher than most users would want.

Nevertheless, the use of a contract to this end is in simpler cases practicable and is, for example, becoming extensive in local government in contracting out subsidized or otherwise unprofitable services,[68] though even then it may be hard to capture all relevant dimensions of quality, and moreover the contract period had better be short since quality requirements may well alter with time.

A rather different development of a similar notion is that made in the United States under the name of a social contract or compact.[69] The periodic renegotiation of such a contract with a utility becomes a broader discussion of the goods, services and quality levels that will be provided and their prices. Superficially, this may seem similar to the contract implicit in RPI–X, since one cannot rationally set a value for X without predetermining possible adjustments in the quality levels to which any give X value relates.[70] However, there is potentially a difference between selecting desired levels of quality in the light of what a regulator believes customers would freely choose – the approach of economic regulation – and the negotiation of a social contract between a regulator and a utility. Instead of periodically reviewing the return on capital of a utility and of being drawn into detailed discussions of capital investment and other corporate policies in order to determine the scope for adjustments to quality levels, as under the social contract approach, the RPI-X regulator reverses the process. He considers various aspects of quality under the present system and discusses what financial incentives the company would require to reach various levels of improvement. If it fails to meet its side of the resulting bargain, there could be revenue claw-backs and other penalties; if it over-fulfils its targets, it could earn a bonus.

In principle, the approach of the independent regulator to quality under this regime could be consistent with economic regulation, but there is a temptation for him to reflect in it non-economic values. Moreover, the more he does this – unsupported by market research or other objective evidence of what consumers want that they would be ready to pay for – the greater the difficulty he could find himself in of negotiating prices for the quality standards he tries to agree or impose, which could lead him into a relationship with the monopoly that is dangerous to his independence. And this difficulty will be compounded if through the use of access charges he is able to finance this increase in social costs by a levy on many other firms. In succumbing to this temptation he will be drawn into a position of responsibility for the costs of the social obligations he imposes, as well as criticized for the effect on other consumer prices and possibly even on the viability of the regulated firm. Thus quality can be treated in a way that is consistent with economic regulation, but its treatment can be such as may distort it.

9.4 Reflecting the consumer's interest

Where there is competition, the consumer is protected by his ability to leave one supplier for another; where there is not, either he buys from the monopolist or not at all. Therefore it is unsurprising that special laws, regulations and arrangements have grown up to protect the customers of natural monopolies. As we have seen, some such protection is written into statutes and licences; but the consumer's interest cannot be reflected adequately in those ways.

One supplementary protective measure would be to rely on the regulator to be the interpreter of the consumer's interest, to monitor all of a monopoly's activities from that standpoint – for example, approving all price changes as in the consumer's interest, given the other obligations he and the monopoly have. An economist naturally interprets economic efficiency as in the consumer's interest and therefore believes that any moves, including price changes, which increase economic efficiency are in that interest. Indeed, in economic theory it is a formal corollary of an improvement in economic efficiency that consumers in aggregate are better off from it, if one abstracts from passing judgement on the distribution of income.[71] A situation is efficient if no consumer could be made better off without some other being made worse off by the same amount or more. This conception of the consumer's interest justifies the marginal-cost pricing requirements that economically minded regulators attempt to introduce; and while the ethical underpinnings of these have long been debated among economists – one does not have to believe that economic efficiency so defined is the sole economic good – it can be regarded as a convenient expression of a pro-consumer policy. (The universe of consumers implied by it, however, is that of all consumers, not just those served by the natural monopoly in question. But we shall abstract from this complication until section 5. For it is only likely to make a material difference for a weak natural monopoly or where there is a divergence between social and private costs.)

In this role, a consumer-regarding regulator would conduct research and undertake surveys to determine consumer attitudes; and in particular what they would pay for.[72] (Consumer surveys and other market research could help a regulator to an unbiased view. In particular he may form a clearer view of the needs of the less-articulate and less-organized consumers.) Thus he might argue that it would be efficient for the natural monopoly to provide goods or services which it does not provide at present or with different quality or other characteristics. (Such quality requirements might be lower as well as higher.) But is further machinery needed?

It is observed in chapter 11 that regulatory capture by the regulated industry has been persistent and that the most common reason for the (occasional) overthrow of such regulatory capture has been surges of active consumer resentment – which have, however, tended to die down when, or even before, the immediate objective has been secured. A regulator is less likely to want, or be able, to yield his discretion to the firm (or firms) he regulates if he is under a countervailing influence from consumers (and from competitors). Yet the forceful expression of consumer power is rarely spontaneous. And any moderately competent monopoly ought to be able to avoid the building up and expression of the levels of customer outrage that existed during the British Telecom quality crisis in 1987 (provided it is earning enough money to be able to maintain the quality of its operations and has not been starved of capital, as British Telecom had been by government); any monopoly ought to be able to develop machinery to handle day-to-day complaints so as to stop them gaining enough momentum to erupt into a sustained press campaign. But that is not the same as ensuring customers their rights by law and by the terms and conditions of the licence. The regulators' annual reports are full of claims that monopolies often do not treat their customers well.

Nations vary greatly in the scope their political arrangements give to consumer politics. In the United States the more relaxed laws of libel help: but as important are the much looser ties of party allegiance; and the consequential greater independence of individual legislators which makes them a worthwhile target of pressure groups, including those of consumers. While such differences between the United States and Britain help explain the comparatively widespread consumer apathy in Britain, British governments have also nurtured consumer interests less. Ministers have in general seen themselves as in touch with consumer feeling. And their civil servants have seen it as their duty to forecast movements in consumer attitudes before they become disturbing. That the focus of consumer pressure groups has had to be ministers and civil servants rather than legislators has meant that they have had to rely more on argument than agitation unless sure of their ground.[73]

This difference in attitude towards consumers is well reflected in the unremarkable history of nationalized industry consumer consultative committees.[74] Under a variety of names, these bodies, established by the nationalization statutes, were intended to give consumers a voice. Under exceptionally vigorous chairmen, they occasionally made their mark; but usually they were useful safety valves for complaints rather than powerful pressure groups. They were indeed of most interest to the industries they were monitoring, who could normally gain their acquiescence by giving them but modest attention. And they were helped in this by an extraordinary arrangement by which – ostensibly to save public money – the industries supplied their premises and staff. (It is hard to see this as other than a cynical provision to secure their capture.) Having therefore few resources and little information, the committees did not generally command respect; and their inadequacies tended to reinforce ministers and civil servants in their prejudice that they understood consumers better than the committees did. Yet, as we have seen, the interest of the consumer was only one among many that influenced ministers; rarely was it decisive except in some crisis of poor-quality service. Thus the nationalized industry consumer consultative committees were frequently a disappointment.

It is against this background that one must judge the attempt in the privatization statutes to make consumer representation more effective.[75] In every case (except that of gas, where consumer representation at first remained much as it was), the regulator is given the power to choose chairmen and committee members; he is required to appoint some subordinate committee – for example, one for each region and possibly for certain classes of consumers – but he may appoint others to reflect specialist groups of consumers.[76] The combination of the regulator and the consumer committees could be formidable; each can gain from the other. And this ought to make regulatory capture by the industry less likely.

The committees have a role in overseeing the handling of complaints, which are dealt with by their staff.[77] Though they need not deal with individual complaints themselves, they are aware of what is being complained about and of the company's record in dealing with such complaints.[78] The committees are consulted on codes of practice and on whatever matters the regulator has to handle – including price changes – which he believes are of consumer interest. In the case of water, for example, they have been consulted on the various pricing methods that could replace water rates – which as presently levied are a charge or tax for water and sewerage based on property values. If they believe that a regulator is not reflecting the consumer's interest, they have opportunities to make this known to him. And they may sit in public, which would mean that aggrieved consumers could approach them directly. The main difficulties that they would seem to have to meet are how to acquire enough technical knowledge of the industry to be useful without compromising their independence from producer interests; how to persist in representing the consumer's interest despite the apathy that so often marks the individual consumer when there is no crisis affecting him; and how best to deploy influential arguments on a wide range of matters when their information, experience and resources will be more limited than those of the industry.

But whom do these consumer representatives actually represent? However chosen, undoubtedly some committee members will identify with particular groups – the poor, the elderly, the disabled – or regions. They may well see uniform charges, for example, as a privilege to be held on to. They may castigate companies for poor services but with insufficient regard to cost. In short, they may be expected to be a force pushing regulation into social, and away from economic, matters. If the legislative intention was to avoid this and to confine the consumer committees' attention to the grievances of the consumer in a context of economic efficiency, then the statutes could have been plainer.[79]

Recently, Labour Party thinking has suggested altering the system of natural-monopoly regulation that has developed during the 1980s through replacing the Monopolies and Mergers Commission by an overall body more representative of all consumers which would undertake all its functions.[80] Its main justification is to make regulatory capture less likely – or, rather, to ensure that there is capture by consumers. However, the last state is hardly to be preferred to the first. Consumer bodies in practice do not escape political influence. Often, as political pressure groups, understandably they define their role as political. Their concern is not economic efficiency, and they do not see it as part of their concern to give due weight to producer interests or directly to competition. Moreover, they do not perform their functions in the quasi-judicial manner described in the last chapter. Thus, to replace the Monopolies and Mergers Commission by a body representing all consumers would be to replace a body which uses its discretion in a quasi-judicial way to determine whether certain regulatory offences have been committed by a body which one would expect to behave like a pressure group. In so far as the Commission exists to improve economic efficiency – a plausible interpretation of most of its duties – it is acting for consumers in an economic sense. If the Labour Party's intention were merely to make that plainer, then there need not be a difference. Otherwise, the result would be to increase the power of consumer politics over economic regulation. And though the channels of influence would be different the resulting intervention need be no more coherent and conducive to efficiency than was that of ministers in the affairs of nationalized industries.

To place a regulator in a position where representations are made to him by producers and informed consumer representatives but in a context in which the key regulatory offences are economic would be an ideal arrangement in the design of an economic regulatory system. The views of such consumer representatives on prices could help the regulator give an opinion on proposed price changes and on quality. As Joskow and Schmalensee have said, 'regulation provides a natural forum for individual and collective expressions of dissatisfaction.'[81] Where there are economic reasons for an adverse price change, the regulator would hope that the consumer representatives would still be persuaded of the economic case for what the producers propose. And the vital issue of deciding what quality levels consumers would pay for if they had the choice could be canvassed more easily with their help (though individual complaints are bound to command much of their interest). However, against all these factors, which would institutionalize consumer concern so as to prevent regulatory capture, must be set the certainty that consumer representatives will not always be moved by the purely economic interests of consumers and are in practice likely to give some undue weight to minority interests, including the non-consumer interests about to be discussed – making a widening of economic into social regulation more likely. Nevertheless, it is the regulator who decides, helped by the advice of such committees; they are not juries reaching verdicts. In short, consumer committees should be a powerful support for economic regulation, though they can deflect the pursuit of its objectivees.

9.5   Divergences between social and private interests

Thus far, economic regulation has been said to be needed because competition cannot avoid the market failure caused by natural monopoly and asymmetric information. But there are other types and causes of market failure whose correction is part of economic regulation in so far as its purpose is to increase overall economic efficiency.[82] These causes of failure are divergences between private and social costs which result from inadequacies in the price mechanism where prices cannot perform their function of clearing the market efficiently. Among those that are important for the regulation of natural monopolies are those caused by the 'externalities' that result from congestion, environmental pollution and accidents. For example, coal-fired power-stations emit local and atmospheric pollution which actually or potentially causes damage to a widely dispersed population and to the natural environment, the social cost to those affected being greater than the private costs to the producers of making and emitting pollution. By contrast, the water industry in purifying water is correcting the divergences between social and private costs caused by the producers of effluent. The water industry can more accurately be described, not as producing water, since the water is always there, but as purifying water from various pollutants so that it may be used again. While in principle the cost of this pollution can be assessed, its effects are generally diffused and its actual attribution to particular sources often impossible.

It would logically be possible for the correcting of such divergences between private and social costs to be treated entirely as part of economic regulation. The behaviour proscribed could be defined as acting in specified circumstances in a way that fails to take account of the social costs of one's actions which to a material extent fall on others, and the role of an economic regulator could be extended to cover the regulation of this sixth key economic regulatory offence, *externality inefficiency*, without departing from economic regulation. In effect, this would mean extending the regulator's constituency, from consumers, however widely defined, to include those affected adversely by the incorrectly priced environmental, safety or other outputs or inputs which have those consequences. An economically efficient solution, if it could be found, would be one that relied on estimating those costs and charged each source of pollution, for example, for the damage it caused.[83] To make such regulation consistent with economic efficiency, the relevance of what is sometimes called total economic efficiency must be defined. That considers the impact of a firm on the efficiency of all other parties affected by a firm. It allows for the fact that such unpriced environmental consequences need to be corrected by appropriate taxes, charges or regulations if a fully efficient solution is to be implemented.[84] An implication of such a definition is that objectives such as safety and environmental enhancement are to be pursued through economic regulation only to the extent that they increase total economic efficiency, and no further.

Nearly from the beginning, the natural monopolies have been regulated in the interests of safety. More recently, airports, railways, electricity and water have been seen to raise increasingly important environmental issues. Both legislation and licences reflect safety and environmental concerns.[85] The proceeds of the electricity and water flotations were greatly reduced from what was originally expected by the realization that massive investment was needed to improve the environmental quality of these industries. Discussion of these issues could again lead to a book within a book. But there has been ample discussion elsewhere, and here discussion will be confined to a few issues that illuminate the regulatory problems.

Electricity and the environment Electricity pylons have long been objects of environmental concern. Lines have often been forced underground or via alternative routes, at substantial extra cost to the electricity consumer. But the arrangements for these are well understood and have been carried forward on a similar basis after privatization – as have like arrangements for telecommunications and gas.[86] Of increasing importance are the relative effects of different forms of generation on atmospheric pollution. Rationally, regulating this requires not only a clear understanding of the effects on climate and health but also an economic analysis of the costs and benefits of various policies to limit those effects. This should lead to an international political decision – if there is international agreement – or separate national political decisions on what is to be done. All this can only be done by governments or agencies whose scope is far greater than that of a natural-monopoly regulator. However, it could be his role to secure as far as possible that the regulation affects different forms of operation in such a way as to secure the most efficient patterns of generation given these environmental policies.

Water pollution This is more difficult, for with water there are even more forms, sources and recipients of pollution. Aside from transport cost, the main cost of supplying water is the removal of pollutants from it so that it may be reused. If it were not for difficulties in determining the source, and measuring the quantity, of pollution, the most rational way of charging for water would be to base charges on the cost of removing the pollutants introduced by each polluter, from household to chemical plant.[87] Again, an economically efficient solution would involve balancing the cost of purification against the costs imposed by the use of water with various types of pollutants and degrees of pollution; and then rationally assessing the cost of inducing pollution control by polluters as against the cost of the water or sewerage authority removing the pollutants itself. The problem is, however, complicated by the fact that some of those who cause, or are affected by, pollution, do not do so as users of the water as supplied through the system – fishermen, farmers, bathers and yachtsmen, for example, both create and are affected by pollution as they pursue those activities. Nevertheless, economic efficiency is likely to be best served by bringing this within the same system of economic regulation.

Nuclear safety Nuclear safety could have been subject to economic regulation: that is, those responsible could have adopted cost-benefit methods in an attempt to establish as far as possible what an economically efficient solution might be; so that modifications to nuclear power-station designs or to existing stations could have been adopted where the expected benefits would have exceeded the expected costs. Such a calculation could not have been made without assuming a value for a human life (as also holds in some cases for pollution), an issue which itself inspires considerable moral controversy.[88] The choice of such a value must be a political one in a political context. It is, however, generally reasonable to assume that all human lives are equally valuable in all circumstances, unless there is a clear reason for a difference. Politicians normally draw back from asserting that different lives should be given different values, though insurance companies sometimes do not – related, for example, to differences in wealth and income. Sometimes it is maintained that there are some causes of death where a human life should be given a high value because of the greater political or managerial responsibility for those deaths, as when it is argued that rail safety should be to a higher standard, and therefore reflect a higher value for a human life, than road safety. Or where deaths are peculiarly painful or long drawn out. Or where they potentially occur in large enough numbers to constitute a catastrophe, which is a justification to some people for higher values in fixing standards of nuclear safety. (Here though, the calculation of the value for a life implied by dividing, for each measure adopted, the number of lives it is expected will be saved, by the net cost of the measure commonly reveals inconsistencies in treatment – for instance, can any rational argument explain why the value for a life implied by some marginal improvement in nuclear safety may be of the order of tens of millions of pounds while that implied by improvements in road safety may be less than half a million?[89] What matters for regulation, however, is that if, from ministers or from another designated source, a regulator is told what value or range of values to use, he can then determine economically efficient limits to human and environmental damage for the industry he regulates. Moreover, he can – again given that guidance – design a framework which allows nuclear and other forms of operation to be treated consistently in this regard, so that individual operations and those who own them can then compete efficiently.

These illustrations only have to be given for it to be obvious that such integrated economic regulation is not practised in these or in any other cases in Britain. There would seem to be several reasons for this:

1 In many cases, separate specialist regulators were appointed before the economic regulators were.[90] (The railway inspectors go back to the 1840s.)[91] This has not been so in the United States, where the economic regulators have in general preceded the environmental regulators.

2 Frequently, but not always, the concerns of these inspectors range over a much wider span of industry than over a single natural monopoly. This is perhaps the strongest argument for multiple regulation – it would be a stronger argument if there were a determined effort to get consistency in the application of, say, safety or environmental regulations from one industry to another. A disadvantage of multiple regulation is that it may lead to serious economic inefficiency.

3 There is a long tradition of making such inspectors independent of ministers and, though not invariably, of executive agencies, which is understandable given the political pressures the first, and the economic pressures the second, will be under.[92] But that argument should not apply to independence from an economic regulator, who himself requires a similar independence (for reasons that have already been given).

4 Safety, environmental and other non-economic regulators need a different specialist knowledge from that of an economic regulator, knowledge commonly held to be more scientific and technical. Yet an economic regulator who cannot tap and use the relevant technical and scientific knowledge will be at a serious disadvantage (just as much as a manager in a natural monopoly would be). Moreover, the essential actions of someone who sets safety or environmental standards are, consciously or unconsciously, economic, in that setting a standard at one level or another means applying some measure or measures of benefits against costs.[93]

5 There would also seem to be an administrative belief that separate areas of responsibility require separate regulators. Among other reasons for this is the belief that it prevents an undue concentration of power.

While integrating this other regulation into economic regulation should have a positive effect on efficiency, there are two roles for an economic regulator in regard to non-economic regulation worth considering even where this does not happen. There is a passive role in that a regulator needs to consider the effects of changes in the standards other regulators propose on the profitability of the firm or firms he regulates. Indeed, in the water industry an increase in standards set by the EEC must be among the more likely reasons for an untimely need to renegotiate X in order to raise prices to service the additional capital needed. Such a negotiation should not be entirely passive: in the consumer's interest, and bolstered by such help as his consumer's committees give him, the regulator should attempt to secure the minimum increase in capital expenditure, and therefore prices, needed to meet the new standards. He may also consider the equity of such standards as they fall on the regulated firm and any unregulated firms which are its competitors within the orbit of the standard-setting authority. He may be expected to protect and defend the interests of his industry if he believes that the proposed standards or changes in standards are economically inefficient. Such activity could be among the most important of the activities of the economic regulators of electricity and water. Indeed, given the absence of competition in the water industry, the provisions of the water statute and licence can rationally only be explained by this being a main reason for its privatization and independent economic regulation. Necessarily, such activity differs from an economic regulator's other roles: he is not enforcing a licence; and is relying more on publicity and persuasion, because many of the key decisions belong to others.

But there could be a more active role. We shall see how in the United States the strongest motive industries had for deregulation in the 1970s was to reduce the burden of environmental, safety and other social legislation because of the financial burdens it placed on them. The expectation, as we have seen, is that an economic regulator should in general accept such regulations as given.[94] But if they are irrational, inefficient or damaging to competitiveness he may protest. And indeed, such regulations can go too far on the basis of any reasonable cost-benefit analysis, the outstanding example being nuclear generation, where an over-willingness to respond to any suggestion for making nuclear reactors more safe, however small the increase in the probability of saving human life and disproportionate the costs, has priced out for at least a generation the most environmentally safe method of generating electricity. The environmental and safety criteria regulators are statutorily required to use criteria which actively encourage such inefficiency. As the prospectuses of the electricity generators recognized, the possibility of unexpected and inefficient levels of pollution control is among the greater uncertainties overhanging the industry.[95] And in the case of water the position would seem to be even worse since there are several regulators, many other bodies and ministers, who together have ample powers, set out in the Water Act, 1989, and elsewhere, to load costs onto the water undertakings without having to quantify the benefits or attempt to contribute to any economically efficient solution.[96] Thus, if government or any other authoritative body wished to require more environmental, safety or other costs than are economically efficient, there would be a prima facie case for its paying for them. In the end, then, an economic regulator cannot expect to determine the regulations which constrain his industry – that responsibility lies with others and the regulations may easily apply also to firms he does not regulate – but he can, taking into account the interests of both producer and consumer and remaining open to persuasion from environmental lobbies, use his independence and discretion to decide on the most efficient balance.

None of this is an infringement of the overall conclusion of this chapter, which is that for an economic regulator to broaden his scope into social regulation makes it harder for him to be an effective and acceptable economic regulator. If he departs from various aspects of economic efficiency as his aim, sooner or later politicians will modify, or take away, his discretion. This is as true of his treatment of externalities as of any other aspect of his job. He should consider his objectives in relation to any divergence between private and social costs or benefits purely in economic terms as an aspect of economic efficiency, leaving to others the political or social judgements involved (which should be focused as narrowly as possible on such necessarily political or moral matters as underlie the valuation of a human life).

In conclusion, the jagged interfaces and duplication of regulatory agencies affecting the same industry are a matter of concern. Because the motives of the non-economic regulators are so different from those of the economic regulators and because the profitability and competitiveness of the industries concerned mean so little to them, they can place heavy, even crippling burdens on firms, which may have an adverse effect not only on their international competitiveness, where relevant, but also on that of the firms that they supply. Yet there seems to be no strong case for pursuing safety and environmental goals beyond what is efficient as defined within a framework of total economic efficiency. Or, to put it in another way, there are political and social judgements that have to be made – in particular, in safety and much environmental regulation, they centre, as we have seen, on the value to be given to a human life (and various restrictions on the quality of life through disease and disability) – but as these judgements are political and social there is nothing to be said for handing them over to regulators, and especially not to separate ones. There would, then, seem to be a strong case for integrating non-economic regulation with economic regulation, including that bearing on this sixth key economic offence, placing the whole of regulation as it bears on an industry in the hands of a single regulator or regulatory body so that a consistent and economically efficient policy can be developed. Thus, the nuclear inspectorate and the relevant part of the pollution inspectorate would become part of the Office for Electricity Regulation, as would the relevant safety inspectors. The regulatory activities of the National Rivers Authority and the relevant part of the pollution inspectorate would become part of the Office of Water Services. And so on. To argue that this would increase their chances of regulatory capture – such regulators, it has been said, have been captured by their industries in the past – would be wrong. They would become part of, and strengthen, regulators whose effectiveness depends on their retaining their independence. And to argue that they would lose their independence to economic regulation would be to misunderstand the problem. Higher environmental and safety standards are not an absolute good. Following the statutory criteria here can result in standards that may yield such marginal returns in terms of improvements to safety and the environment that their cost, and the level of damage that that inflicts on competitiveness are unacceptably high.

However, even if British regulation were so modified and unified, there would still be standards set in Brussels without apparent regard to cost-benefit analysis. That problem also needs to be addressed. There is, moreover, a higher-level function to be performed: to try and achieve some consistency between standards as applied to different causes of accident, pollution or other externalities. It is arguable that this is similar to other functions performed by review or appeal bodies. But to consider which form of review or appeal body would be appropriate would take us too far from the subject-matter of this book. What seems to have happened, to a limited extent in the case of electricity and rather more in that of water is that ministers have been given overriding duties and powers to set and alter such standards. The drawback is that this possibility of consistency could also provide an opportunity for ministers to intervene more destructively in economic regulation. Neither are ministers, as has already been argued, the best instruments for achieving consistency. But the present confusion of institutions is likely to lead to both high costs and not necessarily appropriate standards. And this incoherence is among the areas of weakness in the new British system.

9.6   The social regulator and political accountability

In an early statement of intention, Sir Bryan Carsberg stated his position on social regulation in terms which are consistent with the arguments of this chapter:

> I do not think it would be appropriate for me to seek to impose a balance of prices in a way that is motivated primarily by a desire to achieve some particular redistribution of income . . . nor do I think my powers would permit me to do this. I must limit my studies to economic factors and to such matters as the adequate provision of adequate services in rural areas and for elderly and disabled people – matters explicitly referred to in my duties under the 1984 Act. I do not believe . . . that I could properly put forward a proposal for a rule that all people on low incomes should be given telephones free of rental: such a proposal would involve arbitrary judgements about matters of income redistribution and my making it would involve the usurping of the proper role of government . . . [97]

While regulation could be purely economic in intention and practice, it is not. While an economic regulator could see his social and political role as passive, enforcing what he is required to do and managing the erosion of social obligations so far as he can while competition undermines the cross-subsidization that finances them, he could instead adopt a more active role as a social and political policy-maker.

Why is this objectionable? Generally in Britain the independence from the political process of the regulator has been stressed. He has the power in general to give what weight he chooses to any interest mentioned in the relevant statute or licence; to preserve and protect any aspects of the status quo should he decide to do so, unless expressly stopped from doing so, preserving any non-economic quality, pricing or other policy inherited from before privatization; and to interpret widely his duties, which are set out in abstract terms which generally include some notions related to fairness, the environment and other non-economic matters. The breadth of the discretion has two implications. The first is that so broad is it that he can always find reasons for his decisions. As Stephen Breyer has said, 'The effect of having many standards . . . is virtually the same as having none at all', giving freedom to the regulator.[98] The second is that it means that he can find reasons among his duties for engaging in a wide range of political or social policy-making on his own initiative.

Thus, he has the opportunity of drawing into the negotiation some non-economic concessions whenever he negotiates a new value for X or deals with an economic offence. As so often, what is important here is the question of degree. There are signs that regulators have fought not just to preserve the existing rights of the disabled or those who cannot pay their bills but to extend them.[99] This can come cheap but may not. One can try to draw a line between imposing new social obligations, or extensions of existing ones, at small cost (or indeed as with the introduction of liability to damages where there could be a reduction in cost) and imposing or extending social obligations at a substantial cost – while remembering that the accumulation of small burdens can lead to a substantial burden. But the regulator has the power to overstep that line, and if he does so the result may be that his discretion will be constrained or removed.

Before returning to the reasons that may lie in questions of legitimacy and accountability, we shall look at the operational reasons why a regulator's discretion may sooner or later be jeopardized by unwise extensions of social regulation. Besides the possible unsustainability of the resulting cross-subsidization, leading to regulatory failure, a second reason is that, in comparison with economic offences, it is more difficult to provide and monitor the data relevant to social offences, especially on the routine basis recommended in chapter 7. In principle, a regulator has the power to call for any information he regards as relevant, but the provision of the more qualitative data that tend to be relevant to social offences may be harder to insist on than that for economic ones. At best, he is likely to find himself intruding deeply into company affairs if he is to obtain genuine satisfaction on these matters. Moreover, the regulated firms will claim, as they did of the similar ministerial interventions in the affairs of nationalized industries, that over and above the financial cost of producing such data, there is excessive effort required from, and disruption of, management. A third operational reason is that the six key economic regulatory offences that have been described are complementary in so far as a firm may be convicted of any of them with consistency – they are separate but non-conflicting offences. But, as we have seen, one of the simplest non-economic regulatory offences – the prohibition of discrimination – usually conflicts with economic efficiency. And non-economic objectives often conflict both with each other and with economic objectives. For instance, treating one social group differently – say, rural dwellers or the disabled – may conflict with a policy of uniform charges, which may itself conflict with economic efficiency. Thus, the more a regulator considers social objectives while entering into a social contract, renegotiating X or interpreting a licence, the more he has to use his discretion in deciding what weight to give to each objective; and the more it is appreciated that he intends to behave like this, the greater the pressure he will be under from various interests to adopt their values, and what pleases one, will displease another. The difficulty is knowing how this may develop. To some extent, the stress given to the disabled in the privatization statutes reflects the effectiveness of a particular lobby over a period of time, while the inclusion of environmental duties in the later statutes reflects pressures which were not as strong earlier. Thus, in the future other interests may well press their claims. So the social offences could multiply – bringing about greater incoherence and preventing regulators achieving the consistency which ought as far as possible to be the hallmark of regulation and which the regulated need for the efficient planning of their industries.[100] And such incoherence could become as inimical to efficiency as it was for the nationalized industries; and for similar reasons (chapter 3).

There is a fundamental difference between a ministerial social contract such as has been adopted since 1976 for British Rail and a regulatory social contract. This difference has a contingent and a necessary aspect. The contingent one is that, whereas the minister in the British Rail example supplies cash to buy the social services which he requires the railways to provide in addition to what it is profitable for them to provide, a regulatory social contract does not rest on a cash subsidy, any social requirements being financed by the pattern of cross-subsidization the regulator imposes on, or agrees with, the regulated industry, which, as has already been argued, must distort production efficiency and competition. It is a contingent difference because a minister could force cross-subsidization rather than use cash – as has happened – and a regulator could raise 'taxes' or be voted cash to use to subsidize his contract.[101]

In principle, a ministerial contract is one which could be with either a privatized or a public body. But it is often argued that ministers could get these services as well, or even better, provided by private as by public enterprise.[102] (Much local government privatization is of this kind; but, except for some bus services, it is not subject to economic regulation as described in this book.) The analysis of this problem is the same as for any franchise. It depends on how easy it is to define the price, cost and quality characteristics of the services to be provided, as well as on the likelihood that government will wish to alter the specifications after the contract has been made. Whether independent economic regulation is then practical is likely to depend in practice on how dominant is the revenue from the contract. Even in the private sector, there is a marked difference between the independence of a firm with many customers and that of a tied supplier. But in the public sector there is the additional problem that ministers are accountable for public monies spent in this as in other ways. Thus, where the viability of an enterprise depends on government subsidy to the extent that nuclear generation, some parts of the railways and London Transport are, it is doubtful whether privatization could make much difference to the extent of likely political intervention.

The necessary aspect to the difference between these two types of social contract derives from the different political and legal positions of the officials involved. Whether he is a social or an economic regulator, a regulator under the British system is largely formally unaccountable (other than to the law), whereas a minister and his civil servants are accountable to Parliament and the electorate. This marks a crucial division of responsibility. The formal case for limiting regulators to a few offences which can be reasonably well described – as has been attempted in this book – even if they cannot be defined precisely, is that a certain consistency in each regulator's policy towards economic regulation can then be developed, but it also justifies the discretion, or lack of accountability, that that development requires. Therefore, the multiplication of offences through a social contract, in some cases negotiated rather than based in statute or licence, vaguely defined and not easily monitored, not only makes such consistency impossible, but also shifts the regulator into an arena where political accountability is expected – which in a democracy means direct or indirect accountability to an electorate.

In a sense the problem does not arise where regulators are themselves elected, as often happens with state regulators in the United States.[103] Then they are to be expected to be responsive to the wishes of those who elect them as far as the law allows, and may be expected to behave in a similar way to elected officials in any other branch of local government. In other words, the outcome will not be economic regulation. Indeed, this arrangement is no more likely to be conducive to that, or coherent (except where it is disciplined by the courts), than were relations between ministers, civil servants and nationalized industries. Where regulators are not elected, the same development can occur but will not have the same sanction.

US regulatory statutes, from earliest times to the 1970s, have been characterized by the vague remits and wide discretion they have given, characteristics which have often encouraged political lobbying; but it is only in recent years that there has been a swing in regulatory appointments from lawyers to politicians.[104] Yet such a development is not in itself surprising. An aspiring politician may hope in the United States to increase his chances of election or promotion in federal, state or local government by the favourable publicity he gets as a regulator. He may make a contract which is favourable to business or residential users, the poor, the disabled or a particular community, possibly giving less weight to other groups. And in doing this, he may define his political platform for the future. Yet, even if it could be assumed that he defines his interest solely as helping himself or the party to which he belongs, or wants to belong, to gain a majority vote, that the voters are well informed and that the utility in question is at the centre of their interests, one may be concerned about the outcome; for what matters to the majority may be the preservation of uniform charges or other policies which discriminate against businesses or various minorities.[105] As always in a democracy, minorities and unfranchised organizations may lose out. But since in fact utilities are unlikely to be of dominant interest in an election, what a regulator has to offer to help win it may be something to please a particular minority. Moreover, where an election or the political aspirations of a regulator are focused on one part of a utility's area, weight may be given to the interests of that locality against those of the rest. In general, what in the heat of an election are perceived to be the interests of the electors may be very different from what rational inquiry would suggest that they are and – a distinct point – different from the objectives of economic regulation.

However, one should not assume that the political aspirations of a regulator – in any country – coincide with vote maximization. He may have Virginian or Chicagoan ambitions (to be described in chapter 11). He may be anxious to use his regulatory power, not to win a particular election, but to secure his own advancement within a party. And this may mean conferring favours on particular interests other than those he might have favoured were he primarily in pursuit of a majority, including possibly those of the regulated industry. Or he may directly or indirectly be interested – in countries where this is possible – in increasing his own income through a political career. It may seem as if a periodic review of X or of a rate of return is a clumsy and inconvenient method of furthering his own interests; but to strengthen his hand he may negotiate a contract which has various trigger points at which particular issues are reconsidered by him, increasing his opportunities for self-interested intervention. Moreover, complaints and minor offences also give any regulator recurrent opportunities to intervene in his own, or another's, political interest. In the limit, even an appointed regulator might be as able to serve short-term party and personal political objectives, at the expense of economic efficiency and the customer, as any minister who was responsible for a nationalized industry.

Of course, such a development would be extreme. One does not have to postulate that an appointed or even elected regulator lets political opportunism dominate his regulatory behaviour. However, the more it is accepted that political and social considerations are relevant to regulators, the more people with an interest in a political career will offer themselves for regulatory posts.[106] Even if that were not so, to reach conclusions on regulatory matters regulators need to either follow their own political ideals or mirror those of others. And these may not conduce to effective or consistent regulation. Among the various role-models they could adopt are those of the minister, the party politician or party official, and the civil servant serving a minister: in each case, the priorities of the role-model are likely to vary often quite rapidly, making it difficult to achieve consistency. Again, at present most of a regulator's staff in Britain are on secondment from government departments: while this lasts, their influence on the regulator will reflect both their own experience as advisers to ministers and current ministerial aspirations, especially if they expect to return to a government department.[107]

Whatever the causes, politicization in the United States has not made for more effective regulation. Rather regulation spreads to deal with new issues because they arise as problems for the regulator. As has been observed: 'For many years state public utility commissioners were virtually ignored by the public, the press and the academic community ... Public utility commissions in the 1980s are beleaguered regulatory bodies that cannot seem to cope with the policy dilemmas confronting them.'[108]

In any country where privatization and the establishment of regulation go together, there is another potential source of politicization of the regulator. That threat may come from ministers attempting to regain some of the influence they had over the industries when nationalized. It will be the stronger where, as in Britain, ministers' powers under the law have contained a large element of discretion. The danger is that ministers and their officials will use, misuse or abuse powers given them for a different purpose. Therefore among the strongest powers that could potentially affect the regulator's independence are central government's own:

(1) There are first the powers that survive in Britain because privatization is not complete. Substantial shareholdings allow a government to resume powers the Thatcher and Major governments have disclaimed, as well as make it easier to build up a majority stake. Smaller shareholdings make getting majority shareholdings more expensive and harder, but not impossible. Government may retain rights to nominate board members, or may retain 'golden shares', which enable them to exercise formal powers to prevent foreign control or takeover, but which may also be used to exert informal pressure.[109]

(2) The tradition of British relations between ministers and public enterprises involved the practice of ministers' relying on their formal powers as little as possible. They remained in reserve as the sanction for the informal pressures that were actually used. Or, what comes to much the same thing, powers to do certain things

were used to exert pressure to get other, unrelated things that ministers actually wanted. In all the privatization statutes, ministers retain many powers which could be used in such a way, besides those which have already been discussed as directly related to economic regulation (chapter 8). As George Jones has shrewdly observed: 'Promises and self-denying ordinances of politicians are not to be relied on. In what they regard as a pressing national emergency, they will turn to whatever instruments they find to hand and use them to promote what at the time they see to be the national interest.'[110]

(3) In the Electricity and Water Acts, 1989, there are also powers with specific social connotations, mainly related to the environment. For example, in the first, the Secretary of State, as well as the regulator, in performing his general duties has duties to promote research into, and the development and use of, new techniques, to promote energy conservation and to protect the environment.[111] And the second of these acts has similar provisions. In all the acts ministers also have important powers in relation to approving or modifying codes – for example, in relation to the environment and recreation under the Water Act, 1989. Moreover, under that act, the Secretary of State has copious powers with respect to quality – and these could conflict with the regulator's exercise of his duties.[112]

Although in general since privatization ministers have as expected refrained from intervention, in at least one case a regulator has been put under pressure to control a particular service that a minister found morally distasteful even though there was no basis for believing either that the minister had the right to attempt to exert such influence, or that it was a natural interpretation of the licence that the regulator was intended to reflect it. In that instance, one is not far from one aspect of Morrisonianism: the expectation that, then the chairman, now the regulator, should consult with a minister on whatever happens to interest that minister.[113] Indeed, the privatization statutes generally provide that the regulator should advise ministers, and not simply on regulatory matters.[114] It would seem that ministers are likely to turn to regulators for policy advice because the old civil service divisions that dealt with the industries have been disbanded. And the fact that their staffs are seconded civil servants makes it more likely that they will come to behave in this regard as if they were civil servants.[115]

A more worrying possibility is that, interpreting a general election or by-election, in George Jones' terms, as a national emergency, ministers will use their influence to persuade regulated industries to behave in ways which are not in the firms' self-interest but which ministers believe will bring them electoral advantage, or which, if in the firms' self-interest, are still inconsistent with the behaviour of a profit-seeking industry pursuing economic efficiency as constrained by the terms of its licence.

A more fundamental threat is that, either through the use of its existing powers or through legislation, a new government will try to reintroduce something like the old relationship between ministers and the nationalized industries. If attempted without legislation, much depends on whether the regulated firms wish to slide back into the old relationship. If they do not, the protection given them by the Companies' Acts against a shareholder considering any interests other than the commercial interests of the company may have to be tested, as may the legislation bearing more directly on privatized and regulated firms. Whatever the results of such testing, there can be no doubt but that a government could increase its powers over them through legislation, and reintroduce the old politicization as a result. The arguments against such a destruction of the new regime are implicit in much of what has been said in this book. Among the main points are:

1 The shortcomings of the old relations between ministers and nationalized industries, which in their essentials are likely to return if relations between ministers and industries again become discretionary, even without nationalization.
2 The certainty that, if there is a return to such a relationship, shareholders and other private capital will only stay in such a firm if they in effect get a guaranteed return. That would imply rate-of-return regulation in a form which deprives the regulated firm of all risk and converts it into a cost plus operation. There would then be no incentive for it to be efficient. That situation would arise if ministers' powers were such as to jeopardize a regulated firm's ability to make profits.
3 Past experience suggests not only that the firms would become inefficient again, but that their customers would lose from higher prices and lower quality because of inefficiency. The attempt to give customers great influence and redress through regulators would also be jeopardized.

In general, if a regulator indicates his willingness to stray outside the field of economic regulation into the arena of politics, this will be reflected in a greater expectation that he will consult with ministers and take their advice. Much depends on the political system; but in Britain a minister will then expect his political and social aspirations to be reflected in those of a regulator as in those of a civil servant. (The same is expected of independent government bodies whose heads are appointed by ministers.) But whether or not a regulator follows a ministerial lead in these areas, he will be criticized by those politically opposed to his decisions. Moreover, if there is a change of minister or government, then the regulator will be expected to change his social and political values accordingly. And this may be hard for him to do quickly, and will again lead to inconsistency. Or he may be unwilling to change. If he has independent political ambitions or allegiance, conflict is bound to occur. In the British system in particular one is up against a way of proceeding which is generally inimical to independence on these matters. Formally and informally powers are often devolved to persons, agencies, boards, committees and other bodies who theoretically gain a large measure of practical independence. That independence lasts while the body – or person – is doing well or is otherwise not an object of political attention. However, as ministers show a persistent interest in what they see as its failure, or wish to change its direction, within whatever legal constraints exist, that body will find itself under very great pressure to respond to the new ministerial initiative – to respond, that is, to what is ultimately justified in terms of the warrant of democratic or parliamentary accountability. The courts are not expected so to respond. Neither are inspectors performing their statutory functions, nor are planning or similar inquiries. Neither is the Monopolies and Mergers Commission. They are allowed to have this independence because it reflects their quasi-judicial status and their relatively narrow focus and clear objectives. Similarly, natural-monopoly regulators are most likely to establish an expectation of independence from government, and maintain it, if they stick to economic regulation in a quasi-judicial mode, and do not use their discretion in a way that leads them into areas of policy-making which sooner or later ministers will see as their own concern and interest.

Eventually, if a regulator is seen to be extending the scope of his regulatory area by making independent political or social judgements, his use of his discretion will be criticized. He will be seen, like the Bashaws of Somerset House, as unelected and not accountable yet occupying what is essentially a political position. Such a use of discretion will make a regulatory system vulnerable to change when there is a change of government – at least in a British-style governmental system, where ministers are not likely to be thwarted by the legislature when bringing in the necessary new legislation (in an American-style system, a regulator may be able to play politics for longer).

What is the alternative? As we have seen, social and political obligations may be written into the original privatization instruments as part of the contractual arrangements implied in a flotation or any other kind of sale. They would be open arrangements into which the boards of the new enterprises enter with their eyes open. It would not be unreasonable for regulators to police their observance, and adapt them to changing conditions, providing that the scale of the burden remained proportionate to the firm's scale of activity. The Victorians may have overdone their hostility to retrospective legislation; but there are great dangers in loading retrospective burdens onto private firms, especially if their profitability or competitiveness is thereby jeopardized. There is a danger here that if the prospectus and licence upon which a firm was floated are not taken seriously, and are altered or disregarded without compensation to an extent which materially changes the viability of the firm, its independence will have been undermined to the point where it will be deserted by risk-taking shareholders and will lose the stimulus that profit gives efficiency. As any well-specified social obligations can be achieved through licence amendments, or a direct contract, provided appropriate financial arrangements are made, such a loss of stimulus to efficiency would seem hard to justify. The logical way of imposing a new social obligation would be through a new contract – just as the Select Committee on Nationalised Industries recommended in 1968.[116] Subsidies, that is, should be explicit. Or to put the proposition another way, if government wishes a regulated firm, or indeed any firm, to shoulder a new social burden, it should pay for it through an appropriate contract. To delegate to the regulator the task of achieving the financing of new or extended social obligations through increasing the burden of cross-subsidization means that either the consumer or the shareholder pays; and that, sooner or later, the regulator will find himself losing his independence to the politician. However, if the social obligations are complicated or the political requirements develop or otherwise change, one may question the appropriateness of privatization – which leads conveniently to the topic of the next chapter.

Notes

1 When Secretary of State for Trade and Industry: quoted by J. Hatch in Ramanadham (1988), p. 60.
2 Charles M. Haar and D. W. Fessler, *The Wrong Side of the Tracks*, Simon and Schuster,

1986, cited by Horwitz (1989), p. 54. Hale's opinion, expressed in his treatise *De Portibus Maris*, was cited in a key US regulatory case, *Munn vs. Illinois*, 1876, which said that, when private property is 'affected with a public interest, it ceases to be juris private only', Property becomes clothed with a public interest when used in a manner to make it of public consequence. It was established that such a right of public control existed where there was a monopoly or virtual monopoly. See Horwitz (1989), pp. 59–62. In 1810, Lord Ellenborough and others on the King's Bench decided that a warehouse which was a monopoly had a duty to provide its services for a 'reasonable hire and reward', developing this from Hale's opinion. As in the United States, this was a key case in the development of the offence of discrimination. See Peirce, Allison and Martin (1980), pp. 95–111.

3   Telecommunications Act, 1984 s. 8(1)d; BT Licence, condn. 22, supported by condns 16, 17; Water Appointment, condn. E; Public Electricity Supply Licence, condns 4.2, 4.3, 8A. There are similar provisions in other electricity licences, but not in the Gas Authorisation. The Gas Act, 1986, s. 9(2), does not refer to the contract market. See also the Collum Report's reference to regarding a monopoly as a taxing authority noted in chapter 8 above. Kahn (1990b), p. 5, has suggested that an aim of universal service is to subsidize those in need. As such, it is an inefficient policy.

4   Horwitz (1989), pp. 16–21.

5   While the universal-service obligation for BT is stated in condn. 1 of the BT Licence, the equivalent provision for gas is in the Gas Act, 1986, s. 9, and for electricity in the Electricity Act, 1989 (s. 3(2)a); see also Public Electricity Supply Licence, condn. 8A; Water Appointment, condn. E. British Telecom has a number of universal-service requirements: to provide services in rural areas (condn. 2), information services (condn. 3), maintenance services (condn. 4), international services (condn. 5) and emergency services without charge (condn. 6). All, however, are hedged around with provisos that service is only to be provided when this is 'reasonable', and backed further by the omnibus provisions of condn. 53, which limits BT to doing what is reasonable and practicable. Sections 37 and 40 to 48 of the Water Act, 1989, go into great detail over rights to universal service. Horwitz (1989), p. 7, says that in the USA the old common law principle of the 'obligation to service' has been an essential feature of infrastructure regulation.

6   The fact that a universal-service requirement is not effective without some control over price is clearly stated in DTI (1990), pp. 28–30.

7   BT Licence, condn. 17. The Public Electricity Supply Licence, condn. 8A, in effect defines non-discrimination as implying uniform charges except where there is a cost difference. Strictly interpreted, non-discrimination would seem to imply no differences in the rates of return on different services except where there is a difference in risk, or where a higher return can be justified as a reward to management for greater efficiency. Statutes tend to refer to 'undue' discrimination or preference, where 'undue' is most easily interpreted as 'non-trivial'. Given the current inflexibility of water charges and the difficulties of cost apportionment in the water industry, one is not surprised to find Ofwat (in Ofwat (1990), annex 1) stressing that discrimination there will only be banned if it is 'extravagant'.

8   On British Gas's arguments that not to reflect in prices the cost of costly connections would be discriminatory, see Ofgas (1989), p. 7. On the effect of British Gas's expensive techniques, see Ofgas (1990), p. 41 (also p. 18). In similar vein, Carsberg was right to say that he would resist phone-box closures, hoping that many would prove to be profitable if well managed. They did. See Oftel (1985a), p. 13. The US Department of Transport bizarrely ordered the Massachusetts Port Authority to withdraw a landing charge based on weight and replace it by one based on the number of operations because, it argued, the first was discriminatory, not realizing that the second was also discriminatory, and

that the first could be justified economically by the growth of congestion: Kahn (1990a), p. 346.

9 HM Treasury (1986b), vol. 2, pp. 41–65, discussed many of the problems mentioned in the text. Neither BT nor British Gas had by its licence to provide current cost accounts. Neither did British Gas have to provide separate accounts for separate businesses. This helps explain why cost apportionment was so difficult. British Gas carried on with its pre-privatization current cost accounts, but it determined the conventions used. BT prepared them and presented them to Carsberg, but did not publish them.

10 BT Licence, condn. 30, specifies the obligation of the licensee to ensure accurate and reliable metering. See also Ofwat (1990), pp. 22–5, and studies cited in its annex 7; and Offer (1992).

11 Acworth (1905), pp. 75–98.

12 'Once you abandon marginal cost, it is not *difficult* to find another measure of cost that will serve that purpose; it is hopeless. This is not a question of looking for a black cat in a room in which all the lights have been turned out. *There is no cat there.*' Kahn (1984), p. 12.

13 Uniform rates throughout are prescribed for maintenance of single-line residential users (BT Licence, condn. 25), extended in 1988 to 1993 (Oftel (1989a), p. 24); and for installation (BT Licence, condn. 26), but only if it entails less than 100 man-hours' work.

14 BT Licence, condn. 16; Water Appointment, condn. D; Public Electricity Supply Licence, condn. 7.

15 BT Licence, condn. 17.3, expressly recognizes that there will be a conflict between no-discrimination and unspecified other licence provisions that entail discrimination, giving the latter priority. One of the oddest provisions in the statutes, given the inflexibility of water pricing, is that there should be no undue discrimination in the charges rural water users pay: Water Act, 1989, s. 7(3)a.

16 Ofgas (1990), pp. 7–9. A prime example of what should not be written into a statute. On the changes in the law needed to alter this, see Ofgas (1989), p. 7; (1992), pp. 3, 4.

17 MMC (1988), p. 103, as requested by Ofgas. The argument was that the publication of a schedule open to all who qualified would discourage British Gas from simply pricing to deter competition in any given case; but there was no protection against any schedule being discriminatory, while careful tailoring to individual circumstances might still make it possible for a schedule to be predatory. Ofgas (1991a), p. 3, noted that the new schedules, coupled with the failure of competition to develop, had caused frustration and complaint among large users that the tariff structure was worse than before privatization. Other recommendations were important for competition: see chapter 5 above. There was much evidence presented to the MMC that British Gas discriminated in its prices so as to undercut competitors: MMC (1988), pp. 38, 45, 51, 55. The MMC accepted much of this and asked that British Gas's Authorisation be changed so as to prohibit discrimination in the contract market (p. 106).

18 This was a consequence of the technicality that it was a fair-trading reference to the MMC, so that its implementation was not for the regulator but for the minister. The regulator could have been allowed to enforce its recommendations; but instead the minister required that the regulator and British Gas try to reach agreement, and this prolonged matters. See Ofgas (1989), pp. 1–4; (1990), pp. 9–12, 19–20, 36–7.

19 British Gas argued, against the MMC's view that it should have a uniform price for interruptible gas, that it would lose £150 million a year in revenue from stopping discrimination: MMC (1988), pp. 88, 89. The MMC argued that its profitability on contracts was higher than would have been expected if there had been competition (p. 98); and rejected outright the view that the conditions of its privatization protected it from the effect of a fair-trading action on its profitability (p. 96). British Gas's

expectation that it was entitled to compensatory tariff increases in these or similar circumstances was persistent even though Ofgas flatly denied it: Ofgas (1992), p. 6.

20 British Gas claimed its cost-apportionment methods were based on cost causation: MMC (1988), pp. 75, 76; also pp. 31, 32. However, the cost apportionments it used for pricing were different from those it used for estimating profitability.

21 The Confederation of British Industry told the MMC that gas prices were 20 per cent higher than in other EEC countries: MMC (1988), p. 49. And this claim was supported by others (pp. 54, 55, 97). The adverse differential had increased since privatization. The MMC broadly agreed this (p. 97).

22 While the MMC did not mention this, it did suggest that prices could be brought down if profits were reduced: MMC (1988), p. 98.

23 Oftel (1988a), p. 19. BT put forward B1 routes for acceptance in 1986 and more in 1989. However, digitalization was beginning to erode the cost justification: Oftel (1988a), p. 19; (1990), p. 23.

24 Oftel (1988a), p. 18; BT Licence, condn. 10.

25 Oftel (1987a), pp. 4, 5; (1988a), p. 10. For similar arguments over the extent of cross-subsidy in AT&T, see Faulhaber (1987), pp. 25, 26. DTI (1990) used similar arguments to discourage more rebalancing.

26 As recommended in Littlechild (1983), pp. 34, 35.

27 Oftel (1989a), pp. 11, 12. Beesley and Laidlaw (1991), p. 12, argued the illogicality of this if the Government thought that competition was imminent. In the 1988 RPI-X review, Oftel secured BT's agreement to include operator-assisted services and connection charges in the basket: Oftel (1989a), p. 11.

28 BT (1990b), pp. 27–8.

29 Oftel (1990), pp. 9, 10.

30 Oftel (1988a), p. 10.

31 Oftel (1987b). The network externality is strong in principle but may not be significant quantitatively. BT presented no estimate of it. See also Oftel (1991), p. 6. Limited US empirical work suggests that it may be weak and may be canceled out by the amount that could be achieved by Ramsey pricing, if that were allowed. See Wenders (1987), pp. 65–7, 183–4.

32 BT (1990b), p. 16.

33 BT has relied on cost apportionment to make its case, as for exchange-line rentals, rather than on marginal costs. Because of digitalization, which increases the ratio of fixed to variable costs, the costs of providing calls over different distances have converged, so a long-run marginal cost case for call-charge rebalancing may be more difficult to make. See, for example, Wenders (1987), pp. 63–92. For BT's view that exchange-line rentals were unprofitable by 'normal measures', see BT (1990b), p. 4.

34 DTI (1990), pp. 66–7. In a simple two-part tariff, rentals are likely to make the main contribution to fixed costs.

35 The maximization of revenue subject to constraints implies Ramsey prices – that is, prices inversely proportional to compensated demand elasticities: Ramsey (1927). Two-part tariffs (there is a useful discussion of them in Kahn (1988a), pp. 95–103/I) can be used either as proxies for Ramsey prices or otherwise discriminatorily or to reflect cost differences where these reflect a pattern of fixed and variable cost elements. Thus the difficulty of deciding whether a two or more part tariff is discriminatory or reflects costs, unless the appropriate cost analysis is done.

36 By 1990, BT had recognized the essence of the conflict: 'BT's Licence contains a condition prohibiting "undue discrimination" in the provision of services to customers. In practice, discrimination in tariffing is endemic in telecommunications because of the high degree of cost averaging involved in pricing and because BT has to subsidise services for many millions of customers': BT (1990b), pp. 16, 22–4. BT has not proved

its assertion that about 19 million customers were receiving services below cost or said what the subsidy to those that were cost. Nor does BT distinguish here between joint costs and lack of cost analysis as reasons for cost averaging. One also wonders why BT did not challenge the drafting of the licence condition more vigorously in 1984, if it believed discrimination was endemic in its services. BT's wish to rebalance generally met a hostile public reaction because domestic consumers would suffer. While more sympathetic than most, *The Financial Times*,[21] January 1991, wondered why BT was protesting so much that rebalancing was necessary when for years it had not used the room for manœuvre to do so that it already had. It also objected that BT's supporting cost information needed to be more transparent.

37 BT quantified the levy it would need to compensate it for keeping exchange-line rentals at what it believed were uneconomic levels and the cost to it of the unprofitable services it had to provide. It claimed that on various bases the cost to it was from £1 billion to £2 billion. See BT (1990b), pp. viii–ix. Network externalities provide an argument for keeping exchange-line rentals lower than they would otherwise be: see Wenders (1987), pp. 78–82. But empirically there is likely to remain a strong case for increasing them.

38 BT Licence, condn. 52.

39 Option calling plans incorporate different proportions of fixed charges and variable rates and should therefore appeal to those with different calling volumes and patterns. They may either reflect differences in costs or discriminate. See Wenders (1987), pp. 123–50.

40 While BT had proposed option calling plans to Carsberg as early as 1986, that is, in advance of Mercury competition, he did not approve them until 1991. Carsberg made it clear that he needed it demonstrated that option calling plans did not entail either cross-subsidization or undue discrimination: Oftel (1987a), pp. 5, 6 BT (1990b), p. 5, says that Oftel rejected its case in 1989, and a modified scheme in 1990. DTI (1991), p. 6, accepted BT's case in principle. (In practice, the results will be more complicated because some calls previously made at a higher price will now be made at a lower; but provided the demand elasticity is greater than unity there will still be a net efficiency gain. In a simple non-uniform pricing model it is generally sufficient that the demand curve is downward sloping. Then the only net losers may be competitors.)

41 The option calling plan approximately corresponds to the theoretical requirements for second and third degree discrimination: Pigou (1920), pp. 275–89. US electricity utilities during the 1980s were allowed pricing discretion to forestall competition: Kahn (1990a), p. 328. J. M. MacDonald has argued that the Staggers Act, 1980, in breaking down the old prohibitions against discrimination and therefore allowing competition, has lessened discrimination: MacDonald (1989), pp. 64–5. Kahn (1979), p. 11, argues that the rush of new air fares after deregulation was not discriminatory. Contrast this situation with that of gas in the UK, where the absence of any provision for uniform charges led to the abundance of discriminatory prices for large users which has already been analysed.

42 Telecommunications Act, 1984, s. 8(2); BT Licence, condn. 31. There is also a duty to provide directory enquiries for the blind and disabled (s. 3(2a)). The deaf are covered by BT Licence conditions 32 and 33. See also Gas Act, 1986, s. 4(3); Gas Authorisation, condn. 12; Public Electricity Supply Licence, condn. 20; Water Act, 1989, s. 7(4). The BT Licence required BT to provide maritime emergency services (condn. 41); but it was not made clear that BT should be paid to defray its costs until DTI (1990), p. 78. Oftel (1992a), p. 4, reports Carsberg's sympathy with the view that the deaf should not pay for the extra cost of their purpose-designed special facilities.

43 Public Electricity Supply Licence, condn. 19; Water Act, 1989, s. 49; Water Appointment, condn. H. Persuading British Gas to adopt gentler policies toward those who cannot meet their gas bills was an important priority for the gas regulators over several years. For the saga of the Ofgas campaign to make British Gas more understanding in its procedures to deal with unpaid bills, see Ofgas (1988), pp. 5–9, 12–13; (1989), pp. 4, 12–14,

39; (1990), p. 21. Ofgas's concern (Ofgas (1989), p. 22) about customers' rights affected also British Gas's ability to get warrants to enter homes to effect disconnections, which was greater than that of the electricity authorities under the Electricity Act, 1989, s. 101.

44 This is neither a statutory nor a licence requirement. Presumably it could be regarded as discriminatory, especially since Ofgas has had to concede that British Gas was right to argue that any such rebate scheme for low gas users would be discriminatory, despite complaints that, for many poor and elderly users, standing charges exceeded gas charges: Ofgas (1989), p. 24.

45 Kahn (1988a), pp. 246–50/II. See, for example, the analysis of road and rail competition in G. Walker (1942). Discrimination is accepted on the railways, except on Network Southeast, which helps prove the point.

46 Parris, Pestiau and Saynor (1987), pp. 162, 163.

47 Contrast the more specific obligations defined in the BT Licence (condn. 36) with the environmental duties set out in the electricity and water statutes (mentioned below in no. 85).

48 Coll (1986), p. 192, pointed out that the US government used as evidence of the Federal Communications Commission's inability to regulate AT&T that AT&T chose its own price structure and that this was based on its own policy of cross-subsidization. There was lengthy testimony to Judge Greene on this. On the extent of cross-subsidization within AT&T, see Faulhaber (1987), pp. 25, 26. Rural buses are another excellent example.

49 Telecommunications Act, 1984, s. 3(1)b; Gas Act, 1986, s. ; Water Act, 1989, s. 7(2)b. Arguably, the weaker wording in Airports Act, 1986, s. 41(5), has a similar effect.

50 BT Licence, condn. 19. There has been a parallel development in US telecommunications where a special fund has been set up to permit cross-subsidies to continue: W. Mullane, letters to the *New York Times*, 1983, 132:30, cited by Keeler (1984), p. 120.

51 Access charges amount to an opportunity for all providers to pass through the costs of the services covered at the expense of all who pay the levy. Even if Oftel, as intended, scrutinized those costs, it would be more difficult for the levy payers to achieve efficiency. Oftel scrutiny was a reason why BT rejected access charges. Carsberg has suggested various access charges at various times: for example, to subsidize what he then saw as uneconomic exchange-line rentals (Oftel (1987a), p. 5); or public call boxes (Oftel (1987c)). BT always declined. Beesley and Laidlaw, (1991), p. 10, argued that access charges are unnecessary because a comparable adjustment can be made to a interconnection agreement. Their view would seem to have been accepted.

52 Electricity Act, 1989, s. 33.

53 Kahn (1988b); Keeler (1984).

54 Kahn (1988b), pp. 24, 28.

55 AT&T has however found it comparatively easy to reduce costs and to persuade regulators to adopt devices which have cut drastically the profitability of its long-line competitors: Faulhaber (1987), pp. 130–2.

56 Carsberg recognized the profit incentive that BT had to reduce quality in his first report: Oftel (1985a), p. 13.

57 Massive investment in the gas grid had to be undertaken when natural gas came in: the engineers were able to secure gold-plated standards in the name of safety. This was shown in the early 1980s when there was a possibility of reviving Northern Ireland's old town-gas industry by importing gas through a pipeline from Britain. This would have been profitable if standards of construction had been adopted which were regarded as safe in many parts of the world; but not under the much higher standards of British Gas. See Ofgas (1988), p. 11; (1990), p. 41.

58   One should register here the recognition that in service industries – particularly transport and telecommunications – higher quality in modern times has often become associated with large investment in computer systems. One thinks of the high level of investment by airlines in computer booking systems, alongside flexible fare structures, so as to maximize seat occupancy; or the more than £1 billion investment by BT to bring together data on its customer base, installations and maintenance (only possible after privatization).

59   Carsberg's history of the quality crisis is in Oftel (1988a), pp. 1–4.

60   The issue began with BT's believing that privatization allowed it to stop publishing the quality-of-service statistics it had published while nationalized: Oftel (1986a), p. 12. Carsberg had been trying and failing to persuade BT to provide quality information before the crisis. For other evidence that the crisis was decisive, see Oftel (1987c). On McKinnon's far longer lasting difficulty in persuading British Gas to produce quality performance indicators, see Ofgas (1989), pp. 8, 9.

61   Contrast the Telecommunications Act, 1984, s. 3(2)a, and the Gas Act, 1986, s. 2(a), which are almost the only references to quality, with the Electricity Act, 1989, s. 39, 40 and 42; with the Public Electricity Supply Licence, condns 9, 10 and 21; and with the more stringent requirements of the Water Appointment, condns G and J.

62   Ofgas expressed itself perplexed 'over determining the level of service a customer may be entitled to expect'. It went on to say that the 'standard seems generally very high' but that 'quality of service is in the eye of the beholder.' The regulator produced the rule of thumb that the aim should be the same level of service everywhere. He complained that British Gas had not done any of the things it had been asked to do to clarify its policy on the quality of service it gave its customers. See Ofgas (1989), pp. 8, 9. Even the well-argued DTI (1990) does not pick up this point, referring instead meaninglessly to the Government's aim being 'the widest possible choice of high quality service at the most competitive price' (p. 25).

63   Public Electricity Supply Licence, condn. 10.

64   Some major surveys were commissioned by Oftel, (1987a), p. 25. See also Ofwat (1991a), p. 10.

65   There was mention of the possibility that British Gas might pay penalties for poor service. Interestingly, this was reported as an attempt by British Gas to head off Ofgas: *The Financial Times*, 25 January 1990.

66   Carsberg suggested such a scheme to give BT an incentive to meet complaints: Oftel (1987a), p. 7. Further such measures were agreed later: Oftel (1990), p. 10.

67   Nash (1988), pp. 90–105.

68   For a brief summary, see R. Fraser (1988), pp. 88, 89.

69   Hillman and Braeutigam (1989), pp 73–4, cite one of the best known of these in Vermont as resulting in inefficient prices. On regulation as a contract between the regulator, acting as agent of consumer groups, and the regulated, see Goldberg (1976).

70   Cf. Baumol (1976).

71   There has been lengthy debate whether in the absence of monopoly the test of mergers implied by the Sherman anti-trust act was the maximization of consumers' surplus, or of consumers' surplus plus producers' surplus. A merger may increase the latter and therefore be efficient but reduce consumers' surplus. See the discussion of this problem in the context of regulation in Martin (1989), pp. 49–51, 274–8. But the position can be different with a well-regulated monopoly in which, through RPI–X of rate-of-return control, profits are kept to the minimum necessary to remunerate capital or are supernormal only when increases in efficiency are above normal. In such circumstances one can reasonably call the economic regulation of a monopoly a policy designed to increase consumers' surplus, and so see it as in the consumer's interest. Lewis (1989), p. 244, sees a strong regulator as one who defends the consumer.

72 For such uses of customer surveys, see Oftel (1987a), p. 6; (1988a), p. 4. See the discussion of this in Oftel (1992a), p. 14. Also Oftel (1987a), p. 25; Ofgas (1989), p. 8.

73 That there is as yet in Britain no well-trodden path from pressure-group activity into politics is another reason for the comparatively low level of consumerist activity there.

74 Prosser (1986), pp. 150–75; Kirkpatrick (1988), pp. 215–27; Graham and Prosser (1988), pp. 73–94; Lewis (1989), pp. 236–7.

75 Prosser (1986), pp. 156–7, concludes that directors general and their consumer committees get better information than did nationalized industry consumer consultative committees, except for those of gas, where the past shortcomings persist. It took some years for Ofgas and the Gas Consumers' Council to develop a satisfactory division of responsibility: Ofgas (1987), pp. 5–6; (1988), pp. 13, 14; (1989), p. 21.

76 Telecommunications Act, 1984, s. 54; also BT Licence, condns 27, 28 and 29; Public Electricity Supply Licence, condns 23 and 24; Water Act, 1989, s. 27. The Airports Act, 1986, makes no such provision but empowers the Civil Aviation Authority to investigate complaints (s. 48).

77 Telecommunications Act, 1984, s. 49. Complaints to Oftel trebled during the 1987 quality crisis: Oftel (1988a), p. 9. But in general they went on rising in spite of improvements in quality, becoming a third more at 32,000 in 1989 than in 1988: Oftel (1990) pp. 10, 11. They rose a further 20 per cent in 1990: Oftel (1991), p. 39. The volume of complaints to Ofgas ran much smaller: Ofgas (1991a), p. 37.

78 Dealing with complaints takes up most of the regulator's own time and that of his staff; but, through the press and in other ways, doing so gives him good public and press visibility, providing goodwill to support him in pushing more obscure issues – though unsatisfactory complaints handling may weaken his influence correspondingly.

79 Horwitz (1989), p. 267, notes that many liberals in the USA thought that deregulation would be efficient and equitable: by which they meant that it would entail universal service and no discrimination. The notion that a monopoly customer needs protection because he has no choice – expressed largely through the universal-service obligation and the prohibition on discrimination – can be regarded as behind many interventions that regulators have made. To take but one example, automatic random dialling devices were not approved for connection to the network presumably because customers could not escape to an alternative supplier who could protect them from this: Oftel (1988a), pp. 5, 6.

80 See the reference to a Consumer Protection Commission in Labour Party (1991), p. 21.

81 Joskow and Schmalensee (1983), p. 5.

82 For example, Bator (1958). A recent discussion of types of market failure is Stiglitz (1988), pp. 184–9. Ofwat (1990), annex 2, stresses the connection between environmental costs and economic efficiency.

83 An alternative, which runs into similar difficulties to those mentioned in the previous section, is that environmental, safety and other such interests should also have a right to be listened to in regulatory hearings. Prosser (1986), pp. 95–7, while agreeing that the BT Licence modification process allows for more interest participation than under nationalization, regrets that it falls short in this respect of the United States Administrative Procedures Act, 1946. Such non-consumer groups are generally heard in the USA.

84 Baumol and Oates (1975), pp. 14–54.

85 Safety: Electricity Act, 1989, s. 3(3)d, e; Public Electricity Supply Licence, condn. 25, for employees. Environment: Electricity Act, 1989, s. 3(3); Water Act, 1989, s. 8, 9. Alfred Kahn observes, correctly, that whether an industry is regulated or not should not affect the handling of externalities: Kahn (1988a), p. 194/I. However, governments often see a natural monopoly as easy prey and load disproportionate obligations on it.

86 Telecommunications Act, 1984, s. 10 and schedule 2; Gas Act, 1986, s. 9(3) and schedules 3 and 4.

87   Baumol and Oates (1975), pp. 134–51.
88   There is an excellent discussion of the different approaches to the valuing of a human life, the objections to it and yet its necessity for a rational safety policy or any other policy which affects the chances of dying in Jones-Lee (1989).
89   Jones-Lee (1989) uses the results of various surveys to devise a plausible range of values based on willingness to pay, but such methods cannot be so used to illustrate possible inconsistencies in approach.
90   The Water Act, 1989, s. 1, 4, set up a separate, environmental regulator, the National Rivers Authority as well as Ofwat. See also Kahn (1988a), p. 194/I.
91   Bonavia (undated).
92   Baumol (1977a) has argued that the case for nationalization is greater where there are environmental externalities. If regulation is on the terms set out in this book, that does not follow.
93   On the inefficiencies of badly conceived environmental tools, see Hahn (1989), pp. 131–89.
94   Ofgas's role in relation to gas safety has developed by arrangement with the Health and Safety Executive, the safety regulator: Ofgas (1987), p. 2.
95   For an analysis of a situation where there is separate regulation of natural monopoly and environmental objectives, see Baron (1985), where the conclusion reached is that the public utility subject to both is the probable gainer in that it will be allowed to charge higher prices.
96   Water Act, 1989, s. 1, 125–35 and 143–50, on the National Rivers Authority. There are also relations with other authorities and the numerous powers of the Secretary of State for the Environment.
97   Oftel (1986a), pp. 10–11. Ofwat (1990), p. 10, also says that water charges should not reflect social objectives such as those which are part of health and social services policy.
98   Breyer (1982), p. 79.
99   Ofgas (1988), p. 10.
100 BT stressed the need for clear rules to allow it to plan in BT (1990–6), p. 10.
101 As has been argued above, access charges would be a kind of tax.
102 Savas (1987), pp. 247–8.
103 Gormley (1983), p. 28, observes that elected regulators typically become political and polemical. Appointed ones tend not to.
104 Gormley (1983), p. 24, says that in the USA, especially at state level, few economic regulatory agencies have their own statute, leaving regulators discretion to increase the scope of their intervention to cover non-economic issues; see also McCraw (1981), pp. 18, 19. Kahn (1988a), p. 28/II, has also written of how the scope of regulation widens to deal with new problems. By contrast, if a regulator is only concerned with economic efficiency, and on renegotiation of a price or profit constraint acts so to achieve a reasonable rate of return, then the only difference between classical rate-of-return regulation. RPI–X and the social compact will be that the first will be 'with a regulatory lag explicitly contemplated'.
105 For example, the strong pressure regulators have been under in many states to disfavour chain stores, which has sometimes been reflected in legislation: Keller (1981), p. 91. Or big business: Horwitz (1989), p. 10. On the extent to which local regulators are more likely to go for complex rate structures than are federal regulators, see Romer and Rosenthal (1987), p. 89.
106 Alessi (1975) argues that commissioners stay put and go for a quiet life while civil servants move and act to maximize promotion chances.
107 G. W. Jones (1987), p. 22, has questioned the independence of the regulatory staff given that so many are seconded civil servants.
108 Gormley (1983), p. 6.

109   Graham and Prosser (1991), pp. 141–50; and more generally on government powers after privatization, ibid., pp. 138–78.
110   G. W. Jones (1987), p. 23, sees the privatized industries as particularly vulnerable to pressure because they are 'recently public' (p. 24).
111   Electricity Act, 1989, s. 3(3), 99(1).
112   Water Act, 1989, s. 10; on the minister's powers with respect to quality, s. 51–5, 60, 62, 65, 67, 104–24. Under s. 38 the Secretary of State can prescribe performance standards in relation to water on a recommendation by the regulators. Moreover, a water licence may contain any direction or condition he may want (s. 14(1)2). And there are further powers, enabling the minister to deal with emergencies, as there are under the Electricity Act, 1989.
113   P. Reed (1985) has argued that in the early days ministers sought to overcome the independence of the Civil Aviation Authority. Besides BT's voluntary agreement to keep exchange-line rental increases to RPI+2, one may note British Gas's agreement to show to government all its plans to import gas as these develop, though the Gas Act, 1980, gave it the right to import as it chose: MMC (1988), p. 14. And British Steel was widely criticized for making steelworks closures in Scotland without consulting government, though there was nothing in its licence to require this.
114   Airports Act, 1986, s. 31–34; Water Act, 1989, s. 26(4). The water industry argued in 1991 that Ofwat sought to influence water companies' balance sheets to deter them from putting up charges so much, because of political pressure: *The Times*, 28 November 1991. While it must be doubtful whether the companies needed to respond to this pressure, regulators are sensibly affected by public reactions to price increases which reflect pre-flotation generosity rather than productivity improvements. See also *The Financial Times*, 4 September 1991, p. 18, and 2 October 1991, p. 22.
115   The history of Chatline and Talkabout illustrates a possible way out of such dilemmas. There was ministerial and public indignation that British Telecom carried services, some of which were said to be obscene and others of which enabled teenagers, among others, to run up huge bills for which the telephone customers, usually parents, then had to pay without any warning having been given of how large these bills were likely to be, or any means of preventing access to such services through their telephones: Oftel (1987a), pp. 7, 8; (1988a), pp. 4, 5; (1989a), pp. 29, 30; (1990), p. 13. This tangle of social and economic problems was put to the Monopolies and Mergers Commission, which in its recommendations concentrated on the economic problems: there should be a licence modification to secure itemized billing as soon as possible; the customer should be told when the charges to his account exceed a predetermined level; and customers should be able to bar premium-service calls as soon as this was technically possible. See MMC (1989). It avoided passing judgement on the issues of obscenity, noting merely that this was an offence under the Telecommunications Act, 1984, and that BT had set up a committee to monitor the content of allegedly obscene services. Although it described the censorship arrangements as satisfactory and did not make any recommendation, the MMC did not say or deny that making a recommendation on this matter was outside its remit as an economic regulator: ibid., pp. 76, 77.
116   SCNI (1968), vol. 1, pp. 150–63; also Foster (1971), pp. 36–40.

Part 3

Conclusions

10

Does ownership matter?

> The alternative to minute external supervision is supervision from within by men who become imbued with the public obligations of their trade in the very process of learning it. It is, in short, professionalism in industry.
>
> R. H. Tawney (1921)[1]

Can public enterprise be regenerated without change of ownership? What can privatization alone provide? Can public enterprise reform sometimes create more efficiency? In this chapter the argument comes round full circle to questions avoided when British privatization was born.

When privatization of public enterprise has progressed in Britain to a point where two-thirds of those employed in it at the end of the 1970s had been privatized or otherwise left the sector, such questions may seem pointless. One reason for asking them is analytical: to help decide what is the peculiar contribution of privatization as distinct from that of other associated reforms. But another is that in many countries the choice remains real.

Section 1 asks what changes in the external framework within which public enterprise operates would be needed to let them achieve the efficiency now expected from privatized bodies, while section 2 considers what changes are needed in their internal behaviour. If such changes can be made, section 3 asks what, if anything, privatization provides as an additional stimulus to efficiency. Section 4 considers arguments for and against privatization in less developed countries, while in section 5 areas are discussed in which privatization is not, at least as yet, necessarily an adequate substitute for reformed public enterprise.

10.1 The external prerequisites of efficient public enterprise

This section addresses the narrow question what changes in the framework of public enterprise control would allow it to be as efficient as is expected of privatization. Because this is the question, one is in fact recapitulating the changes which privatization is expected to achieve, to consider how far they can be made without change of ownership.

The overriding objective

The most revolutionary change needed is in objectives. In chapter 7 it was argued that complex, unclear and participatory objectives were incompatible with realizing the scale and scope economies of large enterprises. Section 5 of this chapter considers the consequences of that for the future of public enterprise. But immediately what would seem to follow is that one must start with the assumption that all but small public enterprises are to be given the clarity and singleness of purpose of private enterprise. Therefore we may assume, as was implied in Mrs Thatcher's general position in commending privatization, that economic efficiency or, where there is a difference, profitability is to be given overriding weight, the relevant statutes being altered so that the powers and duties of public enterprises conform to this.[2] However, as we saw in chapter 6 there is a difficult point here. Where the two criteria lead to different outcomes an economist will prefer economic efficiency, a businessman profitability. The difficulty will be more acute for a privatized, but regulated, firm, whose board, naturally and logically, will have profitability as its objective unless it can be constrained to choose economic efficiency. Yet experience suggests that public enterprises also are resistant to adopting economic efficiency, preferring the language of profitability in so far as they feel either criterion is relevant to their behaviour. Public enterprise reform as described in this chapter will make the choice between the two criteria acute. The difference will matter most where adopting economic efficiency will lead to losses because of increasing scale or scope economics. The economist's compromise of Ramsey pricing is often ruled out for monopolies because of the common legal prohibition of discrimination.

In the pasts, except in the few cases where they were Companies' Act companies or had public-dividend capital, public enterprises could not hand over any surpluses or profits to the Treasury. Rather, they had to plough them back into the business in so far as they did not pass them on to consumers through lower prices or to workers through higher wages. The only alternative was to repay outstanding debt, which was what the more prosperous nationalized industries did in the early 1980s because the Treasury was anxious to reduce public borrowing. This was the consistent logic of the Morrisonian public trust, where surplus profits did not go to the shareholders. (Indeed, it has a far older history, going back to the seventeenth century: for the use of state-given monopolies to raise money for the Crown without going through Parliament was a cause of the English Civil War; a profitable public enterprise continued to be regarded as taxation without representation.[3])

In Britain, the litigation pursued by foreign airlines against the British Airports Authority and the Government in 1980 and 1981 on the ground that they were unlawfully in breach of their statutory obligations in raising prices to meet government-imposed financial targets (referred to in chapter 4) had the effect of alerting the Treasury to possible defects in the old legislation. As a result, at the end of 1984 it put out a consultation paper (which for various reasons did not lead to amending legislation).[4] Its principal recommendations would have altered nationalized industry duties in the required direction. The traditional requirement that nationalized industries at least break even taking one year with another was to be replaced by ministers' having the power to set financial targets, after consultation with the board but without its being the board's absolute duty to meet them. In order that they could be set meaningful and realistic targets, reflecting reasonable improvements in performance, public enterprises were to be given capital structures which reflected a medium-term view of their financial circumstances and prospects, with an appropriate 'debt to public dividend' ratio. Public-dividend capital would then have had the same function as equity in a private company. Thus the nationalized industries might then have been expected to raise their dividends in line with the real value of their assets, like private firms. However, while this would have been preferable to the existing regime in that it would have allowed public enterprises to make profits and achieve the positive financial targets that were the ambition and centrepiece proposal of the 1978 White Paper on nationalized industries, the underlying approach had a serious drawback. Superficially, the negotiation of a financial target may look like a negotiation of X in RPI–X, but it is not comparable if the incentives are missing. If they are, the industry, other things being equal, should rationally prefer a lower to a higher target because it would mean that less effort would be required to reduce costs or increase revenues, while government, representing both shareholders and customers and having to take account of both short- and long-term political imperatives, has divided interests. While a financial target may persuade or cajole a public enterprise into greater efficiency, it is not an inducement to maximize profits.

One reason why the Consultation Paper was not implemented was the realization that converting nationalized industries into Companies' Act companies, but retaining 100 per cent of the shares in public ownership, was a simpler and more familiar approach.[5] Indeed, it was already being adopted, though in a piecemeal way and only as a preparation for privatization. And it had the advantage over the previous arrangement of giving the enterprise the clear duty to maximize profits for its shareholders. (What incentives it needs actually to do so is another matter, to which we shall return.) Different countries will have their own conventions for the setting up of private companies. Nevertheless, it may be assumed as a working principle that the reform of a public enterprise in the interest of greater efficiency may be achieved by giving it the same structure as a private company, but with ownership remaining in the hands of the State.

Competition

Should profitability become the guide, the reformed public enterprise would remain inefficient unless there were already competition or the certainty of a rapid increase in competition extending over all its goods and services.

In most countries there are nationalized industries which do, or could easily, experience competition from other state or private enterprises. A powerful reforming measure would be to remove all barriers to entry, making public enterprises contestable (chapter 5). Monopoly power may be curbed through breaking up state enterprises when the resulting stimulus to efficiency should exceed the loss of economies of scale or scope. Thus the National Bus Company was fragmented, at first creating local monopolies but then, because they were contestable, making it somewhat easier for local competitors to enter and harder for the incumbents to deter them through predation. A policy on mergers will be needed to prevent mergers thereafter, except where they would demonstrably create the efficiencies of natural monopoly. For competition to develop fairly, no enterprise should be allowed to act predatorily. That means banning cross-subsidization and ensuring that any surviving social burdens are equitably borne and financed and that the possibility of deficit financing is eliminated.

In countries where there is no market economy, or where it is restricted to only a few sectors, so that there are many public enterprises which are not monopolies, it will be harder to establish competition, because of the greater difficulty of preventing predation. Even where the optimal size of enterprise is large enough for there to be a few or only one efficient enterprise, reducing tariff barriers and otherwise creating an open economy may create the competition needed.[6] And even if it is decided to do this last gradually, firms in such countries would be wise if they evaluated their opportunities and themselves as if they had to operate in the world economy.[7]

Interconnection

In Britain, the competition through interconnection that privatization partially achieved in telecommunications and more fully in the electricity supply industry, and could have won in gas, could have been achieved without privatization by having competing public (and private) entities use a separately owned network. One can also imagine public (and private) firms competing with the owner of a network on its own network – though there is the disadvantage with this that it makes the monitoring by the regulator of predation by the network owner more difficult (chapter 5).

Yardstick competition

It was argued in chapter 5 that this is not real competition. Yet it is a useful procedure. And such national and international comparison would be as useful in helping improve economic efficiency in the public regulated sector as in the private one.

Economic regulation

Where significant competition is impossible, there must be regulation to stimulate economic efficiency; and where a competitive market does exist or is to be created, fair-trading laws to prevent not only predation but also mergers where these result in unnatural monopolies or market domination unjustified by economies of scale or scope are required. And, again, such regulation is as relevant to reformed public enterprise as it to private enterprise. When a country which has not had a market economy or has protected and distorted it behind tariff walls begins a policy of public enterprise reform, it is important that, whether or not this leads to privatization, an active fair-trading agency should be established. As protection is removed, an agency is needed with the powers and discretion to enable it to create and police competitive markets.

Such economic regulation of reformed public enterprise could be done by government departments. Public enterprise in Britain has been, so to speak, 'regulated' through the political and administrative relationships existing between sponsoring ministries and public enterprises. However, these relationships have been embedded in muddle, confusion and short-term political expediency. The case for a separate economic regulator is analogous to the case for a separation of powers described by Montesquieu, who, somewhat simplifying the truth, saw the separation of the legislative, executive and judicial arms of government as the strength of the British constitution, giving each a desirable independence from the others.[8] And the case for an independent economic regulator (or, rather, regulators, since there are advantages, as has been argued, in the fair-trading regulator's covering all commercial enterprises, public and private) is that such independence is necessary for economic efficiency: not to subordinate economic regulation to the courts is not only to reduce its legalism and cost, but also, above all, to give the regulator the necessary discretion.

Arguably, the State has a five-fold function in relation to reformed public enterprise. Separating these roles should mean that whatever part is responsible for each could act consistently according to its distinct objectives within a clearly defined framework of law. The performer of the first would represent the State as shareholder or owner, whose interest would be that the enterprise should be as profitable as possible. The second would be concerned with public or other unprofitable services, and its aim would be to persuade, or pay, the enterprise to achieve the government's long-term policy objectives, probably on a contractual basis. The third would involve the regulating of safety, environmental and other externalities and would probably be carried out by several agencies dealing with different kinds of externality (though the concentration of many of them under the Health and Safety Executive would represent a move towards their coordination which could result in their behaving more consistently). And the fourth would be the economic regulator. The fifth, that of the political decision-maker, would be the one most likely to give rise to aims that conflict with the main objective of the reformed public enterprise. For ministers also have short-term interests and policies, as members of a government and as politicians, which lead them to intervene with adverse effects on profitability. Some reasons for intervention can be countered by establishing stronger consumer committees as part of the regulatory regime (as has usually resulted from the UK privatization statutes.) But, for macroeconomic and other reasons, ministers will still intervene in the running of a public enterprise if they have the powers to do so. Inevitably, and possibly deliberately, any legal separation of powers as has just been outlined will limit the leverage ministers have to pursue their informal objectives. But that is in any case implied by a decision to give public enterprise the overriding objective of profitability or economic efficiency. Such a legal separation and restriction of powers could be done without privatization.

A further argument for separating what were usually functions of the same minister comes from the qualities and interests that are normally found in competent and effective ministers. It will be a rare minister who takes as much interest in the performance of a public enterprise as does a chairman in a private holding company (and he would be neglecting his more important tasks if he did so). Indeed, among the politicians who are candidates for ministerial office it will be rare to find one with the aptitude or interests to act as the active ministerial chairman of a state holding company. (Some of those who have believed that they had such an aptitude have plunged into not always fortunate business careers after politics.) More common will be a minister with the interest to embark on a new social policy which uses a public enterprise as its paid instrument – for example, a bus, rail or energy policy – though once this has been established subsequent ministers are less likely to be keen to carry on actively monitoring performance under this social policy. Ministers, that is, are rarely managers. But, then, why should they be expected to be? They have other talents and interests. Moreover, effective control consists in taking corrective action: ministers may be able to find advisers, civil service or temporary, who can advise them when corrective action is needed and what form it should take; and contracts with those running public enterprises which spell out the consequences of success or failure in advance will also help. Nevertheless, in all difficult situations strategic judgement and judgement about people will also be needed. And any given minister may or may not be equipped for this. In principle, then, anything that independent regulation can do for private industry it can also for public enterprise. But the relationships between ministers and nationalized industries remain a form of regulation, alternative to that between a regulator and a private or public enterprise.[9]

Ultimately, the efficiency argument for privatization as against the reforming of public enterprise turns upon what follows from substituting private shareholders for a government shareholder. Shareholders in privatized firms may be assumed to put commercial interests first, for that is the essential feature of privatization *per se*. In so far as greater economic efficiency increases profits, they should be a force for greater efficiency, though as has been argued this is not always delivered in practice. The motives of regulation and private shareholder should be distinct. The regulator represents the public interest, however that is defined, against the commercial interest wherever there is a conflict between the two – all this provided that there is not regulatory capture. Yet if the State is to be regulator, shareholder and client, among the other roles that have been mentioned, that implies either incoherence in performance or distinct parts of government performing the various roles; and in both cases there is bound to be a greater possibility that the separation of the interests will be blurred. Moreover, government as shareholder will give more weight to non-economic factors than would a diffused body of private shareholders. Other things being equal, government as 100 per cent shareholder will have an influence which on balance is less likely to support economic efficiency. It is also likely to undermine the independence of the regulator, weaken economic regulation and promote short-term political objectives.

Regulatory offences

The six key economic regulatory offences, and the three social regulatory offences, denominated and defined in the previous chapters of this book are as relevant to a publicly owned body, whether or not a monopoly, as to a privately owned one.

Monitoring

The reforms already described make the pursuit of profit or economic efficiency possible, but not inevitable. Appropriate measurements are needed to check whether performance is improving. An obligation to maximize profits or economic efficiency cannot itself be monitored: to prove that an enterprise would have made more money by following some other course of action is practically impossible for a private or public holding company. Hence both kinds of companies have developed the notion of establishing various financial and other performance targets which as quantitative expressions of objectives can be monitored. And just as a holding company may agree more-detailed targets and objectives with those who run its subsidiaries, so may government agree the same with boards – or attempt to impose them. In recent years, government has indeed given considerable attention to devising financial targets and performance indicators.[10] However, they have not been conspicuously successful and there have been long periods during which particular nationalized industries have had no financial targets or performance indicators set. While part of the problem has been a lack of incentive for public enterprises to settle such targets, another source of fundamental difficulty has been that the sponsoring department has tried to increase or impose targets and to do so without sufficient economic warrant. Thus, it has often seemed important to sponsoring departments to publish, for public-relations reasons, a high target which is not achievable, rather than the highest realistic target; or to use the negotiations over targets to get industries to accept social obligations on other ministerial policies at the expense of a lower target. Such motives are unlikely to sway a private holding company. And for the reasons discussed in chapter 7 what matters for the efficiency of public enterprise is that it sets itself targets which are demanding, and which are then understood and accepted by government. Of course, the more that competition separates the winners from the losers, the less necessary it is to set such targets, though autonomous enterprises will still want to set themselves targets.

Just as governments have tended to impose targets – often based on insufficient information – rather than reach agreement on them, so there has been a parallel tendency to regard the monitoring of nationalized industry efficiency as primarily an arm's length function to be conducted by externally devised criteria. In chapter 7 the problems that arose from this were discussed – the objectives of the reviewing bodies were not substantially the same as those of the bodies they reviewed and the information required to monitor performance was not estimated and audited on a regular, routine basis. Nevertheless, as we have seen there often is a difference between an enterprise aiming at profit and a system of economic regulation aiming at economic efficiency, a difference which needs to be handled with tact and discretion.

Management information

If the objectives of a public enterprise are to be monitored, even if only indirectly, then there must be confidence in the information by which they are to be monitored and indeed set. In competitive private-sector markets, analysts can establish, at relatively low inflation rates, a reasonable view of the prospects of a company from the share price and from the accounting and other information provided by the company, the threat of acquisition deterring firms from undervaluing their assets. Often historic cost accounts systematically overstate the real return on capital, especially when assets are long-lived, but the consensus seems to be that it is not worth producing current cost accounts at low rates of inflation, though boards may find it useful to have some current-cost calculations to reassure them that they are putting enough into reserve to maintain their operating capital, and after takeovers, flotations and substantial fund-raising it is not uncommon for firms to produce modified historical cost accounts in which various asset classes are revalued. The Report of the Byatt Committee gave a number of reasons for its being more important for nationalized industries to produce formal current cost accounts: preeminently, the absence of competition and the need to compete in the market for capital.[11] If there is no independent stock-market check upon the value of an enterprise, its place needs to be taken up by an accounting system which attempts to measure changes in the enterprise's real value. In chapter 7 that conclusion was also argued to be correct for privatized natural monopolies, as long as they are immune from effective competition. For the same reasons, current cost accounts remain the most appropriate source of routine information for all state-owned enterprises whether natural or artificial monopolies, whose overriding objective is economic efficiency. The ideal is a periodic current-cost valuation of the enterprise on the lines proposed in New Zealand. As we saw, what was proposed there is the logical step beyond what was recommended in the Byatt Report, and is also what is correctly suggested by Rappaport to be private-sector best practice.[12] If discounted cash flow techniques are appropriate for forecasting the effects of its investment upon an enterprise, so are they for measuring the consequences of all other significant changes altering its overall net worth. If the current cost accounting is appropriate and well done, and if the forecasts made are conceptually consistent with the accounts as well as made on the basis of clear assumptions, then control should be easier.

Secondary objectives

Most private-sector mission statements and similar documents contain references to objectives other than the making of profits. Often these concern the management style which the company intends to use: it will be a 'good employer, 'environmentally sensitive', 'socially responsible' and so forth. Such objectives may or may not act as constraints upon management's ability to make profits. But the general belief is that pursuing them will in the end mean more profits not less. That is, an enterprise which takes care of its work-force, pleases its customers, maintains quality, is good towards its suppliers, enhances the quality of local schools and other local infra-structure and helps provide opportunities for the unemployed where it operates may sacrifice profits in the short term but should gain in the long term. However, some firms have spent too much on philanthropy, to the point where they have been taken over or have otherwise failed before any long-term benefits have materialized. As we have seen, some regulated monopolies when privatized have had to maintain social obligations even where unprofitable. As competition develops there are ways in which the cost of such social obligations can be shared between competitors, as was considered in chapter 9. And these could be adapted for use in the case of public firms as well.

Sustainability

As with the privatized enterprises, what is crucial is that social obligations do not make a reformed public enterprise unsustainable. They should be either voluntary and accepted as contributing to long-term profitability, or credited when the rules governing the profit a natural monopoly is allowed to earn are set, or paid for by pooling between competitors, or paid for directly.

Ministers' powers and explicit subsidy

While it would always be possible for a minister to use whatever powers of persuasion and patronage he may have to induce such a reformed board to fall in with his wishes, the reforms so far set out here, and others to be mentioned below, would greatly reduce his influence. Then a minister's powers need be no different from those of any trust or trustee acting for pensioners or investors; or, alternatively, could be likened to those of a holding company with a duty to reflect its share-holders' interest. Ministers should not have powers to give any directions to such enterprises which affect their profitability without compensation, except possibly in a national emergency. Thus, a minister might be empowered to require a state-owned enterprise to provide an unprofitable service, or a service at an unprofitable price, provided that it is paid an economic subsidy by central or local government or some other body.[13] Such a requirement has been embodied in the New Zealand legislation already mentioned:

> Non-commercial activities: Where the Crown wishes a state enterprise to provide goods or services to any persons, the Crown and the State enterprise shall enter into an agreement under which the State enterprise will provide the goods or services in return for the payment by the Crown of the whole or part of the price thereof.[14]

When one considers other ministerial powers under a reformed public enterprise regime much depends on whether the industry is competitive or a monopoly. Ministers may expect in some cases to need to intervene in the interests of national security, as many privatizations allow; but where or when the costs are significant one would again expect these to be paid for, especially if such a burden could distort competition. As was argued earlier, where there is monopoly ministers may investigate consumers' complaints or delegate this task to consumer councils or a regulator; but where there is competition, so that consumers may choose, such an outlet should be less necessary. Again, with a monopoly one should expect there to be requirements to provide universal service and not to practise discrimination; but they will also become less relevant as competition develops. Ministers will still have patronage, and they will be able to threaten, or use, the weapon of adverse publicity. However, in general, ministers will be less likely to succeed through using those persuasions than under the old relationship, except where publicity will not reflect badly on their motives – that is, when what they want from a reformed public enterprise is publicly defensible.

Freedom to optimize factor mix

Most of the freedoms that reformed public enterprises will relish will follow from the restrictions to be placed on ministerial powers. If ministers are confined to exercising the financial powers of a holding company and are required to get the State or some other body to pay for any appreciable social services to be carried out by such enterprises, then both their interest in day-to-day intervention and their power to intervene in that way will decline. Implied in this model of relations is, for example, the assumption that public enterprise is as free to use its resources, including labour, as efficiently as private enterprise, so that it may get rid of surplus labour and otherwise optimize the factors used in production; and that the State has developed either fiscal or monetary mechanisms to the point where public enterprise is not used for macroeconomic policy, for which it is always a poor instrument.

Freedom to diversify

In Britain, the scope of each nationalized industry has commonly been restricted to the narrow objectives of the business, except where odd activities have been inherited from previous, private undertakings which nobody has bothered to sell off. Other countries, particularly in the Third World but also Italy and Spain, have a very different policy of using their state-owned holding companies and enterprises to develop new initiatives.[15] During the 1980s, the British government got rid of most subsidiary nationalized industry activities, so that those public enterprises remaining are even more narrowly focused. Although this reduction in scope has been recent, attempts by Labour governments in the past to use nationalized industries to start up new activities always ran into opposition. The nationalized industries themselves sometimes wanted to avoid the financial losses which they often saw as both inevitable with such undertakings and the reason why they were being asked to take on the activity in the first place. And rival producers invariably complained that they would experience unfair competition because the nationalized industries did not have the reliable accounting systems to prove that they were not cross-subsidizing these new activities, and might not have been careful if they had.

If public enterprises are to be given more freedom to diversify, especially if they have monopoly power, it is reasonable that they should be required to prove that they are not cross-subsidizing except in the short run. This means that any new business of any consequence begun by them should be set up as an arm's length subsidiary or division with its own accounts (as in similar circumstances under the privatization licences). Moreover, as with privatized natural monopolies, their competitors need to be protected from predation (chapter 5). Thus, any period before the new business is to get into profit should be specified in advance and the outcome monitored. Subject to such safeguards, freedom to diversify could be given to reformed public enterprises. However, this will not involve the granting of a simple, unconstrained freedom. The purpose of diversification is either to achieve economies of scale or scope through vertical or horizontal integration, or to reduce risks by building up a portfolio of businesses where the collective risk is less than that of the separate parts. Now, government as shareholder may have an interest in deciding how far its investment is protected from organizational failure caused by increasing market power in the first case, while it may prefer other ways of hedging risks in the second. Therefore, the change that is relevant is the replacement of any legal or other formal prohibition on diversification by whatever powers of diversification government as a holding company chooses to delegate. Moreover, experience with privatization suggests that there is often a period during which the management may be keener to diversify than it would be if it felt that its own money was at risk. And during such a period it may make mistakes. Thus, it may not be wise to give any freedom to diversify to a management whose own income is not at risk.

Freedom to raise capital

So that a public enterprise may not be disadvantaged in competition with private enterprises, it must have free access to as much capital as it can demonstrate it will employ profitably. In that respect it should be in the same position as a subsidiary of a successful holding company with a strong balance sheet. As we have seen, in Britain there has long been a tendency to assume that nationalized industry borrowing must carry a government guarantee and that therefore government should have the right to control the volume of that borrowing.[16] However, neither assumption is secure: nationalized industries could issue stock or borrow from banks on their own credit, and even if they did not that need not imply government control over their borrowing.

To guarantee public enterprise debt is to acknowledge that the external, internal and financial disciplines within which a public enterprise works are insufficient incentives to stimulate its management to be profitable. Indeed, the existence of such a guarantee undermines such discipline. Where there is discipline such public enterprise borrowing should be of no greater concern to government than is private-sector borrowing. The model to which one is aspiring is analogous to a partial management and worker buy-out whereby all managers and permanent staff have shares in the enterprise, as well as other incentives to maintain an efficient and profitable business. The remainder of its capital as a public enterprise could be a mixture of government equity and fixed-interest loans – the exact sources depending on the arrangements natural to the country in question. Indeed, such a solution would not rule out even a private-equity stake, though its rationale would have to be considered closely. However, what is essential is that the State does not give borrowing freedom to a public enterprise unless those who manage it, and also those who operate it, share its risks through appropriate incentives to the point where they identify its interests with their own.

A public enterprise's powers and duties defined in a contract or licence

The basis upon which such a public (or mixed) enterprise can operate is as capable of being set down in contract, franchise, licence, or planning agreement as is that for a privatized natural monopoly. Indeed, it would be a mistake not so to set it down, since that is the only way of avoiding the muddles of past nationalizations. For reasons which were explored in discussing the shortcomings of railway legislation in the nineteenth century, it would not be sensible to lay it down in a statute.

Thus the conclusion of this section is that a public enterprise could be operated within a framework that allowed it to pursue profitability or economic efficiency without privatization. What is needed is so different from the way in which nationalized industries have been run that it would involve as radical a set of reforms as does privatization. Indeed, to a large extent the reforms that are needed are the same.

10.2 The internal prerequisites of efficient public enterprise

If a clear contract or licence is one prerequisite for efficient public enterprise, as it is for an efficient regulated private one, then the second lesson for public enterprise from privatization is the vital role of incentives. Reformed public enterprise without appropriate incentives will not be efficient. Perhaps the most fundamental mistake of the process of nationalization devised in 1945 was that no attention was paid to incentives. Instead, there was a naïve reliance on the call of the public interest as a sufficient motive. Alleged under-payment in the public sector has been a repeated source of grievance; but that is not the real issue to be faced in the provision of appropriate incentives. This is to make rewards commensurate with risks, which for the managers and workers of public enterprise reformed on the lines set down here are as great as in the private sector.

Incentives to boards

The reforms that have been outlined above would make possible the setting of meaningful objectives which could then be monitored as required on the basis of current cost accounts as well as under effective mechanisms of control. But such an apparatus in itself need not achieve results. Public enterprises will need incentives to pursue profit and their other financial objectives actively. And to be efficient these must operate in such a way as to align remuneration with the achievement of the required objectives.

The price the State must expect to pay for requiring boards to undertake the extra duties it lays on them and to take the consequential risks should be substantially higher pay. But if that high pay is to be efficient then a substantial part of it should be incentive-based, related to the performance of the board, collectively and individually.[17] Determining what the best way of doing this is would be too detailed a task for this book, but an appropriate, and in any important case a not overelaborate, basis for fixing the compensation of the executive head of a regulated public enterprise would be for an estimate of the net worth of the enterprise to be made when he is appointed, which could then serve as the base line for profit-related increases – and which could also serve for agreeing the departing compensation of his predecessor. Something of the kind was attempted when Sir Ian MacGregor joined and left British Steel and then British Coal as chairman. And Sir Ronald Dearing's appointment in 1981 as chairman of the Post Office also involved an arrangement for part of his pay to be profit related.[18] Members of the board who head parts of the business which are separately accountable could have their objectives set and their compensation fixed similarly. And members whose functions are more staff than line could have part of their compensation related to the performance of the whole business and part to the achievement of personal objectives. One supposes that often there need in fact be no special estimate of net worth. Instead, the appropriate quarterly or annual accounts will be used. Indeed, if better and more-regular accounts are published on a current cost accounts basis, the less necessary a special estimate for the chairman or anyone else will be. Besides being used for fixing compensation, the same information should be used to enable, or perhaps even to require, a minister to remove a chairman, board members or even a complete board if agreed objectives are not met. Such a discipline would be similar to that which is starting to be faced by private firms' directors in similar circumstances. And it may be noted here that it is important that a government should not be inhibited from replacing the board, or any members of it, by such contractual arrangements as it has with existing board members. Such contracts should specify the circumstances in which they may be replaced, which should include a significant failure to reach agreed financial objectives.

It is vital that board members' salaries and also their other remunerations are really related to their contribution to improving profitability. In the privatized companies after privatization, these rose steeply, leading, especially in the recession years of 1990–2, to a public outcry. A fundamental mistake often made by the boards of newly privatized companies was to assume that the issue was simply one of raising public-sector salaries to private-sector levels: a matter of parity or equity. Rather, the case for higher salaries was that the boards and managers were taking on more responsibility – that is, in general, more risk – than before. Where privatized bodies found themselves at once in competitive markets, that increase in risk could be immediate and substantial; but the risks in a privatized monopoly while it remains so need not be much greater than in a public one. Board-remuneration committees rarely made this distinction. In the longer term, increases and reductions in remuneration should depend on the contribution made to profitability or in some circumstances to the checking of losses. (It is seldom sensible simply to relate increases in board pay to overall profits, irrespective of how difficult or easy they were to win; and there are occasions when stemming profits decline is as deserving of reward as is increasing profits.) The 1990–2 recession found the chairmen of many private and some privatized companies increasing their salaries enormously, even where there had been a decline in profits (though often this was because of a lag between earning and reporting profits). And the remuneration increases of the chairmen of other privatized companies were apparently more the result of the underpricing of the issues of their shares in the time of privatization, or of favourable negotiations with the regulator, or of booming external demand, than of tangible managerial contributions to profitability. It is important for all companies but would be particularly so for reformed public enterprises that board-remuneration committees should be able to demonstrate to shareholders and publicly that the greater part of any increase in remuneration is limited to what is warranted by the successful efforts of management.

Incentives to other managers

It is not sufficient for the board alone to receive such rewards. Managers at all levels and all (permanent) members of the work-force should, first, be paid at market rates and, secondly, receive a proportion of their pay based on appropriate rewards. And there should be no political or other artificial constraints on this. But of all changes needed in a monopolistic enterprise none requires more intelligence and determination in carrying it through. Setting the objectives of any manager generally implies thinking through the objectives of all and how they interact. This is particularly true of the interconnected entities that so many natural-monopoly enterprises are. To split them up into 'profit centres' whose managers do not control all the revenues and costs would be a travesty. Most component parts of most such enterprises are, in the jargon, *net contribution* centres where managers control only some of the revenues and costs, the remainder being controlled by others. Effective incentives require that remuneration is mostly aligned with the revenues and costs that those thus remunerated can influence.

Incentives to employees

It is not inconsistent with public enterprise to permit employee shareholdings. This is clearly so where a public enterprise is converted into a Companies' Act company, since the State can maintain control while allowing a minority shareholding to be taken up by the enterprise's employees. But even if some different form of public ownership were established, the necessary provision that dividends be paid in some form to the State would seem compatible with a proportion of that dividend going to any part of the work-force which has subscribed capital.[19] If there is to be public-dividend capital, as the Treasury's 1984 proposals provided, some part of this could be allowed to be subscribed in this way so as to motivate the work-force. The inequity and comparative inefficiency of not allowing this in the public sector are increasing, for the proportion of private-sector employees in such schemes rose from 14 per cent in 1980 to 25 per cent in 1984,[20] and has presumably continued to rise since. Moreover, share ownership is only one method of profit-sharing. In 1984, 20 per cent of private-sector employees were in other profit-sharing schemes and 15 per cent received a value-added bonus. In all, some 40 per cent of private-sector workers were in one or more such schemes.

In principle, income which varies with profits will achieve several desirable ends. It will motivate individuals to work harder and better. It will increase their sense of belonging to a firm. And it will reduce unemployment because income will fluctuate over the business cycle. If this does not work in practice – and evidence that establishments where employees share profits are significantly more profitable has been scarce – among the reasons may be that the firm is not well organized, so that employees work in an environment in which neither they nor their supervisors know how to work more effectively. This may be even more relevant for public enterprise. For if the culture of the firm is not conducive to the efficiency of management, neither will it be to that of the employees. Nevertheless, well-devised share ownerships and other profit-sharing and bonus schemes should be helpful, and there is no practical reason why public enterprise should not participate in them.

Equivalents to receivership and bankruptcy

A public enterprise going into receivership if it cannot meet its obligations is a possibility that should be allowed for. Moreover, there is no reason in principle why a government, and any other shareholders, in such a case should not be treated as are the shareholders in a commercial bankruptcy. What needs to be changed is the expectation that a public enterprise cannot go bankrupt. Then the shareholders would know what to expect and would be able to assess their risks accordingly. There may still be surprise because as the (main) owner government should have been able to change the management to avoid this outcome. But no more or less than with private shareholders, this seems an insufficient reason for a government not allowing a public enterprise to go bankrupt. A stronger reason is that in most cases the government will want the enterprise to continue, especially if it is a natural monopoly or utility providing essential goods or services.[21] In that case it will be criticized if it allows the shareholders to receive less than a 100 per cent in the pound – even if it has had to buy the assets at some lower price to restart the business, with in effect a substantial write-off. Yet some of those shareholders will be the board members, managers and workers who collectively caused or allowed the bankruptcy to happen, while most of the rest of the shares will be owned by government, which had not used its powers of stewardship to avoid it. The bankruptcy of a public enterprise not allowed deficit finance would be equivalent to the cancellation of a franchise given to the board. Part of the reconstruction of a public enterprise after its bankruptcy would involve considering what arrangements would motivate new and surviving managers and the work-force. The disciplines and incentives given ought to make bankruptcy an unlikely event. And the contracts with chairmen and other board members should be drawn up so as to avoid unnecessary difficulty and expense.[22]

What form of capital reconstruction may also be needed is an important issue: the incentive that is needed is one which will motivate individuals to avoid their removal on grounds equivalent to bankruptcy, not the discipline of bankruptcy itself. If management action, however competent the management, is not able to pull the business into profit again, then it will not be more unreasonable than in the private sector for there to be a capital reconstruction in which the holdings of taxpayers, managers and work-force as equity shareholders, and stockholders, may lose all or part of their capital value.

It is a widespread but little discussed premise that a privatized enterprise, particularly a natural monopoly, will be allowed to go bankrupt. The water legislation in particular has detailed provisions for ministers to replace a failed enterprise in such an eventuality. There are no similar provisions in other cases, but would British Gas or British Telecom be allowed to fail, its licence going to another firm if it mismanaged its affairs to the point of bankruptcy after whatever attempts it had made itself at reconstruction? It would, however, be wise if the monopoly privatization statutes were to provide mechanisms to ensure continuity of supply for an essential monopoly good or service. The procedures just mentioned can be seen as performing a similar function for reformed public enterprises. Moreover, as was argued in chapter 6 it is important that the independent regulator avoids a situation where he can be blamed for such a failure – for example, through a severity in the RPI–X formula that he cannot defend. And this holds for both reformed public enterprises and privatized firms.

A conclusion of chapter 5 was that an established public enterprise monopoly has to go through a process of debureaucratization if it is to achieve competitive efficiency. And as has already been observed many have achieved this even before privatization and even in some cases before privatization was contemplated. As John Kay observed in 1987, 'the most marked productivity gains have been made not in the privatization candidates but in the traditional nationalized industries – posts, steel, rail – where no privatization was (then) in prospect . . . Each of these industries has experienced senior management changes which have introduced a more commercial and a more abrasive management style'.[23] Before believing that this proves that old-style public enterprises can become efficient if allowed to, one should not forget the inducements of prospective financial rewards that these managements had to prepare their firm in these ways for privatization even if it was not then in prospect, as well as the further advantage to their firm's balance sheet of clearing up inefficiencies before privatization. Yet even competition and regulation may bring about the regeneration of an enterprise too slowly or not at all. Moreover, the principle of the survival of the fittest does not imply that any particular firm will survive. And it is a rash government that is indifferent to the fate of its largest enterprises, especially where they are monopolies. A lesson from the failure of nationalized industries to perform well economically in Britain and in other countries is that even wealthy countries cannot afford to have many substantial inefficient, loss-making enterprises, especially if the quality of the services they provide deteriorates, or does not rise in line with private-sector quality. In order to avoid such economic inefficiency and low quality, incentives are necessary. And that remains valid whether public enterprise reform is contemplated or privatization. But the presumption is that one can give as much incentive to all who work in the public enterprise as makes unnecessary any additional stimulus that would come from the shareholder pressure for efficiency that privatization would bring in larger measure. It is once more an empirical question whether this is likely under any given set of institutional arrangements.[24]

Another lesson from the past is that, above all the other changes listed, the most important is that public enterprise reform like privatization often requires a revolution in the industry's culture before it can become effective. If that does not happen and the industry is not already efficient, there must be a chance that the enterprise will be less able to respond to the competition that emerges. Indeed, culture change is perhaps a *sine qua non* of efficiency. A second moral is that it at least seems possible that such a transformation could be achieved without privatization if governments were prepared to find the right people, give them appropriate objectives, freedoms and incentives, and then back them against political interference.

10.3   Public enterprise reform or privatization?

But do these reforms provide a believable alternative to privatization? Almost nowhere yet has there been as fundamental a reconstruction of public enterprise without change of ownership as in New Zealand. But though 'corporatization' there had been the first intention there has since been privatization. And attempts to introduce far milder changes have come to grief. Thus, it may seem prudent to conclude that public enterprise reform to such an extent is politically impossible. Yet privatization comprehends reforms as fundamental as these and arguably more in addition. So why should the one be politically impossible and the other not? Is there some underlying reason for this, or could public enterprise reform also be about to come into its own; for privatization too had seemed impossible until it happened? Or are there different circumstances in which the one is more practical than the other?

As we have seen, while many who have written on privatization have seen increased competition as the main cause of its success – to a greater extent than is warranted – others, particularly Michael Beesley and Stephen Littlechild, have maintained that privatization should promote efficiency even if there is no increase in competition.[25] This contention rests on two kinds of argument. The first is that regulation is more effective than ministerial and departmental control. A substantial proportion of this book is intended as a demonstration of the truth of that proposition. However, that requirement can be met by separating the economic regulation of public enterprise from ministerial control. The second is that privatization has the edge over any possible public enterprise reform because of several supposedly unique features. Those features would seem to be six:

The process of privatization   This process entails fundamental thinking about the organization to be privatized. The importance of this has already been discussed in chapter 4. By comparison with the reviews and investigations of public enterprise, the process of privatization has been more thorough in what it unearths. But this is a once and for all advantage; and no doubt a commitment to reform within the public sector could lead to an equally thorough organization investigation, though it did not happen when nationalization took place in Britain (chapter 3). Certainly, the preparation for a sound current-cost valuation of an industry if properly done must be thorough.

Taxpayers' risk   Ray Rees has pointed out that privatization leads to less distortion of the taxpayer's forced investment portfolio.[26] A shareholder chooses his own portfolio as he pleases so as to reflect his personal assessment of risk and aversion from it; but as a taxpayer he is forced to invest in certain enterprises as well as to pick up their losses through increased taxation, whose incidence may be unpredictable, creating an investment portfolio significantly different from the private one that as a rational investor he would have formed. This is of practical significance where such forced investments and unpredictable additions to taxation are substantial because public enterprise is pervasive. Behind this point there is an issue that mirrors one discussed in the previous section. It is tempting for politicians to off-load risks onto the taxpayer, since doing so encourages risk-taking by public enterprises and makes them readier to agree to political demands, making this often seem an attractive proposition. Indeed, in many countries this is a motive for widespread public enterprise. And it may result in the combined deficits of public enterprises absorbing a substantial part of taxation. But as has already been argued, the taxpayers, though they have no real choice over the risks they thus take, do not have to be forced to accept them even if there is no privatization: a reformed public enterprise may shoulder much of its own risk. And it ought to if it is to be trusted to raise capital freely.

Financial market disciplines   Although the valuation of the company by movements in its share price is potentially an important check on a privatized enterprise's performance, the periodic current-cost valuation of an enterprise as proposed in the New Zealand legislation provides in principle an equivalent or even a better valuation. However, it is so elaborate in the data it requires as not to be undertaken often. Moreover, a current-cost valuation requires a host of subjective judgements where it is possible to have wide differences of view and to make forecasting errors. It was argued in chapter 7 that it would be helpful to involve the regulator here. He needs to use his specialist knowledge to test in detail the assumptions that the industry has made in conducting such a valuation. Ultimately – as the more recent privatization legislation allows – he has to be satisfied that the conventions and assumptions used are the most appropriate and that he has enough powers to ensure that satisfactory accounts are produced for regulatory purposes. Whoever regulates public enterprise could have the same powers.

A stock market valuation is achieved with less effort, and it may vary continuously both to reflect changes in general market conditions and to respond to factors affecting the particular company. And although stock market valuations also reflect subjective judgements they have the strength of being a compromise between the competing views of many people in the market with different degrees of knowledge and different attitudes towards risk. Occasionally, they may reflect false perceptions of the company; but provided that it does not depart from honesty a company can persuade analysts and others that they are wrong and hope to alter the direction of the influence they exert upon its shareholders. However, acquiring the habit of constantly being aware of the share value and worrying about unexpected changes in it does not come easily. Moreover, ex-public enterprises may often be surprised by how indirect is the interest of the shareholder. At annual general meetings the monopoly's shareholders present rarely question the company's profitability. As we saw earlier, they behave like customers, asking the company to raise quality or otherwise spend more money in the customer's interest or to keep prices down rather than to take actions which will increase profits. Furthermore, like journalists, financial analysts tend to specialize. Even the largest companies are unlikely to have more than one or two knowledgeable about their affairs and investing a substantial proportion of their time getting to know the business. A perceptive senior official of a just-privatized concern has remarked that on a day-to-day basis he was less aware after privatization of the pressures to maintain and improve financial performance. Under the old regime, when there were annual price rounds, wage renegotiations or negotiations over financing limits, the sponsoring department in part assumed the mantle of the customer, sometimes energetically. This was always balanced by its also adopting another voice, a hard financial one. Even more the Treasury put the financial case on every issue. After privatization the clamour on behalf of the customer – to keep prices down and quality up, as well as to invest in new goods and services – intensified, but there was no one to provide the depth of financial analysis or the day-to-day severity of the departmental economic advisers and of the Treasury, even if, as we have suggested, they or the minister they advised usually lacked tenacity.

Financial markets can be deceptive. Again like journalists, the financial institutions and analysts tend to stay quiet while there is no news. But if there is a sudden strong suspicion that all is not well, they crowd into view, plying their questions and their comments. Then it may be difficult for a firm to change the market's opinion of it. Time is no longer on its side. Privatized industry management often has had no experience of the intensity of this pressure. One day an ex-public enterprise will be shaken to find how quickly pressures to change policies and top people can be raised to a point where they are irresistible. And changes made or attempted to correct market perceptions then are more painful and constrained than if they had been made earlier. Acquisition and mergers are also likely to provoke intensive questioning if analysts think that they could have an appreciable effect on the share price. Once again this is likely to be a more effective discipline where there is already competition. Where a privatized body retains monopoly power, the discipline of the share price is less powerful. But in either case even a moderately competent management ought to be able to avoid any undue swings in the share price. Perhaps the greatest danger from this standpoint is unwise diversification, but if the privatized enterprise can avoid this it should be reasonably safe. Of course, dull, safe management may disappoint the stock market's original expectations and this may lead to some downgrading of the stock, but the stock market is used to utilities and knows how to handle them.

Takeover   The possibility of a hostile takeover effects a fierce discipline and provides a powerful incentive to good management because a takeover usually leads to many changes near the top. Some of the largest privatizations have been of companies so large that the threat of takeover is remote. And in many cases a golden share or other restrictions on shareholdings are in force permanently or temporarily. Yet Britoil has disappeared into British Petroleum, against the Government's wishes.[27] And French water companies have bought their way into English ones and are interested in acquiring privatized water authorities when they can. This discipline of takeover is not affected by the finding that most takeovers do not improve the net worth of an enterprise. It is the fear of takeover that is the spur to management at least as much as the reality.[28] However, it will have the least effect on the large privatized natural monopolies – even without golden shares, they are likely to be too large to be taken over.

Though individual shareholders may behave like customers and financial disciplines upon a company often seem light, undoubtedly the financial markets expect a satisfactory rate of profit improvement for a firm and will facilitate takeovers where managements do not realize asset values.

Proceeds   In principle, the choice between reforming a public enterprise to make it efficient and its privatization is the choice between a profit stream and its equivalent capital value. If a government wanting economic efficiency were confident of its ability to deliver efficient public enterprises, it should, from that point of view, be indifferent between the two. Sometimes there has been a lingering hostility to profitable public monopolies as involving taxation without representation. But in general a far more important recent motive for privatization has been the need for cash or foreign exchange – or to avoid putting further investment cash in. (If this were all there was to it, then Harold Macmillan, the Earl of Stockton as he then was, would perhaps have been justified in his gibe that engaging in privatization was like selling the family silver.[29])

Irreversibility   The most important effect of privatization is that the changes it brings about become practically irreversible. While reformed enterprises remain publicly owned, the possibility is much greater that a change of government, or even a change of heart by the same government, will undermine the safeguards, with a return to the old interventionism and confusion. Even with privatization, as it is at present constituted, government retains substantial powers that it could use or abuse to constrain the regulated industries' profitability (chapters 8 and 9). And if government is a majority shareholder or retains a substantial minority of shares, it could change its mind and intervene even though Conservative ones since 1979 have said that they will not do so.[30] If it is true that politicians will be inclined not remain distant from public enterprise and that sooner or later a new generation of politicians may try to recapture the patronage that comes with intervention or have other reasons for wishing to intervene again, then there must always be a real danger that public enterprise reform will not be permanent.

Privatization is less reversible not only because the legislation needed to reverse it would be more complex, and because in some cases the bodies have disappeared into other firms or acquired overseas ownership, but also because too many interests have been created that are opposed to renationalization. This last reason may be looked at by way of a comparison. Many on the Right in recent years have played with the idea of building economic elements into a 'constitution'. Brennan and Buchanan, for example, have used John Rawls' arguments to support the proposal that there should be a 'tax constitution' under which taxation may be no heavier than it would be if any voter might at random occupy any position in the income distribution.[31] And there have been similar requests that a balanced budget be written into the US Constitution.[32] All such attempts seem rather desperate since they amount to a minority trying to persuade a majority to give a protected legal status to that minority's interest.[33] By comparison, privatization, because of the breadth of the interests it appeals to, is expected to achieve a similar change without raising constitutional problems. Earlier it was argued that Madsen Pirie's political arguments did not provide the explanation of why privatization happened in Britain in the 1980s, that the changes they envisaged need not be consistent with increasing net benefits to consumers (chapter 4). Nevertheless, it is those political changes which make it unlikely that privatization will be reversed.

To conclude this section: one ought to be as able to achieve efficiency through public enterprise reform as through privatization. However, simply to renationalize a grid or network without such reform on the grounds that it is necessarily a monopoly, and that therefore its ownership does not matter economically, is to ignore the incentive issues this chapter has stressed. What is required is that everyone engaged in the management, operations and financing of the enterprise should have sufficient incentive to be efficient at every margin that matters. But that does not entail privatization. While the preparation for public enterprise reform could be as thorough and revealing as is that for privatization and even under public ownership most risks could be shifted from the taxpayer to those who manage and work for the enterprise, more powerful arguments for the superiority of privatization over public enterprise reform are the exposure of the enterprise to the disciplines of the financial markets which it alone can give and the discipline of (possible) takeover. However, this means that where the financial markets are poor, non-existent or themselves subject to political influence, the force of these arguments can decline to vanishing point (and in any case these disciplines may be less effective over large monopolies). The most powerful of such arguments are, first, that it will realize cash or foreign exchange, an argument which tends to be most influential during a national economic crisis; and, secondly, the greater irreversibility of privatization, which makes it less likely that there will be a reversal of objectives and of government behaviour – though a government might achieve a similar reversion of power by capturing regulation as through its powers of ownership.

10.4 Privatization versus public enterprise: overseas

Among the main reasons why privatization came in Britain was the vital import-ance of an arguably theoretically irrelevant factor: the overwhelming presentational need to show that public expenditure was falling when it was actually rising. One cannot assume that in other countries sooner or later history will follow a similar course, though the fact that privatization has occurred and is, in various ways, suc-cessful in Britain has itself given overseas governments the confidence to follow the example, if in a more deliberate, less accidental way. However, even though history will never quite repeat British experience, one may be able to deduce some plaus-ible generalizations from that experience. In fact, there seem better reasons for concluding that public enterprise in its present forms will yield to something else in many countries, than to be confident that it will yield to privatization, or re-formed public enterprise as defined earlier in this chapter, though one can perhaps say something about the circumstances in which each will be the more probable outcome.

In its essentials the public enterprise malaise described in chapter 3 is to be found in many other countries: literature on both advanced and less-developed countries seems to suggest that similar difficulties have developed.[34] It is still a common assumption that substantial reform of public enterprise is politically impossible. No one defends the status quo as ideal, but any change from it offends some interests too much. And though its nature will vary between countries, what one observes in many countries is that the balance of interests involved here is part of what binds the political system together. Politicians are ready to tolerate the public sector's relative inefficiency where the private sector is strong and do not expect path-breaking efficiency from it in countries where the private sector is weak. In India for example in 1984/5, 91 out of 207 centrally owned enterprises made losses.[35] In return, they expect the public sector to solve a range of economic and political problems for them; to act as their agents and, in some countries, as a source of jobs for themselves, their relations or their partisans. In many countries industrial and domestic consumers do not mind or perhaps even notice the inefficiency of public enterprises as long as their products and services are cheap and reasonably reliable. Public-sector deficits met by the taxpayer are a means acceptable to both consumer and politician of (appar-ently) keeping prices down. Those who run public enterprises do not expect all the financial rewards of commerce; but they enjoy other rewards. They are protected by monopoly and trade barriers from competition and undue pressure to improve their efficiency. They may derive professional satisfaction from high professional and tech-nical standards or standards of public service. Their political experience and their influence on the economy give them protection from intolerable political inter-ference. And in many cases they may be content with their relatively low financial rewards because of an attendant public recognition or the pride of rising to the top of an organization entered when young, or because they see such a career as leading to national political eminence. Moreover in other cases the actual financial rewards may be higher than the formal remuneration. Bureaucrats may also have developed good working relations with those who run public enterprises. Diplomacy and dexterity are needed to mediate between ministers, boards and the public. Exerting enough influence to satisfy the politicians while protecting the boards from more intervention often requires administrative talents of a high order. There are also the lesser pleasures of advising on appointments and of making criticisms. Personal relations are also closer and more interesting than they normally are within the private sector. Workers may be disappointed in so far as they once had expectations of more control and of participation in management; but jobs are usually secure and pay attractive. And through patronage and promotion high-fliers may carve out interesting careers quickly. Trade union leaders find the public-sector labour-force among the easiest to recruit from among and to lead. And it is generally a solid and cohesive part of the trade union power-base. Suppliers have often found public enterprises good for secure and profitable relationships. They are often less touched with the financial niggardliness which may survive in the civil service. And they are often looked to as among the first of those who will, as far as the rules allow, contribute to good causes and sponsor research. Even private-sector leaders, though often contemptuous of what they see as public-sector ways, will towards the end of their careers not spurn the prospect of a safe berth there with honour. Provided that not too many of the people involved in the public sector are unduly self-seeking, lazy or unprincipled so that defects become unendurable or the level of corruption becomes scandalous, the taxpayer will not notice the weight of the inefficiency he is bearing.

There is no modern business sector in many of the less-developed countries,[36] political intervention and economic protectionism having created or sustained an economy in which the private sector is no more efficient than the public sector and in which a business's survival depends as much on its managers' political skills in getting permits, quotas and government orders as on their entrepreneurship and management ability. Local capital markets are often either non-existent or imperfect, imposing little discipline upon firms and usually unequal to raising funds for privatization.[37] And importing capital from overseas creates political and foreign-exchange problems for the importing company as well as risks for the suppliers of capital. Moreover, the process of privatization can in such countries be yet another opportunity for corruption.

Often the private sector in less-developed countries is composed of small family firms engaged mostly in trading, distribution and light industry. In India, for example, almost without exception even the largest firms are under the control of family dynasties. In many such countries, therefore, the public sector still tends to be the nursery and showplace of modern business management, despite all its shortcomings – a tendency that is reinforced by the shortage of educated business leaders.[38] This is reversed in more-advanced countries where private-sector management is seen as superior to that in the public sector. But such a difference in attitudes may seem less surprising when it is recalled that not many years ago, when British industry and commerce were also dominated by family firms of all sizes, family control often used to be held responsible for bad management in the private sector.[39] Family members had little incentive to prepare themselves for management. Yet managers from outside the family were an underclass whose aspirations generally had, for dynastic reasons, to be limited. Professional management was a creation of the 1920s.[40] In 1921, one apostle of public ownership, R. H. Tawney, in his best-seller *The Acquisitive Society* could write about managers as an industrial proletariat . . . Their opportunities for promotion may be few and distributed with a singular capriciousness. They see the prizes of industry awarded by favouritism, or by the nepotism which results in the head of a business unloading upon it a family of sons whom it would be economical to pay to keep out of it . . .[41]

And he went on to ask them to consider the comparative benefits of public owner-ship:

Under which system, private or public ownership, will they have the most personal discretion and authority over the conduct of matters within their professional competence? Under which will they have the best guarantee that their special know-ledge will carry due weight, and that they will not be overridden or obstructed by amateurs?[42]

That such arguments for public ownership could be plausible in Britain until after the Second World War should help us understand why in many countries where private-sector management has not commonly achieved the professionalism and influence that it has in advanced countries enthusiasm for public enterprise reform may still exceed that for privatization. It should also remind us that nationalization in Britain need not at the time have been quite the retrogressive step it can now so easily seem with hindsight. Instead, there may have been a dialectical progression in which nationalization helped raise professional and management standards above what they were in the private sector in the 1930s, before in its turn best-practice management in the British private sector started to outclass that in the public sector.

Moreover, in many countries nationalization has been part of a deal to reduce economic conflict. The historian of corporatism in Britain has pointed out that nationalization in Britain in the 1920s and 1930s should be seen as one of a number of measures to 'rationalize' or protect flagging industries: cheap government-supported facilities for decaying staple industries; tariff protection for iron and steel; moves towards imperial preference and the setting up of agricultural marketing boards.[43] All these were argued through in such a way as to bring about a delicate balance between the interests concerned. Though they were in restraint of trade, what at the time seemed plausible economic reasons were used to defend them. And similar arrange-ments to limit what seemed at the time to be destructive competition were adopted in the 1930s in the United States and other countries with advanced economies. Many historians and economists have observed how it is often more convenient for polit-icians to induce nationalized industries to benefit particular areas or consumer groups through pricing policies or in other ways than it is for them to pass laws to this effect.[44] In many less-developed countries a comparable stage in economic growth came later and brought similar attempts to limit 'destructive' competition.

In Britain corporatism was a way in which employees, through trade unions and the Trades Union Congress, and employers through their various associations, found ways of working with the State to blunt the harsher workings of the competitive process. Before the early 1930s, the intellectual justification was generally that it better enabled what was called 'rationalization', that is, the finding of ways of buying out the smaller firms in a market so that they left it or willingly submerged their identity in larger firms.[45] Later, the justification was Keynesian: the belief that through demand management one could avoid some of the costs of the competitive process – a form of economic management which evolved into collusive arrangements between the State, Capital and Labour to underpin various kinds of prices and incomes policies.[46]

Some such form of corporatism as a defence against market forces has developed in many countries. In some, the public sector has also provided an estate off which some politicians, their firms or backers could live, resulting in a form of corruption – not found in Britain – which has further cemented public enterprise into the formal and informal structure of the State.[47]

Above all, where savings have not been easily mobilized, government finance for public enterprises has been a way of ensuring that certain activities got at least minimal capital for development. It has been argued that in many countries only the State can mobilize sufficient capital for large industrial units – a belief long sustained by aid-agency support for such projects. If replacement sources of savings are not forthcoming at home or abroad – and they have not as yet always been mobilized for privatization – privatization may result, where capital markets do not work, in a dearth of capital for erstwhile public services. One may also note that there are countries where public enterprises are, exceptionally, efficient without the disciplines of public enterprise reform.

Other arguments which in many countries were used to justify nationalization may be presented as directly related to the distribution of income and wealth or as otherwise political. Not without justification, concentrations of power in the hands of private monopolies were seen as exploitative of consumers and employees. Therefore attempts were made – as in the 1956 Indian Industrial Policy Resolution – to devise forms and instruments of state ownership which would redistribute such power. One can also find, as sometimes in Africa, attempts to use nationalization to prevent particular tribes or racial minorities from holding on to what seemed excessive power.

When privatization comes to be considered, similar or reverse considerations frequently arise. Often they are presented in the form of a discussion about property rights. To whom does the enterprise and its assets belong? Who ought to get what? But implicit in the argument of this book, and particularly of this chapter, is the view that from the standpoint of economic efficiency this is not the most useful, and may be a damaging, way of setting up the problem. Rather, one needs first to ensure that all the factors of production used by an enterprise are remunerated at their opportunity cost to the enterprise. Because the enterprise is unlikely to be perfectly efficient, its labour-force, including its board and other managers, need incentives in their remuneration which will lead them to raise their productivity in ways which lead to greater profitability for the firm, assuming, that that is its overriding objective. What combination of base pay, overtime earnings, and performance-related pay will achieve this is an empirical question, one depending on the circumstances of the enterprise. Property rights, that is, broadly, shareholdings for management and work-force, as well as for those who provide capital and possibly some other assets, may well be part of the optimal package of incentives.

When such a package has been designed there may, or may not, be surplus value which in formal economic terms is yielding rent or monopoly profits. Who should own the property rights to that is not an economic issue, but a political one. One may try to deal with this historically by claiming that certain parties have a legal or moral right to all or part of this surplus value. Or one may treat it as a current political decision not bound by precedent. In the second case, the most natural interpretation is that it belongs to the State, which has the choice of either keeping that part of the income stream – reformed public enterprise – or selling it – privatization. To give it to any other minority, including the managers and employees of the firm, is a political act of redistribution. By assumption, given the argument we have been through, it does not need be given to the management and work-force in order to provide them with sufficient incentives. Moreover, to give them property rights over monopoly profits has a number of dangers. First, like any other monopoly, there will be a tendency for this to lead to increasing or retaining organizational inefficiency, as has been argued earlier in this book. Secondly, managers and employees will be then over-remunerated, if judged by the standards of the market-place, which will act as a disincentive to optimizing the size of the labour-force. Thirdly, if competition erodes monopoly profits, remuneration will fall, which will not be helpful when productivity improvement becomes more essential to the enterprise's viability. Fourthly, and more worrying than any of these, the various parties will have been given property rights which either immediately or over time will more than exhaust the enterprise's output – repeating the error of so many nineteenth-century railways, which would have become unsustainable without the intervention of government to protect them by conferring monopoly power – one way in which liberalization can reverse into its antithesis.

So strong therefore is the position of public enterprise in many countries, so embedded within the body politic, that the forces that can change it have to be exceptionally strong. Moreover, even where there is a perceived need to create a market economy, as in many Third World and Eastern European countries, creating a market economy out of a planned economy is itself a great challenge. Valuing a concern for privatization cannot then be based on the historic or replacement cost of its assets. The value of any given enterprise will depend on the steps that will be taken to create markets as well as on their timing. A practical alternative would be to value firms as far as possible as if their outputs were sold, and any imported inputs bought, at world prices. Such revaluations would not require privatization; but to find realistic bases for valuing assets may not always be possible until tariff barriers and other restrictions on the economy are actually removed.

What seems to have precipitated change in many countries has been similar changes in market forces. In the discussions after the lectures in India from which this book has grown, I found that there was scarcely an issue or experience of nationalization in Britain which did not strike a chord.[48] While some of this identity of perception is explained by a common administrative tradition, much of it seemed to echo a general truth, that in all countries state enterprises have often been set up to meet similar ends and have been based on comparable compromises. Even so, while the reasons why Britain became disillusioned with its nationalized industries were understood, some who took part in the discussions thought that privatization was not a credible alternative. Partly this was because they thought it politically unacceptable in their own circumstances; but, at a more fundamental level, it was also because adopting the traditions and behaviour of the private sector seemed to them an unconvincing move, especially where the market is rudimentary, heavily dependent on the State, constrained by numerous regulations or protected and distorted by tariff barriers.[49]

The tendency of public expenditure to increase as a proportion of Gross National Product, which has been experienced virtually everywhere, while not in itself a cause of economic inefficiency, has increased pressures for privatization. Goods and services for which demand is increasing most rapidly could be those that are most commonly produced by the State. Indeed, health, education, defence, the police, environmental enhancement and protection, water and sewerage are usually among them. Moreover, it could be the case that they are also most efficiently produced by public production. Now, it is this, of course, that is in dispute, but even if it were true there could still be a mismatch between what consumers and taxpayers want and what public suppliers provide. Because of monopoly and of financial support by the taxpayer, public production is determined, as to both quantity and quality, by political and producer interests; add to this an increase in redistribution between income groups because of a political consensus to this end, and the net result is a lack of balance between the social wage – that is, the benefit derived from public expenditure, including expenditure subsidizing public production – and the burden of the taxes to support that expenditure for any given individual.[50]

Such an imbalance became of greater concern from the 1970s onwards because of declining economic growth rates in many countries. An increased burden is less noticed if one's personal income net of taxes is increasing. But inflation and aspects of anti-inflationary policy altered income distribution; and as a result many became resentful of the burden of public expenditure and therefore more critical of it.

But more fundamental in bringing about a movement towards privatization has been the increase in international trade, which in most countries has increased competitiveness to levels which have been not been experienced since the nineteenth century. Falling international transport costs have greatly increased the extent of markets and have made it possible for Far Eastern countries to exploit their economic advantages. In Britain – perhaps to a greater extent than in most other countries – monopolies and cartels had been allowed to develop in this century protected by barriers, quotas and transport costs.[51] The fall in transport costs has greatly reduced the possibility of hiding behind such barriers. In Britain exports have stayed more or less constant as a proportion of Gross Domestic Product throughout the century; but imports increased to 25 per cent at which level they stayed during the 1970s and 1980s. This greater exposure to competition made those who produce traded goods and services more critical of public producers whenever they attempted to raise prices to cover costs, especially during the recession of the early 1980s. 'Why should local taxation or nationalized industry prices go on rising inexorably?' they asked. One often hears that greater openness in international markets has made it harder to pursue national macroeconomic policies; the same is true of microeconomic policies where these have attempted to insulate industries, public or private, from market forces. Even in India and China, where economic isolationism has been particularly strong, the costs of autarky have become increasingly visible, while in the Soviet Union they became revolutionary.

However, it is a massive leap in the argument to believe that the response to such economic difficulties in countries with large public sectors and in particular to poor performance in the public sector will, or should, always be privatization – despite the British experience, and the edge privatized enterprise can have over reformed public enterprise, let alone over unreformed public enterprise.[52] To believe that privatization is the only solution would be to fall again into the fallacy that one can never learn from experience. One of the lessons of the 1980s in Britain was that, as privatization showed, levels of efficiency which had seemed impossible were in fact possible. Another lesson should be that the control of nationalized industries – again, assuming that economic efficiency is their main purpose – can be drastically improved. To believe otherwise would mean believing that there are inevitable trends and patterns in human history which make its course predictable: that human activity only alters society in ways that are predictable. Much political rhetoric has been a source of such notions of historical inevitability and has also used them persuasively. No one to my knowledge has attempted a theory which sees the privatization of public enterprise as an inevitable stage in some Darwinian progression towards a capitalist Utopia or Marxist progression to the eventual downfall of capitalism, but little ingenuity would be needed to concoct either. Yet a theory of privatization that set out to explain why public enterprise is a lower stage of development than a private company and cannot return would be historically unwarranted and metaphysically confused. More to the point, though it would be invidious to quote them, right-wing politicians and thinkers often argue as if privatization were part of some irreversible movement which will blaze around the globe from its original site in Britain. In reality, the prediction of social and economic events cannot be precise, especially that of their timing. No general hypothesis will explain the persistence of public enterprise in so many countries outside the United States. The sophistication of the regulatory regime that this book has suggested is appropriate for privatization may not be realized, or even in some cases intended, in other countries – even allowing for the fact that different governments and legal systems will quite properly involve detailed departures from it. And a poorly regulated privatized natural monopoly may result in a situation which is far from efficient.

The case for reforming a public enterprise rather than privatizing it should be decided at one level by how determined a country is to keep it publicly owned, by the relative efficiency of its own public and private sectors, and by its commitment to economic efficiency and – one might add – to the pursuit of long-term non-economic objectives. If in general a country's private sector is efficient and able to conduct a natural monopoly efficiently, if efficiency is the main aim and if there is as much competition as possible, or where there is not, if there is effective regulation, then it will be difficult not to prefer regulated privatization. However, neither fundamental public enterprise reform nor a full scale privatization programme may become politically attractive unless there is a sustained economic crisis, probably coupled with a crisis in the public finances. Even more than the inefficiency of the public sector, the claims of that sector's deficits on the public finances and of its investment programmes on public borrowing may become so excruciating as to far outweigh the pleasures of continuing with the status quo. An important prediction seems to follow from this: that in such circumstances privatization will win hands down, because it is at just such times that the governments of weak economies will most value the proceeds from privatization.

The kind of upheaval in any country that is likely to lead to the introduction of either fundamental public enterprise reform or thorough-going regulated privatization is likely to be cataclysmic because the new concentration on economic efficiency that would be involved would represent a substantial shift in power and wealth, one which in many countries could fairly be called revolutionary. While the process can be eased, as we have seen, by various measures to win support, if it is to be effective there will be losers, of which the greatest are likely to be those who habitually gain from corporatism: politicians as a class, civil servants, trade union leaders and various lobbyists. The irony in this is that such an upheaval is likely not only when a country's economic difficulties are so great that striving for economic efficiency becomes of paramount importance (very often it will be trade and budget deficits which will be the trigger of this), but when corruption is imposing such costs upon the country that there is real support for a clean sweep (though one cannot rule out the possibility that there is support for privatization or reform as a source of new forms of corruption). As we have just seen, in such circumstances privatization will be more probable than fundamental public enterprise reform, because of its positive effects on public finance, but one always hopes that there will be far-sighted statesmen who will see that a programme of public enterprise reform may also avoid an economic cataclysm now while building the foundations of future growth.

However, one must face the fact that all countries have been slow to introduce anything remotely corresponding to fundamental public enterprise reform, except New Zealand – and there it was superseded by privatization. This may be because a clear analysis of what is required is lacking. Indeed, it may be that only immersion in privatization will lead one to consider what in principle could be achieved by public enterprise reform.

In the long run, the future of privatization will depend most of all on the extension of competition and the success of regulation. This last is the territory which was insufficiently considered in the early stages of privatization. It has been the main topic of this book, but both the competition and the regulation required of public enterprise if it is to be efficient are no different in principle from those needed for a regulated, private, natural monopoly.

10.5 Public enterprise and privatization where economic efficiency is not the overriding objective

If one is to consider how far the results of privatization can be achieved without privatization, one must first determine what its primary objectives are. If they are concerned with the distribution of political power – the kind of objectives that Pirie listed, and which were discussed early in chapter 4 – then they cannot be achieved without privatization. If, on the other hand, they are political in almost any other sense, then the case for either corporatization or privatization is weaker. This is most obviously true, as was maintained in chapter 7, if the objectives politicians have for public enterprise are multiple or shifting or both. Then the structures of nationalization Britain has been privatizing out of existence can be a practical compromise between allowing key activities to follow private-sector motivations entirely and effecting day-to-day political control. If nationalization had not satisfied at least the short-term objectives of generations of politicians, the nationalized industries would not have remained in public hands for so long. From such a standpoint, which was almost common ground among sensible people before 1979, neither privatization nor the type of public enterprise reform described above is needed. Indeed, those who in the past have argued for the reform of public enterprise have tended to regard a multiplicity of objectives and a departure from profit maximization as not only inescapable features of it but also its justification.[53] Such objectives have been diverse not because a single politician has had multiple and shifting objectives, though that is commonly true of individual politicians, but because they have been the product of a political process mediating between different politicians, who have themselves been under diverse political pressures.[54] Hence the confusion over objectives and responsibilities which has been blamed repeatedly for nationalized industry inefficiency. Reformers have therefore concentrated on trying to devise machinery for clarifying and better implementing these diverse objectives, in the belief that they could then be achieved with greater efficiency.

Thus, to continue with nationalization often seems most appropriate where economic efficiency is not the overriding objective – where the aim is to divide rather than to increase the surplus. Nationalization is a way, however economically inefficient, of sharing that surplus between various policies and parties. In some countries, the basis for this will have become consistent and stable over time, either because the same ministers and governments stay in power for many years or because the civil service or a dominant political party is strong enough to achieve such stability. In others, it will be more inconsistent and less stable, which is itself likely to make state enterprise less efficient. One assumes that a minister and his department in their relations with state enterprises will act so as to achieve political support, recognizing that among the support that may be needed could be that of the enterprise itself, if it is politically powerful; but in more-corrupt circumstances the minister and those in his department may have their own personal, family and tribal objectives as well.

Some of the reforms short of privatization that were attempted from the 1950s to 1970s in Britain and which were described in chapter 3, as well as some of the reforms listed in this chapter, could be achieved while retaining a shifting multiplicity of objectives. But, while such changes should improve efficiency, they cannot achieve the clarity of objectives needed to provide clear guidance to management. As was argued in chapter 7, the parties concerned represent different interests and therefore have different primary objectives. They can agree to compromise over actions and secondary objectives but not over primary objectives. And as long as unreconciled objectives remain what is at work is inevitably a political process. If the management of public enterprise is seen primarily as such a political or otherwise representative process, accountability will necessarily run in several directions – indeed to all interests represented in the policy-making process. It has been contended in this book that it is not possible to devise a really satisfying apparatus of accountability unless multiple, shifting objectives give way to a single, stable, overriding one.

Another argument advanced in chapter 7 was that one cannot successfully undertake privatization, or the comprehensive corporatization described in this chapter, with any single, stable, overriding objective other than profitability, or economic efficiency. One can specify objectives such as passenger-mile maximization per unit of subsidy or Qualy – one can adopt numerous mechanisms from the private and nationalized sectors. And they should improve efficiency. But one cannot in practice achieve the maximization of such objectives, redefining both allocative and organizational inefficiency in ways which are consistent with those objectives, because the accounting methodology and, derived from that, the management techniques needed to provide a rigorous basis for controlling, monitoring and incentivizing non-profit-making public enterprises do not exist.

Often the best we can do for these other, non-commercial objectives is to give contracts or subsidies for their attainment to a commercially driven organization – which of course only transfers back to the subsidizer the problem of how he sets objectives, and monitors and controls them. As has been argued in chapter 9, unsustainability can be avoided, where the costs of any such multiple objectives are not negligible, if somebody, usually government, pays subsidies to the enterprise to the extent that all its activities may become profitable. Therefore, in principle it may be possible to continue to realize non-profit objectives with privatization of supply.

Some critics have argued that government can get a better service from private firms than from public agencies because private firms will do anything at a price while public agencies may resist such requests, especially if they expect to have to meet the costs involved from their own resources.[55] But whether the arrangement is with a private or with a public firm it does not solve the problem that there remains a conflict between the objectives of the supplier and those of the client. One can of course, as we have seen, specify a contract,[56] but there are problems in doing so, similar to those discussed in relation to franchising in chapter 3. Such contracts are easier to specify for short periods, for enterprises whose capital investment is either not long-lived or not specific to that industry and where the quality of the good or service required can be clearly described and priced. Above all, it requires that the public client does not change its mind over what it wants from the provider. Where such difficulties are severe, successful privatization may be difficult. There are private firms, especially in the defence industry, which could not continue in business if it were not for government subsidy, in the sense that government could get the service or similar products from other, usually foreign, companies at a lower price if it so chose. However, as many Third World countries have found, a private firm which substantially depends on the public sector for its business is likely to lose its real independence whatever its ownership.[57] Where a nationalized industry is substantially a vehicle for subsidized social services which survive as an act of political will – the railways and London Regional Transport are perhaps the outstanding examples in Britain – a more effective continuing relationship has always seemed easier between a government department and a public enterprise, unless and until a government is ready to specify much more clearly than has been customary with public enterprise, and in contractual form, what levels and quantities of goods and services it wants supplied.

There are therefore areas where both privatization or fundamental public-sector reform as described in this chapter may result in as many problems as they solve: those where the objectives are not profitability or economic efficiency. Where objectives are capable of being clearly defined and expressed and there is the political will to give their expression some permanence, it should be possible to create management and financial structures, techniques and information, to enable organizations with such objectives to enjoy economies of scale and scope. But, by assumption, there will be bodies with other, more-variable objectives for which this is not possible. Similarly, neither privatization nor public enterprise reform as defined above is possible where the contract between client and supplier becomes too complex for efficiency.

The case for retaining public enterprise is greatest where its objectives cannot be converted into profit-making terms and where comparatively simple contracts with privatized or corporatized bodies cannot be used to attain required social and political objectives.

If the overriding objective of a public or privatized enterprise is to be profitability, or economic efficiency, then almost the same changes are required for reforming the traditional control of nationalized industries as are required for privatization. But privatization provides not only further stimuli to economic efficiency that public enterprise reform may not, or cannot, match, but also the prospect of irreversibility Nevertheless, ultimately the choice between public enterprise reform and privatization may well depend on the greater political possibility of achieving one rather than the other, and this will depend on local circumstances, though it can also be said that in general the introduction of a programme of privatization or corporatization is in most countries more likely to depend on the existence of sustained and acute economic crisis than on politicians' becoming sufficiently interested in the merits of either as means of contributing to economic efficiency; and that during such a crisis the proceeds of privatization are likely to give it favour over corporatization. There is also, however, a considerable risk that, whichever is chosen, it will not be accompanied by the other measures needed to make it efficient.

Notes

1 Tawney (1921), p. 187.
2 Moore (1986a). Reformed public enterprise as about to be described may be expected to be profit-seeking, though in principle it may be required to pursue economic efficiency where there is a difference – they will only be the same in the absence of market failure. The approach taken in this chapter may be contrasted with that taken by Bos and Peters (1991), pp. 26–52, who assume that, because of their more complex goals, public organizations, by comparison with private ones, necessarily provide more complex principal-agent problems.
3 Russell (1990), pp. 161–84, has said that the long-standing financial embarrassment of the Crown, caused by a steep rise in the cost of war and the refusal of the Commons to increase taxes to match, was a cause of the Civil War. Whenever it could, despite recurrent statutory prohibitions, the Crown raised money or recompensed its servants by establishing monopolies, sharing the profits with the monopolist.
4 HM Treasury (1984).
5 A similar approach was adopted in the State Owned Enterprises Act (New Zealand), 1986. In this act, the most far reaching model for pubic enterprise reform (without any original intent to privatize), the reformed public enterprises were set up as Companies' Act companies but with all shares owned by the Crown. Uncommercial activities required by ministers were to be paid for by the State. In the event, the New Zealand government also began to sell shares in these enterprises, mainly because it needed the money.
6 Kay and Thompson (1987), p. 193. See also Bishop and Kay (1988), which stresses the need for competition and argues for the possibility of economically efficient public enterprise reform.
7 It is convenient that the theory of shadow prices worked out for investment appraisal in protected less-developed countries is relevant, *mutatis mutandis*, to the evaluation of firms there for privatization or public enterprise reform: Little and Mirrlees (1969); Dasgupta,

Sen and Marglin (1972). For an adaptation of that cost-benefit analysis to privatization, see Jones, Tandon and Vogelsang (1990). For a different approach, see Ickes (1990).

8 Montesquieu (1748), bk. 11, ch. 6. On the present connection between the sovereignty of Parliament and the separation of powers, see A. W. Bradley (1989), pp. 25–52.

9 Rees (1986), p. 19, rightly sees 'privatisation . . . as the transition from one institutional mode of dealing with the failure of the market mechanism to allocate resources efficiently to another. Regulation by government department . . . is to be replaced with regulation by a quasi-governmental public agency.' But the advantages of doing this do not depend on privatization.

10 Cf. NEDO (1976); Prosser (1986); A. J. Harrison (1988).

11 HM Treasury (1986).

12 Rappaport (1986), *passim*.

13 Beesley and Littlechild (1986), pp. 18– .

14 State Owned Enterprises Act (New Zealand), 1986, s. 7.

15 Holland (1972), *passim*, but esp. chs 11 and 12.

16 SCNI (1968), vol. 1, pp. 135–7; vol. 2, qu. 334; Kelf-Cohen (1969), pp. 196–7; Grieve Smith (1982), who urges particularly the vagaries of government policy as making such a guarantee essential.

17 Waterson (1988), pp. 54, 55; also Rees (1986); Waterson (1991). It is theoretically possible to provide incentives which encourage the pursuit of objectives other than profitability – for example, economic efficiency. But since they constrain profitability they will be resisted by rational profit-seeking firms. For the regulator to get information to discover whether the firm is doing what he wants and to prove that it is not overriding his incentives with others of its own will be difficult: see Waterson (1988), pp. 73ff., for a useful summary account; also Berg and Tschirhart (1988), pp. 505–20.

18 Likierman and Bloomfield (1987), p. 116.

19 Blanchflower and Oswald (1988); K. Bradley and A. Gelb, (1986).

20 HM Treasury (1984), p. 6.

21 The Water Act, 1989, s. 11(4), specifically provides for government to step in to provide continuity in supplying an essential service if a water undertaking should fail.

22 It has been said that the Heath government learnt that not assuming a government guarantee involved it in more trouble and expense when the Mersey Docks and Harbour Board went bankrupt than it would have been involved in if it had assumed one.

23 Kay (1987), p. 26.

24 Vickers and Yarrow (1985), pp. 6, 7, are right to point out that, however strong the incentives, the misuse of the government's shareholding could facilitate state control, but such misuse is an abuse of the Companies' Acts.

25 Beesley and Littlechild (1986), p. 44.

26 Rees (1986).

27 Graham and Prosser (1988), pp. 82–6.

28 Rees (1986), p. 23.

29 Quoted in Veljanovski (1987), p. 3.

30 Littlechild (1981). George Jones believes that New Zealand corporatization will not work, because where the Crown owns ministers will interfere whenever they choose to do so: G. W. Jones (1987), p. 26.

31 Brennan and Buchanan (1977).

32 Buchanan, Burtin and Wagner (1978). On the problems raised by economic constitution making, see Heald (1983), pp. 270–4.

33 See the papers in McKenzie (1984).

34 One reason for believing that the problems are similar in British commonwealth countries and others influenced by the British administrative tradition is that there was once an almost slavish copying of British legislation, institutions and regulations in such countries.

35 Aylen (1987), p. 15.
36 Sandbrook (1988), pp. 162ff.
37 Commander and Killick (1988), pp. 111–17.
38 Savas (1987), p. 25.
39 Hannah (1983), pp. 128–32; May (1972), pp. 178, 179.
40 Hannah (1983), p. 78.
41 Tawney (1921), p. 207. C. A. R. Crosland in *The Future of Socialism* (1956) was following this tradition when he said that the divorce of management and ownership which James Burnham had pointed out in his *Managerial Revolution* had made private ownership irrelevant: Morgan (1985), p. 140.
42 Tawney (1921), pp. 202, 204.
43 Middlemas (1979), p. 178; also Hannah (1979).
44 Crew and Rowley (1989). On how the diseconomies of the central-planning process tend to create large monopolies and both exit and entry restrictions, see Ickes (1990), pp. 59–60.
45 Hannah (1983), ch. 3.
46 Middlemas (1979), pp. 174–213.
47 Sandbrook (1988), *passim*.
48 On the prerequisites of privatization in developing countries, see Aylen (1987), pp. 21–30.
49 Jones, Tandon and Vogelsang (1990), ch. 1 and *passim*.
50 See Savas (1987), p. 19.
51 Hannah (1983), ch. 4.
52 Cook and Kirkpatrick (1988), pp. 27–31; Aylen (1987), pp. 27–30.
53 Garner (1988), pp. 27, 28; Commander and Killick (1988), pp. 108–9; Savas (1987), p. 108; Bos and Peters (1991).
54 SCNI (1968), vol. , p. 189.
55 Wilson and Reichal (1977).
56 There has been a long history of planning agreements between government and state enterprises in France, agreements which led to greater clarity about objectives than in Britain but which were still often broken by acts of government policy. Such agreements tended to be more successful with private than with public firms. But they ran into difficulties as well when what government wanted was not economic efficiency. See Green (1982).
57 Graham and Prosser (1987) argue that contracts, where an important source of income to private firms, could be used to help governments gain control over them in a wide sense, citing, for example, the case where the British government remains BT's largest customer.

11

Can the regulator's independence be preserved?

> In the history of no country has there been such a barefaced sacrifice of the public interests for the benefit of private associations who, without any efficient restraint or restriction, have been suffered to monopolise, and for their own selfish purposes to employ, the means of communication of a great industrial nation.
>
> James Morrison (1848)[1]

In chapter 9 it was concluded that a regulator is more likely to keep the independence he needs in order to use his discretion if he narrows his task down as far as possible to economic regulation; if, having inherited from the past a weight of social obligations, he manages them until competition increases to the point where it eliminates the need for his role as a natural-monopoly regulator rather than himself become a social policy-maker; if he defines the consumer's interest, and safety, environmental and any other external interests, in a context of economic efficiency; and if he leaves to ministers what is theirs, while they leave economic regulation to him.

Yet it has been argued by some economists that even on these conditions regulators will lose, if they ever had, their independence, and even that this is a demonstrable truth. That will be denied here. Rather, it will be maintained that the histories of how regulators have lost, or have never had independence, yield lessons for the design of regulatory systems which may help regulators to increase their independence and retain it longer.

The practical reasons that make it necessary to give regulators discretion mean that one cannot then secure that their discretion is used in any predetermined way. This is a central dilemma of economic regulation. Ultimately, one supposes, having set up a regulatory framework which tries to establish the limits of that discretion and having chosen a regulator, one will leave the regulator to use it, unless he is changed, where that is possible, or the legislation is altered. The probability of such a legal change and its outcome for regulatory capture will depend on current political circumstances.

Section 1 contrasts some normative theories of regulation, particularly that which underlies this book, with some predictive theories that maintain that regulators are necessarily captured by the industries they regulate. That hypothesis is tested in section 2 against the facts, especially those of recent US deregulation. An alternative theory is considered in section 3 which allows weight to be given to political factors. Section 4 denies that regulators necessarily lose their independence. There can be scope for discretion. However, such theories do yield useful insights for the design of regulatory systems. Section 5 sets out some ways in which regulatory capture can be kept at bay in the new British system.

11.1   The purpose of regulation: the Chicago theory

Can one devise a plausible theory of regulation to explain the motives, and therefore the decisions, of those who have regulatory discretion? Different disciplines have advanced their own theories: historical, legal, political scientific, organizational theoretic, economic.[2] Thus an economist will generally see the normal purpose of regulation as improving economic efficiency; a political scientist will be more interested in how regulation responds to politics and politicians; and a lawyer will be more concerned with how far a system of regulation conforms to, or departs from, what he regards as a workable legal process.

While commentators with different academic backgrounds may understandably approach a problem of common interest with different ideas on what kinds of explanation may work, the first question for all of them must be why a theory is wanted. A first distinction here is between normative theories, whose purpose is to tell, or perhaps persuade, regulators what they should do, and those theories whose purpose is to explain and predict what actually happens.

The best-known normative theory of regulation is the 'public interest' theory.[3] It so happens that historically it has had an important role in both UK nationalization and US and UK regulation. As we have seen, the Morrisonian concept was that the objective or norm of a nationalized industry was that it should use any surplus it might make to serve the public interest.[4] And US regulatory agencies, especially those established in the 1930s, were also given the overriding objective of serving the 'public interest'.[5] In Britain, until 1979, the political performance of the nationalized industries, despite rumblings, was generally acceptable to ministers. The Morrisonian solution was that the boards of nationalized industries should decide what they meant by the 'public interest' in consultation with their sponsoring ministers. The discretion of the US regulatory agencies was greater in that they did not have to consult with the President or officials over its interpretation; and though the scope for interpretation was limited by the courts they still allowed considerable discretion. In neither case therefore can 'public interest' theory sensibly be called a genuine normative theory, since the relevant statutes gave the phrase no definite meaning. It was an 'empty box'.[6] It could be used to justify any reasonably dignified objective that a nationalized industry or regulatory agency pursued, though unlike the UK nationalized industries the US regulators had to develop and defend publicly an interpretation of the public interest, because of the public nature of their hearings and the possibility of appeal.[7]

The notion pursued in this book that the overriding purpose of economic regulation should be economic efficiency is also a normative one: the discussion here of the criteria for a well-designed system of regulation outlines what regime of economic regulation is needed to achieve economic efficiency, while the appraisal of

British regulatory legislation contrasts that legislation with the requirements of effective economic regulation. But throughout the book there are observations, intended to be predictive rather than normative, on the likely consequences in practice of pursuing various regulatory policies within given regulatory frameworks, though unlike some other theories to be discussed it assumes that legislatures, ministers and regulators have some freedom to choose their behaviour, and that those who design regulatory frameworks have some freedom in the constraints they place on that behaviour.

That the regulatory powers and duties the law lays down will be freely adopted by those to whom they are given, and will be exercised disinterestedly, is the assumption upon which white papers and legislation are drawn up and by which the issues raised by them are mostly discussed. However, one cannot be satisfied with a normative theory of regulation, whatever its content, without considering what is likely to happen in practice, for that may well involve radical departures from the public interest, however that is defined.

Among those who discuss policy there is often the greatest reluctance to depart from normative theory. Yet no historian would write history without at least considering explanations which rely on other than disinterested, obedient behaviour by the major parties concerned; and, as we shall see, since Stigler's seminal 1971 article many economists have gone further to assert that, whatever the form of the regulatory system and however regulators behave, their behaviour can be predicted, which, if true, would make much of the discussion of the aims and intended consequences of regulation and legislation a waste of time. The behavioural theory which has had most support over many years has been the theory of regulatory capture by the regulated industry. It began in political science and public administration.[8] The evidence to support the notion that a regulator will be captured by the regulated industry has been of several kinds:

1   Evidence of intent, of which among the earliest and most notorious example was the often-quoted letter of Attorney-General Richard Olney to the President of the Chicago, Burlington and Quincy Railroad in which he tried to dissuade railroad leaders from exterminating the fledgeling Interstate Commerce Commission by urging them instead to 'utilize' the agency.[9]
2   Evidence that regulators often came from, and returned to, the industries they regulated which, it was argued, gave them a tendency to identify with the industry.
3   As US regulators often were practising lawyers at those times in their careers when they were not regulators, or regulatory officials, self-interest provides a plausible reason for their prolonging the length of regulatory proceedings and enlarging their staffs, as has happened in the United States. One does not need to look further to explain the apparently inexorable tendency of regulatory – or for that matter, judicial – proceedings to lengthen.
4   It also tends to be the case that the longer the proceedings and the more established the rights any party has to put in as much evidence as it chooses, the more likely it is that the regulated industry will get its own way, because it has the most information and resources.
5   Observations, several reported in this book, that the regulatory outcome was

consistent with supposing regulatory capture. A regulated industry has many incentives to capture a regulator. And it can attempt this by influencing the relevant legislation, by securing the appointment of a sympathetic regulator, by influencing the proceedings and by using any machinery of appeal from it.

There are several variants of the theory. There is *life-cycle* theory, which tends to suggest that a regulatory body may start by using its discretion independently, but will progressively be captured.[10] Then there is *conspiracy* theory, which sees the initial legislation as inspired by a conspiracy between the regulated and other interests at the expense of the consumer.[11] Its presumption tends therefore to be that there has been capture from the start. In 1940, H. M. Gray had noted that big business had championed regulation where attempts to restrict competition through mergers had failed them, and from this he developed his conspiracy theory of regulation.[12] In 1969, T. Lowi had advanced an influential version of the capture theory that said that the problem was that regulators were given conflicting goals which could only be met by their ceding discretionary power: 'administrative discretion became a form of bargaining that favored the powerful and the organized'.[13] Finally, various *Marxist* theories take this in another direction by postulating that the function of regulation is to preserve the capitalist system by buying off potentially damaging opposition. Although those variant theories are useful in the insights they suggest into the workings of capture, they need not detain us. Though these are sensible interpretations of many of the facts that were visible to participants or commentators, generally they do not amount to a testable theory or hypothesis in that they do not define rigorously the circumstances in which there will be regulatory capture. At times one theory seems most illuminating. At other times, another.

The first rigorous contribution here was that of the Chicago economist George Stigler, who in 1971 said that, 'The central tasks of the theory of economic regulation are to explain who will receive the benefits or burdens of regulation, what form regulation will take and the effect of regulation upon the allocation of resources'.[14] He was led to his theory by empirical studies in which he was involved which had concluded that a regulated industry is no more efficient than an unregulated industry, nor are its prices lower.[15] His 1971 theory, which in 1976 was developed and given a more formal expression by another Chicago economist, S. Peltzmann, had three main strands.[16] The first tied the analysis to market failure. Where there is natural monopoly or another failure of competition, there will be a monopoly profit, which in an unregulated situation belongs to the monopolist. Initially the legislature and then, by delegation from it, the regulator are given a legal monopoly to decide what is to be done with that profit. The regulated industry therefore has an economic incentive to attempt to influence the legislation setting up the regulatory regime and defining the regulator's power so that the regulatory framework established is as favourable to the industry as possible. Thereafter, the same incentive leads it to attempt to influence the regulatory agency's activities as much as it can. Indeed, the various interested parties compete with each other to influence legislators and regulators in their favour. At all levels there will be 'markets' for regulation.

While this explained the nature of the arena and of the contest to be fought there, the second strand to the theory made a prediction of the outcome. This was that the regulator will as a rule be captured by the regulated industry, because the latter has most to lose or gain. A rational industry is ready to spend up to the full extent of its monopoly profits to retain at least some of these profits, of which it is in the interest of the legislators who have the power to enact regulation to make as good an estimate as they can so as to be able to appropriate as much of them as possible. If it were possible for those legislators to deliver a non-discretionary system which would otherwise secure the monopolist his full profits, a majority of them would negotiate with the monopoly and in the limit pocket just short of that total monopoly profit, leaving the monopoly with no supernormal profits. If for technical reasons the legislators cannot deliver such a system, then they will get less, corresponding to the value of what they can deliver. For the natural monopoly will need to retain enough monopoly profit to be able also to influence the regulator, when established, to use his discretion in the monopoly's interest. He, too, is an income maximizer. If he does not share in the profit, he too has no incentive to favour the monopoly. Provided that the value of the favours that he and the legislators receive does not exceed the monopoly profit, the monopoly's investment is worthwhile. By an argument which goes back to Ricardo, providing that the concern earns at least normal profits it remains rational for the monopoly to continue to produce the output that it would produce if its monopoly profits were not taxed away.[17]

The third strand was pure Chicago in that it added the further prediction that the outcome, regulatory capture, would be economically efficient. Whether the regulator or the legislature received a cut or not, the output and prices of a regulated industry would be virtually the same. The difference would be in the distribution of income between the parties only. Alternatively, it may be argued in the tradition of Williamson (chapter 5) that regulation will be a more efficient method of organizing transactions between consumers and firms, as well as between firms, in a natural monopoly market than either internalizing them within a larger, free-standing monopoly or leaving them as external transactions between firms of unequal market power.[18]

Taken together the three strands of the argument depend on strong assumptions characteristic of the Chicago school of economists. First, all interests concerned – the monopoly, the legislators, the regulators, even the consumers – are assumed to be pure examples of economic man. That is, they are assumed to be income maximizers. For example, according to this view of the world, politicians may seem to want political support, for instance help in getting votes or political advancement, but that is a veil: they are using both as a means to help maximize their cash incomes, given the talents they have. It follows from this assumption that the monopoly is perfectly efficient: there is no X-inefficiency or organizational failure.[19]

Secondly all parties are assumed to have rational expectations. That is, it is assumed that they use all available information in order to put the most accurate value on the discounted value of the monopoly profits which are under negotiation. Because they are as well informed as possible, given the available information, and learn from experience, their valuations do not differ much.

Thirdly, in the earlier formulations of the theory regulation is assumed to be costless. If the costs of regulation are non-existent or negligible, then it follows from the first two assumptions that, while the distribution of monopoly profits between the parties will be different if there is regulation, economic efficiency will not be affected. But if there were substantial costs of regulation they would reduce the efficiency of the industry. Stigler had recognized the possibility of such costs but had treated them as small and therefore negligible. Peltzmann pointed out the implications of recognizing the unreality of this last assumption.[20] There are the costs of the regulatory process itself both for the regulator and for the regulated. And there are also the costs for all parties and for the legislature in devising a regulatory framework. Moreover, the form of regulation itself is likely to have a distorting effect on the efficiency of the industry. Even so, in the formulations of the theory by Stigler, Peltzmann and Becker,[21] the presumption was that regulatory capture by the regulated will be a more efficient outcome than any other, whether or not it involves substantial regulatory costs. Indeed, it was maintained that this had to be so or that an alternative would have been chosen.

Paradoxically, the implicit conclusion of this version of the Chicago theory, which started off as hostile to regulation, as to most other forms of government intervention, was conservative and as such against any deliberate change. Underlying the Stigler analysis was the perception that where there is natural monopoly there is no other more efficient possibility. Thus, given his assumptions, even though there will usually be some efficiency losses through less-than-optimal pricing policies, in general the issue where there is regulated natural monopoly is not how to increase efficiency but how the profits, the benefits, are to be shared. This view, which was only implicit in Stigler's 1971 article, and therefore did not affect his wider reputation as an opponent of regulation, became clearer in articles by Peltzmann and perhaps clearest, because of his opposition to the conservative conclusion, in articles by Posner.[22] The underlying defence of a status quo, including regulation, in Stigler's classic 1971 article was easily missed. The general effect of the Chicago theory was to reinforce the campaign against regulation.[23] Hence Posner, on the other hand, was explicit in his opposition. He believed that the regulatory process, particularly restrictions on entry, stops regulated markets from being efficient and from responding to changes in demand and technology. He argued that the costs of monopoly are deadweight costs without any corresponding benefit. And regulation does not merely transfer income from shareholders to politicians and regulators; it reduces, and its abolition would increase, even optimize, economic efficiency.[24]

11.2 How and why American deregulation occurred

The strength of the Chicago theory, and to some extent its ability to explain facts, was tested by the deregulation movement in the United States in the 1970s and 1980s. Two political scientists who have analysed that movement, which started to receive effective political backing in the mid-1970s, described four stages in its realization.[25] There had to be first the capture of substantial elite – that is, mainly academic and professional – opinion, which meant, practically though paradoxically, the growing acceptance of Chicago-influenced ideas about regulation. This initial movement then needed political, even presidential, support. When that was achieved, regulatory appointments were made which resulted in substantial deregulation – though without legislation. To deregulate further, and permanently, there also had to be acceptance by a majority in Congress.

By the early 1970s, it could be written that, 'I know of no major industrial scholarly work done by an economist or political scientist or lawyer in the past ten years that reaches the conclusion that a particular industry would operate less efficiently and equitably [without] than with regulation'.[26] Opposition to the regulatory system among economists had started in the late 1950s and early 1960s. Just as Acworth and his band of regulatory economists, mostly at the London School of Economics, had been isolated from other British economic thinking, so the much larger numbers of American economists interested in regulatory commissions had been separated from the economic mainstream.[27] They were to be found in odd corners of most American universities and business schools, but writing for different journals, lecturing to different students and compromising with the incoherence of the processes they were appraising. This last they had to do if they were to have any influence on the regulatory agencies. Much of their time was spent indeed giving evidence to them as expert witnesses. Again as in Britain, they derived their intellectual lineage from the so-called 'institutional' school of economists – men like Ely, Commons, the Clarks and Wesley C. Mitchell.[28] This school held the perfectly reasonable belief that good economics starts with the attempt to gain a deep understanding of the nature and operations of the institutions being examined; but they failed to develop theories from this that were capable of generalization. Instead, they slipped into a patchwork of pragmatism. And on the main battlefields of economics they had been worsted by more-theoretical schools, first the neo-classical and then the Keynesian. By the 1950s, regulation was one of their last strongholds. They were finally defeated there because of the explosion in the number and quality of professional economists in the 1950s and 1960s at the same time as, under the methodological influence of the philosopher of science Karl Popper, the view gained ground that, as in the physical sciences, progress in economics depends on the testing of well-thought-out hypotheses.[29] Economists trained in the use of analytic and statistical techniques were keen to quarry new areas for their PhDs and began to ask questions that had previously been taken for granted. For example, if regulation is intended to be in the consumer's interest then in general one would expect regulation to be correlated with lower prices and more efficiency. Is this found to be the case? One investigation after another found no evidence that regulation in fact had led to greater efficiency and some that it had not.[30] Some economists believed that the regulatory agencies (like government departments in Britain) could be persuaded through the power of reason to do better.[31] They deplored the concentration of classical regulation on the issues of a fair rate of return, non-discriminatory pricing, the avoidance of wasteful competition, the protection of smaller players and so forth as fundamentally non-economic though dressed up as economic. In their place they urged regulatory commissions mainly to establish how prices stood in relation to marginal cost.[32] The main difficulty for those who held this position was the same as that for their counterparts in Britain urging the adoption of marginal-cost pricing for nationalized industries: it was hard to get the data to establish what marginal costs were; or indeed to agree on definitions.[33] The relevant data were not normally produced and where they were they were generally regarded as confidential. They were not produced by normal accounting systems. As a result, arguments before regulatory commissions about marginal costs could become as lengthy, inconsistent and arbitrary as had been the arguments about fair value.[34]

Thus, towards the end of the 1960s the emphasis shifted from imposing marginal-cost pricing towards a greater reliance on competition, to be achieved through freedom of entry. Indeed, during the 1960s several economists attacked all prohibition on entry.[35] There were many regulated industries in which there were a large number of firms which quite wrongly had been treated as natural monopolies. The outstanding examples were airlines and trucking. There were also industries where it was obvious or arguable that bits of them were not an essential part of the core natural monopoly or where technical progress was undermining the case for natural monopoly. Examples of the last were telecommunications, radio and television. In discussing this issue, more careful attention than had been given before was directed to defining the essential properties of natural monopoly.[36] Many economists followed W. J. Baumol and maintained that removing barriers to entry, attending to marginal-cost pricing so as to avoid predatory behaviour, and checking periodically to ensure that rates of return are not excessive are all the regulation needed where natural monopoly exists.[37] Where it does not, the whole regulatory apparatus can be dismantled.

Some went further than this, arguing that all regulation is unnecessary provided that freedom of entry is restored.[38] All that is achieved by limiting the rate of return on the natural monopoly is the blunting of incentives to enter that market. There is nothing inefficient about an early entrant into a market earning 'excessive' returns, provided that anyone can enter to compete those profits away. Moreover, the very existence of high profitability is an incentive to technical and managerial innovation. It had been, for example, with IBM; and many had tried, and some had succeeded, in challenging its supremacy. The policy of limiting the profits of a successful monopoly had, they argued, always been misconceived. Doing so had been no more than a political act, born of envy. To the counter-argument that this ignored the possibility, indeed the fact, of organizational failure of the kind that Oliver Williamson had described, the robust answer was that the right way of dealing with that is through the possibility of takeover: no natural monopoly should be immune from that threat.

Some members of the Chicago school, which tended to support that kind of argument, also argued against any anti-trust legislation. And the same line of thinking that in the 1970s had maintained that no government macroeconomic policy could work or would be attempted given rational expectations argued that the offences pursued by regulatory agencies, even predation, were equally the results of irrational behaviour. No rational firm would, for example, bring its prices below marginal cost to drive out predators unless it were in its long-run interest to do so.[39] And that would only be so if it were a more efficient firm than any newcomer. If the incumbent were to engage in predatory pricing without being more efficient than the newcomers, in the end the newcomers could win if they held on long enough, and even if one newcomer failed another, more efficient firm could replace it and win. Thus, in the absence of substantial sunk costs, social obligations and any artificial restriction on the pattern of prices, the most efficient solution should prevail without any regulation.

These economic arguments for deregulation tended to be normative. Economists and other critics of regulation argued as if the federal and state legislatures only had to be persuaded either to correct regulatory imperfections which had arisen from mistakes, accidents or perhaps the malicious or corrupt activities of some of the players in the regulatory game or to deregulate altogether. It was Stigler's achievement – he became a Nobel Prize winner – to question the assumption of the inexplicability in terms of rational behaviour of the imperfections of regulation, replacing that with the view that one can reach an understanding of why regulation occurs as it does by analysing it as a market in which the various players use their power to serve their own interests.[40] To appeal to regulators to behave in a more enlightened manner is, therefore, a waste of time. But as we have seen while he, and some of his associates, gradually reached the conclusion that regulation must be presumed to be efficient, he gave ammunition to many in their battle against regulation.

The view that the greatest incentive to become a regulator lay with those who had an interest or ambition in the industry concerned became commonplace. And indeed, there was no shortage of empirical evidence that a high proportion of regulators did pursue their later careers in the industries they had regulated.[41] By contrast, the representation of the interests of consumers was diffuse and therefore hard to shape into a political force. Thus it would have been surprising if regulatory decisions had not favoured the regulated. But while the economic arguments were the arguments that had mainly converted the professionals, not only economists, to the belief that regulatory reform or even deregulation was needed, lawyers had their own concerns with the regulatory framework, as had political scientists. Despite the Administrative Procedures Act, 1946, many lawyers felt that the procedures of regulatory agencies were commonly still arbitrary and legally defective.[42] And political scientists were concerned by the unrepresentative constitutional position of many powerful agencies, most only subject to elective politicians through their power of appointment and through legislation. Together they combined to create a large and effective group of critics.[43]

Among the factors which made this American revolution possible were a number which had weakened the regulatory process itself and therefore the regulated industries' attachment to it. For many of these the inflation of the 1970s was responsible.[44] Previous regulatory commissions, as we have seen, were able to project current expenditure and revenues on a simple linear basis. General regulatory reviews could be infrequent, because economic circumstances did not alter fast enough to affect industries or their customers severely. And it had not mattered that the agencies had insisted that the industries did not increase charges to reflect capital expenditure until the investments were producing returns. High rates of inflation strained these arrangements. The industries in these inflationary circumstances asked their agencies for more-frequent price reviews.[45] But as they had found no agreed method of inflation accounting, the result was either congestion in the review process or an arbitrary speeding up of the process. Many utilities ran into cash-flow problems and found it difficult to fund capital expenditure for the first time.[46] And at the same time attempts to keep prices down through prices and incomes policies meant that there was a political reluctance to allow rate increases.[47] Subject to political pressures, many regulatory agencies placed a disproportionate share of the price increases they allowed upon industrial consumers, who had fewer votes, fuelling their resentment and encouraging a backlash from them.[48] And because different agencies, even those regulating the same industries, were under different political and consumer pressures, their treatment of their industries became increasingly idiosyncratic and inconsistent (though always explicable in Chicago terms as the outcome of some combination of economic interests working through the political process).

The problem was at its worst in the electricity and gas industries. In the case of electricity it was compounded by the technical failure of nuclear power, where costs escalated many times not only because of rising interest rates but even more because of the apparently endless respecifications of nuclear power-stations required after Three Mile Island,[49] some power-stations as a result never being completed. At the same time, increases in oil prices disorganized the economics of power still further.[50] And gas utilities were similarly affected – by increases in the price of natural gas. Many oil and gas producers and distributors found that they had more new investments coming on than were needed at the new higher prices. The confusion pleased nobody. By precedent, utilities could only have been prevented from earning a reasonable return on all their investment if it could have been shown that its increased cost was a result of their mistakes, but nobody could reasonably have foreseen the effect of Three Mile Island or predicted the oil and gas price increases. However, political pressures did not allow all this extra cost to be passed through to the consumer, so that the outcome was an increase in the number of rate cases and a variety of fudges which left most power utilities with reduced real returns and less ability to fund investment.[51] And the industries were not helped by economic recession and changes in industrial structure reducing the demand for power below that they had initially forecast.

Another cause for dissatisfaction with the regulatory process was the opinion that most regulatory agencies did not adapt quickly enough to reflect technical change in the regulated industries.[52] This was most true in telecommunications, radio and television. This failure was perhaps resented most by unregulated firms that saw opportunities from the pursuit of which they were barred. But it also seemed deadening to the more technically progressive managers in the regulated industries themselves. And the growing fear of Japan's competitive ability in the United States and overseas strengthened this dissatisfaction.[53]

However, despite all these causes for disillusionment, in no case did a regulated industry prompt the deregulation that occurred, or, in its earlier stages, support it.[54] The influence of this disillusionment was more indirect. It made the regulated industries less effective as lobbyists in Washington, despite their resources.[55] It meant that Senators and Congressmen were more aware of the stresses and strains upon the regulatory system. It has been said that the failure of the Interstate Commerce Commission to avert the financial failure of the old and prestigious Pennsylvania Railroad in 1971 was a landmark in this regard.[56]

Of possibly more lasting importance was the growth of consumerism. Under Ralph Nader's leadership from the late 1960s, consumer representatives complained effectively that regulatory agencies were captives of their industries and that they did not give enough weight to the consumer's interest, in terms of lower prices, safety and a good environment.[57] Their initial efforts attacked both the people and the procedures involved. The people were vilified as mere political appointees whose main career before and after could well be in the industries regulated. And the consumerists were effective in persuading the courts and Congress to ensure that the procedures were altered so that consumer interests might be represented at hearings.[58] This further complicated and lengthened regulatory proceedings, increasing the uncertainty of the outcome. And what emerged was again likely to be inconsistent, because of differences in the receptiveness of different regulatory agencies to these consumerist pressures. Regulatory decisions thus became more obviously the result of the various and varying strengths of different pressure groups, that is, the result of a political process.[59]

Growing interest in the environment and safety had still wider effects. Between 1970 and 1981 the number of pages in the Federal Register increased in total from about 400,000 to over 1 million.[60] Most of this reflected new environmental and health and safety regulations. Many impinged on existing regulatory agencies directly since they had to take them into account. In other cases, new regulatory agencies were set up to administer them. Some twenty new federal regulatory agencies were created in the 1970s, or from a quarter to a third of the total number.[61] And the estimated total cost of regulatory activities to the economy increased from some 66 billion dollars in 1976 to about 100 billion in 1979.[62] The fact that many of the new agencies, and indeed some of the old ones with new responsibilities, now had to interact with other agencies making decisions which affected theirs (and vice versa) added to the incoherence of the outcome.

All this influenced the regulated industries' attitude to the regulatory process. The cost to them of the new consumer-inspired regulations made them anxious to support reforms which they hoped would reduce that cost, as well as less inclined to support the status quo, triggering during the 1970s a flow of funds from industry into right-wing think-tanks. However, these think-tanks' analyses tended to damn those parts of the regulatory system which the regulatory industries favoured while having less effect in limiting the increase in the development of consumer protection.[63] On this, the most that was achieved was a requirement, varied in form, introduced by Ford, Carter and Reagan that new regulations be supported by some form of cost-benefit analysis or impact study – which proved but a weak deterrent.[64] Despite the effort made by business, there was no environmental or safety deregulation for many years and even what was achieved at the end of the 1980s was limited. Thus the deregulation that regulated industries wanted, and lobbied for, they did not achieve. And what they got was of most interest to that small part of industry which gained new competitive opportunities.[65]

Another effect of the criticism of the regulatory framework was that for the first time there was a power in the regulatory process – the organized consumer movement – at least equal in its influence to that of the old regulated industries. An interesting and important issue is whether that equality of power is likely to continue. If it does it will prevent a renewal of regulatory capture by industry. And in so far as consumer politics remain influential regulation will not yield completely to deregulation. As Lester C. Thurow has said, reliance on regulation in the United States 'springs from our lack of other kinds of government involvement'.[66] Regulation appeals to a lawyer-dominated society. It also appeals to politicians because adding to lists of regulations is easy and can be made politically visible. Problems tend to arise later, with implementation.

Another reason for deregulation in the 1970s was a revulsion against the growth of government – and not only among Republicans.[67] As in Britain, successive administrations found it hard to cut the rate of growth of public expenditure. While in Britain that turned attention to privatization (which was impossible at the federal level in the United States because there were almost no public enterprises to privatize), regulation became the main target in the United States.[68] The fact that there were eighty-seven federal regulatory agencies, by some counts, as well as hundreds of state ones, and that there were, for example, eight regulating transport alone was marvellous material for political speeches, as were such facts as that, in its cases against MCI and Litton, AT&T supplied 12 million pages of documents, from which MCI's and Litton's lawyers had sifted 2 to 5 million pages as possibly relevant.[69]

While these factors account for general changes in political attitudes towards regulation, offsetting the importance to politicians of the regulatory agencies as sources of income, influence and jobs, they do not explain why particular deregulations took place when and in the way that they did. There were five deregulations of consequence: airlines, trucking, railroads, telecommunications and financial securities.[70] In the first three of these the course of events was similar. In 1974, Senator Edward Kennedy was Chairman of the Senate Subcommittee on Administrative Practice and Procedure, and was looking for a subject that would attract publicity.[71] Stephen Breyer, a professor of law at Harvard and later a federal judge, who became a staff member of that subcommittee, persuaded him, not without difficulty, that airline deregulation was a winner. A mass of academic work had been done demonstrating to the satisfaction of the interested academic community its futility and excessive cost. Preparation for the hearings was massive. Vast documents were produced. Questionnaires were sent in many directions. Considerable lobbying was done at various federal agencies and the White House in order to secure support. And the hearings were stage-managed effectively. The main result of such hearings was that they provided a rigorous test of the academic findings. Academics had suffered because they could never get enough data and because the bodies they criticized were under no obligation to reply. Before the Senate, both airlines and the Civil Aeronautics Board (CAB) had to reply. They were often shown to be wanting. The impression that emerged was of a process of regulation operating in the airline industry's interest, a process whose principles and decisions the CAB members often were unable to explain or justify. Clever stage-management gave these hearings wide publicity in the press. And President Ford cooperated by developing a government attitude which was strongly pro-competitive.[72] The outcome of this first stage was the emergence of a political consensus that deregulation was needed, despite the opposition of the airlines themselves. The next stage occurred on two levels. Within the Senate a bill was prepared which led eventually to the 1978 act which provided for airline deregulation and the termination of the CAB.[73] Outside it, President Ford and then President Carter made in their turn pro-competitive appointments to the chairmanship of the CAB (of which more later).

Senator Kennedy also presided some three years later (1977–8) over the same subcommittee when it considered the trucking industry.[74] And that scrutiny too led to deregulatory legislation and the appointment of a pro-competitive agency chairman. Congress was also involved in unearthing facts about telecommunications.[75] In that case, however, the industrial lobby was powerful enough to be able to prevent the passing of any legislation in favour of deregulation, though it could not secure any new legislative protection for the industry.

Successive US presidents were committed to regulatory reform and greater competition but Gerald Ford was in the almost unique position of being a man who became president without having had to give commitments to secure votes. Early on, he developed a strong resistance to industrial lobbying which defended the regulatory status quo, and kept it up even when those around him warned him that other presidents had stood out against the same interests at their peril. Ford helped prove them wrong, making it easier for Carter and Reagan also to stand up to such forces, though there were many occasions still where they had to knuckle under to the remaining strength of powerful regulated interests.

Airlines and trucking had the advantage from the point of view of those seeking their deregulation – airlines in appearance only – that they were not natural monopolies but 'structurally competitive' industries (in which competition was not allowed). While the railroads were local monopolies on their own, they had been subject to increasing competition, mainly from road transport, to the point where – some fifteen years later than in Britain – the industry realized that it lost more than it gained from traditional regulation. Thus the passing of the Staggers Act in 1980, which deregulated the railroads, was an exception to the rule that the industries did not approve deregulation.[76] Competition had been frozen in each case by legislation of the 1930s, when it was believed that 'unregulated competition would be destructive of the quality, continuity, reliability and safety of service as well as unacceptably discriminatory among various groups of customers.[77] Just as in Britain it has proved easier to privatize structurally competitive industries, so in the United States it has been easier to deregulate such industries.

What is striking to an Englishman is the exhaustive and admirable thoroughness of the research and analysis that were done in the United States, and arguably had to be done, to destabilize established political positions on matters of regulation. No act of Parliament, certainly no privatization statute, has been supported by one hundredth part of the same research and analysis in published form. Without question, the research that was done to analyse the case for, and forecast the consequences of, privatization has been meagre by comparison (though very substantial, pioneering research was done by several firms of consultants both during and after the passage of the privatization statute to make electricity interconnection possible). One result of an apparent need for greater research to underpin American legislation of a radical type is that it makes fundamental change more difficult, though the outcome should be more satisfactory. It is also relevant that such analysis had to be concerned with the distributional consequences of policy changes. That increases the chances of political disagreement and reduces the likelihood of agreement on deregulation.[78]

Arguably the most important function of Congress in promoting deregulation was the blaze of publicity it gave to such analyses and findings – that publicity which Charles Francis Adams had regarded as the real medium for regulation. The actual deregulation of the airlines was mostly achieved by the conversion of the regulatory agency itself through the appointment of two pro-competitive chairmen to head the Civil Aeronautics Board: John Robson by President Ford and Alfred Kahn by President Carter.[79] The very ambiguity of the original enabling statute of the CAB, which required it to pursue the 'public interest', gave them the legal power to change course dramatically towards deregulation.[80] A deregulating chairman of a regulatory agency was helped by the fact that over the years the chairmen had come to dominate the regulatory commissions, principally because of their greater access to staff resources and their ability to set priorities.[81] The main task of a deregulating chairman was still to persuade his fellow commissioners, enough of his staff and indeed the industries regulated to cooperate with him in his own wish to effect practical deregulation by making decisions which reduced the protection given incumbents. At the CAB, Kahn, a brilliant teacher and chairman, was masterly in changing attitudes there and preparing it for its own demise.[82] He argued for pricing freedom and freedom of entry. A number of decisions broke down the old cartels and agreements. Fares fell. And utilization increased. The notion that commissioners and staff would always identify with the regulated industry, because that was where their career prospects lay, was shown to be false. Many of the staff either saw part of their career as being in universities or research institutions or, if they did not, had been sufficiently influenced by the growing weight of elite professional opinion against regulation as practised. And most of the commissioners saw their careers elsewhere – in law, politics or academia.

It was the use of regulatory discretion to get deregulation started that helped give confidence to Congress to pass the 1978 act which provided for the end of the Civil Aeronautics Board. Since the termination of the CAB in 1982 there has been no economic regulation of airlines except as provided by general anti-trust laws. But the result has not been quite as predicted. A new hub-and-spoke operation pattern has emerged where, from each major airport, a major airline tends to dominate the flights, a main route having a hub at each end whose dominant airline will provide some competition for the one at the other end along the route. While it is arguable that the economics of this form of operation will make it difficult for other airlines to compete, it is possible that potential competition from free entry will keep costs and fares down to competitive levels. But it is also possible that in some shape or form regulation will have to be revived to police a new pattern of collusive monopoly if that emerges. Nevertheless, as Alfred Kahn himself has pointed out, the fact that not all of what has resulted has been as competitive as he and others hoped does not mean that the status quo ante was better.[83] It was not. What has been achieved through deregulation is a more efficient and lower cost industry.[84]

Deregulation of the trucking industry also began with academic analysis which concluded against regulation.[85] Senator Kennedy's examination of this and other evidence at hearings in the later 1970s was similar to what had happened in the case of the airlines, though it attracted less publicity, which may explain why trucking deregulation did not go as far. The intellectual case was also similar: high barriers kept new entrants out; old and artificial rate structures provided a 'high quality, high-cost' service with low utilization – high quality for which there was no evidence that the customer was ready to pay. And, again, opposition to deregulation from within the industry was almost 100 per cent. But the trucking industry was better organized to resist than the airlines had been. And in this case what mattered was not so much publicity as the conversion of a regulatory agency, the Interstate Commerce Commission (ICC), through the appointment of a new chairman, Darius Gaskins, who in his quiet way was as effective as Kahn and his colleagues had been in the CAB.[86] He also used his discretion to deregulate actively. As a result, so confusing were a series of new ICC piecemeal decisions coexisting with earlier decisions, that ultimately the main force for deregulation became the industry itself when it decided that it could not plan ahead given the transitional uncertainties. The outcome was quick: the Motor Carrier Act, 1980. Thus the deregulation of trucking occurred within five years of the Ford administration's first announcing it as its policy in 1975. The trucking interest had used all its influence to try to persuade Congress to pass a bill more favourable to it, employing massive lobbying to that end; and it did secure several amendments which were presented to the industry as preserving 'the basic concept and principles of economic regulation'. But the victory was an empty one. Regulation had all but gone: though some anti-competitive standards were retained, there was in general a removal of obstacles to entry.

Telecommunications differed from the other industries mentioned because it was plainly a natural monopoly.[87] Because AT&T dominated the industry and was enormously influential in Washington, deregulation took place over a longer period. What was intellectually important here was the realization that, though there was a natural monopoly in telecommunications, it did not cover all aspects of the legal monopoly that AT&T enjoyed. As early as 1968 the courts began to take away its legal monopoly over the provision of terminal equipment. And in 1969 a rival, MCI, was allowed to introduce competitive long distance services. There was as yet, however, no deregulation as such, since the Federal Communications Commission (FCC) insisted on continuing to control entry, to set standards and in general to employ the full apparatus of classical regulation. Moreover, at all stages AT&T fought the introduction of competition, using its enormous influence in Washington and employing its vast resources to battle in the courts. It was not until 1980, when the FCC stopped regulating 'enhanced services' which used computer technology, that it withdrew from any aspect of regulation. It also then deregulated the provision of terminal equipment, from the simple to the most complicated. And it became less interested in rate control. Again it is arguable that the regulatory body, in using its discretion to effect deregulatory or pro-competitive measures, was a more important agency for deregulation than was Congress, especially as Congress was unable to agree on any legislation which would determine the extent of competition or the limits of regulation in this field. When none of the bills that AT&T had tried to get through Congress in the 1970s, bills which were in many important respects anti-competitive, were passed, AT&T had no alternative but to come to terms with the increasingly pro-competitive attitude of the FCC. At the same time however the Justice Department was preparing a court action to break up AT&T as a monopoly trust, using as its justification AT&T's refusal to interconnect with other operators, its delaying tactics and its predatory behaviour. From then on it was a matter of negotiation, until in 1982 agreement was reached in the courts that AT&T would be broken up geographically, into regional operating companies, leaving AT&T's rump whose main business was long lines, where it was to be in competition with other long-line operators. Throughout these negotiations there had been deadlock in Congress. It was the FCC, the Justice Department and, most decisively, the courts which between them had brought about major structural change and deregulation in the industry.

While there are those who would argue that generally the movement towards deregulation has been a success, deregulation has been less fundamental outside the industries mentioned.[88] Attempts to deregulate, or rather to regulate more consistently or economically, the natural gas industry ran into disagreement in Congress. Despite a willingness to reform, President Carter's efforts ended in an economically unsatisfactory compromise. It is true that during the 1980s large customers became able to buy large quantities of gas at a discount from suppliers outside their normal franchise area; and the Federal Energy Regulatory Commission from 1987 has encouraged transmission companies to act as common carriers. And similarly there has also been a growth in electricity generation by companies other than the utilities, the deregulation of some bulk power sales and the requirement in some states that local electricity companies get supplies additional to those they themselves generate, by competitive tender. But while some aspects of gas, and electricity as well as oil, regulation have changed, principally because of the effects of inflation, oil and natural gas price increases and anxiety over nuclear safety, the basic form of rate-of-return regulation remains the same, and it is hard to maintain that there has been any material increase in competition. Such deregulation of broadcasting as has occurred has mainly been in the interests of the industry itself, in that it has got rid of constraints upon quality.[89] The regulatory agencies in telecommunications have continued to operate in the old way despite the break-up of AT&T.[90] Various attempts were made to cut out federal government control of wages in the construction industry, which operated through legislation that required the federal government to set minimum wage rates for federally aided construction. But legislative change proved impossible. In the end, deregulation came through the courts, allowing that the executive had discretion over whether or not to fix these minima. Despite attempts to cut support prices for milk during the 1970s, the farming interest was able to put up an effective resistance. No deregulation of shipping has been achieved. David Stockman, as Director of the Bureau of Budget, tried to introduce the cost-benefit analysis of air pollution control measures, but public opinion made it clear that it did not want environmental deregulation. Later, President Reagan made some progress in introducing economic tests for air pollution regulations, but the real effect of this was small.

Derthick and Quirk concluded, and subsequent events seem to have confirmed, that deregulation was easiest where the industry was structurally competitive, where it was fragmented and where it was possible to achieve enough deregulation through the appointment of willing regulators for some legislation to be seen by the industry itself to be needed to rationalize arrangements which that partial deregulation had made unsatisfactory to it.[91] However, unless the issue provided publicity and political capital that made it attractive to Senators, Congress was unlikely to alter the law. And indeed, arguably the greatest gift that Congress itself had to offer to the deregulatory movement was publicity at the pre-legislative stages. It would only legislate when the preparatory work had been done by others to the point where no strong defensive lobby survived. In the United States, where the industry concerned has remained strong and the regulatory agency has not brought about partial deregulation, it has proved impossible to pass legislation against the opposition of an industrial lobby, which shows how entrenched in Congress vested interests supporting the regulatory status quo have become – reminding one of the strength of the railway interest in Parliament in the nineteenth century. Such deregulation as has been achieved has been largely the result of a coalition between business and consumer interests who saw deregulation as a common means to different ends. Thus the deregulation that has been achieved has been partial. The main deregulations had been achieved by the mid-1980s, though one must not underrate the further progress made.[92]

There is a simple explanation why Britain initiated regulation while the United States deregulated. While Britain had nationalized, the United States had taken the alternative route of imposing substantial, heavy and frequently irrational economic regulation upon the same industries and on others. US regulators went far further than the regulation of natural monopoly and the prevention of unfair trading, into spurious economic regulation and palpable social regulation. The common intention behind recent British regulation and American deregulation has been to seek the minimum regulation natural monopoly and predation make necessary, though in regard to the situation in the United States that bald statement over-simplifies the interests of the various coalitions concerned.

11.3   Regulatory capture: the Virginian theory

Derthick and Quirk have suggested that the theory of regulatory capture by the regulated cannot explain what has happened in the United States since 1975.[93] We are here faced with the surprising result that an apparently well-supported theory yields a prediction which limits strictly the possibilities of change, yet that prediction is then defeated by change.[94] In every industry that was deregulated, almost every re-gulated firm was opposed to deregulation.[95] Thus, it is implausible that the regulated firms could not have outbid the resources of other interests to avoid deregulation if whether or not deregulation occurred depended on such an auction. They had much more at stake. Yet their undoubted lobbying was ineffective. What then is left of the original prediction? The deregulation of American public utilities that occurred after 1975 seems a genuine counter-example to the theory of regulatory capture - as were the contemporary privatizations in Britain – and as a result falsified the Stigler-Peltzmann version of the Chicago theory. Or, more strictly, the theory that there is a market for regulation as, for example, put forward by Stigler survives as a tautology but the further conclusion that capture is necessarily by the regulated has been falsified by those events. For that reason Derthick and Quirk, and Horwitz, were right to maintain that the economic theory of regulation in its simpler Chicago forms has been discredited.[96]

However, there is another way in which the Chicago theory has often been shown to be incomplete. Regulatory capture by the regulated can be achieved – but at a cost that is far from fully explicable in terms of the theory that predicts it. For example, early Victorian railway legislation seems to provide as plain an example of such re-gulatory capture as one can find. Here the regulatory 'market' operated mainly in Parliament: the railway companies had to get an act of Parliament to build a line since, to be able to obtain the land that they needed, they had to get compulsory-purchase powers; and not only was Parliament packed with railway directors, but the landed interest – which arguably had most to gain from the generous compensation paid for land bought for railway development – was overwhelmingly represented in both Houses.[97] And as a result of the strength of the landed interest in Parliament the compensation paid for land was greater than it would have been without the need for such a 'purchase' – leading to the high costs of over-capitalization which contemporaries observed. Thus far, what happened was consistent with the Chicago theory. But these costs were not the only price the railways paid for securing or retaining their legal position. We have seen how even the final, emasculated version of the 1844 Act contained a cornucopia of social provisions: the parliamentary train for the poor, a requirement that railways carry at special rates the mails and troops in certain circumstances. Yet one cannot reasonably argue that the then unfranchised, would-be users of cheap workman's trains had the financial muscle to 'purchase' these concessions in the 'market' of Parliament. To take an extreme example, there were furious and nearly successful arguments in the House of Lords – supported by Gladstone in the Commons – that the cheap trains should not run on Sundays, because of the damage they would do to workmen's souls by tempting them away from church (even though ordinary passenger trains ran on Sundays). That cannot be explained in terms of the financial interests of those concerned. Neither was it in the financial interest of the ministers responsible for defence and the posts to 'purchase' the duty of railways to carry troops and the mails at special rates against the stronger financial interest of the railways to avoid such duties. What gave some political urgency to the carriage of troops was that there had been a number of times in the previous thirty years – the Massacre of Peterloo, the Rebecca Riots and the revolutionary threats of 1830 – when contemporaries had believed that the country was on the brink of revolution. And in 1844 itself Chartism was on the increase. Anti-government feeling was building up to the point where there was a serious fear that the revolutionary currents that swept through Europe might be successful in Britain as well. Since there was no proper police force, troops were needed to meet these threats and trains were seen as a means of getting them to the scene of any riot quickly. Thus there were political reasons for contemplating imposing social obligations on the railways, but they did not put commensurate cash in the pockets of any party. (One can, of course, always say that the fear of the economic consequences of revolution explains the willingness to force the railways to carry troops – though there would be greater difficulty in explaining in Chicago terms the unwillingness to extend to Sundays the obligation to run a cheap train – but this would be to push the theory towards tautology.)[98] And much the same can be said of the safety measures that Charles Francis Adams was able to force on the Massachusetts railroads.

Towards the end of the nineteenth century, progressively more social obligations were placed on railways in Britain and America, and on other utilities. And yet again it is implausible to argue that this was done by vested interests with a longer purse to purchase these obligations than the industries had to resist them. Instead, one has what appear to be quasi-contracts where monopolies have bargained with legislators or regulators to retain some elements of monopoly profit for which they have had to pay by undertaking to meet various social and political obligations. Because of the growth of party discipline and the decline in private bills, Parliament changed from being a legislature in which MPs' individual votes mattered into a debating chamber. This meant that lobbying Parliament was no longer an effective method of regulatory capture, and that the prices it exacted for natural-monopoly legislation were increasingly social. But in the United States, Congress retained some of these characteristics of Parliament in the nineteenth century, in that the political and financial interests of individual Senators and Congressmen remained more important than party interest.[99] Until the last twenty years or so, while the consent of Congress to measures sought by the regulated industries was vital, and the obtaining of that consent had to be addressed by the traditional means available to the American lobbyist, the price Congress exacted for it was not generally acquiescence in the imposition of social obligations on the regulated or social duties on the regulator. Moreover, because the regulated industries in the United States have been distanced from politicians by the setting up of regulatory commissions, politicians have had less leverage thereafter with which to impose social obligations. What has mattered more in deciding the content of regulation has been who has captured the regulator. Again, the simple capture theory, which has been often borne out, is that it has been easy for the regulated industries to do this. They have done it by deploying superior information and resources before the regulator. And they have used legal procedures – usually when they have appealed to the courts they have won because the law is a conservative force mindful of the interest of property. But they have also been able to further the personal interest of regulators.

But, depending on how they are selected, regulators may have other pressures upon them. Peltzmann presumes that they are elected, which is sometimes true, and supposes that they have to get and retain political support: in which case, the regulated industries are likely to have to pay some political, rather than a purely career or financial, price for capture.[100] Becker sees pressure groups at work influencing voters and those who have been voted or appointed to office. Thus, how regulators are appointed, and therefore where their career ambitions lie, will affect the extent of capture and the kind of price that must be paid.[101] Civil servants and politicians will behave differently from lawyers and from those whose ambitions are more straightforwardly with the regulated industries – though, while the mechanics will be different, one may assume that there will always be ways in which regulated industries and other pressure groups may act so as to influence, even capture, regulation. Yet as soon as one tries to reformulate the Chicago theory to cope with legislatures, committees of legislatures, the executive, elected or appointed regulators – as soon as one tries to reflect in it the actual complexity of politics and administration – its predictive power evaporates: insights may remain and ingenious rationalizations can always be attempted, but generalization is elusive.

Another economic theory of regulation, deriving from the Virginian school of political economy, helps explains the burden of social obligation.[102] It agrees with the second and third strands of the Chicago theory, but then goes on to dispute the first. In the strictest Chicago version, legislators may aim to maximize votes and so ensure their return to power, but their personal wish is to maximize their income or wealth.[103] The Virginian theory allows other motives. In the more complex versions, both legislators and regulators are allowed to be seeking to maximize utility functions variously weighted in terms of expected votes or even ideology, as well as cash.[104] Thus a natural monopoly may be able to give up comparatively little cash, yet give politicians or regulators a return of greater value. By this argument – which can easily be extended to nationalized industries – regulated industries have a gift of particular value to make: they can use their powers of cross-subsidization to favour particular groups of interest to politicians by reducing prices or improving quality more than would be achieved by market forces.[105] And they can do this without the publicity or hassle of legislation.

By comparison with the Chicago theory, this theory involves a gain in realism. Historians and political scientists can recognize its close affinity with 'pressure group' theories of politics.[106] The formulation and enactment of the legislation needed to establish a regulatory framework and thereafter the activities of a regulator can be seen as occasions for 'markets' in which different interests compete for favours using whatever favours they have to offer in exchange. Trade continues until the marginal value to the politicians and regulator of the obligation assumed by the regulated industry equals its marginal financial cost to the industry. If the parties concerned trade obligations for cash rather than cash for cash, both sides will be better off: the regulated industry will gain because, by assumption, the value of the cash and non-cash benefits to politicians and regulator exceeds the cash costs to the industry of providing them, which the politicians and regulator must be better off from the transaction or they would not have engaged in it. (All this trading has, however, a price in lost economic efficiency, measured by comparison with what would occur in an unregulated market – a useful insight.)

Yet though this theory involves a gain in realism it loses in predictive power. The proponents of such a theory easily find themselves in a situation where, whatever the regulatory outcome, it can always be rationalized as the achievement of a political equilibrium between the various interests, an equilibrium in which no interest can be made better off without some other being made worse off because, if that were not so, then by assumption there would be a different outcome. Because one does not know what weight to give in each case to money, votes, ideology and other factors, some of which cannot be measured at all, one has no measures of comparative efficiency. And even where one can quantitatively compare the outcome with economic efficiency because the other factors can be expressed in terms of money, one does not know whether the relative economic inefficiency found is a dead-weight loss or the rational outcome of political forces, implying an efficiency alternative to economic efficiency.

The Chicago school's view is from its standpoint optimistic: Stigler, Peltzmann and Becker have argued that the outcome of regulation is generally not very inefficient; but even if regulation is a considerably less than efficient means of dealing with market failure, as Posner has argued, if one removes regulation then, according to Chicago assumptions, so strong are everyone's economic instincts that most of the inefficiency caused by regulation will be swept away. And the Chicago theory has been elaborated ingeniously to explain diverse regulatory phenomena as consistent with its principles of economic rationality and its conclusion of economic efficiency.[107] Moreover, many economists have used the basic Chicago approach of assuming that any regulatory outcome is the result of the interplay of economic interests to come up with ingenious and not implausible rationalizations of the status quo. However, though it is always possible to find some rationalization of any set of regulatory circumstances which is consistent with basic Chicago principles, as the explanations become more intricate it usually becomes progressively more difficult to resort to the praiseworthy Chicago practice of measuring the costs and benefits to the various parties involved so as to test the hypothesis. Thus the plausibility of the explanation proposed tends to turn on that of the underlying assumptions of economic rationality: that all parties are income maximizers and have rational expectations.[108] And there is always a danger of tautology in such explanations. If regulation is assumed, because it exists, to be the most efficient method of dealing with these examples of market failure, then it can easily be maintained that what is, is efficient. Anomalies are then explained away as some party's rational reaction to particular circumstances. As one of the ablest of the Chicago economists has written, 'the methods used to accomplish any given end tend to be the most efficient available in the public as well as in the market sector . . . This approach leaves little room for economists to suggest improved methods in the public section.'[109] This easily slides into a further tendency to explain away change similarly: what changes are needed to maintain economic efficiency are those which occur; whatever occurs is what is rational, needed and inevitable. In the limit, this can remove all point from the discussion of regulatory systems. Where the conclusions of the Chicago school assume such inevitable economic rationality of the status quo, however, and in whatever directions it changes, their analysis becomes *ex post* explanation and cannot influence the course of events. And they have a further difficulty in interpreting the economic efficiency of arrangements in countries with different constitutional and legal systems, some less democratic. Are all to be characterized as economically efficient? If not a higher analysis is required – but has not been supplied – to decide how one distinguishes between constitutional arrangements which allow economic efficiency and those which impair it.[110]

By contrast with Chicago optimism, the Virginian school is pessimistic. As sure as the Chicago school that economic efficiency is desirable, they observe a world in which the political equilibrium in the regulatory arena, reached through the interplay of pressure groups, departs markedly from the economic efficiency that would be achieved by market forces, yet because, by assumption, it serves the needs of those who have political and economic power it is in the normal course of events invulnerable to change. As several Virginians have noted, this theory can also easily justify the status quo, however inefficient it is: whatever is, is what is desired. And the most relevant conclusion that follows from this theory is that it is almost impossibly difficult to carry out planned changes towards greater economic efficiency. In F. H. Bradley's sceptical gloss on Candide, 'This is the best of all possible worlds and every evil in it is a necessary one.'[111] Such pessimism has led some Virginians to believe that the only way to achieve the liberation of market forces from the strait-jacket of vested interest is through crisis or revolution.[112] British privatization has been instanced as evidence of this: the argument being that it is only because of acute economic crisis that it happened.[113]

11.4   Is an independent regulator possible?

If one means by a theory of regulation a conceptual framework for the analysis of regulation, then the Chicago and Virginian notions of the regulatory arena as a market-place in which various parties bargain for the favours the legislature and other arms of government, including regulators, provide powerful rival methodologies which up to a point ask the same questions. And both have taught a lesson in demanding high standards of proof. The Chicago tradition in particular has made a great contribution to economics in this respect. However, demanding such a high standard of proof in the context of a structured theoretical framework that tries to capture the general functioning of regulatory behaviour can be disabling since, especially with regard to past events, it is easier to formulate rigorous explanatory hypotheses than to test them rigorously so as to supply the required empirical proofs.

Such hypotheses are hard to prove except to those predisposed to accept the assumptions made.[114] Moreover, where they are applied to explain more-complicated, particular circumstances – as they need to be – their structural form often becomes more complicated and less easily reducible to their basic form. As a consequence, any results tend to lack the generality that was the source of the attractiveness of the original theory. In such circumstances, either no theory succeeds or there is a tendency to fall back upon *a priori* reasoning: a Chicagoan will assume to be true whatever outcome seems most consistent with the assumption that all parties behave like economic man, while the Virginians will find most convenient whatever explanation seems to fit best their belief that the cause of economic efficiency is persistently undermined by politics. But is the only alternative to a rigorous explanation a form of explanation that will not enable one to make predictions that will be useful for the design of regulatory systems and to help guide regulatory behaviour?

In fact one has reason, in addition to those that have been given, for rejecting theories that depend on such narrow explanations of human behaviour. Both the Chicagoan and the Virginian theories can be interpreted as removing discretion from both legislatures and regulators. Yet one has no need to accept such regulatory determinism: Carsberg, McKinnon, Byatt, Littlechild and the Civil Aviation Authority do not have to be seen as puppets or dupes of impersonal forces. There are two reasons why one should not assume that regulation in the future will be as it has been in the past. The first derives from Popper's argument against historical inevitability, the belief there are universal laws of history. His argument, which seems irrefutable, is that, first, one cannot deny, both rationally and given the available evidence, that the course of human history is affected by increases in human knowledge;[115] secondly, there is no rational way of predicting what form the growth of human knowledge will take – we cannot know what we do not yet know – so we cannot know what effect the growth in human knowledge will have on history. We have therefore to reject any notion that there are immutable historical laws or explanations; or that there are predetermined courses of human development. Thus even if it were true that regulation has always been captured by the regulated, the growth of human knowledge may lead to the break-up of that pattern of behaviour.

In that spirit, Derthick and Quirk argue that American deregulation of the 1970s and 1980s was a triumph of economic ideas propagated by an elite and taken up by politicians.[116] However, there are various difficulties with this as a complete theory. First, the relationship between ideas and events is always complicated, so that to infer causation without explaining why times should have been propitious for certain ideas to be effective tends to leave the exact train of causation unexplained. Then, as a particular example of that difficulty, there is an unmet need to explain why some industries were deregulated and not others, when the same ideas were at work in both. Moreover, one can find no sufficiently influential campaign of ideas to explain comparable changes in Britain in the early 1980s – or in the United States in 1880s and the 1930s, when there also seem to have been discontinuities in the regulatory system. To say that an unpredicted change in behaviour may come about through a growth in human knowledge is in fact not the same as saying that the agent of change will be a campaign of ideas. There are many other ways in which experience can alter the behaviour of those who are the agents of change.

The second reason for challenging the assumption that the future pattern of regulatory behaviour will be the same as in the past is that capture has not always occurred. That being so, can one say anything about the circumstances in which the regulatory framework, or proposed changes in it, or the regulator will not be captured by the regulated industry? It is possible that there is no valid general theory and that one has to rely on normal historical explanations – that is, each one of these and other major changes in regulatory systems may well be explicable, but the explanations may be different in each case. There is nothing wrong with this. Indeed, one can feel fairly certain that the more one is driven to explain more fully the particular episodes of regulatory change which have been discussed in this book the more the explanations will become historical: that it will be found that particular individuals, unique combinations of circumstances and chance are vital parts of the explanation. As the historian H. A. L. Fisher said: 'Men . . . have discerned in history a plot, a rhythm, a predetermined pattern . . . I can see only one emergency following another . . . only one great fact with respect to which, since it is unique, there can be no generalisations.'[117] The disadvantage with this is that, if no generalization can be made, prediction is impossible even in terms of probabilities.

Nevertheless, even if we could do no better than this, we would still have an apparently robust theory of regulation: regulatory capture is the norm – and the fact that the regulated industry normally has much to gain from capture is a sufficient, *a priori* reason for believing that there will always be a persistent tendency to capture – but occasionally there are episodes of major change which cannot be explained in terms of capture theory. On these lines Horwitz has what he calls a *dysfunctional* theory of regulation. Such major changes are to be explained by some major failure in the regulatory system, which may have external causes or causes from within its own operations or both. (One has to avoid truism here: it is easy to argue that any significant change must be caused by some dysfunction. Horwitz is plainly talking of major changes.)[118] On this basis he analyses four main episodes in American regulatory history.

1   During the nineteenth century, the tendency in United States regulation was towards *laissez-faire*. Previously, it had been to confer exclusive charters on local monopolies, which took on obligations of universal service and also frequently of dividend limitation in return for compulsory-purchase powers over land. What was dysfunctional with respect to that tendency was that early court judgements had tended to exclude new rivals where it could be argued that this would reduce the incumbent's profits through competition. This view of the prior property right of the first entrant was overturned by a classic decision in Boston. The Charles River bridge had been a successful, and had become a very crowded, toll bridge. In 1827 it petitioned to close another bridge a mile upstream that was cutting into its profits. That second bridge had been built on the presumption that the public had the right to break up a monopoly even though that monopoly was grounded in a contract established in law. The defeat of the Charles River bridge in the courts led to a presumption afterwards always in favour of competition even if it meant violating a legal contract. That was plainly an example of the overturn of 'capture by the regulated' in the interests of both bridge users and, by extension, the customers and owners of other utilities.[119] This can be rephrased in Stigler's terms as the following hypothesis: the Charles River bridge owners were able to capture their regulator, the courts, until congestion on the bridge became so severe and prolonged that the mass

of customers were raised to a height of activity in which they were willing and able to exert more pressure on the legislature than were the bridge owners.

2   In general, during the rest of the century utilities captured their regulators – though there were exceptions, as there was, it has been argued, when Adams presided over the Massachusetts Board. An important reason for this on the railroads was the activity of the judiciary in developing the argument that the states had no right to regulate interstate commerce. In the absence of congressional interest in federal regulation, the courts took on this function. Developing notions of property rights enshrined in the Constitution, they gave primacy to the right of a regulated industry to earn a satisfactory return on its capital, a stance conducive to regulatory capture. What had proved dysfunctional by the end of the 1880s was that there was massive resistance by Western farmers to the discriminatory rates the railroads imposed on them to make the most of geographical differences in their monopoly power. Not only was this seen to be unfair, but it also brought many farmers to bankruptcy. Their protests were intensified by economic recession and helped by the strong representation of the Western agricultural interest in Congress. The result in 1887 was the Interstate Commerce Commission. But before one concludes that this represented an overthrow of capture by the regulated, one must take account of the fact that for fifteen years or more the Commission was unable to be effective, principally because the judiciary overruled its implementation of what it thought to be its legislative mandate. There has been much debate over how far the legislature was captured before the setting up of the Commission – but whatever the case here the 1887 Act altered only the form, not the fact, of regulatory capture. In Stigler's terms, the intense interest of the small number of railroads in capturing the state regulators and the courts may have been overborne temporarily by the concentration of a mass of farmers near to destitution using their political power to out-vote the railroad interest. But others have alternative explanations: the railroads may have expected that they could use the courts to neutralize the Commission and may have believed that this was preferable to the greater costs and uncertainty of continuing to handle the state regulators.[120]

3   In the 1930s, economic recession brought in the Roosevelt administration, under which many new regulatory agencies were created and old ones altered, constituting a major change in the regulatory system. In most cases the objective was to improve the profitability of key industries by limiting competition through restricting entry or by other means. Higher prices were needed, it was thought, to preserve jobs. What had been dysfunctional from the standpoint of an industry had been the inability of the older style of regulation, or of freedom from regulation, to enable it to achieve profitability in a deep, persistent slump. For a time after their creation or alteration, some of these agencies used their discretion inconsistently and to serve a range of objectives which were not always to the liking of the regulated industries. But it was the form, not the fact, of regulatory capture that had changed – and the Administrative Procedures Act, 1946, confirmed that capture.

4   Because the regulatory system could not cope with the high rates of inflation of the 1970s, the attractiveness of regulation to the regulated industries was gravely weakened, though they still resisted fundamental changes in it. Also, regulators tended to react to inflation by increasing prices to domestic consumers less, because they had votes, than to industrial consumers, who therefore reacted against

Conclusions

regulation. And in several regulated industries, technical progress encouraged rival firms to want to make an entry, increasing the pressure from within business for deregulation. But all this was overshadowed by the reaction of industry generally to the much increased burden of environmental and other social regulation placed on it in the 1960s and early 1970s. That led to ample funding of think-tanks to develop strong criticisms of regulation. Eventually, an alliance of consumerist forces, who saw regulatory capture as the enemy, with business interests who attacked regulation played a large part in effecting substantial deregulation in a few industries, largely against the opposition of the industries themselves. This was not consistent with capture theory. In Stigler's terms again, the concentrated interest of the industry concerned was countered by, amongst other forces, a temporary concentration of previously more diffusely represented consumer interests.

A difficulty in making comparable studies of the main regulatory episodes in Britain over the same periods is that historians have not given as much attention to them as such. Nevertheless:

(1) Chapter 1 indicates that the early history of railway regulation, when Parliament attempted to the regulatory body, was one of capture and, to the extent that some railways found it difficult to be profitable, of regulatory failure as well.

(2) Economic recession in the 1860s increased the opposition of many traders to railway rates. While the density of the railway network in Britain and the smallness of the island meant that railways could not have as strong a strangle-hold over traders as their counterparts had in the United States, there was still powerful resentment against the discrimination that did occur. In particular, home producers felt that their goods were discriminated against by comparison with imports. However, the first railway commission in 1873 was effectively captured by the industry, using its command of Parliament, and helped by judicial behaviour (chapter 2).

(3) Those adversely affected by railway rate policy and by what they saw as the inadequacies in railway services continued to fight. During the 'Great Depression' of 1873–96, the agricultural industries were particularly badly affected and they blamed some of their problems on the higher rates they paid for the carriage of their goods by railway by comparison with American imports. A change in political alignment which meant that the railway industry ceased to have as much influence on the Liberal Party led to the 1894 Act, which ended the capture of the regulatory commission by the railways. (To some extent this decline in capture was paralleled by the growth of municipalization in other regulated utilities, though it must be doubtful whether regulatory capture did not persist in spite of this change in ownership. Though it was consumer interests that occasioned municipalization, once that had happened, generally the local authority stopped representing the consumer effectively.) As in the United States, traders, not just farmers, felt disadvantaged enough by the railways to concentrate their political power against them. However, it took a long time for them to be successful, and even then it may have been an empty victory: given the low level of railway profitability, the freezing of railway rates in return for permission to amalgamate may have seemed to the railways a worthwhile deal (chapter 2).

(4) The failure of the railways to capture their regulator after 1894, certainly after the turn of the century, was one reason why there was no strong movement towards expanding regulation in the inter-war period. Another reason for the absence of such a movement was that the recession of the early 1930s did not lead to an election of a radical government, as it did in the United States. Transport depression did lead to an expansion of regulation from the railways to cover motor transport, with the same intent as in the United States of limiting entry and increasing profits at the expense of consumers; but this extension of regulation was not paralleled in other industries. However, such regulation as there was – for example, in the electricity industry – was said by many at the time to have been largely captured by the industry concerned. A similar Stiglerian analysis may apply here as to the situation in the United States at the same time (chapter 2).

(5) The large-scale extension of regulation postponed from the 1930s was subsumed in the nationalization programme of the late 1940s. In all cases, except that of iron and steel, it is arguable that there were strong elements within the industries themselves that were keen for them to be nationalized. This was an example of a change in the form of regulatory capture, rather than a departure from it. In Stigler's terms, the returns to managers and even owners were likely to be greater under nationalization, given the economic circumstances (chapter 2).

(6) The 1980s campaign for privatization, and a change to a more American form of regulation, is not easily explained in terms of the theory of regulatory capture. As in the United States, there was a weakening of the regulatory structure because of inflation during the 1970s. In some industries domestic consumers, again as in the United States, tended to benefit relative to industrial consumers, though in others the relation was reversed. And there was again an interest, though a rather weaker one, shown by new suppliers with new technology in entering markets possessed by the old natural monopolies. It cannot be argued, however, that there was a similar consumerist campaign to alter the nature of regulation – in this case, to reverse nationalization. Neither was the elite opinion that was in favour of major change widely influential. If the argument put forward in chapter 4 is correct, most weight in the explanation of why such change occurred has to be given to macroeconomic policy, at least in the early stages of privatization.

No simple theory would seem to explain, or take account of, all these events and circumstances. Nevertheless, the tendency to regulatory capture is, as we have seen, persistent. One reason for major changes in regulation has been a failure of the existing regulatory regime to adapt to a major change in economic circumstances, usually recession but also more recently high rates of inflation. Where this has been the case, the regulated industry has had an incentive to attempt to alter the system of regulation, in its own interest; but it has usually had to pay some social price for this, and for a time may have found that it lost some contol over the system. Otherwise effective opposition has come from consumers, or consumer representatives, and, to a much more limited extent, from rival suppliers, sometimes with new technology. The interesting and vital question here is whether recently the interests of these two 'opposition groups' have become more durable, so that they can prevent recapture by the regulated.

Once new competitors or consumer groups have got their way, there is a tendency for such loose coalitions to collapse and for capture by the regulated to recur- perhaps, though not necessarily, on a basis which continues to be more favourable to these other interests than before. But it is possible that the growth of sustained consumerism and environmentalism, as well as a general greater rapidity of techno- logical change in internationally competitive markets, has altered the regulatory balance for good. The difficulty then will be to forecast how a regulator will use his discretion when there is such a balance of interests with their attentions focused upon him.

There is also the possibility of recapture by government, particularly in British circumstances (chapter 9). In the 1970s and 1980s, Congress was exhorted to control regulation in the interests of public policy, and tried to do so; but the outcome was seldom what the regulators' critics desired, because Congress avoided passing laws which practically defined regulatory discretion any more closely than previously.[121] In Britain, a more likely route to recapture is through ministers' relying on their remaining powers in the regulatory field and on the tradition of their influence under the old regime of control. Ministers might do this if they do not appreciate, or have forgotten, that under the new regime regulators are intended to have far greater inde- pendence, because of their quasi-judicial role. They might be under pressure from critics who want to put right what they see as regulatory shortcomings. They might want to step in to resolve conflicts between regulators or between regulators and other public bodies. And they might have their own political purposes to pursue. All this seems more likely than that ministers should wish to restore the old relationship they, or their predecessors, had with nationalized industries, which involved them in frequent intervention. However, it is also not impossible that the heads of some privatized industries might themselves invite such a return to the old ways of doing things if they find the market too difficult for their own or their firm's survival – this would be a different form of regulatory capture by the regulated industry.

To try to produce a satisfactory theory to explain all past changes and predict future ones would be over-ambitious, yet something further can be said beyond noting the general tendency to regulatory capture:

1 There is a tendency for major change to occur after a period of regulatory decline or failure, usually after a period in which the system has been unable to cope with changes, generally ones external to it. Why such failure happens is vari- able and not susceptible to easy generalization beyond the general proposition that the situation has become dysfunctional.
2 There is a not-invariable tendency for a major agent of change to be a revolt by a large body of consumers, whose motives may range from fears for their own livelihood to more general environmental concerns. At times they come to feel sufficiently strongly about a matter to be able to muster their normally diffusely represented interests to mount an effective campaign against a regulatory system or an arrangement within it.
3 After a major change against the regulated industry's interests, the industry will work, often successfully, to restore its position, though it may take some time to reassert its capture.
4 Whenever there is a change or modification of a regulatory system, further social

or other non-economic obligations tend to result which cannot easily or naturally be explained by the supposition that all parties are income maximizers.

5 The forms of regulatory capture by the regulated are manifold. There are occasions when the desire for a return to a quiet life may lead a regulated industry to seek to embrace something not unlike the old relationship of a nationalized industry with ministers, whatever the cost in terms of profitability and economic efficiency – though there are other reasons as well for believing that regulatory capture by government is as much a threat to regulatory independence as is capture by the industry, especially where the regulated industry had previously been a nationalized industry.

6 One of the closest and most quoted approximations to a historical generalization is that power corrupts and absolute power tends to corrupt absolutely.[122] Within its small but not unimportant compass, the discretion of an effective regulator tends to be absolute. This is one, but not the only, reason – another is the resourcefulness of the regulated – for supposing that the seeds of decay are present in any regulatory system, even one which was set up with a high probability of disinterested behaviour.

11.5   Reinforcing regulatory independence in Britain

While one can see why the interests of the regulated industry make attempts at capture worthwhile for it, it may be possible to devise a regulatory system that is more robust when it meets with such attempts than such systems have been in the past. And to that end it would seem in place to suggest here some ways in which the independence of the new British system of natural-monopoly regulation might be better protected.

To suggest that aspects of the system could have been better designed does not mean that their immediate reform is desirable. A good innovation is one which has the capacity to overcome any shortcomings it may have, develops to meet unexpected challenges and heals its own wounds without further legislative change. By those standards, the first years of the new regime have been promising. Moreover, as has already been argued, neither a legislature nor a government when asked for reform provides just what it has been asked for. And it is in any case possible that the discretion available to the regulators will allow them to do a satisfactory job in promoting competition and determining and dealing with regulatory offences without changes to the system. At present this seems most likely to be true of gas regulation, even though it is the weakest part of the specialist regulatory system; less so of bus and coach regulation, because there is no specialist regulation. Also, reforms which require only administrative change are easier to effect than those that need legislation.

Least needs to be said about protection from the courts, as long as the British tradition of administrative review holds and the European Commission or Court does not intervene in matters of fact or interpretation, or question merits. As was argued in chapter 8 (where it was also suggested what procedures might be appropriate), it is in the interests of the regulators themselves to adopt defensible procedures that keep the courts out and to avoid recourse to an equivalent to the US Administrative Procedures Act, 1946.

In all the regulated industries the regulator's independence would be better protected if his position approximated to that of the Director General of Oftel. He should have discretion over the interpretation and enforcement of the licence, which should cover all the monopoly activities of the regulated firm.[123] Where he cannot agree modifications to the licence with the firm, appeal should lie to the Monopolies and Mergers Commission, without ministers' being able to prevent or modify such an appeal, or bar or modify the MMC's conclusions or interfere with the regulator's implementation of the MMC's recommendations, except on such grounds as that of national emergency.[124] With similar provisos, it might not be unreasonable if appeal also lay to the MMC on interpretations of a licence by the regulator or on his decisions on what constitutes a breach of licence, though only if the MMC, after being approached, were persuaded that there were reasonable grounds for appeal, and one would only expect such a right of appeal to be granted where there were important issues of principle at stake. With such appeals there should be no doubt that, while the regulator may have some discretion in implementing MMC recommendations, he must broadly follow and certainly not exceed them. It might be helpful if the MMC or some other body were to carry out occasional reviews across all relevant regulatory bodies, perhaps of their handling of particular offences, to see what lessons could be drawn from this. Their recommendations would not have retrospective force, or limit regulatory discretion in the future; but parties before regulators might well draw attention to them in future proceedings.

Relations between the Monopolies and Mergers Commission and the regulated natural monopoly, and between the Office of Fair Trading and the specialist regulator, should be the same in each industry when they exercise their powers in relation to the fair-trading laws. Broadly, the specialist regulator should exercise such powers in consultation with the fair-trading regulator.[125] There is no harm in the role of the fair-trading laws in regulation being latent, as it is for airports, provided that they come into play when there is reasonable suspicion of a fair-trading offence.[126]

The basic economic regulatory offences as described in this book should be regarded as the relevant economic offences in all cases. It would seem that essentially the same offences are often expressed variously in the different statutes and licences.[127] But this need not cause concern provided that in practice their meaning is developed in a reasonably consistent way, given the circumstances of each industry. It would be desirable if the provision in the Water Act, 1989, requiring that the burden of proof on the desirability of merger be on those wanting it were extended to other industries to cover mergers, acquisitions, and other, informal arrangements which might be used for extending unnatural, rather than natural, monopoly, as well as to allow for demerger.[128] This would place on regulated firms the requirement to demonstrate that larger size is in the public interest. However, this should be relaxed when competition has developed, in accordance with the principle of competitive necessity.

The Water Appointment, the industry's licence, should be the model for the others in the provision of accounting information. Current cost accounts, as far as possible designed to provide information useful for determining the regulatory offences, should be required of all regulated undertakings if they are monopolies or dominant firms.[129] Where there is sufficient competition, published accounting information should conform to no more stringent requirements than for other companies. Whether competition is sufficient could be decided by the regulator, but with a right of appeal to the Monopolies and Mergers Commission. Where the regulated firms and their regulators fail to agree over the forms of accounts to be provided and the accounting policies to be used, there should be a right of appeal to a tribunal, or arbitrator, with relevant professional competence. And it would increase the ability of regulators to renegotiate X in the RPI-X formula in the consumer's interest and to take other actions in that interest, if they were given the resources to enable them to exchange information with, and to perform joint analyses and surveys on comparable bases with, regulators with similar responsibilities in other countries.

Where there is interconnection, the owner of a grid or network used by others could gain an advantage by limiting its capacity in total or in part, especially if the owner is also a user of the grid or network, competing with others. One way of trying to stop this would be to give the regulator the power to ensure that sufficient capacity is provided – but that would be strongly interventionist.[130] A better solution would be to give the regulator the power to require that he be supplied with, and the power to scrutinize, all capital expenditure plans relevant to interconnection. He should then, without divulging information which needs to be kept confidential, hold hearings on the adequacy of these, so that other parties may express an opinion on their adequacy. He might then prepare, even publish, his own views on their adequacy and present these to the owner of the grid or network. However, he should not impose his views; the provider should decide on its own levels of investment. The interests of the other parties would be best safeguarded if the provider is placed under a liability to damages sufficient to compensate for lost profits should provision prove inadequate, as long as other parties give sufficient notice of their needs.

As far as possible the social offences regulators consider should be limited to those related to the existence of monopoly, and they should be considered only as long as the regulated firms remain monopolies: excess profits, failure to provide universal service, and price discrimination. In a dispute over whether competition has reached an adequate level of contestability, it would be reasonable to allow an approach to the Monopolies and Mergers Commission on appeal. It would also be best for regulatory independence if social obligations were to be kept to the minimum required by economic efficiency. While it may be properly among the regulator's duties to sustain social obligations written into the statute or licence, there should be some indication in the licence of what is to happen if declining profitability through competition undermines the regulated firm's ability to sustain those obligations.

The extension of the consumer committee apparatus to the gas industry might give its regulator greater strength to stand up to it than under present arrangements.[131] It should be understood, preferably by its being described in such terms in the licence, that the function of these committees in advising and helping regulators derives from the absence of competition. Their duty is as far as possible to simulate the choices consumers would make in a competitive market.

In order to ensure that monopolies do not abuse the RPI-X provisions by allowing quality levels to fall below what consumers might be expected to want to purchase freely in a competitive market, regulators should be empowered to secure the regulated industries' liability to commensurate damages if they fail to reach the appropriate quality levels.

The provision of such a mechanism will stimulate consumer concern and involvement. And because such a provision for damages cannot be disregarded in practice, it is likely to be important for preventing regulatory capture, as much by ministers as by regulated firms. Further to the end of preventing political capture, it could be made clearer in any new legislation that any statutory or ownership powers in the hands of ministers are not to be used in such a way as to interfere with the regulators' independence, or, as noted above, with the process of appeal to the Monopolies and Mergers Commission, or with the implementation of its findings, except where there is a clear national emergency or public-interest reason, tightly defined. There should be machinery to ensure in particular that environmental, safety and other externality regulation is to be taken in principle no further than is economically efficient; and that any values involved in this which are necessarily political should be clearly stated so as to help achieve consistency in their use. There should be a review of the ministerial powers that are set out in the relevant statutes, especially those that could be used for unwarranted intervention in the regulatory process. Those that are not justified by reference to national emergency or some other clearly defined ministerial function external to natural-monopoly regulation should be eliminated; and the wording of the rest should, so far as may seem necessary, be strengthened, so as to prevent as far as possible their misuse where the regulatory process is concerned. Where there are overlapping regulatory jurisdictions, time will tell whether it is necessary to clarify those jurisdictions.

Ministers would be wise not to expect or encourage regulators to develop a social or political policy, reserving that for themselves while expecting to pay for any additional social obligations which regulated firms agree to adopt or which are imposed by legislation, except where legislation requires consumers to pay and this is carried through in a way which neither distorts competition nor destroys the regulated firm's profitability.

Where there is a need, as with some telecommunications value-added services and with broadcasting, to review the quality of what is carried and is accessible to the general public, or even to censor it, that should be done by separate bodies rather than that the regulator should be drawn into questions of taste or censorship. Such bodies might have an advisory role similar to that of the consumer committees, though on matters of censorship the expectation should be that the regulator will act on their advice.

A specialist economic regulator should be established for the bus and coach industries on the ground that they are, or are liable to become, natural monopolies. And there should be no question but that mergers leading to monopoly locally should be disallowed, despite the small geographical areas concerned. A bus and coach specialist economic regulator should have the same duties and powers, and relationships with the Office of Fair Trading and the Monopolies and Mergers Commission, as have other specialist economic regulators.

The workload of the Monopolies and Mergers Commission has increased substantially during the 1980s. Natural-monopoly regulation has been only a small part of this, but one may predict that such references will become more common. As its workload grows, it will remain important for the Commission both to maintain, and indeed improve, its record for consistency and to ensure that its procedures are equal to the new demands placed on it (chapter 8). That record might be improved if there were more full-time members, or members who stayed longer on the Commission. Consistency in natural-monopoly cases may be helped by the Commission's maintaining a core of members with experience of specialist regulation. Natural-monopoly cases are more likely than most others to affect many parties, so that, as the number of such cases increases, it will become increasingly important to ensure that proceedings are fair between parties. There is a strong possibility that through one route or another the EC and the European Court will on occasion be brought into natural-monopoly proceedings. Thus, thought needs to be given as to how these intrusions can best be dove-tailed into such proceedings.

While the Director General of Fair Trading and the other specialist regulators should be kept separate from each other and from the Monopolies and Mergers Commission, there would be an advantage if they developed some aspects of a common administration. In order to encourage a career within regulation, there has been common recruitment to, and promotion within, the regulatory staffs of the Office of Fair Trading and bodies engaged in the economic regulation of natural monopolies. That could be extended to other bodies, like the financial regulators, where in general the economic offences concerned overlap. This would provide career paths which might involve staff moving from one regulatory body to another. To the same end, and to help avoid regulatory capture, regulators, like judges, might be allowed to go on beyond the normal civil service retirement age of sixty. They might occasionally move into each other's posts. And it might also be desirable that some, especially towards the end of their careers, should move on, on a full- or part-time basis, to become members of the MMC, though there might reasonably be restrictions on how many, and on who once there might hear an appeal concerning a natural monopoly.[131] Not more than a small proportion of the regulatory staffs should be on secondment from the civil service.

Finally, in order further to ensure that regulators have a practical independence from the industries they regulate, it would be wise if it were mandatory that neither they nor more than a small proportion of their staffs should have been employed within any firm they regulate at any time during the previous, say, five years, or should join or receive remuneration from any such firm for a further such reasonable period. The only exceptions might be those with scarce technical knowledge, provided that they do not become the regulator.

Notes

1   J. Morrison (1848), p. 97.
2   Derthick and Quirk (1985), esp. ch. 7; Horwitz (1989), ch. 2.
3   Horwitz (1989), pp. 23–6. Weber (1947), p. 340, referred to official enforcing 'law without hatred or passion and hence without enthusiasm'.
4   H. Morrison (1933), *passim.*
5   Note what AT&T's counsel said when before Judge Greene after the agreement to break it up: 'It may be hard for a lot of people to believe it, but for a hundred years, the company has been based on the notion of public service. A lot of Bell people cried this

morning, and not because they are going to make any more money . . . The problem is, what does this do to the public? . . . And the message that has been coming out from Congress and the courts is "this is none of your business. The market protects the public interest. You are being arrogant, in thinking you even have a responsibility to consider it." ' Quoted in Coll (1986), pp. 341, 342. AT&T had equated 'the public interest' with cross-subsidy: ibid., pp. 273–4.

6   Horwitz (1989) p. 9. Few US regulatory agencies have specific statutory provisions which define their behaviour: Gormley (1983), p. 24. Therefore US regulation as much reflects a failure to establish contracts between the State and the regulated industries as did nationalization. Its coherence, which is not to be exaggerated as there is much diversity in regulatory interpretation of the public interest, derives from the courts and the Administrative Procedures Act, 1946.

7   Breyer and Stewart (1985), pp. 127–30; also Bernstein (1955), p. 264, for his comparison between USA and UK. The notion of the 'public interest' is still employed in the crop of new UK licences, though in subordinate positions. And it remains important for the fair-trading laws. The most determined practical attempt to give content to public interest theory was made by economists outside the regulatory system who equated the public interest with economic efficiency. On both sides of the Atlantic, as we have seen, a literature developed to persuade the various parties that this should be the aim of public or regulated enterprise. And in both cases they were led to advocate the employment of marginal-cost pricing.

8   Derthick and Quirk (1985), p. 8; Horwitz (1989), pp. 27, 28.

9   Bernstein (1955), p. 265.

10   Ibid.

11   E.g., the view that the 1887 Interstate Commerce Act was the result of pressure behind the scenes from the railroads, who publicly appeared to oppose it: Kolko (1963).

12   Gray (1940).

13   Lowi (1969). See Horwitz (1989), p. 31. However, it has been said that contrary to rational expectations the 'substantial discretionary authority delegated by Congress to a regulatory entity is non-increasing with increased uncertainty and conflict of interest': McCubbins (1985), p. 722.

14   Stigler (1971) in Stigler (1975), p. 114.

15   Stigler and Friedland (1962). For a more recent view of the effect of regulation on prices, see Joskow and Rose (1989), pp. 146–8.

16   Peltzmann (1976).

17   Where there is more than one regulated firm confronting a regulator, those regulated firms will have an economic incentive to act as a cartel in their efforts to negotiate to retain as much as they can of their joint monopoly profit. Their ability to do this will be the less the more they are in number or the more they are competing with each other. Ibid., pp. 217–24; Posner (1974), pp. 344–7. They will not be as successful as one firm and the distribution between them of monopoly profit will depend on their relative power. If a regulated firm is faced by more than one regulator, and those regulators are independent of each other, then they should be less able to extract monopoly profit.

18   On regulation as an economically efficient process, see Williamson (1976).

19   Stigler (1971).

20   On how transaction costs and imperfect information make it conceptually possible for regulation to be inefficient, see Noll (1989), pp. 1,258, 1,259; also Posner (1969).

21   Becker (1983).

22   Peltzmann (1976); Posner (1969), (1974) and (1975). In his comments on his 1971 article in his 1975 book and in his introduction to that book Stigler made this view explicit: 'A policy adopted and followed for a long time . . . could not usefully be described as a

mistake': Stigler (1975), p. x; also pp. 137–41. Becker (1989) made a very clear statement to the same end, using a rational-expectations approach. Keeler (1984) is an interesting and illuminating extension and use of the Peltzmann model.

23 On the Chicago paradox, see Keeler (1984), p. 104.

24 Crew (1989) says that several articles of Posner's from 1969–76 were influential in promoting deregulation. The influence of the Chicago school in making US anti-trust concentrate on entry barriers and horizontal concentration has been profound: see Eisner (1991), pp. 103–7.

25 Derthick and Quirk (1985), p. 147. See also Kahn (1982), pp. 247–63, on how deregulation happened; also Horwitz (1989).

26 Noll quoted in Derthick and Quirk (1985), p. 54. See also Pierce, Allison and Martin (1980), pp. 71–3; Horwitz (1989), pp. 35–8.

27 Acworth (1905) did not mention one mainstream economist in his footnotes.

28 McCraw (1984), p. 227.

29 The influence of Karl Popper is particularly marked in that long-lived economics textbook by one of his pupils, Lipsey (1963), esp. ch. 1. I confess to the same influence.

30 Surveyed by Joskow and Rose (1989). On the increased influence of economics on anti-trust in the United States, and of Chicago thinking among economics schools, see Eisner (1991), pp. 107–111.

31 Derthick and Quirk (1985), pp. 35–9.

32 Kahn (1988a), pp. 65–70/I. A balanced case for basing regulation pre-eminently on marginal-cost pricing is to be found in Kahn's lecture to the American Economics Association: Kahn (1979). See also Kahn (1978) for detailed applications.

33 Kahn (1988a), pp. 70–86/I.

34 See, for example, McCraw (1984), pp. 239–43; Pierce, Allison and Martin (1980), pp. 407–43.

35 McCraw (1984), p. 228. Eisner (1991), pp. 103–17, in his discussion of the influence of Chicago thinking on anti-trust shows the importance of its attitude towards barriers on entry.

36 For example, Baumol (1977b); Sharkey (1982).

37 'The New Policies are based on the theory that both trucking and aviation markets are in the absence of regulatory intervention, naturally contestable': E. E. Bailey (1981), p. 179.

38 See the Chicago school, as characterized by Kahn (1988a), pp. 327–8/II; also Coase (1960). As is explained in chapter 5 above, successful contest ability also depends on the absence of substantial sunk costs.

39 See the discussion in chapter 5 above.

40 Stigler (1971) in Stigler (1975), p. 125: 'A representative cannot use or keep office with the support of the sum of those opposed to: oil import quotas, farm subsidies, airport subsidies, hospital subsidies, unnecessary navy shipyards, an inequitable public housing programme and rural electrification subsidies.'

41 On revolving doors between industry and regulatory agency, see Horwitz (1989), pp. 27, 37ff. See the evidence on the large numbers of FCC commissioners entering the communications industry: ibid., p. 237, n. 16. And note that Kenneth Cox, who in 1969 as a FCC commissioner voted for MCI's first application, joined MCI the day after his term expired: Coll (1986), pp. 204, 205.

42 Breyer (1982), pp. 2–3.

43 Derthick and Quirk (1985), pp. 29–35.

44 Kahn (1978), pp. 4–5; Kahn (1988a), pp. xxiii–xxviii and p. 2; McCraw (1984), pp. 237–9, 277; Horwitz (1989), p. 198. Derthick and Quirk (1985), pp. 20, 21, argue that this is an implausible explanation, for there is no evidence that any regulated industry argued or lobbied to this end. However, it is sufficient to argue that they were

weakened by the effect of inflation, both financially and in terms of self-confidence, so as to be less effective in retaining regulatory capture.

45 Joskow (1974). Kahn (1988a), pp. xiii–xxviii; Kahn (1982), p. 257.
46 Kahn (1988a), p. xxiv; Kahn (1978), pp. 6–7.
47 Derthick and Quirk (1985), p. 56.
48 Horwitz (1989), pp. 203–6, 214.
49 Weyman Jones (1989), pp. 279–99.
50 One result that might seem ironical in Britain was that, because they could more easily bear the risks, the proportion of investment made by publicly owned utilities increased during the 1970s relative to that made by privately owned ones: Joskow and Schmalensee (1983), p. 19.
51 For an interesting analysis of the effects of Chernobyl on regulatory attitudes, and therefore on electricity-utility viability, see Eckel and Vermaclen (1989), pp. 183–201.
52 Derthick and Quirk (1985), pp. 20, 21.
53 Tunstall (1986), p. 27.
54 Derthick and Quirk (1985), p. 147; Horwitz (1989), p. 17. United Airlines eventually came round to supporting airline deregulation: Kahn (1990a), p. 331.
55 Horwitz (1989), pp. 238, 239. For AT&T's failure to get its 1976 Consumer Communications Reform Bill through Congress despite intensive lobbying, see Coll (1986), pp. 92–100.
56 Derthick and Quirk (1985), p. 38.
57 Breyer (1982), pp. 348–50.
58 Nader Report, 1960, quoted in Clarkson and Muris (1982), pp. 137, 138.
59 Tunstall (1986), last chapter.
60 Breyer (1982), appendix 1.
61 Pierce, Allison and Martin (1980), p. 84; Joskow and Noll (1981).
62 Weidenbaum (1980); also Tunstall (1986), p. 11. Inevitably, any such figures are widely disputed.
63 Horwitz (1989), p. 207.
64 Derthick and Quirk (185), pp. 30–2; Horwitz (1989), p. 209.
65 Horwitz (1989), p. 6.
66 Thurow (1980), pp. 122–39. In a legalistic environment, he observes, environmentalism naturally leads to regulation, but that is found difficult to implement. Long fights follow.
67 Lipset and Schneider (1983), p. 33.
68 Derthick and Quirk (1985), pp. 53–7.
69 Breyer and Stewart (1985), p. 130; Kahn (1988a), p. 92/II; Tunstall (1986), p. 103.
70 Kahn (1990a).
71 Breyer (1982), pp. 317ff.
72 Derthick and Quirk (1985), pp. 46–50. While Ford and Carter were pro-competitive, this seems less clearly so of Reagan. Most of his cabinet were pro-AT&T. On the one occasion that the issue came to him, his conclusion was opaque. As White House chief of staff, James Baker decided to support divestiture on the tactical ground that standing up for AT&T would be more damaging to Reagan. See Coll (1986), pp. 211–22, 225–9.
73 Airline Deregulation Act, 1978.
74 Derthick and Quirk (1985), p. 66.
75 Horwitz (1989), pp. 238, 239.
76 Kahn (1990a), p. 331.
77 Derthick and Quirk (1985), p. 131.
78 Ibid., pp. 250–1.
79 Ibid., p. 149.
80 Horwitz (1989), p. 9. However, Alfred Kahn believes that the airlines might have

successfully challenged his use of his discretion to allow free entry if the Airline Deregulation Act, 1978, had not got through Congress in time: Kahn and Reach (1979), pp. 106–12.

81 Derthick and Quirk (1985), p. 63; McCraw (1984), p. 22.

82 Stigler alleged that the CAB had not allowed a new route since it was created in 1938: Stigler (1975), p. 117. This was later denied by Kahn: Kahn (1978), p. 7.

83 Kahn (1988b). It has been argued that the growth of natural monopoly since deregulation proves that regulation distorts natural monopoly: Bailey, Graham and Kaplan (1985), p. 196

84 Arguably, as in the British bus industry, where the outcome was in many respects similar, it would have been more competitive if the anti-trust authorities had shown on inclination to challenge mergers and predatory practices.

85 Derthick and Quirk (1985), p. 67.

86 Ibid., p. 149.

87 Ibid., p. 18; Coll (1986), *passim*.

88 Kahn (1988a), his optimistic introduction to this 1988 edition; Poole (1982), p. viii; Kahn (1990a).

89 Horwitz (1989), p. 262.

90 Ibid., pp. 274–8; Kahn (1990a), p. 326. See also Faulhaber (1987), pp. 77–8, on Bell's disillusionment with the idea that it would benefit from deregulation.

91 Derthick and Quirk (1985), pp. 238–45; Horwitz (1989), p. 6.

92 Horwitz (1989), p. 287. Despite disappointment over the extent of deregulation, some was still continuing: Kahn (1990a), pp. 327, 328.

93 Derthick and Quirk (1985), p. 93; Fainsod (1940). Posner (1974) has admitted the practical difficulty of proving regulatory capture by the regulated.

94 See Popper (1945), vol. 2.

95 Derthick and Quirk (1985), p. 147.

96 Also Keeler (1984). J. Q. Wilson also argued that the existence of environmental regulation disproves regulatory capture by the regulated: Wilson (1976). In a crude sense it does; but see the strongly critical review in Shepsle (1982).

97 Alderman (1973), *passim*; Williamson (1983), ch. 2.

98 McLean and Foster (forthcoming).

99 Fiorina (1982) argues that Congress changed from being dominated by parties in the nineteenth century to what it is today. It was then more like Parliament in this century. However, Congress in its own terms is more effective than was Parliament in the nineteenth century, because of the size of its staffs.

100 Peltzmann (1976).

101 Becker (1983).

102 A useful summary is Crew and Rowley (1989), pp. 5–20.

103 Peltzmann (1976), p. 212.

104 Becker (1983), p. 392, had maintained that voters were not a force independent from pressure groups. On the difference between Becker's pressure group theory, which tends to believe that the outcome is economically efficient, and the Virginian, which does not, see Crew and Bowley (1989).

105 See the devastating analysis of this in Kahn (1978), p. 4.

106 This is particularly marked in Olson (1965).

107 Among the most useful of the theoretical results achieved has been its hypothesis concerning the cross-subsidization that is common in the pricing polices of regulated (and nationalized or ex-nationalized) industries: Crew and Rowley (1989), pp. 7–8. Such an explanation can arise through postulating that some groups of consumers are able to use their blocking power effectively to outmanœuvre the superior resources of larger

groups; or find it easier to combine their influence. Keeler (1984) has an illuminating application to railroads, airlines and telecommunications.

108 Cf. Stigler's statement that the purpose of empirical investigations is not to test the theory of utility-maximizing: Stigler (1975), pp. 139–40. This was in response to Posner's observations on the Stigler version of the theory that 'the economic theory is still so spongy that virtually any observation can be reconciled with it': Posner (1974), p. 348, where he also observed the difficulty of proving capture.

109 Becker (1983). Note Stigler's earlier observation: 'Until we understand why our society adopts its policies, we will be poorly equipped to give useful advice on how to change those policies. Indeed some changes . . . presumably are unattainable without a fundamental restructuring of the political system which we are unable to describe.' Stigler (1975), p. xi.

110 To explain deregulation by the growth of dead-weight costs is not easily made consistent with theory, since it begs the question of why this should develop to be destabilizing: Becker (1989), pp. 19–22.

111 F. H. Bradley (1930), p. xii.

112 Becker (1989), pp. 23–5, commenting on his (1983) argument that, as political pressure groups act rationally and efficiently, this always amounted to a defence of the status quo, noted that international comparisons sometimes led him to doubt this. There was some evidence that pressure groups act more efficiently in a democracy.

113 Crew and Rowley (1989), p. 17.

114 On the difficulties of both historical and economic explanation, see Fiorina (1982), pp. 37ff. There are difficult specification problems as one moves from simple to complex theories.

115 Popper (1957), pp. ix–xi; also Popper (1945), vol. 2, p. 268.

116 Derthick and Quirk (1985), pp. 35–9, 238, 239. Another explanation of the need for discretion arises from the increasing need to specialize, which leads to delegated authority: Eisner (1991), p. 7.

117 Fisher (1945), vol. 1, p. vii.

118 Horwitz (1989), pp. 54, 58.

119 Goodrich (1967), pp. 377–90.

120 Kolko (1963).

121 McCubbins and Schwartz (1984).

122 Berlin (1954), p. 74.

123 This is not to argue that a single agency should replace either the Office of Fair Trading and the natural-monopoly regulators or just the natural-monopoly regulators. To do either would be to lose the advantage of concentrated specialist knowledge and would be more likely to lead to inconsistency for reasons already stated. The CAA grants licences: Airports Act, 1986, s. 38. In the other industries they are granted by the minister, who may delegate the duty to the regulator: Telecommunications Acts, 1984, s. 7(1); Gas Act, 1986, s. 8(1); Water Act, 1989, s. 11; Electricity Act, 1989, s. 6.

124 Telecommunications Act, 1984, s. 13(6); Gas Act, 1986, s. 24; Water Act 1989, s. 16(1); Electricity Act, 1989, s. 12(2); and, in somewhat different form because mandatory, Airports Act, 1986, s. 43(3).

125 Gas Act, 1986, s. 34(4); Water Act, 1989, se. 28(1); Electricity Act, 1989, s. 43; also Airports Act, 1986, s. 56, if the situation arises.

126 Airports Act, 1986, s. 41(6).

127 Perhaps the most obvious deliberate difference is between the one condition in the Gas Authorisation (condn. 9) and the very large number of conditions in the BT Licence and the Public Electricity Supply Licence; less obviously deliberate would seem to be the differences in the treatment of discrimination.

128   Water Act, 1989, s. 29, 30.

129   The BT, British Gas and airport licences do not require the publication of current cost accounts. The electricity and water licences broadly do.

130   Water Appointment, condn. L.

131   Telecommunications Act, 1984, s. 54; Gas Act, 1986, s. 32; Water Act, 1989, s. 54; Electricity Act, 1989, 2.

12

Privatization, monopoly and the design of regulatory systems

These like the frogs of Egypt, have got possession of our dwellings and we scarce have a room free from them: they sup in our cup, they dip in our dish, they sit by our fire; we find them in the dye-vat, wash-bowl, and powdering-tub; they share with the butler in his box, they have marked and sealed us from head to foot.

Sir John Culpepper, MP (1641)[1]

These concluding remarks are divided into observations on monopoly and the suitability of privatization and nationalization (section 1), and on the need for regulators (section 2); conclusions on what is likely to lead to regulatory failure (section 3); suggestions on how, in general, a defensible regulatory independence may be preserved (section 4); some more general requirements for an effective regulatory system (section 5); and some general conclusions on the new British form of regulation (section 6).

12.1 Monopoly: nationalization and privatization

What Sir John Culpepper said of monopolies before the start of the English Civil War, an MP could have said 340 years later of nationalized industries, with no greater exaggeration. They also permeated the economy and were mostly set up as monopolies. The policy of allowing private monopolies granted by the State had been devised by the Crown to raise money at the expense of the consumer, by passing the House of Commons' prerogative to vote all taxes; but it had also become a way of compensating underpaid public servants and of effecting public policies at no expense to the Crown.[2] Similarly, in many instances the nationalization of industry became a way of creating monopolies to spend money at the expense of consumers and, indirectly through deficit finance, of taxpayers, also without recourse to the House of Commons. There was, however, a significant difference in ends. To revert to the distinction between the Chicago and Virginian schools made in the previous chapter, the first policy was often inspired by a wish to raise cash without paying a political price for it in the Commons; through the second, what politicians mainly sought to avoid paying a political price in Parliament for was, not cash, but influence in kind over public enterprise behaviour. Yet there is a historical link between them, though a minor one, that helps to explain this difference in ends. Remote though it may seem, it was the victory then of Parliament over the use of monopolies, and other ways of imposing taxation without representation, that established a principle which would have reinforced the disinclination of the founders of the nationalized industries to set them up so as to make money even if they had wanted that. Not only, because the English language was never more vigorous and direct than at the time when he spoke out, Culpepper's words strongly remind us that monopoly was of greater concern to our ancestors than it is to us. High transport costs had created a patchwork of local natural monopolies. And to this the financial needs of kings and the cartelizing tendencies of urban guilds added a large number of unnatural, that is, legal, monopolies. Accelerating towards the end of the eighteenth century and in the early nineteenth century, a great movement of deregulation – which owed more to changes in transport technology than to changes in the law – slowly got rid of most of these; and out of this movement modern attitudes to natural monopoly, and the first machinery for dealing with it, were born. However, as we have seen, that machinery failed, and decayed into nationalization.

Public ownership had its substantial individual achievements. Given the management techniques of the time, neither the electricity nor the gas grid could have been built without it. Nor would anything have been gained by maintaining the fiction that the railways which were merged and nationalized in 1948 had previously been competing with each other in any meaningful sense. Moreover, industries like coal and iron and steel did improve their efficiency for a period after nationalization, because of the manifest failures of previous private enterprise to provide management careers open to talents, to hold back from cartelization, or to engage in active competition and productivity improvement.

Nevertheless, one cannot avoid a harsh verdict; for whatever its comparative advantages over the patchy and chaotic regulation it generally succeeded, at least in Britain, nationalization failed to develop a regime well enough designed either to promote economic efficiency or to promote efficiently other well-defined economic or political objectives. With hindsight one can see why this happened; and why would-be reformers failed. When it came to dissolving many of these industries into private-sector firms, they were seen to be what the seventeenth century and later Adam Smith would have called artificial, or merely legal, monopolies, though as often making a loss as a profit. Of course, there were developments in the management of public enterprise; but judged by the standards set out in this book it is hard to quarrel with the view that they did not achieve what was needed, or match the advances at the same time actually made, or potentially made, in private-sector organizational and management techniques.

In many countries from the mid-1970s on there were stirrings of protest against the inefficiencies of modern monopolies and other public or regulated private enterprises. As in the the eighteenth century, changes in technology, principally in transport and communications, supplied actual or potential competition and were as influential as any movement of ideas in bringing about deregulation, which occurred much more quickly in many countries than it had, in the eighteenth and nineteenth centuries. Particularly in Britain, privatization was rapid: the start was delayed until after the first years of the Thatcher administration but was remarkably complete by the early 1990s.

Yet I have argued that the belief that private-sector ownership must be more efficient than public ownership is mistaken, if only because the latter can learn from the errors of the past. And in chapter 10 the main elements of such a programme of public enterprise reform were set out. Nevertheless, there are positive arguments for preferring privatization if the overriding objective is economic efficiency (or profitability). One is that one would do better to harness the well-tried forms of private enterprise and the profit instincts of private shareholders rather than invent a different apparatus and range of incentives to the same end. A second is that financial market disciplines do provide extra stimuli to efficiency – though these only apply where there are workable financial markets, and may not even then be much of a threat to the large natural monopolies. A third is that one has to expect politicians to have ends other than economic efficiency; and, even if one political generation puts economic efficiency first, the passing of time and new exigencies of state make it likely that there will eventually be political interference that will subvert the primacy of that end. In that way, and generally, privatization is less easily reversible. British experience indeed supports that view that the more-ambitious reasons politicians have had for creating or intervening in state enterprise have seldom succeeded or, where they have, could as well have been achieved by regulated private enterprise with modern techniques of management and interconnection – sometimes with clearly defined unprofitable activities subsidized by government. And it suggests that most political intervention has been short term, and not easily justified from the standpoint of efficiency or of any other long-term policy.

Conversely, the main circumstances in which public enterprise may be preferred are where the public purposes that government wants undertaken are too complicated to be contractually expressed. This may be either because those public purposes are short-term and never properly and consistently defined at all, or because, while long term and potentially consistent, not enough intellectual effort has been applied to their definition. While in principle enterprises with such purposes could be efficiently run provided that their objectives are well defined and commensurate, the relevant accounting and management techniques have not been developed to the point where comparable scale and scope economies can be developed as for profit-making enterprise.

Just as the Long Parliament outlawed monopolies – not for the first or last time – so the Thatcher government shed nationalized industries. The full story, step by step, of how that happened has not been attempted here, but already we can see that it will be unlikely to fit easily into any of the standard economic explanations. Privatization was not plausibly an example of regulatory capture at birth: it was not willed by the industries themselves. It was not the result of a formidable outburst of consumer resentment – which has been the commonest cause of profound regulatory change. It is hard to argue that it was driven by a campaign of ideas or by the determination of ministers, though both may have been factors. It had many causes, but the most immediate seems to have been serious macroeconomic difficulties interacting with some conventions of British public finance.

Despite the formal similarities between the various privatization statutes and licences, what is remarkable is that the British entities privatized are so diverse in many important respects. There have been the large number of public enterprises listed in chapter 4 that raised no special regulatory concerns. Among those that did British Telecom is an ex-government department with a history of prices poorly aligned with costs, practising cross-subsidization to achieve uniform prices geographically. British Gas practised a different pattern of cross-subsidization to achieve uniform prices geographically and discounted contract gas prices. Social obligations are less important for it, as they also are for electricity. The objectives of airports are more straightforwardly commercial: they have used prices to optimize airport use and raise enough money for expansion. The form of electricity's privatization means that strict regulation is required to make interconnection competition effective and to prevent subsidized nuclear energy distorting competition further than government interests require. Water regulation is a new form of administration rather than a regulatory regime for a commercial activity: environmental and health issues have become so important, costly and liable to change that they impose severe constraints on commercial operations. Yet despite these differences it has been possible to set the privatized industries within a broadly similar legislative framework.

If one asks why privatization went further in Britain than the deregulation movement went in the United States, the difference between the functions of Parliament and Congress stands out as the main factor involved. The strength of party allegiance in Parliament makes legislative change easier: once the Thatcher government had determined on privatization, it was brought about more steadily than deregulation was, or could have been, in the United States, where in general the legislative inertia of vested interests is greater. There were victories for deregulation there on a scale which could not have been expected a few years previously, but it was far from complete: that inertia was strong enough to make complete deregulation only sure of success, as in airlines, where the regulator was abolished. The industries that have been deregulated in the United States have been similar in their characteristics to those privatized without regulation in Britain. (The deregulation of the railroads may seem an exception. But American railroads do not form a network as do Britain's railways: neither has regulated competitive interconnection been achieved there.) Moreover, as from 1992 it is the UK Government's intention to deregulate and in part privatize the railways.

An important difference between the two eras of deregulation distinguished above was that, in the earlier, the theory of natural monopoly had not been widely enough accepted. There are hints of an adequate theory in Adam Smith, but toll roads, which were the natural monopolies most evident to him, did not draw from him an analysis which could cover the utilities which were to become important from early in the nineteenth century. James Morrison did work out such a theory. And Gladstone in the early versions of his railway bill produced a form of natural-monopoly control which was consistent with Morrison's analysis – it was based on similar insights into the nature of natural monopoly and into the desirable characteristics of a system to control it. But Morrison did not explicitly integrate his theory into Adam Smithian and Ricardian economics, so failing to give it lasting expression. The final form of the 1844 Act abandoned Morrison's principles and insights, and with the passing of years came to be seen, rightly, as the progenitor of the inferior method of dividend control. As such it is still remembered. The reform of the regulatory machinery in the United States has been more elusive because of the weight of the second, Gladstonian, that is non-Morrisonian, tradition. For example, even though the Bell System has been broken up, the old machinery and methods of its regulation remain, though individual regulators have used their discretion to depart from classical regulation. And in the background stand the courts with their well-established procedures and precedents. As a result it seems difficult to find a lasting mean in the United States between regulatory capture and complete abandonment of regulation. It is because this inheritance in the United States is such a deterrent to finding satisfactory methods and institutions for regulation that it is desirable to look for an alternative. The new British system has the advantage that it can draw on the insights of modern natural-monopoly theory, which in its essentials is close to James Morrison's theory of railway monopoly.

12.2   The case for regulation

Arguments have been advanced on empirical, practical grounds that, if a regulatory system is cumbersome and expensive, total deregulation may be best, a line of reasoning that may also be based on the theoretical arguments of the Chicago school. Yet the case for the regulation of natural monopoly remains strong. Where natural monopoly exists, one cannot rely on market forces. Where competition is absent, well-designed and effective regulation can stimulate firms to greater efficiency. Competition can in some cases be increased by making available access to networks and nodes; but that does not avoid, indeed it confirms, the need for the effective regulation of the competitive behaviour of natural monopoly in the consumer's interest. This is also needed because of the growing importance of internal knowledge within a firm; the advantage of balancing risks across international markets; the need to take rapid advantage of technical progress and product innovation in as many markets as possible before the resulting goods and services become obsolete; and the ever-increasing ability of information and other modern management systems to help the effective management ever-larger units. Together these imply that national economies will often lose international competitiveness in many industries if they insist on more than one home-based firm supplying goods or services into their home markets. But if unregulated in their home markets such dominant firms can secure differential advantages which may undermine the efficiency and competitiveness of their suppliers and of the producers of substitute goods and services at home; and more generally of competitors abroad. Moreover, economic efficiency requires that countries adopt consistent approaches to economic regulation. One can already see supra-national economic regulation becoming more significant within the EEC, as well as transatlantic battles between US and European systems of regulation. And the growing importance of environmental, safety and other external factors will make still more essential regulatory oversight which is consistent with economic efficiency. Thus, it is difficult to believe that regulation is unnecessary, unless one has the extraordinary confidence in market forces some Chicago economists have had, or believes that any available system of regulation must be so bad that its absence must be better.

12.3   Regulatory failure

If a regulatory system is to survive, it must be able to avoid or overcome most of the types of 'failure' that it will be heir to. 'Regulatory failure' – a commonly used term – is susceptible of many definitions, their precise formulation depending in part on the interest from whose standpoint the system is said to have failed. Regulatory failure can be seen as a state of affairs in which some party is trying to effect a change in the system to remedy either a derogation in its ability to reflect their interest or its failure to do so in the first place. If the remedy is not available from the regulator, the party in question will turn to the judiciary or the executive, the choice depending on the extent of their discretion or ability to provide a remedy, before attempting legislative change, which in general is the most difficult to achieve. There are various kinds of regulatory failure which may lead to fundamental change.

There is failure from the standpoint of a privately owned regulated industry where at worst it does not continue to be profitable enough to maintain its capital. This may be because of the arrival of new technology; a marked increase in competition; or major changes in economic circumstances to which the regulatory mechanism does not adapt, for example, inflation. Nevertheless, there may be a change in regulatory behaviour sooner or later which will lead to regulatory capture again. In Britain from the 1840s to the 1890s there were successive adaptations of this kind. And in the United States there were successive adaptations from the period of the state commissions of the mid-nineteenth century until the 1970s. Thus, regulatory failure from this standpoint occurs when the system fails to adapt, in so far as such adaptation could restore profitability; or where the regulatory system is itself the cause of such unprofitability.

Because its objectives are not as well defined as those of a privately owned regulated industry, one cannot easily define regulatory failure from the standpoint of a nationalized industry. Indeed, it is a shortcoming of nationalization that a nationalized enterprise may never feel a failure, whatever the size of its deficit or its failure to control costs or quality, provided that it is not seen to be in crisis from outside.

One kind of failure from the standpoint of the regulator arises when he cannot regulate. There was such a failure in Victorian times until the 1870s because there was then no effective regulation. Later, in both the United States and United Kingdom, the courts at times reduced regulators to impotence. And under nationalization, ministers often failed to achieve their objectives, political as well as economic. One also has to recognize the possibility that under all regulatory regimes, including the new British one, ministers may use or abuse any powers they have to obstruct or go round the regulator, or to convert him into their agent.

Another kind of regulatory failure arises when the regulator no longer commands enough political support for him to be comfortable continuing. He may have been captured by the regulated industry without undue protest in the past but now begins to find that he is under other, outside pressures to act against the demands of the industry. He may have the will and the discretion to respond to those new pressures, as Alfred Kahn and Darius Gaskins did when they altered course with no more powers than their predecessors had, and deregulated. If, on the other hand, he does not choose to use the discretion which he has to do so, he may find himself replaced, if that is possible; or the courts, an Administrative Procedures Act, the legislature or some other agency may constrain his freedom. And whether he is willing to change or not the constraints on his discretion may have to be altered if he is to regain political support.

From the standpoint of other parties, regulatory failure exists when they feel that a regulatory system does not reflect their interests (or the interests of those whom they claim to represent), to the point where they are prepared to try to muster and deploy effective power to change that regulatory system. If they escalate their campaign from the regulator to the courts or the legislature, there may be more scope for change, but at a higher cost, both directly and in terms of the concessions that they may have to make. Two of the three main examples of the overturning of regulatory capture have been as a result of the opposition of those excluded from the regulatory compact: the repeated onslaughts of dissatisfied commercial railway customers in Britain and in the United States in the 1880s and 1890s (though the outcome was often unsatisfactory for them); and the opposition of consumer representatives and environmentalists in the United States in the 1970s.

Regulatory failure is often defined in a different sense, by comparison with a norm. Thus, a regulatory system which has objectives that either in principle or in practice differ from those of profitability or economic efficiency will spell regulatory failure to an economist. But it is in these circumstances (among others) that an economist should be humble, recognizing that a system which does not achieve his exacting standards may be better than nothing, even from the standpoint of economic efficiency.

12.4   Avoiding regulatory capture

Capture of the regulator by the regulated industry has the advantage that the industry will contrive matters so that it remains profitable if this is technically possible. Since in most countries monopolies require legislation, they will have to pay some price to those who grant them their privileges. In most circumstances this will be at some expense to their own profits. Where the situation approximates to that postulated by the Chicago school of economists – what many would judge to be that of a corrupt society – the legislators, or whoever else has the power to grant legislative instruments or licences, will, directly or indirectly, themselves be financial beneficiaries. In other circumstances – approximating to the wide range of situations covered by the Virginian theory – the price will have more to do with electoral and other political goals than with money. To analyse the consequences in any given situation requires an understanding of the objectives and relative power of the various interests concerned in a particular country. For example, nationalization generally reflects a situation in which effective power is shared by ministers, the board of the industry and its employees. While it is possible that the effect of the difference in strength of the various interests will result only in a change in the distribution of surplus between them, very often their interaction results in a state of economic inefficiency from which the consumers and some others – such as those adversely affected by the environmental and other external impact of the industry – are losers. (If the inefficiency is sufficiently great by comparison with the levels of efficiency which could have been achieved, it is even possible to imagine a situation in which some among the ministers, board and employees are also net losers.) A privately owned regulated industry which captures its regulator may be inefficient for similar reasons.

Thus, to be fully defensible, a system of economic regulation must not be captured either by the industry or its employees or by politicians or by other particular interests, or sets of interests. The first question therefore to be asked of a regulatory framework is whether it has been designed in the cause of a particular interest, or set of interests. However, even if it has been so designed, it may work to the extent that there is no serious substantial opposition to it, as was true of US regulation and British nationalization for many years, though not, for example, of UK railways regulation before 1948, which ultimately satisfied no one. Even a captured regulatory agency will know that it must buy off other interests by paying sufficient attention to their concerns for them not to be angered enough to mount a campaign against it.

A number of conclusions have been reached in this book on how best to avoid or at least check regulatory capture:

1 Experience suggests that it requires an independent regulator who retains substantial discretion to interpret and decide regulatory offences.

2 The adoption of elaborate, court-like procedures, and a right of appeal to the courts on merits and the interpretation of the law, are likely to favour the regulated industry.

3 The adoption of procedures by a regulator which protect natural justice without leading to over-elaborate and costly proceedings is likely to check regulatory capture. Such natural justice may be protected by a right of appeal to a court.

4 If there are to be appeals on merits and interpretation of the law they should preferably be to a similar regulatory body with similar discretion and procedures.

5 The more firms within an industry a regulator regulates the less likely he is to be captured by any one of them, except where one is dominant or they are able to make common cause against him because their interests are complementary.

6 The more influence on a regulator that is given to interested parties other than the regulated industry the more likely it is that he will strike a balance between those interests and those of the regulated industry, preventing or checking capture by any party.

7 As important as any other is the consideration that ministerial and other political influences must be constrained as far as possible to roles that do not allow them to have opportunities to impose uncompensated burdens on regulated industries with a significant effect on their efficiency. Though the way in which it works is different, political capture can be as great a threat to the consumer's interest as capture of the regulator by the industry. In countries where governments traditionally have strong discretionary powers, it is a more likely outcome.

8 The interest that most needs to be built up is that of the consumer. One needs an apparatus to reflect the consumer's economic interest intelligently, since consumers tend to be apathetic. But one should not make them dominant, as that could lead to regulatory failure.

If a regulator is in a position where he has to mediate between opposing forces, he needs the discretion to allow him do so. In making his choice he will be aware that, if he goes too far in favour of any one interest, he risks losing the political support on which he depends; but within this limitation he may well be able to show bias if he chooses, and that opens up the possibility that a regulator serving his own interests – for example, aiming to pursue a career within a regulated industry – may misuse his discretion. A more venial route to the same end may simply be by way of the fact that a regulator, even if he is mediating between opposing interests, is still likely to see more of the industry he regulates than of the other parties. Moreover, whatever resources and information the regulator has, the industry will have more. Similarly, a regulator whose career ambitions lie within government may veer towards serving its interests. In such ways, his discretion may be captured sooner or later even without his knowing it.

The difficulty of aligning the interests of the regulator with the public interest begins with the problem of deciding what the public interest is. Although deciding what is expressed in law is the conventional method of deciding the public interest, the fact that precise regulatory offences cannot be established means that this is not a useful method in a regulatory context. Hence its usual replacement in the regulatory statutes by a requirement that the regulator decide the public interest. To this may be attached a list of criteria that he is to consider in reaching his decision; but, as he has the discretion to decide what weight he gives each, this is not a restriction on his judgement. It is thus this inability to express the public interest in the field of regulation in a set of laws or rules that bind the regulator that brings one to the difficulty of ensuring that a regulator serves the public interest, however defined.

In such circumstances, a reasonable, though vague, requirement (noted earlier) is that the regulator of a natural monopoly must mediate between two or more interests. He must allow the regulated industry a sufficient return for it to provide and, if appropriate, expand its range of goods or services profitably, as much as a competitive firm would in otherwise similar circumstances. He must protect consumers from higher prices and lower quality than are necessary for the efficient provision of its goods or services, and from higher quality than they would be willing to pay for if they had the freedom to choose. In the interests both of the consumer and of economic efficiency, he must see to it that the economic regulatory offences, preferably those described in this book, are not committed, or left unpunished if they are. And he will also be required to deal with some, one hopes not too many, social regulatory offences. From all this one can extract a negative view of a regulator's performance with respect to the public interest. A regulator is not serving it if he identifies exclusively or preponderantly with either consumer or regulated firm, or if it is apparent that he allows other interests to intrude into his mediation where he is not required to do so by statute. Similarly, he may be criticized if he allows one criterion to dominate in his decision-making when there are several he is required to consider; or if he allows some unlisted criterion to have an evident influence upon his conclusions. Because neither he nor any other party has perfect information, no one can say precisely where in the middle ground the public interest lies. Thus, a regulator may choose positions there more or less favourable to one interest than to the other or others without any possibility of anyone's demonstrating conclusively that he is biased; and the more criteria he is required to use and the more interests he has to weigh, the less can the use of his discretion be criticized.[3] But it is possible on occasion to say where on that ground the public interest does not lie.

An economist would argue that as far as possible, the best outcome is whatever approximates most closely to economic efficiency. However, he must accept that the law may require the regulator to be influenced by other criteria and by specific social obligations. Whether these are so great as to lead in any given industry to what is best described as capture is question of judgement. As we have seen, economic theories of regulation tend to assume, not unreasonably, that the personal interests of a regulator (and possibly of his staff) will dispose him to veer to one end or other of the middle ground; and, given the superior resources of the regulated industry by comparison with those of the consumer, the usual prediction is that regulator and the regulatory process will veer towards the industry's interests. Economic theory generally argues in favour of giving any agent a financial incentive or property right as an inducement to achieve his principal's objectives. But here it would not be possible to engage the services of the regulator as 'agent', using in this way material incentives to engage his self-interest and induce him not to veer too far from that centre; for one wants the regulator to be as far as possible disinterested, and not directed through his self-interest by the interests of 'principle' (a minister, for example) which are themselves equally open to material suasion and therefore to capture (bringing the argument full circle).[4]

Another approach to the question of how to ensure that a regulator serves the public interest is to recognize that economic thinking naturally analyses the power of a regulator to serve his own interests in terms of the absence of competition.[5] The regulator has been given a monopoly; and like any other monopolist he takes what advantage he can from monopoly. Some economists have suggested that the answer is to introduce competition into regulation. As in any other market, regulators would compete for business. Parties would select the regulator that gave them most satisfaction. But in any ordinary sense that does not seem a gain. If there were several competing regulators and a party could choose which regulator to appear before, the eventual outcome might well depend on which party moved first and was therefore able to select a favourable regulator. The outcome would presumably be chaotic unless there was mutual agreement that one regulator was preferred by all parties. But it is hard to believe that some procedure could be devised in each case to select the regulator likely to choose the compromise most acceptable to all parties.[6] In the United States many regulated bodies have more than one regulator, distinguished by differences in territory, procedures and subject-matter. And sometimes there are elements of competition between them or between different officials of the same agency. Yet it is arguable that this multiplicity has been responsible for many bad regulatory decisions.[7] All this does not lead to a clearer definition of the public interest through competition, but generally to confusion and inconsistency.

The judicial system itself provides a form of competition, because there is a sense in which lawyers and courts may compete in their interpretation of the law. Competing interpretations of the law are argued by counsel on both sides and thereafter through an appellate structure to the highest court if necessary. And even then an action in another, related matter may start up sooner or later which leads to a reinterpretation of the same law. In some circumstances such a process of clarification may lead the legislator to revise the law. If the public interest could be set down in laws which were then subject to a process of interpretation, then whenever there was conflict there would be a means, which might be called competitive, by which a regulator could be prevented from giving too personal or vested a judgement. But, as we have seen, regulatory issues cannot be expressed as rules or laws for the most part with precision, so competition in this form cannot achieve an approximation to a disinterested expression of the public interest. A disastrous example of an attempt to give too great a precision to an economic concept was that given to discrimination on the railways after 1894 when at last, following some years of confusion, it became clear that discrimination was any price difference or change that a railway could not justify by an attributable cost increase or quality difference. As we have seen, precision here was gained in this industry at the cost of economic and commercial nonsense. Thus, this way of depersonalizing judgements available to the judiciary is not available to the regulatory process.

Another form of competition is where a regulatory commission has a number of commissioners who take decisions collectively. They may be presumed to have different views of the public interest: some of them perhaps being closer to the consumer and others to the regulated industry. However, this does not seem to have prevented many US regulatory agencies from being captured by the industries they regulate. Moreover, it is more likely to lead to inconsistency in approach. As with juries, it seems easier to use several minds to reach agreement on fact where the law is clear than where it is not; and to reach agreement on fact rather than on what the law – the rules – should be. The new model UK regulation prefers single to multiple regulators, and in the United States most commissions over time have adopted a pattern in which the chairman tends to dominate. The advantage is that a single regulator in office can, if he is able and consistent, devise and develop a consistent policy in decision-making in a way which, at least to himself, plainly locates his exact position in the middle ground, even if he cannot express to others its superiority over some other series of consistent decisions; and there is no reason to believe that a panel of regulators will have such an inner, if inexpressible, consistency. This reflects an old truth that the more a position requires the use of discretion, the more it requires a single mind.[8]

There would seem to be no gain therefore in introducing any means by which the power of the regulator is shared either by appeals to the courts over merits and interpretation of the law, or by introducing competition into regulation, whether by providing competing regulators or by establishing or combining regulatory bodies so that several regulators decide collegiately. If regulatory policy is to be developed consistently, then the best procedure would seem to be to set up a single regulator; but he needs to be exceptionally able, and single-minded enough to carve out a policy which he knows to be consistent. Because of the size of the middle ground within which he can make a defensible decision – for example, in his attempts to find a fair return or a reasonable value for X, or to decide whether a price change is predatory – he must weigh subjective probabilities. And, assuming that he is conscientious, he has to reach a series of judgements which he is himself persuaded is balanced between the parties. If in any instance he makes a mistake, he must decide whether to lean in the opposite direction on the next occasion or still look for the centre of the middle ground.

Nevertheless, in order to strengthen the position of regulators in the face of possible criticisms on the ground of arbitrariness and to curb any excesses, there do need to be some appeals procedures if natural justice is to be seen to be done, though means also need to be found to prevent too many or vexatious appeals. The principles already discussed suggest that appeals should be to a tribunal that acts with similar discretion and flexibility to that of the first-tier regulator, not to a court. That is, it should be another body specializing in economic regulation.[9]

A further form of competition in regulation is the limiting of the term or franchise of each regulator. At the least, an unsatisfactory regulator who is felt to have abused his discretion can then be removed. However, one cannot of course stop politicians removing or keeping regulators for quite different reasons (as the reasons for continuing with or removing nationalized industry chairman have often had nothing to do with their commercial effectiveness). Moreover, replacing one regulator by another will alter regulatory decisions and policy more than replacing one judge by another will alter legal judgements, just because of the extent of that defensible middle ground of discretion: even equally able regulators may strike a different balance between the interests of parties and give different weights to various criteria, not because of any change in the law or government policy but because they have the freedom to do so.

However well designed a regulatory regime is, the chances of capture or failure will increase with time. It is not easy to maintain a succession of regulators of quality. And with time the chances that even able regulators will find themselves in an inconsistency, will have the forecasts upon which they make their decisions falsified or will be outmanoeuvred by the regulated industry must increase. The regulators may not maintain enough publicity to keep consumer and other public opinion on his side. And politicians may use their powers to constrain his judgement, or threaten unpalatable change to gain his assent to their proposals. Nevertheless, it is a leading contention of this book that regulation as defined here, and adapted to national traditions, is preferable both to regulation by the courts and to political control.

12.5   An effective regulatory system

It has been a key strand in the argument of this book that, while the underlying economic principles and therefore the regulatory offences should be relevant in all economies, how the offences should best be expressed, monitored and controlled can only be decided in the context of the constitution, laws and political habits of the individual country. Each country needs to find its way of achieving the following desiderata:

the progressive extension of competition whenever that is possible;
definitions of regulatory offences which enable regulators to concentrate on the critical economic issues;
independent, impartial regulators;
enough information to be made available on a routine basis to enable the regulator to do his job without protracted, inconclusive wrangles over data;
appropriate penalties the regulator can enforce;
procedures that conform to natural justice without being legalistic;
an appeals system that as far as possible obeys the same discretionary spirit in its procedures;
enough discretion for the regulator to develop and use specialized knowledge;
distance from parties who are likely to want to intervene to secure political aims;
such social obligations as the regulated industry has or acquires being financially sustainable by it.

It is also always important to take into account who has the greatest interest in ensuring that the regulated industry is economically efficient and to ensure that they as well have a place in the regulatory proceedings. And the interests of consumers and of actual and potential competitors and suppliers stand out in this respect. However, in neither case is their representation without difficulty. Although consumers gain from the lower prices and higher service quality that economic efficiency provides, unfortunately consumer representative bodies tend to be more interested in quality than in lower prices or economic efficiency *per se*. The difficulty here with potential competitors and suppliers is that they generally do not have the interest to bring pressure to bear until they have actually decided that their entry into the market is possible – they are not interested in making a heavy investment before that. Moreover, if they are economically rational, they will always be asking whether collusion with the incumbent, or being bought out by it, is not a more profitable policy. Nevertheless, entrenching consumer interests and the interests of actual and potential competitors and suppliers within the regulatory process so that they cannot be ignored is probably the single most effective means of ensuring that the regulator gives due weight to those interests, as it will also be for environmental and other external interests.

The development of regulation has not been reflected in steady progress towards well-defined contractual obligations. The Victorians placed great weight on the sanctity of contractual obligations, especially on those to be found in the relevant private acts. But that was undermined by corporatist interventions from around the turn of the century until, under nationalization, the absence of formal contractual relations was counted a virtue. However, for successful regulation some document or documents are needed in which the obligations of the various parties are recorded so that they may be identified, administered and enforced. Various reasons have been given why statutes are unlikely to be sufficiently consistent or detailed on their own for this purpose. Experience suggests they need to be backed up by a licence or franchise: a document which in well-defined circumstances should be reviewed and may be altered without recourse to the legislature.

As far as possible such contracts should be flexible enough to cope with all likely changes in economic and technological circumstances. Past regulatory systems have been seriously flawed by their inability to cope with inflation, for example, or deep recession; neither have they generally shown any need to recognize that technical change can alter the practicality of competition. But there are limits to the complications that can usefully be reflected in contracts.

Under the new British system a vital ministerial role is the issuing of such contracts or licences. But others could have this role. Whoever does largely controls increases in competition since the increasing of competition in general requires the issuing of licences. It has been argued that it is important to do this quickly; not to be over-impressed by arguments for delay; and in particular to encourage technical advances which are likely to make more competition possible. All this is especially important in gas and telecommunications, where the privatization legislation restricted competition. Yet such further competition will be resisted by the regulated industry, and rightly from its standpoint; it has every incentive to attempt capture to prevent it, at least in the blinkered short run. Moreover, those who grant licences may have their own reasons for wishing to restrict competition.

An important issue here – the significance of which has been underplayed in Britain – is the extent to which one should go back to the view that, as contracts, such legislation and licences should be immune from retrospective intervention. The general principles seem clear. There should be immunity from legislation or other retrospective intervention which damages the profitability of a natural monopoly without compensation except in the context of a general measure which affects others similarly, though even then it is wise to consider the effect on profitability.

12.6 Conclusion: the new British regulatory system. Lessons for elsewhere.

The new British regulatory system has developed a general consistency while learning from its own brief experience. Unconsciously or not, it has taken several steps to lessen the chances of capture by the regulated industry. It has avoided legalistic processes and appeal to the courts. And with perhaps one exception it has recognized that new possibilities of competition should be encouraged. Will it be said that in the 1980s the regulation of natural monopoly came to be established on a better and more permanent basis than earlier systems, that the new system is more capable of organic development and of adapting to changing circumstances, is less likely to become fossilized? Despite improvisation under pressure what has emerged does seem to have avoided many of the shortcomings of the past, British and American. It has thrown up administrative techniques of imagination and ingenuity. It has given the regulator the powers to determine and pursue the appropriate offences. And it has given him more power over information than has been usual. In almost every case it has limited ministerial powers to matters which should not give ministers much opportunity for day-to-day intervention in the industries, or in how a regulator performs his duties. And above all it has realized, again without obvious explicit recognition, that an absence of precise laws or rules, and the use instead of discretion, is necessary for effective regulation: it has given the regulators the greatest possible discretion in the interpretation of the licences and, for the most part, the independence to use it.

It would be wrong to go overboard in praise of the new system. It has, as we have seen, a number of shortcomings. Nevertheless, in the end, whatever reservations one may have about the desirability of independent economic regulation, or its continuing possibility, while it lasts and avoids as many imperfections as it can, it is better than what has hitherto been tried – better than relying on anything approaching the normal relationship between ministers and public enterprise and better than economic regulation by, or dominated by, the courts. That indeed has been the contention of this book.

Notes

1   W. Cobbett (ed.) *Parliamentary History*, vol. 12, p. 656, cited by Tanner (1928), p. 76.
2   Russell (1990), pp. 176, 177.
3   Breyer (1982), pp. 78, 79.

4 This view derives from Coase (1960).

5 Alessi (1975).

6 While it is possible to imagine competition between regulators converging to a stable solution, it would, I think, mean that it is always possible for a party getting an unfavourable decision from one regulator to go to another and so on until the cost to that party exceeded the benefit. Such a system would mean that the outcome would be decided by the length of a party's purse.

7 Wenders (1987).

8 Another way of putting the same point is Robert Solo's 'Composite choice, emerging out of a diversity of interests and premises, is without a specific point of reference save in the weight of counterbalancing forces. The process of corporate force cannot be the expression of a unitary purpose, a reasoning mind and an integral ideology': Solo (1980), pp. 38, 39.

9 Reference to the Monopolies and Mergers Commission has been avoided where possible by licensees because of the strong possibility that the Commission might widen the investigation; the demands it will make upon management time; the publicity that may ensue; and the fear that an inquiry may unearth something which the organization either wants keeping quiet or does not itself know about.

References

Abel-Smith, B. (1964) *The Hospitals: 1800–1948*, Heinemann.

Accounting Standards Committee (1986) *Accounting for Changing Prices: A Handbook*, CCAB.

Acworth, W. M. (1905) *Elements of Railway Economics*, Clarendon Press.

(1912) *The State in Relation to Railways*, Royal Economic Society, P. S. King.

Albert, W. (1972) *Turnpike Road System*, Cambridge University Press.

Albu, A. (1963) 'Ministerial and parliamentary control', in Shanks (1963).

Aldcroft, D. H. (1968) 'Efficiency and enterprise in British railways, 1870–1914', *Explorations in Entrepreneurial History*, vol. 5, no. 2, pp. 158–74.

Alderman, G. (1973) *The Railway Interest*, Leicester University Press.

Alessi, L. de (1975) 'An economic analysis of government ownership and regulation', *Public Choice*, vol. 19, pp. 1–42.

Anscombe, G. E. M. (1957) *Intention*, Blackwell.

Areeda, P. and Turner, D. F. (1975) 'Predatory pricing and related practices under Section 2 of the Sherman Act', *Harvard Law Review*, February, vol. 88, pp. 697–733.

Aristotle (1946) *The Politics of Aristotle*, ed. E. Baker, Oxford University Press.

Armytage, W. H. G. (1951) *A. J. Mundella, 1825–1897*, Ernest Benn.

Ashworth, M. A. and Forsyth, P. J. (1984) *British Airways*, Institute of Fiscal Studies Report Series No. 12.

Averch, H. and Johnson, L. L. (1962) 'Behaviour of the firm under regulatory constraint', *American Economic Review*, vol. 52.2, no. 5, pp. 1,052–69.

Aylen, J. (1987) 'Privatisation in developing countries', *Lloyds Bank Review*, no. 163.

Bagehot, W. (1933) *The English Constitution*, (1st edn. 1867), Oxford University Press.

Bagwell, P. S. (1968) *The Railway Clearing House*, Allen and Unwin.

(1988) *The Transport Revolution: 1770–1985*, Routledge.

Bailey, E. E. (1981) 'Contestability and the design of regulatory and anti-trust policy', *American Economic Review*, May, vol. 71, pp. 178–89.

(ed.) (1987) *Public Regulation: New Perspectives on Institutions and Policies*, MIT Press.

Bailey, E. E., Graham, D. R. and Kaplan, D. P. (eds) (1985) *Deregulating the Airlines*, MIT Press.

Bailey, S. (1931) *A Critical Dissertation on the Nature, Measure and Causes of Value*, (1st edn. 1825), Hunter.

Baldwin, R. (1987) 'Civil aviation regulation', in Baldwin and McCrudden (1987).

Baldwin, R. and McCrudden, C. (1987) *Regulation and Public Law*, Weidenfeld and Nicolson.

Banister, D. (1985) 'Deregulating the bus industry – the proposals', *Transport Reviews*, vol. 5, pp. 99–103.

Barker, T. and Savage, C. I. (1974) *An Economic History of Transport in Britain*, Hutchinson.

Barnato, M. (1981) 'Nationalised industries and government controls', *Public Money*, vol. 1, no. 3, pp. 16–17.

Baron, D. P. (1985) 'Non-cooperative regulation of a nonlocalised externality', *Rand Journal of Economics*, vol. 16, pp. 553–68.

Bator, F. M. (1958) 'The anatomy of market failure', *Quarterly Journal of Economics*, August, pp. 351–79.

Baumol, W. J. (1975) 'Payment by performance in rail passenger transportation: an innovation in Amtrak's operations', *Bell Journal of Economics*, vol. 6, pp. 281–98.

(1977a) 'Towards a theory of public enterprise', *Atlantic Economic Journal*, vol. 12, pp. 13–19.

(1977b) 'On the proper cost tests for natural monopoly', *American Economic Review*, vol. 67, pp. 808–22.

Baumol, W. J., Bailey, E. E. and Willig, R. D. (1977) 'Weak invisible hand theorems on the sustainability of multi-product natural monopoly', *American Economic Review*, vol. 67, pp. 350–65.

Baumol, W. J. and Klevorick, A. J. (1970) 'Input choices and rate of return regulation: an overview of the discussion', *Bell Journal of Economics*, vol. 1, pp. 162–90.

Baumol, W. J. and Oates, W. E. (1975) *Theory of Environmental Policy*, Prentice-Hall.

Baumol, W. J., Panzar, J. C. and Willig, R. D. (1982) *Contestable Markets and the Theory of Industry Structure*, Harcourt Brace Jovanovich.

Becker, G. S. (1983) 'A theory of competition among pressure groups for political influence', *Quarterly Journal of Economics*, vol. 98, pp. 371–400.

(1985) 'Public policies, pressure groups and deadweight costs', *Journal of Public Economics*, vol. 28, pp. 329–47.

(1989) 'Political competition among interest groups', in Shogren (1989).

Beesley, M. E. (1981) *Liberalisation of the Use of British Telecommunications Network*, HMSO.

(1990) 'Collusion, predation and merger in the U.K. bus industry', *Journal of Transport Economics and Policy*, September, vol. 24.

Beesley, M. E. and Foster, C. D. (1965) 'Victoria Line: social benefit and finances', *Journal of the Royal Statistical Society*, series A, vol. 128, pp. 67–88.

Beesley, M. E. and Laidlaw, B. (1989) *Future of Telecommunications*, Institute of Economic Affairs Research Monograph No. 42.

(1991) *Competition and Choice: Telecommunication Policy for the 1990s*, Institute of Economic Affairs Inquiry No. 21.

Beesley, M. E. and Littlechild, S. (1986) 'Privatisation: principles, problems and priorities', in Kay, Mayer and Thompson (1986).

Berg, S. V. and Tschirhart, J. (1988) *Natural Monopoly Regulation: Principles and Practice*, Cambridge University Press.

Berlin, I. (1954) *Historical Inevitability*, Oxford University Press.

Bernstein, M. (1955) *Regulating Business by Independent Commission*, Princeton University Press.

Bishop, M. and Kay, J. A. (1988) *Does Privatisation Work? Lessons from the UK*, London Business School.

Blanchflower, D. G. and Oswald, A. J. (1988) 'Profit-related Pay: Prose discovered?' *Economic Journal*, September, vol. 98, pp. 720–33.

Bocherding, T. E. (ed.) (1977) *Budgets and Bureaucrats: The Sources of Government Growth*, Duke University Press.

Bonavia, M. R. (1971) *Organisation of British Railways*, Ian Allan.

(1981) *Railway Policy Between the Wars*, Manchester University Press.

(1986) *Railways and Some Politicians, 1845–1945*, Charles Cluster Memorial Lecture.

(1987) *The Nationalisation of British Transport*, Macmillan.

(undated) *The Role of Government in the Field of Railway Safety and the Work of the Railway Inspectorate*, memorandum.

Bonbright, J. C. (1961) *Principles of Public Utility Rates*, Columbia University Press.

Bos, D. and Peters, W. (1991) 'Principal–agent approach on manager effort and control in privatised and public firms', in Ott and Hartley (1991).

Boyson, R. (ed.) (1971) *Good-Bye to Nationalisation*, Churchill Press.

Bradley, A. W. (1989) 'The sovereignty of Parliament in perpetuity?' in Jowell and Oliver 1989.

Bradley, F. H. (1930) *Appearance and Reality* (1st edn. 1893), Oxford University Press.

Bradley, K. and Gelb, A. (1986) *Share Ownership for Employees*, Public Policy Centre.

Braeutigam, R. R. (1989) 'Output policies for natural monopolies', in Schmalensee and Willig (1989).

Brech, M. and Whiteman, J. (1982) 'Financing nationalised industries: a third way', *Public Money*, vol. 2, no. 3, pp. 13–17.

Brennan, G. and Buchanan, J. M. (1977) 'Towards a tax constitution for Leviathan', *Journal of Public Economics*, vol. 8, pp. 255–74.

Breyer, S. G. (1982) *Regulation and its Reform*, Harvard University Press.

(1987) 'Judicial review of questions of law and policy', in Bailey (1987).

Breyer, S. G. and Stewart, R. R. (1985) *Administrative Law and Regulatory Policy*, Little, Brown.

British Transport Commission (1955) *Modernisation and Re-equipment of British Railways*, British Transport Commission.

Brittan, S. and Riley, B. (1978) 'A people's stake in North Sea oil', *Lloyds Bank Review*, April.

Brown, L. N. and Garner, J. F. (1983) *French Administrative Law*, Butterworth.

Brown, S. J. and Sibley, D. S. (1986) *The Theory of Public Utility Pricing*, Cambridge University Press.

BT (British Telecom) (1990a) *Annual Review*, British Telecom.

(1990b) *Competitive Markets in Telecommunications*, British Telecom.

Buchanan, J. M. (1977) 'Why does government grow?' in Bocherding (1977).

Buchanan, J. M., Burtin J. and Wagner, R. W. (1978) *The Consequences of Mr Keynes*, Hobart Paper No. 78, Institute of Economic Affairs.

Buckland, R. (1987) 'Costs and returns of the privatised industries', *Public Administration*, vol. 59, pp. 239–41.

Burk, K. (1988) *The First Privatization*, Historians' Press.

Butler, D. and Kavanagh, D. (1988) *The British General Election of 1987*, Macmillan.

Button, K. (1988) 'Contestability in the UK bus industry', in Dodgson and Topham (1988).

Button, K. and Swann, D. (eds) (1989) *Age of Regulatory Reform*, Clarendon Press.

Buxton, N. K. and Aldcroft, D. F. (1979) *British Industry Between the Wars*, Scolar Press.

Cain, P. J. (1972) 'Railway combination and government', *Economic History Review*, vol. 25, pp. 623–31.

(1973) 'Traders vs. railways: the genesis of the Railway and Canal Traffic Act of 1894', *Journal of Transport History*, NS, vol. 2, no. 2, pp. 65–84.

(1976) 'Railways and price discrimination: the case of agriculture, 1880–1914', *Business History*, vol. 18, no. 2, pp. 190–204.

(1978) 'The British railway rates problem', *Business History*, vol. 20, no. 1, pp. 87–99.

(1980) 'Private enterprise or public utility? Output, pricing and investment on English and Welsh railways: 1870–1914', *Journal of Transport History*, 3rd series, vol. 1, no. 1, pp. 9–23.

Cairncross, A. (1985) *The Years of Recovery*, Methuen.

Cannan, E. (1927) *History of Local Rates*, P. S. King.

Central Statistical Office (1988) *Annual Abstract of Statistics*, HMSO.

(1990) *Annual Abstract of Statistics*, HMSO.

Chadwick, E. (1859) 'On different principles of legislation and administration', *Journal of the Royal Statistical Society*, vol. 22, pp. 381–420.

Chandler, A. D. (1962) *Strategy and Structure*, MIT Press.

(1977) *The Visible Hand: The Managerial Revolution in American Business*, Harvard University Press.

Checkland, S. G. and Checkland, E. O. A. (eds) (1974) *The Poor Law Report of 1834*, Pelican Classics.

Chester, D. N. (1975) *The Nationalization of British Industry: 1945–51*, HMSO.

Clapham, J. H. (1926) *An Economic History of Modern Britain: The Early Railway Age*, Cambridge University Press.

Clarkson, K. W. and Muris, T. J. (1982) 'Letting competition serve consumers', in Poole (1982).

Clegg, H. A. and Chester, T. E. (1953) *The Failure of Nationalisation*, Blackwell.

Cleveland Stevens, E. (1915) *English Railways: Their Development and Their Relation to the State*, Routledge.

Coase, R. H. (1960) 'The problem of social cost', *Journal of Law and Economics*, October, vol. 3.

—— (1979) 'Should the Federal Communications Commission be abolished?' in Siegan (1979).

Cohen, W. M. and Levin, R. C. (1989) 'Empirical studies of innovation and market structure', in Schmalensee and Willig (1989).

Coll, S. (1986) *The Deal of the Century*, Atheneum.

Commander, S. and Killick, T. (1988) 'Privatisation in developing countries: a survey of the issues', in Cook and Kirkpatrick (1988).

Conservative Party (1983) *Election Manifesto*.

Cook, P. and Kirkpatrick, C. (eds) (1988) *Privatization in Developing Countries*, Wheatsheaf.

Coopers & Lybrand (1988) *Privatisation*, Coopers & Lybrand.

Cornell, N. W. and Webbank, D. W. (1985) 'Public utility regulation: can it ever protect customers?' in Poole (1985).

Cournot, A-A. (1838) *Recherches sur les principes mathématiques de la théorie des richesses*, Hachette.

Coyne, J. and Wright, M. (1982) 'Buy-outs and British industry', *Lloyds Bank Review*, October 1982.

Craig, P. P. (1989) *Administrative Law*, Sweet and Maxwell.

Cramer, C. (1989) 'Natural gas pipelines', in Nowotny, Smith and Trebing (1989).

Crew, M. A. (ed.) (1987) *Regulatory Utilities in an Era of Deregulation*, Macmillan.

—— (ed.) (1989) *Deregulation and Diversification of Utilities*, Kluwer.

Crew, M. A. and Rowley, C. J. (1989) 'Towards a public choice theory of monopoly regulation', in Crew (1989).

Crosland, C. A. R. (1956) *The Future of Socialism*, Jonathan Cape.

Crossman, R. H. S. (1976) *Diaries of a Cabinet Minister* vol. 2: *Lord President of the Council and Leader of the House of Commons 1966–8*, Hamish Hamilton/Jonathan Cape.

Cushman, R. E. (1941) *The Independent Regulatory Commissions*, Oxford University Press.

Dasgupta, P., Sen, A. K. and Marglin, S. (1972) *Guidelines for Project Evaluation*, United Nations.

Dasgupta, P. and Stiglitz, P. (1980) 'Uncertainty, industrial structure and the speed of R and D', *Bell Journal of Economics*, vol. 11, pp. 1–28.

Davies, E. (1913) *The Case for Railway Nationalisation*, Collins.

Davis, E. H. (1986) 'Express coaching since 1980' in Kay, Mayer and Thompson (1986).

Davis, J. (1988) *Reforming London: The London Government problem 1855–1900*, Clarendon Press.

Davis, K. C. (1969) *Discretionary Justice*, Louisiana State University Press.

Day, P. and Klein, R. (1987) *Accountabilities*, Tavistock.

Demsetz, H. (1968) 'Why regulate utilities?', *Journal of Law and Economics*, vol. 11, pp. 55–65.

—— (1971) 'On the regulation of industry: a reply', *Journal of Law and Economics*, vol. 79, pp. 356–73.

Department of Economic Affairs (1965), *National Plan*, HMSO.

Department of Transport (1984), *Buses*, HMSO.

Derthick, M. and Quirk, P. J. (1985) *Politics of Deregulation*, Brookings.

Dicey, A. V. (1914) *Lectures on the Relation between Law and Public Opinion in England during the Nineteenth Century* (2nd edn.: 1st edn. 1905), Macmillan.

(1959) *Introduction to the Study of the Law of the Constitution* (1st edn. 1885), Oxford University Press.

Dodgson, J. S. (1989) *Privatising Britain's Railways: Lessons from the Past*, University of Liverpool, Discussion Papers in Economics No. 59.

Dodgson, J. S. and Topham, N. (eds) (1988) *Bus Deregulation and Privatisation*, Avebury.

Donoghue, B. and Jones, G. (1973) *Herbert Morrison: Portrait of a Politician*, Weidenfeld and Nicolson.

Dornbusch, R. and Layard, R. (eds) (1987) *The Performance of the British Economy*, Clarendon Press.

Douglas, N. J. (1987) *Welfare Assessment of Transport Deregulation*, Gower.

DTI (Department of Trade and Industry) (1990) *Competition and Choice: Telecommunications Policy for the 1990s: A Consultative Document*, Cm. 1303, HMSO.

(1991) *Competition and Choice: Telecommunications Policy for the 1990s*, Cm. 1461, HMSO.

Dunleavy, P. and Rhodes, R. A. W. (1986) 'Government beyond Whitehall', in H. Drucker et al., *Developments in British Politics*, vol. 2, Macmillan.

Dunsire, A. (1991) 'Organisational status change and performance', in Ott and Hartley (1991).

Eckel, C. C. and Vermaclen, T. (1989) 'Financial fall-out from Chernobyl', in Crew (1989).

Ede, H. W. et al. (1925) *Modern Railway Administration*, Gresham.

Edwards, C. (1897) *Railways Nationalisation*, Methuen.

Eisner, M. E. (1991) *Anti-trust and the Triumph of Economics*, University of North Carolina Press.

Estrada, J. et al. (1988) *Natural Gas in Europe*, Pinter.

Evans, A. (1988) 'Hereford: a case study of bus deregulation', *Journal of Transport Economics and Policy*, vol. 22, pp. 283–306.

(1990) 'Competition and the structure of local bus markets', *Journal of Transport Economics and Policy*, vol. 24, no. 3, pp. 255–81.

Fainsod, M. (1940) 'Some reflections on the regulatory process', in C. J. Friedrich and E. S. Mason (eds), *Public Policy*, Harvard University Press.

Farrer, T. H. (1883) *The State in its Relation to Trade*, Macmillan.

Faulhaber, G. R. (1975) 'Cross-subsidisation: pricing in public enterprise', *American Economic Review*, vol. 65, pp. 966–77.

(1987) *Telecommunications in Turmoil*, Ballinger.

Finer, H. E. (1933) *English Local Government*, Methuen.

(1941) *Municipal Trading*, Allen and Unwin.

Fiorina, M. P. (1982) 'Legislative choice of regulatory forms: legal process or administrative process?', *Public Choice*, vol. 39, pp. 33–66.

Fisher, H. A. L. (1945) *History of Europe*, (1st edn. 1938) Eyre and Spottiswode.

Foot, M. R. D. and Matthew, H. C. G. (1974) *The Gladstone Diaries: 1840–47*, vol. 3, Clarendon Press.

Foreman Peck, J. (1987) 'Natural monopoly and railway policy in the nineteenth century', *Oxford Economic Papers*, December, pp. 699–718.

Foster, C. D. (1959) 'Some notes on railway costs and costing', *Bulletin of the Oxford Institute of Statistics*.

(1963) *The Transport Problem*, Blackie.

(1971) *Politics, Finance and the Role of Economics: An Essay on the Control of Public Enterprise*, Allen and Unwin.

(1983) *Public Sector Accounting and Research*, Deloittes, Haskins and Sells.

Foster, C. D. and Beesley, M. E. (1963) 'Estimating the social benefit of constructing an underground railway in London', *Journal of the Royal Statistical Society*, series A, vol. 126, pp. 46–92.

Foster, C. D. and Golay, J. (1986) 'Some curious old practices and their relevance to equilibrium in Bus Competition', *Journal of Transport Economics and Policy*, vol. 20, no. 2, pp. 191–216.

Francis, J. A. (1851) *A History of the English Railways: 1820–1845* (reprinted 1968), Longmans.

Fraser, D. (1973) *Evolution of the British Welfare State*, Macmillan.

Fraser, R. (1988) *Privatisation: the U.K. Experience and International Trends*, Longmans.

Friedman, M. (1977) *From Galbraith to Economic Freedom*, Institute of Economic Affairs Occasional Paper 49.

Fromm, G. (ed.) (1981) *Studies in Public Regulation*, MIT Press.

Gaitskell, H. T. N. (1956) *Socialism and Nationalisation*, Fabian Tract No. 300.

Galt, W. (1844) *Railway Reform*, Pelham Richardson.

(1865) *Railway Reform*, Longmans Green (much enlarged edn. of Galt (1844).

Garner, M. (1988) 'Has public enterprise failed?' in Ramanadham (1988).

Gerwig, R. (1962) 'Natural gas production: a study of the costs of regulation', *Journal of Law and Economics*, October, vol. 5, pp. 69–92.

Gilbert, R. J. and Newbery, D. M. (1988) *Regulation Games*, Centre for Economic Policy and Research Discussion Paper No. 267.

Glaister, S. (1991) 'UK bus deregulation: the reasons and the experience', (May 1991), *Investigaciones Economicas*, vol. 15, no. 2.

Glaister, S. and Collings, J. J. (1978) 'Passenger mile maximisation in theory and practice', *Journal of Transport Economics and Policy*, vol. 12, no. 3, pp. 304–32.

Glaister, S. and Mulley, C. (1983) *Public Control of the British Bus Industry*, Gower.

Goldberg, V. P. (1976) 'Regulation and administered contracts', *Bell Journal of Economics*, vol. 7, pp. 426–48.

Goodrich, C. (1967) *The Government and the Economy*, Bobbs-Merrill.

Gordon, L. (1938) *The Public Corporation in Great Britain*, Oxford University Press.

Gormley, W. (1983) *Politics of Public Utility Regulation*, University of Pittsburgh Press.

Gourvish, T. R. (1988) 'The rise of the professions', in T. R. Gourvish and A. O'Day (eds), *Later Victorian Britain: 1867–1900*, Macmillan.

Graham, C. and Prosser, T. (1987) 'Privatising nationalised industries: constitutional issues and new legal techniques', *Modern Law Review*, vol. 50, pp. 16–51.

(1988) 'The privatisation of state enterprises', in their *Waiving the Rules*, Open University Press.

(1991) *Privatising Public Enterprises*, Clarendon Press.

Gray, H. M. (1940) 'The passing of public utility concept', *Land Economics*, February, vol. 16, pp. 8–20.

Green, D. (1982) 'Government and industry in France', *Public Money*, vol. 2, no. 2, pp. 27–31.

Gregg, P. (1973) *Social and Economic History of Britain 1760–1972*, Harrap.

Grieve Smith, J. (1982) 'Nationalised industries: private capital', *Public Money*, vol. 1, no. 4, pp. 7–8.

Grigg, J. (1978) *Lloyd George: The People's Champion*, Eyre Methuen.

Gwilliam, K. (1989) 'Setting the market free', *Journal of Transport Economics and Policy*, vol. 23, no. 1, pp. 29–45.

Gwilliam, K., Nash, C. A. and Mackie, P. J. (1985a) 'Deregulating the bus industry in Britain: the case against', *Transport Reviews*, vol. 5, no. 2, pp. 105–32.

(1985b) 'A rejoinder', *Transport Reviews*, vol. 5, no. 3.

Hadley, A. T. (1890) *Railroad Transportation: its History and its Laws*, (1st edn. 1885), Putnam.

Hahn, R. W. (1989) 'Economic prescriptions for environmental problems: not exactly what the doctor ordered', in Shogren (1989).

Halévy, E. (1928) *Growth of Philosophic Radicalism*, Faber and Faber.

Hammond, E. Helm, D. and Thompson, D. (1986) 'British Gas: options for privatisation', in Kay, Mayer and Thompson (1986).

Hannah, L. (1979) *Electricity Before Nationalisation*, Macmillan.

   (1982) *Engineers, Managers and Politicians*, Macmillan.

   (1983) *The Rise of the Corporate Economy*, (1st edn. 1976), Methuen.

Harris, K. (1982) *Attlee*, Weidenfeld and Nicolson.

   (1988) *Thatcher*, Weidenfeld and Nicolson.

Harrison, A. J. (1981a) 'Privatising nationalised industry: a progress report', *Public Money*, vol. 1, no. 1, pp. 58–61.

   (1981b) 'British Gas showrooms: what the argument is about', *Public Money*, vol. 1, no. 3, pp. 29–37.

   (1982) 'Liberalising British Telecom', *Public Money*, vol. 2, no. 4, pp. 15–20.

   (1983) 'Competition and privatisation: some radical options', *Public Money*, vol. 3, no. 3, pp. 29–32.

   (1988) 'The framework of control', in Whitehead (1988).

Harrison, G. W. (1987) 'Experimental evaluation of the contestable markets hypothesis', in E. E. Bailey (1987).

Harvey-Jones, J. (1988) *Making it Happen*, Collins.

Hawke, G. (1969) 'Pricing policy of railways in England and Wales before 1881', in M. C. Reed (1969).

   (1970) *Railways and Economic Growth in England and Wales, 1840–1870*, Clarendon Press.

Hawke, G. and Higgins, J. (1983) 'Britain', in P. O'Brien (1983).

Hayaki, M., Serier, M. and Trapont, J. M. (1987) 'An analysis of pricing and production efficiency of electric utilities by mode of ownership', in Crew (1987).

Hays, S. P. (1981) 'Political choice in regulatory administration', in McCraw 1981.

Hazlett, T. (1985) 'The curious evolution of natural monopoly theory', in Poole (1985).

Heald, D. (1983) *Public Expenditure*, Martin Robertson.

   (1985) 'Privatisation and the problem of control', *Public Administration*, vol. 63.

Heald, D. and Steel, D. (1981) 'Nationalised industries: the search for control', *Public Money*, vol. 1, no. 1, pp. 13–19.

   (eds) (1984) *Privatising Public Enterprises*, Royal Institute of Public Administration.

   (1986) 'Privatising public enterprises: an analysis of the Government's case', in Kay, Mayer and Thompson (1986).

Helm, D. (1987) 'RPI–X and the newly privatised industries: a deceptively simple regulatory rule', *Public Money*, vol. 7, no. 1, pp. 47–51.

Henney, A. (1987) *Privatise Power: Restructuring the Electricity Supply Industry*, Centre for Policy Studies.

Hicks, J. R. (1932) *Theory of Wages*, Clarendon Press.

   (1939) *Value and Capital*, Clarendon Press.

   (1959) *Essays in World Economics*, Clarendon Press.

Hillman, J. J. and Braeutigam, R. (1989) *Price Level Regulation for Diversified Public Utilities*, Kluwer.

Hilton, G. (1982) 'Ending the ground-transportation cartel', in Poole (1982).

Hinde, W. (1987) *Richard Cobden*, Yale University Press.

HM Treasury (1961) *Financial and Economic Obligations of the Nationalised Industries*, Cmnd. 1337, HMSO.

   (1967) *Nationalised Industries: A Review of Economic and Financial Objectives*, Cmnd. 3437, HMSO.

(1978) *The Nationalised Industries, 1978*, Cmnd. 7131, HMSO.

(1980) *The Government's Expenditure Plans 1980/1 to 1982/4*, Cmnd. 7841, HMSO.

(1981) *The Government's Expenditure Plans 1981/2 to 1983/4*, Cmnd. 8175, HMSO.

(1984) *Nationalised Industries Regulation: Consultative Proposals*, 20 December 1984, HMSO.

(1985a) *Capital Expenditure and Finance: A Consultation Paper*, July 1985, HMSO.

(1985b) *Economic Progress Report*, June–July 1985.

(1986a) *Economic Progress Report*, July–August 1986.

(1986b) *Accounting for Economic Costs and Changing Prices*, (the Byatt Report), HMSO.

(1988) *Public Expenditure Survey*, HMSO.

Hobsbawm, E. J. (1967) *Industry and Empire*, Weidenfeld and Nicolson.

Holland, S. (1972) *The State as Entrepreneur*, Weidenfeld and Nicolson.

Horwitz, R. B. (1989) *The Irony of Regulatory Reform: The Deregulation of American Telecommunications*, Oxford University Press.

Howe, Sir Geoffrey (1981) *Privatisation: The Way Ahead*, Conservative Political Centre.

Hutchinson, G. (1991) 'Efficiency gains through privatisation of UK industries', in Ott and Hartley (1991).

Hyde, F. E. (1934) *Mr Gladstone at the Board of Trade*, Cobden Sanderson.

Ickes, B. W. (1990) 'Obstacles to economic reform of Socialism', *Annals of the American Academy of Politics and Social Science*, January, pp. 53–64.

Jaffer, and Thompson, D. (1986) 'Deregulating express coaches: a reassessment', *Fiscal Studies*, vol. 7, pp. 45–68.

Jones, G. W. (1987) *Privatisation: Reflections on the British Experience*, Institute of Policy Studies.

Jones, L. P., Tandon, P. and Vogelsang, I. (1990) *Selling Public Enterprises*, MIT Press.

(1991) 'Net benefits from privatisation of public enterprises', in Ott and Hartley (1991).

Jones, W. (1962) *Licensing of Domestic Air Transportation*, Civil Aeronautics Board.

Jones-Lee, M. W. (1989) *Economics of Safety and Physical Risk*, Blackwell.

Joskow, P. L. (1974) 'Inflation and environmental concern', *Journal of Law and Economics*, October, vol. 17, pp. 291–327.

(1979) 'Public Utility Regulatory Policies Act of 1978', *Natural Resources Journal*, April, vol. 19, pp. 787–809.

Joskow, P. L. and Noll, R. G. (1981) 'Regulation in theory and Practice: an overview', in Fromm (1981).

Joskow, P. L. and Rose, N. (1989) 'Economic effects of regulation', in Schmalensee and Willig (1989).

Joskow, P. L. and Schmalensee, R. (1983) *Markets for Power*, MIT Press.

Jowell, J. L. (1986) 'Implementation and enforcement of law', in L. Lipson and S. Wheeler, *Law and the Social Sciences*, 1986, Russell Sage Foundation.

(1989) 'The rule of law to-day', in Jowell and Oliver (1989).

Jowell, J. L. and Oliver, D. (1988) *New Directions in Judicial Review*, Stevens.

(eds) (1989) *The Changing Constitution*, Clarendon Press.

Kahn, A. E. (1978) 'An economist at work on utility rate regulation', *Public Utilities Fortnightly*, 5 Jan.; 19 Jan.; 2 Feb.

(1979) 'Applications of economics to an imperfect world', *American Economic Review*, Papers and Proceedings, vol. 69, no. 2, pp. 1–13.

(1982) 'The political feasibility of regulatory reform: how did we do it?' in L. Graymer and F. Thompson, *Reforming Social Regulations*, 1982, Sage.

(1984) 'The uneasy marriage of regulation and competition', *Telematics*, vol. 1, no. 5.

(1988a) *Economics of Regulation* (1st edn. 1970, 1971), MIT Press.

(1988b) 'Surprises of deregulation', *American Economic Review*, vol. 78, no. 2, pp. 315–22.

(1990a) 'Deregulation: looking backward and looking forward', *Yale Journal of Regulation*, vol. 7, no. 2, pp. 325–54.

(1990b) 'Telecommunications, competitiveness and economic development – what makes us competitive?', *Public Utilities Fortnightly*, 13 September.

Kahn, A. E. and Roach, M. (1979) 'Commentary: a paean to legal creativity', *Administrative Law Review*, winter, vol. 31, pp. 97–114.

Kahn, A. E. and Shew, W. B. (1987) 'Current issues in telecommunications regulation: pricing', *Yale Journal of Regulation*, vol. 4, pp. 191–256.

Kahn Freund, O. (1939) *The Law of Inland Transport*, Stevens.

Kanter, R. M. (1984) *The Change Masters*, Allen and Unwin.

Kay, J. A. (1984) 'The privatisation of British Telecommunications', in Heald and Steel (1984).

(1987) *The State and the Market: The UK Experience of Privatisation*, Group of Thirty.

Kay, J. A., Mayer, C. and Thompson, D. (eds) (1986) *Privatisation and Regulation: The UK Experience*, Clarendon Press.

Kay, J. A. and Silberston, Z. (1984) 'The new industrial policy – privatisation and competition', *Midland Bank Review*, spring, vol. 8.

Kay, J. A. and Thompson, D. J. (1986) 'Privatisation: a policy in search of a rationale', *Economic Journal*, March, vol. 96 pp. 18–32.

(1987) 'Policy for industry', in Dornbusch and Layard (1987).

Kay, J. A. and Vickers, J. (1988) 'Regulatory reform in Britain', *Economic Policy*, October, vol. 7, pp. 286–351.

Keeler, T. E. (1984) 'Theories of regulation and the deregulation movement', *Public Choice*, vol. 44, pp. 103–45.

Keith-Lucas, B. (1980) *The Unreformed Local Government System*, Croom Helm.

Kelf-Cohen, R. (1969) *Twenty Years of Nationalisation*, Macmillan.

Keller, M. (1981) 'The pluralist state: American economic regulation, 1900–1930', in McCraw (1981).

Kellett, J. R. (1969) *The Impact of Railways on Victorian Cities*, Routledge.

Keynes, J. M. (1931) 'The end of laissez-faire', in his *Essays in Persuasion*, Macmillan.

(1936) *The General Theory of Employment, Interest and Money*, Macmillan.

(1981) *Activities: 1929–30*, Royal Economic Society, vol. 20, Macmillan.

Kirkpatrick, J. (1988) 'Representing the consumer', in Whitehead (1988).

Knowles, L. C. A. (1926) *The Industrial and Commercial Revolutions in Great Britain during the Nineteenth Century*, (1st edn. 1921) Routledge.

Kolbe, A. L. and Read, J. A. (1984) *The Cost of Capital: Estimating the Rate of Return for Public Utilities*, MIT Press.

Kolko, G. (1963) *The Triumph of Conservatism*, Free Press.

Kreps, D. and Wilson, R. (1982) 'Reputation and Imperfect Information', *Journal of Economic Theory*, vol. 27, pp. 253–79.

Labour Party (1991) *It's Time to Get Britain Working Again, Labour's Election Manifesto*.

Layton, W. T. et al. (1977) *Britain's Industrial Future*, Liberal Party/Ernest Benn.

Lee, L. W. (1980) 'A theory of just regulation', *American Economic Review*, vol. 70, pp. 848–62.

Leibenstein, H. (1966) 'Allocative efficiency vs. X-efficiency', *American Economic Review*, vol. 56, no. 3, pp. 392–415.

Lerner, A. P. (1944) *The Economics of Control*, Macmillan.

Letwin, O. (1988) *Privatising the World: A Study of International Privatization in Theory and Practice*, Cassell.

Lewis, N. (1989) 'Regulating non-governmental bodies', in Jowell and Oliver, (1989).

Liberal Party (1928) *Britain's Industrial Future: Report of the Liberal Industrial Inquiry*, Ernest Benn.

Likierman, A. (1981) 'Financial targets', *Public Money*, vol. 1, no. 1, pp. 5–6.

(1988) 'Public enterprises', in *Public Domain*, Public Finance Foundation.

Likierman, A. and Bloomfield, S. (1987) 'Whither nationalized industries?' *Public Domain*, Public Finance Foundation.

Lipset, S. M. and Schneider, W. (1983) *The Confidence Gap*, Free Press.

Lipsey, R. G. (1963) *An Introduction to Positive Economics*, Weidenfeld and Nicolson.

Little, I. M. D. (1953) *The Price of Fuel*, Oxford University Press.

Little, I. M. D. and Mirrlees, J. A. (1969) *Manual of Industrial Project Analysis in Developing Countries*, OECD.

Littlechild, S. (1981) 'Ten steps to denationalisation', *Journal of Economic Affairs*, vol. 2, no. 1, pp. 11–19.

(1983) *Regulation of British Telecommunications Profitability*, Department of Industry.

(1986) *Economic Regulation of Privatised Water Authorities*, HMSO.

Locke, J. (1947) 'An Essay Concerning the True Original, Extent and End of Civil Government', in E. Barker, ed., *Social Contract*, 1947, Oxford University Press.

Lowi, T. (1969) *The End of Liberalism*, Norton.

Lowry, E. D. (1973) 'Justification for regulation: the case for natural monopoly', *Public Utilities Fortnightly*, November, vol. 97.

Lubenow, W. C. (1971) *The Politics of Government Growth: Early Victorian Attitudes toward State Intervention 1833–1848*, David and Charles.

MacDonald, J. M. (1989) 'Railroad deregulation, innovation and competition', *Journal of Law and Economics*, vol. 32, no. 1, pp. 63–95.

Mackie, P. and Preston, J. (1988) 'Competition in the urban bus markets: a case study', Institute of Transport Studies, Leeds.

Majone, C. (ed.) (1990) *Deregulation or Re-Regulation?*, St Martin's Press.

Mankiw, G. B. and Whinston, M. D. (1986) 'Free entry and social inefficiency', *Rand Journal of Economics*, vol. 17.

Marquand, D. (1988) *The Unprincipled Society*, Jonathan Cape.

Marshall, A. (1920) *Principles of Economics* (1st edn. 1890), Macmillan.

Martin, S. (1989) *Industrial Economics*, Macmillan.

Mathias, P. (1983) *The First Industrial Nation* (1st edn. 1969), Methuen.

Matthew, H. C. G. (1986) *Gladstone: 1809–1874*, Oxford University Press.

Matthews, R. C. O., Feinstein, and Odling Smee, (1982) *British Economic Growth: 1856–1973*, Clarendon Press.

May, T. (1972) *The Economy: 1815–1914*, Collins.

Mayer, C. and Meadowcroft, S. (1986) 'Selling public assets', in Kay, Mayer and Thompson (1986).

McChesney, F. S. (1987) 'Rent extraction and rent creation in the economic theory of regulation', *Journal of Legal Studies*, vol. 16, pp. 101–18.

McCraw, T. K. (ed.) (1981) *Regulation in Perspective*, Harvard University Press.

(1984) *Prophets of Regulation*, Harvard University Press.

McCubbins, M. D. (1985) 'Legislative design of regulatory structures', *American Journal of Political Science*, vol. 29, no. 4, pp. 727–48.

McCubbins, M. D. and Schwartz, T. (1984) 'Congressional oversight overlooked', *American Journal of Political Science*, vol. 28, pp. 165–79.

McCulloch, J. R. (1849) *Principles of Political Economy*, (1st edn. 1825), A. & C. Black.

McGee, J. S. (1958) 'Predatory pricing: the Standard Oil (N.J.) case', *Journal of Law and Economics*, October, vol. 1, pp. 137–69.

McKee, J. W. (ed.) (1976) *Social Responsibilities and Business Predicaments*, Brooking.

McKenzie, R. B. (ed.) (1984) *Constitutional Economics*, Lexington Books.

McLean, I. and Foster, C. D. (forthcoming) 'The Political Economy of Regulation', *Public Administration*.

Merrett, A. J. and Sykes, A. (1963) *Finance and Analysis of Capital Projects*, Longmans.

Middlemas, K. (1979) *Politics in Industrial Society*, Andre Deutsch.

Milgrom, P. and Roberts, J. (1982) 'Predation, reputation and entry deterrence', *Journal of Economic Theory*, vol. 27, pp. 280–312.

Mill, J. S. (1852) *Principles of Political Economy* (1st edn. 1848), J. W. Parker and Son.

Millward, R. (1986) 'The comparative performance of public and private enterprise', in Kay, Mayer and Thompson (1986).

Milne, A. M. and Laing, A. (1956) *The Obligation to Carry*, Institute of Transport.

Mitchell, B. R. (1969) 'The coming of the railway and United Kingdom economic growth', in M. C. Reed (1969).

MMC (Monopolies and Mergers Commission) (1981) *Central Electricity Generating Board*, HMSO.

(1987) *Manchester Airport, Civil Aviation Authority*, November 1987, HMSO.

(1988) *Gas*, HMSO.

(1989) *Chatline and Message Services*, HMSO.

(1991) *BAA plc, Civil Aviation Authority*, Civil Aviation Authority.

Molyneux, R. and Thompson, D. (1987) 'Nationalised performance still third rate?' *Fiscal Studies*, vol. 8, no. 1, pp. 48–72.

Montesquieu (1748) *De l'esprit des lois*.

Moore, J. (1986a) 'Why privatise?' in Kay, Mayer and Thompson (1986).

(1986b) 'The success of privatisation', in Kay, Mayer and Thompson (1986).

Morgan, K. O. (1985) *Labour in Power*, Oxford University Press.

Morrison, H. (1933) *Socialisation and Transport*, Constable.

Morrison, J. (1848) *Influence of English Railway Legislation on Trade and Industry*, Longmans.

Mulley, C. (1983) 'The background to regulation in the 1930 Road Traffic Act', *Journal of Transport History*, 3rd series, vol. 4, no. 2, pp. 1–19.

Nash, C. (1988) 'British Rail and the administration of subsidies', in Whitehead (1988).

National Audit Office (1984) *Departments of Energy, Trade and Industry, and Transport: Monitoring and Control of Nationalised Industries*, HC 553, HMSO.

(1988) *Department of Trade and Industry: Sale of Government Shareholdings in Rolls-Royce plc*, 1988, HMSO.

NEDO (National Economic Development Office) (1965) *Investment Appraisal*, HMSO.

(1976) *A Study of UK Nationalised Industries*, HMSO.

Nelson, J. C. (1950) 'Patterns of competition and monopoly in present day transport', *Land Economics*, vol. 26, no. 3, pp. 232–48.

(1959) *Railroad Transportation and Public Policy*, Brookings.

Niskanen, W. A. (1971) *Bureaucracy and Representative Government*, Aldine Atherton.

Noll, R. G. (1989) 'The politics of regulation', in Schmalensee and Willig (1989).

Nowotny, K., Smith, D. B. and Trebing, H. M. (eds) (1989) *Public Utility Regulation*, Kluwer.

Oakeshott, R. (1983) 'Privatisation and worker buy-outs', *Public Money*, vol. 3, no. 3, pp. 15–18.

O'Brien, D. P. (1970) *J. R. McCulloch: A Study in Classical Economics*, Allen and Unwin.

O'Brien, P. (ed.) (1983) *Railways and Economic Development of Western Europe*, Methuen.

Offer (Office for Electricity Regulation) (1991a) *Annual Report 1990*, HMSO.

(1990/91) *Report on Distribution and Transmission System Performance*, Offer.

(1991b) *Report on Pool Price Inquiry*, December 1991, Offer.

(1992) *Metering: Consultation Paper*, January 1992, Offer.

Ofgas (Office of Gas Supply) (1987) *Annual Report: 1986*, 25 February 1987, HMSO.

(1988) *Annual Report: 1987*, 2 March 1988, HMSO.

(1989) *Annual Report: 1988*, 1 March 1989, HMSO.

(1990) *Annual Report: 1989*, 12 February 1990, HMSO.

(1991a) *Annual Report: 1990,* 12 February 1991, HMSO.

(1991b) *New Gas Tariff Formula: Economic Aspects,* Ofgas.

(1992) *Annual Report: 1991,* 11 February 1992, HMSO.

OFT (Office of Fair Trading) (1991) *The Gas Review,* OFT.

Oftel (Office of Telecommunications) (1985a) *Annual Report: 5 August to 31 December 1984,* 3 July 1985, HMSO.

(1985b) *British Telecom's Price Increases November 1985: A Statement by the Director General of Telecommunications,* 16 December 1985, Oftel.

(1986a) *Annual Report 1985,* 25 June 1986, HMSO.

(1986b) *Review of British Telecom's Tariff Changes: Report by the Director General of Telecommunications,* November 1986, Oftel.

(1987a) *Annual Report 1986,* 1 July 1987, HMSO.

(1987b) *British Telecom's Quality of Service Statement,* 14 July 1987, Oftel.

(1987c) *Telephone Service and Price Statement,* 7 November 1987, Oftel.

(1988a) *Annual Report 1987,* 4 May 1988, HMSO.

(1988b) *The Regulation of British Telecom's Prices: A Consultative Document,* 27 January 1988, Oftel.

(1988c) *Control of British Telecom's Prices Statement,* 7 July 1988, Oftel.

(1989a) *Annual Report 1988,* 23 May 1989, HMSO.

(1989b) *BT's September 1989 Price Changes Statement,* 20 July 1989, Oftel.

(1990) *Annual Report 1989,* 27 June 1990, HMSO.

(1991) *Annual Report 1990,* 23 May 1991, HMSO.

(1992a) *Regulation of BT's Prices,* 30 January 1992, Oftel.

(1992b) *Cost of Capital,* 30 January 1992, Oftel.

Ofwat (Office of Water Services) (1990) *Paying for Water, a Consultation Paper,* Ofwat.

(1991a) *Annual Report: 1990,* HMSO.

(1991b) *The Cost of Capital: A Consultation Paper,* 2 vols, July 1991, Ofwat.

(1991c) News Release, 18 June 1991.

O'Leary, M. C. and Smith, D. B. (1989) 'The contribution of economic theory to the regulatory process', in Nowotny, Smith and Trebing (1989).

Oliver, D. (1988) 'The courts and the policy-making process in judicial review', in Jowell and Oliver (1988).

Olson, M. (1965) *The Logic of Collective Action,* Harvard University Press.

Ostergaard, G. N. (1954) 'Labour and the development of the public corporation', *Manchester School,* vol. 22, pp. 192–226.

Ott, O. F. and Hartley, K. (eds) (1991) *Privatisation and Economic Efficiency,* Edward Elgar.

Pannick, D. (1988) 'What is a public authority for the purposes of judicial review?' in Jowell and Oliver (1988).

Panzar, J. C. and Willig, R. D. (1977) 'Free entry and the sustainability of natural monopoly', *Bell Journal of Economics,* vol. 8, pp. 1–22.

Parris, H. (1965) *Government and the Railways in Nineteenth-Century Britain,* Routledge.

Parris, H., Pestiau, P. and Saynor, P. (1987) *Public Enterprise in Western Europe,* Croom Helm.

Pawson, E. (1977) *Transport and Economy,* Academic Press.

Peacock Committee (1986) *Financing the B.B.C.,* Cmnd. 9824, HMSO.

Pelling, H. (1984) *Labour Governments: 1945–51,* Macmillan.

Peltzmann, S. (1976) 'Towards a more general theory of regulation', *Journal of Law and Economics,* vol. 19, pp. 211–40.

Pierce, R. J., Allison, G. D. and Martin, P. A. (1980) *Economic Regulation: Energy, Transportation and Utilities,* Michie, Bobbs-Merrill.

Pigou, A. C. (1920) *Economics of Welfare,* Macmillan.

Pirie, M. (1988) *Privatisation: Theory, Practice and Choice,* Wildwood House.

Plato (1952) *Statesman*, translated by J. B. Skemp, Routledge and Kegan Paul.

Pollins, H. (1969) 'Aspects of railway accounting before 1868', in M. C. Reed (1969).

Poole, R. W. (ed.) (1982) *Instead of Regulation*, Lexington Books.

(ed.) (1985) *Unnatural Monopolies*, Lexington Books.

Popper, K. R. (1957) *The Poverty of Historicism*, Routledge and Kegan Paul.

(1945) *The Open Society and its Enemies*, Routledge and Kegan Paul.

Posner, R. A. (1969) 'Natural monopoly and regulation', *Stanford Law Review*, vol. 21, pp. 548–643.

(1974) 'Theories of economic regulation', *Bell Journal of Economics*, vol. 5, pp. 335–58.

(1975) 'The social cost of monopoly and regulation', *Journal of Political Economy*, August, vol. 83, pp. 807–27.

(1976) *Antitrust Law: An Economic Perspective*, University of Chicago Press.

Pratt, E. A. (1908) *Railways and Nationalisation*, P. S. King and Son.

Preston, J. (1991) 'Competition policy and the British bus industry: the case of mergers', unpublished.

Prosser, T. (1986) *Nationalised Industries and Public Control*, Blackwell.

Pryke, R. (1971) *Public Enterprise in Practice*, MacGibbon and Kee.

(1981) *The Nationalised Industries: Policies and Performance since 1968*, Martin Robertson.

(1987) 'The comparative performance of public and private enterprise', *Fiscal Studies*, vol. 8, no. 3, pp. 68–81.

Ramanadham, V. V. (ed.) (1988) *Privatisation in the United Kingdom*, Routledge.

(ed.) (1989) *Privatisation in Developing Countries*, Routledge.

Ramsey, F. P. (1927) 'A contribution to the theory of taxation', *Economic Journal*, vol. 37, pp. 47–61.

Rappaport, A. (1986) *Creating Shareholder Value*, Free Press.

Redwood, J. (1980) *Public Enterprise in Crisis*, Blackwell.

(1984) *Going for Broke: Gambling with Taxpayers' Money*, Blackwell.

Reed, M. C. (ed.) (1969) *Railways in the Victorian Economy*, Augustus M. Kelley.

Reed, P. (1985) 'Taking regulation out of politics: the case of the Civil Aviation Authority', *Public Money*, vol. 5, no. 2, pp. 27–30.

Rees, R. (1968) 'Second best rules for public enterprise pricing', *Economica*, vol. 35, pp. 260–73.

(1986) 'Is there an economic case for privatisation?', *Public Money*, vol. 5, no. 4, pp. 19–26.

Ricardo, D. (1962) *Principles of Political Economy and Taxation* (1st edn. 1817), Cambridge University Press.

Robbins, D. and White, P. (1986) 'The experience of express coach deregulation in Great Britain', paper presented to Fourth World Conference on Transport Research, May 1986.

Robbins, L. (1952) *The Theory of Economic Policy*, Macmillan.

Roberts, D. (1979) *Paternalism in Early Victorian England*, Rutgers University Press.

Robinson, C. (1987) 'A liberalised coal market?' *Lloyds Bank Review*, April.

Robinson, J. (1948) *Economics of Imperfect Competition* (1st edn. 1933), Macmillan.

Robson, W. A. (ed.) (1937) *Public Enterprise*, Allen and Unwin.

(1951) *Justice and Administrative Law* (1st edn. 1928), Macmillan.

(1952) *Problems of Nationalised Industry*, Allen and Unwin.

(1962) *Nationalised Industry and Public Ownership* (1st edn. 1960), Allen and Unwin.

Romer, T. and Rosenthal, H. (1987) 'Modern political economy and the study of regulation', in E. E. Bailey (1987).

Russell, C. (1990) *The Causes of the English Civil War*, Oxford University Press.

Sandbrook, R. (1988) 'Patrimonialism and the failing of parastatals: Africa in comparative perspective', in Cook and Kirkpatrick (1988).

Sanders, E. (1987) 'The regulatory surge of the 1970s', in E. E. Bailey (1987).

Sappington, D. E. M. and Stiglitz, J. E. (1987) 'Information and regulation', in E. E. Bailey (1987).

Savage, C. I. (1959) *An Economic History of Transport*, Hutchinson.

Savage, I. S. (1985) *The Deregulation of Bus Services*, Institute of Transport Studies, Leeds.

Savas, E. S. (1987) *Privatisation: The Key to Better Government*, Chatham House.

Scherer, F. (1980) *Industrial Market Structure and Economic Performance*, 1980, Chicago University Press.

Schmalensee, R. and Willig, R. D. (eds) (1989) *Handbook of Industrial Organisation*, vol. 2, Amsterdam.

Schwartz, B. (1949) *Law and the Executive in Britain*, New York University Press.

(1987) *Lions over the Throne*, New York University Press.

SCNI (Select Committee on Nationalised Industries) (1959) *British Railways*, HMSO.

(1968) *Ministerial Control*, HMSO.

Senior, Nassau (1836) *Outline of the Science of Political Economy*, Encyclopaedia Metopolitana.

Serpell Committee (1983) *Report: Railway Finances*, HMSO.

Shackle, G. L. S. (1967) *The Years of High Theory*, Cambridge University Press.

Shanks, M. (ed.) (1963) *Lessons of Public Enterprise*, Jonathan Cape.

Shannon, R. (1982) *Gladstone: 1809–1865*, Hamish Hamilton.

Sharkey, W. (1982) *The Theory of Natural Monopoly*, Cambridge University Press.

Shepherd, W. G. (1965) *Economic Performance under Public Ownership*, Yale University Press.

(1966) 'Marginal cost pricing in American utilities', *Southern Economic Journal*, July, vol. 33, no. 1, pp. 58–70.

Shepsle, K. A. (1982) Review of Wilson (1976), *Journal of Political Economy*, vol. 90, no. 1, pp. 216–21.

Sherrington, C. E. (1928) *Economics of Rail Transport in Great Britain*, Arnold.

Shinwell, E. (1955) *Conflict Without Malice.*

Shleifer, A. (1985) 'A theory of yardstick competition', *Rand Journal of Economics*, vol. 16, pp. 319–27.

Shogren, J. F. (ed.) (1989) *Political Economy of Government Regulation*, Kluwer.

Sidgwick, H. (1887) *Principles of Political Economy* (1st edn. 1883), Macmillan.

Siegan, B. H. (ed.) (1979) *Regulation, Economics and the Law*, Lexington Books.

Simon, H. A. (1957) *Models of Man*, Wiley.

Sked, A. and Cook, C. (1979) *Post-War Britain: A Political History*, Penguin Books.

Smith, A. (1802) *Wealth of Nations* (1st edn. 1776), Cadell and Davies.

Solo, R. A. (1980) *The Positive State*, Southwestern Publishing.

Sopengels, P. S. (1982) 'Strategic firm behaviour under a dynamic adjustment process', *Bell Journal of Economics*, vol. 11, pp. 360–72.

Spence, A. M. (1975) 'Monopoly, quality and regulation', *Bell Journal of Economics*, vol. 6, pp. 417–29.

Spencer, H. (1883) 'Railway morals and railway policy', *Edinburgh Review*, 1854, reprinted in his *Essays: Scientific, Political and Speculative*, vol. 2, 1883, Williams and Norgate.

Sraffa, P. (1926) 'The law of returns under competive conditions', *Economic Journal*, vol. 36.

Starkie, D. and Thompson, D. (1986) 'Cross-subsidy', *Public Money*, vol. 5, no. 4, p. 5.

Stigler, G. J. (1971) 'The theory of economic regulation', *Bell Journal of Economics*, spring, vol. 2, pp. 3–21. (Reprinted in Stigler (1975).)

(1975) *Citizen and the State*, Chicago University Press.

(1976) 'X-istence of X inefficiency', *American Economic Review*, March, vol. 66, pp. 213–16.

Stigler, G. J. and Friedland, C. (1962) 'What can regulators regulate? The case of electricity', *Journal of Law and Economics*, October, vol. 5. (Reprinted in Stigler (1975).)

Stiglitz, J. E. (1988) *Economics of the Public Sector*, Norton.

Swann, D. (1988) *The Retreat of the State*, Harvester.

References 435

Sykes, A. (1985) 'BGC privatisation – the case for a re-think', memorandum, July 1985.

Tanner, J. R. (1928) *English Constitutional Conflicts of the Seventeenth Century*, Cambridge University Press.

Tawney, R. H. (1921) *The Acquisitive Society*, G. Bell.

Taylor, A. J. (1972) *Laissez-faire and State Intervention in Nineteenth-Century Britain*, Macmillan.

Telser, L. G. (1969) 'On the regulation of industry: a note', *Journal of Political Economy*, vol. 77, pp. 937–52.

Thomas, D. (1986a) 'The union response to denationalisation', in Kay, Mayer and Thompson (1986).

(1986b) 'Easier to sack', *Public Money*, September, vol. 6, pp. 9–10.

Thompson, D. (1988) 'Privatisation: introducing competition, opportunities and constraints', in (1988).

Thurow, L. C. (1980) *Zero Sum Society*, Basic Books.

Travis, C., Lamb, D. R. and Jenkinson, J. A. (1913) *Elements of Railway Operating Economics*, Railway News.

Tunstall, J. (1986) *Communications Deregulation*, Blackwell.

Turpin, C. (1989) 'Ministerial responsibility: myth or reality?' in Jowell and Oliver (1989).

Turvey, R. (1968) *Optimal Pricing and Investment in Electricity Supply*, Allen and Unwin.

Utt, R. D. (1991) 'Privatisation in the United States', in Ott and Hartley (1991).

Utton, M. A. (1986) *Economics of Regulating Industry*, Blackwell.

Veitch, G. (1930) *The Struggle for the Liverpool and Manchester Railway*, Daily Post Printers.

Veljanovski, C. (1987) *Selling the State: Privatisation in Britain*, Weidenfeld and Nicolson.

(1990) 'The political economy of regulation', in P. Dunleavy et al., *Development in British Politics*, vol. 3, Macmillan.

Vickers, J. and Yarrow, G. (1985) *Privatisation and the Natural Monopolies*, Public Policy Centre.

(1986) 'Telecommunications: liberalisation and the privatisation of BT', in Kay, Mayer and Thompson (1986).

(1988) *Privatisation: An Economic Analysis*, MIT Press.

Vincent, J. R. (1978) *Disraeli, Derby and the Conservative Party*, Harvester.

Wade, W. (1982) *Administrative Law*, Clarendon Press.

Walker, G. (1942) *Road and Rail*, Allen and Unwin.

Walker, M. (1988) *Privatisation: Tactics and Techniques*, Fraser Institute.

Waterson, M. (1988) *Regulation of the Firm and Natural Monopoly*, Blackwell.

(1991) *Regulation and Ownership of the Major Utilities*, Fabian Society.

Webb, S. and Webb, B. (1920) *English Local Government: The Story of the King's Highways* (1st edn. 1913), Longmans.

(1922) *Statutory Authorities for Special Purposes*, Longmans.

Weber, M. (1947) *Theory of Social and Economic Organisation*, tr. T. Parsons, Hodge.

Weidenbaum, M. W. (1980) *The Cost of Regulating Government Business*, US Congress, Joint Economic Committee, Subcommittee on Economic Growth and Stabilisation.

Wenders, J. T. (1987) *Economics of Telecommunications*, Ballinger.

Weyman Jones, T. (1989) 'US and UK Energy Policy', in Button and Swann (1989).

Wharton, R. (1988) 'Efficiency reviews and the role of the MMC', in Whitehead 1988.

White, P. (1990) 'Bus deregulation: a welfare balance-sheet', *Journal of Transport Economics and Policy*, September, vol. 24, pp. 311–32.

Whitehead, C. (ed.) (1988) *Reshaping the Nationalised Industries*, Policy Journals.

Wickwar, W. A. (1938) *The Public Services*, Cobden-Sanderson.

Williams, A. (1985) 'Economics of coronary artery bypass grafting', *British Medical Journal*, vol. 291, pp. 326–9.

Williams, P. L. (1978) *The Emergence of the Theory of the Firm*, Macmillan.

Williams, P. M. (1951) 'Public opinion on the railway rate question in 1886', *English Historical Review*, vol. 65.

Williams, T. (1908) 'No combination without regulation', *Annals*, vol. 32.

Williamson, O. E. (1976) 'Franchise bidding for natural monopolies', *Bell Journal of Economics*, vol. 7, pp. 73–104.

(1983) *Markets and Hierarchies* (1st edn. 1975), Free Press.

(1987) *Antitrust Economics*, Blackwell.

Wilson, J. Q. (1976) 'The politics of regulation', in McKee (1976).

Wilson, J. Q. and Reichal, P. (1977) 'Can the Government regulate itself?' *Public Interest*, winter, vol. 46, pp. 3–14.

Wilson, W. (1913) *The New Freedom*, Doubleday.

Wiltshire, K. (1987) *Privatisation: The British Experience*, 1987, Committee for Economic Development of Australia.

Wiseman, J. (1969) *Rebirth of Britain*, Pan Books. (Reprinted in C. Veljanovski, *Privatization and Competition*, 1989, Institute of Economic Affairs.)

Wright, M., Chipton, B. and Robbie, K. (1989) 'Management buy-outs', *Public Money and Management*, autumn, vol. 9, no. 3.

Yamey, B. S. (1972) 'Predatory price cutting', *Journal of Law and Economics*, vol. 15, pp. 129–42.

Young, G. M. (1953) *Portrait of an Age* (1st edn. 1936), Oxford University Press.

Index

Index

workhouses, 231
working capital, 113
  see also External Financing Limits (EFLs)
working conditions, 11, 54–5, 57, 94, 232, 233
write-off, 349
Wytch Farm oilfield, 131, 132

X (RPI–*X* rule)

revision of, 26, 27, 212–18, 251–3, 293, 296, 314, 317, 337, 397
value, 207–9, 272–3, 277, 298, 300, 303–4, 306, 416
X-inefficiency, 91, 151, 241

yardstick competition, 5, 134, 338
  break-up, 177–9
Yarrow, George, 129, 252